Bobby A. Wintermute, David J. Ulbrich
Race and Gender in Modern Western W

Bobby A. Wintermute, David J. Ulbrich

Race and Gender in Modern Western Warfare

Foreword by Dennis E. Showalter

DE GRUYTER
OLDENBOURG

Despite our best efforts we were not able to track down the copyright holder of some images printed in this book. If you recognize one of this images as work of your own, please contact the publishing house.

ISBN 978-3-11-047745-0
e-ISBN (PDF) 978-3-11-047746-7
e-ISBN (EPUB) 978-3-11-058879-8

Library of Congress Cataloging-in-Publication Data
Names: Wintermute, Bobby A., author | Ulbrich, David J., author.
Title: Race and gender in modern western warfare/Bobby A.
Wintermute, David Ulbrich.
Description: First edition. | Berlin; Boston: De Gruyter, [2018]
Identifiers: LCCN 2018020560| ISBN 9783110477450 (print) | ISBN 9783110477467
(e-book pdf) | ISBN 9783110588798 (e-book epub)
Subjects: LCSH: Women and war–History. | Masculinity–History. | Armed
forces–Minorities–History. | Sociology, Military–History.
Classification: LCC UB416 .U43 2018 | DDC 355.0081–dc23 LC record available at https://lccn.
loc.gov/2018020560

Bibliographic information published by the Deutsche Nationalbibliothek
The Deutsche Nationalbibliothek lists this publication in the Deutsche Nationalbibliografie;
detailed bibliographic data are available in the Internet at http://dnb.dnb.de.

© 2019 Walter der Gruyter GmbH, Berlin/Boston
Cover image: Drills – Civilian Bodies – Women – Women's machine gun squad police reserves,
New York City, RG 165, American Unofficial Collection of WWI Photographs. © The National
Archives/International Film Service
Typesetting: Integra Software Services Pvt. Ltd.
Printing and Binding: CPI books GmbH, Leck

www.degruyter.com

Foreword

Since the study of history has been reshaped and redefined by the Three Horse-men (Horsepersons?) of CLASS, RACE, and GENDER, military writing has been particularly influenced by this development. Its conventional, operational and institutional focuses have been fundamentally challenged by a "new military history," by now itself three quarters of a century old, that uses warfare as a back-ground and framework for the study of everything else, from politics to cookery, from social structure to theology.

The relationships of these approaches remain subjects of discussion and debate, ranging in tone from collegial to consternation. Issues involving class has been fully integrated, indeed welcomed, into operational/institutional history. A question raised from antiquity in almost all cultures is whether some men by virtue of their occupation, position, or character objectively less or more suita-ble as combatants? In particular, understanding the experience of mass war as it extended from 1789 to 1918, and arguably to the present, has made this a compre-hensive central issue, one providing a structural and intellectual synergy to many a book and article.

Unlike class, the interrelationships between race/gender and operational/ institutional perspectives are fraught with discrepancies. This is in spite of Joanna Bourke's perceptive argument in *Wounding the World* that "War and peace are no longer highly differentiated zones in British and American societies"—and by extension other industrial/electronic societies as well. War may have become "fun" as Bourke mordantly asserts—but where gender identity is concerned the fun remains differentiated. Specifically—and centrally—gender identity remains fundamentally dichotomous at war's sharp end of ground combat, where women are unquestioningly accepted only in the esoteric field of combat science fiction. Even there, women are presented as literal superheroines or in terms of supra-normal abilities along the lines of Joss Whedon's Buffy the vampire slayer or the women of S.M. Stirling's dystopian Draka culture. Even in David Drake's *Hammer's Slammers*, the most successful gender-blended combat Special Force's physical and psychological specifics are ignored or sidestepped. Michael Grant has recently published an alternative history series in which American women were draft-eligible in World War II. *Front Lines* is, however, essentially *Hammer's Slammers* with Garands instead of AFVs—successful on its own terms only if the matrix is accepted as a given.

The current cultural approach to race has an opposite problem: If gender is encysted, race tends—intentionally or not—to define works in which it is included, whatever may be their intention. Consideration of melanin and epicanthic folds

https://doi.org/10.1515/9783110477467-201

overshadows the themes of war and warmaking. William A. Bowers et al., *Black Soldier, White Army: the 24th Infantry Regiment in Korea*, published in 1996 by the official Center of Military History, is a classic example. Counterpoints include the histories of the Second World War's 92nd Division in Italy by W. M. Hammond and Daniel Gibrom. It is no insult to these solid works to suggest their operational elements are on the whole obscured by racial themes and memes. Useful examples can also be drawn from popular culture. The "Magnificent Seven" as reconfigured for the 2016 remake of the 1958 original significantly reshape the story line and its subtext. Group identity and intersectionality are sufficiently influential to maintain this pattern —probably to enhance it across the cultural and intellectual boards.

Bobby Wintermute and David Ulbrich step into these historical and historiographic contexts in *Race and Gender in Modern Western* Warfare. Their book is the outgrowth, in part, of their individual monographic studies the U.S. Army Medical Department and U.S. Marine Corps biography. Both authors have likewise drawn heavily on their experiences and teaching techniques gleaned from more two decades as instructors in online programs at Norwich University and in brick-n-mortar institutions like Queens College-CUNY and Rogers State University.

Their book is welcome because it does exactly what the two authors say it does: presenting the overlapped and intertwined relationships of racial and gender identities to warmaking. There is a refreshing absence of the polemics and cheeseparing that inform too many works on tactics and gender. Quite the contrary, the authors resist temptations to engage other scholarly works in fine points of debate and arcana, yet at the same time they do not sacrifice main themes vital to a process of grafting new perspectives onto an old matrix. Rather than make gender and race the foci of their structure, Wintermute and Ulbrich use the operational and institutional frameworks that enable synthesizing new ideas and data with their conventional counterparts, and that enables editing that INTEGRATES race and gender with warmaking, as opposed to using warmaking as a backdrop for discussions of race and gender.

Wintermute and Ulbrich bite the bullet in affirming the position that warfare is a sufficiently established, structured, complex matrix that any fresh perspectives will be best understood when considered within the established matrix, as opposed to innovative material being privileged as demanding complete revision. A major problem of the relationship between the "new military history" and the "traditional" approach was (and in good part is) the question of "who's the windshield and who's the bug." Instead of a distracting and unwinnable struggle for mastery, this book offer not so much a dialectic but a synergy enabling both "new" and "traditional" perspectives to demonstrate strengths, shortcomings, and errors.

Wintermute and Ulbrich bite another bullet in emphasizing *modern western* warfare. Aside from the fact that their own scholarly works spring from these temporal and regional areas, race and gender have been correspondingly significant in western work on war, whether or not the authors' or practitioners' self-reflection included notions of race or gender. Cultural assumptions embedded in traditional military history need to be teased out of the texts in ways exemplified by this book.

The text is well executed. Wintermute and Ulbrich merit praise for having the intellectual self-discipline to separate race and gender where appropriate. Too many of the works of this kind tend to link the "Revisionist" subjects at the expense of clarity. The reference apparatus for understanding the historiographic trends is also solid—thus, making the book a valuable guide to further study. The work's format, structure, and compact size makes it a natural choice as collateral reading for courses in military history and war in society, enabling new approaches to be readily plugged into standard syllabi without risking the "cuckoo in the nest" syndrome. Adherents of the traditional approaches will appreciate this possibility; and general readers will appreciate the work's wider contributions to the seminal issues of race and gender as they relate to wars and the societies THAT fight those wars.

Dennis E. Showalter

Preface

Background

This book had its genesis over a decade ago. It evolved out of years of publishing, teaching, and developing courses on the intersections of warfare and cultural constructions of identity. The creative process has been an odyssey of historiographical discovery for both of us. *Race and Gender in Modern Western Warfare* (*RGMWW*) is intended to introduce readers to some of the most critical scholarship in the War and Society field. In so doing, the histories of race and gender can enrich military history and vice versa.

In brief, *RGMWW* accepts that state-sanctioned and non-governmental violence are integral, albeit tragic, parts of the human condition, and that conflicts always result in suffering made more horrific by embedded cultural markers. We cannot deny that there will always and should always be a prominent place in the larger field of military history for "battle and leader" studies. Even so, by incorporating cultural history – in particular the history and theory associated with gender and race – the future of military history as an intellectual discipline residing on the cutting edge of the larger historical profession can be assured.[1]

With these premises as a backdrop, our book examines why constructions of gender and racial identities are transformed by war, and why they in turn influence the nature of military institutions and conflicts. By focusing on the modern Western world, this project begins by introducing the contours of race and gender theories as they have evolved and how they are employed by historians, anthropologists, sociologists, and other scholars. We blend chronological narrative with analysis and historiography as our books takes readers through a series of case studies, ranging from the early nineteenth century to the Global War of Terror. The purpose throughout is not merely to create a list of "great moments" in race and gender in military history, but rather to fashion a meta-landscape from which readers can learn to identify for themselves the disjunctures, flaws, and critical synergies in traditional memory and history of what has hitherto been portrayed as a largely monochrome and male-exclusive military experience. Indeed, our introductory text fills a void because its addresses race and gender as inquiries more than merely sub-categories of the "New Military History." In recent years,

---

1 For two very recent examples of cutting edge cultural methodologies in military history, see Matthew S. Muehlbauer and David J. Ulbrich, eds, *The Routledge History of Global War and Society* (Routledge, 2018); and Kara Dixon Vuic, ed., *The Routledge History of Gender, War, and the U.S. Military* (Routledge, 2017).

https://doi.org/10.1515/9783110477467-202

several military history textbooks have strived to stretch the limitations of the traditional "great battles perspective."[2] In addition to Jeremy Black's works in this area, there are a few other historiographic treatments, such as Robert Citino's article "Military Histories Old and New: A Reintroduction" in *American Historical Review*, Matthew Hughes and William J. Philpott's anthology *Palgrave Advances in Modern Military History*, and most recently Stephen Morillo and Michael F. Pavkovic's textbook *What is Military History*, that target broader audiences and demonstrate how military history stands as a legitimate field of academic research and philosophical discourse.[3]

Yet there is no extant treatment of the balances how and why race and gender are contingent constructions of identities in modern warfare. *RGMWW* directly addresses these shortcomings and thus becomes the benchmark for future syntheses of race and gender into the historical study of warfare. As such, our text could be assigned in surveys of modern military history in Europe or the United Sates, courses on war and society, seminars on the World Wars or imperialism, and graduate colloquia on military, race, or gender historiography. Our text could likewise serve a primer for public and uniformed audiences who want or need to address questions about race and gender absent elsewhere. Too few traditional military history monographs, let alone textbooks, expose readers to the ideas of Joan Wallach Scott, Mady Wechsler Segal, Barbara Ehrenreich, Cynthia Enloe, Jean Bethke Elshtain, Joanna Bourke, George Frederickson, Joshua Goldstein, or Benedict Anderson.[4] No doubt for many the reason is a question of relevance;

---

2 For example, see Wayne E. Lee, *Waging War: Conflict, Culture, and Innovation in World History* (Oxford, 2015); and Matthew S. Muehlbauer and David J. Ulbrich, *Ways of War: American Military History from the Colonial Era to the Twentieth-First Century*, 2nd ed. (Routledge, 2017).

3 See; Jeremy Black, *Rethinking Military History* (Routledge, 2004); Jeremy Black, *War and the Cultural Turn* (Polity, 2011); Robert M. Citino, "Military Histories Old and New: A Reintroduction," *American Historical Review* 112:4 (October 2007), 1070–1090; Stephen Morillo with Michael F. Pavkovic, *What is Military History*, 3rd ed. (Polity, 2017); and Matthew Hughes and William J. Philpott, eds., *Palgrave Advances in Modern Military History* (Palgrave McMillan, 2006).

4 Joanna Bourke has published several relevant books, including the seminal *Dismembering the Male: Men's Bodies, Britain, and the Great War* (University of Chicago Press, 1996), and more recently *Wounding the World: Hoe the Military and War-Play Invade Our Lives* (Virago, 2014); Joan Wallach Scott, "Gender: A Useful Category of Historical Analysis," *American Historical Review* 91 (December 1986): 1053–75; Mady Wechsler Segal, "Women's Military Roles Cross-Nationally: Past, Present, and Future," *Gender & Society* 9 (December 1995): 757–75; Barbara Ehrenreich, *Blood Rites: Origins and History of the Passions of War* (Metropolitan, 1998); Jean Bethke Elshtain, *Women and War* (Basic Books, 1987); George Frederickson, *Racism: A Short History* (Princeton University Press, 2002); Joshua S. Goldstein, *War and Gender: How Gender Shapes the War System and Vice Versa* (Cambridge University Press, 2001), Edward Said, *Culture*

that is to say, convinced of the power of the narrative form, or instinctively skeptical of any attempt to impose cultural imperatives on their own form, or untrained in modes of analyses required to grapple with race or gender, many conventional or traditional authors hesitate to go there. Among these, John Lynn stands as one notable exception. Fortunately for our craft, the growing War and Society field is following Lynn's "marching orders" from that now twenty-one-year-old article he published in the *Journal of Military History*, which was followed in 2008 when he published a monograph on women in early modern European warfare.[5]

RGMWW thus opens students and scholars interested in military history to discoveries that war, military institutions, and traditions are far more than place-holders for operational narratives, gripping though these may be. They move beyond realizations of the timelessness of warfare with its full fury and horror to further understand why those who practice and study conflicts are so committed to preventing it from breaking free from the constraints that attempt to hold it in check. Students look at soldiers, sailors, marines, and airmen in any era; and, thanks to the microscopic lens of cultural analysis, they see a little bit of themselves and their world residing in the persons and places of the distant past. And as the United States and its allies enter, at the time of this writing, the seventeenth year of combat operations in the Middle East, the need to understand the limits and costs of military power and the wages of war are more important now than ever. For us, adding analyses of race and gender into the methodological mix yields pivotal insights into experience and conduct of warfare, and into the epistemological reasons for what historians have chosen to ignore or emphasis in scholarship.

It seems like almost yesterday when we began teaching an online summer course on Race and Gender in Military History for Norwich University's Masters of Military History (MMH) program in 2007. The class was conceived as a modest introduction to twentieth century conflicts viewed through the two lenses of race and gender theory. This arrangement benefitted from guaranteed regular enrollments. At the same time, though, there was no assurance that any student would take the course or its subject matter seriously. This was a period, in the 2000s, when concepts of race and gender were still being dismissed or discounted by many people pursuing degrees in the field of military history. "Don't Ask, Don't Tell" (DADT) was the law

---

and Imperialism (Vintage, 1994); and Benedict Anderson, *Imagined Communities: Reflections on the Origin and Spread of Nationalism* (Verso, 1998).
5 John A. Lynn, "The Embattled Future of Academic Military History," *Journal of Military History* 61:4 (October, 1997), 777–789; and John A. Lynn II, *Women, Armies, and Warfare in Early Modern Europe* (Cambridge University Press, 2008).

of the land, and resistance toward women entering the combat support branches (let alone the combat arms specializations) was still high, even several years after the opening of the Iraq War. Despite the tremendous effort within the American military since the end of the Second World War to eliminate racial discrimination, the toxic residue of the Jim Crow Army continued to survive, albeit increasingly in the shadows. The practice of profiling and dehumanizing America's enemies with tired old racial tropes continued to flourish as evinced by cultural slurs and assumptions about America's enemies in Middle East.

Looking back, we expected that the course might wither and die, considering the general preferences for operational history among the student base in the MMH Program at Norwich.

We were wrong.

For several years, the Race and Gender course attracted a full roster of students, young and old, male and female, active duty and reservists and civilians. Many students professed that they entered the course because of the limited offerings for this final academic seminar stage. Others did so because they thought the work load would be smaller than for a more "traditional" military history course. Some assumed that the course would be an exercise in politicized agendas that had little bearing on the outcome of battles or motivations of combatants. Not everyone took to what they considered watering down of the traditional histories of warfare. We both recall the encounters with skeptical students who rebelled against the very idea that race or gender *matters* for the military historian. A few students could not make the leap, instead allowing their pre-existing cognitive and philosophical perspectives to distract them from engaging their chosen fields of study in new and stimulating ways.

In almost every case, however, our course succeeded in convincing our students that "this stuff matters" – that cultural frameworks, along with awareness of class and ideology, do enhance our understanding of conflict and the structures of military institutions and traditions. Most students soon recognized their blind spots and misperceptions, and then buckled down for the duration of the seminar. In these early years, the Race and Gender in Military History course was both a demanding experience and a tremendous opportunity for us as freshly minted Ph.D.'s in history. More than anything else, teaching the course validated how important, indeed *imperative,* it was to bring a fresh appreciation for social and cultural methodologies of history to students primarily interested in more traditional approaches to military history. Even though so many of American military personnel taking this course were living through history in the making and serving in the most diverse military force in American history in terms of gender, ethnicity, religious observance, and sexual orientation, these students may have never considered the multifaceted historical dynamics that underpin their own experiences. A history course geared toward war and the military experience, privileging how racial and gendered stereotypes, modalities, and perceptions affect the context of conflict and violence, while also determining policy and doctrine, was something completely new to this segment of students.

The combination of many successes and a few failures prompted us to expand the scope of the Race and Gender in Military History course to a full eleven-week seminar for Norwich, which we created in 2009. Along the way, Bob Wintermute revised the course further, adapting first it into a fourteen-week undergraduate seminar, and then a graduate seminar, for use at his home institution in the City University of New York. New readings and assignments followed in regular revisions. This course has thus proven to be a living, growing experience, evolving as new trends in scholarship emerge.

Intent

After years of creating, writing, and revising the course, we decided the time was right to develop a textbook based on the Norwich course. This book, *Race and Gender in Modern Western Warfare*, familiarizes readers with why and how cultural constructions of identity are transformed by war and how they in turn influence the nature of military institutions and conflicts. Beyond the topics of race and gender in the title, our book delves into issues of sexuality, ethnicity, class, health, ideology, and others to demonstrate that studying race and gender requires additional modes of analysis.[6]

The book largely emphasizes the Western perspective in matters of war and society related to race and gender. We are both by training Occidentalists and Modernists – that is to say, our frames of reference are tied to Western and American historical experiences ranging from the mid-nineteenth century to the twenty-first century. Thus our focus on the Modern Western warfare is a deliberate choice, but not one that seeks to celebrate or privilege Western societies predicated on delusional premises about inherent superiority. Quite the contrary, we accept the premise that modern Western warfare is fraught with atrocities, genocides, and other horrifying wartime acts that nullify any claims to exceptionalism. Moreover, Non-Western or Pre-Modern warfare should certainly not be ignored. Both deserve the attention of specialists trained in those frameworks,

---

6 For a monograph that blends the histories of race, health, culture, medicine, progressivism, gender, sexuality, imperialism, and the U.S. Army into a single "war and society" study, see Bobby A. Wintermute, *Public Health and the U.S. Military: A History of the Army Medical Department, 1818–1917* (Routledge, 2010).

who can engage the roles of race and gender, as well as the correlating constructions of sexuality and ethnicity, in shaping historical memory. Far more so, that is,
than two scholars trying to say something meaningful far outside their fields and
consequently doing more harm than good by risking the reinforcing of ingrained
prejudices. We don't want that outcome![7]

What we can say with certainty is this: Variations of the "West is Best" truisms
and "Might Makes Right" polemics appear so often in books and classrooms as to
become predictable and, worse still, dangerous. The interpretations sometimes
expose readers to apologists for neoconservative interventionism, hagiographers
of great (wealthy, male) commanders, cheerleaders for consensus interpretations,
proponents of the New Imperialism, devotees to "lost cause" myths, deniers of
genocides, and others. Such narratives can be traced as far in the past as Herodotus' prejudiced cultural portrayal of the Persians.[8] This is not to say, however,
that such interpretations completely ignored race and gender. To wit, one needs
only look to the most extreme case of Adolf Hitler's Germany to see how these two
identities were contorted to legitimize the superiority of Nazi "self" versus the
inferiority of the non-Aryan "other."[9]

These approaches share some common threads. They fail to address their
ideological, methodological, and sometime xenophobic premises regarding
race and gender because any careful scrutiny might make their conclusion feel
uncomfortable or expose their epistemologies as fabrications. Indeed, opening
up candid inquiries relating to race and gender can hardly be answered, let alone
be asked, by those historians so entrenched in tropes of Eurocentrism or American exceptionalism. In addition to blind spots in logic and evidence, ignoring
race- and gender-conscious considerations could likewise mean risking defeats
in real-world conflicts or failures to establish any stable peace that follows those
conflicts. Either case can have tragic consequences.

---

7 For expert surveys of the historiography of non-Western war and society, see Kenneth M.
Swope, "War and Society in East Asia," Richard A. Ruth, "War and Society in Southeast Asia,"
Kaushik Roy, "War and Society in South Asia," Eileen Ryan, "War and Society in the Middle East
and North Africa," Bruce Vandervort and Marilyn Zilli, "War and Societh in Sub-Saharan Africa,"
and Ellen Tillman, "War and Society in Latin America," all in Muehlbauer and Ulbrich, *The Routledge History of Global War and Society*.
8 Two examples of books offering interpretations from European and American exceptionlist
biases are Victor Davis Hanson, *Carnage and Culture: Landmark Battles in the Rise of Western
Power* (Doubleday, 2001); and Max Boot, *Savage of War of Peace: Small Wars and the Rise of
American Power* (Basic Books, 2002). Both authors are also neo-conservative in their outlooks.
9 Chapter 6 on the Second World War on the Eastern Front delves into the twisted racial and
gendered discourses espoused in Nazi Germany.

In the face of entrenched traditional military historiography, our book unmasks several incomplete, if not flawed, assumptions embedded in European and American perceptions of "self" in conflicts with the "others," vis-à-vis phobias, platitudes, and stereotypes of race and gender. Several case studies demonstrate how and why these notions decisively influenced the causes, conduct, and consequences of wars. We devote several chapters, for example, to the comparative racisms and sexisms in Pacific War and the Eastern Front during the Second World War, and to the Vietnam War and the Mau Mau Rebellion during the Cold War. Apart from redressing several interpretative voids in military historiography, our book also serves as a call for those scholars specializing in race and gender to grapple with the roles that wars have played in the ebb and flow between cultural change and continuity.

Put simply but not simplistically: race and gender have affected wars and the societies that fought them. And the inverse is true because wars and the societies that fought them have also altered the constructions of race and gender. These intertwined causal relationships were rarely tidy or rational – too often resulted in different degrees or kinds of race- or gender-based discrimination and sometimes with appalling consequences. Even so, causal relationships did and do exist just the same. Herein lies the discourse that our book tries to dissect and analyze.

Another point here: it is not possible, let alone desirable, to attempt to examine all relevant case studies and every condition related to race and gender as applied to military history. Both of us made hard choices when it came to deciding which case studies to include, and which to omit. Those making the cut, as it were, reflect our own particular interests, biases, and training. Ideally, readers will use this text, not as the final word on the intersection of race, gender, and war, but rather as a tool to help raise awareness of how and why specific themes and conditions described herein may be used to evaluate similar examples within the scope of any particular interest or specialty.

Content

On to the book *Race and Gender in Modern Western Warfare* itself. Chapter One serves as an introduction to the theoretical and applied foundations of race and gender as conceptual tools for military historians and other types of historians. Broad definitions of both race and gender are placed within their historiographical contexts. By introducing key concepts from critical voices in the development of race and gender studies, readers are presented with the analytical tools to examine their own perceptions of the military past.

Chapter Two presents race and gender as historical and social constructions that determine and are affected by events taking place around them. The focus here is on the nineteenth century, although some of the discussion occurs a century or more before, chronologically. Largely European in its scope, the chapter introduces concepts like the so-called "Cult of Domesticity," gender inversion and martial masculinity, Lamarckian evolution, racial hierarchies, and anti-Semitism as social concepts

Chapter Three turns to race and gender as critical facets of the nineteenth century's New Imperialism. After surveying the theoretical connections between the three concepts, closer attention is focused on the British case study in India, and its connections to military institutions and martial masculinity. In addition to considering the Contagious Diseases Act of 1864 as a strictly gendered imperial policy, issues of racial exceptionalism in India and Africa are considered, including the "Martial Races" construct. Racial exceptionalism in the United States is discussed as well, with Western Expansion introduced as an expansive imperialistic policy at the expense of Native Americans and other groups. These threads of racial exceptionalism and masculine supremacy are followed through the Spanish-American War into the Philippines and ultimately, China.

Chapter Four offers a detailed exploration of gender ideologies and constructs active in the First World War. After setting up the common and unique aspects of gender politics and identity in each of the major combatants, it examines wartime nationalism and masculinity during the conflict's first two years. *Elan Vital*, morale and motivation in the trenches, and the issue of atrocities in Belgium are among the factors considered. In a separate discussion of the second half of the war, labor and gender come into focus, including the evolving role and responsibilities of German women in an ever more desperate home front. Additional sections are devoted to sexuality and the state, the place of discipline in the Allied armies, the male body as a contested space, and the issue of homosociality and perceptions of same-sex wartime liaisons as introduced through popular culture.

Chapter Five, in its focus on race and the First World War, counters the conventional argument that so much literature and historiography has characterized this conflict as one dominated by evolving concepts and perceptions of gender roles and identities. Actually the war was just as clearly defined by concepts of racial and ethnic exceptionalism and prejudice. Following a short introduction to the different concepts regarding national identity promoted in each nation, the chapter considers the role of non-white troops and ethnic white minorities in England, France, the United States, the Ottoman Empire, and Germany as means of clarifying racial assumptions among Caucasians in the upper tiers of cultural hierarchies.

Chapter Six is devoted to a pair of case studies – the Nazi-Soviet War with the parallel war against Europe's Jews during the Second World War; and the Asia-Pacific War from 1931 until 1945. For many decades, popular authors and scholars alike have built careers and reputations by espousing the "Good *Wehrmacht*" thesis and playing to public obsession with the armies of the Third Reich and their purported "coolness." Debunking this myth reminiscent of the American Civil War's "lost cause" trope stands among most distressing challenges facing modern military historians. Using cultural constructions of race and gender as lenses for analyzing policies, attitudes, and actions of the German state and its military provide invaluable means of stripping away the layers of romanticized half-truths. The other case study in Chapter Six turns to evaluate race and gender in the Second World War on the Asian continent and the Pacific basin. John Dower's thesis in *War without Mercy* paved the way for more than three decades of scholarship building on his argument that racism affected the conduct of all levels of war and experience in these regions. Subsequent studies have also noted the prominent effects of gender on the home and battle fronts. Although delving mostly into Japanese and American perspectives, the roles of race and gender of the Chinese, Koreas, Filipinos, and British also receive due consideration. The calculated appropriation of racist and chauvinist dogmas made the conflict in Asia and the Pacific as brutal in scope and context as the conflict on the Eastern Front in Europe.

Chapter Seven shifts to comparative examinations of the belligerent nation's home front experience vis-a-vis gender, race, and sexuality. The United States, the United Kingdom, the Soviet Union, German, and Japan are filtered through Mady Segal's sociological model of military necessity to determine the erosion of their respective gender norms during Second World War. Race relations likewise underwent significant wartime changes in these nations, some for better, others for worse. In the cases of gender and race, however, the changes within hierarchies or adapted roles were affected by internal values and external military exigencies.

Chapter Eight picks up with America's post-war efforts to return to normalcy and the attendant racial, gender, and sexual conflicts in the U.S. military establishment and American society as a whole. The beginnings of national movements for Civil Rights and Women's Rights can also be seen. Meanwhile, this normalcy was then unexpectedly plunged in another war in Asia. This reignited the challenges of juxtaposing race and gender in a war against the supposedly inferior yellow race. The rising threats of communism and Soviet Union added ideological and military factors to existing racial, gender, and sexual tensions that evolved into what history has labeled the "Cold War."

Chapter Nine briefly summarizes some general historical models of decolonization that may or may not emphasize race or gender in explicit ways. Then the chapter turns to a pair of case studies in decolonization: The Mau Mau Rebellion in Kenya during the 1950s, and the Vietnam Wars in Southeast Asia from 1945 to 1975. The British leadership, although infected by racism, did not miss the fact that exploiting gender roles in Kenya could hurt the Mau Mau's efforts to gain independence from the Commonwealth. The same could not be said for the French and Americans who, blinded by stunningly high degrees of racism and chauvinism and by unwavering faith in technology and firepower, underestimated the Vietnamese ability to mobilize and fight a war of liberation and unification. Indeed, theirs was a "total war" effort versus the French and American "limited war" efforts. This chapter also explores racial and gender influences on politics and culture internal to the U.S. military and American society during the turbulent decade of the 1960s.

Finally, apart from compiling conclusions about race and gender in modern warfare, Chapter 10 forms as an epilogue for the entire book: picking up with the U.S. military in the post-Vietnam years, commenting on the racial and gender factors in recent genocides, and examining the impacts on race and gender constructions during seemingly endless conflicts in the Middle East. All these topics remain controversial and fluid because changes occur in military and civilian institutions so very quickly and often without warning. Race and gender, together with ethnicity and sexuality, have played complex, if confusing, parts in how and why wars are fought in the post-modern and post-colonial eras.

ACKNOWLEDGEMENTS

As we bring this preface to a close, it would be very bad form if we did not acknowledge those people and institutions that helped inspire, direct, and challenge us through this long process. We wish first to express our appreciation to Jim Ehrman, John "Doc" Broom, Andrew Liptak, Hugo Evans, Ben Sipe, and the late Lars Nielsen at Norwich University for their endless support, trust, and encouragement as we developed the course and wrote this book that grew out of that course. We need to make mention of the dozens of students enrolled in the "Race and Gender in Military History" courses over the last decade, all of whom challenged our thinking, questioned our premises, and deepened our perspectives. Joanna Bourke and Dennis Showalter provided insights at just the right times as we worked to bring our project to fruition. Both of us must thank Elise Wintz, Rabea Rittgerodt, and Andreas Brandmair at De Gruyter Press for their enthusiastic support, patience, and encouragement throughout the publishing process, and to the scholarly referees who offered suggestions for improving our book.

Finally, we are grateful to our respective home institutions of Queens College, City University of New York, and of Norwich University, USA, for ongoing assistance.

Bobby Wintermute recognizes his colleagues for their moral and intellectual support – Peter Conolly-Smith, Kristin Celello, Julie Sneeringer, Satadru Sen, Kate Antonova, Bryan Cooper-Owens, and so many more of you. Bobby also thanks the people in his life, who gave moral and emotional support. There are so many of you, but the greatest thanks to: Carol "Cleo" Lowinger, Sandra Sinicropi, the Lawless Family, Louis and Tamsen Monnoleto, Matthew Muehlbauer, Richard Immerman, James Westheider, Mary Procida, Pete Hester and Lisa Roth, Scott Cullen and Mary O'Brien Acciani, Fiona Lipscombe, and Yvonne Vance. And a last thank you to the two souls who continue to inspire Bobby to succeed and try harder every day: Russell F. Weigley and Priscilla Bulford Wintermute, you are missed.

David Ulbrich gratefully acknowledges his colleagues, friends, and mentors including Eugene August, Alex Roland, Glenda Riley, Abel Alves, Tory Dickinson, James Westheider, Jay Lockenour, Beth Bailey, Paul Thomsen, the late Lawrence Birken, and the late George Kren. At critical times, they challenged David – an otherwise traditionally-trained, conservative-minded military historian – to expand his inquiries into the past by using gender and race consciousness as means of gleaning a more complete understanding of warfare and peacetime. Lastly, David is grateful to his brother Tom Ulbrich and sister-in-law Pat for providing advice, support, and a wonderful place to enjoy holidays and vacations.

Bobby A. Wintermute – Trenton, New Jersey
David J. Ulbrich – Barre, Vermont

Contents

1 Western Warfare as a Crucible for Constructions of Race and Gender

Scope and Conceptual Frameworks

The concepts of race and gender as categories of social and biological differentiation have become so ingrained in our lives that many take their perceived legitimacy for granted. In both cases, the terms have developed their own taxonomies of meaning, with different levels of value and definition attached to them. "Gender" has come to signify both the physical aspects of identity based upon sexual characteristics, as well as the behavioral norms associated with each sex as assigned by society and nature. In turn, "race" identifies biological difference related to several physical aspects, including skin color, stature, hair type, and other physical indicators, as well as language groups, cultural norms and practices, physical predisposition to certain illnesses, and other less-readily identifiable factors. At their core, both "race" and "gender" exist as terms used to connote subjective difference – real and imagined, for good and for ill – between sectors of the human population. In turn, this creation of difference, the categorization of an "us" and an "other," is critical to the establishment of formal and informal social and cultural roles. These roles are in turn accorded certain legitimacy, forming the bedrock of power relationships and hierarchical entitlements in societies. In other words, we perceive ourselves and those like "us" in certain ways because of certain social categories and geological characteristics, while also perceiving "others," because of their different social categories and biological characteristics. We all see ourselves and others through particular lenses tinted by racial, gendered, and behavioral assumptions, which affect our beliefs, actions, and policies to varying degrees.

"Race" and "gender" are absolutely central to our understanding of ourselves and our relative statuses in society. In their most basic sense, they are unchangeable characteristics and markers not only signifying basic physical difference, but also a complex skein of real and imagined social roles both rooted in tradition and are constantly in flux. While these roles are generally recognized and understood, all too frequently this takes the form of uncomfortable stereotype and imagined identity. Perhaps it is a signal difference of Western cultures that these roles and norms are constantly debated and renegotiated, in recognition of the impacts of technology and information on our society. Or maybe it is a process that is older than our own short-lived perceptions of identity based on national origin.[1]

---

[1] For more on constructions of self and others, see Anderson, *Imagine Communities*. See also Linda Colley, *Britons: Forging the Nation, 1707–1837*, rev. ed. (Yale University Press, 2009); George

https://doi.org/10.1515/9783110477467-001

On the whole, race and gender exist on at least three planes of cognitive perception. First, they are both related to physical conditions and factors. Gender identity in large part is related to the possession of specific sexual organs and physical conditions; and racial identity is also largely related to the possession of specific physical characteristics related to the point of inherited biological origin. Second, aside from the immediate effects of these physical characteristics, there are no other significant emotional and cognitive differences between the sexes and different racial types. Third, those differences which are identified and presented are *socially* and *culturally* constructed – in essence, the various "characteristics" and "identities" associated with race and gender are created by societies to reflect cultural norms and power relationships.[2] In short, "race" and "gender" are socially constructed forms of identity that, while tied to the perception of physical difference, more accurately reflect both individual and communal negotiations of status and value in specific cultures.

Based on the assumptions fleshed out in this introduction and applied in later chapters, *Race and Gender in Modern Western Warfare* fills a gap in existing literature associated with three fields: the histories of race, gender, and war. Building upon the intellectual foundation of the "war and society" and "new military history"[3] schools, we seek to craft a synthetic primer for understanding how social constructions of identity are transformed by war, and how they in turn influence the nature of military institutions. Largely focused upon Western case studies, we begin by introducing to the contours of race and gender theories as they have evolved and are employed by

L. Mosse, *Nationalism and Sexuality: Respectability and Abnormal Sexuality in Modern Europe* (Howard Fertig, 1985); Frantz Fanon, *Black Skin, White Masks* (Grove Press, 1998); and Michael Billig, *Banal Nationalism* (Sage, 1995). Nationalism is an ism that can be as powerful in its influence of actions and attitudes as racism or sexism.

2 For theoretical overviews of race and gender, see Ivan Hannaford, *Race: The History of an Idea in the West* (Johns Hopkins University Press, 1996); Frederickson, *Racism*; Judith Butler, *Gender Trouble*, 2nd ed. (Routledge, 1999); and Judith Halberstam, *Female Masculinity* (Duke University Press, 1998).

3 A long-running commentary, if not debate, about "war and society" and the "new military history" can be found in Russell F. Weigley, ed., *New Dimensions in Military History: An Anthology* (Presidio Press, 1975); Richard H. Kohn, "The Social History of the American Soldier: A Review and Prospectus for Research," *American Historical Review* 86 (June 1981): 553–67; Edward M. Coffman, "The New American Military History," *Military Affairs* 48 (January 1984): 1–5; Peter Karsten, "The 'New' American Military History: A Map of the Territory, Explored and Unexplored," *American Quarterly* 36 (1984): 389–418; John Shy, "The Cultural Approach to the History of War," *Journal of Military History* 57 (October 1993): 13–26; Jeremy Black, "Determinisms and Other Issues," *Journal of Military History* 68 (October 2004): 1217–32; Morillo with Pavkovic, *What is Military History?*; and Citino, "Militaries Old and New," 1070–90.

historians, anthropologists, sociologists, literary critics, and other groups.[4] We then apply a mixed chronological narrative and analytical historiography to a series of case studies, ranging from nineteenth century conflicts through the Global War on Terror. Exploring how and why constructions of race and gender existed before, transformed during, and resettled after specific conflicts provide useful springboards to understanding critical fault lines of race and gender identity and perceptions. Military conflicts function like seismic ruptures, rendering said fault lines visible, laying bare deeper cultural and social assumptions. Accordingly, this book should not be viewed as an attempt to simply create a list of "great moments in race and gender during wartime." Rather we hope to help our readers envision a meta-landscape in which they may identify for themselves disjunctures, flaws, and critical synergies in the traditional memory/history of a largely monochrome/male-exclusive military experience. Considering that war is accepted as the most complex and perhaps most significant human interaction, it is remarkable that so much of its history in the West has been predicated on its being a singular gender-based phenomenon, with little consideration of the impact of ethnic and racial based motivators for accelerating the level and breadth of violence toward enemy combatants and civilian communities. The final chapter considers the current challenges that Western societies face in imposing social diversity and tolerance on statist military structures, in the face of both strong public opposition (at times) and ongoing military conflict.

The Origins of Race

What is "Race"? Is it a legitimate classification schema, or is it a flawed tool for assigning difference according to rules and factors established by one group seeking to preserve a status quo against others? In his book *"Race" is a Four-Letter Word,* anthropologist C. Loring Brace adopts a two-tiered method of accounting for real physical difference and the cultural need for assigning difference.

---

4 For other examples of how anthropology, sociology, psychology, ideology, biology, or literary criticism can be used to enrich the study of warfare, see also Ehrenreich, *Blood Rites*; Eric J. Leed, *No Man's Land: Combat and Identity in World War I* (Cambridge University Press, 1979); Elshtain, *Women and War*; Paul Fussell, *The Great War and Modern Memory* (Oxford University Press, 1976); Samuel Hynes, *The Soldier's Tale: Bearing Witness to a Modern War* (Penguin, 1998); J. Glenn Gray, *The Warriors: Reflections on Men in Battle* (Harcourt, Brace, and Company, 1959); George L. Mosse, *Fallen Soldiers: Reshaping the Memory of the World Wars* (Oxford University Press, 1990); Modris Eckstein, *Rites of Spring: The Great War and the Birth of the Modern Age* (Houghton Mifflin, 1989); Andrew D. Evans, *Anthropology and War: World War I and the Science of Race in* Germany (University of Chicago Press, 2010); and Goldstein, *War and Gender*.

He is careful to note that, with few exceptions, "race" was an unknown concept throughout much of human experience.

Drawing on ideas of British biologist Julian Huxley in the 1930s, Brace rejects the use of "race" as a categorization of real physical difference in human beings. Instead he substitutes the term "clines" – itself a term used to demarcate degrees of variation in specific physical traits – to identify how human beings fit into different groups and subgroups separated by what are actually minor biological differences. These physical characteristics include, but are not limited to, skin color, tooth size, blood type, hair color, and the presence of a sickle-cell hemoglobin factor. Prior to the Age of Exploration, these various clines were almost overwhelmingly geographically centered in specific regions of the globe; and thus accounted for a perceptual differentiation between human populations that would later form the context for racial classification.[5]

Yet there remained the issue of differentiating populations from each other. Certainly, the Ancient Greeks and Romans considered themselves superior from other groups on the basis of race. Plato and Herodotus described the Greeks as a people separate from outsiders – "barbarians" being a term introduced to describe all non-Greeks – on the basis of their language, religious and cultural practices, and forms of governance. However, these differences were usually based upon cultural behaviors and perception, not physical difference.[6] What of the differences identified in the Old Testament, related to the divine punishment assigned the descendants of Noah's son, Ham, following his attempt to shame his drunken, naked father? It appears Judeans and early Christians alike viewed this as a metaphysical parable, with Ham's progeny interpreted as heretics and heathens, not sub-Saharan Africans.[7] But then what of Roman identification of the Gauls, Celts, Germans, and other so-called barbarians as being inferior? Again, the emphasized difference was not predicated on racial characteristics, but on cultural factors – specifically the absence or weakness of legal and political institutions (by Roman standards) in these areas as dictating their lesser status.[8]

It becomes clear, therefore, upon closer study that "race" – as a classification scheme based upon physical difference alone – was an unfamiliar concept in the

---

5 C. Loring Brace, *"Race" is a Four-Letter Word: The Genesis of a Concept* (Oxford University Press, 2005), 5–12. See also John P. Jackson and Nadine M. Weidman, eds., *Race. Racism, and Science: Social Impact and Interaction* (Rutgers University Press, 2005).
6 Julie K. Ward and Tommy Lee Lott, *Philosophers on Race: Critical Essays* (Wiley-Blackwell, 2002), 3–4.
7 *Genesis* 9:21–27 (New International Version); and Hannaford, *Race*, 95.
8 Hannaford, *Race: The History of an Idea*, 85. See also chapters in Meriam Eliav-Feldon, et al., eds. *The Origins of Racism in the West* (Cambridge University Press, 2009).

Ancient World. Even in the Middle Ages, race was not considered a significant factor establishing identity; religion served as a more precise defining "us" and "them." Not until the Age of Exploration do we see racial identity begin to be defined as a means of categorization and classification.

A second factor is the idea that individuals had relatively little contact with others outside of their own communities. For centuries most people lived very stationary lives, isolated on their farms and villages. With the exception of a small group of traders, pilgrims, and soldier-sailors, only rarely did individuals, let alone large groups, travel more than a day's distance from their homes. Accordingly, before the onset of the Age of Exploration, the overwhelming majority of humankind shared a rather homogenous view of the world and its inhabitants. Aside from dialect and root language differences (which were far more common in the Middle Ages than we would expect today), religious identity, and the obvious class differences, Europeans considered the world to be populated largely by persons with shared features and physiology. While there were accounts of persons and communities different from the Western European norm, these were treated as exotic travelogues, exaggerated by the teller to emphasize the fantastical experience of a world beyond the reach of the many.

As noted, religious identity stood as a clear mark of difference, and thanks to the perennial conflict between the Muslim and and Christian worlds, became the chief indicator of difference in Medieval Europe. Terms like "Saracen," "Muslim," and "infidel" – all signifying Islamic *religious* identity – insinuated into the language of Western Europe as signifiers of difference from a perceived norm of religious conformity. Considered heretics and apostates, Islamic peoples across the Mediterranean and North African basin were targeted by Christian soldier and priest alike for conversion, enslavement, even massacre on this slim margin of cultural difference.

Interestingly, even in the face of direct exposure to persons of different physiological type, Europeans did not acknowledge any sense of racial difference. Marco Polo, Ibn Batuta, and other travelers made no distinction of racial differentiation in their encounters throughout the Mideast, India, Asia, and beyond. As Brace notes in his study, this should not be taken as a mark of the observer's lack of sophistication: "In fact, quite the opposite; and one could suggest that they actually recorded a more accurate picture of the world than the one that has subsequently become accepted because they were forced to see it as it is, rather than skip steps. ... The world of human biological variation, then, was perceived as a gradual phenomenon and not one comprised of discrete or distinct units."[9]

---

9 Brace, *"Race,"* 21.

The first step toward defining race as a concept followed hard on the heels of the discovery of the Americas. What was to be made of the inhabitants of this New World, a people living in ignorance of the rest of the world, apparently free of original sin, yet also embracing the most demonic practices in the Spanish Catholic imagination? Were these people even subject to the rules of the Church – and thus candidates for salvation and grace – or were they animals in human form, to be exploited and treated as beasts of burden and nothing more? In the end, the decision was left to the Papacy, which decided the Native Americans were men after all, making them dependent subjects of the secular kingdoms who claimed the land upon which they lived.

The Pope's decision could not have come at a more inconvenient time for the New World's Spanish and Portuguese conquerors, who were realizing tremendous profits from their exploitation of Indians in silver and gold mines, salt mines, and sugar plantations. Ultimately, the Papal order was ignored in all but the most basic contexts. Throughout Spanish and Portuguese America, local indigenous peoples were either enslaved directly or subjected to near-complete peonage. Critics such as the Franciscan missionary Bartolomé de las Casas sought to preserve some sense of humanitarian dignity and rights for the dwindling indigenous population, often to no avail.[10] The quandary over the future status of the Native Americans was not restricted to Spain and Portugal. After their own entrance into the great game, English and French colonial administrators in the Caribbean and North America struggled to define the status of the Indian peoples in their own spheres of control.

Compounding this issue was the perceived poor health and high mortality of Native American laborers. As observed by numerous analysts, including historian Alfred Crosby and more recently, biologist Jared Diamond, the common diseases of Europe – measles, diphtheria, tuberculosis, and smallpox – burned their way through the Americas like a Biblical scourge. By some accounts, up to eighteen million Indians died between 1490 and 1650 of these diseases, which depopulated entire sections of the North and South American continents.[11] The survivors fared poorly as well. Many tribes preserved their culture through an elder-based oral history tradition. In some cases, such as the Catawba people of the Carolinas, disease and famine effectively eradicated centuries of culture and identity, so great was the death toll among the tribal elders. Bereft and rootless, the Catawba

---

10 Joseph L. Graves, *The Emperor's New Clothes: Biological Theories of Race at the Millennium* (Rutgers University Press, 2003), 28.

11 See Alfred Crosby, *The Columbian Exchange, Biological and Cultural Consequences of 1492* (Greenwood, 2003), 35–63; and Jared Diamond, *Guns, Germs, and Steel: The Fates of Human Societies* (W.W. Norton, 1997), 211.

were eventually assimilated by the Cherokee and Creek nations.[12] Other tribes were eradicated altogether, subject to the combination of disease and overwork in European colonial work projects. The prospect of such apocalyptic catastrophes lingered into the nineteenth century – witness the fate of the Mandan tribe in the 1830s. Once considered one of the major tribes in the upper Great Plains, they were virtually annihilated by a wave of diseases, culminating with a smallpox epidemic in 1837. Reduced to a handful of people, the survivors merged with the neighboring Hidatsa Sioux in the aftermath of the outbreak.[13]

Facing annihilation and marginalization at the hands of an ever-growing colonial presence along the North American fringe, some tribes adopted a hostile outlook toward the new European arrivals. In 1622, the Powhatan tribes launched a series of raids on English setters' farm communities outside of Jamestown in the First Tidewater War. Similar violence broke out against English settlers in the Massachusetts Bay Colonies after the 1637 Pequot War. Yet as military historian John Grenier notes, these early extirpative conflicts were not driven by racial intolerance to ever more brutal conduct.[14] However the no-quarter character of frontier combat, and the stakes of total survival for both sides in the face of an implacable foe, certainly would facilitate the ready incorporation of a racialized ideology of hatred and distrust. Historian E. Wayne Lee pursues this line in his book *Barbarians and Brothers: Anglo-American Warfare, 1500–1865*. A century and a half of ever-escalating conflict between the colonizing English and the indigenous tribes of Eastern North America fostered a growing dynamic of hate that translated into racial intolerance. Warfare entered a context of atrocity extending beyond mere rage to encompass mutilation, desecration, and wanton violence against noncombatants. Lee observes that:

> essentially, by the middle of the eighteenth century at the latest, white American society had come to presumptively "authorize" a level of wartime violence against Indians that it simply did not sanction against European enemies. This social authorization generated an atmosphere of permissiveness that assured individual soldiers that they would not face censure from their peers for such violence. It did not *require* that they act violently, but it swept away the restraints that might otherwise govern individuals' choices about violence.

---

12 Colin G. Calloway, *New Worlds for All: Indians, Europeans, and the Remaking of Early America* (Johns Hopkins University Press, 1997), 142–43.

13 Donald R. Hopkins, *The Greatest Killer: Smallpox in History* (University of Chicago Press, 1983), 271–74.

14 John Grenier, *The First Way of War: American War Making on the Frontier, 1607–1814* (Cambridge University Press, 2005), 11.

> This absence of restraint opened the door for acts of violence even when the leadership's calculations of necessity or notions of honor suggested mercy and forbearance.[15]

Such an evolved world view predicated on violence followed a prolonged and ultimately frustrating encounter in which, despite the presence of mutually acknowledged similarities and shared self-interests, the overriding signifier was permanent and irreconcilable cultural difference. By the mid eighteenth century, Anglo-Americans viewed the Indian not only as a savage living in a state of nature, but also as a barbaric, heathen race, separate and distinct from white culture, and thus, a legitimate target of extreme violence. Cultural difference recast as grounds of racial-oriented difference sanctioned a course of ethnically-based violence that would persist until the turn of the nineteenth century.[16]

Colliding with material exploitation, disease, and war was the onset of a new effort in European culture to quantify and classify the natural world as part of the Enlightenment. As natural science began to assert its primacy over superstition, folk practice, and religious-sanctified practice, individuals like Sir Isaac Newton, René Descartes, and Carolus Linneaus set out to impose boundaries and order on the hitherto divine randomness of nature. In the logic-governed worldview promoted by the champions of the Enlightenment, everything in the world fulfilled a role and purpose. Nature was not a capricious mistress, governed by divine whimsy and chance. Quite the contrary, it was a massive system of cause and effect, in which everything served a purpose. Adopting the Aristotelian schema of classification, Linneaus sought to rescue nature from the chaos of randomness that had constrained it since the collapse of Rome.

Not until 1758, in the tenth edition of his work *Systema Naturae*, did Linnaeus consider the place of humanity in his grand schema. In linking humanity to primates and bats, Linnaeus established the context of classifying mankind along a hierarchical ranking of value and worth governed by science. Linneaus classified all of humanity along four distinct axes of development – *Homo sapiens europaeus, Homo sapiens asiaticus, Homo sapiens americanus,* and *Homo sapiens afer.* Each name matched the general location and set of physical clines common to the residents thereof. Interestingly Linnaeus took things a step further, linking physical location to the four Galenic humors. Europeans were sanguinary – governed by their blood. As melancholics, Asians were ruled by their black bile – allegedly reflecting their cautious nature. In turn, American Indians were choleric and Africans bilious in temperament.[17]

---

15 Wayne E. Lee, *Barbarians and Brothers: Anglo-American Warfare, 1500–1865* (Oxford University Press, 2010), 225.
16 *Ibid.*, 226–27.
17 Brace, *"Race,"* 26–27.

Equally significant is how Linnaeus' scientific classification helped define the general systemic hierarchy that would govern racial perspectives through the twentieth century. This was not accidental. Following the rules of taxonomy laid out in the Old Testament, which placed man atop all beasts, which in turn were created to serve his needs, Linnaeus set Europeans atop a hierarchy which followed the imagined contours of divine Creation. Not only was European man assigned pride of place on the base of his Christian identity, Linnaeus and other Enlightenment writers viewed applied technology, sophistication of dress and culture, and the conceptualization of individual and collective liberties and rights as evidence of primacy and place in the natural order.[18]

What is Race?

Perhaps the better question is *when* did the concept of "race" take root in Western society. Like all complex questions, there is no single answer – no single "ah-hah!" moment pointing to the start of the system. Several factors come together by the seventeenth and eighteenth centuries to make it easier to accept race as a conceptual system of hierarchical classification. But these factors come together at different points and in different contexts to establish its differing aspects as a point of identity and establishing racial boundaries to social status and power. The advent of such racism, according to historian George Frederickson, drew heavily on the sense of difference it fostered and provided a rationale for abuse of power against other races. He observes in modernity that the "nexus of attitude and action range from official but pervasive social discrimination at one end of the spectrum to genocide at the other."[19] As will be seen in subsequent chapters, this translation of belief into action can be particularly horrific when latent and obvious racism is marshaled to support war efforts or to justify war crimes.

The first serious efforts to conceptualize racial differences within human beings followed the efforts of Enlightenment scientists to identify the source of the physical differences between different peoples and cultures. Beginning in the seventeenth century, a variety of polygenistic explanations are offered by biologists and other scientists. These schemes were predicated on the simple premise that human species all developed from different simultaneous tracks. As newer scientific theories of biological development and diversity appeared, the polygenist method acquired new popularity and a broader scope, reflecting the

---

18 *Ibid.*, 28–30.
19 Frederickson, *Racism*, 9.

desire to further sub-categorize humanity on the basis of ever more specific and complex criteria. Thus, by the appearance of Charles Darwin's theory of natural selection in 1859, humankind was divided into at least two distinct species, with various sub-genuses. The more sophisticated and higher species, the polygenists reasoned, were the various "white" races (European, Asian, Indian, Malays, Amerinds, and Polynesian), while "black" races (African, Papuan, Aboriginal, Hottentot) were perceived as more animalistic and less developed.[20]

The polygenist scheme was more complex than it appears at face value, particularly when placed alongside the traditional monogenist doctrine of race that was more prevalent outside of the scientific community. Accordingly, monogenism is rooted in the premise that all humans were descendants of Adam and Eve. Any physical difference between peoples was the result either of divine intervention or some other moralist consideration. Yet while monogenism was considered the norm through the mid-nineteenth century, the polygenist view became ever more prevalent as individuals sought to contextualize the scope of physical differences between peoples. In short, man was *too* diverse in his appearance and physical characteristics to come from a single biological pair, regardless of the theological implications. Significantly the polygenists gained support *because* of the complexity of their schema; the idea that mankind originated from different biological paths was appealing to many Enlightenment and Romantic Era thinkers *because* it necessitated a complex and impersonal divinity to manage the process.

With polygenism becoming an accepted "fact" by the dawn of the nineteenth century, the scientific argument for race was in place. Yet other considerations were also at stake to imbue race with a social and cultural legitimacy that would help it become entrenched in the Western worldview. The first factor to be considered was the linkage of technology to identity. As the West expanded its global reach in the sixteenth and seventeenth centuries, explorers, soldiers, and other participants were consistently impressed by what they perceived as a tremendous gap between themselves and the people they encountered. From the start of exploration, Europeans sought out equals with whom to treat and trade. Yet in case after case in the Americas, and then later in Africa and the Pacific, European explorers and traders were disappointed to encounter indigenous peoples scraping a bare subsistence in a lush environment of plenty. Add to this the absence of evidence of complex architecture, engineering, and law; explorers came to the New World seeking Princes, and found savages. Making matters worse was the amoral behavior – by European standards – of the local people. Beginning

---

20 Brace, *Race*, 40–41.

with small scale evidence of cannibalism and sacrifice among Caribs and Arowak tribes, this escalated to include the wholesale ritualistic bloodlettings in Tenochtitlan, and only stoked the perception that "they" *couldn't* be like us. After asserting hegemony in the New World, Europeans brought their growing sense of technology as a mark of cultural sophistication and physical advancement with them to other Old World encounters in Africa, the Middle East, and Asia. By 1800, technology represented something much more than the advantage accrued from a system of applied engineering. It had become suffused with a moralist aspect, evidence of the innate superiority of Europeans over those cultures which were less fortunate. Might therefore made right.[21]

A second consideration was tied to the exploitation of individual and collective identity to facilitate the production and acquisition of capital. In short, the division of labor between white Europeans and non-whites in the New World and later Imperial settings depended upon racial hierarchy. After his second voyage to the New World, Christopher Columbus was appointed governor of Hispaniola. From the onset of his regime, slavery was central to European control and exploitation of the island. The first slaves were captive Taiho and Carib Indians, a status guaranteed by their alien cultural practices – such as ancestor worship, animism, and ritual cannibalism – as well as their physical difference. The pool of native labor was soon exhausted, however, by the toll of new epidemic diseases introduced by the Spanish. A new source of labor was needed, and the void was soon filled by Portuguese slave traders. Practicing since the mid-fifteenth century along the West Coast of Africa, the traders were soon in great demand. Unlike the Indians, Africans were less affected by the mortal ravages of smallpox and other diseases. By the mid-1500s, sugar processing replaced mining as the chief industry of the Spanish Caribbean. African labor was ideal for the industry, as shown by the extent to which Africans were imported as slave into the New World. Forty-one percent of all slaves imported to the New World by 1700 were imported to Portuguese Brazil, while another forty-seven percent were introduced to British, French, and Spanish colonies in the Caribbean. Most estimates indicate that for every white colonist who came to the New World between 1519 and 1820, between 2.5 to four Africans arrived as slaves.[22]

---

21 See Michael Adas, *Machines as the Measure of Men: Science, Technology, and Ideologies of Western Dominance* (Rutgers University Press, 1990); and Daniel R. Headrick, *The Tools of Empire: Technology and European Imperialism in the Nineteenth Century* (Oxford University Press, 1981).

22 David Ellis, *The Rise of African Slavery in the Americas* (Cambridge University Press, 2000), 9, 11–12; The Gilder Lehrman Institute of American History. "History Now: Historical Context: Facts

African slavery was present in English colonies almost from the beginning of settlement. In 1619, a Dutch privateer pulled into Jamestown with a cargo of Africans captured from a Spanish ship in the Caribbean. The captain sold the English twenty Africans in exchange for enough food and water for their journey home. Yet at the start the English were reluctant to embrace total slavery, as the first group of slaves and many that followed through the turn of the century were sold as indentured servants. The transition from the indenture system to a system of race-based slavery would take place over the course of the seventeenth century. Initially, Africans who satisfied their indentures could own and manage property in Virginia and other colonies, yet gradually colonial courts began revoking this land, claiming that because their owners were "negroes, and thus alien" could not own land. Meanwhile, laws were passed elsewhere, first in Massachusetts in 1641, then in the other colonies, that legalized slavery. In 1662, Virginia introduced a law establishing the descendants of a slave born in the New World were likewise slaves, and followed up in 1705 with another law stating "All servants imported and brought in this Country ... who were not Christians in their Native Country ... shall be slaves. A Negro, mulatto and Indian slaves ... shall be held as real estate."[23] This brief timeline shows the gradual process by which the subjugation of a people for the purpose of exploitive labor on the sole basis of their physical difference – increasingly identified as a racial difference as new concepts of racial categorization appear. Once introduced into the Western consciousness, the scientific concept of race as a schema of classifying humanity based upon positive and negative values was very quickly adopted as a means to order society into a hierarchy of privilege and exploitation.

There were other contexts by which to view race, however, outside of the exchange of labor. One concept introduced by American philosopher Samuel Stanhope Smith combined the divine origins of monogenism with an environmental determinist outlook on racial variation. Not only were different human races descended from a single source, the traits separating them could readily disappear as they lived in close proximity to each other in the same environment. This concept of reversible racial difference would fall out of favor by the nineteenth century, however, as the Romantic ideal of Nature and emotion triumphed over the Reason of the Enlightenment.[24] Across Europe and the young United States, a new focus on natural truths transcending the limits of reason also transformed

---

about the Slave Trade and Slavery," https://www.gilderlehrman.org/content/historical-context-facts-about-slave-trade-and-slavery (Accessed February 5, 2018).
23 Robert S. Cope, *Carry Me Back: Slavery and Servitude in Seventeenth Century Virginia* (Pikeville College Press of the Appalachian Studies Center, 1973), 14.
24 Brace, *"Race,"* 52–53.

the meaning of race. For the first time, the scientific theories of difference at the heart of race were charged with the emotive power of ideology, giving rise to a new way of thought. Thus racialism – the premise that humanity is subject to a natural division of racial archetypes – begins to give way to "racism" – the imposition of a social and moral hierarchy of value and legitimacy based upon racial characteristics. Coming chapters will consider how race further evolved in the nineteenth century as a tool to legitimize white dominance over other non-white cultures and peoples via slavery, imperialism, and other schemes. More tellingly we will examine how specific case studies reveal a growing anxiety among whites as the boundaries of encounter between the races come ever closer to the Euro-American homeland.

What is Gender?

In recent decades, the word "gender" has often been substituted for sex, as in male or female genders. The study of gender history deals with social or psychological distinctions between masculinity and femininity as well as the political, economic, legal, religious, and behavioral ramifications of those gender-specific differences over time. Throughout most of human history, it was understood that men should occupy public, political, and military spheres in society. They should be fathers, husbands, providers, and protectors of the women. Men often exercised absolute authority over those women in their families and in larger social groups. Scholars have employed the terms *patriarchy* or *paternalism* to describe this control by males over females, children, and other dependents. Women, on the contrary, were expected to remain in the private, familial, domestic, and sometimes moral spheres. Accordingly they were expected to be mothers, wives, and nurtures.

These trends notwithstanding, gender has not necessarily followed linear or progressive paths over the centuries in Europe and the United States. Constructions of gender have been in constant negotiation among competing groups because of factors such as society, culture, morality, politics, economics, industry, environment, ideology, religion, and warfare. Assumptions regarding gendered emotional, intellectual, and biological traits also played significant roles. These factors and assumptions can reinforce one other or discount one another as changes occur in society or culture might affect or be affected by changes in economics or industry. For example, cultural values and legal statutes often restricted women to particular activities or stations in life as in the practices of adolescent female foot-binding in China, ritual widow immolation in certain castes in India, and the exclusion of women from leadership roles and political processes in Christianity, Christianity, Judaism, and Islam. All these examples point to the devalued, marginalized, or controlled status of women in which they lacked legal, familial, religious, or political standing.

In an example relevant to this book, the peacetime prescription against female combatants may or may not be overturned in wartime because of military necessity. In the twenty-first century in the United States, for example, distinctions between men and women can be seen in gender restrictions on their respective military service. (It is worth noting that similar restrictions and limitations on women relative to men can be found in the civilian world in the workplace.) Only recently have women been granted access into ground combat specializations, and they continue to remain exempt from selective service registration. Such integration that has occurred has followed a lengthy public debate over several long-standing gendered presumptions. Assertions about upper-body weakness or menstrual cycles, for example, have been used as justifications for excluding women from military service and physical labor in general. Likewise worries loomed about extraordinary sexual and physical abuse of female prisoners of war.[25] Several chapters on gender in this book contextualize and debunk many such assertions and worries about women's supposed inferior soldiering capabilities. At the very least, those detractors' arguments will be shown to be driven as much by biases as by facts. These biases reveal much about culture, the men in authority, and notions about masculinity and femininity.

Historically, open gender integration in combat roles has occurred as contingency or culture has permitted. In cases like the Soviet Union, Israel, and in North Vietnam, women broke through barriers and serve in occupations and units usually reserved for men. Elsewhere in less-developed social settings or during periods of upheaval, women experienced more equity with men and enjoyed greater opportunities to contribute in more diverse ways. Women on the American frontier took on greater familial responsibilities as wife and mother relative to the man as husband and father. Frontier women needed to perform their traditional feminine roles as well as help in the more masculine tasks of tending crops and livestock or repelling Native American attacks. British women on the colonial frontier in India crossed similar gender lines by learning to use firearms and participating in diplomatic and political arenas, neither activity of

---

25 See Presidential Commission on the Assignment of Women in the Armed Forces, *Women in Combat: Report to the President, November 15, 1992* (Brassey's, 1993); "Women at Arms: G.I. Jane Breaks the Combat Barrier. *The New York Times*, August 16, 2009, http://www.nytimes.com/2009/08/16/us/16women.html?_r=1 (Accessed February 5, 2018); and Mady Wechsler Segal, "Women's Military Roles Cross-Nationally: Past, Present, and Future," *Gender and Society* 9:6 (1995): 757–75.

which could have been achieved in the home country. Herein can be seen gender bending to ensure family survival when the husbands and fathers and men of the family could not guarantee their safety. This circumstance lasted only so long as dangerous threats existed or as colonial relations persisted. Once these ended, however, those women too often were forced to return to their accepted gender roles as wives and mothers, despite their real and perceived advances.[26] Herein one can see gender on the "frontier" as a process. The same logic could be applied to warfare. Wars provided liminal spaces and periods of gender flux in which the barriers could be broken and later might be repaired during the post-war peace.

Distinctions between the genders have also been established because of commonly-held assumptions about psychological attributes, intellectual capabilities, biological functions, and sexual proclivities of men and women. In the Athens of Aristotle, for example, men were seen as worthy of participating in public debates, running for government office, and serving in phalanxes, all duties of male citizens. Conversely, Athenian women were relegated to the private sphere, valued as little better than child bearers and viewed as irrational beings.[27]

Masculine roles and activities tended to be more valued when contrasted with feminine roles and activities. The overwhelming majority of available historical evidence focuses almost entirely on works written by and for elite men, which in turn left women as well as lower-class men with lesser or no voices. Different roles and activities entailed implicit or explicit value judgments and attendant hierarchical distributions of power, prestige, or resources. Although Plato did not devalue women like Aristotle and most Greeks, he did devalue men of average or lower mental capacities. Plato believed that only the philosophers possessed the wisdom to rule. All other men were relegated to servile status in an authoritarian meritocracy, and were thus ignored.

These biological and cultural assumptions about gender and their derivative justifications for gendered distinctions have been remarkably similar to those of racial and ethnic stereotypes. Early nineteenth century descriptions of African-American slaves as docile, unintelligent, obsequious, and childlike could likewise be applied to Caucasian women in the United States. Of course, depending

---

26 See Glenda Riley, *Frontierswomen: The Iowa Experience* (Iowa State University Press, 1981); and Mary Procida, *Married to the Empire: Gender, Politics and Imperialism in India, 1883–1947* (Palgrave, 2002).

27 Kirk Ormand, *Controlling Desires: Sexuality in Ancient Greece and Rome* (Praeger, 2008); Jennifer Larson, *Greek and Roman Sexualities: A Sourcebook* (Bloomsbury, 2012); and Thomas Van Norwick, *Imagining Men: Ideals of Masculinity in Ancient Greek Culture* (Praeger, 2008).

of class and station in life, other adjectives for women, such as emotional, frivolous, and weak, could be added to this list of demeaning descriptors.

Although gender inequality existed throughout human history, significant change in the established normative gender roles and opportunities for women have occurred during the last two centuries in the United States and Western Europe. Women gained greater equity with men because some individuals overturned preconceptions about the cultural and biological differences between the genders. These actors tended to be middle or upper class in background and thus enjoyed more leisure time than those toiling in fields or factories. This progress has been slow, uneven, contentious, and often painful. Other men and women, however, opposed these challenges because they undermined traditional mores. Their opposition believed that changes in the established gender roles could potentially upset the entire social fabric, ranging from familial relations to political elections and economic standings. Because so many of these also hailed from the middle or upper classes, they wanted maintain status in their own families, as well as their control over all classes society. Fear of loss of power and position were as much motivators for opposition to gender equality as anything else.

Such anxieties took shape in social upheavals and military conflicts that helped drive the societal changes that included a gradual evolution toward gender equality. The French Revolution and the World Wars heralded new political structures, economic systems, and gender constructions. Among other factors, these paradigm-shifting conflicts fed off the energy of *nationalism*. Not unlike a virus or pseudo-religious belief, nationalism can infect people with patriotic fervor and arouse them to incredible levels of self-sacrifice and service to their nation-states. This ideology achieved its greatest influence beginning in the French Revolution and Napoleonic Wars.[28] Nationalism can also employ tropes of gender (and racial) difference to maximize identity and increase allegiance to the nation-state. Nationalism can cross gender barriers as well as class, racial, religious, and regional barriers to unite people. It can also employ tropes of gender (and race) to increase identity and allegiance to the nation-state. Nationalism's power reaches its zenith in times of perceived or real need during an enemy invasion, which, as will be seen in several chapters, can transform gender (and race) roles and relations.

---

28 See Joan B. Landes, "Republican Citizenship and Heterosocial Desire: Concepts of Masculinity in Revolutionary France," in *Masculinities in Politics and War: Gendering Modern History*, ed. Stefan Dudink et al. (Manchester University Press, 2004), 96–115; Robert Nye, *Masculinity and Male Codes of Honor in Modern France* (University of California Press, 1998); and John A. Lynn, *Bayonets of the Republic: Motivation and Tactics in the Army of Revolutionary France, 1791–1794* (Westview, 1996).

No less dramatic than the French Revolution and the World Wars was the Industrial Revolution in the nineteenth century. It served as another catalyst for transformations of gender roles, family relations, and social and political structures – as well as the eventually as a primary catalyst for global warfare in the twentieth century.[29] New machinery and technology reduced the centrality of physical strength in labor processes, and simultaneously more and more people moved from agricultural-based jobs in rural areas to industrial-based jobs in urban areas. The urban living and working environments caused permanent changes in the ways people viewed themselves and their worlds. These transformations shook the long-standing cultural hegemony enjoyed by middle-and upper-class Europeans who gradually lost their control of gender relations and roles.

Gender Historiography

For centuries the practice and subject of historical writing was primarily concerned with the affairs of men of high economic, political, and social status. Conversely, the history of women as a distinct social group emerged haltingly in the nineteenth and early twentieth centuries in what has been called the "first wave" of women's history. Many of these studies were hagiographic and ethnographic in nature, primarily dedicated to identifying great women in history. Some historians, such as Mary Beard in her 1946 book titled *Women as Force in History*, attempted to analyze the roles of women relative to those of men. In so doing, Beard asserted that women had also always made active and important, albeit often ignored and subordinated, contributions in society.[30]

Militating these ground-breaking, revisionist interpretations writing women into the past were stubbornly-held traditionalist social norms in the United States and Europe. Allegiance to the male-dominated family and nation-state during the first half of the twentieth century reflected in the dominant historiographical paradigm that still focused on great men in history. Exceptionalist narratives by Frederick Jackson Turner in 1890s up through Samuel Flagg Bemis in the 1950s, for example, consistently ignored women as historical actors.[31]

---

29 See John Horne, "Masculinity in Politics and War in the Age of the Nation-States and the World Wars, 1850–1945," in *Masculinities in Politics and War: Gendering Modern History*, ed. Stefan Dudink et al. (Manchester University Press, 2004), 41–59.

30 Mary Beard, *Women as Force in History: A Study of Traditions and Realities* (Persea Books, 1946).

31 Glenda Riley, "Frederick Jackson Turner Forgot the Ladies," *Journal of the Early Republic* 2 (Summer 1993): 216–30.

Meanwhile, some social critics contested these traditional gender roles and family structures. They found roles as housewives and homemakers to be stifling because these offered little fulfillment and few chances for personal development or empowerment. In her 1949 book *The Second Sex*, French feminist Simone de Beauvoir urged women to break away from the traditional gender paradigm which relegated them to inferiority. Ending this paradigm required that women be willing to eschew their roles of wives and mothers for more independent roles in families, politics, society, and commerce. Such new constructions of gender would, according to de Beauvoir, benefit not only women but also men because both would be liberated from restrictions set by traditional gender paradigms.[32] Writing fourteen years later in *The Feminine Mystique* in 1963, American feminist Betty Friedan labeled the traditional construction of gender as the "problem that has no name."[33] In ongoing inequity that included race, the post-Second World War years did not bring to fruition the hopes of equality among blacks or other racial and ethnic minorities. They received little respect or help from the white establishment, despite their storied records and great sacrifices during the Second World War. In the post-war decades, some American women, African Americans and minorities grew restive or militant because they wanted to enjoy more equally the privileges and protections of full-fledged citizenship.[34]

Ideas of Friedan, du Beauvoir, and others filtered into the "second wave" or feminist wave of women's history emerging in tandem with "new social history" in the 1960 and 1970s. Both interpretative lenses were influenced by the women's rights movement, the Civil Rights movement, and the anti-war movement. The scholars, some also activists, saw many forms of inequality, exploitation, and manipulation in American society; and they sought redress to these problems by empowering underrepresented, exploited, or ignored groups. Their studies highlighted the inherent historical value of women as byproducts of their interpretation. Like scholars studying social history, women's historians focused on everyday experiences and on struggles of women.[35] To these could be also added influences of race, region, religion, and other socially or culturally defined distinctions that created multiple economic, social, and political hierarchies.

---

32 Simon de Beauvoir, *The Second Sex*, trans. H. M. Parshley (1949; Knopf, 1953). See also Gisela Bock, *Women in European History*, trans. Allison Brown (Blackwell, 2002), 233–55.

33 Betty Friedan, *The Feminine Mystique* (Norton, 1963), 15.

34 For the standard histories of women and African Americans in the post-war United States, see Elaine Tyler May, *Homeward Bound: American Families in the Cold War Era* (Basic Books, 1988); and Harvard Sitkoff, *The Struggle for Black Equality*, 1845–1980 (Hill and Wang, 1981).

35 For an ground-breaking article, see Gerda Lerner, "The Lady and the Mill Girl: Changes in the Status of Women in the Age of Jackson," *American Studies* 10 (Spring 1969): 5–15.

Writing in 1997, historian Linda Gordon explained the influence of feminist ideology at length:

> Women's historians usually approach their scholarship from a feminist perspective. The definition of "feminism" is contested and has changed throughout the history of the women's rights movement. I use it here, in its most inclusive and historical sense, to mean those who disapprove of women's subordinate status, who believe that women's disadvantaged position is not inevitable and can be changed, and who doubt the 'objectivity' in history as it has been previously written in a male-dominated culture. But just as the women's movement is composed of different tendencies, so has women's history become a field of debate as well as consensus. There are many "feminisms." The common denominator among women's historians is the insistence that gender must be an important category of analysis. Women's historians do not expect to agree or always to produce the answers expected by feminist political activists. They do, however, insist that scholarship take into account the different situations of men and women, and they criticize scholarship that draws its evidence exclusively from male sources and then interprets that evidence as representing the entire society.[36]

By the 1980s, historians of women branched out from the feminist waves into what could be called *gender* history. While this approach maintained women possessed historical value, its practitioners also added men and masculinity into their analyses. They showed that understanding feminine roles, activities, and perspectives of the past necessitated understanding masculine roles, activities, and perspectives. Gender historians have concentrated on the intertwined social and cultural underpinnings, manifestations, and ramifications of both genders, masculine and feminine.

Appearing in 1986, Joan Wallach Scott's groundbreaking article "Gender: A Useful Category of Analysis" stands as a prime example of gender history. Although most of her article discusses women in history, she does not treat women and men in separate historical vacuums. She draws on earlier waves of women's history, yet she moved beyond those to deal with literal and figurative symbols and language for women as well as men. Scott does not succumb to misandry like some feminist historians who blame men, masculinity, and male-dominant paradigm for so many problems, but she does not shy away from criticizing men and their oppressive behavior when warranted. Scott's article is so important because it treats constructions of masculinity and femininity as foils for each other, yet also points to similarities between the genders.[37] In years since it appeared, several historians have followed Scott's model in men's history and

---

36 Linda Gordon, "U.S. Women's History," in *The New American History*, rev. ed, ed. Eric Foner (Temple University Press, 1997), 259–60.
37 Scott, "Gender," 1053–75.

the history of masculinity. These scholars have utilized the methods of gender history to better interpret masculinity as a cultural construction.[38]

Scott's article is still more relevant when applied to the field of military history. Too often non-military historians ignore or give short-shrift to wars in their writings and classes. They fail to understand that wars affect the societies that fight them, just as much as societies can affect the ways war are fought.[39] Conversely, Scott stakes a critical point of departure for gender studies to be extended into war studies, when she writes that:

> The subject of war, diplomacy, and high politics frequently comes up when traditional political historians question the utility of gender in their work. But here, too, we need to look beyond the actors and the literal import of their words. The legitimizing of war – of expending young lives to protect the state – have variously taken the forms of explicit appeals to manhood (to the need to defend otherwise vulnerable women and children), of implicit reliance on belief in the duty of sons to serve their leaders of their (father the) king, or of associations between masculinity and national strength.[40]

This call for greater application of gender analysis of men in "war, diplomacy, and high politics" represents an incredibly rich area of inquiry. Such explorations can be seen implicitly or explicitly in works by scholars of warfare like Peter Karsten, John Lynn, Robert Nye, Mady Segal, Craig Cameron, and Joshua Goldstein. These authors knowingly or unknowingly have followed Scott's lead. The history of wars and the people who fought them represents the ultimate crucible to study masculinity, femininity, and sexuality.[41]

---

38 Peter Stearns, *Be a Man: Males in Modern Society* (Homes and Meier, 1990); E. Anthony Rotundo, *American Manhood: Transformations in Masculinity from the Revolution to the Modern Era* (Basic Books, 1993); Robert Griswold, *Fatherhood in America: A History* (Basic Books, 1994); George L. Mosse, *The Image of Man: The Creation of Modern Masculinity* (Oxford University Press, 1996); and Gail Bederman, *Manliness and Civilization: A Cultural History of Race and Gender in the United States, 1880–1917* (University of Chicago Press, 1997).

39 In Eric Foner's revised *The New American History* appearing in 1997, none of the sixteen chronological or thematic chapters dealt with military history as a distinct historical field, nor was there a separate chapter on military history. This book was published under the auspices of the American Historical Association and can be understand as a measurement of the state of history as scholarly field.

40 Scott, "Gender," 1073.

41 Peter Karsten, "Introduction," *The Military in America: From the Colonial Era to the Present*, rev. ed., ed. Peter Karsten (Free Press, 1986), 1–3, 18; John A. Lynn, "The Embattled Future of Military History," *Journal of Military History* 61 (October 1997): 777–89; Craig M. Cameron, *American Samurai: Myth, Imagination, and the Conduct of Battle in the First Marine Division, 1941–1951* (Cambridge University Press, 1994); Robert A. Nye, "Western Masculinities in War and Peace," *American Historical Review* 112 (April 2007): 417–38; Segal, "Women's Military Roles Cross-Nationally," 757–75; and Goldstein, *War and Gender*.

2 Race and Gender in the Nineteenth Century

Introduction

Historically the nineteenth century offers a long period of relative cultural normalcy divided by short episodes of intense change that inform the careful development of a specific racial and gender consciousness on the eve of the modern in the early twentieth century. European global imperial hegemony was fueled as much by racial ideology and the alleged prerogatives of white manliness as economic expansion, strategic politics, and military technology. In the wake of imperial expansion, entire societies in Africa, the Indian Subcontinent, Southeast Asia, and China were brought to heel beneath an ideological precept that devalued non-whites as mere chattel for sustaining European metropoles. Indigenous women living the periphery found themselves marginalized in two hierarchies: as non-white women, they suffered racial discrimination similar to men in their nations, groups, or tribes; and as females in their indigenous communities, they also experienced the gender-based discriminations.

In the Western Hemisphere, the epicenter of change was the young United States. Vibrant and expansionist, America's nineteenth century was an era fueled by both consensus and disagreement over racial doctrines and practices. Signal moments like the abolition of slavery and the acquisition, settlement, and exploitation of new territories were charged with racial conflict and disharmony. Race became the central idea of the American Republic, dictating the status of new arrivals from Europe in a carefully delineated hierarchy of status and power, justifying the mistreatment and exploitation of Native Americans and African Americans, while also dictating the exclusion of Asians as a "threat" to the nation's white majority. Likewise, economic and industrial expansion exposed the fragility of American white male male identity, fostering an escalating sense of anxiety over the meaning of maleness in the industrial era. By the end of the century, modernity became a catchphrase not only for material prosperity and style, but for the corrosive degeneration of maleness as well. The expanding influence of women – especially those from the middle class – in public life only fueled these anxieties, creating further cultural disjuncture. This forms the backdrop against which we examine war and military institutions in the nineteenth century.

https://doi.org/10.1515/9783110477467-002

Gender and War before 1865

Before considering how gender informs an understanding of the past, the prevailing worldviews regarding gender relations in the specific period and place under examination must be defined. This process generally entails adopting a theoretical framework as the lens through which to assess the values of past communities. Consider, for example, the influence of *spheres theory* on the formation of gender roles and identity. First described by Aristotle in reference to the public and private elements of Greek society (*polis* versus *oikos*), the concept of distinct yet symbiotic social spheres of activity, influence, and deference assigned to the genders continues to evolve in the Enlightenment and Industrial Revolution. Alexis DeTocqueville commented at length on the social isolation of American women after marriage, describing how "the inexorable opinion of the public carefully circumscribes woman within the narrow circle of domestic interests and duties and forbids her to step beyond it."[1] The concept further developed by German social theorist Jurgen Habermas in his influential work, *The Structural Transformation of the Public Sphere*. Accordingly the idea of social spheres represents areas where individuals exercise behavior and create identity within a group context. At its most basic level, Habermas describes the intersection of the *Private* and *Public Spheres*. The private sphere encompasses the social space where individuals negotiate and interact to their most immediate benefit – in short, the needs of the individual and the family. Alternatively the public sphere represents the area where individuals speak, work, and interact to the advantage of the community – the educational, political, business, and legal arenas. Habermas further proposes that sphere theory can be used to map out the contours of power hierarchies between different groups on the basis of class, ethnicity, gender, and other categories of differentiation.[2]

This model is particularly useful when applied to pre-twentieth century gender relations. Both men and women existed within the public and private spheres; however, for the most part the roles and opportunities for women to act

---

1 Alexis de Tocqueville, *Democracy in America*, Book Three, Chapter Ten., trans. Henry Reeve (Reprint; Barnes & Noble, 2003), 574. See also Carol Berkin, *First Generations: Women in Colonial America* (Hill and Wang, 1997), 11–14, 62–64; Kathleen M. Brown, *Good Wives, Nasty Wenches, and Anxious Patriarchs: Gender, Race, and Power in Colonial Virginia* (Omohundro Institute of Early American History and Culture and the University of North Carolina Press, 1996), 3–4, 13–15, 24–27; Mary Beth Norton, *Separated By Their Sex: Women in Public and Private in the Colonial Atlantic World* (Cornell University Press, 2011); and Laurel Thatcher Ulrich, *Good Wives: Image and Reality in the Lives of Women in Northern New England* (Vintage, 1991), 8–11.
2 Jurgen Habermas, *The Structural Transformation of the Public Sphere: An Inquiry into a Category of Bourgeois Society* (MIT Press, 1991).

in both public and private society were dictated and defined by men. Over centuries, a number of cultural ideologies were constructed to support and foster a male-centric social framework in which men, on the exclusive basis of their sex, were endowed with certain gender-identity advantages over the allegedly weaker feminine sex. In time, gender historians would identify some of the most prominent (and pernicious) concepts as being part of the so-called *Cult of Domesticity*, or *Cult of True Womanhood* for women and an attendant *Cult of the Nationalist Male* for men.

In essence a social construction imposing limits upon the legitimate behavior, aspirations, and virtues of women in the face of the cultural changes wrought by industrialization and commercialization, the Cult of Domesticity was firmly established in cultural artifacts – writing, music, art, etc. – consumed by an ever more influential middle class. Ultimately the Cult of Domesticity influenced how nineteenth century middle-class society perceived women as exclusive members of the private sphere. Women were discouraged from entering higher education, for example, as the study of advanced disciplines was considered an overtaxing endeavor. Women were also discouraged from business as the handling of money was considered at its base a masculine task. Though given the general responsibility of handling money for domestic purposes, running a business was certainly considered out of the question for the proper woman. Similarly, women were discouraged from seeking release from the daily routine of housework in activities that may prove too strenuous in nature. Music halls were dangerous, since there they ran the risk of coming into contact with "fallen women." Strenuous exercise – like bicycle riding – was risky as well, since the activity might excite the passions. Instead women were increasingly directed toward light social activities – church affairs, home music recitals, etc. Finally, women were actively discouraged from taking on any save the most grass-roots political activism. Voting, political action, office-seeking, etc., were all considered outside the realm of the female public sphere, and were hence essentially masculine in nature.

Women who challenged the Cult of Domesticity generally faced two outcomes: social ostracism and the medicalization of their own identity. In the first case, women who vocally and directly confronted the limits of their public sphere by agitating for social change were ridiculed, arrested and generally shunned by male society. For example, Women's Christian Temperance Union activist Carrie Nation became a subject of regular lampooning in the press as a dangerously unbalanced and violent agitator. Susan B. Anthony, co-founder with Elizabeth Cady Stanton of the American Equal Rights Association, Equal Rights Association, was repeatedly arrested through the 1870s and 1880s on charges ranging from disturbing the peace, violating voting laws, and other offenses. National Birth Control League founder Margaret Sanger was forced to leave the United

States following her conviction on obscenity charges related to mailing family planning information. Another case was that of suffrage activist Alice Paul, who was regularly assaulted, spit on, and shouted at by male passersby during her six-month picket of the White House in 1917. These cases and many others indicate the extent to which Western male society viewed eroding the precepts of the Cult of Domesticity as a threat to their own gender identity and its prerogatives in the nineteenth and early twentieth centuries.[3]

More common however was the organized effort to define female activism as symptomatic of a deeper medical condition. By casting women's actions in the context of a medical disorder, it was possible to redefine their very access to the world outside of the private sphere. Key to this was the constructed diagnosis of *Hysteria*. At its root, the condition was used to identify female mental and emotional states. First coined by Hippocrates, in the nineteenth century hysteria was used as the foundation of a new medical condition, used frequently to describe women who acted outside their legitimate sphere. Victims of the diagnostic labeling were subject to frequent hospitalization, water and manual manipulations, dietary treatment, pharmacological treatment, primitive psychoanalysis, and in the most extreme cases, surgical interventions including hysterectomies, trephinations, and lobotomies. According to American physician Silas Weir Mitchell, one of the chief advocates of female hysteria,

> Today, the American woman is, to speak plainly, too often physically unfit for her duties as woman, and is perhaps of all civilized females the least qualified to undertake those weightier tasks which tax so heavily the nervous system of man. She is not fairly up to what nature asks from her as wife and mother. How will she sustain herself under the pressure of those yet more exacting duties which nowadays she is eager to share with the man.[4]

Women were not the sole target of a medicalized gender identity. In addition to diagnosing female hysteria, Mitchell also appropriated hysteria to define male depression and nervous breakdowns. He coined the term *neurasthenia* as a male-centric term to explain these problems among his male patients, who experienced a value-assessment on the basis of their diagnostic association with hysteria, a gender-charged term at this point, indicating the subject suffered from a female-like ailment. Curiously however, unlike hysteria, which was considered

---

3 Starting points for examining women in the context of gender relations include: Bonnie S. Anderson and Judith P. Zinsser, *A History of Their Own: Women in Europe from Prehistory to the Present*, rev. ed. (Oxford University Press, 1999); and Merry Wiesner-Hanks, *Gender in History: Global Perspectives* (Wiley-Blackwell, 2010).
4 Silas Weir Mitchell, "Wear and Tear, or Hints for the Overworked," in *Short Works of Silas Weir Mitchell* (BiblioBazaar, 2008), 40.

essential to the female identity, neurasthenia was portrayed as a physiological condition, related specifically to the "wearing out of the nerves" attendant to the accelerating pace of modern life, which produced a hysteria-like reaction in men. Rest, an iron-rich diet, and strenuous exercise were offered as essential remedies for the neurasthenic, less they experience greater stress and the potential of a life-altering gender identity inversion.

The nineteenth century rise of nationalism as a dominant ideology transcending class also translated into a significant marker affecting gender identity. If one considers nationalism as a concept that facilitated the diffusion of political power from the upper to the middle class, it stands to reason that gender mores and behaviors were similarly transformed. Such is the case made by cultural historian George Mosse, who considers the nineteenth century rise of nationalism as a signal marking the rejection of the libertinage and other moral excesses of the Enlightenment aristocracy. Following the example of the French Revolution, the Romantics movement emphasized the Nation as a surrogate lover for European middle-class males. The state was imbued with all the virtuous characteristics of the feminine ideal; prompting a reconsideration of male conduct. As politics became the primary obligation of the enfranchised man, respectability was the paramount expression of middle-class maleness. In essence the new political man shared his attentions with two lovers; one the filial helpmate residing at home; the other the maternal/maidenly construction that was the new nation-state. Respectability, Mosse offers, was the primary defining characteristic of the Western middle-class male in the public sphere, and which was considered the primary virtue that set him apart from the debauched upper class and the degenerate worker. As Mosse explains:

> Nationalism is perhaps the most powerful and effective ideology of modern times, and its alliance with bourgeois morality forged an engine difficult to stop. ... It reached out to liberalism, conservatism, and socialism; it advocated both tolerance and repression, peace and war – whatever served its purpose. Through its claim to immutability, it endowed all that it touched with a "slice of eternity." But however flexible, nationalism hardly wavered in its advocacy of respectability.[5]

The flip side of Respectability was moral deviance. Just as bourgeois stability was perceived as a virtuous signifier of prosperity and political legitimacy, gendered conduct outside of the mainstream was seen as a sign of moral degeneration. The open expression of active sexuality, masturbation, the pursuit of multiple partners, homosexuality, and other behaviors were all taken as proof of an

---

5 Mosse, *Nationalism and Sexuality*, 9.

abnormality that rendered the individual unfit for polite society. Such persons became social and political outriders, pariahs who represented how the lack of personal control rendered individuals unfit in the moral judgment necessary for exercising political power. Victims of their own base lusts, they were to be shunned, lest their conduct infect others in society.

Women as a whole were also considered both victims and agents of their own corruption in the Respectability schema. Condemned as shallow, frivolous, and immature, women were as a rule considered disqualified from exercising a public political voice. Left on her own, the unrestrained female would distract the Respectable male from his obligation to the state, contributing the decay of both. Thus Respectability demanded female submission to the control of the confident and strong male.

Here the Cult of Domesticity served a dual purpose; as a pathway to an idealized perfect femininity of of submissive purity in the home, it also signaled a new, symbolic – albeit passive – role for women. In the new Nationalism of the nineteenth century, women took their place as the iconic representation of the state: moral, virtuous, strong, and nurturing – all elements of the "Respectable Nation." Likewise, the domesticated middle-class woman provided the moral backbone for their menfolk engaged in the serious public work of government and commerce. Though deprived of true independent power, they became the figurative head of the domestic sphere, standing as guardians of the hearth, serving in their own way the needs of the state.

If the Cult of Respectability empowered the middle-class Nation-State, and further validated the separation of genders in public and private, how did it affect the most public expression of masculine identity, military service? For the first time in history, war was valued in both a pragmatic light and as a moral signifier of gender. The perverse logic of eugenicism dictated that left alone, communities risked becoming overwhelmed with the degenerate offspring of morally and physically corrupted families. Alcoholism, venereal disease, drug abuse, miscegenation, and incest were all presumed vices of the lower classes. In the absence of some mechanism to cull the weaker offspring, social scientists and eugenicists feared they would continue to breed and given time, cause the overall degeneration of the national community. War, however, provided the means not only to implement state policies for the betterment of all citizens, but it also supplied a safety valve for preventing the degeneration of the community. Some sons of the upper- and middle classes would die; such was the tragic cost of war. But the greater number of losses would occur among the debased poor, saving the national community from its inevitable fate. Such an outlook is obviously warped; the prospect of war as an exercise in racial Darwinism, "cleansing" the racial community by force of arms. Yet it was an outlook shared across borders, from the United States across the Atlantic to Great Britain, across the Continent to the Russian Empire. By the close of the nineteenth century, this outlook of war as a regenerative force began to lose some of its appeal; yet it remained influential enough to help justify the opening of the First World War a generation later.[6]

And yet war also offered an opportunity for moral regeneration among the survivors, especially those in the middle class. As the nineteenth century progressed, fears mounted throughout the West of the transformative effects of modernization and industrialization. Young men, particularly those coming of age in the second half of the century, occupied a world in which the daily pressures of a wage-based existence combined with the hectic pace of urban life to corrode the core of their masculinity. Even if the individual remained temperate in his pursuits, he ran the risk of "running down" over time, of falling into a degenerative state that if not remedied could affect the physical strength of future offspring and again place the long term eugenic health of the nation into risk. War – or at least, military service – was considered a remedy for this neurasthenic decay. For a middle class given to sedentary ways, military service offered a revalidation of the individual's maleness. And war – though a very rare experience in *fin de siècle* Europe and America – was held to be a natural tonic for the nation's youth. As George Mosse summed up in *Nationalism and Sexuality*, "War was an invitation to manliness... a test of courage, maturity, and prowess that posed the question, 'Are you really a man?'"[7] For a generation raised on accounts of their parents' and grandparents' martial glory, war became the elusive object of their desire, the one rite of passage that wealth and prosperity could not provide.

Women in Arms: Gender Inversion and Martial Identity

What then of women bearing arms? Over the last twenty years gender and women's historiography has shown greater interest in identifying cases of martial women – cross-dressing females who bore arms and adopted a male identity in order to serve alongside men. The trend was hardly new; accounts of women donning men's clothing to fight go back at least to the iconic tale of Jean d'Arc. In his own study of the early modern European army, military historian John Lynn notes how, while rare in numbers, actual cases of female transvestite soldiers fighting alongside men were seen in as representative of the larger contest

---

6 See Richard Hofstadter, *Social Darwinism in American Thought* (University of Pennsylvania Press, 1944); and Thomas C. Leonard, *Illiberal Reformers: Race, Eugenics, and American Economics* (Princeton University Press, 2017).
7 Mosse, *Nationalism and Sexuality*, 114.

between genders for legitimate roles and identities. Female soldiers were viewed as an inversion of reality, and hence an example of the dangers to the normative gender culture prevalent in the West. Lost in the artistic portrayals of female soldiers as Amazons – a somehow sexless martial virago archetype – was the more common and realistic image of women serving as members of a community in danger during sieges. Here was the normative – albeit hidden – role for women in combat during the early Modern era. Ranging from digging entrenchments or building ad hoc projectiles and grenades to be used against the besieging army, to operating the cauldrons of hot oil along city walls to carrying ammunition to the defending garrison, women were expected to take an active defensive role in sieges.[8]

As readers consider the evolution of gender identity in nineteenth century military communities, they should first examine the baseline of shared experience and expectations dominating Western perceptions. Far from an exclusive preserve of masculinity, early modern European armies were complex communities. Female camp followers accompanied armies since the middle ages, not only cooking, cleaning, and tending for the wounded, but also occupying places within a complex social hierarchy, ranked on the basis of their relationships with men.

Again, John Lynn offers a simple breakdown of camp women into "prostitutes, 'whores,' and wives" – classifying women on the basis of their legitimacy as partners in the eyes of the church and the extent to which they used their own bodies as a commodity.[9] Atop the hierarchy were the lawful spouses of soldiers, who in some cases were encouraged to accompany their spouses. By the eighteenth century they were the only class permitted in military camps. Once welcomed in camps, prostitutes were eventually banned for moral, medical, and morale-based reasons. Not only were they recognized as carriers of disease, but they were also considered to be a source of fighting and dissatisfaction in the regiment. Nevertheless, while banned from camp, prostitutes shadowed armies and camps well into the nineteenth century, plying their trade from tents, brothels, and taverns on the camp periphery. Less clear was the status of the unwed partners of soldiers. In the parlance of the sixteenth and seventeenth century, such women were described as "whores" – a harsh label, intended to signify their sexuality along with their status as free partners to their chosen mate.[10] Regardless of their status, however, all three

---

8 Lynn *Women, Armies, and Warfare*, 164–66, 202–208.
9 *Ibid.*, 67.
10 *Ibid.*, 68–76.

Figure 2.1: "The Heroine of Monmouth" – Molly Pitcher – was actually a composite of several women present at or around the Battle of Monmouth who, as camp followers, generally stayed clear of combat. Yet in moments of great stress or need, female camp followers could step forward alongside male soldiers, as seen here in this nineteenth century woodcut.
Source: Library of Congress. Reproduction Number: LC-DIG-pga-09083 (digital file from original item); LC-USZC2-2573 (Color Film copy slide) LC-USZ62-655 (B&W film copy neg.).

classes actively participated in both the mundane daily habits of an army on the march or in camp and as essential material and psychological supports during and after battle.

The women lived and worked in military encampments, which existed as unique social communities independent of the civilian societies to which they were beholden. The women of a camp offered more than sexual release; they created a sense of normalcy in a world dominated by men trained in and organized for the purpose of conducting organized violence. Camp women often served as informal intermediaries with local communities, negotiating for food and services in peacetime, and joining in the ruthless pillage of villages and farms in war. Though restrained from direct participation in the exclusive male sphere by social fears of gender inversion – the reversal of normal gender roles and the dominant status of maleness – women also acted as litter bearers, nurses, ammo bearers, and water carriers in battle. Even more critical was their palliative role in helping individual soldiers reconcile the emotional toll of combat and war, while running the risk of being similarly afflicted themselves.[11]

As social venues pre-disposed to hyper-masculine activity and behavior, military camps were by their nature violent places. Military service in the pre-modern era was a harsh experience even in peacetime; many enlisted men were given to fighting over the slightest provocation or disagreement with their fellows. Accordingly, camp women were both the direct subject and the indirect (and at times, direct) object of violence. As casual domestic violence directed toward the female spouse was generally accepted as the norm in civilian society, so too was it accepted in the domestic military sphere. Indeed, domestic partners and prostitutes who violated the social norms associated with their place in the camp could be subject to vicious beatings, not only at the hands of their partner, but by officers and non-commissioned officers as well. Some transgressors – generally women who had cuckolded their partners – were handed over to the male camp hirelings for their pleasure.[12] Yet women also enjoyed some agency and power as well, as they could (and often did) use their influence over their partners to address perceived slights and wrongs from others in the camps. So long as they did not violate gender norms separating men from women as combatants by bearing arms – and thus inverting the presumed natural order of gender identity – camp women exercised no small amount of agency as advocates for their partners in the domestic order of camp life in the early modern era.

The case of female soldiers became more significant during the American Civil War. While there is no real way to quantify just how many women took up arms, it seems clear that hundreds served on both sides of the conflict. It is enough to prompt historians to consider their service as something more than the act of an eccentric woman. Accordingly as a group, these were women who challenged the norms of a society which advocated distinct spheres for men and women. Not only did they lift the restrictions locking them into a domestic role, their actions stand in direct opposition to the social parameters of political identity accorded women since the American Revolution. The martial women of the Civil War were not engaged in an eighteenth century exercise of gender inversion – overturning social and cultural norms for the sake of breaking into a hitherto unknown realm of experience. As historians DeAnne Blanton and Lauren M. Cook note in their 2002 book *They Fought Like Demons: Women Soldiers in the American Civil War*, "Their transvestitism was a private rebellion against public conventions. By

---

11 *Ibid.*, 94. See also Holly A. Mayer, *Belonging to the Army: Camp Follower and Community during the American Revolution* (University of South Carolina Press, 1996).
12 *Ibid.*, 103–104.

Figure 2.2: Camp followers like Sutler Mary Tippee, with Collis Zouaves (114th Pennsylvania Regiment), were a regular part of campaigning armies since the Middle Ages. As a civilian merchant attached to the regiment, Tippee remained within the normative constraints of nineteenth century gendered identity, even as she adopted elements of the uniform (the shell jacket, belt, and revolver holster) for her own use.
Source: National Archives and Records Administration, College Park, MD. National Archives Identifier: 520202. Local Identifier: 79-T-2148.

taking a male social identity, they secured for themselves male power and independence, as well as full status as citizens of their nation. In essence, the Civil War was an opportunity for hundreds of women to escape the confines of their sex."[13]

Female service constituted a direct action against the political and cultural restrictions placed upon their gender, at the same time they were obtaining economic and social freedom through their actions. Although literary scholar Judith Butler does not consider combat in her book *Gender Trouble*, her explanation of

---

13 DeAnne Blanton and Lauren M. Cook, *They Fought Like Demons: Women Soldiers in the American Civil War* (Louisiana State University Press, 2002), 5. See also Nina Silber, *Gender and Sectional Conflict* (University of North Carolina Press, 2008).

men in drag can be applied to the case studies of martial women during the Civil War. To Butler, cross-dressing men imitate or parody femininity and thus take on feminine personas as an effort to further solidify the boundaries of gender as a dualistic construction: "In imitating gender, drag implicitly reveals the imitative structure of gender itself – as well as its contingency."[14] Butler's work can also be applied to nineteenth century women as soldiers. By imitating the exclusive masculine role of combat soldier, they transcended their normative essence as feminine women – and hence drew greater attention to the stark differentiation separating the genders with reference for organized violence. This can be taken beyond the ritual of imitation and parody, since unlike the facile context of gender bending inherent in drag, martial women represented real actions occurring outside normative femininity – manifest in acts of "transvestitism" as described by Blanton and Cook.

And yet the context of female masculinity is actually less surprising when one also considers the varying degrees of male identity in practice in the Northern United States at the time of the American Civil War. When the convenient device of a single male identity is discarded and the reality of a multi-varied Northern male identity hinging upon class, religion, ethnicity, and region is accepted, the many contradictions in antebellum maleness become less confusing. East Coast urban elites expressed their male identity in ways that were completely at odds with the patterns of masculinity exhibited by men from the Upper Northwest states. Likewise, Irish Catholic immigrant men entertained a much different maleness than either the Pennsylvania Dutch or the Kansas Jayhawker. Nineteenth century America remained very much a place of transient populations and identities, and these varying representations of manhood would remain key signifiers of resistance to cultural assimilation. And yet this individuality in maleness was accepted and understood by the men serving in the Union Army. Historian Lorien Foote's study of Northern manhood in wartime, *The Gentlemen and the Roughs: Violence, Honor, and Manhood in the Union Army*, identifies a distinction between Northern and Southern perceptions of masculinity following these lines. Whereas Southern male identity was generally homogenous in nature due to the rural agrarian culture common throughout the region (as well as the unifying role slavery played among white males in the region intertwined senses of martial virtue and masculine honor), Northern identity was far more diverse, a reflection of the different class and ethnic conditions there.[15] Tensions were common as working-class farmers and urban day laborers interacted with educated upper- and

---

14 Butler, *Gender Trouble*, 186–187. For more on women crossing normative cultural borders into military service, see Halberstam, *Female Masculinity*.

15 Lorien Foote, *The Gentlemen and the Roughs: Violence, Honor, and Manhood in the Union Army* (New York University Press, 2011), 3. For the southern gentleman, see Bertram Wyatt-Brown, *The*

middle-class officers and private soldiers who were outside their normal social milieu. Hence legitimate authority and deference were subject to constant negotiation, against an ever-shifting backdrop of competing ideals of masculinity. Thus the presence in letters and memoirs from Northern soldiers and officers of seemingly contradictory positions on appropriate male behavior. Individuals simultaneously or concurrently expressed their male identity through the careful moral restraint of religion, business, and family, as well as the more physical and exuberant expression of athletic and martial conduct. When cultural norms attendant to ethnicity and region were included, a rich and complex fabric of Northern masculinity takes shape within the Union Army.

This complexity worked against itself over the course of the Civil War to promote a more restricted and carefully constructed universal male ideal, Foote continues. As men from different backgrounds and communities served together as soldiers, the incongruities of what passed for male identity jarred many observers. As Foote concludes:

> Northerners assumed that manliness in civilian life should naturally produce model citizen-soldiers whose manhood would carry northern armies to victory. At a time when it seemed so important that northern men *be* manly, however, it became clear that no consensus existed as to what that meant. As the soldiers and officers of the Union Army looked around them, they were able to articulate the differences between their understanding of manhood and the competing versions they saw all around them. Indeed, during the war men were able to define manliness by pointing to their comrades as good examples of what it was not. Army life exposed in a very unsettling fashion the conflicts between northern men over how to define the attributes essential to manhood and how to recognize manliness in other men.[16]

Over time, masculinity was measured not in what one believes and standards one held for himself, but instead in what one's comrades and peers did that was *not* manly.

Nineteenth Century Race Theory (1800–1860)

The concept of race experienced a dramatic shift in the first half of the nineteenth century as two distinct theories explaining biological diversity captured the popular and scientific imagination. At one end of the period resides the evolutionary doctrine of Jean Baptiste Chevalier de Lamarck. Rooted firmly in the

---

Shaping of Southern Culture: Honor, Grace, and War, 1760s-1890s (University of North Carolina Press, 2001).

16 Foote, *Gentlemen and the Roughs*, 4.

enlightenment physical histories of Newton and Lavoisier, in his own 1809 book, *Philosophie Zoologique*, Lamarck reasoned environmental factors stimulated subjective responses in living organisms, which in turn set in motion the evolution of sub genii and species over time. These organisms react to some impulses by adopting habits as a general response to environmental stimuli, which acquire over constant repetition the force of a second nature. In time this habitual response affects the physical shape and form of organisms, causing limbs to atrophy or grow over generations, or even causing the appearance of new organs to satisfy drastic new needs and impulses.[17]

Applied only sparingly to human evolution, Lamarck noted his theory did account for the basic physical changes in superficial racial characteristics. Rather than offer a direct value assessment on the relative worth and flaws in different species, Lamarckianism reinforced the basic concepts of racial difference as stemming from changes in the original monogenist pair. Evolution was far too long and impersonal a process to be subjected to the whim of human values, though it did offer a scheme to contextualize race as the outcome of an environmental experience that was bound to promote change. Combined with other ideologies and theories, Lamarckian evolution would experience a series of applications and contexts far outside of the author's original intention.

The second biological theory appeared in 1859. Charles Darwin's own theory of natural selection grew out of decades of field study and deep consideration back home in England, and while related to the precepts identified by Lamarck, constituted in their whole a fresh consideration of the question of how life evolved over time. Whereas Lamarckian evolution presented a positivist view of how species evolve toward a higher ideal, with each step an improvement upon the last, Darwinian natural selection was a harsh, cold rule of life as eternal struggle. Species did not evolve along a strictly linear path; they responded to varying stimuli, and in the end, those best suited for survival, often at the expense of others, prospered. Where nature was a partner to evolution in Lamarckianism, to Darwin nature was an obstacle, if not a challenge, that threatened frail life. Yet the process of natural selection could be and was manipulated by man to suit his own needs. Dogs, cats, cattle, and other domesticated animals served as proof that species could be manipulated to fulfill specific needs and labor niches far different from that of their original stock in nature.

Each theory exerted its own influence on the concept of race. In a sense both Lamarck and Darwin offered explanations for racial differences that served both the monogenists and polygenists; nature served as the impetus for promoting

---

17 Benjamin Ginzburg, *The Adventure of Science* (Simon & Schuster, 1931), 293–99.

physical changes that would in turn form the basis for racial distinction. In some circles Lamarckianism gained greater credence, in part because of the positivist viewpoint it offered for evolution as an agent of progress. In the Lamarckian racial context, whiteness was presented as the ideal state of human evolution, with different races ranked beneath Northern European whites in order of their relative state of development. Hence race was assigned value or lack thereof, reflecting the social order of the day. The majority of *racial hierarchies* followed the same general trend:

Table 2.1: Typical racial hierarchy classification, circa. 1850.

Anglo-Saxons, Scandinavians, Germans, Dutch
Balts, French, Bohemians, Moravians, Russian Slavs
Celts (Non-Irish), Walloons, Hungarians, Poles
Spaniards, Italians, Greeks, Non-Russian Slavs
Arabs, Egyptians, Jews, Chinese, Japanese, Persians
Irish, Burmese, Pathans, Sikhs, Moguls
Native Americans, Bengalis, Bedouin, Polynesians
Sub-Saharan Africans
Bushmen, Aborigines

As the above table indicates, racial identities began to parse along ever-more specific lines in the nineteenth century, reflecting the demarcations of power, privilege, education, and access to improvement. As the century progressed into a scramble for imperial possessions in Asia and Africa, the number of ethnic identities assigned a place on the chart would become ever more detailed, reflecting the nature of the encounter between Europe and the rest of the world.

After the introduction of the theory of natural selection, the discourse of race took on a darker tone, however. Race was now subject to the harsh rule of natural selection, which brought new implications for struggle between the races. Whereas in the Lamarckian view, race presented a ladder of progress to whiteness, Darwinism showed race as an eternal struggle for dominance, in which whiteness was under constant assault by lesser races. The implications of Lamarckian and Darwinian ideas on race relations are best summarized by George Frederickson in his work, *Racism: A Short History*. He presents the idea of racism occupying two intertwined discourses: difference and power. Accordingly the purported sense of difference provided rationale for "stronger" races to exploit and control other, allegedly "weaker" or "inferior" races. As Frederickson notes, "the nexus of attitude and action range from unofficial but pervasive discrimination at one of the spectrum to genocide at the other."[18]

---

18 Frederickson, *Racism*, 9.

Figure 2.3: A typical early twentieth-century diagram outlining a perceived racial hierarchy. Beginning at the upper right with the "Americo-European," the gradations of racial identity are ranked according to their perceived merits and worth, with the "Bushman" appearing just before the "Prehistoric Man."
Source: Frontispiece to James W. Buel, *Louisiana and the Fair: An Exposition of the World, Its People, and Their Achievements*. Volume V. St. Louis: World's Progress Publishing Company, 1904. Newberry Library. Chicago, Illinois.

The Mexican War and the American Civil War (1846–1865)

The Mexican War (1846–1848) stands out in the conventional history of the United States as the great test of Manifest Destiny. Here the American Republic, eager to push its boundaries to the Pacific Ocean, waged a war against a militarized Mexican dictatorship. Following a handful of victories and missteps in Northern Mexico, the U.S. Army's commanding general, Winfield Scott, landed an amphibious force at Veracruz and launched a remarkable campaign of maneuver that brought his small force of hardened Regulars to the center of Mexico City within a few months. Consequently, the popular narrative reduces the war to a small contest in the larger context of American expansion.

This conventional account does not address other relevant issues such as the deeply-seated racialized perspective of the primacy of Anglo-Saxon whiteness in contemporary American views of the war and the Mexican people. Indeed, it must be stated that at its core, nineteenth-century Manifest Destiny was built upon the idea that whiteness was the dominant racial identity in North America. Versions of this exceptionalist narrative persisted well into the twentieth century, extending beyond the continental United States into the Pacific Basin and into Asia. Taking his cue from Benedict Anderson's *Imagined Communities*, historian Gary Gerstle explains that nations are "invented political and cultural entities whose power rests not only on the acquisitions and control of territory but also on their ability to gain allegiance and affection of large heterogenous populations that reside in their borders." Gerstle defines race exclusively as a social construction, an invented identity he calls "racial nationalism" that was employed by leaders to bind white America together in a struggle against "other" races. Real warfare represented the ultimate expression and self-fulfilling justification of this imagined struggle, as war sharpened not only national identities, but racial consciousness as well.[19]

Gerstle applied his model to the global conflicts of the twentieth century, but it is equally effective when it is used to contextualize the Mexican War. America was destined to control the course of political affairs in the New World because its Anglo-Saxon/Germanic racial identity lent itself toward expansion and dominance. Mexicans of all degrees of racial identity were deemed inferior to the martial republican virtues contained within white Americans. Save for a small elite resident in Mexican cities and descended from the original Spanish *conquistadores* and other subsequent arrivals from Spain, Americans saw Mexicans

---

19 Gary Gerstle, *American Crucible: Race and Nation in the 20th Century* (University Press, 2001), 4–6, 17.

as product of centuries of intermarriage between all local races – whites, Native Americans, and African slaves. Contemporary accounts and descriptions of the average Mexicans were quite harsh: they were seen as lazy, immoral, diseased, and besotten with drink. After generations of alleged miscegenation, Mexicans were seen as incapable of self-governance following the purportedly superior model of white American republicanism. Instead they were viewed as an illiterate mob, ready to be led by the small white Spanish elite – itself considered to be beneath Anglo-Saxon Americans because of centuries of inbreeding and overexposure to the tropical climate.[20]

Viewed in this light, the Mexican War actually stands out as an American conflict framed within the context of race – specifically the inherent superiority of whiteness as compared with other racial and ethnic populations co-habiting the North American continent. Even republicanism itself was considered beyond the reach of Mexicans, who were viewed as inherently disposed toward corrupt absolutism if left to their own devices. Many Americans considered war to be the first step in the gradual absorption of Mexico by the United States, which itself would stand as the beginning of a process of whitening all of North America itself.[21] Consider the various Caribbean filibuster expeditions of the 1850s; when seen outside of the lens of race, they lose all sense of proportion to each other, and exist as a collection of half-hearted schemes undertaken by radical dreamers and schemers. Nor are they exclusively efforts to spread a Southern institution of slavery beyond its existing confines – in fact, the support of Northern Democrats for both the Mexican War and the filibusters that followed reveals a broader support for the movement outside of the slave-owning South. However when examined as part of a cultural movement aimed to promote the advance of white Anglo-Saxon American political power on the heels of the success of the Mexican War, the filibusters become part of a larger movement predicated on the political and cultural superiority of whiteness in North America.

Of course the Mexican War did not enjoy universal domestic support. Widespread opposition to the war was voiced throughout Whig circles in the industrializing Northeast and the free soil Old Northwest. At the center of Whig

---

20 [Richard H. Coolidge] *Statistical Abstract on the Sickness and Mortality of the Army of the United States ..., From January, 1839 to January, 1855* (A.O.P. Nicholson, Printer, 1856), 358, 415, 423; and [Richard H. Coolidge] *Statistical Abstract on the Sickness and Mortality of the Army of the United States ..., From January, 1855, to January, 1860* (George W. Bowman, Printer, 1860), 212–213. See also Amy S. Greenberg, *A Wicked War: Polk, Clay, Lincoln, and the 1846 U.S. Invasion of Mexico* (Alfred A. Knopf, 2012), 131–133.

21 Mark E. Neely, Jr., *The Civil War and the Limits of Destruction* (Cambridge: Harvard University Press, 2007), 17.

opposition were concerns over the rise of Southern political influence on the heels of the spread of slavery into the territories to be acquired from Mexico. However some Whigs joined Nativist groups in opposing the war on racial grounds – specifically the prospect of large numbers of Mexicans joining the United States as political equals. Opponents of Manifest Destiny charged President James K. Polk's administration with seeking to degrade the whiteness of the American republic by bringing into the country a large number of Mexicans, all viewed as the degenerate outcome of centuries of miscegenation between the Spaniard and Native Americans and escaped slaves.[22]

Regardless of the political and regional divisions over the war, common notions of racial superiority unified white Americans when it came to the actual news of fighting from the Mexican frontier. Amy S. Greenberg describes how Americans celebrated accounts of victories that "'sustained nobly the character of the Anglo-Saxon race.'"[23] While political division over the issue of war with Mexico was generally tolerated (grudgingly, of course), there was no such split over the performance of American troops in battle. Whig and Democratic newspapers and politicians applauded the martial deeds of the armies in Mexico. By sustaining the cherished ideal of American martial prowess – one which was frequently championed by all parties – they helped buttress the concepts of Manifest Destiny and American Exceptionalism sweeping the popular imagination and the political landscape.[24]

The greatest legacy of the Mexican War was the American Civil War. More frequently historians view the crisis decade of the 1850s in American politics as a mere interlude between the wars. Indeed without the immediate controversy over the fate of slavery in the new territories, it is hard to imagine the Civil War as taking place in the absence of the earlier conflict. It goes without saying that the debate over the causes of the Civil War remains quite involved and active; yet it is also a matter of fact the fate of slavery, initially in the territories, but ultimately within the Union itself, rest at the core of the war itself. In all of their pronouncements about state's rights and speeches in favor of secession, Southern fire-eaters

---

22 See Gene M. Brack, "Mexican Opinion, American Racism, and the War of 1846," *Western Historical Quarterly* 1:2 (April 1970), 161–74; Reginald Horsman, *Race and Manifest Destiny: Origins of American Racial Anglo-Saxonism*, rev. ed. (Harvard University Press, 1981); Paul Foos, *A Short, Offhand, Killing Affair: Soldiers and Social Conflict during the Mexican-American War* (University of North Carolina Press, 2002); and Amy S. Greenberg, *Manifest Manhood and the Antebellum American Empire* (Cambridge University Press, 2005).
23 "The Fields of Palo Alto," *Cleveland Herald*, June 2, 1846, quoted in *A Wicked War*, 120.
24 Greenberg, *A Wicked War*, 120.

made clear their commitment to preserve their "peculiar institution" as an essential feature of their very existence.[25]

This rationale is fully expressed in the various Declarations of Cause for secession issued by Southern states as justification for leaving the Union. Mississippi, for example, asserted that "Our position is thoroughly identified with the institution of slavery – the greatest material interest of the world.... a blow at slavery is a blow at commerce and civilization.... There was no choice left us but submission to the mandates of abolition, or a dissolution of the Union, whose principles had been subverted to work out our ruin."[26]

South Carolina's delegates presented a grim forecast as justification for secession:

> On the 4th day of March next, [the Republican Party] will take possession of the Government. It has announced that the South shall be excluded from the common territory, that the judicial tribunals shall be made sectional, and that a war must be waged against slavery until it shall cease throughout the United States.

From the slaveholders' perspective, the guaranties of the Constitution will then no longer exist; the equal rights of the States will be lost. The slaveholders will no longer have the power of self-government, or self-protection, and the Federal Government will have become their enemy.[27]

In Texas, the assembly claimed slavery and white supremacy as an indisputable fact, sanctioned by divine will:

> We hold as undeniable truths that the governments of the various States, and of the confederacy itself, were established exclusively by the white race, for themselves and their posterity; that the African race had no agency in their establishment; that they were rightfully held and regarded as an inferior and dependent race, and in that condition only could their existence in this country be rendered beneficial or tolerable.

> That in this free government *all white men are and of right ought to be entitled to equal civil and political rights*; that the servitude of the African race, as existing in these States, is mutually beneficial to both bond and free, and is abundantly authorized and justified by the experience of mankind, and the revealed will of the Almighty Creator, as recognized by all Christian nations; while the destruction of the existing relations between the two races,

---

25 See James M. McPherson, *Drawn with the Sword: Reflections on the American Civil War* (Oxford University Press, 1996), 16–17; Russell F. Weigley, *A Great Civil War: A Military and Political History, 1861–1865* (Indiana University Press, 2004), xxxvi, 7–9.
26 "Declaration of Causes of Seceding States," Civil War Trust Website, https://www.civilwar.org/learn/primary-sources/declaration-causes-seceding-states Accessed November 3, 2017.
27 *Ibid.*

as advocated by our sectional enemies, would bring inevitable calamities upon both and desolation upon the fifteen slave-holding states.[28]

Without slavery, the Southern way of life – one sustained economically on chattel labor exploitation, and culturally on defusing glaring inequities between the plantation owning elite and the plurality of the rural poor laborer and petty land-owner classes – would cease to exist.

Another issue often examined by historians is the role African Americans played in the conflict after the issuance of War Department General Order 143 in May 1863, establishing a "Bureau of Colored Troops" to manage the recruitment, pay, and training of former slaves and freedmen in segregated units under the command of white officers. Thanks in no small part to the 1989 film *Glory!* the story of the 54th Massachusetts Volunteer Infantry Regiment became a convenient case study for the experiences of over 180,000 troops; by May 1865 one-tenth of the entire Union Army in arms. Though marked by over-romanticized portrayals of the relationships between freedmen, students, contrabands, and escaped slaves and their white officers, *Glory!* does provide a valuable service in pointing out that the overwhelming number of whites in the Union Army had little use for the blacks in its service.

Rampant racism, many times at the hands of the Irish soldier in uniform – himself a victim of virulent racism from Nativists – confronted the members of the United States Colored Troops (USCT) at every turn. Paid less than whites until June 15, 1864, often outfitted in shoddy, inferior uniforms and given less savory food than their white counterparts, members of the USCT also suffered from generally poor leadership, as regimental commanders were increasingly drawn from the pool of low quality officers. Any welcome by white soldiers and officers was frequently superficial, if not jaded: if blacks wished to take the place of others as potential casualties, so much the better.[29] Nor did their troubles end there. The presence of black troops on the battlefield was decried by many Confederates as a war crime indicative of the hatred the Union had for the secessionist South. From their first serious engagement at Battery Wagner on July 18, 1863, through the April 12, 1864 capture of Fort Pillow in Tennessee, to the abortive July 30, 1864,

---

28 *Ibid*. Emphasis in original.
29 James McPherson, *The Negro's Civil War: How American Negros Felt and Acted During the War for the Union* (Pantheon Books, 1965), 193–203; and William A. Dobak, *Freedom by the Sword: The U.S. Colored Troops, 1862–1867* (Skyhorse Publishing, 2013), 5, 9. See also Joseph T. Glatthaar, *Forged in Battle: The Civil War Alliance of Black Soldiers and White Officers* (Louisiana State University Press, 2000); and Ian Michael Spurgeon, *Soldiers in the Army of Freedom: The 1st Kansas Colored, The Civil War First African American Combat Unit* (University of Oklahoma Press, 2014).

Crater assault at Petersburg and beyond, blacks in the blue uniform of the United States Colored Troops routinely faced certain death even if captured by Confederate troops. Outraged by the prospect of fighting armed blacks, Southern soldiers often refused to acknowledge the surrender of blacks, and at times exercised their rage by mutilating both dead and wounded black soldiers. Nevertheless despite the outrages committed against them, there are few accounts of USCT soldiers seeking revenge against the enemy.[30]

A most peculiar phenomenon has appeared in recent years that indirect affects the notion that slavery dominated the discourses on the Civil War. Not surprisingly, it has gained support among neo-Confederate revisionists who wish to de-emphasize the racist context of the war – specifically proponents of "black Confederates" exercising personal agency to enlist in small numbers in state regiments. Revisionist historians eager to recast the Civil War as a contest over the power and influence of the federal system over individual states have seized upon sketchy rumors and incomplete oral histories of elderly former slaves who served with the Confederate Army to create a mythic image of the black slave willfully taking up arms to defend his own state of bondage alongside his white overseers and masters. While the rational mind boggles at the prospect, it must be acknowledged that some 60,000 to 100,000 slaves did accompany the Southern armies as laborers, cooks, bodyguards, servants, grooms, and teamsters. As one account notes, one could well debate whether these men were rightfully accorded the status of "soldier" or not.[31] Perhaps; yet a formal review of the accounts offered as evidence of military service in combat reveals a premise sustained by apocryphal secondary and even tertiary accounts. There are no pension records related to African Americans in Rebel mufti; there are no Union accounts of capturing or burying black Confederates armed with anything more serious than a spade. And what of Southern resistance to the prospect of arming blacks? The very mention of which in a personal letter to Jefferson Davis cost Major General Patrick Cleburne the chance of ever exercising command of a formation larger than a division. While blacks did accompany their masters into their regiments as servants, or were purchased outright to serve as laborers and cooks, there is

---

30 John David Smith, *Black Soldiers in Blue: African American Troops in the Civil War Era* (University of North Carolina Press, 2002), 136–40, 157–58, 181–87. See also Gregory J.W. Urwin, ed., *Black Flag over Dixie: Racial Atrocities and Reprisals in the Civil War* (Southern Illinois University Press, 2005).

31 J.H. Segars, "Prologue: Black Southerners in Gray?," *Forgotten Confederates: An Anthology About Black Southerners, Journal of Confederate History* Series, Vol. XIV, ed. J.H. Segars, et al. (Southern Heritage Press, 1995), 1–7, quote on 3.

nothing save the most apocryphal evidence to verify if they did indeed take up arms against the Union.

Of more pressing interest to scholars is the question of *why* the defeated Confederates failed to adopt a sweeping post-war insurgency struggle against the Union. Considering how the war had become more destructive after 1863, culminating in the despoliation of the Shenandoah Valley and William Tecumseh Sherman's march to the sea, and not to mention the complete social transformation expected of the white-dominant South in defeat, the absence of an insurgency phase stands out as an anomaly.

Part of the credit no doubt must fall to General Robert E. Lee's conceptualization of war; like so many other officers trained in West Point, Lee viewed war along the lines of a Jominian contest between armies, not peoples. To extend violence against the civilian population was bad enough – as shown in his own disdain for Major General John Pope's actions north of the Rappahannock River in the summer of 1862. Likewise the issue of *francs-tireur* – soldiers waging war in civilian mufti – was one Lee objected to. Influenced in part by his training, here Lee could also pull from his own experiences in Mexico. As a member of Major General Winfield Scott's expeditionary force, Lee witnessed first-hand his commander's effort to restrain the violence along his line of march by forcing a harsh discipline on his troops in order to avoid any provocation that might send the Mexican population into armed rebellion against its American occupiers. Impressed by the extent of Union strength, and recognizing the absence of any benefit for a defeated and occupied South in armed rebellion, Lee counseled tolerance and forbearance to the South.

Gender in the Second Half of the Nineteenth Century

After the Civil War, a renewed emphasis was placed on the issue of masculinity, as American society became increasingly obsessed with the prospect of a regressive manliness. Part of this was due to the war itself; soldiers on both sides were perceived by their children and grandchildren as larger than life figures. Right or wrong, the martial accomplishments of the Civil War generation were held up as examples of an American civic ideal that was fading in the face of material prosperity. Veterans decried the lack of a motivating grand mission for their children; adrift in a sea of consumerism and plenty during the 1870s and 1880s, the postwar generation was lost without meaning and purpose. Young men in turn bemoaned their own lack of a chance to prove their mettle.

Other factors were at play as well. White middle-class reformers decried the growing tide of immigrants, who not only challenged native-born Americans for jobs, but also threatened to undermine contemporary notions of stolid reserved masculinity with one of ostentatious licentiousness born in the saloon. Others feared that, while immigrant men took on the solid manual labor tasks that established the masculine ideal of labor before the war, native-born whites were being pressed ever more readily into "soft" clerical and managerial positions. More and more artists and writers extolled the virtues of the unskilled laborer while demeaning the "effeminacy" of the urban wage laborer. In manner, dress, and language, the "dandy" and the "dude" was transformed in the public's eye from virile masculine images into the effeminate male risking sexual inversion.[32]

Amidst these changes in identity emerged a new iconic image – the white American taming the West, bringing civilization to the limits of settlement, taming a continent one buffalo carcass at a time. Dime novels and popular songs and plays touted the rough and ready culture of the American West as an ideal venue for masculinity. Nevermind the crime-filled anarchy of cowtowns, forget about the venal corruption of rogue capitalism crushing the individual farmer and rancher underfoot – a new male ideal had come to the fore in the great frontier landscape of the imagined American West. One half *conquistador*, claiming land for white civilization, and one half Jeffersonian yeoman, wrestling a livelihood from nature's sometimes cruel embrace, the western male became the American ideal.

In his trilogy on the frontier myth, cultural historian Richard Slotkin lays out a process that included parallel efforts by Americans as they moved west during the nineteenth. Both the environment and the Native Americans living beyond the frontier – the imaginary line between civilization and barbarism – needed to tamed by the white settlers. In one parallel effort, this entailed the physical transformation of pristine woodlands or plains into family farms. The white settlers in the other effort needed to expel the Native Americans living in these areas by force of arms – sometimes on their own and other times by the U.S. Army. Slotkin ties these threads together by introducing mythology to show how the American settlers justified the violence against Native Americans and the transformation of the land by creating the archetypal "frontiersman." As males, these heroic frontiersmen could only subdue the people and the landscape by setting aside civilized practices and then adopting barbaric traits of those Native American adversaries. Then during the latter part of the nineteenth century as the United States successfully conquered the West, those rough frontiersmen evolved into a new archetype that Slotkin terms as the "frontier aristocrats," who turned their attention to exploiting the benefits of industrialization. Yet they could still use barbaric violence when

---

32 See E. Anthony Rotundo, *American Mahood: Transformations from the Revolution to the Modern Era* (New York: Basic Books, 1994).

necessary. After the United States defeated the Spanish in 1898, these American aristocrats turned their attention to new frontiers overseas that needed to be subdued by force, whether they be the Caribbean islands or Vietnam.[33]

Such imagined figures of identity aside however, there was one aspect of American masculinity which coexisted and complemented the Western ideal. For the first half of the century, religion, in the form of piety and submission, was considered a feminine enterprise. Though the final arbitration of God's will was a male-exclusive role, as a nurturing, loving endeavor, religiosity was feminine. Even the person of Christ himself was portrayed in the popular arts of the day (c. 1830–1860) as a figure of tenderness and sacrifice.

After the Civil War, however, this older, benign, and somewhat feminine perspective of religion was considered inadequate. Preachers and ministers decried the loss of men to other pursuits, including sports like baseball, because religion was viewed as part of the feminine sphere. To counter this portrayal, an alternative perspective on religion appeared in the 1860s and 1870s emphasizing the activist message of Christianity in conjunction with the virility of physical strength and exercise. This new movement, identified by some as *Muscular Christianity* became more relevant in the 1880s and 1890s as an alternative to both the perceived degradation of amoral pleasure unleashed in saloons and brothels across the country and to the spread of neurasthenic neuroses among well-intentioned but physically inept middle-class whit men. By co-opting team sports like football, rugby, and baseball, the advocates of Muscular Christianity charged they were saving men "body and soul," and training young men for the "real business" of fighting sin and saving souls.[34]

Nineteenth Century Race Theory (1850–1900)

As the nation recovered from the Civil War, racial ideology actually facilitated reconciliation between the white North and South, albeit at the expense of any hope of immediate social and economic equality for black Americans. While it is

[33] Richard Slotkin, *Regeneration Through Violence: The Mythology of the American Frontier, 1600–1860* (Wesleyan University Press, 1973). Also by Slotkin, see *The Fatal Environment: The Myth of the Frontier in the Age of Industrialization, 1800–1890* (MacMillan, 1985), and *Gunfighter Nation: The Myth of the Frontier in Twentieth Century America* (Atheneum, 1992).
[34] See Susan Curtis, "The Son of Man and God the Father: The Social Gospel and Victorian Masculinity," in *Meanings for Manhood: Constructions of Masculinity in Victorian America*, ed. Mark C. Carnes and Clyde Griffen (University of Chicago Press, 1990), 67–78; and Clifford Putney, *Muscular Christianity: Manhood and Sports in Protestant America, 1880–1920* (Harvard University Press, 2003).

true the slavery question lay at the heart of the conflict, likewise it can be stated that no one in the fractured Union gave any serious consideration of just *what* to do with the four million emancipated slaves at the war's end. Lincoln's untimely death only exacerbated the question of what role the Federal Government should take in providing the basic economic foundation for racial equality. Accordingly, African Americans made only short-term, limited advances during Reconstruction (1865–1877). While guaranteed political equality in the form of the Fifteenth Amendment, few blacks were given the chance to vote outside of areas under direct army control. A small number of black politicians were elected to state and federal office during Reconstruction, but they were all denied a chance to run once their states were readmitted to the Union after 1877. Other anticipated reforms, including land distribution and state-sponsored education, withered away before they could be implemented, first victims of Northern indifference, then Southern vindictiveness.

Reconstruction's failure to address the question of social and economic equality for former slaves bore witness to the pervasiveness of racism in American society. While the subject of humiliating chattel slavery in the South for generations, blacks fared little better in the North. Racist ideologies privileging whiteness were widespread, and even though they were technically free, African Americans faced harsh prejudice throughout the North. Race riots in Northern urban areas became commonplace after 1865, as white laborers resented the appearance of freed blacks as competition for scarce jobs. Irish workers in particular resisted their displacement in the labor markets in the North and the Midwest by cheaper black labor. Indeed, the harsh language and epithets of the slave South found a ready audience in the North. No matter where they tried to settle after the war, freed slaves confronted the sad reality that regardless of their status, they were not welcome anywhere in the recovering Union. Reconstruction for the black man was a sad repudiation of the promises extended during the war.[35]

In no area was this more apparent than in the white backlash against emancipation in the American South. The first example of this was in the formation of the Knights of the Ku Klux Klan in central Tennessee in December 1865. Comprised of Confederate veterans, the Klan's purpose was simple: intimidate and oppress freed slaves through terror. While not considered a true guerilla force by the Union Army, by 1870 the Klan operated as a white-exclusive militia, sometimes using deadly force against blacks who dared to question the "old order"

---

35 See Craig Thompson Friend, *Southern Masculinity: Perspectives on Manhood in the South since Reconstruction* (University of Georgia Press, 2009); and Riché Richardson, *Black Masculinity and the U.S. South: From Uncle Tom to Gangsta* (University of Georgia Press, 2007).

in spirit or deed. Although ultimately labeled a terror organization by Federal courts in 1870, the Klan continued to act as the iron fist behind the white Southern efforts to clamp down on African American equality.

The fading of the first Klan in the 1870s was due primarily to the 1877 end of Reconstruction. With the threat of federal occupation gone, the white Southern mainstream was free to impose greater restrictions on black political and economic fulfillment. The freedom promised to blacks existed in name only by 1890, as successive black codes and restrictive ordnances gave way to an entire culture of repression. The "Jim Crow" laws of the South only masked a growing hatred of black participation in any save an infantilized dependency status. And as the nineteenth century drew to a close, the rule of law gave way to a culture of lynching and murder that was beginning to spread beyond the confines of the Old Confederacy.

At the same time the United States grappled with the question of race following the Civil War, new debates and theories were unfolding on the subject in Europe elsewhere in Western society. Another influential figure in the rise of race theory was Joseph-Arthur, Comte de Gobineau. Identified by some as the "father of racism," Gobineau's ideology helped contextualize a system founded on racial supremacy that not only celebrated the rise of whiteness in the ages of exploration and empire, but also later became the foundation stone of National Socialist racial ideology. The scion of an aristocratic family with links to the Bourbons, Gobineau was by nature both a romantic and a social conservative. Coming of age during Napoleonic France and the fractious Bourbon restoration, Gobineau viewed race as the chief factor in determining global social structures.[36] A monogenist at heart, Gobineau believed all humanity descended from the original biblical pair. However, biological factors (inbreeding) and environmental factors (the debilitating effect of too much time spent in the direct light of the tropical sun, caused mankind to diverge into a collection of races). Descended from the original "Aryan" race, white Europeans of Western Europe were considered the most noble and vital members of humanity. Other races declined in terms of value and worth from this Western European ideal, in a cruel hierarchy of decreasing whiteness, until reaching the lowest state accorded to black Africans and Australian aboriginal people. Once set upon their divergent paths, each racial type had evolved into its own sub-genus, their physical differences becoming set in biology as individual traits.[37]

---

36 Michael Biddiss, *Father of Racist Ideology: The Social and Political Thought of Count Gobineau* (Weybright and Talley, 1970).

37 Edward Beasley, *The Victorian Reinvention of Race: New Racisms and the Problem of Grouping in the Human Sciences* (Taylor and Francis, 2010).

Gobineau's schema of a racial hierarchy dominated by Whiteness was not a static construction, however. A central component of his racial ideology was the prospect of transformative mobility between different subgroups. On one hand, isolation from other races led to stagnation, and the general decline of a race. Likewise a race could be brought low by the degenerative effects of miscegenation – the intermingling of two races through sexual congress. Thus humanity was ultimately doomed, despite its best efforts to avoid it, to the inevitable degeneration of the white race, and by extension, civilization itself.[38] From their first publication in the mid 1850s, Gobineau's theories won a hard core of adherents in the United States and Europe itself. In the last gasps of the pre-war crisis, white Southern slaveholders and their supporters acclaimed Gobineau's *Essay on the Inequality of the Human Races* as a validation for their institution – despite his opposition to slavery on general principle.

In England and France, Gobineau was cited as justification for imperial expansion into Asia and Africa. Meanwhile in the Northern United States, Gobineau's work influenced future race theorists, including Lieutenant Colonel Charles E. Woodruff. A medical officer since joining the Army in 1887, Woodruff considered imperial expansion to be the ultimate bane of American culture and civilization. Race joined with climate as a cruel hazard to the biological integrity of race. The decaying effect of tropical sun, heat, and humidity would readily make itself felt on white American soldiers stationed in the region. Constant exposure through long terms of service or work in the tropics eroded the physical and moral strength of men stationed there. Upon their return home, these men, their racial characteristics affected by their long service abroad, posed a grave risk to the solid health and racial superiority of whites, as their offspring spread the degeneration they had acquired abroad at home.[39] Along with contexts of gender identity, racial ideology and the accompanying fear of degeneration came to define the American dialogue of race and empire.

Perhaps the most influential proponent of Gobineau's theory of racial hierarchies was Theodore Roosevelt. As president from 1901 to 1909, Roosevelt not only possessed strong beliefs on gender and race, but took full advantage of the "bully pulpit" to promote his world view, making him the chief case study for American racial perceptions during the Progressive Era. On one hand a strong advocate for assimilation and the erosion of racial identity, he was also constrained by personal views on the inherent inferiority of other non-European races and

---

38 Brace, *"Race,"* 119–122.
39 Charles E. Woodruff, *Medical Ethnology* (Rebman Company, 1915), 244, 290–304; Wintermute, *Public Health and the US Military*, 130–32.

ethnicities in comparison with his Anglo-Saxon ideal. Despite opening up access to political participation for Italian-Americans, Jews, and other groups, privately Roosevelt held many of the same stereotypes that gripped the country at the time – deriding the influence of Jews in finance, describing Irish politicians as innately corrupt and venal, as well as being pliant tools of the Papacy. A proponent of the "Melting Pot" ideology of social and ethnic assimilation into a singular American identity – "Americanization," in his words – Roosevelt also felt some groups, particularly the Japanese and Chinese, were incapable of full assimilation. Regardless he believed Western (and American) society had a commitment to uplift and promote the advance and elevation of lesser races – including Africans, Filipinos, and Cubans – along the guidelines established by the United States.

This was not to imply that Theodore Roosevelt was highly-progressive on the issue of ethnicity and racial identity in the United States. Rather he was obsessed with the prospect of "race suicide" – the slow yet inexorable decline of a race of men through declining reproductive rates. Following the 1890 census, he was shocked at the purported decline of the old-guard white patrician families in the face of a growing Irish population in Boston. Tying his burgeoning theory of race suicide with the morality of the manly virtues of work, action, and exercise, he considered the overall decline of the "higher races" evidence of a general biological trend. Bar a dramatic increase in birthrates among whites, Roosevelt feared the inevitable decline of the United States. As summarized by Thomas G. Dyer in his study of Roosevelt's racial ideology:

> If the trend were not arrested, higher races might commit "race suicide" and literally die out, leaving no trace of the superior qualities which accounted for the present state of civilization and constituted the best hope for the future. The second possible consequence of racial Reproductive failure would be the frightening prospect that lower races such as Latin Americans, blacks, and East Europeans would swamp the higher orders in the "warfare of the cradle." Abroad, the fecund Russians, rivals in the imperialistic struggle, threatened American interests, and at home the virile blacks with their reproductive powers undiminished by the presence of the white man constituted a menace.[40]

Theodore Roosevelt's obsession with race was hardly unique; rather he stands out as representative of white American concerns with a social construction that was inadequately understood and openly manipulated for the purposes of a narrow section of the population. Moreover the benefits of democracy, Roosevelt believed, could only be achieved and enjoyed by Caucasian males. Other races – including African Americans – and women could never fully reach the

---

40 Thomas G. Dyer, *Theodore Roosevelt and the Idea of Race* (Louisiana State University Press, 1980), 149.

level of intellect, autonomy, or ability of White Americans. Roosevelt refused to cast this as a burden, however; rather he viewed this as both challenge and obligation, promoting a highly paternalistic and hegemonic view of the primacy of male whiteness – "The Strenuous Life" writ large, as it were.[41]

Anti-Semitism before 1900

Anti-Semitism can be traced directly to the classical world. Some historians note the rise of a general anti-Jewish sentiment dating back to the post-Alexandrian Hellenic world in the Eastern Mediterranean. Accordingly Jews and Greeks were engaged in an informal cultural conflict, in which the Hellenes criticized Jews for their failure to fully accept Greek values, while Jews felt disrespected by the Greeks' dismissive attitude toward the older Judean culture.[42] The first century of the Christian Era saw increased tensions between the Jews of the Eastern Mediterranean and the Roman Empire. In some cases – the rioting in Alexandria in 38 CE, for example – the attacks on Jews were as much attempts by local Greek and Egyptian communities to regain civic power over an ethnic rival. Rome's position on the rights of Jews to live peacefully was more problematic, however. By refusing to accept or even acknowledge Roman gods, Jews were frequently perceived to be disrespectful, if not openly defiant and rebellious, of Roman authority. The province of Judea was in a state of constant near-rebellion at this time, with small uprisings being matched with ever-escalating punitive measures by the Roman governor. These tit-for-tat attacks culminated in the Great Rebellion (66 to 70 CE), a bitter uprising that was ended with the Roman sacking and destruction of the second Temple of Solomon in Jerusalem. Uprisings continued until the Emperor Hadrian leveled the city in 135CE, killing thousands and scattering the surviving population across the empire, many as slaves.[43]

The experiences of stubborn defiance and insistence upon preserving their unique identity combined to set in place numerous stereotypes that would in turn form the foundation of anti-Semitism in the late Roman Empire and the early Middle Ages. Vicious rumors and fierce slanders about the disparate Jewish

---

41 Gerstle, *American Crucible*, 51–58. See also Bederman, *Manliness and Civilization*; and Christopher P. Barton, "Tacking Between Black and White: Race Relations in Gilded Age Philadelphia," *International Journal of Historical Archeology* 16 (December 2012): 634–50.
42 Phyllis Goldstein, *A Convenient Hatred: The History of Antisemitism* (Facing History and Ourselves National Foundation, 2012), 7–16; and David M. Crowe, *The Holocaust: Roots, History, and Aftermath* (Westview Press, 2008), 11.
43 Goldstein, *A Convenient Hatred*, 18–21.

community in exile persisted, despite the efforts of more tolerant governors and emperors. The misunderstanding blossomed into full-blown culture clash as early Christians sought as much distance as possible from Jews. Not only were they perceived as responsible for the death of Jesus Christ, they were also viewed as a quarrelsome, bloodthirsty, and money-hungry people. As Christianity became ascendant in the Roman Empire after 315 CE, the reputations of Jews sank lower in the estimation of lay persons and clergy alike. Saints and bishops alike castigated Jews as "Christ-killers," "serpents," and "wicked men" and made their safety ever more tenuous.[44]

Nevertheless European Jews flourished in several disparate and small communities throughout the early and high Middle Ages. Forced into small urban communities by a generally ignorant and intolerant rural poor, Jews survived and even prospered as craftsmen, traders, and bankers. Even amidst the low point of the Crusades, they served as intermediaries and trade conduits between the Latin West and the Islamic World, fulfilling a valuable role through the use of their own cultural ties with fellow Jews in the homeland. Unfortunately Jews remained targets of intolerance in Europe, subject to regular attacks from popes, kings, and commoners. In the eleventh century, for example, as Pope Urban II issued calls for a crusade to reclaim the Holy Land for Christianity, Jewish communities in France, Germany, and Italy were attacked by crusaders en route to Jerusalem. Over the next centuries, legislation and edicts from secular and ecclesiastical authorities went even further in their effort to isolate and punish Jews, until the ultimate indignity of expulsion from Western Europe was accomplished in the fourteenth and fifteenth centuries.

Relations worsened between Jews and Christians during the Protestant Reformation, After realizing Jews were not interested in conversions to Christianity. Martin Luther attacked them as a people stained with the guilt of killing Christ and as idolaters who should be extirpated from Christian society. Luther's written assaults set the tone for future outrages throughout the sixteenth and seventeenth centuries in Central Protestant Europe. Jews fared little better in Catholic Europe. Those remaining in Spain and Portugal following the *Reconquista* became direct targets of Inquisitions, forced conversions, and resettlement in ghettos.

The fate of Jews in Western Europe improved during the Enlightenment. In the spirit of social tolerance and scientific inquiry that marked the age, urban Jewish populations acquired new civil rights and opportunities. As Western

---

44 Dennis Prager and Joseph Telushkin, *Why the Jews? The Reason for Antisemitism, The Most Accurate Predictor of Human Evil* (Touchstone, 1983, 2003, 2016), 77–79; and Goldstein, *A Convenient Evil*, 25–37.

philosophers sought to overturn the religiosity of the Medieval age, many considered anti-Semitism to be as much an artifact of the uninformed and superstitious past as a manifestation of nascent racial classification. Acknowledged as a people made distinct by their religious practice and relationship with the Christian world, some writers, like Denis Diderot and Henri Dietrich Baron d'Holbach, perceived Jews as biologically different from other European peoples. The tone of attacks made against Jews during the Enlightenment focused primarily on their conservatism with regard to religion. Even Emmanuel Kant decried Judaism as the fountainhead of Christian mysticism and superstition: abolish the Jewish faith, and an enlightened Christianity would reign supreme, "the conclusion of the great drama of religious change on earth, where there will be only one shepherd and one flock."[45]

Nevertheless Western Jews continued to assimilate into Western European civil and intellectual society. Individual rabbis like Baruch Spinoza and Moses Mendelssohn promoted the application of historical and scientific methods to the study of the Judaic texts. Following their lead, many Western Jewish families and communities sought new identities as prosperous, educated, secular Jews. Different only in the observation of their faith, these liberals adopted the dress, language, and even diet of their Christian neighbors. As they assimilated, Europe's secularist Jews became ever more guarded of their religious difference, and distanced themselves from their Eastern European orthodox cousins – like them only in religion, not in nationality or race, they argued. Everywhere across Western Europe, it seemed, Jews were becoming accepted as equal members of society.[46]

Such appearances were deceiving and ephemeral because, even in the midst of assimilation, anti-Semitism flourished. As industrialization transformed entire societies, Jews became again castigated via old prejudices disseminated through new methods.[47] Social Darwinists mixed Darwin's views on natural selection with Gobineau's views on race struggle to promote a new doctrine predicated on the quaint nostrum, "the survival of the fittest." True believers like Herbert Spencer and German physician Alfred Ploetz promoted ideas of "racial hygiene," a process of war and government action intended to cull the weak from the strong in order to create a purer race. The culmination was the first use of "Anti-Semitism" in a literary context by Wilhelm Marr in 1879, where Jews were described in a racialized context. It was a short step from Marr's original pamphlet decrying a Jewish

---

45 *Ibid.*, 46.
46 Goldstein, *A Convenient Hatred*, 158–161.
47 Léon Poliakov, *The History of Anti-Semitism*, vol. 4, *Suicidal Europe, 1870–1933*, trans. George Kiln (University of Pennsylvania Press, 2003).

plot to "Jewify" Germany through exploiting economic and social unrest to the nationalist and racist musical musings of Richard Wagner. Not only in his great symphonic works – particularly *Parsifal* and *Die Niebelungen* – but also in his essays on music, Wagner promoted a martial, pure *Völkisch* identity for Germany founded in his friend Gobineau's Aryan ideal, and at immediate risk of corruption at the hand of the perfidious, racially degenerate outsider – in short, the Jew. By the close of the nineteenth century, anti-Semitism was at a crossroads. One road pointed to its inevitable demise as a practical ideology, its bankruptcy proven by their contributions to community development and the national defense. The other road promised to be a hard and lonely path for European Jews, who would be ever more vilified and demonized by culture and circumstance.[48]

The extent to which anti-Semitism pervaded European society can be seen in the much sensationalized Dreyfus Affair.[49] In October 1894, an obscure artillerist, Captain Alfred Dreyfus, was arrested on charges of spying for the German Army. During his court-martial, only circumstantial evidence was brought against Dreyfus. A cleaning lady working in the German Embassy in Paris who also worked with the French Army's Counter-Intelligence arm recovered from a wastebasket a hand-written list of top secret projects, including the army's newest 120mm howitzer. Even with no link to Dreyfus, the military court found him guilty of espionage in December 1894. In turn Dreyfus was publicly humiliated in a formal ceremony stripping him of his braid, epaulettes, and sword, and sentenced to life imprisonment on Devil's Island, the notorious prison off the coast of French Guyana.

Over time it became clear to many that in the absence of proof, the indictment proceeded to avoid embarrassing the French Army. Apparently the decision was made at the highest ranks to convict Dreyfus on the basis of his Jewish descent. Investigative reporters, including the famed novelist Emile Zola and future premier Georges Clemenceau, discovered widespread anti-Semitism in the French Army, as well as confirmation the military tribunal withheld testimony and evidence that would have exonerated Dreyfus. Most damning, however, was the discovery by French counter-intelligence that another officer, Major Ferdinand Walsin-Esterhazy, was a more likely candidate for espionage. A court martial in January 1898 exonerated Esterhazy, although he later admitted to the charges from retirement in England.

---

48 Goldstein, *A Convenient Hatred*, 202–204; and Poliakov, *The History of Anti-Semitism*, 31–66, 306–309.
49 For a recent study, see Piers Paul Read, *The Dreyfus Affair: The Scandal that Tore France in Two* (Bloomsbury, 2012).

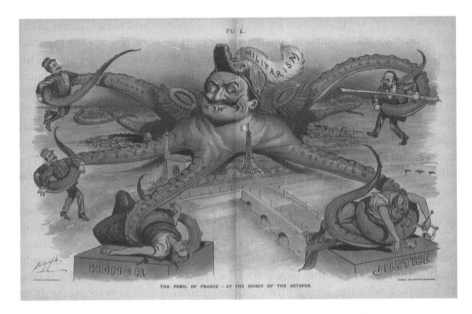

Figure 2.4: "The Peril of France – at the mercy of the octopus." In this case, the octopus represents one of the leaders of the French Army, who in turn represents the growing trend toward Militarism that is spreading across France in the wake of the arrest and conviction of Captain Alfred Dreyfus on charges of espionage. The tentacles spreading across France include "Decepton," "Dishonor," "Forgery," "Assassination," "Corrupton," "Falsehood," and "Blackmail." Ensnared in the tentacles are two military officers, representing Dreyfus and Major Georges Picquart, the officer who obtained evidence that ultimately exonerated Dreyfus. Also caught by the octopus are two females representing "Honor" and "Justice," as well as the author Èmile Zola, holding a pen labeled "J'Accuse." Illustration from *Puck*, Volume 44, Number 1129, October 26, 1898.
Source: Library of Congress. Reproduction Number: LC-DIG-ppmsca-28642 (digital file from original print). Call Number: Illus. in AP101.P7 1898 (Case X) [P&P].

After the Esterhazy trial, Emile Zola published his indictment of the French military in his essay *J'Accuse* in the newspaper *L'Aurore*. A stinging attack on the Army claiming a conspiracy to obstruct justice, Zola's letter provoked strong anti-Semitic demonstrations across France. Mobs broke into Jewish businesses and synagogues all over France, and tensions mounted amidst fear of a possible military coup to restore order. By the year's end however, Zola's charges were revealed to be true, following the jail cell suicide of Major Hubert-Joseph Henry after his arrest on charges of forging documents submitted as evidence against Dreyfus. On the basis of Henry's actions, Dreyfus was retried in August 1899. Found guilty again, and sentenced to ten years imprisonment, Dreyfus was in turn pardoned by President Emile Loubet. In 1906 he was restored to full military rank and awarded the Cross of the Legion of Honor.

The Dreyfus scandal is significant in that it reveals the extent to which anti-Semitism infiltrated various levels of the French Army and French society at the turn of the nineteenth century. Following the incident, the French military took special care to overturn the perception it was dominated by such bigoted officers. Nevertheless, the affair, while exposing the stain of French anti-Semitism, did not completely expunge it. Many Frenchmen would retain their lingering resentment over the Dreyfus Affair well into the twentieth century, waiting only for the opportunity to express their antipathy anew.[50]

Conclusions

For students interested in the nexus of race and gender with military history, the nineteenth century offers a wide range of critical cultural and social points in the development of Western-based values and their global reach. The period discussed in this chapter provides further elaboration on the evolution of racial and gendered concepts of identity, highlighting how they were in many ways cooperative explanatory schemas. Several specific military case studies are examined, particularly with reference to the Western Hemisphere. Yet in many ways, this chapter only scratches the surface of how concepts of race and gender identity affect military culture and institutions and the practice of warfare. This notwithstanding, the practices and concepts discussed here will have a dramatic influence on the spread of Western global dominance (Chapter Three) and the First World War (Chapters Four and Five). As we move into the Imperial case studies in the next chapter, consider the themes of whiteness and racial hierarchies, as well as the importance of martial masculinity and respectable nationalism, and how they combine to facilitate the rise of Western Imperialism.

---

50 Crowe, *The Holocaust*, 64–68.

3 Race, Gender, and Warfare during New Imperialism

Introduction

One of the most divisive and exploitive socio-political systems devised, *New Imperialism* has left a harsh legacy that survives in various forms to this day. Occupying a point in time where raw capitalism was realized at the expense of millions of subjugated persons, imperialism also represents an extreme expression of nationalistic fervor. During its height at the turn of the twentieth century, fully 3/5 of the world's land mass was controlled by another 1/5 (comprising the great powers of Western Europe, the United States, and Japan). A highly romanticized age of bright uniforms, gaudy indigenous costumes, and intricate pageantry, the Age of Empire was also a time of crushing repression, open exploitation, and tremendous disparities of wealth and power. An age when whiteness reigned supreme, the nineteenth and first half of the twentieth centuries bore witness to the rise of scientific racism and carefully regulated gender segregation that not only gave legitimacy to the imperial project, but also set up the great tragedies of the twentieth century. This chapter will examine how race and gender ideologies affected the military structures that helped define imperial boundaries and imposed imperial order globally.

A few basic definitions and points must be laid out first, however. Some of the oldest human social interactions are based on the construction of political and economic structures intended to benefit a core state, or *metropole*, at the expense of subordinate dependent regions, also called *periphery regions* (or colonies). The history of the ancient and medieval world is replete with examples of small militaristic states – Rome, Macedonia, etc. – that grew exponentially stronger through the conquest and subordination of neighboring and regional powers. By the seventeenth century, a select group of Western European kingdoms further prospered by the creation of vast maritime networks, empires linked largely by trade, military conquest, and colonization. The quest for empire, it appears, has always been part of the human condition.

And yet there is a marked difference between the empires of the pre-modern era and those which flourished in the nineteenth and early twentieth centuries. Thanks to a real applied advantage in material engineering – particularly in railroads, ship design, and military arms – Western Europe's direct influence over the rest of the world grew exponentially in the nineteenth century. These technological advantages permitted Great Britain, France, Germany, Russia, the United States, and Japan a real opportunity to create an imperial structure of conquest,

https://doi.org/10.1515/9783110477467-003

expansion, and exploitation that reshaped the world along the lines of Western dominance.[1]

There are at least two good reasons for including the nineteenth century's quest for empire in a study of race and gender in military history. The first is a matter of practicality. The transcendence of Western power that began in the sixteenth century, and which really hit its stride by 1800, was based largely on military capability. Vast empires were carved out in the name of European monarchs by small numbers of professional soldiers and freebooters. After conquest came administration, and again, here military institutions exercised great influence over millions of indigenous subject peoples. The story of empire, then, is much entwined in military history.

The second reason is no less real, although it is heavily rooted in material and philosophical symbolism. The story of Western Imperialism is largely one of coercion and control: that is, after the acquisition of different territories, a great deal of influence and power was exerted to solidify Western political and cultural dominance over a diverse population. In many cases, Western tropes and intellectual constructions were employed to establish a purported racial justification for empire that validated and rewarded whiteness at the expense of other ethnic and racial identities. Likewise, colonized and dominated non-white populations were subjected to presumed verdicts on their purported values and virtues which were cued to gender identities. Thus many subject peoples were effeminized and infantilized at the same time they were being racially classified. Such categorizations made European control over indigenous populations – often with the cooperation of "safe" local ethnicities deemed more "manly/martial" by Western administrators – far easier to maintain. Hence as participants in a cultural exchange intended to facilitate subjugation and control, military personnel became *de facto* arbiters of racial and gender boundaries surrounding and between Westerners and their colonial subjects.[2]

Any serious study of imperialism must begin with British historian and imperialist critic John A. Hobson. In his landmark 1902 work, *Imperialism: A Study*, Hobson portrayed imperialism not as a natural outgrowth of nationalist fervor, like colonialism, but rather as a calculated exploitation of nationalism for economic gain. Unlike the colonial system, which was organized around the settlement of new communities by transported citizens, imperialism thrived through the exploitation of indigenous populations by a small cadre of foreign administrators

---

1 See H. L. Wesseling, *The European Colonial Empires, 1815–1919* (Pearson Longman, 2004), 32–34.
2 See Tracey Rizzo and Steven Gerontakis, *Intimate Empires: Body, Race, and Gender in the Modern World* (Oxford University Press, 2016).

and troops. With political control over a mapped out territory fixed, the energies of the imperial power could be applied toward organizing total economic management of the colony.[3] In the case of the British, for example, trade in all natural resources and commodities was controlled by different companies, each assured of a near-monopoly in their field through Crown charters, granted by Parliament or its agents in the Cabinet offices. While the individual administration of different colonies varied, based upon the size, the history of compliance with imperial authority, and other factors, in all cases colonial administration was directed at maintaining order and ensuring that trade with the imperial core country and its representatives were not disrupted.

Ultimately Hobson rejected imperialism as a morally and economically corrupt institution. Imperial advocates claimed they represented the best interests of the nation and its people, he concluded, while in reality they sought nothing more than to further their own economic interests at the expense of the nation. The misplaced patriotism invoked by imperialists could very rapidly turn against the security interests of the nation, as distant friction points between national or imperial rivals could flare into real war. More critically, Hobson warned, imperialism offered little material return to the state on the massive expenditures in defense and administrative spending it promoted. In the end, he concluded, "Imperialism is a depraved choice of national life, imposed by self-seeking interests which appeal to the lusts of quantitative acquisitiveness and of forceful domination surviving in a nation from early centuries of animal struggle for existence."[4]

Others have followed Hobson's critique of imperialism with their own nuanced challenges to the system. The American humorist Mark Twain objected to American imperialism on moral grounds; what right did a republic born out of rebellion against an empire have acquiring one, he argued at the time of the Spanish-American and Phillipine-American Wars.[5] W.E.B. Dubois directly confronted the racist paradigm at the heart of imperialism; specifically, by extending their control over the globe, Western states created a new global color line, one which imposed submission and subservience on the world's non-white populations, even in their own homes.[6] V.I. Lenin's own critique elevated imperialism to "the

---

3 John A. Hobson, *Imperialism: A Study* (George Allen & Unwin, 1902, 1905; Reprint, Cosimo Classics, 2005), 7–8; 19–27.

4 *Ibid.*, 368.

5 "Mark Twain – The World of 1898: The Spanish-American War," Hispanic Division, Library of Congress. http://www.loc.gov/rr/hispanic/1898/twain.html, Accessed October 8, 2017.

6 W.E.B. DuBois, "The Color Line Belts the World," in *A W.E.B. DuBois Reader*, ed. Andrew G. Paschal (Macmillan, 1971), 263–64.

highest level of capitalism," a condition at which monopolistic free enterprise in the form of finance capital institutions had grown so powerful that it subverted the political will of the state and had set off to divide the world into markets and sources of material on its own.[7] Italian Marxist theorist Antonio Gramsci in turn downplayed the need for total physical control by the state or any other surrogate entity. Instead, Gramsci described a process of cultural imperialism – based on his construction of *cultural hegemony*– whereby social norms dictated to a population acquire the weight of imperial dominance.[8]

Another line of semiotic and cultural criticism has come from feminist scholars. Scholars like J. Ann Tickner argue strenuously for expanding the scope of their field to incorporate non-traditional issues (e.g.: rape, sex trafficking and prostitution, pornography, physical abuse, spousal violence) that have long been associated with the world's nameless and voiceless subaltern populations. Extending this worldview to imperialism, for example, Tickner identifies overt linkages between imperialism and Western-style patriarchy on a global scale: "Western forms of patriarchy spread to much of the rest of the world through imperialism where 'civilized' behavior was often equated with the behavior of Western men and women, particularly behavior based on appropriate gender roles."[9] The feminist perspective was linked with race by the American writer bell hooks, who defines whiteness itself as form of cultural imperialism, one calculated to manufacture control and subjugation through the manipulation of mass media[10] This construction certainly resonates with the image of white males exercising total control over their imperial domains being deconstructed to reconceptualize empire as a "Men's-only Club," a constructed space in which male administrators and capitalists dominated every aspect of life, free of female meddling. As feminist theorist Laura E. Donaldson noted in her book, *Decolonizing Feminism: Race, Gender, and Empire Building*:

> While colonizing nations certainly did employ military or economic coercion to secure and maintain access to satellite markets, they also penetrated colonized societies by means of

---

7 V. I. Lenin, *Imperialism: The Highest Stage of Capitalism* in *Selected Works*, (Progress Publishers, 1963), 667–776. Digitized in Marxists Internet Archive (http://www.marxists.org/archive/lenin/works/1916/imp-hsc/index.htm), Accessed, October 8, 2017.

8 Antonio Gramsci, *Prison Notebooks* (Columbia University Press, 1992), 155–57.

9 J. Ann Tickner, *Gendering World Politics: Issues and Approaches in the Post-Cold War Era* (Columbia University Press, 2001), 88.

10 See bell hooks and Amelia Mesa-Bains, *Homegrown: Engaged Cultural Criticism* (South End Press, 2006).

signifying *practices*, or the production of meaning-effects, perceptions, self-images, and subject positions necessary to sustain the colonialist enterprise.[11]

Indeed, by suborning gender and sexuality to race in the imperial setting, European and American males were free to subjugate all women – whites and colored – by recasting sexuality as a venue through which colonized peoples posed a grave threat to the sanctity of whiteness. As Anne McClintock notes in her book, *Imperial Leather: Race, Gender, and Sexuality in the Colonial Context*, imperialism was not only explicitly about racial and gender segregation and control, it was also present everywhere; the domestic hearth, home, and bedroom were no less imperial spaces than the most distant periphery outpost: "The invention of race in the urban metropole," McClintock writes, "became central not only to the self-definition of the middle class but also to the policing of the 'dangerous classes,'" an agglomeration of various deviants, including the Irish, other imperial persons of color, foreigners, sexual libertines, prostitutes, lesbians, homosexuals, and liberals.[12] The message was clear: western (i.e.: white) women were considered extremely vulnerable in the domestic and imperial setting; their sex rendering them more susceptible to environmental hazards, while their gender and their whiteness made them objects of perverse and salacious indigenous desires.[13] But in the periphery, Western women were nevertheless essential adjuncts to the masculine pursuit of empire. Left to their own devices, white European and American men were doomed to fall victim to their own animal natures, and indulge their lusts with local women and men. Western women thus were an anchor for their male imperial partners and associates, providing a necessary moral refuge from the buffeting forces of sexual desire and moral decline.[14]

And yet as a social construct, gender and Empire occupied other cultural and intellectual spaces among politically and socially active Westerners. Female reformers seeking to establish a political role for their gender in Western politics actively sought to redefine their own status of race and gender superiority over colonial subjects. In the process, they established their own roles as critical intermediaries between imperial master and colonized subject, while also

---

11 Laura E. Donaldson, *Decolonizing Feminisms: Race, Gender, and Empire-Building* (University of North Carolina Press, 1992), 89.

12 Anne McClintock, *Imperial Leather: Race, Gender, and Sexuality in the Colonial Context* (Routledge, 1995), 5.

13 Wesseling, *European Colonial Empires*, 23–24. For case studies, see chapters in Will Jackson and Emily Mantelow, eds., *Subverting Empires: Deviance and Disorder in the British Colonial World* (Palgrave Macmillan, 2015).

14 Ann Laura Stoler, *Carnal Knowledge and Imperial Power: Race and the Intimate in Colonial Rule*, 2nd ed. (University of California Press, 2002), 2, 6.

establishing new power roles outside of the imperial metropole where whiteness was more critical than gender. Male reformers and actors in the imperial project accepted the participation of their female peers – provided they did not overturn the homosocial cultures taking shape in their Western-exclusive enclaves. A frontier ethos took shape across the Western Imperial landscape, in which certain male-exclusive norms – hard drinking, libertarian outlooks on personal rights and the intrusion of law and order, sexual libertinage, and a raw sense of opportunity – set the tone, and only grudgingly gave way to gentility, law, and order.[15]

Another critique ties imperialism directly to racial exceptionalism via long-established and self-sustaining literary motifs in Western culture. First described by the social critic Edward Said as *Orientalism*, such linguistic and hermeneutic concepts continue to be employed to promote Western hegemonic control over those areas deemed "inferior" or "aberrant" in the prevalent discursive modality. In short, artistic and cultural representations of the Orient – the Levantine Mideast and India formed in the eighteenth and nineteenth centuries – assume a life of their own in the public imagination. By defining distant cultures as an exoticized venue rife with corruption, sexuality, and decadence, the objects of this discourse are transformed into mirror opposites of Western society. In turn, these same cultures and regions become acceptable targets for Western domination.[16] As Said described in his follow-up to *Orientalism*, the 1993 book *Culture and Imperialism*, "For the colonizer the incorporative apparatus requires unremitting effort to maintain. For the victim, imperialism offers these alternatives: serve or be destroyed."[17]

Once established, Said's philosophical construct opened up a range of new perspectives on the Imperial dynamic for historians. Technology-focused analysis, by historians like Daniel Headrick and Michael Adas, places imperialism within the context of a material and intellectual contest – the West flourishes on the basis of its applied technology and the absence (or failure) of the colonized to keep pace with the rush of invention. Other historians interested in how the perceived roles of environment and/or biology facilitated Western imperial expansion followed the lead of David Arnold in shifting the cultural focus of Orientalism to a physical focus on *Tropicality*, placing the responsibility for Western exploration and imperialism on the allure of a lush and rich environment that, left unmanaged, would ultimately degenerate the regions inhabitants. Regardless of their position, historians working in both interpretive schemas describe

---

15 Philippa Levine, "Preface," *Gender and Empire* (Oxford University Press, 2004), viii-ix.
16 Edward Said, *Orientalism* (Vintage, 1979).
17 Edward Said, *Culture and Imperialism* (Vintage, 1993), 168.

how Western imperialists believed their own superior science and organization would enable them to bend the physical environment to their will while also transforming the indigene into a productive and pliant subject.[18]

Clearly the historical, philosophical, and literary critiques of imperialism are well established. The challenge for military historians and other scholars working on or teaching imperialism is to balance the physical realities of imperial policies pursued across different colonies or empires with the philosophical critiques of the system. First, how does one reconcile the applied policies of different Western states – Belgium, Great Britain, France, Germany, Italy, Portugal, Russia, Spain, the United States – with each other? What about the differing approaches and policies within an imperial system? How should one compare and contrast British administration of the West Indies, for example, with that of India? Or Kenya? Or Cape Colony? Second, what does the current historian make of, or teach about, the calculated benevolence of Western administrators? Imperialism was not just a simple matter of control and coercion; administrators, engineers, physicians, and scientists all viewed the colonial periphery as a setting to advance their own agendas and programs. In the process, roads, schools, hospitals, clinics, and other civic institutions were brought to the periphery by these agents of empire. Was the resulting benevolent administration a direct policy, or a side effect of the imperial project? Finally, how deep do the currents of coercion and control run in the different imperial contexts and constructs of the era? To what extent was cultural imperialism a means to exert greater power over the indigenous populations of empire, at the same time limiting the expense of overt direct control.[19]

In closing this introduction, it should be apparent that prior patterns for establishing the nexus of race, gender, and the military, while informing elements of our study, are not necessary wholly applicable to the Imperial setting. In the remainder of this chapter, we will examine three different imperial ventures: The British Empire, the American frontier experience, and the post-1898 American Empire, and how the military imperial experience serves as a window into the complex negotiations of race, gender, and identity in the modern age.[20] We close this chapter with a brief overview of the 1900 Western intervention in China,

---

18 Headrick, *Power Over Peoples*; Adas, *Machines as the Measure of Men*; David Arnold, *Colonizing the Body: State Medicine and Epidemic Disease in Nineteenth Century India* (University of California Press, 1993); Crosby, *Ecological Imperialism*; Philip D. Curtin, *Disease and Empire: The Health of European Troops in the Conquest of Africa* (Cambridge University Press, 1998); Wintermute, *Public Health and the US Military*.
19 See Jackson and Mantelow, *Subverting Empires*.
20 French imperial policy and ideology will be discussed to a greater extent in Chapter Four.

in response to the so-called Boxer Rebellion. This exchange not only serves as a high mark for the influence and power of the Imperial experience, but it also reveals the fissures that would inevitably alter these various imperial relationships, as well as the confidence and dynamics of power within the core nations themselves.

British Concepts of Empire: Gender Identity

After the reshuffling of imperial priorities in 1783, following the Treaty of Paris ending the American Revolution, the British Imperial project was tied explicitly to the politics of gender identity. In Britain proper, the long period of peace and prosperity following the Congress of Vienna provoked its own crisis of masculinity. English pride and identity was buttressed by the twin virtues of martial prowess and forbearance in the long war against Napoleon and the heroic deeds of its imperial forces in India. Middle-class prosperity ushered in a new social conservatism, as Anglican and Presbyterian reformers vied with each other to promote a new Christian ethos to govern an immoral industrial empire. Ministers and lay persons both offered a new moral vision for Britain that was deeply motivated by the urge to foster a popular religiosity to transform the nation's institutions into a form fit for global dominance. The *Pax Brittanica* of Queen Victoria's reign was far more than a time of British economic and political preeminence; it was also intended as a venue for the assertion of a new moral masculinity founded according to a *bourgeois* Protestant Christian model.

An immediate target for British moral reformers was the nation's armed forces. At the start of the nineteenth century, the public's opinion of soldiers and sailors was generally negative. While certainly an essential agent of security from alien Continental (read: French) hostility, the general consensus held the military's rank and file at arms' length from civilian society. The reputation of the Army as a sanctuary for the dregs of Britain's jails and poorhouses was not entirely fair, but neither was it unwarranted. Predominantly young rural recruits, the sons of tenant farmers and local craftsmen, the British Army's reputation was set rather by the conduct of the minority of miscreants and criminals who found shelter and employ in its ranks. Even with harsh penalties for misconduct and drunkenness, many soldiers continued to prey upon local civilians and their own comrades-in-arms. Desertion was a perennial drain on the King's regiments, with many repeat offenders. Poverty proved a great motivation for recruiting sergeants, who employed tactics both fair and foul to lure men into service. During the eighteenth century, regular Press Acts were enacted by Parliament to guarantee full enlistment. Pardoned criminals, recovered deserters, and debtors were dragooned into uniform with little ceremony or debate.[21] The Duke of Wellington's assertion that the common soldier was "the very scum of the earth" still speaks volumes of how polite society perceived them. But it is also worth considering the rest of his statement:

> People talk about enlisting from their fine military feeling – all stuff – no such thing. Some of our men enlist from having got bastard children – some for minor offences – many more for drink; but you can hardly conceive such a set brought together, and it is really wonderful that we should have made them the fine fellows they are.[22]

This outlook changed in the mid nineteenth century, however. As British military power was dispersed far and wide across the globe in the name of empire, social reformers sought to transform the army and navy into better representations of British manhood. Camp followers were chased away from army posts at the same time that alcohol access was restricted to the post canteen. Chaplains entered the regimental rolls as vital moral guardians of the private soldier, their influence bolstered by the support of career non-commissioned officers interested in maintaining order and discipline.[23] All of this took place against the backdrop of the rise of Victorian morality across society, itself a response to the prior century's moral laxity. By 1890, the British military was transformed in the public's eye from a cesspit of scoundrels and thieves into an upright guardian of the British Empire's moral and material security. As historian Allen J. Frantzen describes in his book *Bloody Good: Chivalry, Sacrifice, and the Great War*, "The British army became a gathering of 'Christian' as opposed to 'Anglican' soldiers."[24]

And yet the realities of Britain's class system and the economic disparities produced through rapid industrialization and urbanization exerted a persistent drag on British imperial policies and ideologies. Just as France and Germany obsessed over their own birthrates in comparison with their neighbors, British elites worried over the combined bugaboos of low birthrates, high child mortality, and the physical and mental state of the general population. Taken together, these factors constituted a natalist trap that threatened the very material solvency of the Empire itself. If young British males of military service were found unfit in

---

21 Mark Urban, *Fusiliers: The Saga of a British Redcoat Regiment in the American Revolution* (Walker and Company, 2007), 16–18; and Richard Holmes, *Soldiers: Army Lives and Loyalties from Redcoats to Dusty Warriors* (Harper Press, 2011), 302–304.
22 Philip Henry Stanhope, *Notes of Conversations with the Duke of Wellington* (London: 1886), 250.
23 Holmes, *Soldiers*, 249.
24 Allen J. Frantzen, *Bloody Good: Chivalry, Sacrifice, and the Great War* (University of Chicago Press, 2004), 138.

large enough numbers, who would take on the role of security in a global empire where whiteness was held at a premium? Bad enough that the British Army may well face off against competing Great Powers in Africa and Central Asia; could the army control the millions of subject colored peoples under British dominion? This dilemma was brought into sharp relief during the Second Boer War (1899–1902). The early successes of the Afrikaner rebels against the British forces in Cape Colony and the Transvaal revealed that the British Army, for all of its presumed superiority over non-white indigenes in Africa and Asia, was hardly the repository of martial fitness. Underweight and unfit British soldiers drawn from the industrial towns of England struggled to keep up with the demands of field campaigning. Compounding the humiliation was the comparative fitness of Dominion soldiers, particularly from Australia and Canada, to British soldiers. Unlike the British army, Dominion volunteers were largely drawn from rural communities. Healthier and stronger, these volunteers also came with civilian experience in riding, shooting, and in many cases, field craft that the British rank and file did not.[25]

In response the British middle-class establishment joined forces with the Army to promote a militarized form of muscular Christianity among British school-age youth. Since the 1850s, a growing number of Anglican and Presbyterian ministers and lay workers promoted the notion of combining physical fitness with moral fitness. Taking issue with the traditionally cloistered and sedentary approach to religious study and worship, activists like Thomas Hughes and Charles Kingsley promoted a regimen of strenuous exercise, rough team sport, sexual abstinence and moral temperance, and religious study in the English public school environment. If Britain were to take its place as global imperial steward, it needed physically strong and morally resolute men to govern at home and abroad, proponents reasoned. Such fortitude was especially warranted in the face of the moral and physical hazards lurking in tropical postings.[26] Self-proclaimed military affairs experts embraced the muscular Christianity movement as an ideal schema for finally reforming the British Army's rank and file and eliminating the real and imagined scourges of misconduct, drunkenness, and venereal disease infection among the rank and file. Observant Christian soldiers organized barracks-room temperance societies to tout the evils of alcohol, while civilian groups opened dry canteens and sutler shops to offer an alternative to the local pub for enlisted men in their off hours. Membership in fraternal organizations, such as Freemasonry,

---

25 Pat Thane, "The British Imperial State and the Construction of National Identities," in *Borderlines: Genders and Identities in War and Peace, 1870–1930*, ed. Billie Melman (Routledge, 1998), 29–45, 30.
26 See Putney, *Muscular Christianity*.

was permitted on the grounds that it provided a controlled social outlet for enlisted men and officers alike. Games and sporting events – football, cricket, foot races, boxing – were introduced as well, to promote fitness, camaraderie, *esprit de corps*, and moral health.[27]

One thing reformers could agree upon was the idea that sexuality and venereal disease represented the gravest threat to the private soldier's moral and physical health. An important example of how Victorian era society bifurcated gender along moral and physical boundaries can be found in the passage of various Contagious Diseases Acts (CDA) in mid-century. Taking aim at high rates of venereal disease in British soldiers and sailors serving at home and abroad, the laws sought to contain disease by singling out promiscuous women as the vector of infection. Any suspected prostitute was subjected to arrest, detention, physical examination, treatment, and isolation or even expulsion from the communities where they were first discovered. Beginning in 1864, the circle of legitimate isolation and incarceration under the protection of the laws spread from military towns and ports in England, to larger cities in Great Britain and its imperial possessions, to virtually the entire Empire. Two key factors stand out regarding the CDA regime. First, the objectification of women as the origin of infection was a one-way street; that is to say, male soldiers, sailors, and other patrons were considered to be hapless victims, with no practical role in the spread of infection. Save for short-lived moral sanction, men were not adversely affected by the laws.

The second, more indirect, aspect of the CDAs was their relation to the dilemmas of empire and whiteness. Even though the laws were initiated in England, the origins of the Contagious Disease Acts resided in British India and the West Indies. The problem of venereal infection was found to be much greater in Imperial postings, where white military personnel engaged in regular sexual congress with indigenous prostitutes and women. Such close intermingling between the white enforcers and controllers of empire and their different indigenous subjects ran counter to every impulse of the race-conscious British culture of the nineteenth century. Issues of racial intermingling set aside, reformers considered the introduction of alien strains of venereal disease into the home islands a virtual assault on the racial vitality of British whiteness. Difficult to manage as it was, purported new virulent strains of syphilis were seen as a death sentence for the infected, regardless of social class and access to medical treatment. And while gonorrhea was not generally lethal, infection often translated directly into infertility. British natalists therefore considered the CDAs to be a final line of defense

---

27 Holmes, *Soldiers*, 536–37, 579–82.

for the homelands from foreign infection via the arteries of imperial commerce and migration.

The Contagious Diseases Acts were ultimately repealed in 1886. Shortly after they first appeared in 1864, British liberals – particularly women's groups – attacked their legality on the grounds that they provided an indiscriminate tool to coerce all women deemed troublesome by the state. Petitions bearing millions of signatures conveyed the general public's outrage over the prospect of decent people being labeled "public women" and subjected to imprisonment, let alone the intrusion into their most private personal space. However despite the legal rejection of the CDAs, the practices of compulsory inspection, treatment, and incarceration of suspected prostitutes continued without interruption in India and other parts of the British Empire for decades afterwards.[28]

As the British Army became more acceptable to the middle class, further steps were taken to entwine hyper-patriotic nationalism with military fitness. Retired Lieutenant General Robert Baden-Powell, the first Baron Baden-Powell, wrote his 1903 manual, *Aids to Scouting*, after his service in the Boer War. Within a short time, Baden-Powell's book sparked a movement among young boys and girls – almost exclusively from the middle class – that formed the core of the international Scouting movement. By 1909 troops of teenage boys took to the fields and woods of England, tromping across pastures and parkland and practicing their new skills in field craft gleaned from Baden-Powell's revised manual, *Scouting for Boys*. Even as the movement proclaimed its pan-global humanism in the years leading up to the First World War, there was little mistaking the watered-down militarism at the core of scouting. From the uniforms, to the overnight and weekend-long marches, the bivouacs to the pursuit of badges signifying mastery of skills like marksmanship, tracking, and pioneering, the Scouting movement presented its members a relatively safe introduction to the soldier's life.[29]

British Imperialism in India and Africa

Even in the twenty-first century, the mention of British India conjures up visions of British civil servants, soldiers, and their wives passing the time within white-terraced palaces, their every need attended to by faithful Indian *wallahs*; tiger

---

28 Levine, *Gender and Empire*, 127–29; Mark Harrison, *Public Health in British India: Anglo-Indian Preventive Medicine, 1857–1914* (Cambridge University Press, 1994), 72–76; and Judith Walkowitz, *City of Dreadful Delight: Narratives of Sexual Danger in Late-Victorian London* (University of Chicago Press, 1992), 22–23.
29 Mosse, *The Image of Man*, 135–36.

hunts, high tea, and potent gin and tonics keeping ennui and the tropic torpor at bay, the privileged masters of hundreds of millions of more or less loyal subjects. Of course such fantastical images are not only deeply flawed, but wholly ignorant of the reality of the nearly ninety year-long British rule of the Indian subcontinent. Even before the failed 1857 rebellion against the East India Company, British policy and conduct to its subjects and local allies rested upon the premise of total economic exploitation. In planning and in practice, a harsh interpretation of white racial exceptionalism drove British policy at all levels. Social benevolence or physical improvements, no matter how large or important, served the needs of the occupying authority foremost, not the indigenous subject. Public acceptance of the caste system belied the British reliance upon the strict socio-economic stratification it provided, not only to maintain order, but to establish a hierarchy of exploitation at all levels of social interaction.[30] Ann Laura Stoler and Frederick Cooper summarize this best: "'Caste' in India and 'tribe' in Africa were in part colonial constructs, efforts to render fluid and confusing social and political relationships into categories sufficiently static and reified and thereby useful to colonial understanding and control."[31] Classifying and categorizing Indian society along existing boundaries and imagined contours of race, ethnicity, social and religious caste, and culture facilitated the division and isolation of different communities as the British imperial authority felt best. Once fragmented, different groups could be played off of each other, their respective loyalties purchased by the dispensation of petty perquisites and rewards.

For the purpose of this study, the most critical aspect of British racial exceptionalism at play in the Indian subcontinent centers around the creation of the Indian Army. Since European traders established their first trade settlements in India in the eighteenth century, natives were recruited for local regiments. By 1750, the British East India Company made extensive use of these native regiments, and fell into the practice of referring to them as *Sepoys*, a corruption of a Persian/ Moghul term for common soldier. Recruited locally from all over India, membership qualifications varied based upon local preference. No social restrictions were placed on regiments raised in Madras and Bombay, for example; while Bengali regiments were drawn exclusively from Brahman and Rajput communities. Led

---

30 Mrinalini Sinha, *Colonial Masculinity: The "Manly Englishman" and the "Effeminate Bengali" in the Late Nineteenth Century* (Manchester University Press, 1995), 100–103; and Kaushik Roy, *Brown Warriors of the Raj: Recruitment and Mechanics of Command in the Sepoy Army, 1859–1913* (Manohar, 2008).

31 Quote in Ann Laura Stoler and Frederick Cooper, "Between Metropole and Colony: Rethinking a Research Agenda," in Frederick Cooper and Ann Laura Stoler, *Tensions of Empire: Colonial Cultures in a Bourgeois World* (University of California Press, 1997), 1–56, 11.

by European officers – many of them former military officers drawn to Indian service by the promise of easy money and cheap living expenses – the British East Indian Company army grew to just over 200,000 Sepoys and 50,000 British soldiers by 1857.

The Indian Rebellion of 1857 (described contemporarily as "The Sepoy Mutiny") marked the end of the East India Company. By the 1850s, the company had become the de facto agent of British imperial interests in South Asia. Master of the Indian Subcontinent, bulwark against Russian expansion toward the Indian Ocean, and jumping off point for future expeditions into China and Burma, the East India Company was also viewed as an oppressor by many Indian elites. Efforts to restrict the prevalence of high caste recruitment and rituals in the regiments drew deeply suspicious reactions, with some viewing British efforts at control as being part of a larger effort to convert sepoys to Christianity. The extension of new foreign service terms, in advance of proposed expeditions into Southeast Asia, rankled soldiers who had grown accustomed to short (ten to twenty mile) deployments from their home region. Finally limits on promotion and officer status for native sepoys, matched with an increase in newly commissioned British officers, was viewed by some as a further insult. The final straw, however, was the issue of rifle cartridges greased with animal fat of an unknown origin, which was taken by many as a calculated affront to their religion – be it Hindu or Muslim. Sporadic protests in different barracks led to a popular uprising in the Bengal Army, where sixty-one regiments (82 percent of the army's seventy-four infantry regiments) joined the rebellion. The ensuing war between the rebels, who self-identified with the last Mughal Emperor, Bahadur Shah Zafar, and the loyal elements of the East India Company and the British Army, was savage and bloody, with ample atrocities on both sides. By June 1858, the rebellion was crushed, and the East India Company was dissolved, its responsibilities and powers handed over to a new Cabinet department, the India Office. Reprisals and punishments against captured rebels and their leaders continued through 1859, as the British sought to extend full control over the entire region.[32]

The specter of rebellion would haunt the British for the next ninety years in India. The reality of direct imperial administration was that India as a whole was too large for an -all-British occupation force. Such an army would prove deeply unpopular at home and bankrupt the nation. Reluctant to repeat the mistakes of the East India Company, the India Office set about to create a new Indian Army

---

32 Saul David, *The Indian Mutiny* (Penguin Books, 2003), 369–74. See also Rudrangshu Mukherjee, "The Sepoy Mutinies Revisited," in Kaushik Roy, ed., *War and Society in Colonial India*, 2nd ed. (Oxford University Press, 2006), 114–25.

Figure 3.1: Two sepoy officers and one private, circa. 1820. Handcoloured engravings by Frederic Shoberl, *The World in Miniature: Hindoostan*. London: R. Ackerman.
Source: Columbia University Library, New York, New York. Public Domain. (PD-1923).

following the same method as their predecessor, albeit one free of the risk of future mutiny or rebellion. Regiments drawn from the Northern hill country of India – predominantly Garhwali, Gurkha, Kumaon, Pathan, Punjabi, and Sikh recruits – remained loyal during the rebellion. After 1860, these same ethnic groups were redefined as being "martial races" – physically robust and tough people with a long martial tradition who were natural soldiers – and became the exclusive recruitment pool for the new Indian Army. Indeed, historian Heather Streets observes that the martial race ideology was invoked as a response to a series of global events – the 1857 rebellion, Russia's own growing military threat, Irish nationalism, and problems meeting recruitment quotas in Britain – that challenged the imperial dynamic in India and abroad.[33] Even at the time, the

---

33 Heather Streets, *Martial Races: The Military, Race and Masculinity in British Imperial Cultures, 1857–1914* (Manchester University Press, 2004), 1–2.

"martial race" construct was viewed with some suspicion, though it did become assimilated into British culture thanks in no small part to the barracks-hall poetry and prose of Rudyard Kipling. Just as the loyal regiments of the Rebellion were classified as "martial" in disposition and nature, the balance of Bengal and Southern India were recast as being "non-martial" people. The former recruitment pool for the old sepoy regiments was suddenly the home of the "Bengali *babu*" – an effeminized, money hungry, sedentary race of shopkeepers, beggars, and civil servants. Military action and the need to maintain strict control over a subject people saw the transformation of the different nationalities of India along lines dictated by an outside imperial power.[34] Trevor Getz and Heather Streets-Salter offer a cogent summary of this dynamic:

> However violent force was organized or employed, it is worth remembering that its use lay at the heart of all colonial administrations in this period. Few states relinquished their authority to outsiders by choice, and even after conquest it was usually necessary to use violent force to quell unrest and maintain order. Even in times of relative peace, the presence of large standing armies, police forces, militias, or armed civilians kept the threat of violence just under the surface of colonial rule.[35]

The Indian Revolution of 1857 thus takes on a larger global context. Long contextualized as a local rebellion sparked by British indifference to the immediate religious and cultural needs of its client partners, the significance of the event grows when viewed as a part of a larger process. Coercive military force resides at the core of the imperial project, not only at the point of first contact or acquisition, but also in the supplanting of traditional power dynamics by systems favoring the new occupying imperial presence. Even as new client relationships were being identified and forged under the auspices of the "martial races" concept, other elite communities who rejected British control were culturally and politically emasculated in the new India of the Raj. Gendered rhetoric and policies proved effective tools of imperial control. The pattern of Western control over gendered identity continued into virtually every aspect of Indian life. David Arnold

---

34 Sinha, *Colonial Masculinity*, 16–18; Streets, *Martial Races*, 2; and Roy, *Brown Warriors of the Raj*, 36–79. Roy attributes British recruitment policy in India to a multi-varied set of criteria, all tied intimately to the need to maintain imperial control over the subcontinent with a minimal expenditure of force and capital. Martial races ideology was complemented by a distinct – though related – outlook he defines as "anti-martial race ideology." Accordingly, the privileges associated with military service (and close cooperation with imperial policies) were granted on such a limited clan-oriented basis that they essentially created a self-validating system of ethnic exceptionalism (*Ibid.*, 306).
35 Trevor R. Getz and Heather Streets-Salter, *Modern Imperialism and Colonialism: A Global Perspective* (Prentice Hall, 2011), 196.

identifies similar acts of cultural insensitivity in the guise of imperial policy in response to cholera and smallpox epidemics in India. Communities and individuals who rejected vaccination on religious grounds were treated as intransigent and hostile subjects, and were singled out for coercive methods to ensure compliance. Western medicine, therefore, was not only implicitly engaged in the imperial project, those institutions and individuals associated with its practice in India were effectively colonizing the individual and collective body of the Indian.[36]

Figure 3.2: "Pioneer Regiments, 1911 (c)."Watercolour by Major Alfred Crowdy Lovett (1862–1919), 1911 (c).
Eleven figures from the following units: 34th Sikh Pioneers; 12th Pioneers (The Kelat-i-Ghilzie Regiment); 128th Pioneers; 23rd Sikh Pioneers; 64th Pioneers; 61st Prince of Wales's Own Pioneers; 48th Pioneers; 81st Pioneers; 106th Hazara Pioneers; 107th Pioneers. Indian pioneer units repaired roads and bridges, worked on fortifications and trenches, moved supplies and carried out countless other engineering and logistical tasks.
Source: Alfred Crowdy Lovett and Sir George Fletcher MacMunn, *The Armies of India*, Adam and Charles Black, 1911.

The "martial races" construct soon escaped its Indian context. In Britain proper, the term was applied to Scots and Scot-Irish communities that provided large contingents of recruits for the army. Abeyance was offered to the concept in the white

---

36 Arnold, *Colonizing the Body*, 292.

Dominions – Canada, Australia, and New Zealand in particular – both to the descendants of the original settlers and to some of the indigenous peoples they encountered. British Africa, however, presented a variety of contexts that validated and challenged the construct.[37] Some, like the Egyptians, were dismissed entirely as effeminate degenerates, incapable of following simple instruction or showing the initiative needed to wage war successfully. Generally considered inadequate for military service, Adam Dighton observes how "it was thought that the Egyptian male had been 'reared in an effeminate clime' and so did not make a good soldier."[38] British officers soon accepted this biologically determined view as a matter of course, effectively both emasculating and infantilizing the Egyptian male as they became supporting players on the larger imperial stage.[39] This construction speaks toward another element of martial races ideology worth considering; specifically, as Heather Streets notes, "'Martial race' soldiers were not just 'raced', however: they also, significantly, came to be 'gendered' as ideally masculine."[40] Keeping an empire running was clearly a man's job; not only requiring the tacit support of local soldiers and auxiliaries, but needing only the most "manly" of the local communities. By displaying masculine martial virtue, these select groups – Highland Scots, Sikhs, Gurkhas, Pashtuns – were rising above the general trends in their own demographic enclaves. By dint of their military prowess, they were not only more masculine than their peers, they also were essentially placed higher on the imagined yet all important hierarchy of racial classification.

Alternatively other non-white groups, such as the Zulu, Sudanese, and Maasai, were identified as being martial races on the basis of their armed resistance to British encroachment. A special case was also made for the white Boer settlers of the Transvaal. Descended from strict Calvinist Dutch settlers, the Boer proved adept at guerilla warfare at the turn of the century. In the two Boer Wars in in South Africa, they inflicted humiliating defeats on larger and ostensibly better trained regular British forces. After the shock of defeat passed, the British mustered the full weight of its imperial forces to crush the Boers. Within a short

---

37 James O. Gump's *The Dust Rose Like Smoke: The Subjugation of the Zulu and the Sioux* (University of Nebraska Press, 1994) presents a comparative study of two distinct campaigns on the imperial frontier for Great Britain and the United States. Gump argues that study of the two encounters with indigenous peoples offers numerous insights into the process of imperial expansion and the limits of local resistance against it.

38 Adam Dighton, "Race, Masculinity, and Imperialism: The British Officer and the Egyptian Army, 1882–1899," *War and Society* 35 (February 2016): 1–18, quote on 5.

39 *Ibid.*, 17–18.

40 Street, *Martial Races*, 10.

time, however, bitterness changed into grudging respect as the Afrikaners were assimilated into the Empire, and were recognized as equals alongside the other Dominions in political autonomy and military prowess.[41]

American Exceptionalism at Play: Race and the Native American

For generations the conventional interpretation of American transcontinental expansion followed the direction laid out in John Gast's famous 1872 painting of the spirit of American Progress opening up the vast Western wilderness to the promise of civilization and settlement. Shining light onto the wilderness, Progress serves as a feminized surrogate for white Anglo-American culture spreading across the West. Accordingly, only wild animals and savages dwelled in the American interior, interlopers who would either flee from the purifying light of American Progress or die where they made their stand. Regardless of the decision taken, the long night of ignorance, indolence, and sloth were over. Following in the wake of Progress, a new frontier was taking shape, as white homesteaders, ranchers, and railroad men took charge of Nature itself, crafting a New "new world," one which submitted to the powers of reason and commerce. Manifest Destiny was not just a catchy slogan peddled by Irish-American newspaper men. It was an elemental process that would create an Anglo-American paradise, a study in the power of progress for all to observe and embrace: today may still belong to the Old World's kings, princes, and popes; the future would belong to the new American Republic.

Quite the evocative portrayal, and one which has become so ingrained into the American psyche that it is rarely challenged in public settings or popular discourse. Schoolbooks in middle America champion an account of national growth and expansion rooted in myth, fiction, and misrepresentation; and yet, little thought is given toward an alternative narrative, lest it somehow cheapen the burgeoning pride in place and history desired in young people.

Regardless of how one group or another tries to paint it, however, the story of American expansion is one of American imperialism at work. Strip away the patriotic memes and the veneer of false legitimacy accorded to our drive West, and what remains is an account of a remarkably successful imperial drive across a continent. And just as with British, French, Russian, or other nineteenth century case studies, the story of American Empire is one of military conquest, public

---

41 Douglas Porch, *Wars of Empire* (Smithsonian Books/HarperCollins, 2000) 162–68; and Streets, *Martial Races*, 105–107.

betrayal, and shifting borderlands. At the center of American Western expansion is the United States Army, both in its small professional cadre and its much larger volunteer militia components. Reconstituted in 1790, the Army quickly settled into its primary role as a frontier constabulary. Frequently scattered across the Western territories in small forts and encampments, individual infantry companies and cavalry troops served as the symbolic and physical manifestations of federal authority and law and order on the frontier. In this capacity, American military personnel and officers became by default the chief arbiter of peace and conflict in the vast and commonly shifting borderlands between white settlers, Indian tribes, and other foreign governments with claims either competing with or bordering alongside those of the United States.[42]

Before examining the nature of the American military's role as an agent of frontier imperial administration, clarification of the borderlands concept itself is warranted. In many ways a response to Frederick Jackson Turner's frontier thesis, the borderlands concept was first elaborated upon by Turner's student, Herbert Eugene Bolton, in his 1921 book *The Spanish Borderlands*. Here Bolton describes the rise in the eighteenth and nineteenth centuries of a hybridized culture blending different elements from those cultures that came into contact with each other along the fringe of Spanish settlement in the Southwest. From Spanish Florida to Baja California, the entire region was a rich and diverse setting for the intermingling of different cultural norms and identities. The borderlands, as Bolton described the shared space, was a place where representatives from all sides of the cultural divide met to negotiate terms of trade, commerce, and interfamilial relations that transcended formal political positions dictated from the distant metropole. Thus whether in conflict or in peace, the borderlands offered a clear study in how relations on the imperial periphery affected – if not dictated – the shaping of policy at the core. In later decades, Bolton's theory of regional negotiation and shared communities was applied to other case studies, marking out a powerful state of agency for the colonized imperial subjects residing at the tipping point of empire.[43]

One recent example is found in Anne Hyde's contribution to the University of Nebraska Press' multi-volume History of the American West Series, *Empires,*

---

42 David Narrett, *Adventurism and Empire: The Struggle for Mastery in the Louisiana-Florida Borderlands, 1762–1803* (University of North Carolina Press, 2015); and Kevin Adams, *Class and Race in the Frontier Army: Military Life in the West, 1870–1890* (University of Oklahoma Press, 2009).
43 Herbert Eugene Bolton, *The Spanish Borderlands: A Chronicle of Old Florida and the Southwest* (N.P.: 1921; Reprint, Forgotten Books, 2012); Jeremy Adelman and Stephen Aron, "From Borderlands to Borders: Empires, Nation-States and the Peoples in between in North American History," *American Historical Review* 104.3 (1999): 814–41; and Albert L. Hurtado, *Herbert Eugene Bolton: Historian of the American Borderlands* (University of California Press, 2012).

Nations, and Families: A History of the North American West, 1800–1860. Following Bolton's general outline of looking to the interactions of local communities, Hyde rejects the worn-out notion of the Western frontier as an empty space waiting for American settlement and commercial exploitation. Using the example of the fur trade, Hyde describes a rich and diverse series of interactions and trade nexii, each linked through long-standing histories of mutually negotiated interests, frequently sealed through intermarriage. The "blank space" on contemporary maps that was the Antebellum West was far from empty. Long before American settlers arrived on the scene, many parts of the Western frontier were occupied by others – Spaniards (later Mexicans), English and French traders, Russians, and of course, a diverse and complex network of Indian tribes and communities. The notion of the West as a wild, untamed frontier is an Americentric construction, ignoring the many borderland exchanges and cultures that were being established in the absence of white American participation. The same can be said of women's roles and perspectives, regardless of their race or ethnicity. Such accounts are the centerpiece of the "New West" history movement.[44] By recasting the story of American expansion as an intrusion into a pre-existing borderlands culture, long overdue attention is drawn toward the other, non Anglo-American, communities that occupied the region. The residual effect of this approach, however, places American expansion in the perspective of being a hostile intrusion, marked by greedy land speculation, raw exploitation of existing peoples and resources, and the extension of American culture and political control into new territories outside the nation's traditional East Coast core. At the same time, a new cultural exchange was being established between the West's existing inhabitants and the ever-growing number of American migrants. Unlike its predecessors, however, the new borderlands were fluid and changing. Always under pressure from new waves of settlers, this frontier was always shrinking, until it disappeared altogether in the 1890s.

Of course the greatest losers in this new borderland were the Native Americans. Other non-American communities benefitted from their status, wealth, and whiteness to assimilate readily with the new arrivals. After all, these were the same groups who for centuries had staked out their positions in the West through careful intermarriage with powerful trading partners and allies. Some other groups, including the *mestizo* populations of the Southwest who remained on the

---

44 Anne F. Hyde, *Empires, Nations, and Families: A History of the North American West, 1800–1860* (University of Nebraska Press, 2011); Glenda Riley, *Confronting Race: Women and Indians on the Frontier, 1815–1915* (University of New Mexico Press, 2004). For a comparative international study, see Glenda Riley, *Taking Land, Breaking Land: Women Colonizing the American West and Kenya, 1840–1940* (University of New Mexico Press, 2003).

scene after the Mexican War, suffered indignities and insults, often expressed in the crudest racial terms. But even these communities assimilated over time. The Indian, however, remained the eternal intruder in their own country, subjected to constant pressure to submit to the whims of the white interlopers who sought their lands and who claimed a divine mandate over the continent. Uncomfortable as it may be to acknowledge it, the American Indian in the West was the subject of a long and brutal campaign of ethnic cleansing and resettlement, made legitimate by acts of Congress and imposed at all levels of society across the entire country. Until they were confined to carefully laid-out reservations – often on tracts of land generally inhospitable to permanent settlement – the Indian remained a hindrance to America's manifest destiny, a position summarized by Interior Secretary James Harlan in 1866, and later commented on by historian Robert M. Utley:

> "It has been the settled policy of the government . . . to establish the various tribes upon suitable reservations and there protect and subsist them until they can be taught to cultivate the soil and sustain themselves." This goal, of course, was actually only a means to a larger goal: to remove the Indian from the paths of westward expansion and – a consoling legalism – to extinguish Indian "title" to lands on which whites wanted to settle.[45]

Long before the American Civil War, the United States Army's chief role was to deal with the problem of openly hostile Indian tribes. In turning over British claims to territories east of the Mississippi River to the new Confederation, the 1783 Treaty of Paris signaled to the Native Americans residing there the onset of a new cycle of war with the Americans. By the time of the combined Shawnee and Miami victory over an Army expeditionary force along Ohio's Wabash River in 1791, many Indian leaders and tribal councils had come to accept the inevitability of war with the new United States. With white settlement of the Ohio Valley threatening to overwhelm the Indians who lived there, armed violence escalated in scale and tone between the two sides. On the American side, individual settlers and organized militia and Regular Army units alike followed the trend of attacking unarmed camps and settlements that had been the norm since the first encounters between the English and the Indians in the sixteenth and seventeenth centuries – a practice which was repeated by the Indians against isolated white settlements and refugee camps. The savage attacks, counter-attacks, and reprisals between the two sides were entirely the result of a racialized discourse of hatred and ethnic resettlement that was shared by Indians and Americans.

---

45 Robert M. Utley, *Frontier Regulars: The United States Army and the Indian, 1866–1891* (University of Nebraska Press, 1984), 7–8. Quote taken from Commissioner of Indian Affairs, *Annual Report* (1866), 370–72.

On the part of the Anglo-Americans, there is some indication that such violence was accepted as the norm because the Indians were considered to be racially different – and inferior – to the Europeans now competing for their lands. Historian Wayne E. Lee linked this behavior to English conduct during the mid-sixteenth century Tudor conquest of Ireland. Their ethnic exceptionalism and religious hatreds fed a harsh war of civilian reprisals and irregular warfare that lasted for over a century, establishing an informal code of wartime conduct that sanctioned total war against civilian non-Protestant/Christian populations. It was a simple matter, Lee argues, for English colonists to pursue similar warfare against hostile Indian tribes that threatened to overwhelm their tenuous settlements in Virginia and New England.[46] And after becoming accepted practice culturally by the first English colonists in the New World, the savage totality of violence defined Colonial and then American conduct in warfare with Indians ever after. And for their part, the Indians recognized and willingly participated in the escalation of violence with their American counterparts. Unlike warfare with other tribes, which often settled upon resolving blood debts and stronger tribes asserting dominance over weaker neighbors, combat with English colonists (and later the Americans) was aimed at total annihilation. Shawnee war leader Tecumseh captured this spirit in his warnings to a gathering of Creek warriors in 1811, when he urged his audience: "Let the white race perish. They seize your land; they corrupt your women; they trample on the bones of your dead!"[47]

Both sides, it appears, resolved on a course of annihilative war dictated by perceptions and experiences of racial persecution and exceptionalism. And a review of the various Indian Wars after the War of 1812 reveals an overt hatred between the two societies that helped fuel the worse outrages over the next 75 years: Major General Andrew Jackson's attacks against the Creek and Cherokee nations; the Seminole Wars in Florida; the resettlement of the Southern tribes under Presidents Jackson and Martin Van Buren; the Black Hawk War; the Sand Creek Massacre; the Sioux Wars; the Ute Wars; etc. Of course not every participant experienced the same totality of racist hatred – indeed the absence of such a total consensus helped impose some restriction on violence, making the Indian Wars sometimes more of an exercise in ethnic resettlement than of unrestrained ethnic cleansing. But just as the English codes of conduct against Irish rebels in the sixteenth and seventeenth centuries legitimized extreme war against non-English and non-white persons in the New World, American martial violence influenced

---

46 Lee, *Barbarians and Brothers*.
47 Quoted in Robert Wooster, *The American Military Frontiers: The United States Army in the West, 1783–1900* (University of New Mexico Press, 2009), 45.

by racist ideology in the Frontier translated into a sanctioned racialized warfare abroad after 1898.[48]

Theodore Roosevelt and "The Strenuous Life"

When the United States went to war with Spain in 1898, many felt the rugged individualism of the recently closed Frontier could be reborn, and the violent rift between Northerners and Southerners could be healed – all in service of freeing an exploited people from an allegedly corrupt empire. Never mind that the real motivations and conduct of the Spanish-American War were problematic at best. Warfare at its organic level represented the ultimate arena for men to prove themselves as truly masculine in an otherwise emasculated existence. One American following his country's call to duty in 1898 was Theodore Roosevelt, who embodied the notions of masculinity, nationalism, and independence in the United States in that decade and thereafter. As a cowboy, boxer, hunter, politician, Sunday School teacher, Rough Rider, Medal of Honor recipient, and Nobel Peace Prize laureate, Roosevelt can be considered the icon of the ideal Victorian man and symbol of the early twentieth century's *Cult of Manliness* in ways that perhaps only Ernest Hemingway and a few others did.

Born in 1858 and raised in an environment of economic privilege in New York, Theodore Roosevelt did not enjoy a healthy childhood. Although scrawny and asthmatic with poor eyesight, he did not allow this to deter him in the long term. As a young man, Roosevelt left the comfortable confines of the eastern seaboard and moved to a ranch in the Dakota Territory where the fresh air and robust work matured him into true manhood. He would never lose his love for outdoor activities like sports and hunting because he believed these represented keys for good health and proper manliness. Roosevelt thus fit comfortably into the mold of "Muscular Christianity" with its penchants for out virility, courage, strength, competition, endurance, and heroism all in service God, country, and civilization. Against these virtues stood the dangerous vices of laziness, softness, effeminacy, cowardice, and passivity, all which heralded the decline and eventual defeat of any man and his country or civilization.

Nowhere was Roosevelt perhaps more eloquent or forceful in articulating his construction of ideal American masculinity than in his famous speech of 1899

---

48 For two provocative comparative studies, see Gump, *The Dust Rose Like Smoke*; and Edward B. Westermann, *Hitler's Ostkrieg and the Indian War: Comparing Genocide and Conquest* (University of Oklahoma Press, 2016).

Figure 3.3: "The Soldier" – A portrayal of Theodore Roosevelt living up to the ideals of "The Strenuous Life" during the charge up San Juan Hill in Cuba, 1898. Taken from William Wallace Denslow's *When I Grow Up*, a children's book published in 1909.
Source: British Library, London UK © British Library Board All Rights Reserved/Bridgeman images

known as "The Strenuous Life." Roosevelt argues for traditional gender relations and roles, as well as for specific types of child rearing that could benefit the American family and the nation as a whole:

> A healthy state can exist only when the men and women who make it up lead clean, vigorous, healthy lives; when the children are so trained that they shall endeavor, not to shirk difficulties, but to overcome them; not to seek ease, but to know how to wrest triumph from

toil and risk. . . . When men fear work or fear righteous war, when women fear motherhood, they tremble on the brink of doom; and well it is that they should vanish from the earth, where they are fit subjects for the scorn of all men and women who are themselves strong and brave and high-minded.[49]

The correlation of men with war and women with motherhood demonstrates Roosevelt's conception of what ideal activities should be associated with each gender. For his part, he strived to live a manly life, whether as a father and husband or as a leader of men in combat and President of the United States.

Roosevelt's speech on "The Strenuous Life" also revealed his attitudes about race and culture. His ambitions for the Caucasian race, for Caucasians living in the United States of America, and for western Christian democracy to dominate the globe can be seen the following:

> The problems are different for the different islands. Porto Rico is not large enough to stand alone. We must govern it wisely and well, primarily in the interest of its own people. Cuba is, in my judgment, entitled ultimately to settle for itself whether it shall be an independent state or an integral portion of the mightiest of republics. But until order and stable liberty are secured, we must remain in the island to insure them, and infinite tact, judgment, moderation, and courage must be shown by our military and civil representatives in keeping the island pacified, in relentlessly stamping out brigandage, in protecting all alike, and yet in showing proper recognition to the men who have fought for Cuban liberty. The Philippines offer a yet graver problem. Their population includes half-caste and native Christians, warlike Moslems, and wild pagans. Many of their people are utterly unfit for self-government, and show no signs of becoming fit. Others may in time become fit but at present can only take part in self-government under a wise supervision, at once firm and beneficent. We have driven Spanish tyranny from the islands. If we now let it be replaced by savage anarchy, our work has been for harm and not for good.[50]

Embedded therefore in his speech were agendas for American politics and foreign policy. Such ideas smack of Social Darwinism and the "White Man's Burden" and of exceptionalism of White Anglo-Saxon Protestant masculinity. Indeed, at risk of being ahistorical, had he lived in today's world, Roosevelt would likely buy into the ideology advanced by the neo-conservatives in the contemporary United States. He would have favored their efforts at nation-building and democratization. In any event, Roosevelt supported territorial imperialism as much as he did cultural imperialism during his life time.[51]

---

49 Theodore Roosevelt, *The Strenuous Life*, 1899. http://www.bartleby.com/58/1.html (Accessed October 8, 2017).
50 *Ibid.*
51 Sarah Watts, *Rough Rider in the White House: Theodore Roosevelt and the Politics of Desire* (University of Chicago Press, 2006); and Bederman, *Manliness and Civilization.*

The Spanish-American War

Long obsessed with domesticating its vast Western territories, the United States was a late comer to the grand imperial game, making its debut in the Spanish-American War. Described by then-U.S. Secretary of State John Hay as "a splendid little war," the contest with an aging Spanish monarchy was for the most part an uneven contest. Separated from its contested imperial possessions by thousands of miles of ocean, the obsolete Spanish fleet was thoroughly outclassed by the new American steel and steam navy. Similarly, the outnumbered Spanish defenders in the Philippines, Cuba, and Puerto Rico also faced off against an active insurgency, while also struggling to survive in the face of crippling tropical diseases. Even so, while the narrative of the Spanish-American War is one of America's ascension to great power status, the story is also a case study revealing the wartime nexus of race, gender, and policy. Historian Kristin Hoganson follows this story in her ground-breaking monograph, *Fighting for American Manhood: How Gender Politics Provoked the Spanish-American and Philippine American Wars*. Moving past traditional explanations for the war, Hoganson places the hyper-nationalist arguments of jingoes favoring war with Spain within the context of a national gendered discourse that served dual purposes: "On the one hand, gender served as a cultural motive that easily lent itself to economic, strategic, and other justifications for war. On the other, gender served as a coalition –building political method, one that helped jingoes forge their disparate arguments for war into a simpler, more visceral rationale that had a broad appeal."[52] Essentially the case for war resided exclusively on gendered constructions, Hoganson argues. Proximal justifications for intervention, such as the *reconcentrado* policy undertaken by the Spanish military governor, General Valeriano Weyler y Nicolau, were cast as an assault on the honor of Cuban women. Likewise, interventionists portrayed the imminent conflict as a moral obligation for American men; just as they would act if a neighbor were sexually assaulted, so too should the United States come to the rescue of the moribund Cuban maiden, under attack by a brutal Spanish overlord. Anti-imperialists and other opponents of intervention were in turn castigated as demasculinized milksops, in the form of either weak-kneed sissies or as cross-dressing inverts, virtual women in all but name.[53]

---

52 Kristin L. Hoganson, *Fighting for American Manhood: How Gender Politics Provoked the Spanish-American and Philippine-American Wars* (Yale University Press, 1998), 8.
53 *Ibid.*, 9, 51, 102–104.

Figure 3.4: "Our Busy Old Women" (From *Puck*, 45:1150 March 22, 1899). The centerfold print shows a mob of anti-imperialist "Old Women" attacking a memorial erected to the McKinley Administration's accomplishments in the recent war with Spain.
Source: Library of Congress. Reproduction Number: LC-DIG-ppmsca-28582 (digital file from original print).

The gendered rhetoric Hoganson describes transcended the immediate issue of war with Spain, however. Throughout America, just as in Europe, imperialists sought to link their cause with arguments for restoring masculinity in the face of its erosion under the pressures of peace and prosperity. Curiously the decades-long stability that existed across Western Europe and the United States after the violent 1860s had become recast as a time not only of material prosperity and economic growth, but also as a time in which normative standards of manhood were in flux. Anxiety over a perceived demasculinization of Western culture expressed itself in a spate of strenuous activity in political affairs. As Tom Lutz noted in *American Nervousness, 1903: An Anecdotal History*, this was nothing less than a dynamic call to imperial expansion in the name of preserving Western masculinity. "The civilized man was being replaced as a middle-class hero by the civilizing man, by the man whose enterprise was expansion . ... American expansionist foreign policy is mirrored by the successful man's attempt to increase his bulk through vigorous muscle-building, conspicuous consumption of casualties, or the making of 'fat and blood' as prescribed by Mitchell."[54] This extended to a tacit support for military adventures abroad, which was seen as an essential remedy for the dissipative effects of modernity on the collective American masculine-oriented vitality; a biological imperative that was also rooted in contexts of race and whiteness.[55] In the immediate absence of war, the whole practice of empire building was increasingly seen as the best pathway for white men to arrest the gradual degeneration of their gender. The tasks of conquering distant cultures and bringing them under the civil and economic control of Western nations became popularized both as a moral obligation – *mission civilisatrice* to use the French term – and as a way to reassert certain dormant tendencies and behaviors through the exercise of conquest and colonization.[56]

As the United States flexed its economic muscle abroad, little wonder that a new generation of American imperialists considered the possibilities of foreign adventures. Historian Louis A. Perez summarized this broader impulse in association with the specific experience of the invasion and subsequent administration of Cuba:

> Precisely because the pursuit of national interest was imagined as enactment of moral purpose, the Americans could plausibly demand the world to acquiesce to the purity of their motives. Having persuaded themselves that they acted entirely out of disinterested motive and selfless intent, in the service of humanity, as agents of order, progress, and liberty, they concluded that other people had no cause to doubt their intentions or oppose

---

54 Lutz, *American Nervousness*, 35.
55 *Ibid.*, 61, 82.
56 See Stephen Kinzer, *The True Flag: Theodore Roosevelt, Mark Twain, and the Birth of American Empire* (Henry Holt and Company, 2017).

their policies. Power thus exercised with the certainty of beneficent purpose could not readily admit the plausibility of opposition. Indeed, to oppose notable intent could only suggest ignoble motive. Those who would challenge the authenticity of American altruism, those who opposed the goals of American generosity, were necessarily evildoers and mischief-makers, misinformed or else malcontents given to doing bad things, and by definition deemed to be enemies of humanity. So fully were Americans in the thrall of the moral propriety of their own motives as to be unable to recognize the havoc their actions often wrought on the lives of others.[57]

These perceptions were actually common across the West, but in the United States, such rhetoric was especially alluring. Considering how Frederick Jackson Turner's 1890 verdict that the Frontier is Closed was accepted with little question, the message of the new imperialists became even more popular. If indeed the great American West was tamed, then the great crucible for a virile American masculinity was likewise lost.

The key dilemma facing American imperialists, however, was the realization that by 1890, there was very little territory left for a simple territory grab. The closest the United States came before 1898 to the great imperial game was the acquisition of Hawaii; and even here, white filibusters were denied their first chance to come under American control, in 1893. Formal annexation would have to wait until 1900. This dilemma returns the argument back to the issue of war with Spain, and how they in turn cast war, alongside empire, as an exercise essential for bolstering the nation's wavering manhood. Proponents of the "strenuous life" like Theodore Roosevelt, Henry Cabot Lodge, army colonel Leonard Wood, and naval captain Alfred Thayer Mahan followed the Lamarckian ideals pursued by European imperialists, redefining war as a rite of passage for the nation's youth.[58] A generation of young American men had grown soft and flaccid in the absence of any vital, life-or-death challenge that would test their mettle and signal the passing from callow youth to virile manhood. In comparison with their parents and grandparents, who in their youth fought in the American Civil War, young people of the Gilded Age were aimless dreamers. In the absence of any significant moral and physical test, America's youth were increasingly susceptible to the various material and earthly pleasures that would lead inexorably to gender degradation. War and empire, vocal adherents argued, combined to become the perfect remedy to stave off national decline. Positivist-oriented biological determinists adopted an action-oriented schema for human development

---

57 Louis A. Perez, *Cuba in the American Imagination: Metaphor and the Imperial Ethos* (University of North Carolina Press, 2008), 7.
58 See Evan Thomas, *The War Lovers: Roosevelt, Lodge, Hearst, and the Rush to Empire, 1898* (Little, Brown, 2010).

that placed violence front and center. "The evolution of the race has been notoriously sanguinary," behaviorist James Rowland Angell wrote, "and we should feel no surprise . . . that under the excitement of actual combat the old brute should display the cloven hoof."[59] Angell was seconded by Sir Ronald Ross, the much-acclaimed discoverer of the malaria insect vector and chair of tropical medicine at the University of Liverpool. War had successfully culled the weak, but it also imposed a deeper respect and appreciation for the social cues – discipline, sacrifice, obedience – that came out of war. Given time, war may well become obsolete, but in the interim, it was an essential tool for human development.[60]

By applying a gendered dynamic to the social and cultural backdrop to intervention in 1898, a new interpretation of the Spanish-American War unfolds. But even in the face of such powerful cultural evidence, the case for America's rise to the global stage being a gendered exchange would be weak were it not for the direct interplay of gendered associations and conducts taking place in the field. And at the same time American soldiers struggled to maintain their manly forbearance and identities, different and yet related contexts over racial identity arose, signaling their close relationship in the wake of Western imperial expansion and control. As noted earlier, the case for war was founded largely in a gendered context, with the United States taking on the role of masculine defender of a moribund Cuban feminine dependency. To a large degree, the Army's V Corps pursued a self-defined "manly course" in its short campaign in Cuba.

The twin issues of gender and race combined on the island of Cuba from the start of the campaign. As V Corps disembarked at Daiquiri and Siboney, the Americans were stunned to discover that the Cuban *insurrectos* were comprised largely of black and creole farmers. Many Americans just assumed the Cubans were Caucasians, on the basis of the Hearst and Pulitzer press editorial cartoon portrayals and the limited contacts with Cuban exiles in New York and Florida. The revelation of the racial dynamic in Cuba only further emboldened American imperialists.[61] A generation earlier, Southern Democrats first promoted the

---

59 Paul Crook, *Darwinism, War, and History* (Cambridge University Press, 1994), 133.
60 *Ibid.*, 138.
61 The American military presence in Cuba began a series of occupation and counterinsurgencies by the U.S. Marines in Latin American that would last until the mid-1930s, all of which the U.S. undertook with the goals of civilizing, Christianizing (Protestantism), democratizing, and modernizing the region. Economic and commercial interests are place critical roles as motivators. For examples, see Gilbert Joseph and Catherine C. LeGrand, eds. *Close Encounters of Empire: Writing the Cultural History of U.S.-Latin American Relations* (Duke University Press, 1998); Mary Renda, *Taking Haiti: Military Occupation and the Culture of U.S. Imperialism* (University of North Carolina Press, 2001); and Ellen D. Tillman, *Dollar Diplomacy by Force: Nation-Building and Resistance in the Dominican Republic* (University of North Carolina Press, 2016).

idea of annexation in order to further the expansion of slavery. Now the appeals were couched in a combination of racial security and paternalist stewardship. Left to their own governance, the racially suspect Cubans would certainly fail to develop the stability needed to promote economic prosperity and political autonomy. This would certainly be true as applied to the other Great Powers, who were portrayed as vultures circling the moribund Spanish Empire. At the same time, American stewardship of Cuba was cast as an essential step toward preventing racial violence and insurrection at home. The prospect of a colored independent state ninety miles from Miami threatened the white hegemonic control over the multi-racial South. In order to preserve a Jim Crow society based on racial segregation, Cuban independence had to be curbed until the white Cuban elite was able to exert its own control over its mulatto and black citizens.[62]

In its final battles at El Caney and San Juan Hill, V Corps directly confronted the inconsistencies of American racial and gender constructions. The perception that war buttressed individual character among young men was shaken by the rediscovery that war creates casualties. Miscommunication and the tropic heat combined with withering Spanish fire to sow confusion among the attacking Americans. At the foot of San Juan and Kettle Hills, black troopers of the Ninth and Tenth Cavalry led the assault on Spanish positions, and were soon joined by other white regiments, including the First US Volunteer Cavalry, led by its executive officer, Lieutenant Colonel Theodore Roosevelt. In the ensuing charge, black and white soldiers were intermingled in the rush to the summit under enemy fire, driving off the Spanish defenders.[63] The battle of San Juan Hill proved decisive, as the Spanish garrison in Santiago would surrender two weeks later, on July 17, 1898, and again demonstrated the fighting abilities of the Army's black regiments. Their moment of glory would be short-lived. After the war ended, Theodore Roosevelt published his own account of the Cuban campaign, focusing its attention on the performance of his own unit. In many ways, *The Rough Riders* was a strong and enthralling account of the Santiago Campaign. But Roosevelt revealed his own prejudices as he downplayed the role of the Ninth and Tenth Cavalry in the battle. The only persons from the regiments to be singled out in his narrative were

---

62 A detailed accounting of the ebb and flow of Cuban planter elite designs for control of the island after the eventual withdrawal of Spanish colonial rule, and the unintended role of American forces in accelerating this process, may be found in Louis A. Perez, *Cuba: Between Reform and Revolution* (Oxford University Press, 1995), 181–83.

63 According to Graham Cosmas, the Spanish were already evacuating their blockhouses on San Juan Hill, their artillery having exhausted their supply of shrapnel shells. See Graham A. Cosmas, *An Army for Empire: The United States Army in the Spanish-American War* (Texas A&M University Press, 1998), 217.

the units white officers, as he gave the impression that the enlisted troopers were less than enthusiastic in joining the assault. When he revised the book in later editions, the Ninth and Tenth Cavalry Regiments parts in the battle shrunk, while the role of the First US Volunteer Cavalry Regiment became more pronounced.

Events in the United States however proved to be just as significant for the future organization and mission of the Army as the Cuban campaign. In the rush to enlist for wartime service, thousands of young men from all over the country volunteered for the duration of the war. So many of the new enlisted men (and their officers, too) were so green and unskilled that a long period of training was deemed in order by Commanding General Nelson A. Miles, a decision further validated at time by the lack of shipping to convey troops for an amphibious landing. Dispatched to rural training camps in Georgia, Florida, and Virginia, thousands of young soldiers threw themselves into the mundane ritual of drill, drill, and more drill, broken up intermittently by work details. Many regiments refused to take part in the most basic sanitary details, such as digging latrines and policing their camp waste. As late summer storms swept over the camps in Georgia and Virginia, filthy waste – some of it infected with typhoid and dysentery germs – washed over the fields. In the wake of the floods, deadly disease outbreaks followed, sending thousands of young men to overwhelmed regimental hospitals.

The typhoid epidemic in the volunteer training camps triggered an immediate backlash against the one agency deemed responsible for the disaster. Volunteer officers and their political patrons moved swiftly to pillory the Army Medical Department as an over-privileged band of weak and effeminate specialists. So long accustomed to cushy peacetime service and the perquisites of garrison living, critics accused the Regular Army's medical establishment of rank incompetence and hysterical behavior in the face of the epidemic. The controversies over the fever camps and allegedly tainted canned beef supplies assumed a gendered connotation, as quartermasters and physicians were both reduced in public discourse to an inferior status, one which was often portrayed as possessing feminized characteristics of incompetency and hysteria. In the case of the Medical Department, however, the response of Surgeon General George Miller Sternberg and his immediate subordinates to the crisis and its aftermath reversed the gender inversion dynamic levied against them. The Regular medical officer was recast as a skilled practitioner of scientific medicine, whose professional legitimacy was denied by the host of amateur volunteer officers who, despite knowing nothing of military sanitation, willfully ignored the recommendations offered by the Army's physicians. Suddenly medical officers were transformed from nurturing mother-like figures into decisive men of action, waging health alongside their line peers who waged war in the name of national security.

After 1898, the medical officer performed double duty for the Army. Much attention has been focused on the work of individuals like Major Walter Reed, Colonel Bailey Ashford, and Major General William Crawford Gorgas in the areas of disease control. Yellow fever, malaria, hookworm infection, and typhoid fever all came under intense scrutiny and new control measures, ranging from vaccines to environmental and cultural transformation. The response to American medical intervention was mixed. On one hand, local elites recognized the inherent value of introducing bold remediation of widespread infectious disease in their communities. On the other hand, however, American medical officers took full advantage of their privileged access and power as members of the colonial administration to intercede in local indigenous cultures in the name of public health and safety. Backed by military force if need be, medical officers introduced basic sanitation into many communities in Cuba, Puerto Rico, and the Philippines, whether the locals wanted it or not. All the while, the same American medical officers acted as ethnographers, classifying and categorizing the indigenous population to further expanding white dominance in the new imperial periphery. Just as in British India, American medical officers sought to employ their knowledge as a coercive force just as they also sought to introduce benevolent (and interventionist) public health reform. Local responses varied; some communities took issue with the intrusion of these strangers into their most private and personal affairs. Regardless, the "men in khaki" rode the wave of public support for their action up to the very eve of the First World War, as they redefined medicine (at least in the military and imperial context) as a bold manly profession.

Pursuing Empire in Asia: The United States and the Philippines

Even as American troops consolidated control over Cuba and Puerto Rico, another expeditionary force was steaming across the Pacific en route to the Spanish-controlled Philippine Islands.[64] The invasion and subsequent pacification of the Philippines was not a casual addendum to an ad hoc war plan. Months before the invasion, the U.S. Navy's Asiatic Squadron, under command of Commodore George Dewey, visited the British port at Hong Kong to take on supplies in anticipation of war with Spain. Such an advance posture was well in keeping with the Mahanian vision – seizing control of oceanic trade routes and compelling strategic decision through strenuous action at sea – but it also put into action

---

64 For best single-volume conventional history, see Brian McAllister Linn, *The Philippine War, 1899–1902* (University Press of Kansas, 2000).

long-standing desires to open up new access to China. Since the early nineteenth century, the fabled China market was the object of many American merchants. Access was limited, however, by the combination of Chinese protectionist laws and the lack of coaling stations across the Pacific from San Francisco. Rather than discourage prospective merchants, however, these obstacles only made China ever more appealing to subsequent generations of American entrepreneurs and missionaries. The final resolution of the long conflict with Native Americans in the 1880s gave rise to a renewed call for expansion – this time across the Pacific to Hawaii and Samoa – to facilitate easier American access to Asia.

War with Spain therefore set America off on a vague, yet predetermined, course of empire acquisition in the Pacific. On June 21, a small squadron carrying American troops to the Philippines paid call at Guam and seized the island from the uninformed Spanish garrison. A larger expeditionary force built around the Army's VIII Corps, under command of Major General Wesley Merritt, embarked for the Philippines on June 27, 1898. By the time VIII Corps arrived at Manila, the city was already besieged by 15,000 local *insurrectos*, under the nominal command of Emilio Aguinaldo. Since his own return to the Philippines in May, Aguinaldo had worked tentatively with Dewey to consolidate control over Luzon. The two armies were allied in name only, as both commanders looked upon the other with disdain and uncertainty. For their part, the Filipino Army of Liberation remained unclear as to American political and military objectives in their homeland, and kept their distance from the VIII Corps after its arrival. Dewey and Merritt, on the other hand, were influenced as much by their own racial prejudices against the non-white Filipino as orders stressing caution from Washington.[65] Like the Cuban and Puerto Rican populations, many Americans considered Filipinos to be incapable of executing the nuanced prerogatives of self-governance. Even as American forces maneuvered into place to commence their own surprise attack on Manila on August 13, a debate over the future state of the archipelago was under way in the United States. Even strong proponents of empire hesitated before the prospect of taking over the Philippines as a whole. Just as some proposed the immediate annexation of the islands as a just reward for the war, others balked at the prospect of taking responsibility for dozens of different non-white ethnic and tribal populations. Despite a history of over three hundred years of Spanish colonial administration, Filipinos were cast as a morally defective, degenerated population of savages, who would become a burden on any American colonial administration. Nevertheless

---

65 Leon Wolff, *Little Brown Brother: America's Forgotten Bid for Empire Which Cost 50,000 Lives* (Doubleday, 1961); Michael H. Hunt, *Ideology and U.S. Foreign Policy* (Yale University Press, 1987); and Paul A. Kramer, "Race-Making and Colonial Violence in the U.S. Empire: The Philippine-American War as Race War," *Diplomatic History* 30 (April 2006): 169–210.

political administrators and military officers promoted a policy of "benevolent assimilation" for the Philippines, painting the American occupation of the Philippines in a positive light, linking imperial control to a civilizing mission, in which the Filipino population were "prepared" for democratic self-rule.[66]

In the end, the imperialists prevailed, setting the United States directly into conflict with the *insurrectos*. Whereas the war with Spain ended within months, the Philippine-American War would last over three years. After a brief experiment in matching the American units in conventional warfare that quickly degenerated into rout, the *insurrectos* reverted to a classic insurgency style of ambush and nighttime raids against isolated American outposts and garrisons. A bitter counterinsurgency ensued, with American forces compelled to apply ever harsher policies against the civilian population in order to isolate the indigenous fighters. Throughout Luzon and other islands, entire villages were moved into *reconcentrados* – concentration camps – to isolate the *insurrectos*. Communities suspected of supporting the rebels saw their food supplies destroyed, while wells and irrigation systems were destroyed, all in the name of denying comfort to the enemy. Most controversially, individuals were regularly tortured to obtain information about the location and strength of local rebels. The "water cure" – a precursor of the waterboarding of the Global War on Terror in the twenty-first century – was a particular favorite. Accounts of the water cure in American newspapers prompted an outcry against the army's prosecution of the war in editorials and on the floor of Congress, but its use came to an end only after the conclusion of hostilities in 1903. Yet, as David Silbey notes in his study of the Philippine-American War, "Torture was never official American policy, but in many places it became de facto American practice."[67]

In the face of such criticisms against the military policies associated with the Philippine-American War, American civil servants and civil affairs military officers undertook a bold social engineering project aimed at transforming the islands into a model American community. Open-air schools and clinics were opened in cities and villages alike, vying with road crews and sanitary engineers building sewers and laying macadam roads over dirt tracks. Newly-arrived missionaries, upon learning that many Filipinos were practicing Catholics, turned their attentions to social reform. Civilian work crews were organized in the style of military organizations to tackle the job of cleaning filthy cities and towns, while wealthy *padrones* were lectured on the health benefits of providing privies and shoes for their tenant farmers. Military physicians detailed to catalog and study the islands'

---

66 Stuart Creighton Miller, *"Benevolent Assimilation": The American Conquest of the Philippines, 1899–1903* (Yale University Press, 1982), 250–51.
67 David J. Silbey, *A War of Frontier and Empire: The Philippine-American War, 1899–1902* (Hill and Wang, 2007), 164.

tropical diseases were surprised at the virulence and scope of disease they confronted, resulting in the formation of the Army Board for the Study of Tropical Diseases as the chief agent of military medical research in the Philippines.

The interest in identifying and eradicating diseases like malaria, plague, and leprosy was not altogether altruistic. Medical science remained locked in a racialized environmental paradigm of disease causation and virulence. As a humid, tropical landscape, the Philippines were considered to be especially fertile breeding ground for debilitating diseases that, if unrestrained, would not only threaten the health of the white Americans living and working there, but could potentially cross the Pacific to infect the homeland. Combating tropical disease at its source was essential, then, to the material security of the United States. Inspired by the dual outbreaks of cholera and bubonic plague in Manila during the first five years of American occupation, the Army Medical Department joined with the Navy Hospital Corps and the US Public Health Service to impose a forward inspection and quarantine regimen on all shipping entering and leaving the islands from abroad. The Philippines became an advance picket line of public health, intended as a tripwire defense line to prevent communicable diseases from reaching American shores from Asia.

Another concern was the effect of long-term service in the tropics on white Americans from a more temperate climate. Military administrators like Major General Leonard Wood, governor of Moro Province, or Lieutenant Colonel Louis Mervin Maus, the Army's chief medical officer responsible for the Philippines, shared the belief that while Americans were physically fit enough to work and thrive in the equatorial climate (provided they remained morally pure and abstained from alcohol and sexual encounters with the local population), they remained nevertheless vulnerable to a variety of conditions that collectively would lead to the genetic degradation of the entire white American race. Over time a new condition – *tropical neurasthenia* – would take shape as the catch-all diagnosis related to the collected nervous and pulmonary distress that was an alleged marker of this degeneration. "Going native" was no casual affair; it signaled the imminent breakdown of the body's actinic defenses against the cumulative effects of tropical light, heat, and humidity, which in turn would render the individual more susceptible to debilitating illness. In short, tropical service was seen – well into the 1930s – as a potential health hazard, and was justification for regular rotation back to the United States or other, more local, temperate regions (i.e.: North China, Hawaii, Alaska).[68]

---

68 See Warwick Anderson, *Colonial Pathologies: American Tropical Medicine, Race, and Hygiene in the Philippines* (Duke University Press, 2006) for specific details about American public health

Within a short time, American eagerness to acquire the Philippines as a new imperial outpost waned, however, as questions of racial exceptionalism and the potential threat to American whiteness came to the fore. Back in the United States, politicians began questioning the merits of assuming control over nearly seven and a half million people of color. As the jingoist rhetoric of 1898 faded in the face of a prolonged guerrilla war, even the most fervent imperialists began to wonder aloud if the Philippines were worth the effort. Others feared for the social impact of close fraternization between young white soldiers and the local indigenous population. Various venal sins were assigned to Filipinos, ranging from rampant alcoholism and drug use to unbridled sexuality. Long exposure to such a people, some warned, would translate into moral degeneration among the young American soldiers stationed there. High rates of syphilis and gonorrhea in volunteer regiments posted to the Philippines during the insurgency were identified as evidence of the potential threat the tropical islands posed to the nation. Moralists like Lt. Colonel Maus saw venereal disease as part of a larger problem. The breakdown of morality in public life created too many opportunities for young soldiers to fall victim to vice in all of its forms. Unrestrained access to alcohol and narcotic drugs in the Army's Asian stations was the source of the high venereal infection rates – nearly 50 percent in the Army's Beijing Garrison by February 1901, for example – leading Maus to comment: "It is my opinion that the majority of degenerates, who enter our services, as expressed by flagrant violators of rules, regulations and orders, deserters, the inept, moral perverts, and venereal debauches, result from the use of alcohol beverages or their hereditary effects."[69]

Another dilemma Americans faced in the Philippines and other new imperial possessions was the potential effect of close fraternization between African-American soldiers and the local population on race relations back in the United States. All four of the Army's colored regiments (9th and 10th Cavalry, 24th and 25th Infantry) and two volunteer regiments – the 48th and 49th US Volunteer Infantry – were posted to the Philippines during the three year long insurrection. During their service, individual black soldiers confronted the awkward realities of waging a counterinsurgency against an indigenous foe who was also deemed biologically and socially "inferior" by their white superiors. Filipino civilians and black American soldiers constructed a posture of mutual

---

activities in the Philippines. See also Wintermute, *Public Health and the US Military*, for additional detail on US Army Medical Department practices and theories regarding tropical service.
69 L. Mervin Maus, "Injurious Effects Resulting from the Moderate Use of Alcohol," *Journal of the Military Service Institute* 54 (January-February, 1914), 1–2, cited in Wintermute, *Public Health and the US Military*, 214.

respect. Many natives were surprised by the presence of persons of color among their new occupiers, while the Americans were likewise interested in the ease with which they were accepted by the Filipinos. Even as black soldiers adopted the same racially-charged language – "goo-goos" and "gooks" – when describing active insurrectionists, they generally avoided such terms in regard to the general population. Indeed, individual soldiers observed with little irony or surprise how the Army's occupation policies were recreating a Jim Crow environment in the imperial periphery, as reported in one letter home from a soldier in the 24th Infantry:

> By the difference in "dealing with us" expressed is meant the colored soldiers do not push them off the streets, spit at them, call them damned "niggers," abuse them in all manner of ways, and connect race hatred with duty, for the colored soldier has none such for them.
>
> The future of the Filipino, I fear, is that of the Negro in the South. Matters are almost to that condition in Manilo now. No one (white) has any scruples as regards respecting the rights of a Filipino. He is kicked and cuffed at will and he dare not remonstrate.[70]

The racial politics of occupation were also noted by white Southern officers, however. First was the now-standard white obsession with an armed insurrection by blacks against white society. Southern officers insisted upon the extension of the same Jim Crow social and political barriers that were taking shape in the United States to the Philippines and other imperial possessions as well, lest black soldiers find common cause with the insurrectionists. Some also worried as to the racial classification of Filipinos themselves, and the implications for race relations if they were seen as favoring one group of blacks (i.e.: Filipino elites) over another (i.e.: African-American soldiers). This dual rationale fostered the insinuation of Jim Crow racism into the United States Army just at the point when the so-called "Buffalo Soldier" regiments were at the height of their respectability and acceptance by civilian society in the aftermath of the Spanish-American War. Promoted by Southerners, the new institutional racism was accepted with little complaint by Northerners eager to lay to rest any lingering resentments from the Civil War and Reconstruction. After over thirty years of serving as a safe refuge for black men seeking steady employment, service, and respect, the Army began walking back from its commitment to African-American soldiers that would reach its nadir after the First World War.[71]

---

70 Willard B. Gatewood, Jr., *Smoked Yankees and the Struggle for Empire: Letters from Negro Soldiers, 1898–1902* (University of Illinois Press, 1971), 241–42, quote on 253.

71 Silbey, *A War of Frontier and Empire*, 108–112; and Gatewood, *Smoked Yankees*, 243–44.

Western Gender and Racial Exceptionalism in China

In closing this chapter on race, gender, and imperialism, it is best to consider the case of China. More than Africa, China was considered the great prize for the Western powers. Vast in size and population, its people viewed as members of a degenerated, inferior race, and under the control of a corrupt and seemingly inept bureaucracy, China was universally presumed to be the last great untapped marketplace. Industrialists and traders from San Francisco to Moscow fantasized over the prospects of capturing special access to over 430 million Chinese, both as consumers and as a source of cheap labor to exploit the countries natural resources. Christian missionaries likewise saw a ripe opportunity for evangelical outreach. Hundreds of priests, itinerant preachers, and lay philanthropic workers spread across China, trading Western medical care and knowledge, education, and civil works for souls.[72]

Since the early 1800s, China found itself in an ever-worsening relationship with foreign powers bent on securing their own concessions from the Manchu Throne. First England, then France, Japan, Russia, and Germany sought secure ports of entry into China – cities along the coastal fringe that would remain under European political control and from which traders and missionaries would spread out across the countryside, taking advantage of the great rivers to travel deep into the interior. This process was exacerbated by a wanton disregard for Chinese sovereignty, as exhibited in the Opium Wars. For decades before the outbreak of war in 1839, Great Britain openly traded Indian opium in China, with little regard for the destabilizing impact the drug trade had on Chinese society. When the Chinese government attempted to ban the sale of opium, the British Royal Navy shelled Chinese ports as troop transports unloaded regiments from India to take control of the blockaded coastal cities. Outmatched militarily, the Qing government sued for peace in August 1842, which required a massive indemnity payment and the concession of full control in several major South Chinese cities, including Hong Kong and Shanghai. A second foreign war over a decade later resulted in similar humiliations, guaranteeing the opening of China further to Western trade despite the government's wishes. Trade and missionary concessions were awarded, as a five million ounces of silver indemnity was paid to England and France.

Western interference in Chinese affairs triggered a cultural and political crisis that lingered through most of the remaining decades of the nineteenth century. Western missionaries contributed to the rise of a quasi-Christian millenialist cult that rose up against the Qing Dynasty. The ensuing Taiping Rebellion lasted four-

---

72 Hunt, *Ideology and U.S. Foreign Policy*, 69–77.

teen years (1850 to 1864), and though put down by the government, proved crippling. At least 20 million Chinese were killed, leaving entire provinces in ruins. Weakened by decades of war, the bankrupted Qing retrenched culturally under the leadership of the Emperor's one-time concubine, the Empress Dowager Cixi. Strong-willed, intelligent, and paranoid, the Empress Dowager was forced to confront the reality of governing a once magnificent empire in swift decline. Even the solutions to China's dilemmas hid potential traps that would further indebt the empire to foreign interests. China had little capacity for raising or organizing sufficient investment capital for modernization, a problem worsened by the grip xenophobic conservatives in the civil service maintained on the bureaucracy. Without access to domestic credit or tax revenue, infrastructure projects like railroads, telegraph networks, and urban electrification required foreign partners. The same was true for the Chinese military, whose modernization hinged on obtaining Western weapons and advisors. From the Opium Wars through the 1895 Sino-Japanese War, the nineteenth century proved to be time of constant conflict and strife for China. Humiliation followed humiliation as Imperial Chinese forces, largely organized and equipped along eighteenth century standards, were handled roughly by foreign armies. Military defeat was accompanied by internal strife, not only in the form of the Taiping uprising, but the interminable press of local bandit gangs and warlords defying imperial authority.[73]

In response to these pressures China pursued two conflicting paths, reflecting the internal power struggles within the Empress Dowager's court. Many noblemen, merchants, and military officers pled the case for expanding trade with the growing tide of foreign ambassadors and ministers. Even if the terms for capital financing and loans were exorbitant, if not extortionate, the immediate results were tangible and beneficial. Foreign companies, like their governments, sought concessions in various forms, including a majority stake, if not outright ownership, of any infrastructure and industrial project they funded. Western military advisors also promised great results, in return for exclusive long-term contracts and treaties between their respective governments. Included in these treaties were even more concessions, ranging from territorial "gifts" to criminal immunity for foreign citizens.[74]

The counter argument favored by many Confucian Mandarins and courtiers, as well as other powerful nobility, was the outright rejection of foreign assistance and the termination of all foreign influence. After all, they reckoned, China was

---

73 See Julia Lovel, *The Opium Wars: Drugs, Dreams, and the Making of Modern China* (Overlook Press, 2015); and Robert A. Bickers, *The Scramble for China: Foreign Devils in the Qing Empire, 1800–1914* (Allen Lane, 2011).
74 David J. Silbey, *The Boxer Rebellion and the Great Game in China* (Hill and Wang, 2012), 9–32.

not only an ancient and august civilization, it was a great power in its own right. Any intrusion or offer of assistance from the West was considered little more than one of many attempts to mislead and defraud the Chinese of their power and sovereignty. After all, since the mid-nineteenth century, Great Britain, France, Russia, and the other European powers at turns attacked, cajoled, and intimidated Chinese compliance with their own trade initiatives. Soon other powers, including Germany and Japan, joined in the great humiliation; even the purported neutral United States entered the fray, claiming amity and cooperation while backing Protestant missionaries in their efforts to proselytize the masses. And yet the court remained deadlocked in debate between reformers and conservatives, with Cixi acting only when her power was threatened.[75]

At the center of the conservative resistance, therefore, rest the secret societies. Lumped together as the "Societies of Harmonious Fists," or "Boxers" by Westerners unfamiliar with traditional Chinese street theater, the various secret societies represented a long tradition of populist political discourse. Responding to the combined pressures of high taxation, poor land policy, drought, and the creeping advance of Western commercial and political influence along the coastal periphery and beyond, the secret societies preached a message of reform and xenophobic backlash to the ordinary peasant. The growing tensions between the Imperial Court, the Western interests in China, and the masses boiled over in an outbreak of violence that led to the isolation of the Western consulates and an informal war during the summer of 1900. Following the assassination of the German consul, Klemens Freiherr von Ketteler, by an angry mob led by Boxers, the Western legations took refuge in the Legion Quarter, initiating a siege by Imperial Chinese Army and Boxer forces that lasted from June 20 to August 14. During this time, a series of multi-national relief forces were assembled at the port of Tianjin. The first attempt to rescue the legations, commanded by British Vice-Admiral Edward Seymour, was nearly annihilated by Chinese government forces, and needed rescue itself on June 25. A larger and more diverse combined force of American, British, Russian, Japanese, French, and German forces assembled and began its own march inland from Tienjin on July 14.[76]

The ensuing conflict between the Western powers, the Chinese Army, and the Boxers set in motion the final days of the Qing dynasty.[77] After a thirty-day march, the relief expedition arrived at the walls of Beijing. Under cover of a nighttime rainstorm, the Western forces broke through the Chinese defenses and entered

---

75 Silbey, *The Boxer Rebellion*, 30–34, 51–52.
76 *Ibid.*, 102–12, 116–31.
77 See Robert Bickers and R. G. Teidemann, eds., *The Boxers, China, and the World* (Rowman and Littlefield, 2007).

the Imperial City, rescuing the beleaguered consulates. The Empress Dowager and her court fled the city in the confusion, leaving Beijing to the Westerners, who embarked on a massive looting spree, with general officers competing with privates and seamen for the choicest items. In a way, the sack of Beijing was only the opening act of a more systematic and brutal subjugation of China by the West. Russian forces took advantage of the Boxer Rebellion to invade Manchuria. European forces spread out across the North China plain surrounding Beijing, looting towns and villages to claim "reparations" for themselves and Chinese Christians who were also attacked by the Boxers. Over the next two years, Japanese forces killed thousands of civilians as they searched for Boxer resistance, while the late-arriving German expeditionary force stalked the countryside, conducting its own campaign of organized pillage and looting in the name of punishing the Boxers. These individual acts and campaigns culminated in the September 21, 1901, Peace Agreement between the Eight Powers and China. An indemnity of 540 million ounces of silver was levied by the West, while sovereignty over Tientsin and its surrounding countryside was given up to the Western powers. The Peace Agreement can be taken as evidence of a shift in the application of Western imperialism. Rather than openly occupying a partitioned China, the consensus solution trended toward exerting trade concessions worth millions from a much weakened and dependent Qing court. This cooperative form of imperialism would prove quite lucrative for the West, and survived the collapse of the monarchy in the aftermath of the 1911 Revolution, even as the Nationalists and Communists railed against China's exploitation.[78]

Another perspective can be gleaned from the narrative of China's humiliation, however. The Seymour expedition's progress north from Tientsin was hampered, not only by the Boxers, but by the well-armed and capable Chinese Army. The Gan Division, under General Dong Fuxiang, was made up of ethnic Muslim Chinese soldiers, equipped with German Mauser rifles and Krupp artillery. After blocking the railroad to Beijing, the Gan Division compelled the relief force to retreat to the city of Tianjin, where the westerners now had to wait out their own rescue. This resistance, and the ongoing fight against the second relief column, provides some evidence that the Chinese soldier was capable of matching European and Japanese forces on somewhat even terms if well led.[79] This last factor, of course, proved to be the sticking point for the Chinese; modern military reforms had only just begun to shape the Army into a more effective force; many generals followed the lead of the Imperial Court's conservatives in actively rejecting

---

78 Silbey, *The Boxer Rebellion*, 226–35.
79 *Ibid.*, 231–32.

Western advisors, preferring instead to retain their own command and control systems. The end result is self-evident; China was humiliated in the field, and entered the new century on a course to chaotic, bitter war and revolution.

Nevertheless the potential for non-white populations to wage a successful campaign against Western imperialism remained quite real, as the abortive Italian effort to subjugate Ethiopia a decade earlier reveals. Here on March 1, 1896, an Italian expeditionary force – some 17,000 men strong – was overwhelmed by over 100,000 Ethiopian warriors on the slopes of Mount Belah, outside the village of Adwa (Adowa). The annihilation of the Italian expedition was considered nothing less than a national humiliation. Nearly forty years later, Benito Mussolini would launch a revanchist campaign to avenge the earlier battle and reclaim Ethiopia as an Italian colony.[80]

In the end, the history of Western Imperialism and the resistance makes for a complex field of study. Traditionally the military historian's perspective has been sought out solely to describe the actual process of doomed resistance and inevitable conquest. However, as this chapter has strived to reveal, the intersection of western and indigenous persons is a place where military institutions and exchanges are central, not merely to the point of conquest, but also to the classification of the subjugated cultures by the victorious West and their administration. In this venue, the incorporation of racial and gendered analyses is absolutely critical for the military historian as they make the case for a more precise and complete study of this moment.

---

80 Porch, *Wars of Empire*, 150.

4 Gender and the First World War

Introduction

From today's perspective, the twentieth century dawned in Europe and the United States as a new era of prosperity and confidence. Successive waves of industrialization, combined with the dismantling of centuries-old mercantilist barriers, had ushered in a state of economic prosperity never before seen. The advance of parliamentary and republican governance helped even the most autocratic regimes avoid the challenge of continental war since Napoleon's defeat in 1815. Imperial contests may not have proven to be the key to unfettered power and prosperity their chief advocates had promised, but the race for colonies in Africa and Asia did serve to create the twin illusions of nationalistic pride and racial exceptionalism. Certainly domestic crises existed to threaten stability and order. Great Britain's Irish Home Rule question vied for prominence in the daily newspapers with the specter of Suffragette violence. In France, the scandals surrounding the tawdry Caillaux affair threatened to bring down yet another government. Working-class challenges in Germany toward the unfettered power of the wealthy and nobility in the emasculated *Reichstag*; the seemingly-eternal problem of Russia's restive masses threatened that nation's stability. In the United States, growing labor unrest was only matched by the dehumanizing racist treatment of non-white citizens. Nevertheless, the era certainly warranted the title it claimed: *La Belle Epoque*, a time of great optimism and prosperity.

All this came crashing down in the warm fall of 1914, as Europeans plunged headlong into most destructive conflict to date in recorded history. Within three years, the United States joined in a conflict so monumental it could only be known for decades to come as "The Great War." A truly global conflict, with combat theaters spanning three continents and all seven seas, ultimately as many as 38 million men were killed, wounded, and missing in more than four bloody years. This chapter traces the dramatic changes in cultural constructions of masculinity and femininity occurring on battlefields and home fronts during the First World War. This conflict witnessed an existential clash between what social historian Peter Stearns terms as an "inertia of change" resulting from the wartime upheaval, and what literary critic Leo Braudy describes as "centripetal forces" coalescing in the traditionalist resistance to change.[1] Seen in this light,

---

1 Peter Stearns, *Be a Man: Males in Modern Society* (Homes and Meier, 1990), 161; Leo Braudy, *From Chivalry to Terrorism: War and the Changing Nature of Masculinity* (Vintage, 2005), 330–31. For Braudy, "centrifugal forces" equated to Stearns "inertia of change."

https://doi.org/10.1515/9783110477467-004

the First World War thus can be evaluated as a series of gendered interactions and social engineering experiments, some deliberately calculated, but others occurring quite by accident.

Overview

In August 1914, the combination of hyper-nationalism and hyper-masculinity infected many Europeans as millions of men rallied to their flags and fulfilled their gendered responsibilities. Reservists reported to their depots, trading their civilian clothes and tools for uniforms and rifles. Young men, caught up in the moment, queued up at recruiting stations, hoping they would have the opportunity to get their licks in before Christmas, when everyone knew the war would be over. Women too adopted wartime roles, some time-honored, others new. As the mobilizations began, young women and their chaperones prowled the streets, challenging fit-looking men to do their duty. In England, said women were armed with white feathers to press on those resisting, to signify their cowardice. Everywhere women also took up the slack on farms, in offices, and later, in factories, replacing their menfolk who were called off to war. By time of the 1916 bloodbaths on the Eastern and Western fronts, most existing assumptions about the relative spheres occupied by men and women in public life were disrupted, as women took on roles that had hitherto been exclusively male preserves in peacetime.

On the front lines, the almost innocent naivete over war faded, the old language of "God, King, and Country" found sadly empty. Consensus is generally lacking, but most historians agree that by 1917, the old social notions of war being a place for heroism and patriotism to rise to the fore were inconsequential. Soldiers fought for their comrades in small primary groups, not for recognition or duty. In France, France, Russia, and the Carpathians, many ultimately refused to fight unless attacked, or embraced mutiny against their generals and ultimately their own monarchs and governments. Home fronts also felt the pinch as governments tried to buoy popular support for war efforts, a task made harder by the interminable rationing and curfews that defined public life. In Germany, housewives took on the role of sustaining the war effort almost single-handedly, not in the factory, but in the lines for ersatz food of ever declining nutritional quality and palatability. Elsewhere in Europe, none of the belligerent populations struggled in the face of starvation in the same way as the German people, but there too, rations were basic, dull, and barely sufficient. For the Allies, the only bright spot in 1917 was the entry of the United States into the war. It would take time, but the infusion of millions of enthusiastic American doughboys would rescue the Western Front and help win the war in 1918. Thanks to the great distance between America and the war, and the relatively short period of time – seven months – that the American Expeditionary Forces (AEF) were engaged in battle there, civilians at home in the United States experienced few of the immediate challenges and hazards that defined the war, leaving the nation's pre-war normative gender roles and spheres relatively untouched.

As the fighting came to an end in November 1918, people across the globe eagerly looked forward to a new day of peace and prosperity. Unspoken amidst the hopes of the exhausted combatant nations was the tacit understanding that the state of gender identity and access to public expressions of agency and potential power would return as much as possible to the prewar norm. Within a few short years, women returned to their earlier state – either as unseen and underpaid laborers working in unskilled jobs, as part of a massive domestic labor workforce, again underappreciated and under paid, or in the home as the subordinate partner in their marital relationships. However, in many areas, the political and social changes wrought by the war proved to be almost insurgent in their collective influence in the 1920s. Throughout much of the Western World, women had finally acquired their long-sought political franchise. And if women could vote, they could also consume. Within a short time, women became highly pursued clients for businesses and marketers, just as they constituted a new potential bloc of voters. This should not be construed as the arrival of a bold new era of gender equality. It was not. But the First World War's greatest effects were perhaps not those imposed upon nations; rather, it was the cultural transformation of everyday life and the respective place of women in society.

Gender Relations and Roles before the First World War

Just as the onset of the twentieth century was heralded as a golden age of progress and stability by its celebrants throughout the West, it also signaled a transformation in class identity for many millions of men and women. The managerial revolution reshaping the foundation of industrial and commercial enterprise was met by the increased relevance of specialization and professional expertise across Europe and the Americas. Male attorneys, doctors, businessmen, managers, and teachers not only comprised a middle class with ever-growing political and consumer power, they also sought to craft new intellectual schemas of power and control within the existing cultural boundaries of religion, class, race, and gender. As more men left behind the world of physical labor and craftsmanship that defined their parents' lives and labors, they acquired new values, goals, and anxieties that placed them increasingly at odds with the Victorian Era culture they were raised in. It is important to note that there was no singular model of

Western male identity that transcended perceived racial, ethnic, or national boundaries. Yet there were some shared expectations of normal male conduct within the private sphere of interpersonal relationships within the home, the public sphere of work, politics, and commerce, and the semi-public/semi-private spheres of male-specific leisure. It is not inappropriate to identify some common tropes of *Fin de Siecle* middle-class male identity. For the most part, they typically worked outside their homes. They continued to exercise legal authority, if not absolute control, over their families. Quintessential and self-identified middle-class male traits included self-discipline, autonomy, trustworthiness, diligence, liberalism, loyalty, restraint, rationality, competitiveness, fair-mindedness, and success. Not only were these men the binary opposites of all other, weaker groups – women, socialists, workers, and racial and ethnic minorities – they were also the ideal defenders of home and hearth, *heimat und volk*, and king and country.[2]

Despite these efforts to retain control of an increasingly tenuous social order, men throughout Europe and North America were almost themselves delusional on the subject of their own status in comparison with the realities of their lives. If at all self-reflective, most early twentieth century men felt increasingly imprisoned by new corporate structures that controlled more and more of their time and activities, and that demanded absolute obedience and conformity. Failure to march lockstep in the business world could mean termination and disgrace – code words for emasculation and impotence. Ironically, these feelings resembled the alienation that Karl Marx wrote about regarding the working class in factories in the nineteenth century. Like the men and women slaving away in sweatshops as little better than machines themselves, so too did bourgeois men find themselves to be white-collar cogs in corporate machines.[3]

This reality left some middle-class men feeling what has been called "status anxieties" or "psychic crises" because their self-identification as men with certain expectations and duties came under assault. The press of modern life, with its demands for fast decision and even faster action, at home and at work, could

---

2 J.A. Mangan and James Walvin, eds., *Manliness and Morality: Middle-Class Masculinity in Britain and America, 1800–1940* (St. Martin's Press, 1987); Mark C. Carnes and Clyde Griffen, eds., *Meanings for Manhood: Constructions of Masculinity in Victorian America* (University of Chicago Press, 1990); Stearns, *Be a Man*; George L. Mosse, *The Image of Man: The Creation of Modern Masculinity* (Oxford University Press, 1996); Rotundo, *American Manhood.*, 178–85; and Karen Hagemann, "German Heroes: The Cult of the Death for the Fatherland in Nineteenth-Century Germany," in *Masculinities in Politics and War: Gendering Modern History*, eds, Stefan Dudink, et al. (Manchester University Press, 2004), 116–35.

3 Stearns, *Be A Man*, 48–50, 106–18; and Rotundo, *American Manhood*, 178–85.

trigger emotional episodes that to the unlearned eye appeared to be hysterical in nature. The logical conclusion one might infer from these episodes was that modern life had a cumulative erosive effect on the male nervous system, creating a generation of emasculated, weak men. Failure thus not only meant the potential losses of status and self-esteem, it also signaled social emasculation. In a study of Canadian masculinity and boy culture in Ontario during the early twentieth century, historian Mark Moss observed that:

> In a climate where the most "important watchwords" were "discipline, efficiency, and development," men sought to revive a manliness that appeared vulnerable. Opportunity to recapture a particulate idea of what real men were about could take many diverse forms: getting back to nature, participating in sports, reading adventure novels, cheering for sports teams, or bonding at the pub – any of these might serve to revise the essential male spirit that was threatened by modernization.[4]

This observation may as well be applied anywhere in the Western world where middle-class fathers feared that their sons might grow up to become soft, lazy, and feminized men.[5] Worse still in the early twentieth-century context, according to literary scholar Leo Braudy and cultural historians George Mosse and Peter Stearns, was the older generation's fear that their male children might become unruly like the proletarian rabble, or decadent like homosexuals. Both unwanted outcomes could turn normative middle-class masculinity into something un-masculine and un-middle class.[6]

Within a short time, the medical establishment, following the lead of American physician George M. Beard, confronted the problem. Looking toward the (at the time) female condition of *hysteria*, these male practitioners crafted a less-gendered term for the condition: *neurasthenia*. Accordingly, rather than signaling the imminent de-masculinizing of the afflicted, the anxieties and near-hysterical states represented the atonic degeneration of the male nervous system under the daily stresses of being a man in the modern world. Simply put, men exhibiting emotional collapse had exhausted their stores of nervous energy through a variety of positive activities – work, family, and social interactions – and negative

---

4 Mark Moss, *Manliness and Militarism: Educating Young Boys in Ontario for War* (University of Toronto Press, 2001), 15.
5 Donald J. Mrozek, "The Habit of Victory: The American Military and the Cult of Manliness," in *Manliness and Morality: Middle-Class Masculinity in Britain and America, 1800–1940*, ed. J.A. Mangan and James Walvin (Manchester, 1987), 220–241; Rotundo, *American Manhood*, 222–46; and Patrick F. McDevitt, *"May the Best Man Win": Sport, Masculinity, and Nationalism and the Empire, 1880–1935* (Palgrave McMillan, 2004), 58–80.
6 Braudy, *From Chivalry to Terrorism*, 349–50; Mosse, *The Image of Man*, 79–97; and Stearns, *Be a Man*, 48–78.

behaviors – masturbation, gambling, carousing. Over time the cumulative toll of nervous dissipation would lead to the degeneration of the individual, and by extension, society at large, as decadence took hold. No worry, though – the prosperity of the modern age made possible a remedy in the form of opportunities for regular physical exertion and competition to restore the worn out nerves to their former vigorous state.[7]

Once pigeon-holed into a medical condition, it was much easier to craft a social response to address the perceived problems of anxiety and masculinity in private and public life. To inculcate their sons with proper notions of manhood, American and European fathers encouraged them to play sports, hunt wild animals, or join the Boy Scouts. They also bought their sons books that glorified the virtues of manhood. The stories by Sir Walter Scott, Rudyard Kipling, and Stephen Crane captured the imagination of so many boys. Published in 1895, for example, Crane's *Red Badge of Courage* traces how the main character – a young Union soldier named Henry Fleming fighting the American Civil War – succumbed to fear and cowardice in his initial exposure to enemy fire in battle. He would later master his unmanly emotions and fight with great bravery. For American boys reading his story, combat thus represented a quest for true manhood. If they could not experience such a manful struggle on the battlefield, reading such war and adventure novels at least allowed them to observe rites of passage, albeit vicariously, artificial, and romanticized, into respectable manhood. In the United Kingdom and Europe, similar works of fiction used motifs of conquest and empire to instill such feelings of competition and dominance over less-masculine nations and races.[8]

Women also experienced a cultural transition during this turn of the century moment, particularly among the middle and upper classes. Throughout almost the entire nineteenth century, the place for women in Western society was defined by social contracts and constructs like the Cult of Domesticity. Women were largely confined to domestic roles in their adult life on account of their inherent grace, innocence, chasteness, and nurturing qualities. Motherhood was thus the noblest calling a woman could aspire to; seeking employment outside of the married home was, for middle- and upper-class women, a potentially subversive

---

7 Tom Lutz, *American Nervousness, 1903* (Cornell University Press, 1991), 3–4.

8 Joanna Bourke, "Gender Roles in Killing Zones," in Jay Winter, ed., *Cambridge History of the First World War*, vol III, *Civil Society*, (Cambridge University Press, 2014), 155–56; Moss, *Manliness and Militarism*, 75–77, 115–31; Amy Kaplan, "Romancing the Empire: The Embodiment of American Masculinity in the Popular Historical Novel of the 1890s," *American Literary History* 4 (Winter 1990): 659–65; and Graham Dawson, *Soldier Heroes: British Adventure, Empire and the Imagining of Masculinities* (Routledge, 1994), 1–11, 45–62.

expression of unnatural independence that in turn threatened to cut them off from family and legitimacy. More and more enterprising women risked their future reputations within their families and communities to seek legitimacy in a number of professional fields that were increasingly cast as suitable for female participation without threatening the dominant patriarchal social order. Nursing, teaching, and social work became considered safe outlets for women seeking meaningful careers of their own, albeit even here with gendered limitations on their authority over male peers and associates. There were exceptions – Marie Curie's work in chemistry and physics, for example, or Jane Addams' pioneering social work – but they were few. Even as educated women joined the ranks of the professional elite, their status as subordinate feminine participants was considered a given throughout Western society at large.

Notions of restricted access to work for women were entirely based upon class consciousness. The Cult of Domesticity was never intended for the working class, save as an unobtainable social ideal that set poor women even further apart from those of higher social status and privilege. Throughout the West, lower-class women were frequently thrust into the workplace to supplement scanty family incomes. Some were able to take on piecework as garment workers without having to leave their houses, but many more were compelled to find work away from home, either as domestic servants, cooks, or sweatshop day laborers. Interestingly, while lower-class women actually utilized their potential as wage earners, their social and economic status in both public and private life remained quite low. Still considered subordinate partners in a paternalist-oriented system of personal and public relationships with men, they were also marginalized on the basis of their lower-class status – even as they exercised greater wage-earning agency than many of their middle and upper-class critics.

It was in the workplace, however, where working-class women experienced the most crushing reminders of their subordinate gendered status. Paid far less than men, women were considered almost as a disposable commodity to be exploited and used until they were either married off or worn out. On the job, women remained targets of opportunity for crude male advances, all while their own honor and purity was dismissed purely on the basis of their social status (or rather, the lack of it). In the United States, ethnicity and race only compounded these issues, as many immigrant and African-American women were victims of abuse from multiple reasons: not only "othered" on the basis of their ethnicity or race, many were automatically cast as "immoral" women on the basis of their class and ethnicity. In teasing out these factors relating to masculinities and femininities, scholars have applied E.P. Thompson's conceptualizations to gender discourses in labor history.[9] In his groundbreaking 1963 book, *The Making of the English Working Class*, Thompson employed a Marxist lens to examine his title subject during the first industrial revolution, from 1780 to 1863. Thompson found evidence about the everyday lives of these "real people," imparted agency to those workers, and depicted "class" as "experience" and "consciousness" manifested in human relationships.[10]

Other historians then expanded on Thompson's rationale in studies of the American working class during the nineteenth and early twentieth centuries. All these scholars found that strictures in financial, social, and political hierarchies created by the *bourgeoisie* did indeed limit working-class mobility and agency, yet the workers did also act as individuals and collectives within those hierarchies.[11] With these social and economic relations as backdrops, the working class developed alternative constructions of gender by the turn of the twentieth century. Male workers struggled against the *bourgeoisie* and their unfettered capitalism through union membership, legal reforms or sometimes radical change trough bloody confrontations. In these scenarios, the factories became the battlefields, while the workers became the disciplined, dutiful, self-sacrificing, heroic soldiers serving causes greater than themselves.[12] Thus gender paradigms evolved for working-class men and women, who comprised the proletariat in nineteenth century vernacular. Many of their families lived barely at subsistence levels. Smoke-belching factory chimneys, the blatant disregard for health and welfare, and the concentration of wealth and position among the few were hallmarks of the burgeoning urban centers in Europe and the United States. Nineteenth century observers like Jacob Riis, Charles Dickens, and Karl Marx offered damning portrayals of the workers' suffering, exploitation, and alienation at the hands of the factory-owning, wealth-controlling bourgeoisie.

Regardless of their class status, ethnicity, or privilege, working women were always portrayed as a potential challenge to the existing male patriarchal system. It was one thing for lower-class women to enter the workplace out of

---

9 For examples, see Joanna Bourke, *Working Class Cultures in Britain, 1890–1960: Gender, Class, and Ethnicity* (Routledge 1993), 1–21, 50–54; and Lara Vapnek, *Breadwinners: Working Women and Economic Independence, 1865–1920* (University of Illinois Press, 2009), 57–79, 127–45.
10 E.P. Thompson, *The Making of the English Working Class* (Victor Gollancz, 1963), 9–12; and Moss, *Manliness and Militarism*, 11–12.
11 David Montgomery, *The Fall of the House of Labor: The Workplace, the State, and American Labor Activism, 1865–1925* (Press Syndicate of the University of Cambridge, 1987); and Herbert Gutman, *Work, Culture, and Society* (Vintage, 1977).
12 Nell Irvin Painter, *Standing at Armageddon: A Grassroots History of the United States, 1877–1919*, reprint. (W.W. Norton, 2008), 37–60; Stearns, *Be A Man*, 99–103; and Laura L. Frader and Sonya O. Rose, eds., *Gender and Class in Modern Europe* (Cornell University Press, 1996).

material necessity for the sake of their families. But when middle and upper-class women sought work beyond the immediate material needs of their own home and family, their actions were considered evidence of a potentially disruptive personality. Conformity with the gendered system was expected, as was befitting the alleged passivity that lay at the core of the healthy female constitution. Doubt, skepticism, and other acts of individual agency were viewed as signs of an insurgent and unhealthy mind and body. Self-empowerment was, save perhaps for the most wealthy and exceptional persons, seen as proof of a moral and physical derangement among women. Many physiological causes were assigned to this dangerous expression of individuality and self-motivation: hyper-sexuality, gender inversion, hysteria, or depression. Regardless of the cause, the danger of active female independent agency grew more visible in the most radical expressions of political activism, free love, and the rejection of comfortable social norms like marriage and family. Women who were most vocal about the daily slights, offenses, and repressions inherent in a male-privileged world were often deemed to be physically ill or deranged. Just as men experiencing anxiety were medicalized in a manner fit with their gendered identity, so too were women who expressed independence and a desire for a level playing field in the workplace and in relationships diagnosed as "hysterical." Their tender feminine sensibilities disrupted by hyperactive sexual organs and other hidden physical abnormalities, such women were deemed to be barely in control of their lives, their personalities unnaturally distorted into an over-emotional and over-expressive state. An entire culture of medical intervention was crafted to manage such women, ranging from isolation and confinement, to carefully moderated diet and exercise; to physical stimulation and deprivation, and ultimately, if warranted, surgical intervention.[13]

During the month of August 1914, these varied constructs of gender identity and conduct proved far more important than other social concepts associated with class and shared ethnic identity that were expected to serve as possible restraints on the slide to war. As calls for mobilization circulated around Europe, they were greeted in European cities by massive crowds eager for war. The pictures of these first heady days are virtually burned into the public memory of the war – especially the images of rapturous crowds in Paris, Berlin, and Munich. Yet as telling as these photographs are, they fail to convey other messages of ambiguity and uncertainty among the witnesses. Since long before 1914, European

---

13 Emmanuel Broussolle, et al., "History of Physical and 'Moral' Treatment of Hysteria," in Julien Bogousslavsky, ed., *Hysteria: The Rise of an Enigma* (Karger, 2014), 181–97; and James E. Moore, "Hysteria from a Surgical Stand-Point," *Annals of Surgery: A Monthly Review of Surgical Science Since 1885*. 28 (August 1898): 177–86.

political elites were concerned socialist and communist elements in the working class might disrupt production or impede war efforts in a genuine crisis. And in the pre-war years, trade unions and socialist parties did criticize any international conflicts, arguing that the crises were generated by the *bourgeoisie* for their own interests, leaving the fighting – and dying – to the rural and urban working poor. Indeed, recent analyses by historians like Michael Neiberg pull away the image of Europeans celebrating the arrival of war to reveal a far more skeptical and worried public. Student and bourgeois rallies anticipating victory are one thing, but a careful dissection of daily newspapers during the final days of the July Crisis, as the prospect of war became more certain, shows deep concern and anxiety throughout European working-class society. Indeed, outside of Germany, where SPD leader Friedrich Ebert committed his party to Kaiser Wilhelm II's *Burgfrieden* in the *Reichstag*, socialist leaders in Britain, France, and Italy were vocally against the war. Whether these leaders – especially Jean Jaures in France or Keir Hardie in Britain – could have swayed public opinion against war will never know, because both men were assassinated within the first year of the war. Regardless, their resistance, and the ambiguity that war news was greeted with outside of the city squares and public spaces, helps diminish the standard interpretation of July and August 1914.[14]

In spite of these anxieties over the prospect of war, the fact does remain that many thousands of men, women, and children took to the streets over the last week of July 1914. Cultural historian Jeffrey Verhey labels these phenomena in Germany as the "curious crowds," the audience crowds," and the "'carnivalesque' crowds," but these words also apply to other nations surging toward war.[15] The image in some ways almost appears as if it were drawn from a satirical weekly magazine: educated and prosperous middle-class citizens, mingling with workers and nobility in support of autocrats, parliamentarians, and republicans. In Germany and France, the nation's powerful trade unions agreed to suspend demonstrations and strikes for the duration of the war, promises which would eventually be forgotten. In France, the political left and labor unions entered into a coalition government with the center-right parties that became known as *L'union sacree* (The Sacred Union). In Germany, the Social Democrats – the largest party in the *Reichstag* – suspended all of its demands for stronger representation to join with the other parties in the Kaiser's invocation of the *Burgfrieden* – the political truce of all parties in the face of war.

---

14 Michael Neiberg, *Dance of the Furies: Europe and the Outbreak of World War I* (Harvard University Press, 2013), 33–35, 109–14.
15 Jeffery Verhey, *The Spirit of 1914: Militarism, Myth, and Mobilization in Germany* (Cambridge University Press, 2000), 72, 82.

Figure 4.1: Crowds cheering the declaration of war in Berlin, outside the Berlin Cathedral.
Source: Library of Congress. George Grantham Bain Collection. Reproduction Number:
LC-DIG-ggbain-16893 (digital file from original negative).

While German and French reservists reported for duty, young men in both countries also followed the example of Great Britain, where hundreds of thousands of men converged on army recruitment centers after the country entered the war on August 4, 1914. Here exhortations for men to do their part to defend British values were cast immediately in gendered terms. Recruiting posters challenged British men to join the cause, lest they explain to their future children why they didn't go to the war; or emphasized how going across the English Channel to fight Germany was a selfless act of defending the honor of British women. In many cases, though, the official recruiting effort was overwhelmed by individual and collective acts by men and women across the country. Young women took to the streets of London and other cities, confronting military age men who were not in uniform, all to shame them into compliance with aforementioned white feathers. Everywhere entire professional, sporting, and neighborhood groups went *en masse* to join up for the war, creating companies of "chums" who relied upon their mutual ties of friendship and association to keep their spirits up through training and deployment to France. Only after the bloody battles of 1916 did the War Office come to realize that allowing companies made up entirely of men from one neighborhood, village, or town to go into battle might not be the best method for keeping civilian morale firmly behind the effort. Before that turning point, two million Britons would enlist in response to the call to arms, creating the core of a mass army for the first time in British history.[16]

The question that remains for those looking back from the perspective of a century after the opening of the war is how so many individuals from such disparate backgrounds and social identities were bound together to support something as destructive and lethal as total industrial war. One possible answer is offered by scholar Barbara Ehrenreich in her book *Blood Rites: Origins and History of the Passions of War*. Ehrenreich traces "nationalism *as* a religion, complete with its own deities, mythology, and rites" from the French Revolutionary wars through the World Wars:

> To acknowledge that nationalism is itself a kind of religion would be to concede that all that is 'modern' is not necessarily 'progressive' or 'rational': that history can sometimes take us 'backward' toward what have come to see as the archaic and primitive. . . It is in times of war and the threat of war that nationalism takes on its most overtly religious hues. During the temporary enthusiasms of war, such as those inspired by the outbreak of First World War, individuals see themselves as participants in, or candidates for, a divine form of 'sacrifice.'[17]

Following Ehrenreich's logic, masculinity and femininity can be situated in her analogues of nationalism to religion and war to sacrifice. Men, true to their culturally constructed and socially ingrained identities, could utilize war as a rite of passage to prove their masculinity, act as protectors of their women against the heathen enemy, and serve as lambs on the bloody altar of patriotism. Leo Braudy adds another outgrowth in the interrelationship among nationalism, masculinity, and war: "In the diffuseness of peacetime, different masculinities might be

---

16 Lloyd S. Kramer, *Nationalism in Europe and America: Politics, Cultures, and Identities since 1775* (University of North Carolina Press, 2011), 7–29, 147–60.
17 Ehrenreich, *Blood Rites*, 204–205. See also Bourke, "Gender Roles in Killing Zones," 167–68.

indulged, but in war masculinity was the core of national cohesiveness, and, not coincidentally, the essence of defining *us* against *them*."[18]

Wartime Nationalism and Masculinity in Europe's War: 1914–1916

In his book, *Tommy: The British Soldier on the Western Front, 1914–1918*, social military historian Richard Holmes decried the effects of one of the most popular platitudes associated with the First World War on future attempts to come to grips with the conflict. "One of the problems with trying to write about the First World War is that most people have already read Wilfred Owen and Siegfried Sassoon, Pat Barker and Sebastian Faulks before you get to them," writes Holmes. "I am certainly not the first historian to complain that it was far too literary a war."[19] In penning this objection to the intersection between history and popular culture with regard to the war, Holmes was largely expressing his concerns with the broad acceptance of two long-standing trends in First World War historiography and literature. First is the "lions and donkeys' approach," popularized by Alan Clark in his scathing treatment of the British Expeditionary Forces in 1915, *The Donkeys*.[20] His portrayal of the British Army's field command as a collection of callow incompetents, who planned battles like Loos with little regard for the lives of the men they sent to certain death, has become a staple of popular histories of the First World War ever since it first appeared in 1962. The second trend Holmes ascribes to the literary war tradition is what Dan Todman has called the "mud and blood" genre of accounts of the war.[21] In this tradition, the war has been reduced to a perpetual travesty of knee-deep mud, corpse-festooned stands of barbed wire, and constant misery. Between these two deeply reductionist tropes, a more accurate and responsible telling of the war and the sacrifices of those who fought, lived, and died in the trenches and on the home front is lost.[22]

The same criticism of the literary war can be applied to efforts to identify how the average soldier experienced the war and how their own mettle was tested by loved ones at home against their own perceptions of the front lines. Thanks in

---

18 Braudy, *From Chivalry to Terrorism*, 378. See also Robert Wohl, *Generation of 1914* (Harvard University Press, 1979), 207, 216–17; Goldstein, *War and Gender*, 264–72.

19 Richard Holmes, *Tommy: The British Soldier on the Western Front, 1914–1918* (Harper Collins, 2004), xvii.

20 Alan Clark, *The Donkeys: A Controversial Account of the Leaders of the British Expeditionary Forces in France, 1915* (Morrow, 1962).

21 Dan Todman, *The Great War: Myth and Memory* (Hambledon and London, 2005), 1–3, 26.

22 Holmes. *Tommy*, xxii–xxiii; and Todman, *The Great War*, 29–33, 40–41.

no small part to poetic efforts like Wilfred Owen, or prose memoirs like Siegfried Sassoon, the English-reading audience is left with an account of the war in which conventional notions of bravery, courage, and sacrifice are turned on their heads. Readers come away from these primary accounts, and others like them, with the impression that the average Tommy in the trenches was a cynical fatalist, possessed of a scathing sense of irony that reduced all prior constructions of male identity in wartime to pale epithets in the face of mass industrial warfare. After July 1, 1916, all pre-war concepts of masculine behavior under fire were swept away, leaving only the bitter fatalism that colors the later memoirs.

As attractive as this literary-based truism may be to generations of writers, novelists, and amateur historians, it is a deeply flawed generalization. Even among the highly educated caste of gentlemen who were commissioned as officers in the first years of the war, military service was viewed as an obligation and duty not to be taken lightly. Indeed, the prospect of fulfilling masculine expectations through combat in the First World War enabled many men to make symbolic and substantive breaks with the adolescent innocence, feminine influence, and soft existences that contemporary writers considered to be prevalent among the generation coming of age in 1914. Under the auspices of warmaking, many of the traits that were encouraged in British public schools, German *gymnasia*, and French *academies* – controlled aggression, competition, loyalty – were embraced as essential manly virtues. Even the prospect of brutal violence against the foe was reduced to just another competitive experience, which the stronger, fitter man was better prepared to survive. Simply put, for many hundreds of thousands of middle and upper-class young men, war represented a masculine adventure, one which not only validated the virtues of their gender, but which culled the weak and unfit, leaving behind those fit and strong men best prepared to lead post war society.[23]

The Death of *Elan*: The War's First Two Years (1914–1915)

If there is any stereotype of combat in the First World War that might challenge the images of tired and filthy soldiers huddled in waterlogged trenches, facing off across the muddy and corpse-ridden No Man's Land, it is the idea of brave yet inexperienced young conscripts marching in parade ground formation against

---

23 H. L. Wesseling, *Soldier and Warrior: French Attitudes toward the Army and War on the Eve of the First World War*, Trans. Arnold J. Pomerans, (Greenwood Press, 2000), 178–179, 182–183; and Michael C. C. Adams, *The Great Adventure: Male Desire and the Coming of World War I* (Indiana University Press, 1990), 57.

well-positioned machine guns. Again, much of this is tied to the impact of the Literary War on popular accounts of the Western Front that were popularized around the time of the fiftieth anniversary of the conflict. Unlike many of the half-truths and maudlin fictions promoted at this time, however, there is more than a kernel of truth to the notion of young men marching lockstep to their doom. In the first years of the war, all of the major combatant armies experienced their own introduction to the realities of modern industrial war and the slaughter it imposed on its participants. In this case, the primary factor was the realization of the limits of an offensive doctrine that was rooted in both national exceptionalism and the perceived value of masculine forbearance and aggression in battle. Simply put, personal bravery – "cram," "guts," "*elan vital*," "the cult of the bayonet" – could carry attackers through the most intense fire to successfully carry the day.

Casual observers generally point toward the French Army's doctrine of "*l'offensive à outrance*" – "the extreme [or excessive] offensive" as the starting point for this outlook. Articulated in a series of staff college lectures by Lieutenant Colonel Louis Loyzeau de Grandmaison, "*l'offensive à outrance*" was intended as a remedy for the erosion of French martial spirit that had followed the Franco-Prussian War. Since 1871, the French General Staff was engaged in a search for the appropriate doctrine that would offset the German material and demographic advantages in the next war. By 1890, military planners had settled on a defense-oriented strategy that would avoid risking open battle save on French terms. Though certainly the more logical choice, to young officers like Grandmaison this decision sacrificed the offensive initiative to the enemy, a decision calculated to bring about defeat. Instead, Grandmaison counseled employing a professional army well-trained in offensive tactics in constant attacks against the enemy. Through training and repetition such men could be conditioned to overcome the fear attendant to battle, to the point where assaults were instinctive. In the event of mass mobilization, the example of this highly-motivated warrior cadre would prove sufficient to inculcate a similar spirit which would translate into victory.[24] When combined with the critical impetus or force – the *elan vital* articulated by philosopher Henri Bergson – employed in this case as an emotive exercise of energy and spirit that could overcome the material weight of shot and shell, the French soldier would acquire a nearly-unstoppable impetus in the attack that would overwhelm the enemy.[25]

---

24 Jack Snyder, *The Ideology of the Offensive: Military Decision Making and the Disasters of 1914.* (Cornell University Press, 1984), 90–91; and Robert A. Doughty, *Pyrrhic Victory: French Strategy and Operations in the Great War* (Belknap Press of Harvard University Press, 2005), 26.
25 Snyder, *Ideology of the Offensive*, 10.

Within two years, Grandmaison's lectures overcame individual resistance within the defense establishment to become the foundation a series of revisions, beginning in December 1913 and continuing through 1914, of army regulations and ultimately to shape the context of French Army doctrine in the case of war with Germany. In the former, the emphasis of combat was now shifted to the offensive, in which all energies were transferred from the defensive stance (employed only to draw the enemy out to offer battle) to the constant, vigorous attack. As historian Robert A. Doughty observes, this attack would be infantry-based and depended upon offering fighting in close quarters:

> The infantry regulations of April 1914 asserted that the 'supreme weapon' of the infantry was the bayonet. After the infantrymen fixed bayonets, they would advance—wearing a blue coat, red trousers, and a blue cap with red top—with their officers leading in the front and with drums and bugles sounding the charge. The attacking troops would supposedly gain a superiority of fire with the rapid and intense fire of the 75-mm cannon and with a hail of bullets from the advancing soldiers. When they closed with the enemy soldiers, they would throw themselves into their ranks and finish the fight with the bayonet and superior courage.[26]

Presuming of course that the resplendent French infantry survived the moment of first encounter with an enemy clad in drab field grey and lavishly equipped with quick-firing rifles of their own and belt-fed machine guns. The French offensive plan for August 1914, Plan XVII, called for the immediate invasion of Alsace and Lorraine, the two provinces lost to Germany in the previous war. Expecting the German defenders to fold under the inexorable force of the French attack, commanders were shocked to discover their men made little headway against the local defenses. The subsequent disasters cumulatively known as the Battle of the Frontiers (August 7 to September 13, 1914) would cost the French Army over 325,000 casualties. Fortunately, the French Army would recover quickly from the shock of the failure of its *elan,* and would successfully halt the German advance on Paris at the Battle of the Marne (September 6 to September 12, 1914).

Though never quite abandoned during the war, *elan vital* and *l'attaque à outrance* represented the dilemma that all armies – not only the French – faced in the prosecution of modern industrial war. In a conflict that pit human flesh against massive quantities of munitions, how could soldiers survive, let alone succeed in executing decision in battle? To virtually all participants, the solution rested on the backs of the infantryman: a moderately to professionally trained conscript

---

26 Doughty, *Pyrrhic Victory*, 28.

or volunteer in peacetime, and a uniformed civilian of ever-growing potential in war. The reliance upon individual character and cultural assumptions of masculine physical and emotional prowess, competition, and internal spirit was universal. In 1904, European and American military liaisons watched Japanese infantrymen launch successive waves of massed infantry assaults on Russian defenses at Port Arthur during the Russo-Japanese War. When the observers reported back to their respective staff colleges, they did not emphasize the relative thin lines and limited resources of the Russian defenders, but rather the remarkable fighting spirit of the Japanese soldier and the success of human wave assaults carried out to completion regardless of the cost.[27]

Over the next decade, general staffs across the world sought to incorporate the aggressive style of the Japanese army into their own troops, a trend that helps explain how Grandmaison's approach was so quickly adopted within the French army. In the Russian army, theorists balanced their own experience during the Russo-Japanese War with a systemic historical analysis of Russian martial accomplishments going back to the days of Suvarov. Looking at their past glories and recent humiliations, the Russian planners came to accept the bayonet over the bullet. More specifically, shock attacks were assessed as the ideal deployment for an army heavy in infantry, as the superior stolid willpower of the Russian soldier was proven indomitable in the face of stronger defenses, time and again.[28] Even as machine gun and quick-firing field artillery firepower became more significant in the Russian Army's field regulations after 1912, the bayonet assault remained the centerpiece of doctrine, which should occur just as "the moral force had shifted in favor of the attack. ... The instruction prescribed that the final assault be 'fast, decisive, and violent as a hurricane.'"[29] While privileging mass and maneuver, Russian infantry doctrine, like that in other European armies, emphasized the importance of individual and collective *elan* in achieving decision.

The British Army placed greater emphasis on marksmanship, putting the lessons of the Boer War into practice. In terms of doctrine, however, the British Army's 1909 *Field Service Regulations* also emphasized the offensive both in application and in spirit. "In retrospect, a ruthless determination to succeed seems to be over-emphasized as against material factors such as weight of fire," J. P. Harris, a recent Haig biographer, notes in his account of his subject's pre-war

---

27 Hew Strachan, *The First World War, Volume I: To Arms* (Cambridge University Press, 2001), 304–305, 463; and Snyder, *Ideology of the Offensive*, 79–81.
28 Bruce W. Menning, *Bayonets Before Bullets: The Imperial Russian Army, 1861–1914* (Indiana University Press, 1992), 211.
29 *Ibid.*, 262; Op cit. *Naztavlenie dlia deistvii pekhoty v boiu. vysohaishe utverzhdeno 27 fevralia g.* (St. Petersburg, 1914), 36–37.

years at the British War Office.[30] Accordingly the British infantry was intended to advance to contact the enemy, and combine suppressive fire with aggressive assaults in order to create the opportunity for cavalry exploitation. In practice, the small British Expeditionary Force pivoted to the defense, first at Mons, and then throughout the "Great Retreat" before the German Fifth Army to the Marne River. Yet the general staff, first under Field Marshall Sir John French, and after December 18, 1915, Field Marshall Sir Douglas Haig, never abandoned its desire to achieve a breakthrough the first line of German defenses, opening up a pathway to "the green fields beyond" for the cavalry. This was expected to be accomplished in large part by the British and Imperial soldier's fighting spirit, in combination with a massive material superiority. Tested at Neuve Chapelle and Loos (in both cases, to miserable defeat) in 1915, the culminating point of this outlook occurred in the July 1, 1916 attack along the Somme River valley. Following a massive seven day bombardment, the British attackers were expected to walk over the shattered German trench defenses. Morale was high, as the attacking regiments climbed out of their own trenches; in some units, the men followed officers kicking a soccer ball across no man's land. By the end of the day, however, the 100,000 British attackers sustained over 57,000 casualties, including 19,240 killed.[31]

One of the more frequently discussed subjects in the historiography of the First World War centers on the German August 1914 offensive against France, the much-discussed Schlieffen Plan offensive. Accordingly the discussions of the German right hook swing through Belgium rest on the viability of the timetable for the attack, and whether or not it offered a realistic timeline for foot infantry to complete its objectives before the French and British defenders recovered from the initial surprise.[32] For the most part the monographs on the Schlieffen Plan offensive go into great detail into the operational and tactical facets of the campaign, but offer relatively little insight into the individual motivation and role of

---

30 J. P. Harris, *Sir Douglas Haig and the First World War* (Cambridge University Press, 2008), 46.
31 Gary Sheffield, *The Somme* (Cassell, 2007), 68. The literature on the British Army's performance on the Somme is voluminous: John Keegan, *The Face of Battle: A Study of Agincourt, Waterloo, and The Somme* (Penguin, 1976); Martin Middlebrook, *The First Day on the Somme* (Allen Lane, 1971); and Jessica Meyer, *Men of War: Masculinity and the First World War in Britain* (Palgrave Macmillan, 2008), 130–36.
32 See Gerhard Ritter, *The Schlieffen Plan: Critique of a Myth* (Wolff, 1958); Snyder, *The Ideology of the Offensive*; Holger H. Herwig, *The Marne, 1914: The Opening of World War I and the Battle that Changed the World* (Random House, 2011); Terence Zuber, *Inventing the Schlieffen Plan: German War Planning, 1871–1914* (Oxford University Press, 2014); Hans Ehlert et al., eds., *The Schlieffen Plan: International Perspectives on the German Strategy for World War I* (University Press of Kentucky, 2014); and Dennis Showalter, et al., *The German Failure in Belgium, August 1914* (McFarland, 2018).

elan in the German Army. Robert Wohl presents a much needed corrective, though his focus is primarily on the state of European youth culture before 1914. Examining the character of the generation of young German men who left school and university to enlist at the onset of the war, Wohl argues that rather than an act of patriotic conformity, this lusty support for war was an act of youth rebellion. This generation not only sought to win the war to preserve German sovereignty and values, they also saw themselves as agents of cultural renewal, who would revitalize public and private life in a stale and vulgar *Kaiserreich*.[33] From here it was a quick leap to the type of outlook evoked by writer and infantry lieutenant Ernst Jünger, who saw the Western Front, with all its hazards and threat of death as the epicenter for the spiritual renewal that he and so many of his peers desired.[34]

More recently, Ann P. Linder reaches a similar conclusion in her book *Princes of the Trenches: Narrating the German Experience of the First World War*. Building off of Wohl's study, Linder examines what motivated so many elite and bourgeois young men to follow the call to war. While granting that significant war enthusiasm existed among bourgeois urban and semi-rural youth, it was not exactly tied to the prior generation's concepts of nationalistic identity. Rather the youth who were called up or volunteered in the frenzied first months of the war followed a rather more romanticized imagined community space that was tied to a more mystical, quasi-historical conceptualization of the German medieval past. While rejecting the definition offered by recent critics of the so-called *Sonderweg* ("special path") in German history like Daniel Jonah Goldhagen, Linder considers this entirely within the context of the German Romantics movement, and which, she notes, provided a "positive model of development, buttressing the Second Empire with an aura of spiritual legitimacy and historical continuity, and supplying conservatives of the Weimar Republic with persuasive arguments for rejecting the 'alien' forms of republicanism."[35]

Those participants cast their service in the first years of the war as an almost religious experience, a children's crusade as it were, in which their youthful idealism and innocence not only carried them as one to the recruiting office or their reservist garrisons, but was also ripped from them in the subsequent slaughters of late 1914 through 1916. The passage from young romantic idealist to embittered *Frontschwein*, while never as complete or systematic as the war's literary legacy portrayed, did have almost mythical elements that were quite real. Consider the

---

33 Wohl, *The Generation of 1914*, 44–48.

34 *Ibid.*, 57.

35 Ann P. Linder, *Princes of the Trenches: Narrating the German Experience of the First World War* (Camden House, 1996), 21–22, quote on 22. See also Dennis E. Showalter's award-winning book *Instrument of War: The German Army 1914–18* (Osprey, 2016).

so-called *"Kindermord von Langemarck"* – the slaughter of the innocents at the battle of Langemarck, in November 1914. The latest in a series of attacks intended to break through the thin British defenses surrounding Ypres, on November 10, some 7,000 young volunteer soldiers were decimated in their assault. As the legend of the attack took shape, the attackers were recast as almost entirely drawn from university and gymnasium student volunteers, who linked arms together, singing *"Deutschland, Deutschland, über alles"* as they marched to their deaths.[36] The legend of Langemarck grew far out of proportion to the actual events of the battle, which actually occurred at the less-German sounding town of Bixschote, and which proved costly but successful. By the 1920s Langemarck was a standard component of rightist and National Socialist accounts of the war, used to promote the twin ideas of sacrifice and slaughter. Yet while Langemarck was largely a mythic construction, it did represent the starker reality of a new war, one in which the material weight of industrial war (*Materialschlacht*) consumed traditional martial virtues (bravery, courage, valor, honor), with ease. In the moment, Langemarck became a metaphor for the process by which thousands of inexperienced young German volunteers and reservists would be squandered in fruitless attacks in 1914 and 1915. Another case of misguided *elan* being relied upon as the sole guarantor of victory.

Any analysis of the first year of the war must contend with the failures of an offensive doctrinal wave based upon the flawed premise that *elan vital* was in of itself sufficient to create a breakthrough victory. Indeed, the high casualties of the first two years of the war can be attributed as much to this emphasis on the primacy of the all-out offensive, brought to fruition by the superior masculine qualities of each participants' soldiers as on anything else. The root cause for the flawed offensives and their ghastly tolls resides in these romanticized views of war as a masculine endeavor. Yet it is also important to consider that the disasters of 1914 through 1916 did not signal the end for *elan*-influenced doctrine. As the war entered its third year, internal motivation and aggressive drive became more important factors in continuing the war. As discipline and morale began to waver on both the Eastern and Western Fronts in the face of even greater material slaughter, new tactical solutions in the French, German, British, and Italian armies sought to emphasize the role of highly motivated elite organizations to carry the day. These formations, be they *Alpini*, *Stosstruppen*, Dominion forces, or *Arditi*, continued to emphasize a superior fighting spirit as a force multiplier in combat against the enemy. In all these cases, infiltration doctrine and new technologies

---

36 Wohl, *The Generation of 1914*, 48; and Holger H. Herwig, *The First World War: Germany and Austria-Hungary, 1914–1918* (Arnold, 1997), 116.

were intended as adjuncts to – not replacements for – the critical *elan* these specialized units possessed.

The Rape of Belgium: The Nexus of Atrocity and Propaganda

Within mere weeks of the first attack on Liege, accounts of German atrocities in Belgium swept through the French and British press, and from there, to the world at large. Initially the outrage was directed toward the violation of Belgian neutrality, preserved since 1839 in a five-power agreement allegedly dismissed by Chancellor Theobald von Bethmann-Hollweg as a "scrap of paper." Presented as an open act of German aggression, the invasion of Belgium was predetermined by the adoption of the Schlieffen Plan by the German General Staff; otherwise the vaunted "strong right hook" aimed at Paris could not have taken place. Within days of the invasion, reports of German attacks on civilians began to circulate. These were not random acts of violence or looting by individual soldiers. Rather they were accounts of summary justice being meted out by firing squads against groups of Belgian men rounded up on flimsy charges of armed resistance. As the assault on the fortress town of Liege stalled, atrocity stories increased, with new, though almost predictable, features: bands of German soldiers assaulting Belgian women, looting, raping, and burning their way through small villages; parish priests and nuns being rounded up and executed in retaliation for unrelated attacks on German soldiers; the mutilation of the dead and the living – the amputation of breasts or hands a particular favorite.[37]

Then came to sack of Louvain, a cultural gem east of Brussels. The city's pride and joy was the library of the University of Louvain, renowned for its collection of medieval manuscripts and incunabula. On the night of August 25, 1914, panicking Germans, acting on rumors of an imminent British attack, set fire to several homes and public buildings, including the library. Over the next few days, 248 civilians were killed, and over 1,500 men, women, and children were deported to a prison camp outside Munster. By the end of the assault, some 1,120 buildings were destroyed, as was the entire university archive and library.[38]

Accounts of Louvain, and other atrocities, soon dominated the headlines in Britain, France, and the US. Within a short time, though, the reports assumed a clearly gendered cast. New stories of German soldiers engaging in an orgy of

---

37 John Horne and Alan Kramer, *German Atrocities 1914: A History of Denial* (Yale University Press, 2000), 23–38, 63–64.
38 Alan Kramer, *Dynamic of Destruction: Culture and Mass Killing in the First World War* (Oxford University Press, 2007), 6–12; and Horne and Kramer, *German Atrocities 1914*, 38–42.

Figure 4.2: "24 August 1914. Louvain. After capturing a Belgian soldier, the enemy hangs him from a lamppost in front of the station… (from the official Belgian Report. J.G. Domergue, 1915)." (Translated by author). Illustration in *Le livre rouge des atrocités Allemandes d'aprés les rapports officiels des gouvernements Français, Anglais et Belge, par l'image* (Paris: Le Magazine, 1916), 20. An example of how alleged and real atrocities in Belgium were presented by the Allies during the war.
Source: Library of Congress. Reproduction Number: LC-USZ62-14437 (b&w film copy neg.).

sexual violence and looting took center stage. Propagandists in Britain quickly took advantage of these accounts to craft a series of recruiting posters that established once and for all the German enemy as the "Hun" – a bestial vandal, seeking to burn civilization down to the ground.[39] After the United States entered the war

---

39 The "Hun" allusion is itself drawn from a speech Kaiser Wilhelm II delivered as the German expeditionary force bound for China departed Bremerhaven on July 27, 1900. "Should you encounter the enemy, he will be defeated! No quarter will be given! Prisoners will not be taken! Whoever falls into your hands is forfeited. Just as a thousand years ago the Huns under their King Attila made a name for themselves, one that even today makes them seem mighty in history and legend, may the name German be affirmed by you in such a way in China that no Chinese will ever again dare to look cross-eyed at a German." Wilhelm II: "Hun": "Hun" Speech, German

Figure 4.3: Reports of German atrocities in Belgium and Northern. France soon acquired a more specifically gendered tone, as seen in this 1918 American poster soliciting support for the Fourth Liberty Loan.
Source: Library of Congress. Reproduction Number: LC-USZC4-4441 (color film copy transparency) LC-USZ62-19905 (b&w film copy neg.).

in April 1917, American propagandists took the imagery even further, recasting the German enemy as demonic murderers, hands and feet dripping with blood, carrying prostate women on their backs as their looted property. The posters carried

History in Documents and Images website. http://germanhistorydocs.ghi-dc.org/sub_document.cfm?document_id=755 (Accessed March 20, 2018).

a clear message: Stop the German before he does to us what he did to Belgium. The Rape of Belgium thus acquired an outsized meaning, beyond the immediate atrocities captured in the Bryce Report (the official British inquiry report into Belgium). Belgium became the surrogate for civilization, as Germany acquired a dehumanized character far out of proportion to its pre-war reputation.[40]

For decades, these narratives have been dismissed as lurid propaganda by historians. The immediate concern has been to restore agency to the academic institution which was a willing participant in the demonization of Germany for wartime necessity. More recently, this took on a new dimension, as historians argued that it was precisely because of these false narratives that the very real news of the Nazi Holocaust was ignored or dismissed as just more propaganda. This argument was co-opted by Holocaust deniers, who claimed that the Final Solution, like the Belgian atrocities of the First World War, was the product of Allied propaganda. By the 1990s, another narrative line took shape that argues the highly gendered representations of the German atrocities helped the Allied cause by presenting a skeptical public with an allegorical narrative to substitute for the more tedious reality of international law.[41]

The historical debate over the veracity of the claims of Belgian atrocities took a sharp turn in 2000. At that time, historians John Horne and Alan Kramer revealed that over 6,500 Belgian and French civilians were killed by German soldiers, while an untold number of women were raped.[42] Much of this was a panicked response to alleged *franc-tireur* activity, and was explained away as such at the time by an unapologetic German High Command (*Oberste Heeresleitung - OHL*). Taken as a whole, the issue of atrocities in Belgium was certainly real, but also subject to an exaggerated level of distortion, not by the Allied governments, but rather through other, unofficial actors. In this regard, the narrative lent itself to

---

40 An exhaustive archive of WWI Propaganda posters is located at: http://www.ww1propaganda. com/. Specific examples of American propaganda demonizing the German occupation of Belgium include:http://www.ww1propaganda.com/ww1-poster/halt-hun-buy-us-government-bonds-third-liberty-loan; http://www.ww1propaganda.com/ww1-poster/keep-these-usa-buy-more-liberty-bonds; http://www.ww1propaganda.com/ww1-poster/remember-belgium-buy-bonds-fourth-lib-erty-loan; (Accessed March 20, 2018). Also see: http://www.loc.gov/pictures/item/2010652057/ (Accessed March 21, 2018).

41 Harry Elmer Barnes, *The Genesis of the World War: An Introduction to the Problem of War Guilt* (Alfred A. Knopf, 1927), 290–298; Isabel Hull, *Absolute Destruction: Military Culture and the Practices of War in Imperial Germany* (Cornell University Press, 2006); Deborah Lipstadt, *Denying the Holocaust* (Plume, 1994), 34; and Nicoletta F. Gullace, "Sexual Violence and Family Honor: British Propaganda and International Law during the First World War," *American Historical Review* 102 (June 1997), 714–47, 716.

42 Horne and Kramer, *German Atrocities 1914*, 196–201.

wild accounts of mutilation and amputation largely because of Belgium's own history of misogynistic and race-motivated mutilation in the Congo over the previous generation. Primed to associate amputations and body desecrations with King Leopold II's administration of the colony, outside observers came to accept the likelihood of similar treatment at the hands of the German invaders. In this regard, the real misery of the entire German occupation of Belgium, described by Larry Zuckerman as the "real" rape of Belgium, is obscured by the imagined narrative. For four years, he writes, Belgian civilians lived under a regime of organized and systemic plunder, wanton destruction, mass deportation, and arbitrary confiscations that created a climate of constant institutional terror from which the country never recovered.[43] All of this was soon forgotten, however, as the more outrageous accounts of German atrocities were disputed.

Deflating Nationalisms and Destabilizing Masculinities, 1916–1918

On home fronts across Europe, women supported their men at war because, as dutiful nurturers, wives, mothers, sisters, and daughters, they adhered to pre-war constructions of femininity. Except for Russia, no serious consideration of sending women into the masculine public, industrial, or military spheres was yet thought necessary. Government-sponsored posters allegorized women's patriotic duty to encourage the men in their lives to volunteer for military service. Willingly offering their sons, husbands, brothers, and fathers to the cause was just another sacrificial duty required of women. They still were passive objects to be protected by their nation's male soldiers. Nevertheless, some middle-class women, including suffragists, saw the war as an opportunity to better demonstrate their abilities to fulfill duties as citizens in hopes of attaining emancipation and equality as citizens.[44]

---

43 Adam Hochschild, *King Leopold's Ghost: A Story of Greed, Terror, and Heroism in Colonial Africa* (Houghton Mifflin, 1999); and Larry Zuckerman, *The Rape of Belgium: The Untold Story of World War I* (New York University Press, 2004), 1–3.
44 Jenny Gould, "Women's Military Service in First World War Britain" in *Behind the Lines: Gender and the Two World Wars*, ed. Margaret Higonnet et al. (Yale University Press, 1987), 114–125; and Nancy M. Wingfield and Maria Bucur, eds., *Gender and War in Twentieth Century Eastern Europe* (Indiana University Press, 2006), 5–10. See also: Susan Grayzel, "Men and Women at Home," in *Cambridge History of the First World War*, vol III, *Civil Society*, ed. Jay Winter (Cambridge University Press, 2014), 96–120; and Laura Lee Downs, "War Work," in *Cambridge History of the First World War*, vol III, *Civil Society*, ed. Jay Winter (Cambridge University Press, 2014), 72–95; Goldstein, *War and Gender*, 318–21, 384–86.

In France, women in the labor force increased from 38 percent in 1914 to almost 50 percent by war's end, entering many formerly all-male chemical, timber, transportation, and manufacturing industries. Their numbers in these vital sectors of France's wartime economy expanded from five percent in 1914 to twenty-five percent in 1918. In Britain women experienced similar gains: female employment in industry nearly doubled from three million women in 1915 to five million in 1918. In both countries, one of the largest employers of unskilled working-class women was the munitions industry, a dangerous occupation in which the "munitionettes" experienced chemical poisoning, industrial accidents, or potential death in assembly line and stockpile explosions, and regular male harassment. The British government likewise established the Women's Army Auxiliary Corps, the Women's Royal Naval Service, and the Women's Royal Air Force to free men up for other combat related duty. No British women in uniform, however, saw combat.[45]

Women in Germany and Russia followed somewhat different paths from those in France and Britain. The German case is described in more detail in the next section of this chapter, but in summary, German efforts to mobilize middle-class women as wartime laborers and military auxiliaries only proceeded in the last two years of the war, and even then were limited by the necessities of providing the basic subsistence needs of the family amidst blockade. Working-class women, of course, were no strangers to industrial labor, but even they were distracted by the food shortages. Russian women, on the contrary, surpassed the other belligerent nations because they received suffrage rights and a few even served in combat units. The most well-known of these Russian female combat units was the so-called "Women's Battalion of Death," an organization intended as much to shame reluctant men into service as it was to serve in the field.[46]

---

45 Antoine Prost, "Workers," in Jay Winter, ed., *Cambridge History of the First World War*, Volume II, *The State* (Cambridge University Press, 2014), 325–57, 332–38; "Nine Women Reveal the Dangers of Working in a Munitions Factory," Imperial War Museum, https://www.iwm.org.uk/history/9-women-reveal-the-dangers-of-working-in-a-first-world-war-munitions-factory (Accessed, March 20, 2018); Vera Brittain, *Testament of Youth: An Autobiographical Study of the Years 1900–1925* (1933; New York: Penguin, 1994); Gould, "Women's Military Service in First World War Britain," 114–25; and Margaret H. Darrow, *French Women and the First World War: War Stories from the Home Front* (Bloomsbury Academic, 2000).
46 Melissa Stockdale, "My Death for the Motherland is Happiness: Women, Patriotism, and Soldiering in Russia's Great War, 1914–1917," *American Historical Review* 109 (February 2004): 78–115; Laurie Stoff, *They Fought for the Motherland: Russia's Women Soldiers in World War I and the Revolution* (University Press of Kansas, 2006); and Karen Hagemann, "Mobilizing Women for War: The History, Historiography, and Memory of German Women's War Service in the Two World Wars," *Journal of Military History* 75 (October 2011): 1060–73.

As casualties mounted in 1915, many of the first waves of volunteer soldiers fell dead or wounded. The German, British, and French took desperate steps to replace these losses. The British government, for example, initiated conscription under the Military Service Acts of early 1916. Both England and France used colonial forces of different races and ethnicities to supplement their military strength. Apart from the manpower issue, European belligerents needed to manufacture and transport massive amounts of food, clothing, weapons, and equipment to the battle fronts. This high level of mobilization required all national demographic, agricultural, industrial, and natural resources to be harnessed. On the home fronts, industries retooled for war and began massive building programs that utilized as much of the nation's resources as possible. Radical measures to manage both the public's morale and the wartime material and political economies were undertaken on both sides, transforming traditional gendered roles and responsibilities in the public and private spheres. As the war drew to a close, revolution was more than in the air – it was happening all across the world. While the uprisings were total in Eastern and Central Europe, in England, France, and the United States, the change was socially transformative, as women began to acquire new political, social, and economic power. The First World War was a singular moment of unprecedented multifaceted change, one that set in motion even more cultural and political shocks that continue to be felt a century later.

Women and the War: The German Home Front, 1916–1919

While all of the major European combatant nations experienced after the costly battles of 1916, Germany's total mobilization melded together the front lines and home to a degree never seen before. As gender historians Karen Hagemann and Stefanie Schüler-Springorum noted in 2002, "'Front' and 'home' were intimately related. An expression of this is the concept of the 'home front', which was created in the very first months of the First World War in German propaganda. Thus the constantly emphasized traditional borders between military and civilian society, between 'front' and 'home' became increasingly blurred . . . ."[47] The bloodlettings of 1916 exacted a grim toll of German soldiers. Verdun cost 330,000 casualties, over 100,000 dead and missing; the Somme was even worse, with somewhere around 500,000 casualties. These were losses that could not be easily made up,

---

47 Karen Hagemann and Stefanie Schüler-Springorum, eds., *Home/Front: The Military, War and Gender in Twentieth Century Germany* (Berg, 2002), ix.

particularly as German troops were dispatched with greater regularity to peripheral theaters and fronts to make up for the shortcomings of its Austro-Hungarian ally. But at the same time, the material demands of total industrial war dictated that more skilled and unskilled labor was required to meet the requisite needs of the war. Artillery pieces, machine guns, grenades, rifles, ammunition, uniforms, metal sheets, rebar, supports (for trench construction), poison gas, submarines – none of these vital elements of the war effort would make themselves.

Thus Germany, which had largely sought to limit direct female participation in the industrial war effort before 1916 was compelled to re-examine its policies. For two years, the civilian government and the OHL agreed that skilled industrial and agricultural workers should receive exemptions from military service, so they might continue work in wartime production. In December 1916, the *Reichstag* reinforced this through the Patriotic Auxiliary Service Act (*Vaterländischer Hilfsdienstgesetz*), obligating all men to engage in war work exclusively. However even this proved insufficient, as more men continued to be needed as replacements for the army, particularly on the Western Front. By Spring 1917, the government revised its earlier attempts to restrict female industrial participation in the war effort. Exemptions that were granted to women who volunteered to work in munitions and armament factories in the Winter of 1916 were institutionalized and expanded by the new Central Office of Women's Labor (*Frauenarbeitszentrale*, or *FAZ*). Soon this bureaucratic office began recruiting middle-class women for service, not only in factories, but also as Red Cross nurses and army auxiliaries working in the zone of communication between the front and Germany proper.[48]

By permitting the mobilization of women into military service, the OHL enacted a massive shift in the German social contract that hitherto restricted women to a clearly subordinate role within the state and its institutions. To be sure, trained female nurses associated with the German Red Cross were long accepted as a pool for the army's medical services; this was but one example of the impact of Florence Nightingale's and Clara Barton's experiences in the Crimean and American Civil Wars. By proving nursing was an acceptable feminine occupation, in keeping with contemporary notions of women as maternal, yet chaste, nurturers, the nursing volunteers these women mobilized provided a professional outlet for middle-class women that became more specialized and formal after the Spanish-American and Russo-Japanese Wars. But this was, even in 1916, a small cadre of professionals. As for other military occupations, even before the war, the German Army was both a male-exclusive domain and the most

---

48 Karen Hagemann, "Home/Front: The Military, Violence and Gender Relations in the Age of the World Wars," in Hagemann and Schüler-Springorum, *Home/Front*, 1–41, quote on 10.

Figure 4.4: Middle-class women in Berlin knitting socks for the front in a doctor's anteroom.
Ca. Winter 1914.
Source: Library of Congress. George Grantham Bain Collection. Reproduction Number:
LC-DIG-ggbain-18336 (digital file from original negative).

influential social institution within the *Kaiserreich*. No one could contemplate, let
alone seriously consider, placing women in uniform to serve as orderlies, clerks,
or cooks, in even the most subordinate roles in the rear-most echelon.[49]

---

49 John Hutchinson, *Champions of Charity: War and the Rise of the Red Cross* (Routledge, 1997);
and Bianca Schönberger, "Motherly Heroines and Adventurous Girls: Red Cross Nurses and
Women Army Auxiliaries in the First World War," in Hagemann and Schüler-Springorum, *Home/
Front*, 87–113.

Once accepted into the military establishment, women proved capable, and eager, supporters of the war effort. But even here, class distinctions interrupted full and fair mobilization. By November 1918 the German Red Cross accepted over 28,000 volunteers as nursing aides – virtually all of them drawn from the middle and upper classes. Knowledge, skill, or experience were not the limiting factors excluding non-middle-class women; rather it was the relatively low pay. Women in factories could earn between two and four *marks* a day, whereas nursing aides were paid only 70 *pfennig*. As Bianca Schönberger notes, the length of the war and the accompanying decline in basic consumer essentials, including food, were the issues at stake:

> In the course of the war, however, a self-selection by social class evolved, particularly after the rapid deterioration of food supplies in Germany. . . . Financial pressure, therefore, kept an increasing number of women from volunteering for the Red Cross, and the commitment to Volunteer Nursing was left largely to bourgeois and noble women as had already been the case before the war.[50]

A similar dynamic existed for the female army auxiliaries. Beginning in the Spring of 1917, female orderlies began replacing their male counterparts in the *Kriegsamt* in Berlin and in the occupied territory administration. Perhaps even more than the German Red Cross, the military was more sensitive to the moral contours of how women could be perceived by a socially conservative civilian public. Volunteers were limited to women between 20 and 40 years of age, who were also subjected to background checks and medical examinations. This helped limit participation predominantly to upper- and middle-class women, with working-class women gaining access to some menial occupations. Professional women and military spouses were largely excluded as a matter of course. By the end of the war, some 20,000 women were thus directly employed by the army.[51]

The war dramatically affected the social fabric of German life in many other ways as well. Family life had long been considered the central facet of stability and order in Wilhelmine Germany, with the traditional distribution of gendered labor and responsibility at its core. Long term enlistment and conscription disrupted the German family in a way that was felt more keenly than in other combatant societies. Here not only were the male heads of the family – and the primary wage earners – withdrawn with no clear end in sight, their female partners were compelled to take on double and even triple the work to maintain the stability at home that underlie the war effort and the unquestioned rule of the state. With

---

50 Schönberger, "Motherly Heroines and Adventurous Girls," 89.
51 *Ibid.*, 90–91.

Figure 4.5: German working-class women clearing streets in Berlin, ca. 1916.
Source: Library of Congress. George Grantham Bain Collection. Reproduction Number:
LC-DIG-ggbain-21222 (digital file from original negative).

the exception of Russia and perhaps Austria Hungary, the remaining European
Great Powers were all dependent upon food imports to satisfy their peacetime
need. After August 1914, however, the Allied blockade effectively cut Germany off
from 53 percent of its imports, creating shortages that soon translated into heavy
rationing and an ever-growing supply of *ersatz* foodstuffs. The blockade, combined with poor harvests and poor planning, soon exerted a drastic reduction in
food supplies. Fats, meat, and potatoes were among the first foods to be rationed;
by the end of 1916, all foods were subject to rationing.[52]

In their new role as the primary *and* secondary providers for their families,
German women (especially urban women) needed to earn wages in jobs that had

---

52 Alan Kramer, "Blockade and Economic Warfare," in Jay Winter, ed., *The Cambridge History
of the First World War*, vol. 2, *The State* (Cambridge University Press, 2014), 460–89, 460–61;
and David A. Janicki, "The British Blockade During World War I: The Weapon of Deprivation,"
Inquiries Journal: Social Sciences, Arts, & Humanities 6 (2014), http://www.inquiriesjournal.
com/articles/899/the-british-blockade-during-world-war-i-the-weapon-of-deprivation (Accessed
March 20, 2018).

largely been closed to them before 1914. Then they had to negotiate the shrinking opportunities to obtain food for their families, a task that became more taxing as food supplies became more scarce. All this was to be done while also remaining – in the absence of their spouses – the moral authority of the household, and the primary liaison in communicating the wartime needs of the state to the hearth, and vice versa. Ute Daniel summarizes the essentiality of the family to the war effort, and the role of female members in both spheres:

> In the First World War, the family, as the 'decisive social institution for managing every-day life,' played an even more central role in the population's physical and psychological doping with existence than previously, and this affected women in particular. Managing everyday life had already been a priority of female family members, and especially wives, before the war. The change that the war induced here consisted 'only' in accentuating the traditional gender-specific division of labor, caused by the often years-long absence of numerous husbands, to a completely new degree under very aggravated circumstances.[53]

The most immediate sign that the family's strength was collapsing under the weight of the war was the drastic decline in birthrates. The primary factor here was obvious – with menfolk at the front, or working double shifts in factories – there was less time for romantic liaisons. But there were other, more systemic factors, at play as well. The long hours female spouses and partners were compelled to spend in queues for food became a greater drain on time and energy. Food shopping had become a female-exclusive area, and one that was demanding more time daily. The declining caloric values of the food that was acquired also meant that many casual activities were ignored or forgotten – and for domestic women, this included reproduction.[54]

The quest for food was no simple matter. Military necessity meant that soldiers and critical industrial workers were provided for first. Rationing schemes were supposed to provide an adequate, albeit bland, diet for all. The failure of the 1916 potato crop hit doubly hard. Not only were humans deprived of a critical source of nutrition, in the ensuing "turnip winter" the feed stock supply of rutabaga and turnips was diverted to feed people, triggering a collapse in vital livestock. Demonstrations for food were nothing new, but in the winter of 1916–1917 they became constant features as working-class women began to express greater anxiety and anger over the scarcity of food. Unable to get away from their jobs and homes long enough to go on the food scavenging jaunts their middle

---

53 Ute Daniel, *The War from Within: German Working-Class Women in the First World War* (Berg, 1997), 127.
54 *Ibid.*, 128.

class neighbors pursued, the so-called "women of little means" (*minderbemittlte Frauen*) took to the streets in Berlin, Hamburg, and other major German cities demanding food.[55]

As the family's cohesion frayed, support for the war also began to run thin after 1916. This was not ignored by the German state. The government was well aware that the collapse of domestic stability was in itself a subversive condition that could grow into a direct challenge to the state's moral authority to lead and prosecute the war. The longer the war continued, with the rationing and lack of genuine emotional and physical contact between spouses and partners, the greater the risk. But here a certain delicacy had to be maintained. Not only were spontaneous actions like food demonstrations, looting, bartering food for personal services, and wildcat work stoppages actions of defiance or impatience with the war and the state, they were also virtually the sole venue for German women to exercise a public voice. The fringes of political activism were increasingly legitimized as a vehicle for political expression in a wartime society where women exercised greater agency than they had ever before.[56]

Regulating Gender and Sexuality in Wartime

As the First World War was a total conflict mobilizing all of the belligerent societies, it was perhaps inevitable that the same social forces mobilized to prosecute the war would be employed to regulate morality. On the one hand, the argument could be (and was) made that immorality would undermine the war effort. This was not exactly a new trend; Britain's Contagious Diseases Act of 1864, as we have mentioned earlier, was established to regulate sexuality while also objectifying women as the exclusive vectors of venereal disease.[57] The First World War, however, coincided with the general expansion of government social reform policies throughout the West. The war became a convenient cover for greater state intervention in the private lives and images of men and women, be they considered generally conforming to prevailing social norms or deviating from them.

Two distinct areas worth considering in this light both relate to prostitution in wartime. Illegal throughout the Western World, prostitution was either treated as a decriminalized minor crime of personal choice or covertly exploited

---

55 Belinda J. Davis, *Home Fires Burning: Food, Politics, and Everyday Life in World War I Berlin* (University of North Carolina Press, 2000), 36–37, 191.

56 *Ibid.*, 97–113, 121–29, 237–239; see also Daniel, *The War from Within*, 128.

57 See Judith R. Walkowitz, *City of Dreadful Delight: Narratives of Sexual Danger in Late-Victorian London* (The University of Chicago Press, 1992).

by unscrupulous state and local officials. Opinions as to the overall toll of prostitution on the participants, and the hazards the practice represented to society at large varied widely. Opponents were unified in their rejection of prostitution on moral and public grounds. The women themselves were usually portrayed as "soiled doves," "white slaves," or "fallen women" – that is to say they were all cast as unwilling victims, coerced or forced into the profession against their will. Prostitution was also seen as a genuine threat to public health as venereal infections were not only frequently lethal, but could be passed on to innocent partners by an infected person. And from the military perspective, venereal disease itself was cast as a force limiter, detracting from the fighting power of individual soldier and, collectively, a unit as a whole. There was also the matter of cost and corruption. Not only did prostitution exact a material toll on state finances through the enforcement of laws against it and the treatment of diseased participant, it also fostered organized crime and civic graft.

Opinions on the military necessity of the institution varied. Continental armies from French, German, Italian, and Austro-Hungarian had a more relaxed position, to the point of not only tolerating brothels in rear areas, but establishing official inspection regimes and segregated houses for officers. The logic offered was that it was far better for the millions of uniformed men deployed in male-exclusive communities to have the immediate outlet of sexual contact to deal with the anxiety, fear, and confusion of war and military service. Otherwise, military judicial and medical authorities reasoned, soldiers could exercise their pent-up frustration in criminal conduct, including sexual intimidation and rape of local women, that would turn the civilian population against the military. Or even worse, if denied access to female prostitutes, soldiers may turn toward "'even more deplorable evils'" – specifically sexual exchanges with other soldiers.[58]

No less significant was the rational calculation that venereal disease also affected the combat readiness of an army. Richard Holmes describes how the British Army's "treatment" policy included isolation in special hospitals for up to fifty days, all this time without pay. All armies maintained prophylaxis stations, where soldiers could line up for inspection and immediate urethral irrigation with salvarsan or some other mercury-based solution. The success of these stations and hospitals was limited. Nearly 417,000 venereal cases were reported by the Royal Army Medical Corps during the war. Official brothels with regular inspections and mandatory condom use was the most effective method of controlling

---

58 Bruce Cherry, *They Didn't Want to Die Virgins: Sex and Morale in the British Army on the Western Front, 1914–1918* (Helion & Company, 2016), 41–47, quote on 46. See also Richard S. Faulkner, *Pershing's Crusaders: The American Soldier in World War I* (University Press of Kansas, 2017), 386.

the spread of infections, but these quickly ran afoul of public opinion at home, where the sanctioned prostitution was still seen as a moral outrage.[59]

The state's tolerance of prostitution did have limits, however. Lisa M. Todd describes how German military and civil authorities railed against prostitution. First was the more traditional objection, the idea that prostitution was an immoral practice, debasing young recruits and conscripts and their older, presumably married, peers. More tellingly, Todd notes, was the presentation of wartime sex as an act of betrayal, in which loose women selfishly traded their body for sexual release, with not thought of the consequences from venereal disease. She writes:

> By conflating sex, disease, morality, military duty and citizenship, Germans on the home and fighting fronts echoed a widespread concern: that short-sighted sexual decisions were damaging military operations, affecting morale and compromising the future health and strength of the nation. In short, men and women who had sex outside marriage were committing "sexual treason" against the wartime nation.[60]

In the wartime total state, individual expressions of desire were not only compelled to conform to the prevalent social conservative morality, they were also regulated as potential threats to the war effort. Germany was not alone in its efforts to impose constraints on sexuality. In Britain sexual repression was incorporated into the Defense of the Realm Act (DORA), passed on August 8, 1914. By introducing military justice to civil society in any circumstance that threatened the war effort at home and abroad, the law created a new category of offenses that deeply intruded into private life. In addition to acts of civil disobedience and dissent, previously common-place activities were judged to be illegal, including such thoroughly British pursuits as lighting bonfires on Guy Fawkes Day, keeping carrier pigeons, or whistling down cabs on busy London streets.[61] Sexuality was also tightly regulated under DORA. Concerned that casual encounters in Britain would disable soldiers who contracted venereal disease, criminal prosecution under the act was extended to single and married women who solicited sex. By March 1918, this also included to spouses as well as single women and prostitutes, as any woman with venereal disease was considered a threat to the war effort.[62] Across the Channel, medical officers conducted regular inspections of prostitutes, isolating and excluding women who

---

59 Holmes, *Tommy*, 483.
60 Lisa M. Todd, *Sexual Treason in Germany during the First World War* (Palgrave Macmillan, 2017), 1–2, quote on 2.
61 Gerard J. DeGroot, *Blighty: British Society in the Era of the Great War* (Longman, 1996), 141, 204.
62 *Ibid.*, 141–235.

defied or were unresponsive to medical treatment. While officers were able to choose from relatively attractive partners, creating the temporary fiction of a meaningful liaison, enlisted men were serviced in assembly line fashion, often in decrepit houses, barns, and even tents. This was in part a reflection of the class systems that existed across European society, but it was also intended to present a moral choice to the other ranks. Was a short, three-minute liaison with an unattractive working girl worth the prospect of a lifetime of disease? While the majority of soldiers felt it was not, the image of long lines outside of military brothels indicates otherwise.[63]

The United States initiated even greater restraints as it entered the war. Prior to April 1917, vice reformers had tried for years to eliminate the brothel cultures that existed alongside military bases and ports. Cities like San Francisco, New Orleans, and New York boasted thriving tenderloin districts, areas where sex was sold at a brisk profit, often with the tacit consent and cooperation of local authorities. Their efforts had failed, largely because the military itself was divided on the issue. Reformers in uniform saw casual sex and alcohol use as a very real force reducer, owing to the impact of venereal disease. Opponents argued how it was preferable for soldiers to pursue sex from prostitutes, as opposed to seeking out other, more vulnerable, young women, or even worse, engage in regular masturbation or sodomy among themselves. During the Mexican Punitive Expedition, Brigadier General John J. Pershing authorized the creation of official brothels, where local prostitutes would receive regular inspection and be ejected if found to be infected.[64]

Maintaining brothels far from the public's eye deep in Mexico was one thing; regulating sexual contact in full view not only of the American people, but the direct gaze of America's moralist President Woodrow Wilson was another. When a letter from French premier Georges Clemenceau offering American troops the use of French army brothels was presented to Secretary of War Newton D. Baker, he is reported to have exclaimed, "For God's sake, don't show this to the President or he'll stop the war!"[65] Baker's shock reflected the mood of the nation's parents and spouses as American men were conscripted and sent off to Europe: keep our

---

63 Cherry, *They Didn't Want to Die Virgins*, 227–28.
64 Wintermute, *Public Health and the US Military*, 185–187. See also Allan M. Brandt, *No Magic Bullet: A Social History of Venereal Disease in the United States Since 1880* (Oxford University Press, 1987); Peter Lewis Allen, *The Wages of Sin: Sex and Disease, Past and Present* (University of Chicago Press, 2000); and Claude Quétel, *A History of Syphilis*, trans. by Judith Braddock and Brian Pike, (Johns Hopkins University Press, 1992).
65 David M. Kennedy, *Over Here: The First World War and American Society* (Oxford University Press, 1979, 2004), 187.

men and sons clean and free from the wages of sin while they were away from home. The War Department was given a range of powers to suppress prostitution at home under the Selective Service Act of 1917, and in combination with the Commission on Training Camp Activities (CTCA) undertook a massive campaign aimed at crushing the casual brothel culture that had existed for so long in the United States. Military police joined local and state police forces in raids on saloons and brothels in small towns adjacent to military posts and training camps across the country, while progressive politicians exercised their influence, backed by the weight of the federal government, in larger cities to close entire districts. By January 1918, almost all of the famous red-light districts in America – including Storyville, the Tenderloin, the Barbary Coast – were gone. Prostitution was not eliminated in the United States – the traffic shifted from public view to become a more-private, secretive trade – but the war did lend itself to fulfill the desires of social reformers and moral puritans alike who sought its end.[66]

Of course the Army and the CTCA realized that shuttering of brothels in the United States would have little impact on doughboys as they arrived in France. Working with humanitarian and religious organizations, the War Department sanctioned the organization of comfort stations across France. Groups like the American Red Cross, the Salvation Army, the YMCA and YMHA (Young Men's Christian or Hebrew Associations), Knights of Columbus, and many others set up rest centers well behind the front where American soldiers could enjoy safe, comfortable activities that were intended to promote morale without the distraction or need to rely upon alcohol or sexual contact with local women. Simultaneously the Army Medical Department imposed a strict regimen of medical inspection and penalties for men who needed treatment, combined with a vigorous public information campaign intended to shame soldiers into abstinence for the duration of their deployment in France.[67]

How successful was the American anti-sex campaign in France? Many soldiers followed the recommendations and orders of their commanding general, John J. Pershing, who having turned his back on his earlier experiences in Mexico, became a staunch advocate of abstinence (even as he maintained a French mistress in Paris). His outlook was summarized in an official release from AEF General Headquarters on April 7, 1918 of Bulletin No. 54:

> Commanding officers will urge continence on all men of their commands as their duty as soldiers and the best training for the enforced sexual abstinence at the front. Instruction,

---

66 Nancy K. Bristow, *Making Men Moral: Social Engineering During the Great War* (New York University Press, 1997), 5–6, 108–113; and Faulkner, *Pershing's Crusaders*, 369–72.
67 Faulkner, *Pershing's Crusaders*, 386–92.

work, drill, athletics and amusements will be used to the fullest extent in furthering the practice of continence. . . . [General Pershing] enjoins upon all members of the A.E.F. the strictest observance of sexual continence.[68]

Thus Bulletin No. 54 sought to limit the spread of social diseases and anticipated declines in morality and masculinity by forbidding American soldiers from engaging in sex for hire. Those who disobeyed these directives and contracted social diseases could face courts-martial because promiscuity undermined the moral standards and reduced the morale and combat effectiveness of their units. Also imbedded in the words of Pershing and excerpts from Bulletin No. 54 were anxieties over how lax morals might negatively affect the American home front in the post-war era.[69]

Even with restrictions and recriminations, American soldiers still sought out sexual services from prostitutes. The Army Medical Department reported 57,195 total cases of venereal infection among members of the AEF in 1917–1918, an infection rate of approximately 3.4 percent. A number of these were doubtlessly pre-existing or represented multiple infections. Nevertheless, the infection rate was significantly lower than that in the British Army (416,891 cases, or 5 percent of total UK and Dominion strength, between 1914–1918).[70] Anecdotal evidence also reveals a thriving trade despite Pershing's efforts to the contrary. One report from St. Nazaire, for example, claimed that 60 prostitutes working in four different bordellos, over the space of ten days, serviced 15,000 Americans in assembly-line fashion, averaging 25 men a day.[71]

Morale and Discipline in the French and British Armies

With the war grinding on into its third year, the question of morale began to rise to the fore within all the combatant's armies. The March 8, 1917 revolution in Russia occurred amidst labor and bread strikes in Petrograd, signaling how widespread

---

68 G.H.Q. American Expeditionary Force, Bulletin No. 54, 7 August 1918, cited in George Walker, *Venereal Disease in the American Expeditionary Forces* (Medical Standard Book Co., 1922), 67–68.
69 *Ibid.*, 66–68.
70 Henry C. Michie, "The Venereal Diseases," in *The Medical Department of the United States Army in the World War*, vol. IX, Communicable and Other Diseases (Government Printing Office, 1928), 264; World War I Centenary, "The British Army's fight against Venereal Disease in the 'Heroic Age of Prostitution,'" http://ww1centenary.oucs.ox.ac.uk/body-and-mind/the-british-army%E2%80%99s-fight-against-venereal-disease-in-the-%E2%80%98heroic-age-of-prostitution%E2%80%99/ (Accessed March 20, 2018).
71 Faulkner, *Pershing's Crusaders*, 386.

war weariness had become. As the Provisional Government's war effort limped along, other warning signs began to appear among the Western Allies. The most significant of these was the mutiny within the French army following the failed Nivelle offensive targeting the Chemin des Dames sector of the German defenses. Introduced by the charismatic General Robert Nivelle, the plan called for a combination of material warfare (the intensive pre-attack shelling and the creeping barrage) to soften up the German defenses, followed by the *poilu*'s swift *elan*-influenced rush into the paralyzed German defenses to achieve the long-sought breakthrough and decisive victory.

Nivelle and his subordinates were optimistic; their soldiers had a clearer vision of what fate awaited them. Onlookers reported how, as they marched to the front, French soldiers bleated in imitation of sheep going to the slaughter. As the Germans had advance notice of the offensive, they withdraw from their forward positions, which in turn were registered for artillery barrages at the first sight of French soldiers entering them. As the Second Battle of the Aisne opened on April 16, 1917, disaster followed. In the first week, over 37,000 French troops were killed; even worse, over 100,000 surrendered. Meanwhile the attack failed to achieve any of its first day objectives; by the time the offensive was called off, the French had advanced only a few kilometers. The attack on the Chemin des Dames was the worse French performance since the Battle of the Frontiers.[72]

Worse was yet to come. Between April 16 and May 15, 1917, twenty-six incidents classified as "collective indiscipline" took place among divisions of the Sixth Army. By June, the number of incidents had grown, encompassing 54 divisions in all. Nearly all the cases were described later as demonstrations against the war, not a call to overturn the state. Only after June 1 did the actions turn violent, more concerning though, was the refusal of several units to return to the trenches. By this time, grumbling about the war among exhausted *poilus* had grown into something much more serious: a mutiny that was spreading throughout the French Army. There was no single cause for the collapse of morale, though the recent failure of the Nivelle Offensive was clearly the catalyst. On one level, the *poilu* felt betrayed by the officers – from General Robert Nivelle down to their company commanders – whom they had trusted for three years. The constant, daily wastage of the war ate away at their spirit until, by April 1917, the dam of discipline holding back their discouragement broke. The leadership of the recently appointed chief of the General Staff, General Philippe Pétain, was crucial to restoring order. Recognizing the legitimate grievances of the mutineers, he issued a number of orders that were intended to improve morale within the army, while

---

72 Doughty, *Pyrrhic Victory*, 344–54.

also promising to abandon the type of all-out offensives that had proven so costly in the past. Pétain already had the reputation of being a commander who cared for the troops under his command. His actions to restore confidence during and after the mutiny only further cemented his status as an almost paternal figure. Relying on persuasion rather than harsh judgment – 40 men were executed for their actions during the mutiny – he also initiated new weapons production that would deliver to the French army a significant quantitative and qualitative advantage over the enemy in the next year. The investment in new aircraft, armor, artillery, and chemical weapons was both a representation of his preference to expend material over manpower in fulfilling a mission and his desire to avoid repeating the experiences of April 1917.[73]

Mutiny was never a serious prospect in the British army, where morale remained generally high throughout the war. One of the keys to morale in the British Army was the relationship between officers and enlisted men in the trenches. While the original cadre of public school volunteers was much diminished after two years of war, the paternalistic interactions between subalterns and their companies continued to keep order in the trenches. As a rule officers were expected to tend to the individual needs of their enlisted men, ensuing their material needs – food, clothing, shelter – were met, and providing small comfort items as they could. Likewise officers fulfilled the role of patron and advocate in case of small infractions and mistakes, either turning a judicious blind eye toward small offenses or meting out fair judgment for minor infractions. Gary Sheffield notes:

> The bond between the subaltern and his platoon was often described in terms of marriage and parenthood. Both nearly capture the idea of a tender, loving relationship. Sharing, to a greater or lesser degree, the hardships of war, it is perhaps not surprising that boys of similar age made friends across the rank and class divide, or that older officers had a thoroughly paternal concern for their men, or sympathized with men of their own age enduring life in the ranks.[74]

For their part, many officers came to view their men as incapable of independent action, establishing a dependency culture within the contours of paternalism. As a result, relations between officers and their men rested on deference – the

---

73 *Ibid.*, 360–69. See also Leonard V. Smith, *Between Mutiny and Obedience: The Case of the French Fifth Infantry Division during World War I* (Princeton University Press, 1994).
74 Gary Sheffield, "Officer-Man Relations, Discipline and Morale in the British Army of the Great War," in, *Facing Armageddon: The First World War Experienced*, ed. Hugh Cecil and Peter Liddle (Leo Cooper, 1996), 413–24, quote on 418.

display of respect and obedience to natural leaders. The challenge for junior sub-alterns was in learning how to earn the respect of their men. Deference was not the same as subservience, it had to be earned as part of a "natural exchange" based on trust and fairness. In this regard enlisted men were far more canny than many of the war's memoirists (themselves frequently subalterns and junior grade officers) understood. Soldiers were quick to identify and distinguish bad officers ("bullies") from good ones ("toff") as they came into companies. Again, Sheffield observes:

> Officers who did not look after their men, who did not show leadership qualities in battle, or who did not behave in a gentlemanly fashion had, in the eyes of the ordinary soldier, forfeited all rights to commissioned status, and the privileges that went with it, including the right to expect rankers to follow them.[75]

Failure to live up to the expectations of the company was no less critical than failing to fulfill the objectives set out by senior grade officers. Indeed, while many company grade officers would come directly from civilian life, the senior hierarchy of the British Army remained for the most part a regular army preserve. Regimental, division, and corps commanders (not to mention the more senior army commanders) came to their positions following years and decades of rising through the ranks themselves. Keenly aware of the paternalistic system based on trust, honor, and deference themselves, they were quick to transfer officers who failed to live up to the same model. This was one reason, perhaps, that the regular army establishment was so concerned with the prospect of "Temporary Officers" – middle-class subalterns and recruits promoted beyond their scale and means – taking up such a large share of the army's company level appoint-ments. By 1917, some 40 percent of British officers were considered Temporary Officers, being promoted from their middles and working-class statuses for the duration of the war. Could such officers, it was reasoned, prove able to fulfill the material needs of their men? Or was it likely that they would fail to consider how rank made earlier relationships between themselves and the enlisted men whom they once served alongside in the trenches? Certainly, there were occasional lapses. Some of the Temporary Officers failed to measure up to the social eti-quette standards that defined their acceptable conduct. Appearing before their men in a state of intoxication, or indulging their own needs and desires before attending to those of their command could quickly undermine their legitimacy and end their commands. In the end, it appears that the Temporary Officers rose

---

75 *Ibid.*, 419.

to the challenge, and that a majority of enlisted men appear to have supported the command prerogatives of such men leading them.[76]

The Male Body as Contested Terrain: Treating Wounds and Trauma

Imagine for a moment that you are standing alongside your best friends, weighed down under a sixty pound pack, waiting for the whistle signaling you over the top to blow. The last seconds tick away as an eternity, as you crouch by the ladder, knuckles white from clenching your rifle. The drumbeat noise and vibrations from the shelling across the 150 yards-long wire and corpse-strewn waste goes on without stopping. For a fleeting moment you think that nothing could survive such a bombardment, but you know better. They always survive. Or you're thinking of home, or anyplace you'd rather be, when the whistle blows. Time to climb the steep angled ladder, and then to step out into No Man's Land. You take a dozen steps into the pockmarked wasteland when the firing from the other side starts, the machine gun staccato barely audible, but the wining muzzle flashes clear as day.

Suddenly, you are slammed in the hip by a brick – or at least that's how it feels. You collapse, unable to stand, thirty yards out in the wasteland, when the shock gives way to numbness and a faint wet feeling running pooling beneath you where you lay. Is it blood, or have you pissed or shit yourself? Now, as you lay in the puddle of blood and filth, the only thing you think of is how you don't have to keep advancing to the enemy's trench. Until a new thought appears, unbidden but inevitable. Is this the end? It is all you can think of as you black out.

The reality of combat in the First World War is a grim topic, even by the inured standards of military historians. For four long years the world was gripped in a monumental contest between nations for uncertain reasons. Combat was an interminable misery, in a Hieronymus Bosch-like landscape realized in mud and death. The loss of life was catastrophic: in 1916 on the Western Front, each side suffering one million casualties – men killed, wounded, captured, or missing. Through all of this, the individual soldier became the literal canvas of destruction upon which the war's cost was written. Joanna Bourke summarized the encounter of man and war best:

> Men could be able-bodied: fortified, forceful, vigorous. Yet, their bodies could also be mangled, freshly torn from the war and competing for economic and emotional resources with civilians . . . They expressed their freedom through their bodies, but were besieged on

---

76 *Ibid.*, 416–17, 420.

all sides by military, medical and educational disciplines which were governed by different aesthetics, economic objectives and moral economies. The corporeal male would eventually become a corpse on some battlefield or mortuary slab, inviting reconstruction through the memories of loved ones.[77]

The First World War extracted a horrific toll, not only on men and women killed during or as a result of combat, but on those who survived as well. The body was subject to a plethora of assaults intended to kill, but which were often incomplete. No aspect of the self was safe from the hand of war. If not killed, one suffered from various injuries that frequently left the survivor a physical and emotional cripple. Amputations, massive resections, facial disfigurements, chronic respiratory injuries – all too frequently the combat encounter ended in a physical disability that would render the victim a future burden to the state. And then there were the men who suffered a traumatic break with reality in this age of mechanized mayhem. In body and soul, the soldiers themselves were the real contested terrain of the First World War, the liminal space that was reshaped and contorted to its limits.

Wounded soldiers may have escaped death, yet they still faced challenges in adapting their maleness to its new condition. For amputees, being a true man had meant being whole and thus physically capable. Initially honored as a living representative of the cost society paid in the war, they were quickly discarded and relegated to the periphery of state dependency. Within a decade of the war's end, these once and future heroes were forgotten, save for the annual observations of the great victory in the United States and the Western Allies, when they were trotted out for the daily celebration. In all countries, the reality of wartime sacrifice was transformed into a costly financial burden in the form of pensions and a lifetime of state medical care.[78]

Although these disabled veterans may have been honored by their countrymen and supported by their governments, they were more likely defined by their own struggle to reconcile their shattered state with the ideal of maleness they had acquired since childhood. It is problematic to quantify these feelings using historical data and primary research. Nevertheless, a quote from Erich Maria Remarque's *All Quiet on the Western Front* points to the possible sentiments of disabled soldiers. One of the characters in the novel had been shot in his knee,

---

77 Bourke, *Dismembering the Male*, 11.

78 See Beth Linker, *War's Waste: Rehabilitation in World War I America* (University of Chicago Press, 2011); John M. Kinder, *Paying with Their Bodies: American War and the Problem of the Disabled Veteran* (University of Chicago Press, 2015); Jessica L. Adler, *Burdens of War: Creating the United States Veterans Health System* (Johns Hopkins University Press, 2017); and Deborah Cohen, *The War Come Home: Disabled Veterans in Britain and Germany, 1914–1939* (University of California Press, 2001).

and amputation of his leg was necessary to save his life. This amputee reacted by saying, "'I've made up my mind'. . . 'If they take my leg, I'll put an end to it. I won't go through life as a cripple.'"[79] This character would take his own life later in the novel. It can be inferred that this soldier with the leg amputation did not see being "crippled" as being normative in the senses of masculinity or masculine roles.

Post-traumatic stress is a timeless condition. Accounts of emotional and nervous breakdowns associated with combat go back to the ancients, and appear in many literary and documentary forms throughout the history of warfare.[80] The literary war trope, however, has claimed combat stress – "Shell Shock" in the English-speaking world's parlance – as being "discovered" in the First World War. As Tracey Loughran writes in a 2012 article, "The centrality of shell shock in imaginings of the First World War is, therefore, highly important because of the place this conflict in the modern (particularly British) cultural landscape."[81] And yet, it can be argued that the greater factor was the visual drama associated with the condition, rather than the literary oeuvre. Evocative poems, songs, and personal accounts set out the context for men with shattered psyches, but actually it was the film representation of the afflicted in rest hospitals, before and after receiving treatment, that established the preferred image of the shell-shocked soldier. Accurate statistics on the number of men who experienced shell shock are lacking. Consider how the condition was recognized and diagnosed in the British and Dominion armies, where some 80,000 cases of shell shock, or, after 1917, "Nervous (Not Yet Diagnosed). However, as historian Jay Winter notes, if contemporary standards for mental health were applied to the British army of 1914–1918, it is not unreasonable to consider 20 percent of all combat personnel would have been diagnosed with some form of combat neurosis.[82]

Leaving aside recent scholarship that suggests many reported cases of psychological incidents were more likely incidents of traumatic brain injury, shell

---

79 Erich Maria Remarque, *All Quiet on the Western Front* (1929; New York: Ballantine, 1989), 242, 269. See also David J. Ulbrich, "A Male-Conscious Critique of *All Quiet on the Western Front*," *Journal of Men's Studies* 3 (February 1995): 235.

80 See Eric T. Dean, Jr., *Shook over Hell: Post-Traumatic Stress, Vietnam, and the Civil War* (Harvard University Press, 1999).

81 Tracey Loughran, "Shell Shock, Trauma and the First World War: The Making of a Diagnosis and Its Histories," *Journal of the History of Medicine and Allied Sciences* 67 (January 2012), 94–119, quote on 97.

82 Stefanie Caroline Linden and Edgar Jones, "'Shell shock' Revisited: An Examination of the Case Records of the National Hospital in London," *Medical History*, 58:4 (October, 2014), 519–45, 524; and Jay Winter, "Shell shock" in Jay Winter, Ed. *The Cambridge History of the First World War*. Volume III, *The State* (Cambridge University Press, 2014), 310–33, quote on 327.

shock cases were the subject of significant debate within the military establish-ment. At issue was whether or not the condition was purely external – that is to say, the result of environmental stresses related to combat itself – or if it signi-fied some hitherto unseen physical or moral weakness in the soldier. This second point was further broken down. Was the internal flaw a case of personal physi-cal frailty? Was it a sign of congenital moral and physical degeneration? Did it conform to the current thought on neurasthenic strain? Or was the patient exhib-iting the signs of gender inversion, manifesting through a hysterical episode? Or what if the afflicted was perfectly healthy, and merely exploiting the dramatic visuals of an emotional collapse as a cover for their own malingering?

Figure 4.6: American doughboys recovering from war neurosis ("shell-shock") at Chateau Chambord, near Blois, France.
Source: NARA II, College Park, MD. National Archives Identifier: 45497410
Local Identifier: 165-WW-261A-17
Creator: War Department, 1789-9/18/1947 (Most Recent).

The above-listed concerns speak less toward the desire to effectively understand and treat cases, and more toward the ambiguity physicians and the military estab-lishment reserved for anxieties and neuroses obtained under fire. Never mind the needs of the patient; the question remained how they were either unconsciously or actively conspiring to fail in completing their duty. Even if the afflicted soldier did not consciously attempt to shirk their responsibilities, their breakdown signaled a collapse of the male psyche that rendered them not only unfit for further service, but as a future burden to families and societies at all. Shell shock was not the wonder diagnosis it has been portrayed as in the popular literary accounts of the war. Rather, it was a stigmatizing condition, a sign of failed masculine virtue and inability to perform their male obligations.[83]

Fortunately for the patient and the practice of medicine, this stark rejection of shell shock as a legitimate condition began to change in the middle of the war. The sheer number of cases appearing in 1916 and early 1917, along with the totality of their symptoms, disqualified malingering. Empathy for the afflicted replaced the punitive-based physical therapeutic regimens, as physicians discovered that rest and reflection were more effective treatments than electro shocks or hydro therapy. The treatment shift follows the rationalization that nervous collapse in the field was acutely similar to the neurasthenic episodes recorded and treated during the war. Therefore, the patient was not a physical or moral degenerate, but was experiencing a natural and rational nervous collapse under the tremendous stresses of industrial total warfare. Shell shock was a modern condition, but only insofar as it was associated with the press of modernity on bodies not accustomed to such energy. As a result, all but the worse cases exhibiting a true psychotic break could be treated and sent back to the front. Masculinity was preserved and duty restored.[84]

Homosociality and Same-Sex Relations in The First World War

The experience of combat and the sense of mutual responsibility to comrades also helped motivate soldiers to perform well on battlefields. They willingly killed enemy soldiers and, even more readily, sacrificed their own lives for their comrades. Outsiders with no combat experiences might find these actions difficult to comprehend. This phenomenon has been called by different names: small unit cohesion, male bonding, primary groups, or, evoking William Shakespeare, the notion of men serving closely together being a "band of brothers." Many scholars across ideological and disciplinary spectra have recognized such closeness of soldiers in units. In *The Face of Battle*, historian John Keegan relates how soldiers connected with their immediate comrades as "equals within very tiny groups."[85] In his psychological study *The Warriors: Reflections on Men in Battle*, combat

---

83 Bourke, *Dismembering the Male*, 107–11.

84 *Ibid.*, 115–123. See also Bourke, "Effeminacy, Ethnicity, and the End of Trauma," 62; Meyer, *Men of War*, 198–207.

85 Keegan, *The Face of Battle*, cited in. Jean Bethke Elshtain, *Women and War* (The University of Chicago Press, 1987, 1995), 207.

veteran and philosopher J. Glenn Gray talks about the community of soldiers and the "I" of civilian life becomes the "we" in military service.[86] Feminist philosopher Jean Bethke Elshtain also explores this collectivist theme among soldiers in that "together with the powerful sacrificial possibilities and idealized war fighting makes possible and crystallizes as a form of male identity."[87] Most recently in 2008, cultural historian Jessica Meyer has tied soldiers' solidarity directly to their masculine identities when she asserts that "To prove oneself a man. . . One had to prove oneself not as an adventurer but as a good comrade."[88]

The concepts of "band of brothers" and the soldiers as "nearer than lovers" have raised questions regarding the intricate balance between homosociality and homosexuality in the male-exclusive environment of the Western Front in the First World War.[89] First it is essential to note that, like so much assumed about the First World War today, the foundations for the premise of the trenches as a meeting ground for tentative gay liaison resides in the British literary tradition. This is not intended to disqualify or delegitimize the expression of same-sex relations in wartime, but the point remains that such actions were far less commonplace than they have come to be portrayed in literature and film.

Two intertwined questions remain: Does engaging in same-sex liaisons in the trenches signify the two partners were homosexual? Or, was the homosexual act a manifestation of some other need or release that could not be otherwise satisfied? Answering these questions in the wartime context dictates an understanding of cultural assumptions that same-sex relations were both clarifiers of normative masculine behavior and sexuality. Whether or not homosexuals adapted their identities and engaged in homosexual behaviors as gay men also show how heterosexuality manifested itself among straight men. The degree to which camaraderie tipped the scales into homosexuality has been debated among scholars, sometimes degenerating into politicized arguments about whether homosexuals were (or are) worthy soldiers or even truly loyal, patriotic. Stepping back from such pointless debates, the facts that some same-sex relations occurred among soldiers and some of them were homosexuals cannot be denied. Moreover, that

---

86 Gray, *Warriors*, cited in Elshtain, *Women and War*, 207.

87 Elshtain, *Women and War*, 207–208.

88 Meyer, *Men of War*, 148. For similar views, see Sarah Cole, *Modernism, Male Friendship, and the First World War* (Cambridge University Press, 2003), 318–55.

89 William Shakespeare made the phrase "band of brothers" famous in the St. Crispin's Day speech by King Henry V in the title role in Act 4, Scene 3. For the full "nearer than lovers" quote, see Remarque, *All Quiet on the Western Front*, 212.

homoerotic symbols or allusions appeared in posters, novels, memoirs, and poetry from this First World War-era likewise cannot be ignored.[90]

Categories of heterosexual and homosexuality could be blurred in the trenches. In *Gender Trouble,* literary scholar Judith Butler explains that gender is "performative." By this, she means that men and women behave in ways that are expressions of culturally-defined masculinity and femininity. For Butler, however, "there is no gender identity behind the expressions of gender, that identity is performatively constituted by the expressions that are said to be its results."[91] She also uses the term "imaginary formation" to describe this phenomenon in which normative – or traditional and acceptable – gender relations exist for men and women. This relationship is, in Butler's terms, hegemonic heterosexuality with its attendant codes of acceptable behaviors as well as unacceptable taboos like homosexuality.[92]

Whereas Butler does not focus to combat or the First World War, her concept of performative identity can be applied to men in combat to add a useful understanding of gender and war. If masculinity and femininity are performances and expressions with no truly gendered identity as their foundations, then men and women living in peace and stability act out their gender roles according to normative expectations. It is cyclic. Men, for example, should protect women because they presumably cannot protect themselves and thus need men to do so. But, subjecting men (and women) to the extreme experiences of combat could create an entirely different environment where peacetime gender performances have no resonance. Soldiers cannot protect themselves. They must kill or be killed. So, borrowing from Butler, the "expressions," "performative identities," and "imaginary formations" of soldiers in the extraordinary environment of combat creates an entirely different set of gendered results wherein acceptable prescriptions for male behavior cease to exist. Thus, in wartime, men must step across the lines of traditional, peacetime, normative masculinity into femininity, and also step across the lines of heterosexuality into homoeroticism or homosexuality. Likewise, women could potentially also find in combat an environment where their traditional submissive and supportive gender identities have no

---

90 Cole, *Modernism,* 138–64; Jason Crouthamel, *An Intimate History of the Front: Masculinity, Sexuality, and German Soldiers in the First World War* (Palgrave Macmillan, 2014), 121–47; and David J. Ulbrich and Bobby A. Wintermute, "Homosexuality," in *History in Dispute, Vol 9: First World War, Second Series,* ed. Dennis Showalter (St. James Press, 2002), 146–53.
91 Judith Butler, *Gender Trouble,* 34.
92 *Ibid.,* 180. See also Halberstam, *Female Masculinity,* 17, 234–41; and Monique Wittig, "The Point of View: Universal or Particular," *Feminist Issues* 3, no. 2 (1983): 63–69.

foundations. Combat and warfare become free zones for blurring and bending of gender identities and sexual orientations.[93]

Conclusion and Epilogue

The post-war period brought attempts at retrenching pre-war gender roles and relations, all to restore the sense of gender normalcy that defined Western society before 1914. Almost all of the millions of women doing war work were sent home to resume their roles of wives, mothers, and homemakers. On a superficial level it appears the First World War did not elevate women closer to the status of men as dramatically as some feminists might have hoped. Nevertheless, the seeds for dramatic, long-term changes in gender roles and relations had been sown. In several nations, women were granted suffrage in part as acknowledgement of their patriotic support and personal sacrifice during the war. Women received the right to vote in Russia in 1917. Britain, Germany, Sweden, Poland, Austria, Hungary and Czechoslovakia all followed suit in 1918. The United States adopted the Nineteenth Amendment to the Constitution, granting women voting rights in federal and state elections, in 1920, the final push for ratification no doubt influenced by the war effort. Among the belligerent nations, only France and Italy were exceptions to the trend of granting suffrage to women. It would be 1945 before French and Italian women could fully participate in the electoral process.

Many feminists heralded suffrage as the culmination of decades of efforts for emancipation and liberation as well as for public recognition that women were full-fledged citizens. Indeed, it was a victory because suffrage gave women a legal forum and political representation to advocate for their gender-specific goals, and to protect their status as citizens. Men, for their part, feared that a unified women's party might dominate political elections. This, however, did not happen in the 1920 and 1930s, because women most often held similar political beliefs and cast votes like the men in their lives.

The end of First World War and the ensuing decade of the 1920s saw other evidence of the changes in the construction of femininity. Women could move out of their private, domestic sphere and move into political, social, and economic areas of the so-called public sphere. In terms of clothing, bourgeois women gradually ceased to dress in the Victorian clothing and hair styles with emphases of

---

93 See Elizabeth Cobbs, *The Hello Girls: America's First Women Soldiers* (Harvard University Press, 2017).

feminine curves and features, and they instead cut their hair short, and started to dress in the more androgynous clothing of the Flapper that allowed freedom of movement. This was a visible representation of a new type of female and new definition of femininity that made aggressive women who smoked, drank, and danced the *en vogue* ideal. Improvements and increased access to contraception likewise gave women more and more independence and power over their sexuality and their bodies, thereby overturning, or at least challenging, the limits placed on them by patriarchal society and female physiology. It should be noted, however, that for most women in Europe and the United States, few benefits could be enjoyed in any meaningful way. Women of the working class or living in rural settings had no spare time or disposable income to participate as in the "Roaring 20s" as "new" women. By the time the Great Depression hit with full force after 1929, many women of all classes or stations could not take advantage of the lifestyle changes or activities.[94]

For men in the United States, and especially Europe, the end of the First World War meant a return to peace and hopefully to normalcy. Combat and military service had proven to be a misleading expression of nationalism and an unsatisfying means of reinforcing masculine traits and virtues. Forgetting the war and its grievous losses and wounds was not so easy. Conceptions about masculine had been undermined and transformed as men came to grips with the fact that old notions of masculinity had cost millions of lives, lost or scarred. During the 1920s, men turned to any number of ideologies and activities as ways to respond to the war's horrors and re-enter civilized, civilian life. Some men shunned violence in favor of pacifism, others embraced authoritarianism on the right or left, others escaped through hedonism or nihilism in life and art, and still others turned to capitalism in search of riches. These and other groups aimed to construct masculinities for themselves. Affluence and frivolity existed on the surface of society, but beneath percolated bitterness and disillusionment. All this would come crashing down when more desperate and dangerous masculinities rose during the Great Depression and in the years leading up to the Second World War.[95]

---

94 See Renate Bridenthal, "Something Old, Something New: Women Between the Wars," in *Becoming Visible: Women in European History*, 2nd ed., ed. Renate Bridenthal et al. (Houghton Mifflin, 1987), 473–98; and Kimberly Jensen, *Mobilizing Minerva: American Women in the First World War* (University of Illinois Press, 2008) 142–64.

95 Glenda Sluga, "Masculinities, nations, and the New World Order: Peacemaking and Nationality in Britain, France, and the United States after the First World War," in *Masculinities in Politics and War: Gendering Modern History*, ed. Stefan Dundink et al. (Manchester University Press, 2004), 238–54; Stearns, *Be A Man*, 157–61; George Chauncey, *Gay New York : Gender, Urban Culture, and the Making of the Gay Male World, 1890–1940* (Basic Books, 1994), 301–30; and Mosse, *Image of Man*, 147–54.

5 Race and the First World War

Introduction

One of the most frequently stated observations about the First World War is how it represents the liminal point between tradition and modernity. The tremendous human sacrifice, combined with the sheer destructive potential of industrial war, totally changed Western culture. Four years of trench warfare so fractured society that it would never truly recover; in place of normalcy, Europe would lead the world into a climate of uncertainty, anxiety, and bitter recrimination that culminated not only in the rise of fascist militarism, but also set the stage for the twentieth century's greater bloodlettings and ideological contests. Were it not for a wrong turn in a crowded provincial city, perhaps all that followed might have been avoided.

Overlooked of course is how the First World War stands out as a foundation for a larger state of continuity between the past and the present. People today generally forget that those who lived through and waged war in 1914 through 1918 shared a racialized outlook on culture, war, and identity. Whether she was a poor English girl working in a munitions factory or a German officer son of the *Junker* class; a French *poilu* observing the march past of North African colonial soldiers or a black American soldier unloading ships in Brest, everyone shared a common outlook on race. As historians delve deeper into the cultural perspectives of the First World War, the extent of race's effects on global society becomes more readily apparent. This is not to say the First World War was a race war. It was a conflict in which racial identity and perceptions influenced the judgment of its players in significant ways and with consequences.

This fifth chapter examines several select case studies in varying levels of detail to highlight this point. In every case, there is room for interpretation, agreement, and disagreement. The point of this chapter is to highlight the cultural and perceptual constant across several Western societies in their wartime encounter. It is not to offer a detailed, day-by-day narrative of the First World War. We encourage readers to think abstractly and conceptualize the war not merely as a material and physical exchange of destructive violence in pursuit of policy, but also as cultural exchanges between participants on both sides of the firing line.

https://doi.org/10.1515/9783110477467-005

Race, War, and European Identity

Even among the European combatants, racialist thinking – partly determined by the pre-war obsession with racial hierarchies – shaped the perceptions major combatants had of themselves and their opponents. This resulted in a bifurcated "self" and "other" relationship rooted in crude stereotypes and misinformation; take, for example, the image of the German soldier as a criminal, beastlike brute, hell-bent on pillage and rape proffered by British and American propagandists during the war. Some perceptions were also associated with prewar trends in forming national and ethnic identities, and were presented as a positive reinforcement of the national community. Such constructions were in turn reinforced through regimental and divisional traditions, such as uniform, badges of identification, mess culture, etc. Consider the Scottish Highland and Lowland Regiments, each of which enjoyed their own unique form of dress (kilts for the Highlanders, tartan trews for Lowland Regiments) and mess rituals, all linked to a highly mythologized Scottish imagined history that presented all Scots as stout fighters, accustomed to privation and harsh climates. In reality, the majority of recruits for the Scottish Regiments were drawn from the urban centers of Glasgow, Edinburgh, and Aberdeen; not to mention the English recruits and conscripts later assigned to the Scots regiments as replacements. By and large, however, racial and ethnic stereotypes can be directly traced to the Social Darwinist perspective of war as a positive experience for the individual and the group participants. In a contest to determine national destinies and to cull the weak, the victor would be that ethnicity most suited to war. Hence the emphasis by combatants to stake out a martial identity.

All of the national armies shared a similar mindset on ethnicity within their larger national identity. In the German Army, everyone "knew" the Prussians were the toughest fighters, while Bavarian and Saxon regiments were "softer," and more willing to offer temporary truces with their opponents when in the line. The *k.u.k* (*Kaiserlich und Königlich*) *Armee* of the Dual Monarchy was a linguist's nightmare, with dozens of languages and dialects drowning out the official military German language – three quarters of the officer corps being drawn from German-speaking families in Austria. Exacerbating the situation was the general rejection of the military as a career by many noble families that had formerly made up the *k.u.k.*'s officer cadre. Geoffrey Wawro notes that one consequence of reforms after the 1866 Austro-Prussian War intended to improve the officer corps, many aristocrats resigned, choosing to pursue their fortunes and status in the civilian finance sphere. For decades after, the officer corps was dominated by lower-middle-class men, more interested in the free education opportunities at the Empire's military schools than in the prospect of long careers of service.[1]

The Austro-Hungarian Army became thus a prisoner of its own diversity, which not only hampered its effectiveness, but also fostered a caste system in which some nationalities – German-speaking Austrians, Magyars, some Bohemians – comprised the slender dependable core of a larger polyglot, unreliable, mass army. They in turn viewed the Italian-speaking Austrians, Slovenes, Croats, Ruthenians, Bohemian and Moravian Czechs, Slovaks, Serbs, Bosnians, etc. as either unreliable from the start of the conflict or marginally effective warriors who needed close observation and control. Regional and religious divisions intensified the mistrust among the groups. Needless to say, these subject peoples reciprocated such attitudes through various forms of passive and direct resistance. Jaroslav Hasek's masterful comic creation, "The Good Soldier Švejk," was far closer to the mark in its portrayal of a Czech conscript whose calculated malingering foils military authority time and again. No doubt the German High Command (*Oberste Heeresleitung* – *OHL*) believed the *k.u.k. Armee* was plagued by thousands of Švejks as it took overall control of the Austrian war effort in 1917. In the end, though, the collapse of order in the *k.u.k.* was no laughing matter. Distrust bred despair amongst the empire's Slavic troops, many confused over why they were fighting Russians in the first place. By 1915, despair was expressed through high desertion rates in the army, and wholesale rejection of military service by many Czech, Italian, and Romanian communities.[2]

More than any of the other combatants, Germany faced a highly diverse range of foes on all fronts it was engaged. This becomes more pronounced as the relationship between the German military and civilian anthropologists is uncovered. As the primary object of battle on four fronts (Western, Eastern, Italian, and Balkan), the German Army had the opportunity to capture thousands of enemy soldiers. Not surprisingly, physical and cultural anthropologists took immediate advantage of the great opportunity afforded by the war to engage in a systematic study of the many prisoners in the military's care. While the stated purpose was to gain greater insights into Germany's enemies that could help the war effort, the more critical lasting result was to shape the course of German anthropology along a more nationalistic – and by the 1920s, a more overtly racist – discourse. Rooted in the liberal scientific tradition identified with the highly influential groundbreaking pathologist Rudolf Virchow, the original anthropologists sought

---

1 Geoffrey Wawro, *A Mad Catastrophe: The Outbreak of World War One and the Collapse of the Hapsburg Empire* (Basic Books, 2014), 22.

2 Graydon A. Tunstall, *Blood on the Snow: The Carpathian Winter War of 1915* (University Press of Kansas, 2010), 13–14.

to validate their belief in racial equality and to debunk biologically deterministic – and, in their eyes, fraudulent – pseudo-science. Accordingly after Virchow's death, an intellectual void existed in German anthropology that was soon filled by the more extreme Social Darwinists. Working in prisoner of war camps after 1915, the new generation of anthropologists were free to study thousands of captives, from dozens of ethnic, tribal, and racial groups. On the one hand, the whole experience was a tremendous boon to physical anthropology. What once required massive funding and years of travel now could be done within the course of a normal workday. Sketch artists and photographers created thousands of images of the many French, British, and Russian colonial soldiers. However the experience also increased German anthropology's reliance on race ideology. Here, the proponents of scientific racism, was not only proof of Western white superiority. Also revealed was the primacy of the German *Volk* over other Europeans. Ultimately this would translate into the creation of a new "race science" – *Rassenkunde* – that would be central to the realization of National Socialist racial policy.[3]

Even so, the Germans were hardly unique among the European combatants in espousing such ethnically-focused perceptions. The French Army's obsession with *elan vital*, *l'offensive a l'outrance*, and red trousers were all contextualized as honoring the incipient Gallic and Frankish spirit resident within all Frenchmen. As the nature of the conflict changed, this identity underwent a subtle shift, recasting the French soldier as a stolid, imperturbable fighter, the *Poilu* ("hairy one") of the trenches replacing the pre-war offensive-minded soldier. Italian soldiers were viewed almost to a man as drawn from stubborn peasant stock, the same general quality as the legionary of the Roman Republic – again despite a large number of urban conscripts. In the case of the Russian Army, the peasant identity of the individual soldier was closer to fact, even with the influx of urban volunteers and conscripts after 1914. Their German opponents marveled at the Russian soldiers' ability to survive, if not flourish, in the face of harsh weather and severe material shortages. The much-feared Russian steamroller of 1914 and 1915 may have proven a deeply-flawed instrument, but the blame rests almost universally at the higher echelons of the officer corps and in a failed political leadership.[4]

---

3 Andrew D. Evans, *Anthropology at War: World War I and the Science of Race in Germany* (The University of Chicago Press, 2010), 4–8, 34–36, 145, 190–91, 223–24.
4 Largely dedicated to frontier defense and internal policing in peacetime, the Russian Army relied on its vast peasant manpower reserves to compensate for shortages in equipment, ordnance, and experienced non-commissioned officers in the event of mobilization. The events of 1914 would prove this insufficient to meet the needs of full war against Germany and Austro-Hungary.

A similar indictment can be levied against the English Army following the embarrassments of 1914 to 1916. As an all-volunteer force, the British Expeditionary Force (BEF) symbolized as a direct link to the English yeoman tradition. As a rule Britons rejected conscription early in the war as an anti-British institution that ran contrary to the nation's values of fairness and community. Not discussed in the opposition to conscription was also a recognition that the British working class may not necessarily stand up to the test of combat, a fear of English racialists since the Boer War. Since the mid-nineteenth century, war was increasingly recast as the prerogative of the upper- and middle classes. By 1914, the British Army had taken on the character of a scouting troop, with its emphasis on exercise, fitness, marksmanship, and fieldcraft. Given the outcome of the Boer War, this should come as no surprise. However as the BEF disappeared in the mud of the winter of 1914/1915, a new force was clearly required to take its place. The first wave of voluntary enlistment – the "New Army" associated with Lord Kitchener – met this need, not only in numbers but also in spirit, as it was comprised largely of middle-class young men who had come of age well-steeped in the Muscular Christianity of the day.

Empire and War – The British Empire

Long before the outbreak of hostilities in August 1914, England and France prepared contingency plans for employing Colonial troops in a general European war. Through the 1880s and 1890s, the question of employing non-whites in direct combat against fellow Europeans was considered at length. In both cases the decision was made within the context of an imperialist ideology of white superiority reliant upon the tacit support of select ethnic groups of indigenous subjects. Within the British Empire the memory of the 1857 Indian Mutiny included recollection of support the Sikh Princes lent the British East India Company. After the mutiny was quashed in the following year, the newly appointed Viceroy of India, acting in the name of the crown, imposed a new policy for recruiting native troops. Following the example of a purported Scots warrior heritage, colonial administrators imposed a similar schema for classifying the peoples of India. On one side were the so-called "Martial Races" – robust, courageous, warlike, and hardy ethnicities who were biologically and culturally predisposed for war. Included in this classification were the Gurkha, Sikh, Rajputs, and Pathans – all

David Stevenson, *Cataclysm: The First World War as Political Tragedy* (Basic Books, 2004), 51–52; and Prit Buttar, *Germany Ascendant: The Eastern Front 1915* (Osprey, 2015), 31–36.

rural tribes centered in Northwest and North central India. In opposition to these groups were the "non-Martial Races" of Bengali and Southern India – in short, the majority of Indians in the subcontinent and many of the more vocal opponents of English domination. Over the next fifty-five years, the British military establishment in India came to rely ever more on the indigenous regiments raised there, not only for policing the immense subcontinent, but also as a strike force that could be employed on the Afghan periphery, Africa, and elsewhere as demanded by the Empire.[5]

By 1910 the Indian Army, resplendent in its multi-varied regional dress and bolstered by its reputation of its performance under the leadership of white British officers, figured ever more prominently in the War Office's plans for European mobilization. Two infantry divisions and a single cavalry brigade of indigenous troops were slated for transportation to England in the event of war in Europe. After the British Government signaled its intent to defend Belgian neutrality on August 4, 1914, the Indian Corps embarked for Europe, arriving in Marseilles in late September, from which it was shuttled directly to the front. The Indian Corps held part of the hard-pressed Ypres Salient through the first winter of the war, and took part in the early battles of Spring 1915.

In the autumn of 1915, the Indian Corps was relieved by British volunteer ("New Army") divisions and was rotated to the Middle East theater. Several reasons motivated this move, including high rates of sickness among Indian soldiers unaccustomed to the cold and wet European winters, the pressing need for soldiers in the new theater of operations, and the Indian troops' alleged propensity for desert warfare. Generally unstated but well understood were concerns about the war's effect upon the firm boundaries of the imperial relationship between British whites and Indians of color. Among the first effects of combat was the winnowing of the Indian regiments' white officers – all careerists with generally high awareness of the cultural issues related to their men – in combat. Replacement officers, no matter how well meaning, proved to be inadequate advocates for their men, particularly with regard to their interaction with British and French civilians while out of the line. Unlike other British imperial troops, the members of the Indian Corps were carefully segregated from white civilians, receiving harsh official and informal punishments if they challenged this status

---

5 See Heather Streets, *Martial Races: The Military, Race and Masculinity in British Imperial Culture, 1857–1914* (Manchester University Press, 2004); Kaushik Roy, *Brown Warriors of the Raj: Recruitment and the Mechanics of Command in the Sepoy Army, 1859–1913* (Manohar, 2008), 80–119; and Lionel Caplan, "Martial Gurkhas: The Persistence of a British Military Discourse on 'Race'," in Kaushik Roy, ed., *War and Society in Colonial India*. Second Edition (Oxford University Press, 2006, 2011), 225–45.

Figure 5.1: Indian troops led by their bagpipes on way to the trenches; scene during the Mesopotamian Campaign.
Source: NARA II, RG 165, Series: British Photographs of World War I, 1914–1918, 165-BO-1385.

quo. At the same time the British military establishment felt growing unease over the "lessons" being acquired by Indian troops in the battlefield. Imperial control of India was predicated upon two distinct assumptions: the innate cultural and biological superiority of white Britons over the vast numbers of Indians, and the sublime segregation of white European women from Indian society coinciding with absolute coercive dominance of colored Indian femininity by the British Imperial establishment. The longer Indian soldiers served in France, where they witnessed – and participated in – the slaughter of white Europeans and ran the risk of engaging in sexual congress with white women, even if prostitutes, the greater the potential threat to British Imperial control in India.

Thus the British leadership gradually deployed first the Indian Corps and later other divisions in the Indian Army to the war's imperial peripheries in the Mideast and East Africa. In July 1915, the Mesopotamian Expeditionary Force, under General Charles Townshend, launched its drive on Baghdad from the port city of Basra. Comprised of a mixed force of British and Indian troops, the MEF failed to break into Baghdad after fighting the Turkish Army to a stalemate at Ctesiphon in late November and withdrew to the small town of Kut-al-Amara. Indian troops also comprised the bulk of the relief force that failed to break the siege before the British surrender in January 1916. Throughout 1917 and 1918, Indian divisions made up the lion's share of the British armies in Mesopotamia and Palestine. In these two areas, they could engage an enemy without the implications of racial equality becoming apparent, because the Turks rated little higher than the Indians facing them in the western-constructed racial hierarchy scheme.

Indians were not the sole non-white ethnic group employed by the British during the war. The small community of West Indian and African transplants were no less spirited in answering Lord Kitchener's call to arms, and were placed in British regiments along with their white friends and neighbors. These men were the exception, however, as the army sought to establish and maintain a segregated Imperial force.[6] In October 1915, the Imperial War Office resolved to raise a West Indies regiment comprised of black soldiers from the Bahamas, Barbados, Grenada, Jamaica, and Trinidad under white officers. The decision followed a debate pitting racial ideology against political expediency. On one side stood white officers and political figures with concerns regarding the ability of blacks to serve on the Western Front. This was balanced by islander popular opinion, where many middle-class blacks and the imperial administrative establishments viewed military service as both obligation and pathway to home rule. After the British West Indian Regiment (BWIR) was recruited to strength, new accounts of official discrimination in Egypt and informal prejudice at the hands of white non-commissioned trainers riled opposition at home to press for an end to such discrimination. Battalions of the BWIR served from 1917 in Palestine, Italy, and the Western Front, proving their ability to withstand combat in the harshest conditions alongside white regiments. Discrimination, however, proved harder to dispel. After the November 11, 1918 armistice, the BWIR's eleven battalions were gathered together at the Italian port of Taranto. Reassigned as stevedores to offset a local labor shortage, the black soldiers harbored mounting resentment at being pressed into manual labor. On December 6, 1918, men from the Ninth Battalion turned on their white officers and went on strike. To the authorities, the strike equated to mutiny. Within days, the unrest spread to other battalions, as did assaults on officers, prompting a strong response. Aside from the 9th BWIR, which was disbanded, the regiment found itself confined to quarters. Sixty soldiers faced charges of mutiny, with one executed as the ringleader.

While an extreme example, the Taranto mutiny highlighted a larger trend race- or ethnic-based bitterness in the Empire. As white soldiers and sailors mustered

---

6 Stephen Bourne, *Black Poppies: Britain's Black Community and the Great War* (The History Press, 2014), 39–55.

out of service, they returned home to find their jobs occupied by women and migrants from across the Empire. Throughout Britain's urban centers, racial tensions mounted as unemployed veterans took to the streets to challenge the new arrivals for their jobs. In Liverpool and Cardiff, black factory and dockworkers were physically assaulted and killed by angry mobs, displaying a taste for lynching generally seen in the American South during the time. After a series of violent race riots, Parliament passed the Aliens Restriction Act of 1919, authorizing the deportation of non-authorized alien laborers, including seamen and factory workers, to their home countries. Save for small enclaves in London and other major cities, for the time being, Britain would remain a white enclave, despite its rhetoric regarding Imperial "community."[7]

Empire and War – France

According to one popular image during the First World War, a besieged France welcomed thousands of colonial soldiers from North and West Africa as brothers in arms, all equals in the struggle against German aggression. Like all popular myths, there is some basis in fact – indeed it is difficult to ignore the recruitment of over 200,000 *tirailleur* Senegalese, *Chasseur d'Afrique*, Spahis and other organizations over the course of the war. This notwithstanding, the myth could not substitute for a more balanced and analytical interpretation of complex and contradictory policies. Similarly the exclusive focus on the combat role of France's colonial troops obscures the deeper threads of race prejudice and formal policy responses after the war ended.

Gauging the scope of French racial ideology with regard to the *force noire* (encompassing all colonial troops from French North and West Africa) is rendered more difficult by the readiness the concept was accepted by the French General Staff. While African troops were employed since 1857 as *tirailleurs* (riflemen or sharpshooters – light infantry regiments organized exclusively for colonial service), the close of the nineteenth century saw a series of new contingencies that further legitimized their use as adjuncts to French Metropolitan white soldiers.

---

7 Glenford D. Howe, "A Wife Man's War: World War One and the West Indies," http://www. bbc.co.uk/history/worldwars/wwone/west_indies_01.shtml (Accessed September 12, 2018); Glenford Howe, *Race War and Nationalism: A Social History of West Indians in the First World War* (Ian Randle Publishers, 2002); Richard Smith, *Jamaican Volunteers in the First World War: Race, Masculinity, and the Development of National Consciousness* (Manchester University Press, 2004); and Bourne, *Black Poppies*, 149–51.

France's ignominious defeat in war with the Prussian-led German coalition in 1871 and subsequent loss of Alsace and Lorraine reinforced fears of demographically-obsessed leaders who viewed war as a total contest between nations. Simply put, not only were there more Germans than Frenchmen in 1872 (40 million versus 36 million), but the disparity would likewise continue to grow as the German birthrate outdistanced French births. It became imperative that France adopt any measure – military alliance, longer conscription terms, and development of colonial military forces – to assist in the inevitable future war with Germany and to ensure an improved outcome. A second factor occurred as the French expanded colonial territory in the late nineteenth century. Between the 1884 Congress of Berlin and 1910, France extended its territorial reach to encompass virtually all of Saharan Africa and over half of West Africa. Yet even as the French tricolour flew over a contiguous expanse of an African periphery easily three times the size of the *Metropole*, ample resistance remained in the form of independent tribes and bands opposed to French rule. What better tool to use to quell indigenous resistance, it was reasoned, than a regular force equipped, trained, and led by white officers, comprised of those ethnic groups who accepted French rule. In its essence, this latter point was just as representative of European Imperialism as the British practice of identifying and co-opting the "Martial Races" of India. Racial schemes of classification – in this case, the nascent science of anthropology – combined with political expediency on the scene to convey support for certain ethnic groups over more recalcitrant communities.

Nevertheless the primary consideration at the French General Staff's offices in Sainte-Cyr remained the future war with Germany. Since the 1870s, the collected organizations established in French North Africa (present-day Algeria, Tunisia, and Morocco), *Zouaves*, *Tirailleur d'Algerie*, and *Goumiers* were organizationally linked to the French Foreign Legion to form the *Armee d'Afrique*. Comprised of French-born settlers, Arabs, and other Islamic indigenous groups, the *Armee d'Afrique* originally served as an expeditionary force in West Africa and Indochina. In 1905 however, its mission expanded to become a ready reserve for use in France in the next war. In 1910 Lieutenant Colonel Charles Mangin wrote a treatise entitled *La Force Noire* calling for the creation of a black West African force along the same lines as the *Armee d'Afrique*. In addition to providing natural warriors who could be molded into soldiers, Mangin also argued the purportedly overpopulated area would provide an endless supply of manpower. However enrolling West Africans was not without risk. Any recruits required special training and oversight, since, Mangin reasoned, black Africans were biologically and culturally inferior to Westerners. Without proper training and strict discipline, he concluded, black troops would break under fire and create greater discipline problems than expected of whites. Essentially Mangin infantilized the very men he promoted as a solution to France's manpower problems. Yet in his view, the innate warrior savagery and brutality of the black West African was considered too valuable an asset to allow the "realities" of race to intrude. Mangin thus fully embraced the "Martial Races" concept, reasoning that aggressive soldiers would more than compensate for their less warrior-like comrades in arms.[8]

Though *La Force Noire* was widely criticized by conservatives in and out of the French military, Mangin's ideas took hold as several regiments of black West African troops were raised under the direction of white officers. Nevertheless, it took a second German invasion to make the black colonial force a reality. The heavy losses of the first four months of the First World War could not be made up by regular conscription levies in France. This manpower shortage led even the most conservative generals and politicians to consider widespread mobilization of West Africans.[9] As Richard S. Fogarty notes in his book *Race & War in France: Colonial Subjects in the French Army, 1914–1918*, French officers were quite direct and matter-of-fact in their reevaluation of the merits in using black troops, citing one account: "'The Senegalese have been recruited to replace Frenchmen, they are cannon fodder [*chair à canon*] to use to spare the whites.' These men had come to France 'in order to be killed instead of and in place of good Frenchmen.'"[10] Such sentiments cut through the veneer of the growing myth of French racial tolerance, indicating the hidden contingency residing at the core of the policy.

Regardless of the reason behind the policy, once the decision was made to open recruitment to black West Africans, it saw implementation in August 1914 when 29,000 *Tirailleurs Senegalais* served in French West Africa and Morocco. Within weeks, four battalions of West Africans were thrown into battle at Dixmude, where they sustained heavy casualties defending their position against repeated German attack. In the next three years, over 180,000 West Africans were recruited and conscripted into the French Army, where they acquired a reputation among the Germans of savage ferocity and brutal atrocity against prisoners. White Frenchmen and their allies, however, developed mixed views of the black West Africans. In April 1915, Senegalese conscripts broke and ran when gassed at Second Ypres. This and similar incidents led the Ministry of War to contemplate

---

8 Charles Mangin, *La Force Noire* (Hachette et Cie, 1911); and Richard S. Fogarty, "The French Empire," in Robert Gerwarth and Erez Manela, eds., *Empires at War: 1911–1923* (Oxford University Press, 2014), 109–129. See also Ruth Ginio, *The French Army and Its African Soldiers: The Years of Decolonization* (University of Nebraska Press, 2017), 5–8.

9 Dick van Galen Last with Ralf Futselaar, *Black Shame: African Soldiers in Europe, 1914–1922*, trans. Marjolijn de Jager (Bloomsbury, 2015), 20–21.

10 Richard S. Fogarty, *Race & War in France: Colonial Subjects in the French Army, 1914–1918*. (Johns Hopkins University Press, 2008), 7.

Figure 5.2: "Journée de l'armée d'Afrique et des troupes coloniales" (poster One) "A day for the African army and the colonial troops." A 1917 poster created to celebrate the accomplishments and service of the French North African colonial forces.
Source: Library of Congress. Reproduction Number: LC-USZC2-3947 (color film copy slide)

Figure 5.3: "Journée de l'armée d'Afrique et des troupes coloniales" (poster Two) "A day for the African army and the colonial troops." A second poster from the 1917 series created to celebrate the accomplishments and service of the French colonial forces – in this case, French Senegalese soldiers.
Source: Library of Congress. Reproduction Number: LC-USZC2-3949 (color film copy slide).

reforming the Senegalese and other colonial units into mixed regiments, comprised of two battalions of colonial troops matched to a single white battalion to stiffen their discipline under fire. Accordingly such plans represented a more circumspect perspective regarding the ability of nonwhites to survive and conduct European-style modern warfare.

Nevertheless the *Tirailleurs Senegalais* acquired some admirers. Their initial advocate, General Mangin, continued to press for their use as shock troops. General Robert Nivelle hoped to take advantage of their acclaimed innate warrior nature to break through the German trench network along the Chemin des Dames. Their failure to live up to the expectations of their officers should not be taken as evidence of inadequacy, but rather that they were no less human than the white *poilus* alongside them. While it appears the common soldier accepted this as a matter of course, French generals responded in typical fashion, seeing instead a racial disposition to malingering and desertion that could only be arrested by greater control. General Philippe Petain, upon taking charge of the French Army after the Nivelle Offensive petered out, pressed for deeper amalgamation of black and white units on the order of one black company to three white companies at the front.

Their performance at the front notwithstanding, French politicians lauded the *Tirailleur Senegalais* as heroes. The black West African in uniform offered proof positive of the success of the white civilizing mission in the French Empire. Here were a people, advocates posed, who absorbed the benefits of French society, language, and culture, with its promise of *liberté, egalité,* and *fraternité*; and they subsequently offered their lives as a sort of blood payment in defense of the Republic and its values. West African deputies in the French Assembly routinely touted the accomplishments of their soldiers in the press, acclaiming them as selfless heroes of the Republic, evidence in flesh that France's Republican ethos transcended race and ethnicity. Individual soldiers, singled out for decoration with the *Croix de Guerre* and the *Legion d'Honneur*, were held up as symbols not merely of heroism, but of the black West African's commitment to defend the *Metropole* against the crush of Prussian militarism. In this short moment, Empire stood alongside democracy as positive values under threat.

Popular writers picked up the drumbeat. In his classic account of the war *Under Fire*, French novelist Henri Barbusse captured the spirit of this official view of the colonial troops:

> Through the twilight comes the rolling hum of tramping men, and another throng rubs its way through.
>
> "Africans!"
>
> They march past with faces red-brown, yellow or chestnut, their beards scanty and fine or thick and frizzled, their greatcoats yellowish-green, and their muddy helmets sporting the

crescent in place of our grenade. Their eyes are like balls of ivory or onyx, that shine from faces like new pennies, flattened or angular. Now and again comes swaying along above the line the coal-black mask of a Senegalese sharpshooter. Behind the company goes a red flag with a green hand in the center.

We watch them in silence. These are asked no questions. They command respect, and even a little fear.

All the same, these Africans seem jolly and in high spirits. They are going, of course, to the first line. That is their place, and their passing is the sign of an imminent attack.

They are made for the offensive.

"Those and the 75 gun we can take our hats off to. They're everywhere sent ahead at big moments, the Moroccan Division."

"They can't quite fit in with us. They go too fast – and there's no way of stopping them."

Some of these diabolical images in yellow wood or bronze or ebony are serious of mien, uneasy, and taciturn. Their faces have the disquieting and secret look of the snare suddenly discovered. The others laugh with a laugh that jangles like fantastic foreign instruments of music, a laugh that bares the teeth.

We talk over the characteristics of these Africans; their ferocity in attack, their devouring passion to be in with the bayonet, their predilection for "no quarter." We recall those tales that they themselves willingly tell, all in much the same words and with the same gestures. They raise their arms over their heads – "Kam'rad, Kam'rad!" "Non, pas Kam'rad!" And in pantomime they drive a bayonet forward, at belly-height, drawing it back then with the help of a foot.

One of the sharpshooters overhears our talk as he passes. He looks upon us, laughs abundantly in his helmeted turban, and repeats our words with significant shakes of his head: "Pas Kam'rad, non pas Kam'rad, never! Cut head off!"

"No doubt they're a different race from us, with their tent-cloth skin," Barque confesses, though he does not know himself what "cold feet" are. "It worries them to rest, you know; they only live for they minute when the officer puts his watch back in his pocket and says, 'Off you go!'"

"In fact, they're real soldiers."[11]

Even as Barbusse applauds the courage and resilience of the colonial troops, he falls back into the comfortable racialized view separating non-whites as an exotic, if not dangerous, "other" when compared to the "normalcy" of French whiteness. Equals in their ability to kill Germans, yet different in the absence of civilized restraint, Barbusse presented the Africans as little more than a terrible weapon fit for use against the treacherous German foe. Other public media was

---

11 Henri Barbusse, *Under Fire: The Story of a Squad (Le Feu)* (E.P. Dutton & Co., 1917), 44–45.

likewise conflicted. War bond and loan posters both celebrated the fighting spirit of *La Force Noire* while also emphasizing their exotic character and unsophisticated nature. Shown often as wild-eyed berserkers, the official portrayal also frequently emphasized their service as part of a colonial compact, in which military service was both an obligation on the part of the colonized, and an expression of confidence on the part of the *Metropole*. Popular advertising followed suit, using colonial troops to promote popular consumer goods. Here ferocious images were tempered with the application of obsequious and paternalist stereotypes: North African *spahis* and *Zouaves* portrayed in high Orientalist style; Senegalese and other West Africans shown as avuncular, child-like exotics; Annamese and other Indochinese and Polynesians presented as docile subordinares, eager to please their colonial masters. The emphasis was always, whether hawking chocolates, coffee, or maudlin sentimentalities, on presenting the Empire as subordinate yet essential components of France.[12]

Such accounts and experiences went far toward establishing the perception that France was somehow more enlightened in its view on race than the rest of the Western world. In the United States, W.E.B. DuBois proclaimed the French as visionaries who had dismantled the color line, and embarked upon a more liberal path toward race which validated blacks and whites equally as men. Fraternization between black soldiers and white civilians was a signal concern for French government and military officials. The ease with which some nonwhite soldiers mingled with white women behind the lines was greeted with anxious concern, especially as military censors intercepted thousands of letters describing their liaisons and containing photographs – some pornographic, some romantic portraits – of white women. The traditional imperial gender relationship, pairing white male conquerors with female indigenous partners, was inverted in the empire's very heart. Accordingly as the war progressed, white females who interacted with colonial troops on a personal, if not intimate, level – nurses, prostitutes, and lovers – were castigated as race betrayers. Likewise where possible, the military exerted its coercive power on soldiers of color who dared to transgress what was in practice a camouflaged, but very real, color line separating them from their intended partners. Individual soldiers were arrested, and often incarcerated for long periods, for non-military essential interactions with white women.[13]

---

12 For examples of the portrayals of French colonial troops, see Dominiek Dendooven and Piet Chielens, *World War I: Five Continents in Flanders* (Lannoo, 2008), 50–87.

13 Tyler Stovall, "Love, Labor, and Race: Colonial Men and White Women in France During the Great War," in Tyler Stovall and Georges van den Abbeele, eds., *French Civilization and Its Discontents: Nationalism, Colonialism, Race* (Lexington Books, 2003), 297–322, 299, 305, 307–309; Annabelle Melzer, "Spectacles and Sexualities: The 'Mise-en-Scene' of the 'Tirailleur Sénégalais'

The employment of *La Force Noire* was greeted with horror by Germans, even before the war. As news of the Mangin Plan spread after 1909, German newspapers attacked it, decrying that the use of black troops in Europe against white soldiers would constitute a war crime. Within two years, the terms "black shame" and "black danger" were regular features in popular accounts. Meanwhile the General Staff dismissed the *force noire* as a silly distraction, considering African troops as poor soldiering material, and ill-prepared to cope with Europe's cold and damp winter climate.[14] After 1914, German outrage over the Allied (in particular, the French) use of colored troops in Western Europe coalesced around three points. First, the deployment of colonial non-white forces was a violation of international law that undermined Europe's Judeo-Christian culture and its innate biological superiority. Second, African troops in particular were purportedly so unruly and uncontrollable that French officers were incapable of imposing discipline or restraint on their charges. As a result, colored troops were free to commit savage acts of barbaric depravity on dead and captured Germans. Third, owing to their alleged lack of restraint and fecund biology, African soldiers were presumed to be predisposed to sexual violence, from rape to *lustmord* (sexual killings). Not only did this raise the prospect of race mingling and degeneration, it also created the climate for a spiraling collapse of civic order under the pressure of corrosive racial intermingling.[15]

After the armistice, colonial troops were dispatched to the French occupied Rhineland in relatively small numbers: approximately 27,000 African soldiers out of 250,000 French troops occupying the Saar- and Pfalzlands in 1923. Naturally German observers condemned their use as part of a larger policy intended to humiliate and provoke them into rash action, while also proclaiming the so-called "*Schwarze Schmach*" as giving colored troops free license to rape and seduce young German women. From the French perspective, while there was some acknowledgment that African colonial troops would indeed rile their former enemies, the primary motivation actually appears to be a more nuanced effort to reinforce the ties between the French *metropole* and its colonial *periphery*. By including Senegalese or Moroccan troops in the occupation force, France was signaling that the colonies were essential parts of the larger national whole. Regardless, the insult to German sensibilities was quite real, both as an exercise that revealed the depths of

---

on the Western Front, 1914–1920," in *Borderlines: Genders and Identities in War and Peace, 1870–1930*, ed. Billie Melman (Routledge, 1998), 213–244, 214–216, 220; and Fogarty, *Race and War in France*, 203–205, 225–229.

14 van Galen Last with Futselaar, *Black Shame*, 23–24.

15 *Ibid.*, 50–51.

German vulnerabilities and defeat, and as a rallying cry to resistance.[16] The Dutch historians Dick van Galen Last and Ralf Futselaar expertly summarized the German perspective on the occupation, and its lingering impact on racial attitudes:

> [. . .] Clemenceau, Mangin, and Diagne wanted to provide the Africans with the image of a victorious fatherland and reward them for their contribution to that victory by deploying them in the garrisoning of enemy territory. They refused to countenance that they were adding to the shame of the occupation by inflicting another defeat on the Germans: occupation by coloured people, right at the moment when control over colored people had been taken away from Germany; this was reverse colonization by people who had been associated with animals in German propaganda since the colonial period.[17]

The humiliation of the *Schwarze Schmach* was short-lived, as the French occupation force shrank after 1923 to ultimately become a mere token presence. The general outrage was also tempered over time as Germany recovered from the stresses of 1920 through 1923. Within a short time, urban *frissonners* would embrace African culture as an artistic form and anthropological curiosity, just as they pursued American jazz musicians. But make no mistake – outside of the avant-garde, and the very limited number of veterans of von Lettow-Vorbeck's German East Africa campaign – most Germans retained enough disgust to allow them to accept even cruder racist projections in the coming decades.

But yet as the war wound to a close, the question of the future of the colonial soldiers in France and within the Empire became more pressing. Again, the French government made bold statements of citizenship and sacrifice by linking wartime service to identity. Such pronouncements did not translate into self-determination back in West and North Africa or Indochina; quite the reverse, actually, as local colonial administrators sought to clamp down on communities which might entertain such notions as their surviving sons returned home, enriched in the knowledge of how to kill white men. A few sons of the Empire remained in France after the war, but only in a narrow sector of roles, including entertainment and politics. Otherwise average citizens themselves made known their own dissatisfaction with colored immigration to France. Demobilized veterans joined with conservative political organizations to demonstrate against factories and other businesses who contemplated hiring West Africans and other colonial peoples. Just as in Britain,

---

16 "Schwarze Schmach" translates directly in English as "Black Shame." Peter Collar, *The Propaganda War in the Rhineland: Weimar Germany, Race and Occupation after World War I* (I. B. Tauris, 2013), 76–93; van Galen Last with Futselaar, *Black Shame*, 139–59.
17 van Galen Last with Futselaar, *Black Shame*, 159. Blaise Diagne was the first black member of the French Council of Deputies, and one-time mayor of Dakar. He advocated for the full extension of French citizenship to all people residing within the French Empire, no matter their racial identity.

then, the postwar policy called for the maintenance of the whiteness as the racial hegemon in the home country. A major difference, however, was that France did so while also maintaining the image of a mythologized – and fabricated – racial harmony that remains powerful even in the twenty-first century.[18]

Race and the American Expeditionary Force

The United States entered the war on April 6, 1917 to "make the world safe for democracy" and to redress innumerable insults and attacks on American neutrality as defined by President Woodrow Wilson. In the process of mobilizing and waging war against the Central Powers, however, the United States also went to great lengths to maintain its cultural outlook on race and whiteness. This policy indirectly targeted the nation's ten million African Americans. At the onset of war, black intellectuals and social leaders hoped their contributions alongside whites in combat would finally give proof of the lie behind Jim Crow, and at the least, comprise the first step toward economic and social equality. Before long however, it was clear the deck remained stacked against them, as the War Department, directed by Secretary of War Newton D. Baker, and the American Expeditionary Force, under the command of General John J. Pershing, actively sought to limit the role of blacks in the war effort to manual labor tasks.

The Regular Army's four colored regiments, the Ninth and Tenth Cavalry and the Twenty-fourth and Twenty-fifth Infantry, sat the war out in isolated garrisons in the Philippines and along the Mexican border. Of the only two black officers in the Army, the higher ranking, Colonel Charles Young, was briefly forced out of service to avoid giving him a combat command. The other, Lieutenant Benjamin O. Davis, Sr., served out the war in virtual exile in the Philippines. Across the American South, draft boards conspired to limit the number of blacks accepted into service. Meanwhile the War Department only reluctantly organized the 92nd and 93rd Divisions around a small cadre of black National Guard units and conscripts, both divisions the AEF would cast aside at the first opportunity. The message would soon become apparent that, if the black man was to serve in the United States Army, it would be in an adjunct capacity as manual labor behind the lines.

With hindsight it is possible to identify the immediate antecedents to this policy. Since 1867, the Army's four colored regiments – the "Buffalo Soldiers" of popular history – performed distinguished service in the nation's frontier wars

---

18 Fogarty, "The French Empire," 109–129.

against various Indian tribes. Chronically understaffed and under the direct command of white officers, the four colored regiments nevertheless garnered a reputation as choice postings for professionally-minded officers. These were not parade ground regiments; but rather they were hard-fighting and hard-driving men who were at home on the march. Their reputation as shock-troops within the Army only improved during the Spanish-American War. Not only did the Tenth Cavalry and Twenty-fourth Infantry regiments take part in the charge up San Juan Hill, they also joined their sister regiments in the bitter counterinsurgency fighting in the Philippines. Later the "Buffalo Soldiers" joined in the 1916 Mexican Punitive Expedition, where a squadron of the Tenth Cavalry under command of Lieutenant Colonel Charles Young saved an isolated company of the Eighth Infantry from being overrun by Carrista forces at Parral.[19]

This distinguished service was matched by an equally long history of mistreatment and abuse by white American society, both within and outside of the Army. In 1881 the Army's first black line officer, Henry Ossian Flipper, was cashiered from service on flimsy pretense. Shortly after arriving at Fort Davis, Texas, he uncovered the loss of commissary funds in his charge as Acting Commissary of Subsistence, and sought to conceal the loss until he could recover the missing money. Unfortunately for Flipper, the loss was soon discovered, and he faced court-martial on charges of embezzlement and conduct unbecoming an officer.[20] The two subsequent black officers lived in quiet seclusion when not in the field at the head of black troops; all the better than to risk confrontation with racist peers. The four regiments were likewise forced into isolation when stationed in some areas. When posted in the North, Midwest, and Northwest states, black regiments generally received good treatment. The same could not be said of the South, where colored soldiers were stationed at their peril. Proof of this can be seen in the 1906 Brownsville Raid and the 1917 Houston Riot. In both incidents, local white bigots antagonized the black troops of the Twenty-Fourth and Twenty-Fifth Infantry Regiments by attacking individual off-duty soldiers in the town.

At Brownsville, insults and personal discrimination greeted the regiment's First Battalion after they arrived at Fort Brown. Tensions between the soldiers and the white community mounted, until their commanding officer, Major Charles

---

19 Young was the first black graduate of West Point following the sad affair involving Lieutenant Henry O. Flipper in 1881. See Brian G. Shellum's two-volume biography, *Black Cadet in a White Bastion: Charles Young at West Point* (Bison Books, 2006), and *Black Officer in a Buffalo Soldier Regiment: The Military Career of Charles Young* (University of Nebraska Press, 2010).
20 See Charles M. Robinson, III. *The Fall of a Black Army Officer: Racism and the Myth of Henry O. Flipper* (University of Oklahoma Press, 2008).

Penrose, confined his men to barracks for their safety. On the night of August 12, a group of men shot up a local bar, killing the bartender and maiming a police lieutenant. After the locals claimed black troopers had committed the shooting, an investigation singled out twelve enlisted men as the perpetrators. Despite the best efforts of the prosecution to secure their conviction, however, the grand jury convened in the case rejected any indictment, citing lack of evidence. In response, President Theodore Roosevelt insisted upon the immediate dishonorable discharge of all 167 enlisted men in the Fort Brown garrison. Even after evidence appeared showing the garrison remained in barracks during the fracas and an independent investigation ruled that the raid was likely conducted by local bigots eager to create an incident that would evict the black soldiers from Fort Brown, Roosevelt refused to reverse his decision. It stood as a matter of record until 1972, when President Richard Nixon reinstated all men into the service and awarded them all, save one survivor, posthumous honorable discharges.[21]

The outcome of the Houston incident proved even more disheartening. On August 23, 1917, the city's police arrested a private in the Twenty-fourth Infantry regiment for interfering with their questioning of a black woman. After a corporal was assaulted when he inquired about the arrest and rumors of his being shot and killed by police spread throughout his company, a column of 150 black soldiers marched into the center of the city. They ostensibly were to keep matters from spiraling out of control. Their efforts failed when confronted by a mob of armed white citizens and police. In the ensuing firefight, eleven white civilians and four policemen were killed, along with an Ohio National Guard captain who was mistaken for a policeman. As a result of the three courts martial that followed, nineteen men – one sergeant, four corporals, and fourteen privates – were hanged, and another forty-one received life-sentences. The tragic incidents in Brownsville and Houston thus not only negatively influenced public and political opinion against the prospect of fielding black regiments in large numbers in Europe, they had the immediate effect of sidelining the four Regular Colored regiments for the duration of the conflict.[22]

So the stage was set for the War Department's disenfranchisement of the Army's black soldiers in the First World War. Responding to the pressure of Southern senators and congressmen adamantly opposed to training blacks to

---

21 Bobby A. Wintermute, "The Brownsville Affair," Alexander Bielakowski, ed., *Ethnic and Racial Minorities in the U.S. Military: An Encyclopedia,* vol. I (ABC-Clio, 2013), 106–109.
22 Bobby A. Wintermute, "Houston Riot of 1917," in Alexander Bielakowski, ed., *Ethnic and Racial Minorities in the U.S. Military: An Encyclopedia,* vol. I (ABC-Clio, 2013), 305–309; and Jennifer Keene, *World War I: The American Soldier Experience* (University of Nebraska Press, 2011), 95–97.

Figure 5.4: Court martial proceedings of 64 black enlisted men from the 24th Infantry Regiment on charges related to the August 23, 1917 Houston Riot. ("Largest murder trial in the history of the United States. Scene during Court Martial of 64 members of 24th Infantry USA on trial for mutiny and murder of 17 people at Houston, Tex., August 23 1917. Trial held in Gift Chapel, Ft. Sam Houston. Trial started – Nov. 1, 1917, Brig. Genl. George K. Hunter Presiding. Col. J.Q. Hull – Judge Advocate, Maj. D.U. Sutphin, Asst. Advocate, Counsel for Defense, Maj. Harry S. Grier. Prisoners guarded by 19th Infantry Co. "C" Capt. Carl J. Gates.")
Source: NARA II, College Park, Maryland. National Archives Identifier: 533485 Local Identifier: 165-WW-127(1).

fight out of a fear that they might wreak their own revenge for slavery and Jim Crow upon their return, Secretary of War Newton D. Baker ordered the sidelining of black conscripts and volunteers into labor battalions. Instead, they would be put to work at home and in France building railroads, loading and unloading ships, driving supplies, and digging trenches and other facilities. When Northern black civic leaders, including DuBois and the new National Association for the Advancement of Colored People, demanded a combat role for black National Guard units from New York and Ohio, Baker assented to their forming the basis for the 92nd and 93rd Divisions. National Guard organizations like the 15th New York Regiment, the Eighth Illinois Regiment, and smaller units from Maryland, the District of Columbia, Connecticut, Ohio, and Massachusetts were matched, not with the Regular Army's four colored regiments exiled as they were to distant posts, but with newly organized regiments of conscripts.

Forming the two divisions was only part of the problem, however, from the perspective of the War Department and senior Army leaders. The first question was who would lead the black troops into combat. A solution was training educated blacks at Fort Des Moines, from which they were sent out to the two divisions to take charge as company commanders. These new lieutenants still faced resistance however. White enlisted men refused to return salutes or accept orders from the new black officers. Likewise some Southern blacks bridled at the prospect of being commanded by educated blacks and offered passive resistance. Rather than force compliance with centuries of military tradition, the War Department let such incidents pass unnoticed, leaving it to the local chain of command. This resolution brought into focus another problem. Unlike the Regular Army in peacetime in which career-minded officers sought assignment to the four black regiments, many senior officers associated with the two black divisions were barely competent leaders and racist in sentiment – most often Southerners – who received their assignments because they "knew how to deal" with blacks. This dynamic became centripetal. Not surprisingly, morale suffered at the hands of such officers, despite the best efforts of other, more paternalistic, officers serving in the National Guard regiments.

For the War Department, the second question was if and under whom the two black divisions would fight. Here again the influence of white Southern politicians was felt. General Pershing, despite having served the Tenth Cavalry Regiment in Cuba, responded to lobbying by racists opposed to allowing blacks to fight alongside whites in France. Pershing "loaned" the 93rd Division to the French Army. This was the only American division so divested by the senior American commander, who otherwise fiercely opposed amalgamation, on the basis that France "needed" manpower and "could handle" black troops effectively. After control was passed in December 1917, the 93rd's four regiments were splintered and attached to individual French divisions for further training and introduction to combat. Over the next year the division's four regiments – the 369th, 370th, 371st, and 372nd – distinguished themselves in combat under French command. Individual soldiers like Privates Henry Lincoln Johnson and Neadom Roberts impressed their French peers and offices with their courage and ferocity. In May 1918 Johnson and Roberts fought off a German patrol with their rifles and in hand-to-hand combat, winning the *Croix de Guerre* in the process. Such actions combined with the larger unit's hard-driving performance under French command earned each regiment a *Croix de Guerre* citation, as well as numerous individual citations and medals, ranging from the *Legion d'Honneur* and the *Croix de Guerre* to the *Military Medal*.[23]

23 Jeffrey T. Sammons and John H. Morrow, Jr., *Harlem's Rattlers and the Great War: The Undaunted 369th Regiment and the African American Quest for Equality* (University Press of Kansas, 2014), 265–70.

Figure 5.5: "Colored Men: The First Americans Who Planted our Flag on the Firing Line, True Sons of Freedom" by Charles Gustrine, 1918. Poster highlighting African-American soldiers confronting German infantry in France, with Abraham Lincoln looking down from heavens. **Source:** Courtesy of the United States Army Heritage and Education Center, Carlisle, Pennsylvania.

The 92nd Division remained under AEF control, but it would certainly have fared better under French control. Commanded by Major General Charles C. Ballou, a Regular Army officer with over thirty years' experience, the 92nd Division underwent an erratic training program in the United States until it was ordered to France in June 1918. Upon their arrival, the division experienced the additional training and seasoning that was normal for American units arriving in the theater. By August the division went into the line, and it performed well enough in its baptism of fire in the area around St. Die. In September, however, the division joined the First American Army in the Meuse Argonne offensive. The 92nd Division's assault on Binarville ended in a marked failure. Ordered to attack an objective shielded by thick belts of barbed wire without wire cutters, maps, or preparatory bombardment, the assault quickly bogged down. Its 368th Regiment alone sustained over 450 casualties. Although the division recovered and took its objective, the entire operation was later cited as "proof" of black troops' inferiority to whites. This judgment categorically ignored the failure of other white units to take their own respective objectives in support of the 92nd Division.

Combat performance aside, black troops experienced widespread prejudice and abuse in the AEF. White officers and NCOs expended a great deal of energy transferring American Jim Crow policies to France. Housed in inferior barracks, transported in substandard freight cars, and supplied with shoddy equipment, blacks were also routinely subjected to harsh personal attacks by individual white soldiers. Black officers faced even greater ignominies because so many white officers and enlisted men rejected the very premise that blacks could be commissioned. Ignoring direct orders and failing to accord superior black officers the most basic of military honors became common practice. Even when their heroism and contributions were acknowledged in official orders and papers like Stars and Stripes, blacks were frequently described in insulting stereotypes – "coal-tar soldiers," "primitive warriors," or "Uncle Sam's lost children," – that undermined their accomplishments.

Racial prejudices extended to the highest levels of the AEF. In August 1918, the French Liaison officer attached to the AEF's headquarters issued a circular describing official American policy regarding African-American troops. After outlining American racial fears regarding French civil and military tolerance for the American black troops, the circular described AEF concerns and requests that the French scale back their kindness, lest the recipients come to expect such treatment when they returned home. To their credit, the French discarded the circular out of hand; yet the fears outlined in the request remained.[24]

After the war's end, the Army undertook measures to further limit African-American participation in future conflict. An Army War College report appearing in 1925 and titled *The Use of Negro Man Power in War* summarized black combat performance and labeled them as inferior and ill-suited for combat, citing as proof the failed Binarville attack conducted by elements of

---

24 "Secret Information Concerning Black American Troops, 1918," printed in Nina Mjagkij, *Loyalty in Time of Trial: The African American Experience during World War I* (Rowman and Littelfield, 2011), 175–77. A facsimile of the original memorandum, as printed in W.E.B. DuBois' journal, *The Crisis* is available at: http://www.slate.com/blogs/the_vault/2016/04/27/_secret_information_concerning_black_troops_a_warning_memo_sent_to_the_french.html (Accessed February 20, 2018).

the 93rd Division. It read like a catalog of negative stereotypes about African Americans that could just have been easily written by an apologist for slavery. This report further limited black enlistment and training in the interwar years, as the Army's four colored regiments were moved into labor and support roles. The day of the "buffalo soldier," for all practical purposes, was over. In addition to being a culmination of racialist lessons gleaned from the First World War, this Army War College report also foreshadowed the attitudes and assumptions about race in the United States military so predominant in the Second World War.[25]

Race and War: The Ottoman Empire

Since the 1860s, the Ottoman Empire was derided as the "Sick Man of Europe," the weakest of the European powers and a long-standing exotic Oriental bugbear whose only real purpose was to frighten young children and titillate older readers. From 1829, the Ottoman Empire's grip on the Balkans, held since the fifteenth century, steadily slipped in a series of wars of national liberation: first Greece; and then Serbia, Montenegro, Bulgaria, and Romania in 1878. A pair of Balkan Wars in 1912 and 1913 further exposed Ottoman weaknesses and resulted in the loss of much of Thrace and Macedonia to the younger Balkan states.

For almost all practical purposes, the war in the Mideast was conducted as if it were a completely distinct conflict. After joining the Triple Alliance within two days of the start of the war in the West, the Ottoman Empire initiated its first campaigns against two of the world's largest empires – Russia and Great Britain.[26] Whereas from the Allied perspective, the war with the Ottomans was expected to be a short affair, given the evidence of the recent Balkan Wars, the Turkish-dominated military and government perceived an opportunity to reverse the general decline the Empire was experiencing since the eighteenth century. Well aware that the British, French, and Russians, as well as the newer Balkan States, antic-

---

25 H.E. Ely, *The Use of Negro Man Power in War,* U.S. Army War College, October 30, 1925, Memorandum to the Army Chief of Staff, p. 7, Franklin D. Roosevelt Presidential Library and Museum. See citation and summary comments at http://www.fdrlibrary.marist.edu/TCGui.pdf (Accessed April 3, 2018).

26 In December 1914, the Ottoman Third Army launched its first Caucasus expedition. Weeks later, on January 14, 1915, the Ottoman Fourth Army initiated its Sinai campaign, targeting the Suez Canal and Egypt. Both campaigns quickly stalled; the Caucasus campaign in particular amounting to a near total rout. Edward J. Erickson, *Ordered to Die: A History of the Ottoman Army in the First World War* (Greenwood Press, 2001), 59–60, 70–72.

ipated further partitions and acquisitions at the Ottoman's expense, the overall consensus in Istanbul was to capitalize on Europe's current turmoil by joining with Germany and Austria-Hungary.[27]

In November 1914, soon after deciding to enter the war, the Ottoman Caliphate declared the conflict to be a *jihad*, calling on all Muslims to join the Turks against the Allies in a holy war to defend the faith. This action has been credited as the signal for the degeneration of the war into a series of harsh actions against non-Muslims, particularly in and around Turkish Armenia. Due to the intercession of religious authority, the ethnic character of the Ottoman policies, not only in Armenia, but throughout the empire, has been obscured. Since the Balkan Wars, relations between non-Turkish and non-Muslim imperial citizens and civil, military, and religious elites had slipped into distrust and perceived rejection of the Empire's legitimacy. Even before mobilization, Armenians, Kurds, Jews, Arabs, and Christians were being marginalized. The onset of war saw the thinly-veiled hostility break out into organized and random acts of ethnic cleansing and genocide. Most frequently cited as victims, Armenians were merely one of the first populations to be rounded up and forcibly transported to encampments in the center of the interior. Following reports of mass desertions by Ottoman Armenian soldiers, and the risk of guerilla operations, the Ottoman military initiated a mass deportation of civilians on May 30, 1915. Many adult males were murdered outright, their corpses thrown into mass graves. As for the women, children, and elderly, many were left to fend for themselves in the crude camps. There, exposed to the harsh winter conditions, denied food and clean water, and subject to random killings by bored guards, they died in the scores daily. Other minorities also suffered persecution in the wartime empire, but the scale of the attacks on Armenians defied contemporary logic.[28] Even before the May 30, 1915 deportation order, hundreds of villages were annihilated by Ottoman militias. Few reports were made regarding the collapse of order on the overland marches to camps deep in Anatolia. Military historian Hew Strachan records a range of estimated dead between 1.3 and 2.1 million, but also takes care to advise not all of the data provided, even from surviving Armenians, is reliable.[29]

Even a century after the war, the encounters between Australian, English, and French soldiers and the Ottoman defenders on the Gallipoli peninsula

---

27 Mustafa Aksakal, "The Ottoman Empire," in Robert Gerwarth and Erez Manela, *Empires at War, 1911–1923* (Oxford University Press, 2014), 17–33.

28 Erickson, *Ordered to Die*, 99–100, 102; and Aksakal, "The Ottoman Empire," 28–31. Particularly hard off were Christian and Arab communities in Lebanon and Syria. Additionally, the onset of a famine in the region was estimated to have starved over 500,000 people in 1915.

29 Hew Strachan, *The First World War* (Penguin, 2005), 110–111.

defines for many Westerners the character and context of the Turkish soldier. For the general English-speaking public, the image of the Turk was locked in a strange, half-exotic, half-alien perspective that filtered its way into the highest corridors of elite society. Fueled by literary accounts like *The Thousand and One Arabian Nights* and *The Lustful Turk*, as well as numerous artistic representations from the likes of Jean Lecomte de Nouy and Frederick John Lewis, the Turkish elite in Istanbul was alleged to be a decadent, corrupt, and slightly effeminized people. Degraded by centuries of prosperity and unchallenged power, they rejected the scientific reason of the West in favor of superstition and dissipation. The image of the lower classes in Ottoman society fared no better. Perceived at that time as an ignorant, benighted people mired in ignorance and indifference, the majority of people living under Turkish control were supposed to be ready to rise up in revolution against their corrupt masters at the first sign. Consequently, when Britain declared war on the Ottoman Empire on October 31, 1914, following the Turkish shelling of Russian Black Sea ports, expectations were high. The general view in the Ministry of Defense was that the Turkish army would cave in at the first hard blow.

This view prevailed among the British leadership and influenced their planning in 1914 and 1915. Key to the Dardanelles Offensive of 1915 were the presumptions that the Turks were technologically inferior to the Allies, and hence incapable of withstanding a naval thrust to Istanbul, and that the Turkish Army would not resist a coordinated attack made by Westerners. Both premises were proven wrong in short order. After British, Australian, and French troops landed on the Gallipoli peninsula, the initial perception was that the Turkish soldier would not fight, again quickly disproven. Meanwhile planning for the British drive on Baghdad undertaken by General Charles Townshend also had little contingency for Turkish resistance. Rather it expected wholesale desertions by non-Turkish conscripts and a general Arab uprising – both of which failed to materialize.

Both plans and their outcomes revealed how racial perception – or in this case, misperception – impair military planning. By failing to accord the Islamic non-Turkish peoples of the Ottoman Empire any sense of commitment or dedication to the ideal of the Ottoman Caliphate, Western planners unwittingly set about creating operational plans doomed to failure. As both Generals Ian Hamilton and Townshend discovered to their dismay at Gallipoli, the Ottoman soldier was quite willing and ready to die for his faith and his nation – even if he had little concept of nationhood in the Western sense. Also overlooked was the prospect that the Turkish soldier and officer could and did learn modern techniques of warfighting quite readily from their German instructors. Their training may not have been of the exact same quality and depth as in Western armies, but it did level the qualitative field between them and the British and associated Imperial forces. In time of course, the British in the Mideast would rout the Turks in Palestine, but this would come only after a long period of stalemate in the region and the gradual buildup of new technological solutions that the Turks could not keep up with – including aircraft, armored car, new artillery, and tanks. During the interim, the British and Imperial forces in Egypt acquired new respect for their Turkish opponents, while still perceiving them as racially inferior and distinct.[30]

Even as the Dardanelles campaign was unfolding, British imperial forces were advancing upon Baghdad in an independent expedition up the Tigris and Euphrates Rivers. Here again, ethnic prejudices and stereotypes affected the conduct of the campaign. British commanders not only dismissed the quality of the Ottoman defenders during the drive upriver from Basra, they openly disparaged the Arab peoples they "liberated" along the way as degenerates and lazy brigands. As the British consolidated their control over the area around Basra, the Mesopotamian Expeditionary Force's commander, Major General Charles Townshend, envisioned a swift riverine drive up the river to capture Baghdad and compel the Turks to surrender in the face of an invasion of Anatolia. Townshend's hubris, combined with the generally poor assessment of their enemy, saw the expedition outrun its supply lines and ultimately be compelled to surrender unconditionally to the Ottoman Army at the city of Kut on April 29, 1916, following a 147 day long siege. Townshend and his staff, and other senior officers, enjoyed a comfortable captivity, the same could not be said for the 12,500 surviving English and Indian soldiers under their command. Here their guards acted on their own sense of cultural and ethnic superiority, starving their captives during the long desert march into captivity. Over 4,200 enlisted men died of starvation and mistreatment during their captivity. When the Ottoman Empire signed its armistice on October 30, 1918, and the surviving prisoners were repatriated into British hands, many remained convinced they were victims of cruel indifference on the part of their captors, who sought "'to demonstrate their victory over the British to as many of their people as possible.'"[31]

Race and War: Germany

The most vexing question for military historians seeking to examine Germany's role in World War I is determining just how the conflict helped shape the course

---

30 Erickson, *Ordered to Die*, 5–8.
31 Peter Hart, *The Great War, 1914–1918* (Profile Books, 2014), 280–288; Erickson, *Ordered to Die*, 151; Charles Townshend, *Desert Hell: The British Invasion of Mesopotamia* (The Belknap Press of Harvard University Press, 2011), 45–49, 252–53, quote on 318.

of German racial policies and related actions later in the 1930s and 1940s under the National Socialist regime. Recently this question has been complicated as historians seek a better understanding of the place of German Jews in the military and civil society between 1914 and 1918. Traditionally German Jews have been portrayed as passive observers of the war, participating insofar as society would permit them, but remaining somehow aloof and distant from the general war effort. Certainly there were individual exceptions – industrialist Walter Rathenau, the wartime chief of the KRA (*Kriegrohstoffabteilung,* the War Raw Materials Office) and chemist Fritz Haber, the dark genius developing German poison gas weapons – but the standard narrative highlighted the ambiguity of Germany's Jewish community during the war years.[32]

This benign interpretation has been overshadowed by recent historians who have discovered, that while many Jews of conscience were concerned by the war – the same true, of course, for German Protestants and Catholics – more were eager to participate and support the war as a means to display their patriotism and secular identity as legitimate members of the *Volk*. Over 100,000 Jewish men, roughly 20 percent of the total population in Germany, served in all branches of the military and in virtually every capacity. This itself is well-established, and has been offered as the primary evidence for Jewish wartime assimilation.[33] But by focusing exclusively on military service, Jews in German society remain as a distaff community, self-identifying and separate from the whole.

As is frequently the case, there is far more to the question of Jewish identity in First World War Germany than is readily apparent. As Tim Grady notes, Jews were "co-constitutive" participants in the war, joining with the larger German community to celebrate and materially support the war effort, at home, at work, at the market, and through the act of planning and conducting its most violent paroxysms.[34] From the beginning of the crisis, Jews took part in the same civic displays of patriotic support, celebrating its arrival as a moment for all Germans to take up arms to defend itself from a cabal of envious foes. Close study of this moment reveals that contrary to popular misperception, German Jews were not almost exclusively social and cultural liberals, opposed to empire and war on principle. Just like any other demographic community, Jews were scattered across

---

32 Alexander Watson, *Ring of Steel: Germany and Austria-Hungary in World War I* (Basic Books, 2014), 369–70. See also Shulamit Volkov, *Walther Rathenau: Weimar's Fallen Statesman* (Yale University Press, 2012); Daniel Charles, *Master Mind: The Rise and Fall of Fritz Haber, the Nobel Laureate Who Launched the Age of Chemical Warfare* (Ecco, 2005); and L. F. Haber, *The Poisonous Cloud: Chemical Warfare in the First World War* (Clarendon Press, 1986).
33 Watson, *Ring of Steel*, 86–87, 369–70.
34 Tim Grady, *A Deadly Legacy: German Jews and the Great War* (Yale University Press, 2017), 3.

the political spectrum, with no shortage of both conservatives and ultra-rightists. Again, Grady notes: "Differences when they occurred – at least until the war's final months – were rarely about the ethics of Germany's war effort, but were rather about the most appropriate method of achieving a German victory."[35] This point is further reinforced when one considers how the majority of Jews – not only those in the highest economic and social circles – experienced life on the home front in a time of total war. Jews stood in the same queues, suffered the same privations, witnessed the same casualty lists, and experienced the same petty inconveniences as their neighbors. They also voiced the same muttered complaints and engaged in the same minor larcenies to meet their basic needs, but at no time was there a collective rejection of the war and its aims until the very last days, when they were certainly part of the larger whole of civil society confronting defeat.

German Jews shared one other experience with the whole of society during the war. As the war began, no small number of Eastern European Jews, some affluent travelers, but many more transient migrants making their way to the United States through Hamburg and other sea ports, were trapped in Germany. Fear of this group as a potential foundation for spying, espionage, and civil unrest spread rapidly, including within among German Jews. From their perspective these outsiders, many observing the Orthodox tradition, were cast as "double outsiders"; not only were they Russian aliens, they also practiced what was, to the largely Reform-oriented Jews in Germany, an archaic and superstitious form of their faith. German Jews proved to be equally scurrilous in their attacks on the trapped migrants, deriding them as primitive, filthy paupers; a potentially dangerous class of outsiders who threatened to overwhelm the communities where they resided. While ultimately almost all of the internees were repatriated back to Russia, the ease with which German Jews showered them with the same vitriolic disgust expressed in the most anti-Semitic channels was not only disturbing. It also reveals how far this community had gone to express itself as members of the national compact.[36] As it turns out, the Eastern Front would become the place where the issues of race and identity would continue to affect German perceptions of the war and their own place in the world. This was not a gradual process. In 1914, many Germans viewed the Russian East as a landscape teeming with Slavs, who were to be kept at arm's length if at all possible. And when Russia left the war on December 3, 1917, German forces occupied an immense portion of territory including Russian Poland, Byelorussia, Ukraine, and the Baltic regions of Lithuania, Latvia, and

---

35 *Ibid.*, 4.
36 *Ibid*, 60–61.

Estonia. Regardless, no true sense of *lebensraum* or a *drang nach osten* really existed in the German political and cultural imagination outside the fantasies of the most strident Pan-Germanists. Yet twenty-seven years later, the armies went marching deep into the Russian interior to fulfill such ambitions. The question is how did the earlier war in the East influence and change German perceptions of Russian and in turn facilitate a second war of conquest and ethnic cleansing.

Historians have taken this topic up in recent years, to different, yet equally provocative, conclusions. On the one hand, where World War I's origins were rooted in nationalism and great power politics, its conclusion was determined by powerful ideological forces that overturned the traditional order. Expressed most virulently in Soviet Communism and German National Socialism, the ensuing contest over the next generation left Central and Eastern Europe in ruins, the regions transformed into "bloodlands" through the actions of the two extreme violent ideological regimes bracketing the area.[37] In his study of German anti-Semitism, *Hitler's Willing Executioners: Ordinary Germans and the Holocaust*, Daniel Jonah Goldhagen examined the German war in the East 1914 to 1918 as just another case of incipient German anti-Semitism and anti-Slavism being expressed through conquest. In Goldhagen's view of a continuity of German race hatred, the First World War is linked directly to the Teutonic Knights invasion of the Baltic region in the fourteenth century. While lacking any immediate persecution of Russian and Polish Jews on the scale of what would follow in the Nazi era, Germans were in turns disgusted and horrified by their encounters with Eastern Jews, making future atrocities in the East easier.[38]

Klaus Theweleit offers a similar outlook in his two volume study of the gendered and racial cultural aspects of fascism, *Male Fantasies*. In the first volume, Theweleit uses eight German Great War veterans' memoirs and letters as evidence for his thesis that Nazism was rooted in misogyny and violence. Accordingly the war in Russia fueled latent anti-Semitic tendencies through individual real and imagined encounters rooted in blood, sex, and violence. These feelings were in turn transformed into a masculinized ideal worldview predicated on war and racial purity.[39]

Less overtly provocative, yet more carefully nuanced, is the perspective offered by Gabriel Vejas Liulevicius in his book *War Land on the Eastern Front: Culture, National Identity, and German Occupation in World War I*. Liulevicius

---

37 Timothy Snyder, *Bloodlands: Europe Between Hitler and Stalin* (Basic Books, 2010).

38 Daniel Jonah Goldhagen, *Hitler's Willing Executioners: Ordinary Germans and the Holocaust* (Vintage, 1997).

39 Klaus Theweleit, *Male Fantasies, Volume I: Women, Floods, Bodies, History*, trans. Erica Carter et al. (University of Minnesota Press, 1987).

examines how the *Oberbefehlshaber der gesamten Deutschen Streitkräfte im Osten* (Supreme Commander of All German Forces in the East), or *Ober Ost*, administered the territories of Belorussia, Lithuania, Latvia, and East Poland under its control. While extremely informative in terms of breaking down the harsh administration of the region by the German military, more telling is how Liulevicius deconstructs the German soldiers' perceptions of the East and how they in turn informed future perspectives of the region. Many Germans were indeed shocked by their first encounter with the Russian peasant and the land. While many Germans did generally shared a self-perception of cultural and materially superior to the Russian Slav, they were not prepared for the sheer debasement of serf poverty they encountered in the occupied East. Likewise first encounters with local Jewish communities, who observed a far more orthodox form of Judaism than that witnessed in Germany proper, were dramatic exercises in crafting identity. When combined with the feelings of awe and amazement at the primeval pine and aspen forests and swamps of Byelorussia, the Ukraine, and the Baltic regions, and, Liulevicius claims, the average German altered his view of the East. Before the war there was a relatively normal environment inhabited by Slavs who were only superficially different from their Western neighbors. Replacing this view was a perceived wilderness of vast opportunity, inhabited by a people so different from the "normative" Western European. In what some Germans saw as the reasonable explanation, the Slavs living there had to be biologically inferior. While not yet considered worthy of annihilation, the German viewed the conquered rural Slavs as ideal chattel labor to work the land on behalf of their new German masters.[40]

Neighboring *OberOst* was occupied Russian Poland. Here the territory was divided into two administrative sectors: the Austrian K.u.K. Military Government in Poland and the German Imperial Government-General of Warsaw. Described by scholars as the "forgotten occupation," the German administration of Poland stands out for the efforts undertaken by the region's Governor General, General Hans Hartwig von Beseler, to create the foundation for a friendly Polish client state. Rather than prepare the area for post-war assimilation and annexation, von Beseler's administration legitimized Polish autonomy and identity through educational reform, unfettered cultural expression, and support for local Polish sovereignty through the election of city councils and a cadre army. As historian Jesse Kaufman observes, this all served two purposes. First, "the 'education' (*Erziehung*), as Beseler liked to put it – of the Congress Kingdom's Poles in the

---

40 Vejas Liulevicius, *War Land on the Eastern Front: Culture, National Identity and German Occupation in World War I* (Cambridge University Press, 2000), 162.

practice of self-government." The second objective "was the creation of an institutional foundation during the war for the state that would be built on it afterward."[41] While von Beseler's project ultimately failed, in large part due to the extent to which the German military exploited the region's economy in the name of the war effort, it represents a key departure from what has become an active trend to link German misconduct in the First World War with the aberrations and atrocities of the next war. Not only is it curious that a German military careerist promoted creating a new Polish state, but that it could prove compatible with an Imperial Germany which included millions of Poles as citizens in Prussia and Silesia. No doubt affected by his own *bürgerliche* upbringing in the suburbs of Berlin, von Beseler's ambitions for a client – albeit independent – Polish state as a buffer against future Russian or Austrian conflict reveals that Wilsonian ideas of self-determination were not an exclusively American progressive ideal.[42] The question for historians and scholars is if the vision for Polish independent status could survive in the face of a more aggressive pan-nationalist strategy linked to the *Ober Ost* plan, given the not unlikely prospect of German victory in early 1918.

While these historical interpretations offer different levels of nuance in their theories of German perception of the East, the inescapable conclusion is that the majority of German soldiers active in the East harbored racialized perspectives of the indigenous Slavic people and the land they occupied. The collapse of November 1918 did not signal an end to German ambitions in the East. For the next three years, a host of paramilitary *Freikorps* companies fought throughout the Baltic region and Poland, either on behalf of the local governments or to promote independent agendas in the region. After 1921, a sizable number of these *Freikorps* men cast their lot with various conservative parties, including the National Socialists. As we will examine in the next chapter, the views created in the Great War would mature into a far more sinister and annihilative plan of racial exceptionalism.

Conclusion

In his 2014 book, *The World's War: Forgotten Soldiers of Empire*, historian David Olusoga presents an interesting assessment of the place of race and ethnicity in the constructed memory of the First World War within the English-speaking

---

41 Jesse Kaufman, *Elusive Alliance: The German Occupation of Poland in World War I* (Harvard University Press, 2015), 4.
42 *Ibid.*, 23–24, 32–33.

world. "Empire, colonialism, race and multiple theatres of war were defining features of this war," he writes. "Yet, bizarrely, the First World War has a unique characteristic that has – among other consequences – come to *submerge* the war's multinational, multi-ethnic, multiracial dimensions."[43] The post-war generation's obsession with the so-called "literary war" – the deeply emotional, ironic war preserved in memoir and poetic form – quickly overtook the memory of the war's globalist context to construct a narrative privileging the sacrifice and slaughter of a generation of Europe's white sons for an ignoble cause. Unmentioned in this view are both the racialized imperative inherent in the literary war narrative and the extent to which it has become the vehicle by which so many recent efforts to understand or portray the war have been predicated on establishing the contours of modern gender identity and the perquisites of masculinity. One need only look at the late 1980s BBC comedy series *Blackadder Goes Forth* for evidence of this preference for gendered narrative. Critically well-received at the time, the Blackadder treatment of the Western Front is entirely a white European, primarily Anglocentric, one. Where other European parties appear, they are punchlines to jokes validating crude English stereotypes about other ethnicities (including Scots and Irish participants in the British experience). Viewers are left with the perspective that the First World War was a horrible conflict that consumed the flower of European manhood, with no clue as to the international and multi-racial character of the war.

And yet, while the First World War does stand out as a landmark moment in gender studies and modernity, this focus is to a degree misleading. By overlooking the war's impact on racial and ethnic identity and the realization of political power by many in the non-Western world residing within the sphere of imperialized subjects, we lose the opportunity to create a more complete and informed narrative of 1914 and its global meaning. This is a multi-layered narrative, in which racial ideology and politics served many concomitant roles. From the European perspective, concepts about racial hierarchies, and the networks of privileges and subordinations inherent in them, served multiple roles. Existing status quos of Western dominance were preserved in the face of massive existential upheaval, a process that also validated the presumed socio-biological imperatives that would continue to define national identity for both noble and insidious purposes in the decades following the war. If the entire concept of race was established to validate a self-serving, global hegemony of Western European material, intellectual, and social privilege, then it is only natural that this construct would be employed to preserve their primacy. Imperialism as a world system exerted total cognitive

---

43 David Olusoga, *The World's War: Forgotten Soldiers of Empire* (Head of Zeus, 2014), 39.

and material influence on the primary antagonists in 1914. It existed to benefit and sustain the Great Powers economically and politically, at home and abroad. Even as it sustained the West, it imposed an all-encompassing racial calculus on its practitioners and subjects, founded in white supremacy and expressed in hyper-nationalist ideology. Racism, both in its expression and the push-back against it, was central to the First World War.

And yet, even as the Great Powers drew upon the material and human reserves of their vast imperial networks, they set in motion forces that ultimately destroyed their claim to global power. It is a mistake to presume this was an immediate outcome of the war. Even as the successful Allied and Associated Powers gathered to dictate the terms of their victory over Germany at Versailles, the appeals of those non-white populations who had given so much during the war for recognition, self-determination, and respect were ignored. Victory belonged to Europeans (and, by extension, Americans and the white English Dominions), not everyone else. And even as the war saw the dismantling of empires in Central and Eastern Europe and the Mideast, it reinforced the political and economic primacy of the United Kingdom and France. Here empire proved to be a critical adjunct to the success of the *Metropole*, and its own justification for expansion at the expense of the losers.

A different fate awaited the three European empires – Germany, Austria-Hungary, and Russia – after the war. Here the power of ethnic identity and self-determination was asserted as justification for the creation of a patchwork quilt of new, small nation-states to take the place of the defeated dynasties. By redrawing the political map of Europe, however, the victors took shortcuts that failed to satisfy the desires of the successor states for full ethnic autonomy. The flawed exercise at Versailles left unresolved issues of nationalism and ethnocentrism that would fester throughout the interwar years. So long as the West enjoyed material prosperity, many grievances – real and imagined – could be ignored. But as the global depression took hold in the early 1930s, ethnic grievance gained new appeal in the hands of racist and nationalist demagogues throughout Europe, even in those states that successfully resisted their dark siren's call. From the historian's perspective, this coming storm of ethnic and racial hatred would eclipse the First World War's own experiences and legacies – at least until recently. Going forward, one can only hope that by giving the story of race and World War I its proper due, we can obtain a greater and better understanding of the twentieth century – and beyond – as a whole.

6 Race and Gender on the Eastern Front and in the Pacific War

Introduction

For decades after the fact, American accounts of the Second World War have placed the conflict within the context of a noble crusade by the Western democracies and two particularly vicious ideologies – National Socialism and Japanese militarism – that presented an existential crisis to stability and the established political order. Even as the greatest savagery in the two global theaters was directed against nations – China and the Soviet Union – residing on the fringes of Western society, for years the historical emphasis on the war was on the heroic struggle to push Germany and Japan back across their vast empires and to crush their armies and populations beneath the massive industrial weight of the Anglo-American alliance. Other nations, including France and the Soviet Union, involved in this great crusade served either as unfortunate victims needing rescue or as side players whose contributions helped tie the Axis down until the English-speaking powers finished the job.

Not only is this narrative generally flawed and incorrect, it also limits the impact of racial and gendered factors in setting the terms and conditions of the Second World War. This chapter is the first of two devoted to the conflict and identifying how race and gender established the Second World War as a uniquely violent conflict that placed greater emphasis on race (and to a similar extent gender) as a *raison d'être* for extirpative violence. Unlike the First World War, civilian populations were acceptable targets for destruction, as witnessed in the Nazi regime's war against the Jews and Slavic peoples in the Eastern Front, and the Anglo-American bomber campaigns against Germany and Japan. The role of anti-Semitism and racism against Slavs continues to be evaluated even long after these factors have been identified and accepted by historians. And while arguments for political expediency have been made and continue to be offered for the Western Allies' actions against Japan, there should be little debate that their scope was also determined in large part by existing racial prejudices and antagonisms. This chapter will thus consider some aspects of the Eastern Front and the Pacific Theater and how the histories of these theaters continue to evolve, even now, nearly 80 years after the war began.

This comparison may no doubt prove to be troubling for some. Placing the Nazi-Soviet war of annihilation alongside the American war in the Pacific against the expansionist and aggressive Japanese Empire may prompt accusations of uneven and unwarranted comparisons – how could any rational observer even

https://doi.org/10.1515/9783110477467-006

contemplate comparing the genocidal racism of the Nazi regime with the more noble war of liberation waged by the United States in the Pacific? And said critics are, on the surface at least, correct in concerns. Certainly the American war in the Pacific was never intended as a war of conflict and extermination in the same context as that pursued by the Germans in the Soviet Union. Nonetheless there do remain several uncomfortable similarities rhetoric of race and the savage nature of combat that are long overdue for consideration. As historian James Weingartner has observed, "The United States and Nazi Germany each regarded at least one of its multiple adversaries in a manner encouraging, if not dictating, a higher degree of brutality and disregard for the laws of war than that shown to more favored enemies."[1] The common denominator in the two cases, Weingartner considers, were the ingrained codes of racial identity and privilege – and their companions, racist intolerance and prejudice – that existed in the United States and Germany. Even though the two nations were bitter foes in the conflict, they shared common outlooks on whiteness and the imperative for dehumanizing their foe that are uncomfortably close.

Racial intolerance alone does not adequately explain the nature of the two conflicts, as the overwhelming weight of recent historiography shows. Western historians have long divided the Second World War in Europe into two distinct conflicts. On the one side, well-illuminated by access to archives, memoirs, interviews, and other primary accounts, is the Western Theater. Here the main protagonists – Germany, Italy, France, England, and the United States – engaged in a bitter, but nevertheless conventional, struggle pitting the democracies against Fascist militarism. In juxtaposition to this conflict was the Nazi-Soviet War – a bitter conflict charged with vitriolic racial undertones pitting two mortal ideological enemies against each other in a contest to the death. Yet even here, amidst the cold reality of over 20 million Soviet deaths, the fighting was divided until recently into two separate wars – the racial atrocities of the Nazi regime, enacted through its *SS* agents and the "clean" war of the outnumbered *Wehrmacht*. According to this narrative, the German Army, obeying with reservations, invaded the Soviet Union at the order of an insane Adolf Hitler. While the war acquired a brutal cast, the *Wehrmacht* managed to avoid being caught up in the worse crimes of the Nazi regime, and fought a noble, if doomed, fight against the collective material weight of the Allies. Loyal to its oath to the end, the German armed forces waged

---

1 James Weingartner, "War Against Subhumans: Comparisons Between the German War Against the Soviet Union and the American War Against Japan, 1941–1945," *The Historian* 58 (March 1996), 557–73, 557.

a skillful defense until the last days, unaware of the greater crimes committed by the *SS* regime in Russia and Poland.

This idyllic narrative served throughout the Cold War as the conventional wisdom of the Second World War in Europe.[2] As it turns out, almost every aspect of this contrived story is false and misleading. Not only did the *Wehrmacht* leadership know about Hitler's plans for occupie Russia and Poland long before the fact, they actively sought out a chance to enlist the Army and other armed services in his warped crusade. German generals did not merely abrogate the rules of war in the Eastern Front, they also ordered their men to participate in some of the worst atrocities in the field. Likewise German enlisted soldiers conducted a vicious war of brutality against their Russian enemies, their actions fueled by years of racial indoctrination and education. In essence, the Nazi war in the East was one of annihilation, motivated and waged largely on the basis of racial identity.[3]

Just as race and gender heightened the savagery of fighting on Europe's Eastern Front, so too did intransigent cultural constructions make combat in the Asian-Pacific War equally barbaric. Both theaters saw death tolls rising into the many millions of combatants and civilians alike. Indeed, hevastness of Pacific Ocean was not unlike the vastness of the western Russian plains. While the two climates were dramatically different, the effects on the fighting men's morale, health, and combat power were likewise similar in degree, if not kind. Not unlike Nazi Germany, the deeply entrenched racism and chauvinism drove the Japanese to commit innumerable atrocities against other Asians, as well as Caucasians from the United States and the British Empire. The feelings of racial hatred among Americans and Europeans directed at the Japanese proved to be no less potent as motivators. No less than the Eastern Front, ideological distinctions pitted the United States and the United Kingdom with their shared white supremacy and imperial heritage against the Japanese, who in turn firmly believed in their own racial supremacy, remained loyal to the emperor, and adhered to a warrior's code of behavior called *bushidō*.

How and why the belligerent nations appropriated race and gender to help secure victory in the Asian-Pacific War is considered in the second half of this chapter. First, it summarizes the pre-war contexts in Japan from 1868 and the United States from 1898 until the 1930s when these nations charted collision course with each other because of tensions on the Asian mainland and in the western Pacific Ocean. Next the issue of Japanese atrocities on the Asian mainland

---

2 For more details, see Ronald Smelser and Edward J. Davies II, *The Myth of the Eastern Front: The Nazi-Soviet War in American Popular Culture* (Cambridge University Press, 2008).
3 Jeff Rutherford, *Combat and Genocide on the Eastern Front: The German Infantry's War, 1941–1944* (Cambridge University Press, 2014), 376.

is considered. In China and Korea, race and gender combined with sexuality to cause tragic outcomes resembling the Germans and Soviets in Eastern Europe. The final section illuminates Japanese and American wartime conceptions of the superior "self" versus the dehumanized "other," closing with analyses of the Battles of Tarawa and Okinawa as examples of racialized warmaking.

Setting the Context – Planning for Operation Barbarossa

In his book *War of Annihilation: Combat and Genocide on the Eastern Front, 1941*, Holocaust historian Geoffrey Megargee establishes a new narrative paradigm through which to assess the June 22, 1941 Nazi invasion of Russia. From the onset of planning for the invasion in the Summer of 1940, Megargee uncovers a distinct pattern of German Army (*Heer*) complicity in the forthcoming brutal and criminal campaign of organized murder of Russian civilians and prisoners of war. As the *OKH* (*Oberkommando des Heeres* – Army High Command) planning staff began outlining the parameters and objectives for Operation *Barbarossa*, expectations for swift German victory ran high. As Megargee notes, this was driven in no small part by a shared racist outlook:

> A fair amount of racism also colored the officers' views: they tended to share Hitler's opinion that the Soviet Union was a state of Slavs dominated by Jews, which could hardly be expected to field an effective force. In comparison with the French, whom the Wehrmacht had just defeated with such apparent ease, the Red Army seemed an easy target. Most generals agreed with Hitler that "a campaign against Russia would be a sand-table exercise in comparison [with the western campaign]."[4]

Such attitudes were hardly mere examples of the mounting hubris attendant to German success in arms in the opening years of the Second World War. They reveal strong tendencies toward dehumanizing the Russian people that exposed an underlying cultural currents in German public thought since at least the mid-nineteenth century. As previously noted in Chapter 5, this broad tendency was further honed and shaped by the experiences of millions of German soldiers and young officers in the First World War, where they encountered Russia and its people for the first time. After Versailles, many officers in the fledgling *Reichswehr* were further influenced by their experiences in the Ukraine as observers or participants in secret joint exercises. This process resulted in the construction of

---

4 Geoffrey P. Megargee, *War of Annihilation: Combat and Genocide on the Eastern Front, 1941* (Rowman & Littlefield, 2006), 24.

marked racist perspectives of Russian incompetence versus German efficiency, coupled with a general anti-Semitism that likewise became institutionalized thought within the German military.[5] This bifurcated spectrum of superior "self" and the inferior "other" was not dissimilar to previous conflicts, nor of future conflicts. In the case of Nazism, however, it played out in destruction and death truly massive in scope and scale.

When the humanity of a projected foe is devalued and marginalized, it becomes easier to project their abuse and misuse in wartime. In the case study of the Nazi invasion of Russia, this is manifested at an early date. As a matter of ideology enacted as policy, Operation *Barbarossa* was an effort to fulfill Adolf Hitler's designs at expanding German territory in the East – acquiring *Lebensraum* to meet Germany's agricultural and expansionist needs. From August 1940, German military and economic planners composed a series of studies and reports that hinged upon the ruthless exploitation of Russian agriculture to fill German granaries – regardless of the effects on Russian and Ukrainian civilians. By February 1941, these proposals coalesced around the so-called "Hunger Plan," the brainchild of future Reich Minister of Food Herbert Backe. According to the plan, Ukrainian and Russian cities would be deliberately starved of their usual grain and meat shipments from the countryside, which would in turn be shipped to the Reich for civilian and military use. Upward of thirty million Slavs were expected to die from starvation in Backe's plan, which he argued was necessary to maintain Hitler's plan for German expansion and pan-European hegemony against Great Britain and the United States.[6]

Although never fully realized, the Hunger Plan was quickly accepted by the Nazis and *Wehrmacht* alike. From both Hitler's and Hermann Goering's perspective, the radical redistribution of food along racial lines not only fulfilled the ideological imperatives of National Socialism, it also fulfilled the immediate wartime requirements of Germany's most recent Four Year Plan. Military logisticians eagerly signed on as the plan promised to help Germany from realizing a repeat of the prior war's last years, when it's armies were subsisting on starvation rations, while civilians were collapsing in bread queues during the blockade. As the Reich's economic overlords planned their rape of Soviet land for German

---

5 David Stahel, "Radicalizing Warfare: The German Command and the Failure of Operation Barbarossa," in Alex J. Kay, et al., eds., *Nazi Policy on the Eastern Front, 1941: Total War, Genocide, and Radicalization* (University of Rochester Press, 2012), 19–44, 22; and George M. Kren and Leo Rappaport, *The Holocaust and the Crisis of Human Behavior*, rev. ed. (Holmes & Meier, 1994), 34, 37.
6 Lizzie Collingham, *The Taste of War: World War II and the Battle for Food* (Penguin Books, 2011), 35–37.

Figure 6.1: "Porträt Staatssekretär *Herbert Backe* in Uniform als *SS*-Obergruppenführer mit Mappe an Schreibtisch sitzend." State Secretary Herbert Backe in the uniform of an *SS*-Obergruppenführer, seated at desk with portfolio.
Source: © BArch, Bild 183-J02034.

benefit, the *Wehrmacht* received a new set of rules of engagement that were far different from those in place in the West.[7]

In the Spring of 1941, Hitler addressed his generals to outline the basic conditions of war in the East. Foremost the war was to be a campaign of extermination directly against the entire Soviet system which he saw as a criminal conspiracy. Therefore its leaders, including commissars and Party members were to be killed outright. Moreover any resistance – no matter how passive or measured – would be met with brutal responses. The war with the Soviet Union was to be unlike any in Germany's recent memory, as Omer Bartov outlines in his seminal book, *Hitler's Army: Soldiers, Nazis, and War in the Third Reich*:

> The German army invaded the Soviet Union equipped with a set of orders which clearly defined "Barbarossa" as a war essentially different from any previous campaign, a "war of ideologies" in which there were to be "no comrades in arms." It is the fundamental contradiction in terms encapsulated in what have come to be known as the "criminal orders" that is so essential to our understanding of the perversion of law and discipline in the Russian campaign. By legalizing murder, robbery, torture, and destruction, these instructions put

---

7 *Ibid.*, 38–39.

the moral basis of martial law, and thereby of military discipline, on its head. The army did not simply pretend not to notice the criminal actions of the regime, it positively ordered its own troops to carry them out, and was distressed when breaches in discipline prevented their more efficient execution. . . . Put differently, the Wehrmacht's legal system adapted itself to the so-called Nazi *Weltanschauung*, with all its social-darwinist, nihilist, expansionist, anti-Bolshevik, and racist attributes.[8]

From the start then, the *Wehrmacht* played the role an active partner in the forthcoming atrocities – not by accident or happenstance, but by design and calculation. In support of Hitler's address, Field Marshall Walther von Brauchitsch, the head of *OKW* (*Oberkommando des Wehrmacht* – Armed Forces high command), issued a series of orders and memos further outlining *Wehrmacht* rules in the East. This order accepted the participation of *SD* (*Sicherheitsdienst* – *SS Security Department*) "Special Detachments" (*Einsatzgruppen*) in the rear echelons of the advancing *Wehrmacht* forces. It also subordinated army *Ordnungspolizei* (order police – support staff to the regular military police) directly to *SS* oversight in identifying and liquidating "Judeo-bolshevik partisans" in the rear areas. In numbers and activity, these *Wehrmacht* personnel, many of them reservists who had worked in law enforcement in peacetime, would outnumber the *SS-Einsatzagruppen* in the East.

Other orders followed that indict the *Wehrmacht's* conduct in the Eastern Front. A May 13, 1941 *OKH* order stripped army units of the normal restraints governing violence against civilian populations, noting that the "special nature" of the Russian enemy would likely translate into constant war against civilian combatants. Even suspected combatants could be rounded up and executed; similarly, collective actions against entire communities were sanctioned. In support of this order, individual army headquarters issued supplemental memoranda and directives expressing justification for this change in the military code of ethics, often in racial terms. As Megargee cites in his book, General Erich Hoepner's own order to the armored troops under his command followed this trend:

[The war against Russia] is the old fight of the Germans against the Slavs, the defense of European culture against the Muscovite-Asiatic flood, the repulsion of Jewish Bolshevism. The goal of this fight must be the destruction of contemporary Russia and therefore must be conducted with enormous violence. Every combat action, in its conception and conduct, must be governed by the iron will to pitiless and complete annihilation of the enemy. In particular there is no mercy for the carriers of the current Russian-Bolshevik system.[9]

---

8 Omer Bartov, *Hitler's Army: Soldiers, Nazis, and War in the Third Reich* (Oxford University Press, 1992), 69–70.

9 Megargee, *War of Annihilation*, 38.

The clearest evidence of *Wehrmacht* complicity in the Nazi ideological war against "Jewish-Bolshevism" can be seen in the June 6, 1941 *OKW* order entitled "Guidelines for the Treatment of Political Commissars." Here all commissars were singled out for immediate execution upon capture – a patently illegal act which, both Megargee and Bartov note, stirred no complaint or resistance among the *Heer* general officers. After first reviewing the order, they willingly passed it on, as Megargee notes, in writing to the Corps level, from which it was disseminated orally to subordinate officers down the chain of command.[10]

A last area which has been generally overlooked by historians is the mistreatment of Soviet prisoners of war. In 1941 alone, the Germans captured over 3,350,000 Soviet soldiers, of whom over two million died, either by execution by the *SS* and *Heer* or from malnutrition and disease, by February 1942. While noted as an inexcusable tragedy and criminal act, the onus for the treatment of Soviet prisoners has generally been laid on the Nazi system itself, with the *Wehrmacht* avoiding any responsibility for what occurred. Scholarship by Megargee and Wolfram Wette highlights the *Wehrmacht* leadership's calculated role in authorizing and participating in the mistreatment of Soviet prisoners. Expressed simply, the *OKW*'s planning staff understood from the onset of the war that the Soviet prisoner was inferior in status and utility than their Western counterparts; hence they would be subject to a lower standard of care. This, combined with the "Commissar Order," amounted to a death warrant for the Soviet prisoner of war. Deliberately denied adequate food and shelter, subject to overwork under the direct oversight of German soldiers, and the target of callous handling and abuse by German *Heer* – not *SS* – soldiers, Soviet prisoners died in the thousands daily from starvation and disease. Overlooked in all of this was one basic fact in 1941 that the Soviet prisoners fell under the direct control and oversight of the *Wehrmacht* in the field. The responsibility for such criminal treatment resides therefore not only with the planning staffs of *OKH* and *OKW*, it also extends throughout the entire organization of the German *Heer* in the Eastern Front.

Despite the fact that *Barbarossa* stalled in December 1941, the war in the East continued to consume German lives, energy, and resources for the next three years, ultimately resulting in the destruction of the Nazi regime. Just as the level of combat ferocity increased, so too did the mutual dehumanization and brutality shown by both sides toward the other. A savage war of no quarter on the front lines was matched by an even more vicious campaign waged behind the lines between partisans and security forces. Fueled by mutual ideological hatred on

---

10 *Ibid.*, 38–39.

Figure 6.2: "Sowjetunion, Süd.- Don/Stalingrad, vor Stalingrad.- Kolonne kriegsgefangener sowjetischer Soldaten auf dem Marsch; PK 694." A group of captured Soviet Red Army soldiers, Don Region near Stalingrad, Summer 1942.
Source: © BArch, Bild 101I-218-0514-30A.

both sides, the escalating levels of violence exerted an oppressive weight on the moral centers of all fighting men engaged in the East. In his work, Omer Bartov credits this climate of hateful war without end as transforming the operational and qualitative edge of the German soldier. The physical vicissitudes of war in the East – bad weather, implausible distance, and their effect on German war material and men – combined with the intangible effects of criminal behavior toward civilians and prisoners to degrade the *Landser*'s effectiveness. By late 1944, the German soldiers serving in the East found themselves hopelessly lost in a moral quagmire of fear, doubt, and hopelessness, betrayed by their own leadership who had led them there in their own warped sense of honor and duty to an insane regime.

The corrosive effect of participating in criminal activity against civilians manifested itself long before the collapse of Army Group Center, though. As *Heer* infantry regiments advanced into Belarus and Ukraine in 1941, temporary detachment in support of *Einsatzkommando* units occurred regularly. Christopher Browning notes in his classic study, *Ordinary Men*, direct participation in the actions targeting Jewish communities was not mandatory, nor was refusal to join in the killing considered a serious breach of military discipline.[11] Yet many thousands of German infantrymen willingly took part in the ensuing massacres and cleaning-up operations, to the point of executing wounded survivors as they struggled to escape the scene.[12] More savagery awaited *Heer* soldiers. When presented with opportunities to enrich themselves at the expense of their victims, many willfully took advantage of their situation. Some took to looting Jewish homes and businesses, even as they were clearing out the occupants. Others looted jewelry, money, and clothing from the dead piled in mass graves. And there were those who used the opportunity to commit wanton sexual violence against female prisoners, Jewish and Gentile alike. Of course the relative absence of documentation, along with the lack of eyewitnesses (let alone victims or participants), makes this a difficult topic for study. Yet there is significant testimony and evidence to not only suggest that sexual exploitation, forced prostitution, rape, and murder took place along the periphery of the Holocaust in the East, but that it was a regular practice for some of the more depraved soldiers and officers. One factor that stands out is the relative lack of prosecutions for sexual assaults within the *Wehrmacht*. Offenders escaped sanction so long as their activity did not have an adverse effect on discipline or the prosecution of the war. As Waitman Wade Beorn concludes, "At the local level, sexuality in the East seems to have operated under a moral code different from that observed in western Europe. German civil authorities (as well as military men) frequently abused alcohol to excess and participated in depraved sexual acts outside the pale of acceptability in the West, where 'fraternization' with racially equal and more familiar partners was easier and more widespread."[13]

The vast distances and condition of the Russian transportation network combined to create another dilemma for the invading Germans – the collapse of reliable subsistence supply for units at or near the front lines. Overconfidence and lack of logistical insight set the stage for the rapid decline in *Heer* discipline as infantry companies took part in systematic plundering expeditions as they marched deeper into the Russian interior. While such actions were initially forbidden by officers, a blind eye was turned when Jewish farms and towns were targeted.[14] Within a short time, however, even these restrictions were lifted as it became apparent that the advancing *Wehrmacht* would need to rely on its own

---

11 Christopher R. Browning, *Ordinary Men: Reserve Police Battalion 101 and the Final Solution in Poland* (HarperPerennial, 1992), 57, 74–75, 170–72.

12 Waitman Wade Beorn, *Marching into Darkness: The Wehrmacht and the Holocaust in Belarus.* (Harvard University Press, 2014), 2–3; and Rutherford, *Combat and Genocide*, 5–6.

13 *Ibid.*, 161–172, quote on 172.

14 Jeff Rutherford, "The Radicalization of German Occupation Policies: The *Wirtschaftssabt Ost* and the 121st Infantry Division in Pavlovsk, 1941," in Alex J. Kay, Jeff Rutherford, and David

wits and coercive force to feed itself. In fact, this sanctioned looting was in accord with Nazi plans for the invasion and occupation of the East. Field requisitions of food and livestock minimized the burden for German farmers and citizens, while transferring it not only to the Russian farmers who were the immediate target of looters, but also to Russian and Polish urban populations. At least farmers could subsist on the potatoes and turnips they raised as fodder for their livestock. Urban folk were so dependent upon external sources of food that they were essentially consigned to starvation in the coming winter.[15] As *Barbarossa's* objectives slipped away, the German military expanded its rapacious hold: "In order to ensure the combat efficiency of its troops, the Wehrmacht confiscated winter clothes and boots, commandeered dwellings, and requisitioned all of the food it could lay its hands on. . . . While the advance of the Wehrmacht in the summer and autumn of 1941 led to hunger throughout northwestern Russia, the region's cities literally starved during the winter."[16]

Wilhelmine and *Reichwehr* Antecendents for German Military Excesses

Studies of the *Wehrmacht*'s conduct and record generally treat the organization as residing in a vacuum. That is to say, there is little effort made to establish a cultural continuity with its predecessor, the Weimar *Reichswehr*, or its less recent antecedent, the Wilhelmine army. In recent years, however, closer attention has been paid to the cultural identities shaped in peace and war that governed the outcome reached in 1941 by the generals serving in the *Wehrmacht*, and in turn was filtered down among junior officers and career non-commissioned personnel. Accordingly the German military was predisposed to accepting the extreme racial hierarchy espoused by the National Socialists, and would become more willing and pliant participants in the planning and execution of Operation *Barbarossa*'s most extreme elements.

In the 1890s, the officer corps was governed by its association with the more conservative and authoritarian elements of German society. Opposed to the Social Democrats and more liberal political parties, the officer corps' stance defended the Hohenzollern dynasty – and thus, the new German state – from the proletarian

---

Stahel, eds., *Nazi Policy on the Eastern Front, 1941: Total War, Genocide, and Radicalization* (University of Rochester Press, 2012), 103–54, 135.

15 *Ibid.*, 137–138.

16 *Ibid.*, 146.

mob bent upon its replacement with a socialist state. In this way the army reflected the general fears of German conservatives. It also followed the conservative lead in expressing an absolute distrust of German Jews. Since its establishment, the German Empire promoted a general tolerance toward Jews in public life, defining them as a religion, not a race. Tolerance was hardly total or complete, however. While German Jews sought to craft a secularized identity for themselves, many of their neighbors continued to hang to the stereotypes of their parents and grand-parents. This was certainly the case among the *Junker* families of Northeastern Prussia that provided the raw stock of officer cadets for the armed services. Under their direction, the army instituted and maintained a personnel policy excluding Jews from joining the regular forces as a career officer. As Wolfram Wette shows in his synthetic study of the *Wehrmacht*'s conduct in the Hitler regime, this policy followed the wishes of Kaiser Wilhelm II, who opposed Jewish presence in the military as an assault on the "Christian morals" he recognized at the core of an officer's identity.[17] In the view of the Hohenzollern Court, Jews were, with very rare exceptions, unfit for direct introduction to the Royal presence because they were accorded responsibility for the liberal, democratic, and socialist opposition. Moreover, the stereotypes held that Jews were poorly suited for military service by their very nature. As bourgeois members of the stolid middle class, Jews were too soft and effeminate for the army – they made better lawyers, shopowners, and artists. Yet as Wette observes, this prejudice did have its limits. By 1911, for instance, 26 German Jews obtained commissions in the German army after they converted to Lutheranism. Religion, not race, was the key to the general German definition of Jewish identity. Once the religious factor was resolved, Jews could readily assimilate into German society in the Wilhelmine period.[18]

The General Staff was surprised then by the rush of young Jewish men to military service in the First World War. Nearly 100,000 Jews served in the German military during the war, of which 12,000 were killed and 35,000 were decorated for valor. The extent and quality of Jewish wartime military service completely refuted of the Wilhelmine standard – a point not lost on those Jews who served, who saw their participation as further evidence of their German identity and cit-izenship. Nevertheless, rightist anti-Semitic propaganda continued to castigate German Jews as unfit for service and untrustworthy. Jews continued to face preju-dice thereafter even as they were in uniform, being denied promotion and access to the officer corps until the last possible moment.[19]

---

17 Wolfram Wette, *The Wehrmacht: History, Myth, Reality*, trans. Deborah Lucas Schneider (Harvard University Press, 2006), 54.
18 *Ibid.*, 34.
19 Tim Grady, *A Deadly Legacy: German Jews and the Great War* (Yale University Press, 2017), 73.

More pernicious was the spread of Rightist views throughout German society. According to the German Right, few Jews served (when in reality 1/5 of the German Jewish population of 1910 was in uniform); instead they allegedly reaped economic gain at the expense of the community at war. This only increased after Quartermaster General Erich Ludendorff and Field Marshal Paul von Hindenburg assumed command of the German Army in 1916. Ludendorff held strong anti-Semitic views, claiming that German Jews avoided military service (despite clear evidence to the contrary) and constituted the core of democratic opposition to the war and the monarchy. His rage was further fueled by his political advisor, Lieutenant Colonel Max Bauer. Everywhere Bauer looked, he saw conspiracy and obstruction of the war effort by German Jews, as he noted in an October 12, 1917 memorandum to Hindenburg, Ludendorff, and Kaiser Wilhelm:

> Lastly there is a huge sense of outrage at the Jews, and rightly so. If you are in Berlin and go to the Ministry of Commerce or walk down the Tauentzienstrasse, you could well believe you were in Jerusalem. Up at the front, by contrast, you hardly ever see any Jews. Virtually every thinking person is outraged that so few are called up, but nothing is done, because going after the Jews, meaning the capital that controls the press and the parliament, is impossible.[20]

Such inflammatory rhetoric from Bauer matched that of other German officers, whose rightist Nationalist identity was threatened by the efforts of the Social Democrats and other liberal parties to bring about a negotiated peace. In their opinion, since many members of the opposition were Jews, the entire movement represented an anti-German conspiracy mounted by Jews in fulfillment of their own political ambitions. Thus at an earlier point than generally accepted, German rightists began exploiting the anxieties of the general population by leveraging their own race hatred against a small Jewish minority who, save for a smaller number of activists, had actively supported the war effort.

After the end of the war, the German military received heavy sanctions in the Versailles Treaty. Denied such heavy weapons as tanks, artillery, and aircraft, the German army was limited in size and scope to a defense force of 100,000 officers and men. Those officers who remained in uniform were not only drawn from the best in wartime, many of them likewise shared the same general conservative values, including varying degrees of anti-Semitism. While some officers did speak out against the general tone of hostility characterizing rightist anti-Semitic speech during the early years of the Weimar Republic, the majority of personnel both openly supported the different Rightist parties and sympathized with the

---

20 *Ibid.*, 58.

assassins of important supporters and leaders of the Republic, including Finance Minister Matthias Erzberger and Walther Rathenau Following the direction of right-wing veterans organizations, the *Reichswehr* implemented a "no Jews allowed" policy, maintaining the "racial purity" of the armed services. Thus a decade before the accession of Adolf Hitler to power, the German armed forces imposed their own racist standards for membership. In the homogenous community of the officer corps, a general disdain for Jews became the norm, with some members harboring even harsher views that matched those espoused by the National Socialists in the 1930s. Before the *Wehrmacht* came into being in 1935, the *Reichswehr*'s officer corps was primed for accepting Hitler's directives with regard to Jews and other "*Untermenschen*."

The Effects of Nazi Ideology on the Military

By 1939, the *Wehrmacht* evolved into a force steeped in National Socialist race ideology. Many of its generals and admirals openly endorsed the Nazi regime's policies with regard to Jewish segregation and the acquisition of new space (*Lebensraum*) at the expense of Germany's neighbors to the east. Likewise the Nazi concept of the *Volksgemeinschaft* – the pure Aryan German community – appealed to many officers. Two of the military services that comprised the *Wehrmacht* – the *Kriegsmarine* (Navy) and the *Luftwaffe* (Air Force) – were small and new enough to be almost completely indoctrinated by Nazi ideology. Even in the *Heer*, the rank and file did not generally question Nazi ideology. Individual conscripts, particularly from strong religious backgrounds or traditionally socialist urban neighborhoods, may well have opposed it privately, but even here more soldiers accepted the status quo rather than stand out as troublemakers. As a result, even before June 1941, German soldiers accepted as a matter of fact the various components of Nazi ideology, including the legitimacy of Nazi race theory.

What comprised Nazi ideology? Though based primarily on the writings of Adolf Hitler in *Mein Kampf*, it was also influenced and shaped further by a number of theorists and advocates, including Joseph Goebbels, Heinrich Himmler, Alfred Rosenberg, Walther Darre, Julius Streicher, and others. While some of its aspects were linked to the revision of the Versailles Treaty, Nazism was overwhelmingly rooted in racial identity and ideology. Just as Jeffrey Herf describes the Nazi system as an exercise in *Reactionary Modernism* – that is to say, it captures and espouses traditional reaction via the methods of modern media and culture – so too was Nazi ideology a bridge between past and contemporary racial theory. By leveraging "modern" eugenicist theory and practice with "traditional" German antipathy toward Jews and Slavs, Nazi ideology imbued old-style racism with the "legitimacy" of science and modernity.[21]

Coined in Britain in the 1880s, and imported to the United States in 1904, eugenics was predicated on recent discoveries in heredity, evolution, and biological diversity. Accordingly the human race, like other animal and plant species, was subject to the laws of nature and mutation. "Bad" and "unfit" progeny – children born with physical or mental deficiencies – were the outcome of poorly considered unions between strong and weak, or two weak, bloodlines. Similarly the offspring of two different ethnic groups could also pose a danger, either as a weaker or more vital generation. Allowed to flourish these children would grow, reproduce, and ultimately threaten the future vitality of their races – either through biological degeneration, acquired imbecility, hereditary sterility, or replacement by a newer, albeit mongrelized, race. In order to prevent this, American eugenicists championed racial segregation, sterilization, and education. Nazi racialists like Walther Darre, Alfred Rosenberg, and Josef Mengele studied American eugenics and adapted its methods and practices to their own vision of a pure Aryan community. As the war progressed, Nazi eugenics became ever more violent and brutal in its practice, culminating in the wholesale extermination of perceived racial and biological threats to the German *Volk*.[22]

Despite the best efforts of *Wehrmacht* veterans and apologist historians to conceal their indoctrination, the extent to which Nazi ideology permeated the ranks of the *Heer*, *Luftwaffe*, and *Kriegsmarine* is staggering. The majority of German enlisted soldiers and junior officers – nearly 80 percent, according to Omer Bartov – came of age under the Nazi regime, and were steeped in the Party's racialized world view.[23] Since they were children, the German *Landser* were brainwashed to believe that ultimate goal of the Nazi Party was the creation of a racially-pure Greater German Reich. Any actions undertaken in pursuit of this goal, no matter how morally repugnant under conventional social standards, would be applauded and rewarded in a National Socialist Germany. Thus the arguments that German soldiers were "duped" by a few "true believers" or casually drifted into isolated cases of malfeasance are discredited by the scope of success of the Nazi educational system. If anything, the younger generation of Germans who comprised the

---

21 Jeffrey Herf, *Reactionary Modernism: Technology, Culture, and Politics in Weimar and the Third Reich* (Cambridge University Press, 1986); and Lawrence Birken, *Hitler as Philosophe: Remnants of the Enlightenment in National Socialism* (Praeger, 1995).

22 See Stefan Kuhl, *The Nazi Connection: Eugenics, American Racism, and German National Socialism* (Oxford University Press, 2002).

23 Bartov, *Hitler's Army*, 56, 109–118, 138.

recruitment pool for the *Wehrmacht* from 1938 through 1945 increasingly shared Hitler's racist message, and they sought every opportunity to put it into practice.

Figure 6.3: " In dem Judenviertel von Lemberg wirkte der Terror [das Foto zeigt deutsche Polizei] bestialisch." Jewish resident of Lvov experiences brutal humiliation at hands of German *feldpolizei* in first days of German occupation.
Source: © BArch, Bild 146-1975-073-02.

The Nazi Way of War – Racialized Conflict without End

As historians seek to classify different national approaches to warfighting, the "ways of war" usage has become a commonplace form. From "American ways of war" to "German ways of war" to "Soviet ways of war," the idiom has become a sort of short-hand for identifying warfighting methods and practices founded upon qualitative and quantitative factor unique to each case study. Such classification schemas do come under criticism as offering an ethnocentric perspective that may be biased in favor or against their subject, yet they do serve a purpose in pointing toward the individual perspectives on warfare as means to policy objectives. With this in mind, it is appropriate to identify a way of war unique to the German National Socialists. Unlike its counterparts (both national and ideological) however, the Nazi way of war was founded on the premise that warfare was a natural process among races, and as such, was a positive expression of the vitality of the *Volk*. Only through conflict could the German Aryan state flourish and prosper, either by the direct absorption of territory or by imposing its will on weaker, and less vital, ethnicities and races. If Carl von Clausewitz was correct in observing that war is policy be another means, then for Hitler and the Nazis, war was racialist policy by another means. For Hitler, the ultimate objectives of the National Socialist state were: 1) to reorder the geopolitical arena with a racially pure Germany at the apex of human society, and with the accompanying unfettered access to natural resources essential for the modern industrial state; 2) to eradicate the chief racial enemies of the *Volk*, specifically the Jew in its varying guises, including the Judeo-Bolshevik and the Judeo-Capitalist; 3) to subjugate other inferior races, including Slavs, Poles, and Africans, to the will of the Aryan nations; and 4) to rejuvenate the German *Volkgemeinschaft* through the successful prosecution of war against weaker neighbors, redressing the injustices of the Treaty of Versailles.

The only way to achieve these aims was through armed conflict, and the German generals willingly subordinated their better professional judgment and personal ethos to these warped designs of evil. When the outcome of the war finally became clear in 1944, rather than overturn Hitler, the General Staff benignly acceded to its own marginalization following the July Plot, acknowledging that the war could only end in the total annihilation of one side or the other. So intertwined were racism and conflict that one cannot be understood without the other.

The Nazi way of war also turns away from geopolitics to emphasize a total struggle between Jewry and the West. Viewed as a parasitical racial identity, Nazi ideologues and race theorists portrayed Jews as a multi-faceted threat to the vitality and power of the Aryan people – the *"Hagen"* opposition of the purer Aryan *"Siegfried."* The twin threats to Germany's ideal of European solidarity – American capitalism and Soviet Russian communism – were presented as flip sides of the same coin. The Nazis considered both systems to be dominated by Jews, bent upon imposing a Jewish hegemony on Europe and the world. The Nazis believed American capitalism to be a morally corrupting force targeting European youth as a vulnerable group, susceptible to the system's materialistic charms. Fashion, film, music, and youth-oriented culture were all the tip of the spear of an American Jewish-Capitalist effort to impose its will on Europe in the long term. While considered the more insidious threat to German National Socialist objectives, it represented a threat that more remote and out of reach of German arms. The Soviet Union, however, presented a different scale of threat and offered greater opportunity for direct action. In the Nazi lexicon, "Judeo-Bolshevism" was more than a casual insult. It reflected the beliefs of Adolf Hitler and his subordinates in a militant Jewish system aimed at creating a classless society that nevertheless would subjugate the West in a bestial occupation by subhuman Slavs and East Asians under the direction of a Jewish Bolshevik leadership.

In essence, so long as the Soviet Union existed, Western Europe lived under the shadow of war with a mongrelized society of racial inferiors inspired by the "promise" of Bolshevism, itself a system advocated, promoted, and practiced by Russia's Jewish elite. The only way to avoid being swept away in the Red flood was for Aryan Germany – the highest and purest representative of the West next to Anglo-Saxon England and the Scandinavian North – to lead the West in a crusade of annihilation in the East. If war was indeed a racial contest, then in the case of Germany versus the Soviet Union, it became a contest of survival in which only one participant could survive. Total war, in which total annihilation was the only outcome, stood as the ultimate object of Hitler's vision of racial determinism.

As Adolf Hitler's perception of racial purity as the chief object of his political vision is examined more closely, it becomes ever more clear that the War against the Jews was, in his view, the "real" war. In short, the Holocaust was both an inevitable consequence of Nazi rule and inseparable from the more "traditional" war effort sustained between 1939 to 1945. From the onset of the war on September 1, 1939, the Nazi system was bent on conducting a war of racial cleansing in the East. Even as the vaunted *Blitzkrieg* was introduced in the Polish Campaign, SD *Einsatzkommando* units, Gestapo personnel, and *Ordnungspolizei* battalions purged Poland of its Christian and Jewish elites. Above and beyond reprisal shootings following civilian attacks against uniformed military personnel, the Army and Nazi Party organizations unveiled a pre-planned campaign of murder – Operation TANNENBERG – deliberately targeting over 50,000 Poles, including at least 7,000 Jews. As historian Alexander B. Rossino observes:

> As the first representatives of the Gestapo and Security Police apparatus in Poland, *Einsatzgruppen* personnel received instructions from [SD Chief Reinhard] Heydrich to implement what he himself described as the "extraordinarily radical" policy of eliminating those segments of Polish society that could challenge German rule. In this sense, Operation TANNENBERG represented an entirely new phenomenon in the history of modern warfare. Although the Nazis regularly employed violence against their enemies, never before had

Hitler charged his *SS* and security forces with so extensive and merciless a mission as the murder of Poland's leading and educated social-political classes.[24]

From Operation TANNENBERG and the "Commissar Order," it was a short step to the formal enunciation of the Holocaust as official Nazi – and *Wehrmacht* – policy. On January 20, 1942, SD Chief and *SS Obergruppenfuhrer* Reinhard Heydrich convened the Wannsee Conference to discuss the prosecution of the "Final Solution" (*Endlosen*) against Europe's Jews. Although not present at the conference, the *OKH* and the *Wehrmacht* were directly affected by the secret discussions. After January 1942, *Heer* units, including first-rate divisions like the 12th Infantry, 18th Panzer, and *Grossdeutschland* divisions, accelerated their own "anti-partisan" efforts.[25] They executed entire populations of some villages, which in turn were burned to the ground. Likewise *Heer* reservists continued to participate in the round-up and execution of Polish and Ukrainian Jews, under *SS* and SD leadership. Equally telling is the lack of resistance from the *Wehrmacht* to the diversion of rolling stock, manpower, and material to the *SS* concentration camp system. From January 1943 until the war's end, the German military divided its efforts between three operational theaters and an internal campaign of organized murder targeting innocent civilians. The military did not only ignore the diversion of resources to this last effort at the expense of the press of Allied forces in the Mediterranean, in Northwestern Europe, and on the Eastern Front. The Germany military also actively supported this internal campaign through the posting of military police detachments in military railway workers in rail transport cars to take part in the transport of Jews to the camps.[26]

The question of rail assets dedicated to the Holocaust again raises the question of military necessity. Historian Yaron Pasher estimates that 40,000 freight cars and up to 3,000 locomotives were dedicated to transporting Western European Jews to the six primary death camps in the East. Another 33,000 freight cars with 2,000 locomotives are also diverted for transporting the victims' looted wealth to Germany. Combined these 5,000 trains would have been sufficient to move seventy-one infantry divisions with their full complement of equipment and

---

24 Alexander B. Rossino, *Hitler Strikes Poland: Blitzkrieg, Ideology, and Atrocity* (University Press of Kansas, 2003), 228.

25 Ben Shepherd, *War in the Wild East: The German Army and Soviet Partisans* (Harvard University Press, 2004), 114–15; Rutherford, *Combat and Genocide*, 231–39; and Beorn, *Marching into Darkness*, 198–205.

26 Omer Bartov, *The Eastern Front, 1941–1945, German Troops and the Barbarisation of Warfare*, 2nd ed. (Palgrave, 2001), 150–51; Browning, *Ordinary Men*, 133–42; and Richard J. Evans, *The Third Reich at War* (Penguin Press, 2009).

transport, from one front to another.[27] Seen in this light, the Holocaust stands out on two counts. First, it reveals the near total absence of strategic planning, particularly with regard to logistics and transport, resident at the very highest levels in the Nazi Regime and the German military. Second, this prioritization of precious rail transport to implementing the Holocaust highlights the extent to which the German military was subordinated to the Nazi plan for eradicating the Jews of Europe. After the transport scheme began in October 1941, the *Wehrmacht* confronted its greatest challenges against enemies on three fronts that were numerically, logistically, and operationally superior. At no time, even in the greatest crises, was the redistribution of rolling stock to conventional military purposes even remotely considered. In fact, the reach of the *SS* death camp establishment extended to seizing trucks and other vehicles used for moving supplies and men.[28] By mid-1944, the German military position had gone well past the tipping point; there was no question for rational observers that the war was lost – it was just a matter of when. This military collapse was fueled by the Holocaust's insatiable appetite for transport, which denied regular supply, reinforcement, and strategic movement to the Reich's defenders.[29] Nazi emphasis on waging total war against Europe's Jews remained the nation's priority, even if it jeopardized military capabilities against the Reich's armed enemies. Thus the Holocaust is revealed as a decisive factor in Germany's ultimate defeat.

After the war's end, of course, the *Wehrmacht*'s generals went to great lengths to distance themselves from the Holocaust. In post-war interviews, memoirs, and campaign narratives, the German generals laid the blame for any crimes against humanity squarely on the Nazi Party and the *SS*. For over forty years, the myth of the "clean *Wehrmacht*" was sustained and bolstered not only by the participants, but by an entire generation of military historians who accepted – often without question – the German narrative. Since the late 1980s, however, a new understanding and appreciation of the *Wehrmacht*'s complicity in the crimes of the regime has developed. The Holocaust cannot be considered as "separate" from the "clean" war of military objectives and operations. Neither may the *Wehrmacht* be seen as disassociated from the "dirty" war of *SS* and SD ethnic cleansing. In the Nazi regime, the Second World War was intended to be a war of racial annihilation from the start; as a lynchpin of the regime, the *Wehrmacht* was likewise engaged in atrocity, in pursuit of the Nazi goal of racial purity, from the beginning of the war.

---

27 Yaron Pasher, *Holocaust Versus Wehrmacht: How Hitler's "Final Solution" Undermined the German War Effort* (University Press of Kansas, 2014), 5–6.
28 *Ibid.*, 268.
29 *Ibid.*, 285–86.

Pretexts for Racial and Gender Identities in Asia and the Pacific

The Asian-Pacific War's many causes hinged on commercial and strategic considerations, as well as on racial and cultural factors, dating back into the nineteenth century. The Europeans and Americans with imperialist ambitions saw each East and Southeast Asia as vulnerable because these regions lacked the modern technologies to resist the more advanced military forces of the West. By the mid-1800s, European powers had carved up much of Asia as imperial possessions, protectorates, or client states. From Western perspectives, these conquests equated to progress for the undeveloped regions of the world. Nevertheless, European and Americans also feared the Asia continent's huge populations that grew much faster than the West. In 1900, China alone boasted nearly 500 million people, a figure larger than the populations of Western Europe and the United States combined. These demographics turned the Chinese and their neighboring Asian masses into a "Yellow Peril" in Western eyes.[30]

Such pejorative references to Asian peoples frequently appeared in European and American books, newspapers, cartoons, posters and other media. An article published in 1904 in the French literary journal *Revue de Deux Mondes* (*Review of Two Worlds*) captured a disparaging tone even in translation:

> The "yellow peril" has already entered the imagination of the people. . . [I]n the setting of conflagration and carnage, the Japanese and Chinese hordes spread out over all of Europe, crushing under their feet the ruins of our capital cities and destroying our civilizations, grown anemic due to the enjoyment of luxuries and corrupted by vanity of spirit. . . The civilized world has always organized itself before and against a common enemy: for the Roman world, it was the barbarian, for the Christian world, it was Islam; for the world of tomorrow, it may well be the "yellow man." And so we have the reappearance of this necessary concept, without which people do now know themselves, just as the "Me" only takes conscience of itself in opposition to the "non-Me": the enemy.[31]

The juxtaposition of "me" and "non-me" can be traced further back in history than Rome, to the Greeks and the barbaric Persians in Herodotus, and to the Israelites and the heathen Canaanites in the *Pentateuch*. The Greeks and Israelites claimed a unique identity for themselves in race, culture, and religion

---

30 See Chapter 3.
31 René Pinion, "Le Guerre Russo-Japonaise et l'Opinion Européene," *Revue de Deux Mondes* 21 (May 1, 1904), 218–19, translated and cited in John Kuo Wei Tchen and Dylan Yeats, eds., *Yellow Peril!: An Archive of Anti-Asia Fear* (Verso, 2014), 124. See also reprinted publications by H.J. MacKinder, Theodore Roosevelt, Albert Jeremiah Beveridge, William Ward Crane, and Jack London c. 1900 in Tchen and Yeats, *Yellow Peril*, 168–77, and 185–88.

that all non-Greeks and non-Israelites could never have. Devaluing these others made them inferior. What anthropologist C. Loring Brace has called "otherism" took on horrific consequences when acted upon during these earlier historical examples and in the twentieth and twenty-first centuries.[32] Asian studies scholars John Kuo Wei Tchen and Dylan Yeats employ the play of words, "Yellow Perilism," to describe the phenomena of how and why Americans and European stereotyped the Asian in negative ways in opposition to their own "culture of white supremacy."[33]

In Western popular culture, characters such as Sax Rohmer's Fu Manchu and Alex Raymond's Ming the Merciless stood as iconic representations of deviously dangerous Asian leaders bent on domination of others. Other charged labels appeared over time, including "world ogre" and "Mongoloid." Among the many distasteful traits attributed in the West to Asian peoples were cruelty, promiscuity, treachery, effeminacy, and laziness. These images and beliefs permeated Western beliefs concerning the Asian, or "oriental," races as they were known in that time frame, and constructed perverse views of their humanity and civility. Such preconceptions not only validated but also encouraged Europeans and Americans as they exploited the seemingly weaker, less advanced Asians in pursuit of imperial and commercial expansion, and as they sought to maintain control of the Asian hordes.[34]

Although most Americans and Europeans considered the Japanese to be racially inferior, Japan attained higher standing than other Asian nations because of its near-miraculous rise to great power status between 1868 and the early twentieth century. However, this assessment of Japanese modernity was not always the case. From 1868 dating back to 1603, the island-nation existed in isolation with neither outside commercial nor cultural interaction. Life there could be best described as pre-modern and feudal because several powerful clans dominated politics, economics, and warmaking. Atop the political system sat the Tokugawa Shogunate, a dynastic clan that ruled Japan as military warlords. Although a Japanese emperor did sit on the throne, he wielded no real political power because of his figurehead role relative to the *shōgun*, or more formally titled as *sei-i taishōgun*. The leading Tokugawa male holding this title controlled the national government, military affairs, the domestic economy, and the patronage system. Just below the *shōgun* in the hierarchy sat Japanese wealthiest families who owned vast landed estates and comprised a class known as the *daimyō*.

---

32 Brace, *"Race" is a Four-Lettered Word*, 265–72.
33 Tchen and Yeats, *Yellow Peril*, 28, 191, 233.
34 Sadao Asada, *Culture Shock and Japanese-American Relations: Historical Essays* (University of Missouri Press, 2007), 35; Tchen and Yeats, *Yellow Peril*, 167, 212–15.

Similar in function and structure to European nobility, the *daimyō* included male warriors known as *samurai*. Not unlike knights in Medieval Europe, *samurai* spent their lives training for combat and fighting in wars, all the while being subsidized by peasants working in agriculture. The *samurai* lived by a code of conduct called *bushidō* – meaning "way of the warrior" in English – that dictated their actions and demanded loyalty, frugality, martial skill, and honor.[35]

Japan's stable, homogenous system started experiencing problems in 1853 when Commodore Matthew Perry arrived in Tokyo Bay with several modern U.S. Navy warships in 1853. Perry's desire to open Japan to international, especially American, trade sent shock-waves through Japan's collective psyche. Some prescient Japanese leaders recognized their nation's vulnerability of the underdeveloped Shogunate in the face of the coming onslaught of American and European imperialists with their advanced weapons and superior industrial capabilities. Those Japanese who embraced modernization supported the reigning Emperor Meiji's claim to power and fought with him against the forces of the more traditionalist Tokugawa Shogunate. In 1868, the defeat of the last *shōgun's* forces restored Meiji as the undisputed ruler of Japan. The new national government took on vestiges of Western democracies including elections and parliamentary representation. Whereas the emperor remained mostly aloof from details of the political processes, the prerogative of most decision-making rested in the *daimyo* who comprised the leadership of Japanese business and politics. The *samurai* likewise dominated the military's officer corps as the armed forces adopted many Western military institutions and ideas.

Emperor Meiji's government initiated changes to transform Japan into a modern, industrialized power on the European and American models. The most gifted Japanese students attended the best universities in the West, and in turn, they brought their new-found expertise in military, maritime, engineering, management, law, and science home to work in those areas and to educate their countrymen in turn. This drive for advances in industry, for example, spurred Japanese domestic manufacturing of locomotives, railroad cars, turbines, and ships, albeit subsidized and supplemented by Western nations. Nowhere was the transformation more marked than in Japan's Army and Navy. Over several decades after 1868, Japan evolved into a regional military power capable of not merely fending off Western imperialist intrusions, but also acquiring territories for Japan's burgeoning empire. Indeed, Emperor Meiji's reign until his death in 1912 saw the rise of militarism that presaged the more conspicuous expansionism of 1930s.

---

35 The best, more recent analysis is Oleg Benesch, *Inventing the Way of the Samurai: Nationalism, Internationalism, and Bushidō in Modern Japanese* (Oxford University Press, 2014), 15–30.

Japan's modernized military won victories in the Sino-Japanese War in 1894–1895 and then the Russo-Japanese War in 1904–1905. Not insignificantly, the latter outcome against Russia stood as the first instance of a non-European, non-Caucasian nation defeating one of Europe's great powers. Meanwhile, Japan's expansionism reinforced extant fears of the yellow peril in the West.[36]

Figure 6.4: Admiral Tōgō Heihachirō and his senior staff on the bridge of the modern Japanese battleship *Mikasa* in 1906. This warship saw action in the decisive Japanese victories over the Russian Navy at the Battles of Port Arthur (1904) and Tsushima (1905).
Source: https://commons.wikimedia.org/wiki/File:MIKASAPAINTING.jpg.

Like so many people in the United States and Europe, the Japanese imagined themselves to be superior to others because they were part of *Yamato minzoku* (Japanese race) who possessed *Yamato damashii* (Japanese courage and dedication). Japanese intellectuals bolstered their supposition about the uniqueness of their race by adopting tenets of Social Darwinism so prominent in the West. Not

---

36 Benesch, *Inventing the Way of the Samurai*, 35–109. For an older yet similar interpretation, see Kozo Yamamura, "Success Illgotten?: The Role of Meiji Militarism in Japan's Technological Progress," *Journal of Economic History* 37 (March 1977): 113–35.

only were the Japanese disdainful of other Asian peoples with what they believed to be different racial makeups, but the Japanese also believed their nation to be ordained for greatness. Herein lay the stimuli for imperialism: The Japanese wanted to avoid being absorbed by the Western powers, carve out their own sphere of influence by military force, and confiscate resources from conquered peoples. If Europeans and Americans stood in their way, the Japanese would fight.[37] Indeed, for one Japanese veteran, the victory in the Russo-Japanese War came from the "the invincible spirit called *Yamato-damashii*, disciplined under the strict rule of military training."[38]

By the early twentieth century, the Japanese peoples' self-imposed identifications coalesced around four concepts: *tennō, kokutai, bushidō,* and *samurai.* As Japan's *tennō* (emperor), Meiji achieved divine status, which in turn intertwined him as institution and figure with the *kokutai* (national polity or state). When combined with myths rooted in Shinto religion and the certainty of their racial superiority, an "emperor ideology" emerged in Japan that would justify horrific atrocities later in the twentieth century. As the code for proper behavior of *samurai* (warriors), *bushidō* obliged them to maintain absolute loyalty and filial piety to emperor and state. Such sacred duties, so deeply instilled in the collective Japanese psyche, took on an ideological force that drove many military men to fanaticism. *Bushidō* legitimized Japan's unique culture and superior race. The code also enabled imperial conquests at the behest of the emperor and led by militaristic officers of *samurai* ancestry.[39] Despite their significant unifying influences, concepts of *bushidō* and *samurai* lacked historical veracity as historian Oleg Benesch contends in this book *Inventing the Way of the Samurai.* The early twentieth-century Japanese propagandists fabricated new discourses that veered away from the older code of behavior for warriors before the Meiji Restoration in 1868. According to Benesch, the newer twisted version of *bushidō,* together with its close connection to *samurai,* became so "widely accepted and fashionable" in early twentieth century Japan that *bushidō* "was adopted by a broad spectrum of institutions and social groups" and was used to provide contemporary symbols "with apparent historical legitimacy stretching back centuries or even

---

37 Benesch, *Inventing the Way of the Samurai,* 71–72, 94–100; and Theodore Cook and Haruko Cook, eds., *Japan at War: An Oral History* (The New Press, 1992), 129.

38 Sakurai Tadayoshi, *Human Bullets: A Soldier's Story of Port Arthur* (Archibald, 1908), 10, cited in Benesch, *Inventing the Way of the Samurai,* 109.

39 Yuki Tanaka, *Hidden Horrors: Japanese War Crimes in World War II* (Westview Press, 1997), 201–12; and Benesch, *Inventing the Way of the Samurai,* 10–13, 71–72, 94–100, 131–44, 201–202.

millennia."[40] This revisionism helped create both a cult of national unity centered on the Emperor and a race-based rationale for the Japanese military's atrocities during the Second World War.

Although militarism and racism gained prominence in Japan during the late nineteenth and early twentieth centuries, another more altruistic trait of humanitarianism ran parallel to these destructive ideologies. This term is rarely associated with the Japanese in this period. Nevertheless, writing nearly a century later, Olive Checkland uncovered evidence of government-sanctioned humanitarian efforts beginning as early as 1877, the Japanese took cues from Europe and the United States and establishing the Japanese Red Cross Society. Boasting 900,000 members in 1903 and 1.6 million in 1913, the group affiliated with Red Cross Societies across the globe. The Japanese Red Cross played integral roles in caring for some 70,000 Russian prisoners of war captured during the conflict with Russia in 1904–1905. Very few were mistreated or died during captivity. Apart from what seemed to be sincere concerns for the Russians' well-being, Japan's government and Red Cross went to great lengths to portray their treatment of POWs as evidence of maturity as a progressive, modern nation in the world. Then, during the First World War, the Japanese cared for some German military personnel taken prisoner in China, and the Japanese Red Cross sent some medical personnel to Europe to care for wounded soldiers.[41] Even so, Checkland recognized how "remarkable" it was that Japan "should embrace Western humanitarianism, based as it was on Western ethics and Christian values, in defiance of the old *samurai* code of battlefield behavior."[42] Tragically, this impetus toward altruism ended with the rise of a new militarist regime in the early 1930s.

While Japan modernized, the United States also took steps to join great power ranks. Throughout the nineteenth century, Americans conquered the North American continent where settlers and soldiers systematically removed or exterminated the indigenous peoples blocking their paths. The popular American expression "Manifest Destiny" cloaked this otherwise brutal conquest in tame connotations like benevolence, duty, and providence. The move west, as well as the correlating struggle to establish civilization, were tied closely to the American psyche and also American masculinity. Then frontier had ended, as historian Frederick Jackson Turner lamented in 1893, once the United States and its territories stretched from the Atlantic to the Pacific Oceans. Implicitly,

---

40 Benesch, *Inventing the Way of the Samurai*, 132.
41 Olive Checkland, *Humanitarianism and the Emperor's Japan, 1877–1977* (St. Martin's Press, 1994), 5–11, 45–78.
42 *Ibid.*, 6.

the loss of potential conquest left American men bereft of worthy challenges to authenticate their masculinity, both in their own eyes and in the eyes of their families and nation. Yet by that decade's end, another frontier opened when the United States fought a war in 1898 ostensibly to stop Spanish imperial oppression in the Caribbean. The quick and decisive victory in the Spanish-American War elevated the United States to great power status. The peace settlement with Spain yielded not only territorial gains in the Caribbean but also in the western Pacific Ocean, with the acquisition of the Philippines and Guam. The Philippines constituted new savage frontier for Americans to subdue, democratize, modernize, Christianize, and civilize. Apart from this process of fulfilling this American version of the "white man's burden," the Philippines gave the United States a marked presence in East Asia and Southeast Asia. Suddenly, American commercial interests, particularly in China, also made the United States a potential threat to Japan's own growing sphere of influence on the mainland in the early twentieth century. Aside mutual suspicion increased, each side began drawing up plans for war with the other. The name for America's was Orange War Plan, with "orange" being the code-named color for Japan.[43]

Before 1914, the critical points of contention between the two rising powers of Japan and the United States focused on commercial opportunities and spheres of influence in resource-rich China. After the final collapse of the Qing Dynasty in 1912 and the subsequent civil war, the Chinese could not hope to control East Asia, let alone defend their own territory against serious challenges. Then following the end of the First World War, strategic differences in Asia and the Pacific between the United States and Japan grew more intense. The conflict devastated Europe's economies and weakened their empires in Asia. As part of the Treaty of Versailles, Japan assumed control of Germany's island colonies in the Pacific Ocean, collectively known as Micronesia. With the European nations and their empires so severely weakened by the conflict, the United States and Japan too their places as the dominant regional powers. Among other interests, their respective leaders disagreed about the degree and kind of military presence projected by each nation in Vladivostok and Siberia during the Russian Civil War.[44]

During the 1920s, Japan eagerly joined the League of Nations and remained a benign member of the global community. Nevertheless, underneath the surface

---

43 See relevant sections in Chapter 3. For analysis of "frontier" concepts in the Pacific, see Peter Schrijvers, *The GI War against Japan: American Soldiers in Asia and the Pacific during World War II* (New York University Press, 2002), 1–98, 217. For analysis of strategic and economic interests, see Asada, *Culture Shock and Japanese-American Relations*, 37–42; and Edward S. Miller, *War Plan Orange: The U.S. Strategy to Defeat Japan, 1897–1945* (Naval Institute Press, 1991).

44 Paine, *The Wars for Asia*, 83–85; and Hunt, *Ideology and U.S. Foreign Policy*, 112–15.

of peace lay tensions with the United States over intensifying competition for commercial benefits in China, perceived slights to Japanese prestige at the Washington Naval Conference in 1922, real limitations to Japan's warship construction at that conference, and bitterness about American immigration restrictions directed against Japan and other Asian peoples. None too thinly veiled bigotry tainted American and Japanese perceptions and actions.[45] Historian of race, Gerald Horne, uses the term "trans-Pacific racism" to describe this reciprocal distrust based on toxic racial assumptions.[46]

All the apparent peace ended in October 1929 with the Stock Market Crash and the onset of the Great Depression. Then, according to conventional interpretations, the United States experienced a staggering 25 percent unemployment by 1932, up from only three percent before the crash. The American economic downturn also spread across the globe, doing severe damage to every industrialized nation. Germany and other European nations suffered unemployment rates as bad or worse than did the United States. Although Japan did not suffer as badly because unemployment rose from four percent in 1929 to seven percent 1932, its economy did shrink significantly in crucial exports when silk and rice decreased by 50 percent. The nation's ruling liberal party fell from power in 1929, and the subsequent transition saw the sitting prime minister and other leaders of his party assassinated, and internal strife increased until ascendant military leaders seized the reins of Japan's government. These high-ranking officers restored domestic order through authoritarian methods. They then started to solve the economic woes by undertaking more imperial expansion on the Asian continent and pouring money, manpower, and other resources into Japan's military.[47]

First in September 1931, the Japanese Army in Korea invaded Manchuria under dubious pretenses of self-defense. After defeating their Manchurian opponents in short order, the Japanese then created a puppet regime they called Manchukuo. Conquering this region provided Japan with needed natural resources, agricultural production, and living space that the island nation could not otherwise obtain Then in 1932, the United States and the League of Nations issued strongly-worded condemnations of the invasion and refused to recognize Manchukuo as an independent state. Such finger-pointing did not phase the Japanese, however.

---

45 Asada, *Culture Shock and Japanese-American Relations*, 37–40.
46 Gerald Horne, *Race War!: White Supremacy and the Japanese Attack on the British Empire* (New York University Press, 2003), 33.
47 Michael A. Barnhart, *Japan Prepares for Total War: The Search for Economic Security, 1919–1941* (Cornell University Press, 1987); and S.C.M. Paine, *The Wars for Asia, 1911–1949* (Cambridge University Press, 2012), 13–49, 123–70.

They reacted by leaving the League in 1933 and exposing the League's inherent limitations.

Throughout the 1930s, Japan watched China spiral further into bloody civil war that pitted Chiang Kai-Shek's nationalist forces against Mao Zedong's communist forces. With this nation divided and weak, Japan hoped to step in and establish control over the country under the auspices of promoting stability and acting on such euphemistic slogans as "Asian for Asians" and later "The Greater East Asia Co-Prosperity Sphere." The accompanying propaganda portrayed its role on the mainland as liberating of those peoples from the control exerted by Western Caucasian empires for centuries.[48] The rhetoric of pan-Asianism obscured unbridled cruelty made still worse by the Japanese self-identity as the superior *Yamato* race, or what historian John Dower labels "racial arrogance."[49] In this hierarchy elevating Japanese to the highest place while degrading others, no moral limits existed to keep them from exploiting those other inferior Asian peoples in any ways they deemed fit.[50]

Gender metaphors can also be located in Japanese assumptions about themselves and, albeit combined with race, their actions on the mainland. Japanese culture had always exhibited a strong sense of paternalism, be it in individual families where the eldest male exercised control, or at the national level where the emperor represented a father-figure to his people. In this construct, other Asians were not merely racial inferiors but also childish subordinates. Either way, they did not merit autonomy nor freedom. Apart from familial roles, normative masculinity played significant roles in exciting, or more aptly inciting, Japanese desires for conquests by force of arms or worse. Their "masculine characteristics," according to historian Sadao Asada, tied directly to the "samurai tradition – of brute force and iron will."[51] This discourse on masculinity can be traced back to Meiji Restoration in 1868. A *samurai* with his blind obedience to the emperor and exacting adherence to *bushidō* comprised idyllic aspirations for a male in the *daimyo* class. He rejected the feminine with its soft, decadent, anxious, materialistic attributes as dictated by Japanese culture mores, but rather he found legitimacy in attaining the warrior's strength, confidence, asceticism, and selflessness. Indeed, the Japanese projected these same feminine traits onto American and

48 David C. Earhart, *Certain Victory: Images of World War II in the Japanese Media* (Routledge, 2007), 258–83.

49 John Dower, *War Without Mercy: Race and Power in the Pacific War* (Pantheon, 1987), 46.

50 Edward Drea, et al., *Researching Japanese War Crimes Records: Introductory Essay* (Nazi War Crimes and Japanese Imperial Government Records Interagency Working Groups, National Archives and Records Administration, 2006), 1–7.

51 Asada, *Culture Shock and Japanese-American Relations*, 34.

European men, thereby casting them as inferior "others," not merely in race but also in gender. Stepping back into the broader context of Japanese history from 1868 into the 1930s, the identities of the *samurai* with their gendered characteristics in *bushidō* helped enable the growth of nationalism, militarism and imperialism, just as the three isms likewise motivated the warriors and their code of behavior. Those same masculine traits and ideologies filtered down the ranks to the common Japanese soldiers, sailors, and airmen who were deeply inculcated by these supposed virtues in pre-service civilian education and military training.[52] According to Oleg Benesch, the Japanese painted the war with China as a "holy war" in which Japan's military performed "sacred military expeditions" and "heavenly task[s]" by spreading their "righteousness" and "beneficence" to the world.[53] Taken as a whole, Japanese adopted their own version of *mission civilatrice*.

Meanwhile, as nervous Americans and Europeans watched the ominous developments in Asia, Japan's territorial ambitions exacerbated the already intense fear of the "yellow peril" in the United States: what if all the Asian hordes united under the Japanese hegemony? In any event, some authors, politicians, and military leaders in both Japan and the West recognized in the 1930s that any conflict between the two potential enemies would quickly degenerate into a race war. Indeed, Japanese propaganda inverted the West's symbology of racial fears by representing Caucasians as the "White Peril" and touting their own goal of liberating Asia from the West's control as a positive good.[54]

By 1937, the time was ripe as a target for more imperialism on the mainland. Japan's leadership believed that Western democracies would not stop further incursions in China. A seemingly minor incident between Chinese and Japanese near Beijing provided the impetus for what expanded into a full-scale war between the two nations. The ongoing war crimes in this conflict rival those of Nazi Germany in Europe in scope and impulse. The rise of Japanese aggression especially in the late 1930s paralleled the decline of their international humanitarian impulses earlier in the century. The Japanese Red Cross was subsumed into the waves of hyper-nationalism and imperialism sweeping in the nation. Instead of assisting foreign victims of disasters, the JRC completely shifted its efforts into supporting military personnel deployed on Japanese imperialist adventures.[55]

---

52 Jason G. Karlin, "The Gender of Nationalism: Competing Masculinities in Meiji Japan," *Journal of Japanese Studies* 28 (Winter 2002): 41–77.

53 Benesch, *Inventing the Way of Samurai*, 181, 202, 212–13.

54 Asada, *Culture Shock and Japanese-American Relations*, 35–37; Horne, *Race War*, 3–15, 140–42.

55 Checkland, *Humanitarianism and the Emperor's Japan*.

Over the next eight years in mainland Asia, Japanese soldiers committed heinous atrocities against Chinese and other Asian peoples with no restraints against targeting soldiers and civilians alike. Rape, torture, murder, and other acts of terror comprised the Imperial Japanese Army's strategy for its treatment of the inferior and weaker Chinese civilians and prisoners of war. Nowhere was this behavior more horrific than in December 1937 in the city of Nanjing (called Nanking at that time). Not only did the Japanese soldiers massacre Chinese by the tens of thousands in Nanjing, but they also raped Chinese women, whether they were prepubescent girls or elderly women. After enduring abuse, many were summarily executed. The numbers cannot be counted with precision, but estimates run between 20,000 and 80,000 aggravated sexual assaults in what history calls the "Rape of Nanking."[56]

Even in the twenty-first century, Japan's government continues to deny that the Japanese military committed so many sanctioned massacres and rapes against Chinese in Nanjing in addition to their later war crimes like the large-scale use of Asian women as sexual slaves or the biological weapons experiences on human subjects during the Second World War. Nevertheless, standing against the official Japanese interpretation are a few revisionist Japanese historians. Among these are Saburō Ienaga and Yuki Tanaka. First published in 1968, Ienaga's ground-breaking book, *The Pacific War, 1931–1945*, describes the gendered violence in Nanjing:

> Rape was an accepted prerogative of the Imperial [Japanese] Army. Gomi Kōsuke, an enlisted man, saw a veteran soldier attack a Chinese woman during a short rest break. To save time, the soldier mounted the woman in full uniform with all his ammunition and gear. He pumped away while she screamed...[57]

The nonchalance of this Japanese soldier's attitude stands as one of the most shocking features of Nanjing. Ienaga then recounts how another

> soldier watching a regiment approaching from a distance could see "patches of white mixed in with the marching column." When the unit got closer, he saw "there were naked women" with the troops. An NCO was admonishing the men, "If you want to get your hands on these Chink broads, you better keep up with the march. Right? Keep your eyes on those Chink bitches and keep going."[58]

---

56 Iris Chang, *Rape of Nanking: The Forgotten Holocaust of World War II* (Penguin Books, 1997); Tanaka, *Hidden Horrors*, 79–81; Joshua Fogel, ed., *The Nanjing Massacre in History and Historiography* (University of California Press, 2000); Sharon Frederick, *Rape: Women and Terror* (Association of Women for Action and Research, 2001), 18–24; and Canada ALPHA, "Rape of Nanking," http://www.alpha-canada.org/testimonies/about-the-rape-of-nanking (accessed 3 April 2018).
57 Ienaga, *The Pacific War*, 166.
58 *Ibid.*, 167.

Figure 6.5: Japanese troops massacre Chinese soldiers and civilians along the Yangtze River and burned the dead in Nanjing, China, 1937. Photograph by Murase Moriyasa.
Source: https://commons.wikimedia.org/wiki/File:Bodies_of_Chinese_massacred_by_
Japanese_troops_along_a_river_in_Nanjing_(Murase_Moriyasa%27s_photo)_01.jpg

Beyond sexualizing and humiliating Chinese women, this eye-witness quote in Ienaga's book pinpoints racism as a significant factor in the Japanese atrocities. They used the word "chink" as a derogatory slur directed at anyone of Chinese descent.

Another revisionist historian, Yuki Tanaka writing about sexual slavery in 2002, links several ideologies together vis-à-vis Japanese sexual assaults of other Asian women. He offers a complex set of queries, if not explanations, that open the doors to further analysis:

It is imperative to closely analyze the symbolic parallel between the violation of a woman's body and the domination over others (enemies) on the battlefield or through colonial institutions. The question that needs to be asked here is why men find it necessary to demonstrate their power in this manner, particularly in a war situation. The structure of the Japanese military organization must be examined in relation to this fundamental question – how its specific structure and ideology created a strong propensity among soldiers to abuse women.... In a broader sense, the ideology of masculinity is intrinsically interrelated with racism and nationalism. The conquest of another race and colonization of its people often produce the de-masculinization and feminization of the colonized. Sexual abuse of the bodies of women belonging to the conquered nation symbolizes the dominance of the conquerors.[59]

The phenomena described by Tanaka applies to Nanjing in 1937. As members of an inferior race, the Chinese lacked value or thus merited no civilized treatment at Japanese hands. The assaults also point to desires among Japanese soldiers for sexual release and physical gratification. They did not commit thousands of sexual assaults only to satisfy their sexual sadism, to exert their power over the women, and act on effects of heightened testosterone and adrenalin, although these were motivation. The soldiers also committed sexual assaults to discredit the Chinese men in their women's eyes and to dishonor nation's male population as a whole. By raping so many women and girls, the Japanese symbolically emasculated Chinese men as fathers and husbands who could not fulfill their masculine duties. Thus, Japanese virility as exhibited in rape included both racial and gendered traits. It is worth noting that the strict discipline ingrained among Japanese soldiers requiring blind obedience took away any self-reflective or autonomy. Thus, the senior Japanese leadership's decision to make rape a military policy reinforce their domination of their subordinates. In effect, this discipline absolved the also individual Japanese soldier from personal responsibility for rapes and other atrocities.[60]

Analyzing these Japanese rapes of Chinese women unmasked significant gendered and racists attitudes. Throughout history, raping and pillaging were tolerated, if not often ignored, as part of the spoils of war due to the victors. As feminist scholar Susan Brownmiller observed in 1975, rape is one warlike act employed to assert power over enemy women. Rape becomes the weapon, and power the motivation. Mary Daly argues that "war" itself is rape because, for instance, the language and objectives of military invasions are cast in connotations similar to

59 Yuki Tanaka, *Japan's Comfort Women: The Military and Involuntary Prostitution during War and Occupation* (Routledge, 2002), 4–5.
60 Y Tanaka, *Hidden Horrors*, 105–111; Dower, *War Without Mercy*, 230, 276; Goldstein, *War and Gender*, 151–58, 369–71; and relevant chapters in Fogel, *The Nanjing Massacre in History and Historiography*.

sexual assault of women by men. Following this logic, targeting enemy women as objects rape and war typologies also represented attacks on enemy home fronts (private spheres).[61] Many other racial, legal, psychological, cultural, moral, or religious contexts likewise shaped the kind or degree of crime, or lack thereof, by which sexual assaults may be labeled in any given war. More recently in 2007, cultural historian Joanna Bourke makes similar connections in her perceptive book *Rape: Sex, Violence, History*. She writes that, "It is easier to sexually abuse and torture the enemy in campaigns where the enemy is regarded as racially and culturally inferior and inferior. Racist discourse meant that women were not really seen as human."[62]

Although not focused on Nanjing in 1937, the preceding observations by Brownmiller, Daly, and Bourke do help expose motivations behind Japanese atrocities in that city. As members of an inferior race, the Chinese lacked value and thus merited no civilized treatment at Japanese hands. It is also worth noting that the strict discipline ingrained among Japanese soldiers requiring blind obedience took away any self-reflective or agency. Thus, the senior Japanese leaders' decision to make rape a military policy also asserted their control over their soldiers. In effect, this discipline infantilized the soldiers and negated their personal responsibilits is for their heinous acts.[63]

Japanese military personnel showed patterns of treating other Asian women as sexual objects. Consider the "comfort women," a term that came from the contemporary Japanese word *ianfu* and was also a euphemism for prostitute. When speaking of these women, Japanese soldiers borrowed a Chinese slang word *pi*, which could be translated into English as the hateful word "cunt."[64] The women and girls of Korean, Chinese, Filipino, Taiwanese, and other Asian descents subsisted as military sex slaves who were lured with promises of legitimate employment or abducted against their will. Then the women found themselves trapped in at least 60 "comfort stations" in east-central China and still more across Japanese-occupied Asia. According to one study, one comfort woman could have sexual intercourse with 30 Japanese soldiers or more on every day. In addition to being sexual objects with no protection from abuse, the comfort women program represented one of the Japanese military's efforts to reduce or control venereal

---

61 Susan Brownmiller, *Against Our Will: Men, Women, and Rape* (Simon and Schuster, 1975; and Mary Daly, *Gyn/Ecology: The Metaethics of Radical Feminism* (Beacon Press, 1978), discussed in Bourke, *Rape*, 13–14, 389.
62 Bourke, *Rape*, 378.
63 Tanaka, *Hidden Horrors*, 105–111; and Dower, *War Without Mercy*, 230, 276.
64 C. Sarah Soh, *The Comfort Women: Sexual Violence and Postcolonial Memory in Korea and Japan* (University of Chicago Press, 2008), 39.

diseases through regulating the health of female sexual partners. Estimates of victims vary widely from several thousand to more than 400,000 women and girls. Precise figures may never be known, but the higher estimates in the hundreds of thousands are certainly legitimate.[65]

American and Japanese Racisms during the Asia-Pacific War

While the Japanese fought in China and Germany expanded in Europe after 1939, most Americans remained isolationist in their attitudes about military affairs and foreign policy. They tended to be disinterested in the problems in Europe and Asia because they needed employment and their families needed food, clothing, and shelter. Besides 3,000 miles of the Atlantic Ocean and 7,000 miles of the Pacific insulated Americans from any dangers posed by Germans and Japanese. The popular views influenced politicians to keep the U.S. military hamstrung by meager budget. Even as late as 1941, most Americans and British still viewed the Japanese through lenses tinted by racism, Social Darwinism, and American exceptionalism, all which predisposed them to underestimate Japanese military capability and planning audacity.[66]

In late November 1941 under a veil of secrecy, six Japanese aircraft carriers sailed thousands of miles across the north Pacific to within 230 miles of Hawaii and launched a surprise aerial attack that devastated American warships at anchor in Pearl Harbor. Next, Japanese forces carried out more stunningly successful operation across the Pacific and Asia over the next six months. These victories confounded Americans miscalculation of Japanese capabilities in 1941: How could this diminutive, unimaginative, primitive "yellow" race with buck teeth, myopia, inner-ear problems, poor training, and inferior military equipment pull off so many great victories against white, obviously superior Americans? Admittedly, some stereotypes like treachery, barbarity, and inscrutability did offer explanations for the Japanese willingness to commit the "dastardly acts" at Pearl Harbor, but these fail to account adequately for many stereotypes of American bigotry that contributed to military miscalculations in the pre-war years and months. After that, a new stereotype of the Japanese soldier as invincible "superman" and unbeatable jungle fighters supplanted that of the inferior Japanese soldier. That

---

65 Kazuko Watanabe, "Trafficking Women's Bodies, Then and Now: The Issue of Military 'Comfort Women,'" *Women's Studies Quarterly* 27 (Summer 1999): 19–31; and Tanaka, *Japan's Comfort Women*,15–32.

66 Horne, *Race War*, 33; Paine, *The Wars for Asia*, 134–35; and Asada, *Culture Shock and Japanese-American Relations*, 37–39.

myth posited tenacity, skill, and brutality as traits, yet it still drew no less on racist attitudes associated with the long-standing "yellow peril" epithet.[67]

The Japanese, on the other hand, possessed no fewer exceptionalist assumptions regarding their inherent superiority vis-à-vis their American adversaries. According to the dominant Japanese view, the Americans were soft, effete, selfish, self-absorbed, decadent, materialistic, and irresolute – in a word effeminate – all of which made the United States an easy target for a pre-emptive strike as Admiral Isoroku Yamamoto had conceived the attack on Pearl Harbor. Many Japanese planners assumed that American material ability and especially moral will to fight would be so damaged by Pearl Harbor that the United States would not recover fast enough to turn the Japanese tide of victories. The traits relating to American temperament, likewise, exhibited racial underpinnings. Unlike the homogenous *Yamato* race with its divine emperor and unique national character, the American people included many races and mixtures of races. No single bloodline ran pure throughout the United States. White Americans intermingled and intermarried with other ethnic and racial groups, resulting in a mongrelized nation. Consequently, Americans became objects of Japanese scorn and contempt.[68]

The Japanese attack on Pearl Harbor certainly did awaken the sleeping American giant. Some six million Americans of all races and both genders flocked to recruiting stations and volunteered for military service in the days and weeks following the attack. They voluntarily enlisted to because they wished to rally to the American flag, to find adventure in faraway places, to find relief from economic hardship, to prove their manhood in combat, to assert their worth as citizens, to seek revenge against the Japanese, to avoid conscription into an unwanted task in an unwanted service, or other reason. Beyond volunteers, another ten million Americans were conscripted under Selective Service. These draftees were not necessarily any less patriotic or worthy, but they did have other complex reasons for waiting to enter the military until drafted.[69]

The dominant American view of the Japanese as invincible supermen persisted for the first months of the Pacific War. Losses at the Battle of Midway in 1942, and on Guadalcanal between August 1942 and February 1943 steadily

---

67 Dower's book contains examples of racially-based assumptions on both sides. See also Craig M. Cameron, *American Samurai: Myth, Imagination, and the Conduct of Battle in the First Marine Division, 1941–1951* (Cambridge University Press, 1994), 95–96, 104–105, 110–25.

68 Horne, *Race War*, 141; Cook and Cook, *Japan at War*, 240–52; Earhart, *Certain Victory*, 258.

69 Chapter 8 examines race and gender in the American experience in more detail. See also Kindsvatter, *American Soldier*, 4–26.

undermined the American assumptions. Thereafter, a more disturbing myth – suicidal fanaticism – replaced the older one. Military historian Gerald F. Linderman observes how

> integral to the evolution of American reactions. . . on Guadalcanal was a complicated, multifaceted transformation of attitudes toward the Japanese as a people. Propelled by the view that the Japanese, in their zeal to destroy both Americans and themselves, had abandoned the value of life, American soldiers came to consider infinitely killable an enemy believed to lack fundamental human attributes. Successive stages in the dehumanization of the Japanese traced a series culture-bound propositions that consecutively diminished the adversary.[70]

This new contemptuous portrayal depicted the Japanese as vicious fighters who made formidable enemies, but who were still an inferior race no better than animals. In addition to the derisive "Japs" and "Nips," other American racial epithets included "monkeys," "dogs," "bastards," "vermin," "apes," "beasts," and "rats," all of which dehumanized that Japanese enemy that had already been labeled as treacherous and cruel. Frequently enough such words as "yellow" or "slant-eye" further racialized wartime rhetoric and imagery. The Pacific War thus took on a degree and kind of vitriolic hatred that far surpassed American views of German or Italian foes in Europe.[71] "Hate is an attitude," according to a psychological study published in 1990. "It is a judgment about an object or person(s) which reflects a negative assessment or dislike. Likewise, hate usually involves emotion." As such, this judgment can become irrational because, as the study shows, hatred "is conditioned on the character of an individual or group experiencing the emotion. There is a continuing readiness to hate. The group or individual will find targets to rationalized that hate."[72] When plugging the events of 1941 and racist attitudes of Americans and Japanese into this study's model, the resulting levels of mutual hatred in the Pacific make sense, albeit in horrific and diabolical ways.

Such wartime films as *Wake Island* and *Why We Fight* played heavily on American assumptions that the Japanese were cruel, treacherous, imperialists with poor eye-sight, buck teeth, and thick accents. At the behest of the U.S.

---

70 Gerald F. Linderman, *The World Within War: America's Combat Experience in World War II* (Free Press, 1997), 161–64, quote on 161.
71 Weingartner, "War against Subhumans," 557–72; Gerstle, *American Crucible*, 210–214; and Ronald Spector, "The Pacific War and the Fourth Dimension of Strategy," in *The Pacific War Revisited*, ed. Günter Bischof and Robert L. Dupont (Louisiana State University Press, 1997).
72 John A Ballard and Aliecia J. McDowell, "Hate and Combat Behavior," *Armed Forces and Society* 17 (Winter 1991): 230–31.

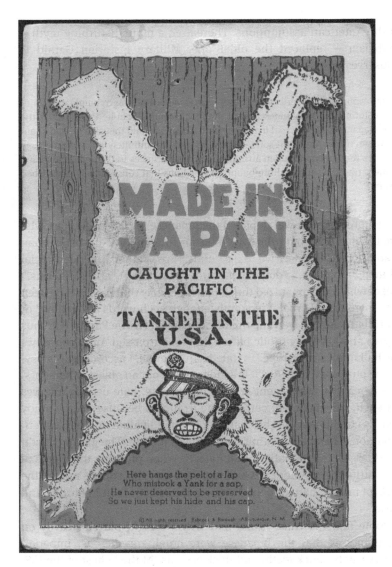

Figure 6.6: An American World War II-era postcard with the disparaging illustration of a Japanese soldier's skin stretched onto a week. In addition to the text in the center of the poster, the fine print reads: "Here hangs the pelt of a Jap, Who mistook a Yank for a sap, He never deserved to be preserved, So we just kept his hide and his cap."
Source: Beck Center, Emory University, copyright expired. https://greatwar.digitalscholarship.emory.edu/postcards/emory:b3jbk

Office of War Information and similar organizations' policies, American propagandists used their enemy's own words and ideas as fodder for their representations. Realities, to include portrayals of Japanese atrocities committed during the Bataan Death March, gave credibility to biased symbolism employed in these films, posters, music, advertisements, cartoons, and other media.[73]

Some examples stand out, including U.S. Marine Corps recruiting pamphlet titled "A Hunting License for Japs" and printed to look like this official document with a seal and authorizing signature. This connection of the Japanese to prey was made obvious to the American people.[74] Elsewhere, popular music captured the anti-Japanese mood in the United States as evinced by two stanzas in "We're gonna have to slap the Dirty Little Jap (And Uncle Sam's the Guy Who Can Do It)" written by Bob Miller:

We're gonna have to slap the dirty little Jap
And Uncle Sam's the guy who can do it
We'll skin the streak of yellow from this sneaky little fellow
And he'll think a cyclone hit him when he's thru it
We'll take the double crosser to the old woodshed
We'll start on his bottom and go to his head
When we get thru with him he'll wish that he was dead
We gotta slap the dirty little Jap

We're gonna have to slap the dirty little Jap
And Uncle Sam's the guy who can do it
The Japs and all their hooey will be changed into chop suey
And the rising sun will set when we get thru it
Their alibi for fighting is to save their face
For ancestors waiting in celestial space
We'll kick their precious face down to the other place
We gotta slap the dirty little Jap.[75]

---

73 Dower, *War Without Mercy*, 98–99, 116–17, 181–200; Cameron, *American Samurai*, 101–105; Christina S. Jarvis, *The Male Body at War: American Masculinity during World War II* (Northern Illinois University Press, 2004).

74 Nakano Gorō, "The Will to Annihilate the American Enemy," in *Rediscovering America: Japanese Perspectives on the American Century*, eds. Peter Duus and Kenji Hasegawa (University of California Press, 2011), 160–64.

75 Copies of lyrics and sound recording, https://www.historyonthenet.com/authentichistory/1939-1945/3-music/04-PH-Reaction/19420218_Were_Gonna_Have_To_Slap_The_Dirty_Little_Jap-Lucky_Millinder.html (accessed 12 March 2018). See also John Bush Jones, *Songs That Fought the War: Popular Music and the Home Front, 1939–1945* (Brandeis University Press, 2006), 133–34.

More than one artist performed this song. Carson Robinson first recorded it in December 1941 shortly after Pearl Harbor. Then, Lucky Millinder released the song in February 1942. These lyrics in "We're gonna have to slap the Dirty Little Jap" revealed well-developed and cleverly-constructed representations of the racially-different enemy. In a bitter irony, Millinder was an African American who performed this song so laced with anti-Japanese and anti-Asian bigotry. The combinations of media-manipulated imagination and front-line reality proved to be effective in arousing American patriotism and fanning hatred for the Japanese.

Japan's government-controlled propaganda also played on perceptions about the American combatants. They believed Americans to be cowards, psychotics, demons, and barbarians, all classic depiction of an inferior "other." American forces surrendering in the Philippines and other captured territories only served to reinforce low Japanese opinions of their foes as unmanly cowards. They portrayed American combatants in other negative ways as seen in translated headlines from 1942 that read "Cruel Devilish U.S. Defense Garrison Massacres Our Detained Countrymen" and labeled Americans as "Enemies of Humanity." *Bushidō* likewise influenced Japanese wartime behavior: what had once been a code mandating benevolence and self-discipline among the *samurai*, now in the Pacific War, became a corrupted code that mandated committing suicide and all manner of brutality in blindly loyal service to the divine Japanese emperor.[76]

All the preconceived biases played out on battlefields where rules of wartime conduct in the Geneva Convention did not apply. Neither side was inclined to ask for or give quarter to their adversaries.[77] Veterans' memories found in William Manchester's *Goodbye, Darkness*, E.B. Sledge's *With the Old Breed* or Theodore and Haruko Cook's *Japan at War: An Oral History Japan at War: An Oral History* revealed commonplace atrocities on both sides. American marines and soldiers felt no compunction when shooting supposedly surrendering Japanese soldiers who might actually attack the American captors once captured, or when bashing in Japanese soldiers' jaws to take their gold teeth as souvenirs. Japanese soldiers felt neither guilt nor dishonor when they executed what they believe to be cowardly American prisoners of war, or when they mutilated the bodies of dead Americans to terrorize their living comrades who might stumble onto them in

---

76 Duus and Hasegawa, *Rediscovering America*, 128–80; Benesch, *Inventing the Way of the Samurai*, 201–12; Earhart, *Certain Victory*, 365–66.

77 Dower, *War Without Mercy*, 10–11, 29–32, 243–44; Cameron, *American Samurai*, 121–25; Schrijvers, *GI War Against Japan*, 143–46, 175–84, 216–18; and Lynn, *Battle*, 222, 232, 256.

the jungle. These examples served to make their respective preconceptions into self-fulfilling prophecies during the conflict.[78]

Two battles in particular – Tarawa and Okinawa – can be seen as turning points in the evolution of attitudes on both sides. At the Battle of Tarawa in late November 1943, some 15,000 U.S. Marines made an amphibious assault against the 5,000 Japanese defending the island. The first day alone saw 1,500 leathernecks killed, wounded, or missing in action out the initial landing force of 5,000 men. By the time the American forces secured the island after four days of savage fighting, the Japanese losses had reached 97 percent of their original garrison, or 4,800 troops killed in action. Fewer than 200 Japanese surrendered. These heavy losses caused an uproar on the American home front, where many believed the battle to be an operational debacle. Moreover, the suicidal fanaticism of the Japanese raised serious concerns among Americans that their forces might not defeat them without experiencing unreasonable losses. The U.S. War Department's *Handbook on Japanese Military Forces* (1944) confirmed these realitie:

> Imbued with the idea of Japanese racial superiority, the Japanese soldier is apt to adopt a superior attitude towards conquered people and to forget the strict instructions given him during military training. Numerous instances of breaches of the military laws have occurred, and evidence shows that crimes of rape, plundering, drunkenness, and robbery have been committed.[79]

The bloody precedent set by Tarawa did not bode well for the future. In every subsequent operation, the Japanese proved their willingnes to fight to the death on Okinawa during nearly three months of fighting from April 1 to June 23, 1945. They made aerial suicide attacks – the *kamikaze* – in heretofore unequaled numbers. Young men were recruited on the Japanese home front to serve as pilots of aircraft. Then they received orders to fly their planes into American warships. In their deaths, the pilots demonstrated unwavering loyalty to their emperor.[80] In the skies over Okinawa, the Japanese made an estimated 1,500 *kamikaze* attacks that damaged dozens of American warships and inflicted some 10,000 casualties.

---

78 Simon Harrison, "Skull Trophies of the Pacific War: Transgressive Objects of Remembrance," *Journal of the Royal Anthropological Society* 12 (2006): 817–36; Kindsvatter, *American Soldiers*, 218–20; Linderman, *World Within War*, 143–73.

79 Joseph H. Alexander, *Utmost Savagery: The Three Days at Tarawa* (Naval Institute Press, 1995); and George H. Roeder, Jr., *The Censored War: American Visual Experience during World War Two* (Yale University Press, 1993); quote from U.S. War Department, *Handbook on Japanese Military Forces*, TM E 30-480 (GPO, 1944), 8–9.

80 Samuel Hideo Yamashita, *Daily Life in Wartime Japan, 1940–1945* (University Press of Kansas, 2015), 127–54.

Back on the ground in Okinawa, the American marines and soldiers fighting on the island witnessed the extent of the suicidal devotion and anti-American indoctrination among the Okinawan civilians. Approximately 100,000 civilians fled the approaching American forces only to buried or entombed in caves on Okinawa. Some jumped off cliffs to their deaths rather than be captured by the Americans, whom they were told would torture, rape, and rape them. This sight of civilians, as well as soldiers, committing suicide or fighting to the death appalled Americans.[81] Racism affected them in what amounted to an unending circular argument: Japanese were "yellow bastards" and racially inferior, because they fought with suicidal fanaticism, because they were "yellow bastards" and racially inferior.

By the summer of 1945, the once-majestic Imperial Japanese Navy and the once-victorious Imperial Japanese Army failed to halt the advances of the American advances. The *kamikaze* attacks could not stem the tide. By late summer, only one more major assault awaited the Americans and their Allies. Operation DOWNFALL, the code name for the invasion of the Japanese home islands.The attackers shuddered to consider how hard the Japanese might fight for their home islands and their emperor. Japanese soldiers were not the only threat; civilians and even women also trained with bamboo spear and explosive devices in preparation to defend their nation.[82] Whereas historians have since debated the possible number of Japanese and American casualties during Operation DOWNFALL, it seems plausible to assume that the Americans and their Allies would suffer at least 500,000 casualties and the Japanese casualties would have reached into the several millions.[83]

With these ominous signs looming, the new President Harry Truman faced a decision point in the summer of 1945. The United States had developed a weapon of incredible destructive power. The atomic bombs could be employed to end the Pacific War quickly, rather than risk imminent invasion. Sometimes underrated, the shrewd and intelligent Truman had many practical concerns to consider. He wanted to save as many lives as possible because he realized that the Japanese

---

81 Earhart, *Certain Victory*, 409–60; Benesch, *Inventing the Way of the Samurai*, 212–13, 239–40. The second section of E.B. Sledge, *With the Old Breed at Okinawa and Peleliu* (Presidio Press, 1981) paints a vivid picture of the horror of combat on Okinawa; and chapter 5 of Craig Cameron's *American Samurai* provides detailed analysis of that battle.

82 For studies of women and gender in wartime Japan, see Haruko Taya Cook, "Turning Women into Weapons: Japan's Woman, the Battle of Saipan, and the 'Nature of the Pacific War,'" in *Woman and War in the Twentieth Century: Enlisted With or Without Consent*, ed. Nicole Ann Dombrowski (Garland, 1999), 240–64; and Yamashita, *Daily Life in Wartime Japan*, 11–34, 127–54.

83 See D.M. Giangreco, *Hell to Pay: Operation DOWNFALL and the Invasion of Japan, 1945–1947* (Naval Institute Press, 2011); and Waldo Heinrichs and Marc Gallichio, *Implacable Foes: War in the Pacific, 1944–1945* (Oxford University Press, 2017).

people would contest an invasion with self-sacrificing zeal. It is also important to note that, because Truman had experienced some of history's most brutal combat while serving as an artillery captain with the American Expeditionary Forces in the First World War, he could fervently wish to avoid more bloodbaths in the streets of Tokyo. The President wanted to end hostilities before the war-weary American people lost heart and bowed to the possibility of a conditional peace. He also saw the atomic bomb as a mean of restraining of Soviet expansion in the post-war world. With all that was at stake, there was little room for a moral dictum against killing civilians in warfare.[84]

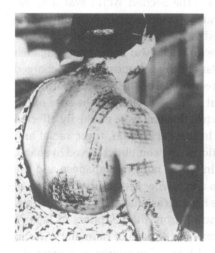

Figure 6.7: The Japanese patient's skin is burned in a pattern corresponding to the dark portions of a kimono worn at the time of the explosion. Japan, circa 1945.
Source: U.S. War Department, National Archives and Records Administration.
https://commons.wikimedia.org/wiki/File:The_patient%27s_skin_is_burned_in_a_pattern_corresponding_to_the_dark_portions_of_a_kimono_-_NARA_-_519686.jpg

In addition to these factors, racism also played a role. The Japanese, civilian and combatant alike, were not seen as worthy of humane treatment. The American fire-bombing of Tokyo and other cities had already killed hundreds of thousands of Japanese early in 1945. So, the prohibition on mass killing of civilians already ended. President Truman believed that using the atomic bombs was necessary

---

84 The scholarly debates over Truman's decision to drop atomic bombs are voluminous. A good starting point is J. Samuel Walker, "The Decision to the Use the Bomb: A Historiography Update" *Diplomatic History* 14 (Winter 1990): 97–114. However, racism is mentioned less often as a factor in dropping the atomic bombs.

because, in his own words, the Japanese were "savages, ruthless, merciless, and fanatic."[85] These descriptions reflected the commonly-held American views of the Japanese. In the end, Truman decided to use two atomic bombs on August 6 and August 9, 1945, based on an intricate combination of political, diplomatic, utilitarian, and, yes, racist factors.[86]

Conclusion

Despite the political contingencies that made the Second World War a global conflict, it would not be inappropriate to categorize it as several distinct wars, distinguished by the extent of violence waged on the grounds of racial exceptionalism, as well as on political expediency. The American war in the Pacific against the Japanese Empire and the Nazi-Soviet War are the two most racially charged conflicts within the larger construct that is recognized as the Second World War. As the examples offered here reveal, tactical and – especially in the case of the Eastern Front – operational elements of the two theaters were markedly affected by racial ideologies and harsh prejudices. In the Pacific War, these racial animosities were shared by both belligerent nations, and combined served to enable a feedback loop of extraordinary violence in which both the Japanese and the Western Allies allowed racial exceptionalism and privilege to nullify the norms of behavior in peacetime civil society. Violence became as much an end as a means in the Pacific War, as the Western Allies moved from the periphery of Japan's occupied territories closer to the Imperial core. In the case of Germany's war in the Soviet Union, racial prejudice combined with anti-Communist fears created a homogenous racial-ideological Russian enemy, which in turn formed the context of an existential conflict from which only one side could survive.

And yet despite their similarities, it is important to note the differences that separate the two conflicts. National Socialist race ideology was the foundation of the Nazi state and, in turn, the paramount consideration in determining the regime's military policies and necessities during conflict with the Soviet Union. In this case, the war was not only inevitable, it was essential to the state itself.

---

85 Truman's Potsdam diary, cited in Dower, *War Without Mercy*, 142. See also William D. Leahy, *I Was There* (McGraw-Hill, 1950), 79.
86 For useful discussions of racism's effect on strategic decisions like the one Truman made, see Spector, "The Pacific War and the Fourth Dimension of Strategy," 41–56; and Stephen E. Ambrose and Brian Villa, "Racism, the Atomic Bomb, and the Transformation of Japanese-American Relations," in *The Pacific War Revisited,* ed. Günter Bischof and Robert L. Dupont (Louisiana State University Press, 1997), 179–98.

This ideological foundation would guarantee the inevitable war between the two totalitarian states – Germany and the Soviet Union – would transcend existing constraints on conflict and create the conditions for the ensuing slaughter. Japanese racial ideology was more focused on the purity of their own race, and their imperative to transform East Asia into their own imperial region. While the Japanese people were held up as the highest and most deserving race, the impulse to exterminate entire rival races was never a factor in the designs of the Japanese military during the long war in China and the Pacific. The horrific violence expressed there was quite real, of course, but it was fueled more by desires to achieve dominance and relieve frustration with Asian resistance to Japanese rule. The intense violence on the American side was likewise fueled in part by racial exceptionalism, but again, there was never – at least not until the initiation of regular strategic bombing of Japanese cities in later 1944 – a truly systematic logic or calculated purpose to American brutality in the war against Japan. As James Weingartner notes in his essay cited at the start of this chapter, "For the United States. . . extermination of the enemy, no matter how appealing it might have seemed to some Americans, was not central to the attainment of the war's objective – the neutralization of Japan as an expansionist force in East Asia and the western Pacific."[87] Save for the firebombing raids late in the conflict and the successful submarine warfare campaign, Japanese civilians were rarely encountered, let alone targeted, by American forces. And unlike the German case, the brutal treatment meted out to the Japanese combatants in the Pacific War was not part of a systematized operational and strategic design. Even so, the violence of the Second World War shall continue to fascinate and influence scholars and readers for decades to come.

Even so, the violence of the Second World War shall continue to fascinate and influence scholars and readers for decades to come. As we turn to the next chapter, our focus will shift, and the place racial and gendered ideologies and presumptions occupied in the so-called "Good War."

---

87 Weingartner, "War Against Subhumans," 573.

7 Gender and Race on the Homefronts in the Second World War

Introduction

Following the Wall Street crash in October 1929, economic distress rippled around the globe, affecting every industrialized nation. Almost no sitting political party or personality survived the crisis; the collapses in consumption, production, and consumer confidence, matched by steep unemployment and extreme stresses on the financial system itself fueling much political distrust with the status quo. In response, over the next decade the new administrations across North America, Asia, and Europe adopted radical economic and political solutions, winning popular support through exploiting public fear, anger, and confusion. Even conventional and long-established social and cultural norms of gender, racial, and sexual identity were altered by the Great Depression. Millions of men across the world lost both their jobs and their traditional role as the primary bread-winner for their families, while women found they were more readily employable, albeit at lower, even exploitive, wages than their male counterparts. In some cases, women took on the role of primary bread-winner, leaving their spouses home with no work, and by extension, no purpose. At the same time, gay men and women continued to exist on the margin of society, devoting great energy to avoid undue attention that might out them as criminal sexual deviants. And of course, non-white families – African American, Asian American, Latino American, and Native American – all continued to live in the shadow of hostile public racism that was accepted as the status quo without question.

In response to this crisis in gender identity and power, several societies embraced a number of regressive and militaristic concepts of masculinity that became more intense nearing the onset of the Second World War. In several cases, an explosion of masculine symbols and opportunities reversed the depression-era tide of aimlessness and joblessness. On some levels, fighting for one's nation became an equalizing statement about manhood, regardless of race or ethnicity. Certainly, they reforged a collective sense of self as warriors as they attained rites of passage and protected their nations and families. For women, however, the conflict required their nations to undertake total war efforts. To live up to these desperate needs, women left their private spheres in their homes and ventured into masculine-typed occupations that they would never have otherwise attained without the Second World War. Even so, women still needed to remain feminine so as to avoid completely upsetting the delicate balance of labor for them and men. Racial and ethnic minorities experienced varying levels

https://doi.org/10.1515/9783110477467-007

of maltreatment ranging from discriminatory government policies to death sentences in extermination camps.

Gender Relations between the World Wars

The Great Depression challenged the pre-existing gendered division of labor and power within families in the United States, Britain, and France. Family incomes declined precipitously as millions of men lost their jobs, their farms, their houses, or their savings. Many were forced to accept government assistance through welfare or workfare programs. Bereft of the ability to be protectors and providers, more than 1.5 million American men became hoboes and took to the roads and the rails to seek employment or escape their dismal existences.[1] Men in Europe faced similar tests of their time-honored privileges as heads of households and of their obligations as providers.

Meanwhile during the interwar period, Caucasian American women experienced some gains despite enduring sexist treatment. Where women were employed in the place of men, they did so for less pay; accordingly their families remained under stress due to loss income. In the workplace, underpaid women also faced constant resentment from their male coworkers, who saw them as potential competition in the face of constant downsizing. Likewise female employees possessed no viable safeguards against exploitation and abuse at the hands of their employers. African American and other minority women were at even greater risk; suffering from chronic high unemployment, where work was available it was menial labor for little pay.

As a result of wide-spread poverty and uncertainty across the United States, marriage rates, divorce rates, and birth rates all declined during the 1930s. British women experienced similar problems to those of American women in terms of unemployment and family relations. France, however, differed slightly from Britain and the United States due to the government's obsession with demographics. Having suffered such grievous losses of their male population in World War I, the French government adopted pro-natal policies: discouraging use of contraception and awarding medals to women who gave birth, for example. Motherhood therefore became a patriotic duty that would hopefully reverse the

---

1 See relevant chapters in Kenneth L. Kusmer, *Down and Out, On the Road: The Homeless in American History* (Oxford University Press, 2002); and Todd Despatino, *Citizen Hobo: How a Century of Homelessness Shaped America* (University of Chicago Press, 2003).

negative trends in France's population. Even with these efforts, however, the birthrate could not replenish the stultifying wartime losses in France.[2]

Among the commonly accepted means to reverse the crippling sense of anomie and irrelevance shared across societies was for men to embrace hyper-masculinity through the Cult of Fascism. In some ways, fascism evolved from the greater desire among men who had participated in the First World War or who were just young enough to miss out of their own opportunity to join in the conflict to recover lost purpose and meaning during peacetime. Or, as cultural historian George L. Mosse observed, "Fascism used manliness both as an ideal and in a practical manner in order to strengthen its political structure, but devotion to a higher cause was at the center of its concept of masculinity."[3] In both its desire to employ violence toward a political end and to subordinate the personal will to the collective goal, fascism served not only as an expression of masculine forbearance, but also reduced masculinity itself into a sad caricature, devoid of nuance and incapable of expressing personal joy. The fascist male was essentially a tool for the most extreme ambitions of the leader, and as such those men remained beautiful yet broken weapons.[4]

And so while many even today dismiss fascism and its most strident version Nazism as being focused exclusively on violence and racial supremacy, such a view is reductionist and ahistorical. Several scholars challenge this view. In identifyinig characteristics of fascism, Stanley Payne notes how the system emphasizes male dominance as a natural social state, to the point of fetishizing the movement as a positive expression of individual and collective "virility."[5] Barbara Spackman clarifies this point on fascism as a gendered discourse, observing that Italian fascism's claims of virility emphasized the idea that such sexualized power was the ideal expression of state identity; hence violence was a natural condition.[6] Thus this ideology is, at its core, a gendered movement expressing itself primarily through violence as means to establish social and political primacy. Klaus Theweleit affirms this interpretation in his multi-volume study of proto-fascist groups within the *Freikorps* and its successors from 1918 through 1930. Inured to violence by the war,

---

2 For overviews, see Laura Hapke, *Daughters of the Great Depression: Women, Work, and Fiction in the American 1930s* (University of Georgia Press, 1995); and Gisela Bock *Women in European History*, trans. Allison Brown (Blackwell, 2002), 183–87.

3 Mosse, *The Image of Man*, 155.

4 *Ibid.*, 178–180.

5 Stanley Payne, *Fascism: Comparison and Definition* (University of Wisconsin Press, 1980), 7, 12–13.

6 Barbara Spackman, *Fascist Virilities: Rhetoric, Identity, and Social Fantasy in Italy* (University of Minnesota Press, 1996), 5, 24.

many men were drawn to right-wing militias through their emphasis on armed resistance against the collective economic and existential threats to the German people. By casting themselves as heroic defenders of the missing umlaut over o, these men established a new gendered role modeled on the popular fiction and memoirs of the war veterans. By making violence central to their political ideology, these early fascists in turn gendered their worldview. Opponents – especially those from the far left – were recast as hostile space, simultaneously feminized and objectified. Only by asserting their own masculine prerogatives as masters of public and private spaces could the new man of the right rescue Germany, and by extension, Europe, from the "red flood" that threatened from the East.[7]

Other historians specializing in the gender and cultural dynamics of the aesthetics and ideals of fascism note that, while the ideology is predicated largely on the exaltation of violence, it also provided a social support network for those who felt a sense of disenfranchisement within society. This actually runs counter to some of our earlier commentators' observations on fascism and its organizations. George Mosse, for example, observes that the Nazi *Sturmabteilung* (SA) rejected social ties that bound its members to any group – even family – over the movement. This was itself representative of how fascism was the "fullest expression of modern masculinity" because it ultimately subordinated family, spouse, and children to the dominant male.[8] Yet such control did not entirely preclude or reject the appeal of family and social charity. Andrew Wackerfuss, for example, identifies the communal aspects of the SA as a significant advantage in the press for new members in the heady streetfighting days of the early Depression. "The SA tried to care for its members, provide social services to its allies, and build networks of support that would enhance its appeal to neighbors while converting its enemies," Mosse writes.[9]

This view of the Nazi stormtroopers as something greater than a homosocial/homoerotic drinking society awash in violence is further elaborated on by Daniel Siemens. Accordingly the SA was central to the ambitions of the Nazi state, and not only during the formative years of struggle before 1933. Portrayed for so many years after 1945 as a criminal racket, ridden with sexual deviants, the SA has largely been dismissed as a legitimate representation of the national will. Yet such an outlook completely overshadows the extent to which the SA both existed as the most primal reminder of the inherent violence of the Nazi state to its citizens

---

7 Klaus Theweleit, *Male Fantasies. Volume I: Women, Floods, Bodies, History*, trans. Erica Carter, et al. (University of Minnesota Press, 1987), 22–24. 232–34.

8 Mosse *The Image of Man*, 166–67, quote on 166.

9 Andrew Wackerfuss, *Stormtrooper Families: Homosexuality and Community in the Early Nazi Movement* (Columbia University Press, 2015), xii.

and as the vehicle by which interested men could claim local, regional, and even national legitimacy as agents of the new masculine-rooted order. Mob violence – both that actualized against armed and unarmed opponents and that inferred through the mere spectacle of ranks of uniformed brownshirts marching through the street – was the means by which individual men acquired purpose and how the Nazi state compelled submission.[10]

But what of the issue of homosexual ties within Fascist organizations. The fact of the June 30–July 2, 1934 purges – "The Night of the Long Knives" – is undisputed. Even if one successfully argued that much of the rhetoric surrounding homosexual activities among senior members was fabricated in order to further legitimize the violent assaults on one's own power base, the lurid image of same-sex liaisons within the SA has become the prevailing historical narrative. Much of this is myth, built around outrageous accusations levelled against the victims by their murderers, and later inflated into the standard historical interpretation by historians eager to cast the Nazi movement as an aberration outside of the general trends of German history.[11] Perhaps more relevant is the prospect that, as a deeply homosocial organization – one that existed almost exclusively outside of female influence and participation, and thus offered male comradeship as a surrogate for inter-sex relations – the SA was more easily cast as being so infiltrated by homosexuals. Some scholars note how this reflects the extent pre-war gender-based social rituals that were disrupted during the First World War. Denied access to normal bourgeois rituals of courtship and marriage by the war, Juan J. Linz argues, young German men instead embraced the notion of a male-exclusive community: "It is hard to judge to what extent the war experience . . . might have made this male political community attractive. The romanticization of the male community with its homosexual undertones in the German youth movement has not escaped attention, and it might not have been an accident that in the SA such tendencies were not absent."[12] Andrew Wackerfuss appears to agree, noting that as the SA built stronger, more cohesive social ties among its members, it is only natural that the organization would become a venue for homosexual expression. Wackerfuss continues: "While the intense emotions of same-sex camaraderie had long been a powerful political force in European history, by this point modern concepts of homosexuality had reached the public's consciousness. It

---

10 Daniel Siemens, *Stormtroopers: A New History of Hitler's Brownshirts* (Yale University Press, 2017), xxvii–xxix, xxxii.

11 *Ibid.*, 171–173.

12 Juan J. Linz, "Some Notes Toward a Comparative Study of Fascism in Sociological Historical Perspective," in *Fascism, A Reader's Guide: Analyses, Interpretations, Bibliography*, ed., Walter Laqueur (University of California Press, 1976), 3–121, quote on 36.

now seemed that those seeking camaraderie also sought sexual relations – and indeed, a series of public revelations established that open homosexuals existed comfortably within the SA."[13] This should not infer that the SA, or fascist organizations overall, were or are more attractive to gay men on the foundation of its all-male exclusivity. Neither the SA nor any of the other myriad fascist groups in Europe and the United States were rife with homosexuals. In this case, the relatively small number of gay men in the SA should be viewed as an outlier rather than representative of the organization. Nevertheless, it is this image, reinforced by the sensationalist accounts of gay orgies on the Night of the Long Knives, that has come to dominate the public imagination. Take aside the tabloid episodes, and the SA appears as an organization, dedicated to radical political change through extreme violence, that also successfully insinuated itself into German daily life as an agent for community.

In Germany as well as Japan, the ascension of the new authoritarian governments meant not only increased spending that stimulated both nations' economies but also increased conservatism in gender and family relations. The two governments demanded traditional, orderly, and strict divisions of gender roles as part of idealized visions for society. In their patriarchal systems, men were expected to be providers and work outside their homes in jobs that helped empower and glorify their nations. They adopted hyper-masculine, -nationalistic, and -racist traits as pure-blooded warriors who would fight, kill, and die without question or quibble. These cultural and ideological constructions of gender mandated that men and women be completely divergent and separate in their roles and activities in family life and in the state as a whole.[14]

Japanese and German women were expected to remain passively supportive wives and mothers in domestic spheres. Women were expected to conform to their purportedly natural maternal roles; any claim to agency and autonomy was linked directly to Bolshevism and amorality. Responses from strong women to the male-dominated public, political, and ideological spheres represented a direct challenge to the newly established militarist and National Socialist regimes. Each nation required complete stability of gender roles and relations in the ultimate service of the state.[15]

---

13 Wackerfuss, *Stormtrooper Families*, xii.
14 Mosse, *Nationalism and Sexuality*.
15 Gail Lee Bernstein, "Introduction," and Yoshiko Miyake, "Doubling Expectations: Motherhood and Women's Factory Work in State Management in Japan in the 1930s and 1940s," in *Recreating Japanese Women 1600–1945*, ed. Gail Lee Bernstein (University of California Press, 1991), 9–12, 267–81.

Nowhere were feminine roles more clearly delineated than in reproduction. In Germany, for example, the Nazi regime undertook systematic programs to indoctrinate women and control the quality and quantity of female reproduction. Pregnancies and births received public recognition in form of the *Ehrenkreuz der deutschen Mutter* (Cross of Honor of the German Mother), which was awarded in different grades according to the number of children birthed by women. And it goes without saying that racial ideology dictated the terms of sexual and family policy. Racial intermingling – not just with Jews, but other purported "inferior" races as well – was forbidden. Nazi Germany took horrific steps in its quest for racial purity, imposing mandatory abortions and sterilization of so-called "degenerate" women of inferior races; all intended to promote the survival and strength of the Aryan *Volk*.[16]

During the interwar years, the Soviet Union presented unique examples of gender roles and relations. Women served and even fought on both sides of the Bolshevik Revolution and the Civil War, with some serving in organized units. In the early years after the Revolution, women attained greater equality relative to men in terms of marriage and divorce laws, in reproduction and maternity rights, and in education. Many of these new laws and policies could be considered privileges and benefits. However, once Stalin consolidated his control, he reversed gender policies and lifted protections of women's maternity and labor rights perhaps because he believed that true women's equality meant that the Soviet women required no special treatment, or perhaps because he was a traditionalist. Later as the social stresses increased in the 1930s and into World War II, Stalin further tried to strengthen Soviet family cohesion as the foundation for the Soviet state by outlawing abortion and abolishing divorce and coeducation, turning back the clock for gender relations to Tsarist Russia.[17]

The Segal Model for Wartime Gender Integration

A precise figure of civilian and military deaths in World War II remains elusive; the most current estimates place the number at approximately 60 million persons, over half of which were civilians. Apart from battlefield operations and extraordinary casualties, all belligerent nations confronted major obstacles as they sought to leverage their industrial economies to the war effort. Virtually every participant

---

16 Miyake, "Doubling Expectations," 267–81; Jill Stephenson, *Women in Nazi Germany*, 3rd ed. (Longman, 2001), 6–25, 109–25; and Bock, *Women in European History*, 218–32.
17 Bock, *Women in European History*, 191–97.

mobilized its available human, natural, and materiel resources, coming as close to "total war" – the full mobilization of society in pursuit of military victory – as any conflict to date in history. As more men went off to war, women increasingly were called on to take their place in the labor force, and, in varying degrees, alongside men in the military. The relaxing of gender role workplace and military service restrictions was met with no small amount of resistance. At least superficially, female employment and military service was rejected on the basis of purported physical weakness and emotional frailty among women. Another factor, however, was the challenge posed to traditional masculine identity. As gender historian D'Ann Campbell notes, many "young men saw military service as validation of their own virility and as a certificate of manhood. If women could do it, then it was not very manly."[18] This attitude proved to be universal, as military necessity in industrial war collided directly with long-established cultural precepts about the masculine exclusivity in war and the industrial workplace.

Not surprisingly, women engaged outside of their traditional domestic or subordinate workplace roles were constantly under pressure, facing open discrimination, insubordination, crude sexual innuendo and harassment on an almost daily basis. Many patriotic women in all combatant nations were slandered in the harshest sexualized language and context imaginable, reduced in public discourse to either hyper-sexualized heterosexual women or predatory lesbians. Both constructions were patently ridiculous – and in their own ways, reflected long-standing Western fears of war as a venue in which sexual inversion threatened traditional gender identities – but this did not stop the rumors from accruing a quasi-legitimacy of their own.

Viewed with temporal distance as a historical construct, these wartime challenges to gender roles offer fertile ground for comparative analyses. Particularly illustrative is the classification model introduced by sociologist Mady Wechsler Segal in 1994. A highly respected specialist in race and gender issues in the U.S. Military, she developed a framework with which to explain the differences in historical case studies related to the mobilization of women in wartime. According to her model, three key factors – social structure, culture, and military – combine to dictate the extent to which gender restrictions are either maintained or eliminated in modern industrial societies. Each of these factors contain a more specific set of markers that combine together to determine the status of the larger factor. For example, the larger military factor is comprised of at least five sub-factors that assign the larger category's status with reference to gender integration:

---

18 D'ann Campbell, "Women in Combat: The World War II Experience in the United States, Great Britain, Germany, and the Soviet Union," *Journal of Military History* 57 (April 1993): 321.

the National Security situation; the state of military technology; the support to combat unit ratio (also known as the "tooth to tail" ratio); the overall force structure; and the military accession policies. A more detailed outline of the three key factors is outlined in Table 7.1:

Table 7.1: Factors that determine extent of female military participation in Segal's model.

Military Factors	Social Structure Factors	Cultural Factors
National Security Situation	Demographic Patterns	Social Construction of Gender and Family
Military Technology	Labor Force Characteristics	Social Values about Gender and Family
Combat Support Ratio	Economic Factors	Public Discourse Regarding Gender
Force Structure	Family Structure	Values Regarding Ascription and Equity
Military Accession Policies		

Source: Segal, "Women's Military Roles Cross-Nationally, 757–75, 759.

In terms of historical case studies, aspects of the target society's situation with reference to the three factors above are placed into context as appropriate. Based upon the overall ranking of each factor in total, it is possible to extrapolate why some societies embraced gender integration in wartime and why others did not. Using Segal's model as a framework with which to assess the extent to which standing gender restrictions on military service were revised, reinforced, or rejected by the major combatant nations, we can more clearly identify and measure how World War II constituted a transformative experience in terms of short- and long-term gender norms in both the public and private spheres.

In many ways the Second World War is the ideal conflict for testing the Segal model. It was a war of extremes, both in terms of brutality and objectives. The Axis Powers doctrines of total conquest and the Allied Powers policies of unconditional surrender together ensured the war would ultimately be a contest of national survival. These extremes were reflected in the varying degrees to which gender norms were either consciously put aside or indirectly subverted by the culture of conflict. Three case studies are presented here to illustrate how the Segal model helps explain the wide range of policy and cultural responses undertaken by the Soviet Union, Nazi Germany, and the United States.[19]

---

19 See B. Fieseler, et al., "Gendering Combat: Military Women's Status in Britain, the United States, and the Soviet Union," *Women's Studies International Forum* 47 (November-December 2014), 115–26.

The Soviet Union

Consider first the Soviet Union, which utilized more women in more wartime activities than any other belligerent nation in World War II. As noted in Chapter Six, the Nazi-Soviet War reached the level of total conflict in every sense of the word, one driven by an annihilative racial ideology that fomented levels of brutality and mutual hatred which in turn rendered the Eastern Front into a charnel house. According to Segal's model, these conditions of ideological brutality and – on the Soviet side, the imperative of national survival – combined with pre-existing policies of social and cultural gender parity to permit the wholesale mobilization of women at all levels of national military service. Millions of women worked in factories, agriculture, or other war-related jobs in order to maintain wartime production, accounting by 1944 for approximately 80 percent of the Soviet labor force. In the best conditions, living standards for women in Soviet war production was difficult, as total mobilization in the Communist state meant that all available resources (save for those claimed by Party *apparatchiks*) were diverted to the war effort. In some areas, however, especially in besieged Leningrad and the battleground city of Stalingrad, where wartime production continued even in the face of immediate combat, male and female workers alike suffered from malnutrition, disease, and other depravations. And amidst it all, the secret police continued to enforce a regime of terror, its actions given greater weight by the war. Even decades after the fall of the Soviet Union, no one really knows how many civilian workers – male and female – died from the fighting, starvation, or from brutal Soviet policies during the war.[20]

In the opening year of the war, the Soviet Red Army was decimated by the Nazi invasion. Often poorly led and generally outclassed by German forces well-schooled in independent tactical operations (*auftragstactik*) and the combined arms tactics generally called *blitzkrieg*, over 5,700,000 Soviet soldiers entered captivity in 1941. An often overlooked immediate effect of this catastrophe was the immediate manpower shortage the Red Army faced as the Soviet High Command (*STAVKA*) sought to make up these losses. As military historian Reina Pennington points out, women were called on in large numbers to fill this gap, and continued to serve through the duration of the war. Soviet women were not simply cast as auxiliary personnel, Pennington notes: "By 1943 Soviet women had been integrated into all services and all military roles, ranging from

---

20 John Barber and Mark Harrison, *The Soviet Home Front, 1941–1945* (Longman, 1991); and Lisa A. Kirschenbaum, "'The Alienated Body': Gender Identity and the Memory of the Siege of Leningrad," in Nancy M. Wingfield and Maria Bucur, editors, *Gender and War in Twentieth-Century Eastern Europe* (Indiana University Press, 2006), 220–34.

traditional roles like medical service, to primarily defensive work in anti-aircraft (AA) defence, to offensive combat roles in the infantry, artillery, and armor, as well as the partisan movement."[21] Women were also a critical addition to shortages in the Soviet Air Force, as female pilots flew over 30,000 combat sorties in both gender-segregated and mixed-gender fighter, dive-bomber, and night-bomber squadrons.[22]

Obviously the Soviet experience was unique because no other nation approached the number – between 800,000 and one million – of women in uniform.[23] Nor did any other nation go so far in eroding the gendered social restrictions that universally distinguished between male-exclusive combat roles and female-accessible support roles. Putting aside the immediate motivations for female participation – government coercion, following spouses, patriotism, revenge, or communist ideology – the Soviet case study does match up almost perfectly against Segal's three-tiered model for female wartime military service. Almost alone of the major combatants in World War II, the Soviet Union practiced and promoted a policy of gender impartiality in the public sphere as a characteristic of Marxist-Leninist ideology. The history of gender organization and access to agency in the pre-war Soviet Union is hardly linear. Immediately following the October Revolution and during the Civil War, Bolshevik programs aimed at expanding the political, economic, and cultural places for women in Soviet society were both complex and frequently contradictory. Earlier when Stalin consolidated power in the late 1920s and early 1930s, the rhetoric of revolutionary gender equality collided with natalist imperatives that sought to restore the hearth and home as the primary venue for the new Soviet woman's organizational and practical skills. Theoretically (and to varying degrees, practically), the Soviet government did not prohibit women from entering what in other societies would be male-specific tasks and roles. As Stalin pushed the Soviet Union in a crash industrialization program in the 1920s and 1930s, women and men alike were employed in heavy labor. Likewise female professionals – doctors, engineers, scientists – took their place alongside men to design the new factories and cities. If in peacetime the Red Army remained a largely male-exclusive

---

21 Reina Pennington, "Offensive Women: Women in Combat in the Red Army," in *Time to Kill: The Soldier's Experience of War in the West 1939–1945*, eds., Paul Addison and Angus Calder (Pamlico Press, 1997), 252.

22 See also Reina Pennington, *Wings, Women, and War: Soviet Airwomen in World War II Combat* (University Press of Kansas, 2002).

23 According to Anna Krylova, 520,000 women served in the Red Army directly, with another 300,000 serving in anti-aircraft units. Anna Krylova, *Soviet Women in Combat: A History of Violence on the Eastern Front* (Cambridge University Press, 2010), 3.

preserve, women did serve in NKVD battalions along the frontier. And as Stalin's vision of a modernizing society coalesced in the 1930s, women were a part of one of the most visible and popular expressions of this new order.

At the same time, popular media created a new role-model, the New Soviet Person. These young men and women were at the vanguard of the revolution at home, working collectively across gender boundaries to create a new wholly integrated society. This was, of course, all taking place in a carefully monitored and guarded environment, in which arbitrary limits could be and were applied to maintain the ratio favoring male gender privilege in peacetime. For Soviet propagandists and leaders, female pilots demonstrated to the world the purported superiority of the new classless workers' paradise, a society in which anything was possible and modernity offered boundless opportunity. In the end, these earlier Potemkin-like exercises at gender balance and fluidity in the public sphere facilitated the conscription of women for full military service with very limited cultural blowback.[24]

The Soviet Union's cultural approach to gender issues and roles also facilitated ready military mobilization for women. At least since the consolidation of power by the Communist Party after the Russian Civil War, the official Soviet stance toward gender separation held the two sexes as equal in political, economic, and social status. This not only applied in the workplace, as described above, but also in university and at home. Women could initiate divorce, and until the mid-1930s, abortions were legal. Unlike the rest of the industrialized world, family planning – including birth control – was taken seriously, while institutional daycare facilities were opened throughout the country. Soviet girls took vocational classes and participated in Komsomol paramilitary training alongside boys, not only learning how to build houses and other more complex structures, but also how to shoot targets, wear a gas mask, first aid, aircraft operation (including piloting), and even parachuting. Though the system often did not work as well as the propaganda portrayed it, the immediate outcome of such policies was a cultural predisposition toward gender parity that facilitated ready wartime mobilization of women.[25]

24 Krylova, *Soviet Women in Combat*, 15–17; Kazimiera J. Cottam, "Soviet Women in Combat in World War II: The Ground Forces and the Navy," *International Journal of Women's Studies* 3 (July–August 1980): 345–57; and Linda Grant De Pauw, *Battlecries and Lullabies: Women in War from Prehistory to the Present* (University of Oklahoma Press, 1998), 239–44.

25 Barbara Alpern Engel, "Women in Russia and the Soviet Union," *Signs* 12:4 (Summer, 1987), 781–796; and Krylova, *Soviet Women in Combat*, 50–53.

Germany

In comparison with the Soviet Union, Germany stood out as a polar opposite in terms of wartime gender integration. Under Adolf Hitler, Nazi Germany promoted a return to traditional pre-World War I family relations with the twist of distinct gender roles as mainstays in *Volksgemeinschaft*. Meaning "people's community," this term entailed the establishment and maintenance of ideological uniformity, Aryan purity, and cultural homogeneity. Women played a conspicuous role in these racial and cultural undertakings, as evinced in a tract titled "The New German Woman" written by Nazi leader Paula Siber:

> Therefore a woman belongs at the side of a man not just as a person who brings children into this world, not just as an adornment to delight the eye, not just as a cook and a cleaner. Instead woman has the holy duty to be a life companion, which means being a comrade who pursues her vocation as woman with clarity of vision and spiritual warmth.[26]

However, the wartime reality of so many German men going to the front lines left many women on the home front with no husbands and no children. The Nazi government attempted to inject these women into the labor force in order to maintain agricultural and industrial production levels. With no husband and little money, they experienced the worst of the ration lines and least desirable rationed items, while the married women with children received the best available goods and services. The childless and single German women, who both needed employment and were encouraged to work, resented those wives and mothers staying at home and enjoying the largesse of Nazi pro-natal policies. Although the single German women did work outside their homes, their numbers accounted for only a fraction of the female population and a fraction of the nation's total wartime labor force. Instead, Germany utilized millions of slave laborers and prisoners of war to supplement its work force and maintain its wartime productions. After all, from the Nazi perspective, *untermenschen* had little value and few uses other than working to death as manual laborers. Only in 1943 would married German women be mobilized and enter the factories in significant numbers, but this change would prove to be too little and too late.[27]

Germany's declining fortunes in the air war and on the Eastern Front occasioned shifts in its military policies regarding gender. In 1943, Hitler allowed

---

26 Paula Siber, "The New German Woman," in *Fascism*, ed. Roger Griffin (Oxford University Press, 1995), 136–38.

27 Bock, *Women in European History*, 218–32. See also Claudia Koonz, *Mothers in the Fatherland: Women, the Family, and Nazi Politics* (St. Martin's Press, 1987).

German women to be trained and utilized in the *Luftwaffe*'s AA crews and search-light crews. Tens of thousands of women served in various capacities in the crews; but, like the women in British AA unit, they were expressly forbidden to fire the weapons because this would violate Germany's strictest divisions between woman and warrior. The continued severe loses of German *man*power in defense against the Soviet onslaught in 1944 drove the Nazi regime to draft women into military service as true auxiliaries, by definition and implementation. In the last year of the conflict, some 450,000 women would eventually wear uniforms and perform many male-only administrative and clerical tasks. As D'Ann Campbell points out, however, these German women were never officially called "female soldiers" and thus never truly destabilized the accepted cultural and ideological gender divisions.[28] Campbell goes on to write that, "Hitler and his advisers firmly believed that [German] public opinion would never tolerate these auxiliaries firing weapons. Indeed, German propaganda warned all women in the auxiliaries not to become 'gun women' (*flintenweiber*). . . the contemptuous term for Soviet women who carried or fired weapons."[29] In Germany's death throes in 1945, a few women took up arms against the Soviets, but these were isolated cases that serve more as minor footnotes to history, rather than as significant changes in Nazism's ingrained prohibition against women warriors.

The United States

Shimmering lines of aluminum aircraft, tended to by swarms of dungaree-clad workers, many female, wielding rivet guns and acetylene torches. Massive hulls of steel, destined for battleships and landing craft, welded into shape by the wives and sisters of workers called into service. Shapely women, claiming the legitimate authority inherent in the uniforms – conductors, bus drivers, traffic wardens – they wore on the job. And everywhere, American women and men of different races and creeds, all working together to win the war against Hitler and Tojo. These are only a few of the images we accept as a matter of fact in the mythology of the "Good War." Not surprisingly, this mythic past has accrued power – witness the iconic image of Rosie the Riveter's rolled-up sleeve – at the expense of reality. If the history of the Second World War is to be one of the larger American community working together to save the world from the dangers of fascist militarism, then the glorification of an idealized domestic war effort is

---

28 Campbell, "Women in Combat," 317.
29 *Ibid.*, 318.

central to this narrative. The reality behind the myth of American wartime mobilization is less selfless than the heroic narrative.[30]

The Second World War witnessed a major transformation in the composition of the American industrial workplace, where women were needed to fulfill the needs of wartime mobilization. The actual number of women belies the popular perception of massive employment; some estimates identify only 12.5 percent of the 33 million unemployed women joining the wartime effort. Of this substantial number – approximately 4,125,000 persons – only 16 per cent – 660,000 women – worked in wartime industries. What was different about the Second World War, however, was the increase in married women entering the workplace. By 1944, married female workers outnumbered single female workers. Again however, this is dwarfed by the number of women who stayed at home.[31] In the end, the American industrial war effort preferred white male labor, then minorities, then women, for employment. Thanks to the massive unemployment preceding the war during the Great Depression – nineteen percent even as late as 1938 – there were ample workers for placement even with conscription to circumvent widespread reliance upon female employment.

Where were the majority of American female workers employed, if not in industry? The two chief areas relying upon female labor were agriculture and the federal government. The sudden spike in relatively high-paying industrial jobs created a massive drain on agricultural labor. In addition to hiring Mexican and West Indian laborers and (after 1942) prisoners of war in the fields, farmers began hiring women. In May 1942 alone, the American Women's Volunteer Services recruited 1,500 women to work during the coming harvest, while the U.S. Agricultural Extension Service instituted a massive training program for 750,000 women in the Women's Land Army. Those women not inclined to hard agricultural labor could find ready employment in the suddenly massive wartime government bureaucracy. Washington, D.C, doubled in population between 1940

---

30 The historiography is surveyed in Sarah Parry Meyers, "'The Women Behind the Men, Behind the Gun,': Gendered Identities and Militarization in the Second World War," in *The Routledge History of Gender, War, and the U.S. Military*, 87–94. Seminal works include Karen Anderson, *Wartime Women: Sex Roles, Family Relations, and the Status of Women during World War II* (Praeger, 1980); Susan H. Hartman, *The Home Front and Beyond: American Women in the 1940s* (Twayne, 1984); D'Ann Campbell, *Woman at War with America: Private Lives in a Patriotic Era* (Harvard University Press, 1984). And, more recent works include Melissa McEuen, *Making War, Making Women: Femininity and Duty on the American Home Front, 1941–1945* (University of Georgia Press, 2011); Donna B. Knaft, *Beyond Rosie the Riveter: Women of World War II in American Popular Graphic Art* (University Press of Kansas, 2012).
31 Michael C.C. Adams, *The Best War Ever: America and World War II.* (The Johns Hopkins University Press, 1994), 70, 123.

Figure 7.1: Unnamed riveter assembling a bomber at the Consolidated Aircraft Corporation, Fort Worth, Texas. While the legend of thousands of "Rosie the Riveters" remains popular, more women were actually employed in agriculture and by the federal bureaucracy than in heavy industry.
Source: Library of Congress.

and 1943, largely on the basis of single women coming into the city to work as clerks, typists, switchboard operators, and secretaries.[32]

Regardless of the precise number or ratio of women in wartime industry, the conditions were generally the same for all. Where they participated directly in the industrial production of wartime material, women faced no shortage of institutional obstacles and informal insults. On average women earned two-thirds the pay of their male coworkers. Likewise women were the target of direct harassment on the assembly line, from peers and supervisors alike. Many men resented the presence of women in the industrial line. Workers who claimed exemptions on the basis that their skills were essential to the war effort feared they could now be replaced and sent off to war. Other men felt that women could cheapen their post-war bargaining power with management, or gain "secret" gender-based

---

32 Carl J. Schneider and Dorothy Schneider, *An Eyewitness History: World War II* (Facts on File, 2003), 96–97.

advantages that would be denied to men. Yet others simply rejected women as coworkers on the basis that their presence somehow emasculated their status as breadwinners. Sexual harassment – both in the form of crude jokes and comments, and overtly sexual provocation – was common.[33] While some women were able to shrug off the advances and crude innuendos of their coworkers, many others suffered silently, unwilling to jeopardize their livelihood – and at times, that of their families – over such actions.

Whereas millions of American women made contributions to the civilian war effort, some 350,000 women volunteered for the armed forces in support roles where they would "Free a Man to Fight." All services maintained female auxiliary branches: the Women's Army Auxiliaries Corps (WAAC) and later the Women's Army Corps (WAC); the Army Air Force's Women's Auxiliary Ferrying Service, which evolved into the Women's Auxiliary Service Pilots (WASPs); the Navy's Women Accepted for Voluntary Emergency Services (WAVES); the Marine Corps Women's Reserve; and the Coast Guard's verbosely named *"Semper Parantus – Always Ready"* (SPARs). Unlike other Allied nations – particularly the Soviet Union – which maintained relaxed recruitment standards, the United States military mandated that all women volunteers possess high levels of education and experience. Most enlisted women possessed at least some post-secondary education, and female officers frequently held advanced degrees. The average enlisted woman was at least six years older than the average male soldier of equal rank, and female officers were sometimes fifteen years older than the male officers of similar rank.[34]

American women's contributions to the war effort belied their small numbers. They did more than merely take dictation or type letters; American women in uniform performed more than 400 separate clerical, logistical, and technical specialties, half of which were previously male exclusive occupations. Women, for example, worked as radio operators, air traffic controllers, engine mechanics, meteorologists, parachute riggers, gunnery instructors, and cryptologists. U.S. Army Chief of Staff George C. Marshall briefly considered fielding mixed-gender AA units, but he backed away from the idea because of likely public and Congressional backlash. In the absence of a dire threat to national security matching that facing the Soviet Union or Germany, it is not surprising the United States excluded women from service in combat units. Cultural discourses and assumptions of female physical strength, physiology, and psychology were never threatened by military

---

33 See Marilyn Hegarty, *Victory Girls, Khaki-Wackies, and Patriotutes: The Regulation of Female Sexuality during World War II* (New York University Press, 2008).
34 De Pauw, *Battlecries and Lullabies*, 247–51.

contingency. Likewise the social pressure of the recent economic collapse of the 1930s was a greater social factor that had some effect on accepted tropes of masculinity. Many American men remained economically displaced at the start of the war – an experience that essentially emasculated them as family providers. No wonder American male-dominant society resisted the intrusion of women into the traditionally masculine-exclusive military sphere.[35]

Just as in the civilian workplace, resentment against female service personnel ran deep. Women in uniform faced numerous insults and slurs against their character, many of them sexually charged. Many women were cast either as promiscuous girls offering sexual favors to male service personnel or as mannish lesbians preying on susceptible young female recruits. Such egregious attacks were not confined to the services; civilians also spread the rumors, shunning female service personnel as suspected sexual deviants. Obviously the rumors were outrageously and patently false – the War and Navy Departments imposed strict moral strictures on their female personnel, who could be discharged without question for any breach. Yet the tenure and vehemence of the attacks offers a window into the accepted gender norms of 1940s American society, that in turn reveals just how much of a challenge to the established order female military mobilization presented. It was disruptive enough that women entered the workforce due to wartime manpower shortages, the social norm held. However, military service – regardless of the role – was traditionally a masculine-exclusive environment. Women entering the service represented an invasion that harkened back to ancient fears of gender inversion; if they were so compelled to enter the man's world of military service, then it was assumed that women were also compelled to adopt male sexual behaviors. The sole juxtaposition to maintain a semblance of balanced gender relations was to classify the women as feminine first and then as service personnel second. And any such individuals in turn represented a drastic challenge to the "normal" public world of clearly defined sexual restraint and family values. Absent the immediate threat to national security, American morality itself, therefore, was seen as being placed at risk by military contingency.

The Segal Model and Its Conclusions

So what then, of the Mady Segal model. How do these case studies inform our understanding of the contingencies of war as they apply to the broad mobilization

---

35 See Campbell, "Women in Combat;" Mattie Treadwell, *Women's Army Corps* (Government Printing Office, 1953); and Holm, *Women in Combat*.

across gender of society? First it must be noted that, with reference to the Second World War case studies, the model itself is not intended to offer an answer as to why women were mobilized – the case studies present that in of themselves. Instead they offer us a means by which to understand how societies at different stages in social and cultural modernity respond to national security threats. By understanding how the three case studies here responded, we can identify scenarios that may result in the relaxation of gender-based norms restricting military service access for women.

The three case studies all represent different socio-political systems and cultural takes on gender identity and the roles assigned to each gender in peacetime and war. If we were to classify the three in order of their ability to accept the ready mobilization of women in wartime (and it must be noted this is not intended as a value assessment), the Soviet Union would rank at the top of the list, with the United States as second, and Germany as third. This is partly based on simple empirical observation. Obviously the Soviet Union's mobilization of some 800,000 women in various combat and support roles places it at the top. Likewise, the German decision to keep women out of the industrial workplace even after Joseph Goebbels' January 1943 Total War speech at the Berlin *Sportzplatz*, and the reluctance to field auxiliaries outside of the clerical capacity – even at the most dire point of national security survival – places it third. But simple observations aside, consider how the three match up using the Segal model:

Table 7.2: The Segal model applied to the three case studies.

Nation	Societal Factors	Cultural Factors	Military Factors
Soviet Union	High	High	High
United States	Medium	Medium	Low
Germany	Low	Low	High

In the Soviet Union, the Societal Factors described by Segal (demography, social structure, economy, and family structures) all may be ranked as "High" in terms of how they provide for gender equity in the public sphere. The same may be said about the Cultural Factors (Gender and Family values, public discourse, and economic necessity) and the Military Factors – in particular, the immediacy and scale of the threat to Soviet political survival. While Germany also faced a dire struggle for survival (one caused by its own actions, of course), Nazi political and cultural ideology presumed women were subordinate members of the hyper-masculine society, and that they should remain in the maternal nurturing domestic sphere. American society, for all of its imagined wartime equality and shared sacrifice, absorbed the workplace mobilization of women, but American were not culturally or socially prepared to permit greater gender equity. The absence of a clear threat to national security survival only reinforced existing gendered role boundaries.

Race and the American Military in Wartime, 1941–1945

Even outside of the extremely violent conduct on the Eastern Front and the Pacific Theater (See Chapters Six), race was a major factor in the prosecution and execution of the war on both sides. Obviously the Nazi regime's ideological hatred of Jews and other alleged inferior groups affected Germany's military policy and strategy. Likewise Stalin's distrust of various ethnic groups in the path of the German Armies in 1942 helped precipitate the mass forced settlements of the Caucasus region. Japanese and American racist ideologies aside, the race-based policies of other European imperial powers in Asia were no less costly and divisive. British insensitivity to the needs of the population of Bengal in the face of the wartime appropriation of grain exacerbated existing food shortages, resulting in a massive famine killing over three million Bengalis in 1943. Meanwhile French colonial authorities in Indochina openly collaborated with Japanese occupiers, while pursuing its counter insurgency against the Vietnamese nationalist resistance. In the United States, the Second World War directly influenced ideologies and policies toward its non-white citizens. Contrary to the imagined construction of a "Greatest Generation" united in pursuit of victory, the American war effort was marked by misperception and misuse founded in a bankrupt racist world view.

In the case of African Americans, the Second World War was only one episode in a long history of injustice. Since the close of the First World War, they had long suffered from the intransigent growing influences of Jim Crow in the United States Army. They made only limited inroads into Caucasian-dominated hierarchy during the First World War, and most of these gains came while fighting under the French flag. The U.S. Army relegated most black soldiers to segregated units that, although preforming essential logical tasks, never saw combat and thus could never measure up to white standards for manhood, valor, and experience. Of the hundreds of thousands of blacks who volunteered and were conscripted, only two provisional infantry divisions – the 92nd and 93rd – were organized under white command. Rejected by AEF commander John J. Pershing, these two divisions acquired a spotty record. The 92nd Division was broken in futile attacks against strong German fixed positions in the Meuse-Argonne, while the 93rd Division fared better after being handed off to the French Army, who employed its constituent regiments alongside French units.

The fate of segregated black units in the Army endured more setbacks because of a series of post-war performance evaluations, memoirs, and official reports. In 1925, an Army War College memorandum criticized the ability of black troops to serve in combat, basing its recommendations largely on the 92nd Division's performance at Binarville in October 1918.[36] Consequently, by 1930, the Army became an increasingly hostile environment for blacks. The four "colored" regiments were pulled from the line (of combat units) and consigned to maintenance and support duties, including cleaning stables for white cavalry regiments and the U.S. Military Academy. Other personnel were detached to serve as orderlies and servants, rather than undergo regular military training. Likewise black National Guard units languished in their states with only minimal federal support and failed to muster together even once for peacetime training during that decade.

In 1937, the U.S. War Department unveiled a plan for mobilization and training that included black troops for the first time since the 1918. Proceeding from a general estimation of African Americans comprising ten percent of a wartime military, the plan called for creating a segregated Negro cadre of reservists who would be fleshed out in wartime with recruits drawn proportionately from the Army's enlistment pool. Resistance from Southern congressional members restricted this plan; the 1940 Selective Service Act, for example, while committed to inducting blacks in direct proportion to the percentage of their population (10.6 percent), provided for the formation of only forty-seven distinct organizations comprised of an enlisted strength of 44,737 men. Except for the pre-existing four Regular regiments, the six National Guard organizations on the books, and two new artillery regiments, all new units would be support and supply formations. Thus even in the face of conscription, African Americans found themselves directed toward menial labor and support functions, rather than service in the combat arms.[37] Such restrictions flew in the face of President Franklin D. Roosevelt's preference for a desegregated military; but given the strength of the Southern faction of the Democratic Party, he was left with little choice other than to going along, unable or unwilling to press further out of fear of alienating Southern Democrats.

When the United States entered the war, it made inefficient use of the African Americans in the Regular Army, whether they volunteered or were conscripted into service. Undersecretary of War Robert Patterson and Special Envoy William Hastie spearheaded efforts to ameliorate the living and working conditions for black recruits, while also seeking to improve training. Their best efforts could not

---

36 AWC 127-25, "Employment of negro man power in war," November 10, 1925 in Franklin Delano Roosevelt Library Library. https://fdrlibrary.org/documents/...doc.../4693156a-8844-4361-ae17-03407e7a3dee (Accessed February 4, 2018).
37 *Ibid.*, 39–40.

blunt the hostility of Southern communities adjacent to the segregated camps. Black soldiers routinely complained of mistreatment at the hands of white policemen and armed civilians. Denied access to the same lunch counters and ice cream shops frequented by white German and Italian prisoners of war, many black soldiers questioned the legitimacy of the war effort. Freedom for whites in Europe living under Nazi repression meant little to blacks denied their own equal rights in the United States. No less oppressive were the institutional and casual racisms in the Army itself. Black officers and NCOs were routinely insulted and ignored by uniformed white bigots. Just like a generation earlier, circumstance and custom forced black officers to navigate a system fraught with bigotry and prejudice. Subordinates refused to obey orders or return salutes, while senior officers actively sought out examples to expose the discomfort and inadequacy of their black junior officers to lead in these situations.[38]

The final indignity came in the wartime assignment of the overwhelming majority of black soldiers to what were euphemistically known as "labor units." Following the recommendations of the 1925 Army War College memorandum, the War Department designated African Americans as generally unfit for combat on the basis of their poor education and an assumed lower capacity for showing initiative and drive essential for high combat performance. Hundreds of thousands of black troops found themselves in construction, stevedore, and trucking units in the rear echelon, where they performed with manual labor jobs considered too menial for whites.

Despite the demeaning treatment at the hands of white officers, black support units ably executed essential tasks throughout the war, as witnessed in the performance of transportation companies ferrying gasoline, ammunition, and other supplies to the front lines in the fabled "Red Ball Express." And their work was not quite so removed from the front as the War Department expected; in Normandy, along the Rhine, on Bougainville, Iwo Jima, and Okinawa, African-American support units worked under direct enemy fire. When given the chance, they took the field to ferret out snipers and machine gunners in their secure underground bunkers. A further chance to take the field came in the ETO in January 1945 with the formation of the "Fifth Platoons" comprised of African-American soldiers under white leadership. To alleviate manpower shortages gripping American infantry companies, the War Department authorized the creation of these extra platoons for attachment to otherwise all-white companies in a few select infantry

---

38 *Ibid.* See also Morris J. MacGregor and Bernard C. Nalty, eds., *Blacks in the United States Armed Forces*, 13 vol. (Scholarly Resources, Inc., 1977); Morris J. MacGregor, *Integration of the Armed Forces, 1940–1965* (United States Army, Center of Military History, 1981); and most recently, Kimberly Phillips Boehm, *War! What is it Good For?: Black Freedom Struggles and the U.S. Military from World War II to Iraq* (University of North Carolina Press, 2012), 20–64.

divisions. Even though the platoons remained segregated, the overall experience of integrated infantry companies helped convince some regimental and divisional commanders of the fallacies of segregation.[39]

When it came to formal combat organizations, however, the War Department's treatment of African-American soldiers was uneven. First, there were the cases of the Army's four regular colored regiments. The 9th and 10th Cavalry Regiments, after making up the core of the 2nd Cavalry Division, were inactivated in 1944, their members scattered among labor battalions in the Mediterranean theater. The 24th Infantry Regiment was dispatched early in the war in April 1942 to the South Pacific, where, upon its arrival, its battalions were sent to different bases where they worked as labor battalions. Not until February 1944 did the 24th Infantry Regiment take to the field as tactical reserve for the 37th Infantry Division on Bougainville. The 25th Infantry Regiment trained and deployed as part of the newly activated 93rd Infantry Division, joined with support units to establish the 25th Regimental Combat Team (RCT). After a short period of training on Guadalcanal, the 25th RCT was deployed to Bougainville in March 1944, joining the Americal and 37th Infantry Divisions in combat against some 25,000 defending Japanese soldiers and sailors. At no point did the 25th RCT lose contact with the enemy, nor did it once break under fire; nevertheless, the unit's white officers voiced scurrilous – and ultimately unverifiable – rumors about the alleged poor morale and other failings of the regiment.

The mistreatment of the four regular regiments and the 93rd Infantry Division pales in comparison with the abuse heaped upon the 92nd Infantry Division. Reconstituted in October 1942, the division was built around a cadre of black National Guard units. The 92nd Division underwent extensive training in the United States under the direction of its commander, Major General Edward "Ned" Almond. A graduate of the Virginia Military Academy, Almond was advanced ahead of his peers to take charge of the Negro division, largely on the basis that as a Southerner, Almond "knew" how to handle and interact with blacks. The decision to appoint him was one of General George Marshall's few mistakes in the Second World War. The 92nd division's new commander soon gained a reputation among his men as a martinet, who was widely disliked. In order to extend his style of control, Almond selected like-minded Southerners as staff officers and senior field subordinates, men who frequently rated low in competence and motivational skills.

---

39 See David Colley, *Blood for Dignity: The Story of the First Integrated Combat Unit in the U.S. Army* (St. Martin's Griffin, 2004).

In August 1944, the 92nd Infantry Division moved into position opposite the Gothic Line adjacent to the 1st Armored Division. After the division was fully consolidated, it went into action along the Serchio River front in November. Following a failed river crossing attempt, the 92nd was hit by a strong joint Italian and German counterattack opposite Castelnuovo di Garfagnana. Despite heavy casualties totaling 2,997 killed, wounded and missing, Almond scapegoated his black troops rather than accept responsibility for his unit's poor performance. Post-combat inspections of the division revealed high levels of distrust among the black troops toward their officers, who in turn expressed their own dissatisfaction with their men. Almond denied these realities even in the face of strong evidence to the contrary, insisting that African Americans were ill-suited for combat, echoing the charges levied in the 1925 Army War College memorandum. Almond subsequently broke up the 92nd Infantry Division, sending one regiment to the rear for additional training, while another was splintered into labor and security battalions. By the time the division returned to the line in late March 1945, it included only a single black regiment; the other two black regiments were replaced with an all-white regiment and the all-Japanese 442nd Regimental Combat Team.[40]

The US Army fielded a handful of other all-black combat units throughout the war, most notably the 761st Tank Battalion, the 827th Tank Destroyer Battalion, and the 555th Parachute Infantry Battalion. While the 761st Tank Battalion performed admirably in battle, collecting eleven Silver Stars and 69 Bronze Stars in its six months in action, other units did not fare so well. The 555th Parachute Infantry, dubbed the "Triple Nickel" by its men, spent most of the war in training and as smoke jumpers – airborne forest fire fighters – in the Pacific Northwest. Attached to the 82nd Airborne Division after Japan's surrender, the battalion was absorbed by the 505th Airborne Infantry Regiment in December 1947. The 827th Tank Destroyer Battalion suffered greatly from its experience in training, during which time it was reorganized four times and led by eight different commanders. By the time it entered the line in France in December 1944, morale in the battalion had fallen to abysmal levels, the nadir being reached on January 6, 1945, when two separate shooting incidents in the unit occurred. Widespread desertion and insubordination bordering on mutiny only compounded the situation, which ended with the 827th Tank Destroyer Battalion being pulled out of the line for reorganization.[41]

---

40 Booker, *African Americans in the Army*, 246–52; and Nalty, *Strength for the Fight*, 172–74.
41 Booker, *African Americans in the Army*, 139–44, 162–66, 288–23.

Another product of military segregation that stood out were the four squadrons – the 99th, 100th, 301st, and 302nd Fighter Squadrons – comprising the 332nd Fighter Group, the acclaimed "Tuskegee Airmen." In January 1941, the US Army Air Corps was an exclusively white-only branch. This policy changed in the summer when President Franklin D. Roosevelt ordered the Army Air Force to institute a flight training program for black officers. The first cadre of thirteen aviation cadets at Tuskegee Army Air Field, Alabama, included First Lieutenant Benjamin O. Davis, Jr., son of Brigadier General Benjamin O. Davis, Sr., and the future commander of the 332nd Fighter Group. After completing its training in March 1942, they deployed to North Africa as the 99th Pursuit Squadron.

Figure 7.2: Tuskegee airmen Roscoe C. Brown, Marcellus G. Smith, and Colonel Benjamin O. Davis, Jr., confer prior to escort mission. Ramitelli, Italy, March 1945.
Source: Library of Congress.

In North Africa, the 99th Pursuit Squadron, under the command of the newly promoted Lieutenant Colonel Davis, Jr., experienced no shortage of mistreatment from whites. The squadron was routinely criticized for poor performance by superiors and was on the verge of being rotated back to the United States as a failure. Lieutenant Colonel Davis convinced a War Department inspector that on-base segregation – ordered by the base commander in North Africa – denied his pilots the chance to learn from other, more experienced white pilots. In the final report, the inspector ruled against transfer, noting there was no qualitative difference between the 99th Pursuit Squadron and other all-white, squadrons in the theater. This report paved the way for Davis' promotion to Colonel and command of the newly organized 332nd Fighter Group. During its subsequent service over Italy, Romania, France, and Germany, the Tuskegee Airmen flew over 15,000 sorties, earning the respect of their peers and the bomber crews they escorted. Despite the later debunking of the claim that they never lost a bomber they escorted, the 332nd Fighter Group record proved no less outstanding and deserving of recognition. On the basis of Colonel Davis' leadership, the performance of the Tuskegee Airmen facilitated the easy assimilation and integration of the Air Force following President Harry S. Truman's Executive Order 9981 mandating the end of segregation in the American military.[42]

African Americans encountered still more institutionalized racism in the U.S. Navy and Marine Corps to include strict limits on advancing in rank and prohibition from service in combat units. To Secretary of the Navy Franklin Knox, Chief of Naval Operations Admiral Ernest King and the Marine Corps Commandant General Thomas Holcomb, the "negroes" (the civil name by which they were known in the 1940s) lacked the capacities for leadership, initiative, and intellect necessary for effective fulfillment of key duties.[43] The Navy and Marine Corps set up policy barriers that kept black Americans from serving in combat units and limiting their upward mobility in rank.

Similar obstacles faced black sailors in the U.S. Navy. In the 1920s, African Americans were rejected entirely from the service, subjects of a recruitment ban that lasted until the Roosevelt Administration. Subsequent recruitment remained

---

42 See William Alexander Percy, "Jim Crow and Uncle Sam: The Tuskegee Flying Units and the U.S. Army Air Forces in Europe during World War II," *Journal of Military History* 67 (July, 2003): 773–810.
43 John W. Davis, "The Negro in the United States Navy, Marine Corps, and Coast Guard," *Journal of Negro Education* 12 (Summer 1943): 347–48; David J. Ulbrich, *Preparing for Victory: Thomas Holcomb and the Making of the Modern Marine Corps, 1936–1943* (Naval Institute Press, 2011), 119–20, 166–67; Routledge M. Dennis, "Social Darwinism, Scientific Racism, and the Metaphysics of Race," *Journal of Negro Education* 64 (Summer 1995): 243–46.

low, no doubt influenced by the Navy's restriction of virtually all black sailors to the Steward's Branch. Here some 5,000 sailors (in December 1941) served in menial roles as butlers, waiters, and personal valets to naval officers, outside of the standard chain of command and authority. Initial efforts to create service opportunities outside of this menial service class foundered over similar obstacles erected in the Army – black seamen lacked the initiative and intelligence to conduct highly technical tasks; the morale and integrity of the service would suffer if ships were integrated; etc. By July 1942, however, the Navy gradually began to open technical specialties – electrician, machinist, signalman, for example – to black sailors. Progress was painfully slow: in February 1943, only 26,909 black sailors were listed on personnel rolls, amounting to only two percent of the entire enlisted establishment. And over two thirds of these men were employed in the Steward's Branch. Ultimately over 164,000 black sailors were enlisted or conscripted for the Navy, including sixty men and women commissioned as ensigns, during the war.[44] And while fewer were sidelined as Stewards, most were employed on manual labor details, generally working at loading and unloading freighters and tenders.[45] A single destroyer escort, the USS *Mason*, was outfitted with an all-black crew, save for officers, in 1944, a gesture toward an indeterminate future for black sea service within an institution that would remain after the war one of the most stubborn bulwarks against integration in the Federal Government.

In the U.S. Marine Corps, no blacks had ever served as Marines before 1942, and long-standing prohibitions also existed against other selected minorities. Nowhere was this race-based discrimination more tellingly routine than in a form letter from Marine Corps Headquarters rejecting an American man of Filippo descent who wanted to join the Corps just days after the attack on Pearl Harbor. The letter answered his request:

---

44 See correspondence by Navy leaders in McGregor and Nalty, *Blacks in the United States Armed Forces*, 13–14; McGregor, *Integration of the Armed Forces*, 62–67; Nalty, *Strength for the Fight*, 185–87; Steven J. Ramold, *Slaves, Soldiers, Citizens: African Americans in the Union Navy* (Northern Illinois University Press, 2002), 182–86; MacGregor, *Integration of the Armed Forces*, 89, 98.

45 While the Navy considered stevedore duties to be non-hazardous, the reality for black sailors was far different. Often led by callous and incompetent white junior officers, enlisted blacks were often employed in haphazard and unsafe conditions. On July 17, 1944, a series of mishaps connected to an informal contest between white officers over whose crew was faster at loading the ammunition tenders they served led to an explosion at Port Chicago, California, that claimed the lives of 250 black sailors and 50 other persons. The ensuing work shutdown protest was quickly deemed a mutiny by the Navy. Some 50 sailors were court-martialed on grounds of mutiny, a decision ultimately overturned by Thurgood Marshall's intervention. See Robert L. Allen, *The Port Chicago Mutiny: The Story of the Largest Mass Mutiny Trial in U.S. Naval History* (Heyday, 2006).

> It has long been the custom of the Marine Corps to accept for enlistment only men of the Caucasian race because of the limited size of the Marine Corps and the diversified duties performed by its members. To make an exception to this policy in your case is not deemed practicable. . .[46]

Other examples of institutional racism can be seen in the Corps as evinced in January 1942, when Commandant and General Thomas Holcomb testified about manpower mobilization to senior admirals sitting on the U.S Navy's General Board. The Commandant cloaked inequitable policies in progressive management terms, stating that "there would be a definite loss of efficiency in the Marine Corps if we have to take Negroes."[47] Holcomb worried that units would lose combat effectiveness if blacks, like Filipino-American applicants, were permitted to join the Corps. His later testimony revealed other fears that training and supervising African-American units would sap his always-short supply of qualified officers and non-commissioned officers. Holcomb closed his remarks to the senior admirals by stating that "the Negro race has every opportunity now to satisfy its aspirations for combat in the Army – a very much larger organization than the Navy or the Marine Corps – and their desire to enter the naval service is largely, I think, to break into a club that doesn't want them."[48] Holcomb thus went so far as to question African Americans' motivations for joining the Corps as less than patriotic because he felt they were only doing so for the sake of attaining membership in an exclusive group, rather for other more legitimate reasons like patriotism.[49]

Sadly, bigoted beliefs were too deeply entrenched in the officer corps and among the senior leaders in the seaborne services. The Marine Corps, for instance, never had any African American to join its ranks. Even if they entered in the Corps or the Navy, the Navy's General Board later agreed that they should not see combat because "their value generally for field service is gravely doubted."[50] Many sources also reveals that, for General Holcomb and Admiral Ernest King, the institutional racism reinforced personal racism and vice versa.[51]

---

46 Major W.E. Burke, USMC, to Louis C. Padillo, Jr., 29 December 1941, MCGC 1939-50, Box 619, RG 127, NACP. See also Jarvis, *Male Body at War*, 131, 135–36.
47 Holcomb, testimony in hearings of the General Board of the Navy, 23 January 1942, Subject: "Enlistment of Men of Colored Race (201)," cited in Henry I. Shaw, Jr., and Ralph W. Donnelly, *Blacks in the Marine Corps* (History and Museums Division, 1975), 1.
48 *Ibid.*
49 See Morris J. McGregor, Jr., *Integration of the Armed Forces, 1940–1965* (GPO, 1981), 100–101.
50 General Board Study of Men of the Colored Race in other than Messman Branch, 20 March 1942, p. 9, File 18E, Holcomb Papers, Box 19, MCURA.
51 For analyses and archival citations, see Heather Pace Marshall, "Crucible of Colonial Service: The Warrior Brotherhood and the Mythos of the Modern Marine Corps, 1898–1934" (M.A. thesis,

In terms of opening the ranks of the seaborne services to minorities during war, President Roosevelt resolved the wartime matter officially in May 1942 when he signed the legislation authorizing the inclusion of African Americans in the Navy and the Marine Corps. Although more socially progressive than many of his contemporaries and certainly influenced by his wife Eleanor also a champion of human rights, the President was also pragmatic. The U.S. needed to muster all available people to fight a global war. It is worth noting that, back in June 1941, Roosevelt set a precedent for such integration measures in his Executive Order 8802, which prohibited employment discrimination and to promote equal opportunity for all races, creeds, colors and national origin in defense-related industries and government agencies. Despite these decisions, however, personal racism among many individuals and in many sectors slowed the process of inclusivity in the U.S. military. While not prepared to defy Roosevelt, senior Navy and Marine Corps leaders regulated inclusion by establishing racist promotion and manpower allocation policies.[52] For the Corps, all newly organized African-American units would be segregated and led by Caucasian officers. No black could receive an officer's commissions. These caveats translated into preserving combat effectiveness of amphibious assault units and other combat formations as all-white entities. Segregation would remain *de jure* in the U.S. military until 1948 when President Truman issued Executive Order 9981; and it would remain *de facto* throughout much of the Korean War.[53]

Meanwhile on the home front, African-American civilians supported the war effort while also struggling to improve their social and political status in the face of tremendous repression. Over three million blacks left the rural Deep South in search of work in the factories of the Northeast, the Great Lakes, and the Pacific Coast. The so-called "Great Migration" proved no easy move for the families seeking a fresh start. Many factories sought to exclude blacks entirely, despite the Roosevelt Administration's efforts to ban workplace segregation in factories fulfilling federal contracts. Many local tradesmen and industrial unions joined in the exclusionary efforts, seeking to preserve jobs for local members. Families seeking housing in the North and Pacific Coast found themselves shunted into

---

University of Hawaii, 2003); McGregor, *Integration of the Armed Forces*, 3–16; Cameron, *American Samurai*, 237; Kennedy, *Freedom from Fear*, 713, 773–74; Ulbrich, *Preparing for Victory*, 119–20, 166–67.

52 Chairman of the General Board to SecNav, 20 March 1942, Knox to Roosevelt, 27 March 1942, and Roosevelt to Knox, 31 March 1942, all in File 18E, all in Holcomb Papers, Box 19, MCURA; memorandum from Holcomb, 25 May 1942, in McGregor and Nalty, *Blacks in the United States Armed Forces*, 416; McGregor, *Integration of the Armed Forces*, 65–67, 99–103; Nalty, *Strength for the Fight*, 187–90, 199–200.

53 A recent overview can be found in Boehm, *War! What is it Good For?*, 20–64.

the worse urban neighborhoods, often without ready access to public transportation or shopping. As bad as the conditions were in the North and Pacific Coast, they did represent improvements of life compared to that of Southern sharecroppers. There state governments strove to restrict black migration, fearing for the negative impact on agriculture in the South. White racists stepped up their mistreatment of blacks, emboldened in their violence by the arrival in the region of Northern blacks who openly questioned Jim Crow. While nowhere near the level of the 1920s, public lynchings continued in the South, often on the most specious grounds and targeting innocent men.

In response to the pressures of Jim Crow and its slow, inexorable march northward following the Great Migration, civil rights advocates sought new legislation and other protections for African Americans, the "Double Victory" against fascism abroad and racism at home.[54] Many black citizens were uneasy about supporting a war against Nazism and Japanese militarism while they remained a second-class caste at home. Indeed, some initially sympathized with the Greater East Asian Co-Prosperity Sphere claim of liberating Asia from white imperialist domination, changing their opinions only as the extent of brutality against non-Japanese persons became apparent. The lingering open racism against African Americans would prove to be one of the "Good War's" most prominent stains. Across the country – not only in the Southeast – African-American service personnel were harassed, denied services, insulted, beaten, maimed, and even killed by white bigots eager to deny black men and women the dignity of equal treatment in the uniform. The only positive outcome of the experience was the awakening of decent Americans – black and white – to the oppressive nature of racism in American society. Having defeated fascism, American civil libertarians were poised to take on Jim Crow in the post-war years.

African Americans were alone among minorities in feeling the effects of Wartime mobilization on the home front. From the forced confinement of West Coast Japanese-Americans, to the use of Native Americans as radio operators in the Pacific Theater; from the prejudice and oppression of Mexican Americans in the "Zoot Suit Riots" of 1942 and 1943, to the faith-affirming experience of American Jews serving in the armed forces – virtually every racial and ethnic

---

54 See Donald Takaki, *Double Victory: A Multicultural History of America in World War II* (New York: Back Bay Books, 2001); Daniel Kryder, *Divided Arsenal: Race and the American State During World War II* (Cambridge University Press, 2001); and Beth Bailey and David Farber, "The 'Double-V' Campaign in World War II in Hawaii: African Americans, Racial Ideology, and Federal Power," *Journal of Social History* 26 (December 1993): 817–43.

Figure 7.3: Group of young "zoot-suiters" boarding a Los Angeles County Sheriff's bus to make their court appearance. June 1943.
Source: Library of Congress. Reproduction Number: LC-USZ62-113319 (b&w film copy neg.)
Item URL: http://www.loc.gov/pictures/item/95504788/

group in the United States experienced a different war.[55] In the end the American war experience rarely matched the common cause image espoused in the consensus narrative. Rather the American war experience was one no less diverse and multi-dimensional as the current day. Hence aspiring and experienced historians specializing in the Second World War are obligated to highlight how the consensus narrative is flawed. As Michael C.C. Adams points out, "Sometimes we conjure up the past in such a way that it appears better than it really was. We forget ugly things we did and magnify the good things. This is wishful thinking, the desire to retell our past not as it was but as we would like it to have been. If

---

55 For context, see Jack D. Forbes, "'Indian' and 'Black' As Radically Different Types of Categories," in *The Social Construction of Race and Ethnicity in the United States*, eds. Joan Ferrante and Prince Brown Jr. (Longman, 1998), 120–22.

the past is remolded too drastically, it ceases to be real history. It becomes what we call myth, or folklore, instead."[56]

When it comes to the Second World War, Americans have fallen all too readily for the mythological interpretation of "Good War." Instead of the reality of a diverse America responding to the challenges of the outside world, restrained by its own systemic issues associated with racial intolerance and gender chauvinism, a mythic grand narrative of the United States as a homogenous society, all fighting together as one to save the world from itself, has taken root and become the prevailing wisdom of the experience. The following case studies offer a sobering perspective on America's great crusade, highlighting the value of using race and gender as tools of analysis.

On February 19, 1942, President Franklin Roosevelt signed Executive Order 9066, setting in motion one of the most tragic missteps in American domestic policy since the founding of the Republic. Bowing to pressure from military authorities and civilian political groups throughout the West Coast, Roosevelt signed away the already tenuous civil rights of over 100,000 first and second generation Japanese-Americans. Despite their professions of patriotism and civic identity as Americans, thousands of families were forced to leave their homes and businesses in California, Oregon, and Washington for confinement in hastily-constructed internment camps for the duration of the war. In their absence, family homes and properties were seized by local authorities and sold for pennies on the dollar, often to neighbors and business competitors. Conditions in the camps, especially those built in the California Rockies, Utah, and the Arizona desert, were initially harsh. In the first months, many families struggled to survive in the face of fuel and food shortages. Conditions were slow to improve. Housing was built on specifications for temporary barracks, which left much to be desired for families living together over prolonged periods of time. Work details were initially few in number, and restricted to basic agriculture and construction details. An appeal of the resettlement order was denied by the Supreme Court in October 1944, citing the President's authority to secure domestic security in wartime by incarcerating enemy aliens. Since Japanese-Americans were formally classified as such in the Alien Enemies Act of 1941 and subsequent Presidential proclamations, the Court held, no law was broken. In a December 1944 decision, however, the Supreme Court ruled the detainment of loyal citizens was unlawful, while in a separate ruling again upholding the internment act. On January 2, 1945,

---

56 Adams, *Best War Ever*, 1.

the internment act was fully rescinded, and all interned families were released during the next year.[57]

The Puerto Rican National Guard activated its 65th Infantry Regiment in June 1940, and immediately set out a training regimen on the island to bring it up to continental National Guard standards. Given the ethnic makeup of the island's population, it was accepted as a matter of course that the cadre would be commanded by a white colonel and subordinate senior officers. In September 1944, the 65th Infantry Regiment deployed to Southern France, from which it occupied positions in the Maritime Alps. In January 1945, the Puerto Rican regiment joined Seventh Army in its drive across Lorraine and Southern Germany.[58] During the next months, the 65th was organized and treated in the same fashion as African-American organizations – with native-born enlisted personnel and junior-grade officers leading platoons, under the direction of white company, battalion, and regimental command grade officers.

By 1941, many young Jewish men and women sought to further their own personal assimilation by pursuing a secularized path to form an American identity. Almost exclusively urban dwellers settling in the Northeastern cities, American Jews understood the overall message of Nazi's race hatred, but were largely unfamiliar with how it was put into practice. After Pearl Harbor, Jewish males joined in the patriotic rush to enlist in the military. Unlike many other white Americans, however, Jews were themselves targets of racial bigotry in the military, particularly in the Southern and Midwestern training camps. Anti-Semitism did not disappear during their service abroad. What did change, however, was the Jewish soldiers' and sailors' willingness to conform to a secular American norm. As American Jews served abroad, they not only directly confronted the full extent of Nazi injustice, they also experienced disparate communities of observant Jews all across the world from India and Australia to England and Italy. A new sense of pride and purpose evolved as they recognized their distinct identity, their faith renewed in the face of extreme hatred and injustice, nourished by the prospect of a post-war community of survivors.[59]

---

57 See Allen Austin, "Eastward Pioneers: Japanese American Resettlement during World War II and the Contested Meaning of Exile and Incarceration," *Journal of American Ethnic Studies* 26 (Winter 2007): 58–65; Greg Robinson, *By Order of the President: FDR and the Internment of Japanese Americans* (Harvard University Press, 2003); and Roger Daniels, *The Japanese American Cases: The Rule of Law in the Time of War* (Lawrence: University Press of Kansas, 2013), 28–79.

58 Booker, *African Americans in World War II*, 160–61.

59 See Deborah Dash Moore, *GI Jews: How World War II Changed a Generation* (Harvard University Press, 2006).

Last Thoughts on the "Greatest Generation" Mythology

Since the 1980s, America's World War II generation has witnessed a dramatic shift in how their actions have been contextualized by and for the general public. In one sense, this was a predictable outcome, as the fiftieth anniversary of the war neared. As the pain of the Vietnam War and the domestic angst of Watergate faded under the bright glare of Ronald Reagan's staged positivism, Americans began to look more closely to their parents' and grandparents' experiences for evidence of a former state of greatness that was somehow free from the moral stain of the recent past. Following the lead of figures like Stephen Ambrose and Tom Brokaw, a flood of new books on the Second World War began to flood best-seller lists. Largely validational, if not even hagiographic, so many of these books offered blameless chronicles of the American GI locked in mortal contest for the soul of humanity with a wholly evil foe. Before long, the new historiography of the war was joined by film and television portrayals that presented American participation in the Second World War as something like a modern-day Passion Play, in which the noble wartime generation – the "Greatest Generation" – willfully gave of itself to deliver the world from evil incarnate. As audiences and readers consumed this fare, a new love of the military and its legacy took shape during the 1990s and 2000s.[60]

Fortunately these sensationalized interpretations to the Second World War have there detractors and critics. Some, like literary figures and veterans Paul Fussell, Joseph Heller, and Kurt Vonnegut, worked from the perspective that war at its most elemental state is one of collective insanity, in which young men and women are sacrificed without concern, all to fulfill the desires of a very select power elite.[61] These accounts are very important corrections to the over-romanticized perspective of the Second World War in American culture and history, but as a rule do not address specific issues associated with race and gender inequalities and misuses. Other more recent efforts have started to

---

60 Stephen E. Ambrose, *D-Day: June 6, 1944, The Climactic Battle of World War II* (Simon & Schuster, 1994); Michael D. Doubler, *Closing with the Enemy: How GIs Fought the War in Europe, 1944–1945* (University Press of Kansas, 1994); Stephen E. Ambrose, *Citizen Soldiers: The U.S. Army from the Normandy Beaches to the Bulge to the Surrender of Germany* (Simon & Schuster, 1998); Tom Brokaw, *The Greatest Generation* (Random House, 1998); and Peter R. Mansoor, *The G.I. Offensive in Europe: The Triumph of American Infantry Divisions* (University Press of Kansas, 1999).

61 Joseph Heller, *Catch-22* (Simon & Schuster, 1981); Kurt Vonnegut, *Slaughterhouse Five, or the Children's Crusade* (Dell Publishing, 1969); Paul Fussell, *Wartime: Understanding and Behavior in the Second World War* (Oxford University Press, 1990); and Paul Fussell, *The Boys' Crusade: The American Infantry in Northwestern Europe, 1944–1945* (Modern Library, 2005).

engage the "Greatest Generation" mythology head on. Kurt Piehler confronts the question of commemoration and memory in his 2004 book, *Remembering War the American Way*, while Michael R. Dolski's *D-Day Remembered: The Normandy Landings in American Collective Memory* takes on what for many remains the chief source of their adulation and neo-militarism. Elsewhere, military historian Eric Klinek calls into question the veracity of portrayals of "great" American soldier, and specifically the millions of wartime replacements shipped over to Europe. Klinek offers a necessary corrective to the usual celebration of American combat effectiveness by arguing that those replacement soldiers filling out units plagued by casualties were not always the superior fighting men.[62] Meanwhile, over the years, both Michael C.C. Adams and Studs Terkel have also received both popular acclaim and negative reviews for their efforts to shine a light on the misdeeds and failings of the "Greatest Generation" during the "Good War." And in some ways their efforts are indeed warranted. The Federal Government (including the War and Navy Departments) and the American people did behave and act on several occasions in ways that are, by contemporary standards, not only embarrassing but overtly criminal. Nevertheless, many readers and critics of the new revisionists miss the point of Adams, Terkel, and other historians who strive to create a more balanced, if rawer, look at World War II and the American war experience. Just as the United States made mistakes and errors in the prosecution of the war against Nazi Germany and the Japanese Empire, it also made great strides and improvements, not just militarily, but socially as well. Many of these advances would not become immediately apparent. Some, like the integration of the Armed Forces, would come a few years later. Others, like the open recruitment of women in the military along the same standards as men, would come a generation later. What is to be noted that even as tremendous social changes were being effected in American society, the United States was a country at war, and that it was able to consider social change at the same time as it contemplated the complete and utter destruction of its enemies.

Perhaps the most important outcome of America's World War II experience is the realization that armed conflict, as a highly socialized endeavor, has the power to wreak tremendous social change. Just as military institutions and war-fighting practices depend upon the mores and limits of civilian society to set the parameters and limits of their prosecution, so too does society respond to the challenges created by war to recalibrate the contours of citizenship and identity in

---

62 G. Kurt Piehler, *Remembering War the American Way* (Smithsonian Books, 2004); Michael R. Dolski, *D-Day Remembered: The Normandy Landings in American Collective Memory* (University of Tennessee Press, 2016); and Eric Klinek, "The Army's Orphans: The United States Army Replacement System in the European Campaign, 1944–1945" (Ph.D. diss., Temple University, 2014).

the subsequent peace. In this way more than any other, perhaps, the warning of George Santayana is realized. Consider, the full context of his famous quote:

> Progress, far from consisting in change, depends on retentiveness. When change is absolute there remains no being to improve and no direction is set for possible improvement: and when experience is not retained, as among savages, infancy is perpetual. *Those who cannot remember the past are condemned to repeat it.* In the first stage of life the mind is frivolous and easily distracted, it misses progress by failing in consecutiveness and persistence. This is the condition of children and barbarians, in which instinct has learned nothing from experience.[63]

If taken in this frame of reference, the great domestic social changes of the late twentieth century take on different meanings. Rather than individualized responses to social tragedies and injustices, perhaps they are part of the American effort to reconcile the Second World War's greater meanings at home after confronting them abroad. If so, then the real dimensions of victory are still unraveling today, over seven decades after the fact.

---

[63] George Santayana, *The Life of Reason: Or the Phases of Human Progress* (Scribner, 1953), 82. Emphasis added.

8 Race and Gender in the United States during the Early Cold War

Introduction

Following the end of the Second World War, the United States and the Soviet Union viewed each other with growing suspicion as a new sort of conflict called the "Cold War" evolved between these two superpowers. Their opposing ideologies of communism and democracy cast long shadows across the globe. The two antagonists did not fight on battlefields in declared wars, but rather they fought each other with ideas and through surrogates in proxy conflicts like the Korea War. This conflict illuminated racial and gender issues on two levels: the clash of Americans versus the North Koreans and Chinese, and confrontation internal to the American military and society.

This chapter traces the evolution of race and gender relations in the United States from 1945 through the 1950s. It examines how Americans tried to readjust to their peacetime lives while remaining watchful for any external threats. They struggled to balance the rising affluence and security against declining individuality and liberty. These paradoxes played out as expressions of ideological and cultural symbols including race, gender, and sexuality. Inside the U.S. military, African Americans made halting institutional, if not always practical, gains in their quests for equality with the Caucasian men in uniform. The Korean War helped solidify their integration into formerly all-white units. Yet, this conflict also strengthened xenophobic attitudes about the yellow race as peril made even more dangerous by the red peril of communism. Meanwhile on the American home front, women did not experience significant improvements in status after they resumed their traditional roles during the post-war years, and blacks found themselves relegated to their pre-war place as second-class citizens such to Jim Crow exclusions and persistent harassment or worse. Increasing resentment among women and minorities about discrimination presaged the coming seismic shifts in American gender and race relations in the 1960s and thereafter.

Gender and Race Between the Wars, 1945–1950

The U.S. military experienced tremendous flux between the end of World War II and the start of the Korean War: The Army shrank from 6 million soldiers in 1945 to 600,000 in 1950, the Navy from 3.5 million sailors to 400,000, and the Marine Corps from 700,000 Marines to 85,000. The newly-established U.S. Air

https://doi.org/10.1515/9783110477467-008

Force stood at 350,000 personnel in 1950. This dramatic demobilization extended beyond the personnel statistics to racial and gender categories because most blacks and women were required to leave military service. As a whole, the United States armed services entered those post-war years without clear policies about what to do with the African Americans and women remaining in the ranks.

Even though the military reduced its personnel by 90 percent, the Soviet Union and communism loomed large as dual threats to the American way of life. Indeed, since it seemed that World War III could break out any time after 1947, the U.S. military needed to find ways to alleviated wartime mobilization problems. One possible solution lay in Universal Military Training (UMT), which called for every adult American male to train and then serve for one year in the reserves. This vision took on more than an explicitly strategic significance because UMT would, according to historian Lori Lyn Bogle, "instill in the American youth the 'spiritual' and 'patriotic' values deemed necessary to maintain a strong national defense and to preserve national historic values."[1] President Harry Truman and other supportive leaders like Dwight D. Eisenhower believed that linking the spiritual fight in the Cold War to the political fight was key to mobilizing a large force in wartime. UMT could help mold an updated version of muscular Christian manhood capable of winning struggles on ideological as well as physical battlefields. Training would likewise inculcate recruits with faith in the primacy of democracy. Heavy-handed indoctrination in anticommunism would intensify later in the 1950s after the Korean War. Despite the perceived moral, ideological, and military needs, legislation enacting UMT failed to make it through Congress to Truman's desk. Too many Americans in labor, religious, and other sectors would not support ongoing reminders of wartime conscription.[2]

Meanwhile, American veterans leaving the military returned to civilian lives markedly different from the pre-war years. No more did most male veterans seek menial employment or suffer privations of homelessness and hopelessness during the Great Depression in the 1930s. Instead, they enjoyed the greatest economic upswing in American history during the ensuing two post-war decades. Millions of male veterans enjoyed the financial and educational incentives of the "G.I. Bill of Rights" (Service Readjustment Act of 1944) by enrolling in colleges or purchasing homes. Others took jobs in factories in rapidly expanding

---

1 Lori Lyn Bogle, *The Pentagon's Battle of the American Mind: The Early Cold War* (Texas A&M University Press, 2004), 46.
2 Bogle, *The Pentagon's Battle*, 29; Christopher S. DeRosa, *Political Indoctrination in the U.S. Army from World War II to the Vietnam War* (University of Nebraska Press, 2006), 51–90; William A. Taylor, *Every Citizen a Soldier: The Campaign for University Training after World War II* (Texas A&M University Press, 2014), 41–89.

the industrial sector. On its face, these years paid the ultimate peace dividends earned by the United States due to its crucial roles in victory in that conflict.

Nevertheless, gender, racial, and sexual tensions remained unresolved and unanticipated beneath the surface of the apparent stability of the post-war era. It is helpful to understand that straight white males possessed what was considered the ideal combination of these three categories, so they could claim the fullest measure of American citizenship. Conversely, women, minorities, and non-heterosexuals fell short when contrasted to straight white men. Thus, the ideals of race, gender, and sexuality, together with legal status, were predicated on excluding or repressing other supposedly inferior groups. Not only did American society shape this value system, but so too did the American state apparatus. Even after seeing the diabolical results of exclusionary, repression practices in Nazi Germany, the United States retained hierarchies.[3]

For women, the end of the war meant the end of wartime employment, either voluntarily or involuntarily. Some four million faced layoffs in manufacturing in 1946 to make room for men coming home from overseas and leaving military service. Most women resumed their roles in households in yet another iteration of the American Cult of Domesticity that required them to be good wives to their veteran husbands and mothers to their children of the "Baby Boom" generation. The five years between World War II and the Korean War saw a popular stereotype of women cheerfully embracing their return to gender normalcy take hold of public consciousness. Nevertheless, during the previous conflict, American women had achieved a higher level of personal independence, a greater amount of financial autonomy, and a keener sense of self-fulfillment that during any earlier time in American history. Many never forgot their wartime experiences, nor would they find their re-domesticated lives to be overly satisfying. Indeed, those post-war years saw a reinvigorated women's right movement seeking gender equality in every area of American life from politics to the bedroom.[4]

For African Americans, the end of World War II seemed to give hope for improvements in their social, political, and legal standings. Then the post-war years, however, failed to bring to fruition their hopes of equality or security. They

---

3 Margot Canaday, *The Straight State: Sexuality and Citizenship in Twentieth-Century America* (Princeton University Press, 2009), 256–57; and Linda K. Kerber, "The Meanings of Citizenship," *Journal of American History* 84 (December 1997): 833–54.

4 Elaine Tyler May, *Homeward Bound: American Families in the Cold War Era* (Basic Books, 1988); Joanne Meyerowitz, *Not June Clever: Women and Gender in Postwar American, 1945–1960* (Temple University, 1994); Robert D. Dean, *Imperial Brotherhood: Gender and the Marking of Cold Foreign Policy* (University of Massachusetts Press, 2001), 66–70; and Elaine Tyler May, *Fortress America: How We Embraced Read and Abandoned Democracy* (Basic Books, 2017), 13–56.

received little respect or help from the white establishment, despite storied records and great sacrifices during the conflict.[5] With the U.S. military demobilization in full swing in late 1945, the few blacks remaining in uniform could not hope for advances in ranks or deployments to desirable stations. Those leaving the military fared badly when returning to civilian life to face ingrained racism, particularly in the southern states where blacks encountered obstructionism and discrimination at best and beatings, assaults, lynchings, and other acts of terror at worst.

One incident in 1946 became the touchstone that helped spur Truman to initiate reforms in race policies. A discharged black veteran named Isaac Woodard boarded a bus for a trip Georgia to South Carolina, still wearing the uniform of a Marine Corps sergeant. At one stop, Woodard was arrested on the trumped-up charge of drunkenness. The Caucasian police officers viciously beat Woodard with nightsticks, leaving him blinded and needing medical treatment. He spent that night in jail without receiving treatment. This incident's racial brutality and miscarried justice exposed bigotry still prevalent in the South and exploded into a major controversy. The Woodward beating was only one of several racially-motivated episodes of white-on-black or black-on-white violence during the late 1940s. Over the next two decades, blacks grew more restive, if sometimes militant, in their pursuit of fully equal privileges citizenship. African-American veterans also joined these grassroots civil rights efforts. Prominent white Americans, including Eleanor Roosevelt and Albert Einstein, added their voices to protests against white racism.[6]

President Harry Truman felt what military historian Bernard C. Nalty called a "gnawing discomfort with the discriminatory practices of the United States."[7] Such disrespect for fellow Americans and their civil rights offended the president's sense of order and morality. From a practical standpoint, Truman could use the African-American segment of the population as a potential source of manpower for the military as would be seen in the Korean War four years later. Ever the political pragmatist, he also recognized he needed African-American votes to win reelection. He could not, however, push legislation through a hostile Congress with so many influential senators and representatives hailing from Southern states. Indeed, the president's risky decision to push for racial integration of the armed forces provoke white Southern democrats to follow then-South Carolina Governor Strom Thurmond and the newly-established "Dixiecrats" in a

---

5 For the standard study of African Americans in the Cold War, see Harvard Sitkoff, *The Struggle for Black Equality, 1945–1980* (Hill and Wang, 1981).

6 Bernard C. Nalty, *Strength for the Fight: A History of Black Americans in the Military* (New York: Free Press, 1989), 204–207, 229–30; and Phillips, *War! What is it Good For?*, 63–111, 167–70.

7 Nalty, *Strength for the Fight*, 247.

third party challenge in 1948.[8] Congress did pass a new Selective Service Act, but this segregationist legislation was not what Truman wanted to sign into law. With no hope of vetoing the act, the president reacted by using his an other option – the executive order – a mandate that carried the weight of law in the Executive Branch and the military. Truman issued Executive Order 9981 on July 26, 1948, which read in part:

> WHEREAS it is essential that there be maintained in the armed services of the United States the highest standards of democracy, with equality of treatment and opportunity for all those who serve in our country's defense. . . . It is hereby declared to be the policy of the President that there shall be equality of treatment and opportunity for all persons in the armed services without regard to race, color, religion or national origin. This policy shall be put into effect as rapidly as possible, having due regard to the time required to effectuate any necessary changes without impairing efficiency or morale.[9]

In the directive, the commander-in-chief championed the leveling and equalizing of the new, unified Department of Defense. While Truman's reform did not call for integration as such, it did lead to its implementation in the U.S. military in 1954 – long before civilian America would achieve similar levels of desegregation. Some military officers, among them Army Chief of Staff Omar N. Bradley, with bigoted beliefs still opposed desegregation of units because they worried that unit effectiveness and combat readiness would suffer by integrating African Americans into Caucasian units. For General Bradley and the Supreme Commander for the Allied Powers General Douglas MacArthur, blacks did not match up to Caucasians in intellect, initiative, discipline, reliability. Many Army officers also did not want blacks to be come officers, let alone commanding fellow whites in units. Thus they dragged their feet on implemented Truman's executive order, with the relatively better results achieved in the new Air Force, and worse results by degrees in the Navy, then the Army, and lastly the Marine Corps.[10]

Like African Americans, women in military service experienced precipitous demobilization in the immediate post-war years. Enlistments into the Women's Army Corps (WAC), for example, halted in August 1945 as did their schools and training. The WAC dropped from nearly 96,000 women in June of that same year

---

8 *Ibid.*, 240–45, 254.

9 Harry S. Truman, "E.O. 9981,"1948, http://www.ourdocuments.gov/doc.php?flash=true&-doc=84&sortorder= (access 30 August 2009). For the most recent analysis of Truman and E.O 9981, see Jeremy Maxwell, *Brotherhood in Combat: How African Americans Found Equality in Korea and Vietnam* (University of Oklahoma Press, 2018), 39–48.

10 Phillips, *War! What is it Good For?*, 111–12, 126–27; and Maxwell, *Brother in Combat*, 77–79.

to 18,000 in mid-1946 and finally to 4,900 by 1949.[11] The other branches' female components faced similar downsizing. After all, they had been expected to serve in World War II "for the duration of the emergency and six months." Once that crisis ended, so too did the desperate need for personnel. Senior military officers and civilian administrators nevertheless puzzled about what to do with the remaining women in uniform in peacetime. The newly-promoted Army Chief of Staff, General Dwight D. Eisenhower, intervened in early 1946 and directed that legislation be sent to Congress to make the WAC a permanent fixture in the Regular Army and Organized Reserve. Two years later, President Truman signed the Women's Armed Services Integration Act into law. This legislation applied to women in all service branches, but its name belied the implications for women. In juxtaposing the meanings of femininity and masculinity with warrior and citizen, historian Margot Canaday argues that "women's integration, in short, did not neuter the traditional martial citizenship, which remained male."[12] In practice, the new WAC resembled its wartime antecedent in function and structure insofar it still subjected women to stricter rules regarding moral behavior. In ways similar in the Second World War, women endured scrutiny about their sexual orientation because of worries about corrupting influences of lesbianism. Questions about motivations of women to enter such a masculine environment remained deeply embedded in this institutionalized paranoia.[13]

The Women's Armed Services Integration Act did nothing so controversial as to integrate women into combat units. In their logistical and administrative roles, women experienced promotion ceilings and assignment limitations that constituted institutional chauvinism. Just as most Americans and their representatives in Congress were not ready to see women as full-fledged "soldiers," so too did American military leaders balk at giving women expanded roles on battlefields or duties with heavy physical requirements.[14]

Unlike blacks and women who entered the post-war era with some gains yet many unrealized hopes, Caucasian American men resumed their civilian

---

11 Jeanne Holm, *Women in Combat: The New Reality* (Wadsworth, 1996), 97–105; and Bettie J. Morden, *The Women's Army Corps, 1945–1978* (Center of Military History, 1990), 409.

12 Canaday, *The Straight State*, 212, and for greater context, see pp. 207–13. See also Tanya L. Roth, "'Attractive Career for Women': Opportunities, Limitations, and Women's Integration in the Cold War Military," in *Integrating the U.S. Military: Race, Gender, and Sexual Orientation since World War II*, eds. Douglas Walter Bristol, Jr., and Heather Marie Stur (Johns Hopkins University Press, 2017): 74–81.

13 Canaday, *The Straight State*, 181–81, 212–13; and Leisa D. Meyer, *Creating G.I. Jane: Sexuality and Power in the Women's Army Corps in World War II* (Columbian University Press, 1996), 100–21, 148–78.

14 Holm, *Women in the Military*, 105–30.

lives with expectations of finding jobs, marrying sweethearts, raising children, and achieving the American dream. The first few years after the war saw their expectations met in soaring job opportunities and living standards that seemed to mark attainment of a straight white middle-class masculine ideal. Men worked forty-hour-a-week jobs, drove sedans, mowed lawns, and lived in new liminal spaces between the urban and the rural worlds called "suburbia." The construction of highways made this suburban living practical because fathers and husbands could commute longer distances between work and home. The first new suburban "frontiers" appeared in 1947 in the planned community of Levittown on Long Island, New York, where families occupied blocks and blocks of houses almost identical in floor plans and architecture. Levittown came to symbolize a homogenous, predictable, sanitized, and racially exclusive atmosphere for those residents. Other suburban communities quickly sprang up on outskirts of urban centers throughout the United States. Even Caucasian men working as wage laborers in factories could also achieve financial success that also allowed them to purchase automobiles and enjoy the middle-class suburban lifestyle.[15]

Although living in Levittowns seemed to correlate with idyllic masculinity, some problems lurked beneath the serene surface. Those millions of American men did not necessarily feel self-satisfied or self-confident while they reaped the benefits of victory over the diabolical Axis enemies. A closer examination of their collective psyche reveals growing status anxiety in men who consciously or unconsciously questioned their masculine prerogatives. Over time, the men found themselves locked into bland white-collar or blue-collar jobs that made them cogs in the corporate wheel, and that created restrictions leaving them living lives of quiet desperation. This phenomenon ran deeper than the privileged men whining in undignified ways about their post-war plights in life. Indeed, they began looking for ways to recapture their glorious war years when they proved their manhood and served a cause greater than themselves.[16]

Writing in 2005, literary scholar Leo Braudy points to the popularity of the western film as one avenue for American men to find reassurance in the age of flagging masculinity. From 1946 to 1951, one out of every five movies was a western; and between 1949 and 1952, half of the 50 top-grossing films came from

---

15 Kenneth T. Jackson, *Crabgrass Frontier: The Suburbanization of the United States* (Oxford University Press, 1987); and Adam Rome, *The Bulldozer in the Countryside: Suburban Sprawl and the Rise of American Environmentalism* (Cambridge University Press, 2001).
16 For contemporary observations, see Sloan Wilson, *Man in the Gray Flannel Suit* (New York: Simon & Schuster, 1955); and William H. Whyte, Jr., *The Organization Man* (Doubleday, 1957). For historical analysis, see Susan Faludi, *Stiffed: The Betrayal of the American Man* (William Morrow, 1999).

this genre. Such Hollywood icons as John Wayne and Alan Ladd starred in formulaic stories that, for Braudy, "fashioned a myth of facing moral decisions on the ragged edged of a civilization, where only guns spoke decisively." Protagonists like Wayne's Captain Nathan Brittles in *She Wore a Yellow Ribbon* and Ladd's Shane in the title role "became the symbolic core of masculinity because [their] struggle with the forces arrayed against [them] was so direct and so personal."[17] When Brittles or Shane did resort to violence to solve problems, the men watching them on screen could live vicariously through their actions. The western film genre supplanted the heroes – or more appropriately heroic caricatures – of Sir Walter Scott, Rudyard Kipling, or Stephen Crane that modeled masculinity in the late nineteenth and early twentieth centuries. In this way, historian James Gilbert finds that American men in late 1940s and 1950s could "refurbish" their masculinity by embracing "fictional idols, charismatic idols, and celebrities."[18] The men could also learn from Brittles and Shane to temper their aggression with stoicism because a stoical mindset could help them cope with their new-found lives of compliance. As will be seen later in this chapter, some Caucasian American men reacted to the onrushing demands of middle-class masculinity by following divergent paths or rebelling against the structure and tedium of the suburban good life.

The Korean War: Fighting on Racial and Gender Fronts

Despite hopes for international harmony, the years between 1945 and 1950 proved to be a tension-filled interlude across the globe and at home in the United States. The Soviet Union emerged from the Second World War in control of Eastern Europe, while the Americans helped rebuild West Germany and Western Europe in their own image. The two superpowers grew further and further apart even as the so-called "Cold War" started at least by 1947. One of the most compelling American statements about the Soviet Union can be seen George F. Kennen's secret "Long Telegram" sent to the U.S. State Department in early 1946 when he was an American diplomat serving in Moscow. Kennan argued that

> We have here a political force committed fanatically to the belief that with [the] US there can be no permanent *modus vivendi*, that it is desirable and necessary that the internal

---

17 Braudy, *From Chivalry to Terrorism*, 497.
18 James Gilbert, *Masculinity in the Middle: Searching for Masculinity in the 1950s* (University of Chicago Press, 2005), 30.

harmony of our society be disrupted, our traditional way of life be destroyed, the international authority of our state be broken, if Soviet power *is* to be secure.[19]

This rhetoric cast the differences between the two superpowers as unequivocal and irreconcilable. With such a hardline stance as a starting point, Kennan then connected the need for unyielding American policy and military reactions to the Soviet threat with the requisite for potent American masculinity. Diplomatic historian Frank Costogliola explains how these gendered motifs related to the Cold War struggle:

> Kennan proposed that the West respond to the monstrous hypermasculinity of the Soviet Union by itself acting more masculine. He urged that the United States "tighten" up, achieve greater "cohesion, firmness and vigor," and approach the Soviet Union with the conventionally masculine virtues of "courage, detachment, objectivity, and . . . determination not to be emotionally provoked or unseated.[20]

American political leaders on both sides of the aisle embraced the masculinist metaphors in the "Long Telegram," which when taken together with Kennan's "X" article published in 1947, represented a realistic threat assessment of the Soviets and communism, as well as the rational prescription for Americans' strategies to deal with that threat. American militarism and nationalism would follow parallel paths in coincidence with containment.[21]

Then an unexpected event shattered the tenuous peace in the international arena when Communist North Korean soldiers invaded South Korea on June 25, 1950. They drove unprepared South Korea and American forces into headlong retreat to a small defensive pocket in the southeastern corner of the Korean peninsula called the Pusan Perimeter. President Truman gained permission from the United Nations to commit American air, ground, and seaborne forces to help the beleaguered Allies in the South and to contain communism. By the fall of 1950, the U.S. and U.N. forces under General Douglas MacArthur's command made a daring amphibious assault at Inchon and subsequently drove the North Koreans back into their home territory as far as the Yalu River near the Chinese border. With the North's collapse imminent, China intervened *en masse* to help their communist neighbor beginning in late November. Some 300,000 troops of

---

19 George F. Kennan, "The Long Telegram," 22 February 1946, in *Foreign Relations of the United States, 1946, Eastern Europe, The Soviet Union, Volume VI* (GPO, 1969), 706, cited in Frank Costogliola, "'Unceasing Pressure for Penetration': Gender, Pathology, and George Kennan's Formation of the Cold War," *Journal of American History* 84 (March 1997): 1333.
20 *Ibid.*
21 *Ibid.*, 1336. See also X (Kennan's pseudonym), "The Sources of Soviet Conduct," *Foreign Affairs* 25 (July 1947): 566–82.

the Chinese military juggernaut stunned the Americans with a surprise attack, sending them on their second retreat back to the south. Meanwhile, MacArthur, in his eagerness to use American air power to drop conventional bombs on the Yalu's bridges and other targets to disrupt Chinese logistics, criticized Truman's decision to fight a limited war in Korea. MacArthur's intransigence and insubordination aroused Truman's ire, so the president relieved him of command in April 1951. Truman then promoted General Matthew B. Ridgeway to direct all U.N. forces in South Korea and the Pacific. Ridgeway proved equal to the task of reinvigorating the demoralized American troops into a force capable of fighting the Chinese to a standstill by the summer of 1951. The conflict evolved into a bloody war of attrition between entrenched outposts for the next two years. Meanwhile, the U.N., U.S., North Korean, South Korean, and Chinese conducted endless negotiations until a cease-fire was called and an armistice signed in July 1953. In all, nearly 6 million American draftees and volunteers served in the U.S. military during thirty-seven months of fighting. Of these, some 38,000 American lost their lives.[22]

Although the preceding narrative tells the conventional story of the Korean War, it fails to address the issues of race relations and racism in that conflict. In fact, this conflict should be considered a "race war," as much as a proxy war between competing ideologies. Few Americans predicted that the North Koreans and Chinese could score initial victories in 1950 or later fight in sustained operations against the mighty U.S. military. Pre-war assumptions about a supposedly inferior race dominated the American mindset between 1945 and 1950, just as had happened regarding the Japanese in 1941. In combat, the Chinese and North Koreans behaved in ways similar the Japanese: the former pair of enemies attacked in wave after wave of infantrymen and seemed impervious to massive casualties; and the latter enemy fought to the death and made massed suicide charges against American lines. Scholars in military history, anthropology, military culture, diplomacy, and Asian studies see continuity in American racism so explicit from the Pacific War to the Korean War and finally to the Vietnam War. The two later conflicts also added ideological factors because, after the North Korean and Chinese achieved their battlefield successes, Americans witnessed the emergence of a dangerous "red peril" that harnessed the Asian hordes in the

---

22 For conventional studies of the Korean War that do not address issues of race and racism, see Allan Millett's *The War for Korea, 1945–1950: A House Burning* (University Press of Kansas, 2005) and *The War for Korea, 1950–1951* (University Press of Kansas, 2010). For treatments that deal with racial issues, see David Halberstam, *The Coldest Winter: America and the Korean War* (Hyperion Books, 2007); and Maxwell, *Brotherhood in Combat.*

service of Marxist-Leninism that was layered over the "yellow peril" so ingrained in the Pacific War.[23]

Commentary during the Korean War offers convincing evidence about how charged a combination of racism and ideology became. One U.S. Army officer recalled in a 1952 book that "countless masses of uniformed robots" had captured him earlier in the conflict, and that "There is a sadism and brutality inherent in many Asiatics, that is not commonly found within men of the better educated areas of the world."[24] These few words drip with derisive stereotypes that reveal several factors denigrating the Chinese. Obviously, the experiences of one American prisoner of war held by the Chinese during the Korean War would not have encouraged less harsh opinions. It is little wonder that vitriol so conspicuous in the Pacific War also appeared in the Korean War. Epithets revealed unambiguous American attitudes regarding Asian peoples, such as demeaning terms like "chinks" and "Chinamen" for the Chinese; or "gooks," "zipperheads," "bucketheads," "kinks," and "underbites" for the North Koreans. Indeed, American slurs barely distinguished between "bad" Asians and "good" Asians like the South Koreans called "biscuit heads." Finally and hardly unexpectedly, the North Koreans and Chinese also utilized deleterious racial stereotypes about Caucasian Americans in their propaganda. Just as in the Pacific War, racism charged emotions and actions on both sides.[25]

Apart from dehumanizing the enemy, racism affected the U.S. military's establishment during the Korean War. In 1950, the U.S. armed services had not yet integrated units in any meaningful ways despite Truman's E.O. 9981 two years earlier. The disregard for African Americans in uniform in 1949 was evinced by their proportions among enlisted personnel and officers:

- 12.4 percent of enlisted soldiers and 1.8 percent of officers in the U.S. Army;
- 4.7 percent enlisted and no officers in the Navy;
- 5.1 percent of enlisted and 0.6 percent of officers in the Air Force; and
- a paltry 2.1 percent of enlisted and no officers in the U.S. Marine Corps.

---

23 Kindsvatter, *American Soldiers*, 301–13; Cameron, *American Samurai*, 228–33; Tchen and Yeats, *The Yellow Peril*, 298–307; Ballard and McDowell, "Hatred and Combat," 234–35; Hunt, *Ideology and U.S. Foreign Policy*, 143–44, 162–68; and Heonik Kwon, *The Other Cold War* (Columbia University Press, 2010), 37–41.

24 Robert B. Rigg, *Red China's Fighting Hordes: A Realistic Account of the Chinese Communist Army, by a U.S. Army Officer* (Military Service Publishing Company, 1952), cited in 302.

25 Christina Klein, *Cold War Orientalism: Asia in the Middlebrow Imagination, 1945–1961* (University of California Press, 2003), 20–70; Susan A. Brewer, *Why America Fights: Patriotism and Propaganda from the Philippines to Iraq* (Oxford University Press, 2009), 141–48, 173; and Cameron, *American Samurai*, 230–33.

Figure 8.1: Painting on a wall of the Sinchon Museum of American War Atrocities depict alleged atrocities carried out by American soldiers during the Korean War.
Source: https://commons.wikimedia.org/wiki/File:DPRK_Museum_painting_1.jpg

Several reasons play into this low figures. Doubtlessly, the military's wheels of bureaucracy turned slowly during demobilization of the late 1940s. Not least among other factors militating against integration was ingrained prejudice. Too many high-ranking white officers believed that blacks were inferior to whites and thus made less competent soldiers. They either actively obstructed or passively stalled integration after 1948. Harkening back to his attitudes about black troops in the 92nd Division in World War II, for instance, Major General Edward "Ned" Almond had not changed his assumption that African-American soldiers were unfit for combat. He held these beliefs while serving as MacArthur's chief of staff and field commander in Korea in 1950.[26] When testifying before the U.S. Senate's Armed Services Committee in 1948, General Dwight D. Eisenhower may have been less stringent than Almond but still made degrading comments: "In

---

26 Nalty, *Strength for the Fight*, 172–73; Halberstam, *The Coldest Winter*, 547–550, 560; and Maxwell, *Brotherhood in Combat*, 80–82.

general, the Negro is less well educated than this brother citizen that is white and if you make a complete amalgamation, what you are going to have is in every company the Negro is going to be relegated to the minor jobs. . . because the competition is too rough."[27] The attitudes of Almond and Eisenhower point to policies firmly imbedded in Army infrastructure. Although military historian James E. Westheider does not focus on the Korean War in his book *Fighting on Two Fronts: African Americans and the Vietnam War*, his ideas can nevertheless be applied in the 1950s. His typologies of racism – "institutional racism," "personal racism," and "perceived racism" – saturated the U.S. armed services from 1945 through the early 1960s and beyond.[28]

Westheider's three racisms are tragically illustrated roles by the story of U.S. Army's 24th Infantry Regiment during the Korean War. When the conflict erupted in June 1950, MacArthur cobbled together units in the Far East and threw them into the breach to stem the North Korean tide during that summer. Among these was the 24th Infantry Regiment, a segregated black unit mostly led by white officers. It deployed to Korea in July 1950 as part of Major General William F. Kean's 25th Infantry Division. The prejudiced Kean held low opinions about the capabilities of black soldiers. In their first combat action, elements of the 24th recaptured the town of Yechon from the North Koreans. Combat effectiveness did not recur in July at the town of Sangju and thereafter. During engagements that fall, cohesion and discipline collapsed in the 24th as many of its soldiers retreated, if not fled pell-mell, from positions at the first sounds of enemy gunfire. It is worth noting that Caucasian units also broke and ran in the face of the North Korean tide.[29] Even so, Kean believed that this single regiment's lackluster performance could cause the ultimate defeat of all U.S. forces in Korea. He was not alone in his opinions, as unequivocally argued in six decades later by historian Kimberly L. Phillips:

> Many in the army subscribed to the idea that race was biological and immutable, especially under combat conditions. Based on long-held racial stereotypes and assumptions about blacks' biological inferiority, some commanders believed African Americans occupied the

---

27 Dwight D. Eisenhower, testimony, U.S. Senate Committee on Armed Services, *Hearings on Universal Military Training*, 80th Cong., 2nd sess., 1948, cited in Lewis, *American Culture of War*, 140.

28 James E. Westheider, *Fighting on Two Fronts: African Americans in the Vietnam War* (New York University Press, 1999), 4–5. This is a seminal work on the topic.

29 William T. Bowers, et al., *Black Soldier, White Army: The 24th Infantry Regiment in Korea* (U.S. Army Center of Military History, 1996); Charles M. Bussey, *Firefight at Yechon: Courage and Racism in the Korean War* (University of Nebraska Press, 2002); and Andrew J. Huebner, *The Warrior Image: Soldiers in American Culture from the Second World War to the Vietnam Era* (University of North Carolina Press, 2011), 100–19.

lowest strata in the hierarchy of races. Wartime and postwar studies by the biological, psychological, and social sciences challenged these pervasive ideas, but racialist sensibilities prevailed and informed the army's convictions about the need for segregation in the foxhole.[30]

The confluence of effective enemy forces, plummeting morale among black soldiers, casualties among the unit's officers, institutional racism of segregation, personal racism of the unit's officers, and perceived racism of unsubstantiated rumors helped create a perfect storm of circumstances – a sadly self-fulfilling prophecy for the racism in the officer corps. The battlefield failures drove the decision in September 1950 to disband the 24th Regiment. Desperate American military manpower shortages in Korea, however, stopped that from becoming a reality.[31]

Back in the United States, the 24th Regiment's dismal combat record in Korea played into the hands of both opponents and proponents of racial integration. For the naysayers, the moribund 24th represented a *fait accompli* that grew out the weaknesses of blacks in uniform. These, detractors argued, would deteriorate further if African-American soldiers mixed with whites in desegregated units. Conversely, according to supporters of racial integration, the regiment's poor combat performance pointed to the need to integrate blacks and whites and provide better training, equipment, and leaders, thereby raising expectations and thus combat effectiveness. Still, other groups on the American home front gravitated toward the controversies of race and racism sparked by the unit's situation. Critics, including vocal civil rights activists Paul Robeson and W.E.B. Du Bois, denounced the war by pointing to the hypocrisy of an oppressed American racial minority group – black soldiers – fighting and dying for Caucasian-led capitalist imperialism against other peoples of color – Asians. This created a credibility gap for the United States that embarrassed President Truman.[32]

Not all senior American officers shared the hidebound personal racism of Generals William Kean or "Ned" Almond. Quite the contrary, General Matthew Ridgway broke with his fellow generals. After he replaced the relieved MacArthur as commander of U.N. and U.S. forces in South Korea in 1951, Ridgway pushed very hard the U.S. Army to integrate. He recalled in his memoir that:

---

30 Phillips, *War! What is It Good For?*, 140.
31 MacGregor, *Integration of the Armed Forces*, 46–42; Nalty, *Strength for the Fight*, 256–58; Halberstam, *The Coldest Winter*, 142–44; and Phillips, *War! What is It Good For?*, 132–36.
32 Lawrence Lamphere, "Paul Robeson, *Freedom* Newspaper, and the Korean War," in *Paul Roberson: Essays on His Life and Legacy*, ed. Joseph Dorinson and William Pencak (McFarland, 2002), 133–41; and Phillips, *What is It Good For?*, 125–27, 154–62.

Figure 8.2: Sgt. 1st Class Elijah McLaughlin (left front) and Cpl. Luther Anderson (right front) lead their squad down a steep hill as they begin a 1,500-yard advance toward another hill north-west of the Ch'ongch'on River, North Korea, Nov. 20, 1950. During the Korean War, soldiers also started serving in combat in integrated units for the first time.
Source: U.S. Army Heritage and Education Center, Carlisle, Pennsylvania.
http://soldiers.dodlive.mil/tag/17th-regimental-combat-team/

> It was my conviction. . . that only in this way could we assure the sort of esprit de corps a fighting army needs, where each soldier stands proudly on his own feet, knowing himself to be as good as the next fellow and better than the enemy. Besides it has always seemed to me both un-American and un-Christian for free citizens to be taught to downgrade themselves this way, as if they were unfit to associate with their fellows or to accept leadership themselves.[33]

The relatively progressive Ridgway's concerted efforts over the next two years of the conflict would account for the integration of some 300,000 African Americans in the Army and eventually extend to the units stationed in Europe and back in the United States. This made the Korean War the watershed for blacks in the U.S. Military. In the meantime, other socially reactionary leaders like Ned Almond continued to stall desegregation. Nevertheless, new units with white and black soldiers serving side-by-side acquitted themselves admirably during the rest the Korean.[34]

33 Matthew B. Ridgeway, *The Korean War*, cited in Lewis, *The American Culture of War*, 140.
34 Maxwell, *Brotherhood in Combat*, 69–72.

Within the sweep of the larger Cold War context, the categories of race and gender became entangled. The Korean War re-energized white American manhood because the conflict put a violent face on what had appeared to be an ideological standoff between 1947 and 1950. The conflict brought with it reaffirmations of the needs for the masculine prerogative of protector and warrior. The Korean War likewise solidified the Cold War into a zero-sum game for every American president from Truman through Richard Nixon. At stake were the freedoms of Americans and other peoples across the globe. Either the United States would triumph over the godless totalitarian communists, or the U.S. would succumb to them in defeat. The future required an absolute stand against this threat as articulated in the concept of containment, which found its voice in the "Report to the National Security Council – NSC-68." The classified document had been drawn up in April 1950 and then adopted as policy by Truman after the start of the Korean War. NSC-68 turned the U.S. into a national security state where stopping Soviet and communist expansion rested atop the priorities for foreign policy. Most American politicians, regardless of party, saw their world through a mono-focal lens that did not allow for grayscale. Americans and their government fused nationalism, militarism, and anticommunism as the United States took whatever measures deemed necessary for security. Among these was the ascendant military-industrial complex that would so strongly dominate defense and domestic policies since the 1950s.[35]

Throughout the Cold War, race became intertwined in other ways and other places across the globe as part of the American strategy of containment. Its application in the international arena did not necessarily support progressive improvement race relations. In one example, race and racism became pawns in the struggle against Soviet influence and communist expansion.[36] In South Africa in the decades after Second World War, successive governments run by the white minority enforced "*Apartheid*" in that nation. Literally meaning "apart-ness," this term became synonymous with racial segregation

---

35 This conceptualization of symmetry versus asymmetry comes from John Lewis Gaddis' seminal *Strategies of Containment: A Critical Appraisal of Postwar American National Security* (Oxford University Press, 1982). For studies of the causes and effects of nationalism and militarism, see William J. Novak, "The Myth of the Weak American State," *American Historical Review* 113 (June 2008): 752–72; for an application in race relations, see Manfred Berg, "Black Civil Rights and Liberal Anticommunism: The NAACP in the Early Cold War," *American Historical Review* 94 (June 2007): 75–96; for a historiographic overview, see Ingo Trauschweizer, "Militarism and Nationalism," in *The Routledge History of Global War and Society*, 296–308.

36 Useful starting points are Thomas Borstelmann, *The Cold War and the Color Line: American Race Relations in the Global Arena* (Harvard University Press, 2001); and Hunt, *Ideology and U.S. Foreign Policy.*

in that nation. Under this harsh system, the black African majority comprised 75 percent of South Africa's population yet lived in separate areas with poorer standards, lower incomes, and inferior education systems than their white counterparts. Such discrimination became part of the fabric of white-dominated culture in what historian George Frederickson has called an "overtly racist regime,"[37] and the foundation for government policies which then-U.S. Minister to South Africa Thomas Holcomb labeled as "oppressive," "undemocratic," and "centripetal in outlook" in the late 1940s.[38] The blacks endured disenfranchisement, incarceration, and deadly violence at the hands of a government determined to keep them in a subservient position in the racial hierarchy. American leaders were fully aware of the oppression of blacks in South Africa, however, they decided not to intervene. The same President Truman, who played such a critical role in integrating the U.S. armed forces, failed to exert pressure on the white government to change its harsh policies. Successive presidents turned blinds eyes to the oppressive policies under Apartheid for many decades. They feared that any bid by the unpredictable black majority for political power might bring with it communist subversion or revolution, neither of which could be tolerated in light of American national security exigencies for a stable South Africa with its vast mineral resources and strategic location.[39]

Gender, Sexuality, and Race on the American Home Front, 1950–1960

The many guises of communism's threat also needed to be contained at home in the United States, where national survival required the maintenance of prescribed roles of men and women, white and black. The primary line of defense centered on preserving the traditional, middle-class, Caucasian family unit as the hegemonic structure in the 1950s. This so-called "nuclear family" had as its head the father and husband who played the roles of provider, protector, and patriarch. His wife, as home-maker and mother of two or three children, consolidated the existence of proper and mature heterosexuality between them. Their family lived

---

37 Frederickson, *Racism*, 101–107, 141–51.
38 Ulbrich, *Preparing for Victory*, 181–85.
39 Thomas J. Noer, "Truman, Eisenhower, and South Africa: The 'Middle Road' and Apartheid," *Journal of Ethnic Studies* 11 (Spring 1983): 75–104; Thomas Borstelmann, *Apartheid's Reluctant Uncle: The United States and Southern Africa in the Early Cold War* (Oxford University Press, 1993), 83–89, 199–202; and Kwon, *The Other Cold War*, 37–38.

quiet, orderly, secure, and domesticated lives – safely containing any possible internal challenges and insulating themselves from any external threats. Census records revealed that 96 percent of American women and 94 percent of men were married during the 1950s. The divorce rate hovered between 20 and 25 percent, which was considerably lower than the 33–50 percent range from the 1970s to the present.[40]

Recent scholarship illuminates how and why some elements in America perpetuated the ideal family. In her book *Prescription for Heterosexuality: Sexual Citizenship in the Cold War Era*, historian Carolyn Herbst Lewis uses the term "heteronormativity" to describe how "gender and sexual performances of heterosexuality constitute[d] the only legitimate expression of self, desire, and identity" in the 1950s.[41] She then argues that the family needed to be preserved at all costs because it represented the bedrock of the American society and nation. Lewis focuses on the American medical profession's prescription (singular) for heterosexuality through not only treatments, but also moral advice given to men and women, by their physicians. In particular, happy couples' sex lives reinforced both partners' psychosexual health and virility. Lewis finds that consumerism and patriotism helped doctors to reinforce the family unit, because good Americans saw it as their duty to purchase products only made in the U.S. and to avoid temptations to buy cheaper communist products. Lewis ties all these strands together with the concept of "citizen parents."[42]

Taking a different tack yet reaching similar conclusions is military historian Lori Lyn Bogle in her book *The Pentagon's Battle of the American Mind: The Early Cold War*. Her analysis reveals how and why the U.S. Department of Defense (DoD) portrayed the U.S. military as the defender of the nation's political entity and, just as important, of the American way of life. The threat of military force deterred Soviet and communist expansion abroad, and the promotion of acceptable social mores inoculated Americans from dangerous moral viruses like weakness, laziness, softness, and purposelessness at home. In latter case, Bogle share a medical imagery with the literal medical practices in Lewis above. Moral viruses could manifest themselves in cowardly unmanly

---

40 Robert L. Griswold, *Fatherhood in America: A History* (New York: Basic Books, 1993), 185–89; Michael Kimmel, *Manhood in America: A Cultural History* (The Free Press, 1996), 250–52; and May, *Homeward Bound*, 23–25.

41 Carolyn Herbst Lewis, *Prescription for Heterosexuality: Sexual Citizenship in the Cold War Era* (Chapel Hill: University of North Carolina Press, 2010), 13–25, 38–39, 75–79, quote on 5.

42 *Ibid.*, 135. See also K.A. Cuordileone, *Manhood and America: Political Culture in the Cold War* (Routledge, 2005).

behavior, sympathizing with communist goals, or participating in homosexual acts. Bogle finds that the DoD carried out a calculated program to mold a "national character that stressed self-sacrifice, obedience, and conformity."[43] Moreover, aside from the value of these traits to a military organization, Truman, Eisenhower, and the DoD used them to create a "civil religion" combining republican virtue and evangelical zeal that could forge a strong national will.[44] Each gender played distinct roles in this civil religion – men as the protector and warrior, and women as the protected and nurturer. Militarism and nationalist thus became intertwined.

One of the most compelling of examples of how American family and gender norms could be harnessed in service of the nation's Cold War goals can be seen in the "Kitchen Debate" in 1959. That summer, American Vice President Richard Nixon visited Moscow where he toured the American National Exhibition. The Soviet Premier Nikita Khrushchev accompanied him as the two leaders walked into the kitchen of an American house on display. It boasted the most modern conveniences purportedly available in every American home. Pausing for a few minutes in the kitchen, the two men debated what contrasting values these conveniences represented. Nixon boasted that, because American housewives could acquire time-saving gadgets like dishwashers, the United States was qualitatively better than the Soviet Union. These conveniences liberated housewives from the back-breaking chores of yesteryear. When Khrushchev pointed out that the American house would only last 20 years and that Soviet houses lasted longer, Nixon retorted,

> American houses last for more than 20 years, but, even so, after twenty years, many Americans want a new house or a new kitchen. Their kitchen is obsolete by that time....The American system is designed to take advantage of new inventions and new techniques.

And a few moments later, Nixon explained how the modern American house symbolized several aspects of his nation's way of life:

> This exhibit was not designed to astound but to interest. Diversity, the right to choose, the fact that we have 1,000 builders building 1,000 different houses is the most important thing. We don't have one decision made at the top by one government official. This is the difference.[45]

---

43 Bogle, *The Pentagon's Battle of the American Mind*, 4–5, 13–15, 55–64, quote 6.
44 See Keith Bates, et al., eds., *Civil Religion and American Christianity* (BorderStone, 2015).
45 Central Intelligence Agency, "The Kitchen Debate – Transcript," July 24, 1959, https://www.cia.gov/library/readingroom/docs/1959-07-24.pdf (Accessed March 24, 2018).

Aside from politicized and ideological discourses, Nixon implicitly appropriated feminine and domestic archetypes as key elements of the good life on the American home front.[46]

Nevertheless, many challenges confronted heteronormativity in the United States during the 1950s. One of these emerged from within the American nuclear family itself. The expectations of husbands/fathers and wives/mothers promulgated by television shows like *Leave It to Beaver* or *The Adventures of Ozzie and Harriet* could be emasculating to men and stagnating to women. The daily activities of Ozzie and Harriet, for example, hardly merited the label of "adventures" in any real sense. Quite the contrary: their everyday lives were humdrum. Nothing could be allowed to upset this domestic paradigm. However, if these television families were so comfortable, then how could there be excitement, let alone danger? These worries according to historian James Gilbert, aroused in men the "horror of suburbs," "dread of conformity," and "fear of being engulfed in trivial mass culture." Living these new monolithic lives, men risked losing their time-honored masculine self-identities as warriors, rugged individuals, and autonomous beings.[47]

Some American men also felt a nagging collective angst that Arthur Miller tapped into in his award-winning play *Death of a Salesman* (1949). The main character, the elderly "Willy" Loman, experienced declining mental health and a failing career that paralleled his increasing bitterness at never attaining the American dream. His cry that, "The competition is maddening" summed up his state of mind.[48] In his youth, he had squandered his talents as a blue-collar carpenter to become a salesman in the middle class. Even Loman's hopes for his oldest son's success in life get dashed. On the face of it, Loman wallows in self-pity, but his depression is caused by hopelessness and helplessness of alienation from his self-imposed and socially-imposed roles and relationships. Such weight drives Loman to suicide, which is his final act committed in hopes providing his oldest son with his life insurance money to start a successful business. Even this goal comes to naught, because the son refuses to enter the business world.[49]

---

46 May, *Homeward Bound*, 19–23.
47 Gilbert, *Masculinity in the Middle*, 7. See also Faludi, *Stiffed: The Betrayal of the American Man*.
48 Cited in Lee Siegel, "Death of a Salesman's Dreams," *New York Times*, May 2, 2012, https://www.nytimes.com/2012/05/03/opinion/death-of-a-salesmans-dreams.html (Accessed March 24, 2018).
49 Arthur Miller, *Death of a Salesman* (Viking Press, 1949). For commentary, see Cuordileone, *Manhood and American Political Culture*, 14–16; Griswold, *Fatherhood in America*, 199–200; and Kimmel, *Manhood in America*, 234–36.

Most men in the 1950s, however, lacked the prescience of the fictional Loman. They dutifully soldiered on through their post-war lives, just as they had done during the Great Depression and the Second World War. They endured one day to the next without much self-reflection, because turning inward and taking stock would doubtlessly have moved them closer to Loman's place. The men bought houses, lived in them long enough to pay off the mortgages, and worked in the same jobs until retirement. Literary scholar Leo Braudy terms this "assimilation."[50] One could also use resignation or surrender or, to borrow a Marxist term, alienation to describe Loman's plight.

Such terms as "horror," "fear," "dread," "assimilation," or "alienation" did not merely apply to men in the 1950s, but rather also to many American women chafing at their socially-dictated homemaking roles. Yes, washing machines, dishwashers, and vacuum cleaners helped reduce the time and physical exertion of house cleaning and other chores in millions of middle-class and working-class homes. Their work however, offered little fulfillment and few chances for personal development in any roles other than wife or mother. Although these feminine-typed activities were worthy roles to play in and of themselves, feminist author Betty Friedan labeled the collective predicament facing women as the "problem that has no name" in her ground-breaking book *The Feminine Mystique*.[51] Women sympathetic to Friedan's message sought to break the bonds of domesticity that kept women contained in their traditional gender roles. They tried to empower themselves by equalizing their perceived, institutional, and legal subsidiarity relative to men. In so doing, feminist activists like Friedan appropriated symbols, not unlike those employed by Marxism: women replaced workers as an oppressed underclass who experienced alienation. This is not to say that feminists were necessarily Marxists or communists. Still, the two messages echoed one another, especially to the untrained ears of social and political conservatives in the 1950s and thereafter.

The disillusionment among women and men with their lots in life extended beyond their kitchens and offices into their bedrooms where female sexuality was not as conventional as popularly portrayed. American biologist Alfred C. Kinsey and several co-authors published two blockbuster books *Sexual Behavior of the Human Male* (1948) and *Sexual Behavior of the Human Female* (1953).[52] Nicknamed the "Kinsey Reports," the authors derived their conclusions from several thousand interviews with women and men that gave insights into the frequency and type of sex acts they performed. Variables included age, class, and

---

50 Braudy, *From Chivalry to Terrorism*, 514.
51 Betty Friedan, *The Feminine Mystique* (Norton, 1963), 15.
52 Alfred Kinsey, et al., *Sexual Behavior of the Human Male* (W.B Saunders, 1948) and *Sexual Behavior of the Human Female* (W.B. Saunders, 1953).

religion. Kinsey and his fellow researchers also delved into taboo topics like sadomasochism and homosexuality to determine the degree to which their subjects engaged in these deviant behaviors. The report's findings indicated that, behind closed doors, both genders were more sexually adventurous than represented in their presumed heteronormative mores. Many more women, for example, engaged in intercourse at younger ages, lost their virginity before marriage, and masturbated to reach organism than was popularly believed. The Kinsey Reports looked at how and why female orgasms occurred, thereby acknowledging that women could find intercourse to be pleasurable and thereby cease playing passive roles therein. Just the mere mention of such concepts in printed pages scandalized many Americans who held fast to traditional sexual practices. The Kinsey Reports also estimated the one in four women engaged in extramarital sex in the first two decades of their marriages, so not even of that bastion of fidelity was sacrosanct. Single, unmarried women were no less of a danger to the sexual status quo in the 1950s because they might seek out physicians to give them contraceptives that allowed them to engage more freely in intercourse with whomever they wished with little fear of consequences from pregnancies. Such lascivious female behavior undermined the strict moral codes of the 1950s, thus constituting severe cultural disorder at, like communism., needed to be contained.[53]

Later in the 1950s, gynecologist William H. Masters and his research assistant Virginia Johnson began decades of research into sexology, the study of human sexuality. Unlike Kinsey who used personal interviews to support his findings, Masters and Johnson looked for patterns of masturbation and sexual intercourse in laboratory settings, where they concentrated anatomical and physiological aspects of sexual behavior. And, like Kinsey, their findings revealed that intercourse could be, if not should be, pleasurable and healthy. Masters and Johnson also tried to identify treatments of sexual dysfunctions like impotence and female frigidity. They later published two seminal works: *Human Sexual Response* and *Human Sexual Inadequacy* in 1966 and 1970, respectively.[54]

Not unlike feminists who felt constricted by their traditional roles others, some American men also rebelled against heteronormativity. Herein lay dual threats to the idyllic way of life in the 1950s: unmarried men on the rampage in

---

53 Lewis, *Prescription for Heterosexuality*, 25, 31–34, 59–61; and Canaday, *The Straight State*, 219–20. See also James H. Jones, *Alfred C. Kinsey: A Public/Private Life* (W.W. Norton, 1997); and for context dating back to the turn of the century, see Lawrence Birken, *Consuming Desire: Sexual Science and the Emergence of a Culture of Abundance* (Columbia University Press, 1989).
54 Lewis, *Prescription for Heterosexuality*,22, 59–65, 147–50; Bailey, *Sex in the Heartland*, 3–8, 77–83; and Paul Robinson, *The Modernization of Sex: Havelock Ellis, Alfred Kinsey, William Masters, and Virginia Johnson* (HarperCollins, 1977).

the society, or still worse homosexuals on the hunt for willing partners or vulnerable prey. Unmarried men ran against the moral grain because they threatened to tear down the masculine orthodoxy with its culturally constructed expectations. Married life provided men with a moral anchor. Among many dangers, male bachelors could sow their wild oats in promiscuous relationships by fathering children without being responsible as fathers to those children. Such untethered men indulged in materialism and hedonism exemplified by Hugh Hefner's *Playboy* magazine beginning in 1953. Its millions of readers embraced a new, alternate constructive of middle-class manhood. They lusted after the ultimate feminine sex object, the curvaceous Marilyn Monroe, who appeared nude in the first issue of *Playboy*. In so doing, the male audience could allay their boredom with their average sex lives by subscribing to a more adventurous, hyper-masculine, albeit air-brushed, heterosexual paradigm. According to the Kinsey Reports, some 50 percent of all married men engaged in some extramarital sexual activities at least once during their marriages. Any concrete connection between reading *Playboy* and having an affair may seem tenuous or incidental, but the fact remains that the magazine's glorification of a morally untethered lifestyle and the married men's proclivity toward extramarital sexual experiences did parallel each other. Other links can be seen between this *Playboy* ethos and Henry Kissinger, who gained notoriety as an expert on nuclear strategy by the late 1950s. He was selected by Playboy bunnies as the man with whom they would most like to go out on a date. These connections among masculinity, sexuality, and the political prowess would later be lampooned in Stanley Kubrick's the 1964 film *Dr. Strangelove or: How I Learned to Stop Worrying and Love the Bomb*.[55]

Such Elsewhere, Angst among single men spilled into the popular culture in Marlon Brando's characters in *A Streetcar Named Desire* (1951), *The Wild Ones* (1953), and *On the Waterfront* (1954). Arguably the most iconic single male was James Dean's fictional "Jim Stark" in *Rebel Without a Cause* released in 1955. Stark, together with another male character named "Plato" and a female character named "Judy," embodied the dissatisfaction of young Americans with their seemingly predestined roles in middle-class, Caucasian families. In particular, the three characters rebelled against their dysfunctional fathers and forsook their affluent, safe lives to become squatters in an abandoned mansion. In an ironic twist in *Rebel Without a Cause*, Stark and Judy become surrogate parents to Plato

---

55 Freedman, "Uncontrolled Desire," 102–104; Lewis, *Prescription for Heterosexuality*, 136; Bailey, *Sex in the Heartland*, 42; and Margot A. Henrickson, *Dr. Sranglove's America: Society and Culture in the Atomic Age* (University of California Press, 1987).

during their stay in the mansion, mimicking what a proper nuclear family should look like, even while challenging that archetype.[56]

Once unleashed, men might choose various means of rebelling like those espoused by Jack Kerouac, Allen Ginsburg, and William Burroughs of the so-called "Beat Generation" or "Beatnik" subculture. Their celebration of non-conformity in their writings went well beyond stereotypical goatees, bongos, and berets. They split with the values of their childhoods ingrained in them by families and society during Second World War and the Great Depression. The Beatnik's liberation likewise foreshadowed the coming sexual revolution and counterculture movement of the next decade. All these cases resulted in Masculine chaos.[57]

During the 1950s, the most sinister threats grew out of same-sex relationships in which male and female homosexuals overturned time-honored tenets of heteronormativity. They trayed from accepted gender roles by engaging in sexual intercourse for pleasure and blurring the lines between traditionally gendered sexual conduct. According to the popular 1950s stereotypes, gay men could be effeminate and submissive, while lesbians could be mannish and aggressive. No more could masculinity be defined in opposition to femininity, and vice versa. Gays were seen as "queer" both literally and figuratively in the contemporary vernacular. In fact, much more degrading terms encumbered homosexuals of both genders with traits of "deviancy," "degenerate," "ambiguous," "inversion," and "perversion."[58]

More scary to Americans adhering to traditional sexual mores were those gays whose public personas appeared to be heteronormative, while they satisfied their uninhibited sexual proclivities occurred behind closed doors. Perhaps most disconcerting were those homosexuals, derisively labeled "sexual psychopaths" in the 1950s psychiatric jargon, who actively converted unsuspecting heterosexuals to their deviant ways. Whether real or imagined, it is sad to note that these behaviors elicited fear and hatred among many Americans.[59]

Accepted mainstream attitudes about homosexuality took on an ideological character during the early Cold War because this deviant lifestyle became conflated with communism. Simply put, just as same-sex relations were believed to be perverted and un-American in lifestyle, so too was communism seen as

---

56 Griswold, *Fatherhood in America*, 185–86.

57 Braudy, *From Chivalry to Terrorism*, 514–18; and Alan Bisbort, *Beatniks: A Guide to an American Subculture* (Greenwood, 2009).

58 Canaday, *Straight State*, 10–13, 36–38, 190–93, 214–15, 227–37

59 Halberstam, *Female Masculinity*, 17, 235–241; Butler, *Gender Trouble*, xi, 34, 185–93; Bailey, *Sexuality in the Heartland*, 59–63; and Freedman, "Uncontrolled Desires," 98–104.

un-American and deviant in ideology.[60] Homophobia coalesced with anticommunism in McCarthyism. An influential public figure between 1950 and 1954, the movement's namesake, Senator Joseph McCarthy of Wisconsin, directed venomous attacks after against any Americans suspected of having sympathies or ties to communism. At the time, his evidence proved to be dubious at best. As the Republican chairman of a special Senate subcommittee, McCarthy conducted witch hunts to identify and purge communists in Hollywood movie studios, the U.S. State Department, and the U.S. Army, seeking to expose those subversive threats. McCarthyism as a phenomenon took shape decades earlier and persisted decades after the senator's fall from power in 1954. Many American political conservatives embraced his ideas, if not always his methods.[61]

McCarthyism's paranoia spread into the realm of morality when his inquisitions focused on suspected gays in what was called the "Lavender Scare," as in the light purple version of the "Red Scare" the combined communism with homosexuality. McCarthy himself left little doubt about his stance when allegedly stated to journals, "If you want to be against McCarthy, boys, you've got to be a Communist or a cocksucker."[62] The senator's supporters painted Truman's State Department as being full of "lavender boys" who were then hounded as suspected gays and branded as soft on communism. For McCarthy and his followers, their moral laxity made them vulnerable to the siren song of communism that offered them sexual licenses unavailable in the heteronormative United States. The communist subversive him-or herself might be both an ideological and a gay fellow traveler. Same-sex trysts could be used as means of blackmailing or turning otherwise seemingly heterosexual Americans. Pejoratives describing the menaces like "inko commie" entered the popular lexicon in the 1950s. Such a bifurcated contest between heterosexual-loyal-American and the homosexual-perverted-unAmerican typologies became a domestic zero-sum game, not unlike that international contest between the superpowers.[63] Senator McCarthy

---

60 Cuordileone, *Manhood and American Political Culture*, 28–29.

61 For a recent overview of McCarthy and his ideology, see Jonathan Michaels, *McCarthyism: The Realities, Delusions and Politics behind the 1950s Red Scare* (Routledge, 2017).

62 Quoted in Edwin R. Bayley, *Joe McCarthy and the Press* (Madison, WI, 1981), 73, cited in Naoko Shibusawa, "The Lavender Scare and Empire: Rethinking Cold War Antigay Politics," *Diplomatic History* 36 (September 2012): 725; as Shibusawa points out in the annotation Footnote 7 in his article, "Bayley's source for this oft-quoted sentence is an oral interview with Charles Seib in March 1976."

63 Several sources find connections between anti-communism and anti-homosexuality: David K. Johnson, *The Lavender Scare: The Cold War Persecutions of Gays and Lesbians in the Federal Government* (University of Chicago Press, 2004), 15–78; Bailey, *Sex in the Heartland*, 58–63; Cuordileone, *Manhood and American Political Culture*, 130–4; Canaday, *The Straight State*, 3, 205,

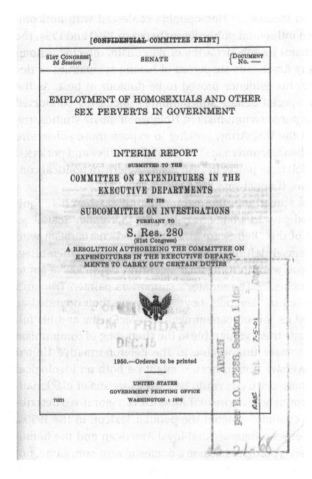

Figure 8.3: On December 15, 1950, a Senate committee released this report, concluding that homosexuals were unsuitable for employment in the Federal Government and constituted security risks in positions of public trust.
Source: Records of the U.S. Senate, Record Group 46, National Archives and Records Administration.

and like-minded Senators Kenneth Wherry and J. Lister Hill needed to expose these communist homosexuals to the American public to justify their persecution of them, and vice versa. "Anticommunist conservatives and anticommunist

256–57; Dean, *Imperial Brotherhood,* 63–67; and Shibusawa, "The Lavender Scare and Empire," 742–44.

liberals alike deplored the 'lavender' threat just as they deplored the red menace," writes historian Robert Dean in his study of gender and American foreign policy. Both sides of the aisle, as Dean explains,

> used the rhetoric of red-blooded masculinity to establish their credentials as a legitimate defense of a genuinely American social and political order. Such language distanced them from suspicion of sympathy with the political and sexual 'other' during a period when guilt by association supplied the favored instrument of countersubversive inquisitors. . . [They] detected danger in the analogy they perceived between the underground communities of communism and homosexuality.[64]

Both represented supreme dangers to the likes of Richard Nixon and John and Robert Kennedy. The Kennedys in particular cultivated their public images of proper American men, patriot, and warrior heroes, whether as a family playing touch football in their yard or as veterans of the Second World War. Moreover, the only person with more anticommunist credentials than Nixon and the two Kennedys was McCarthy himself. His movement, however, was hardly the paragon of heteronormativity because it harbored homosexuals like Roy Cohn, who was McCarthy's chief counsel, and Whitaker Chambers, who was the star witness in the trial of Alger Hiss. In fact, McCarthy also faced accusations of being gay by some elements on the political left.[65]

Ironically, the intimate connection between communism and homosexuality turned out to be primarily an invention of American Cold War propaganda. Contrary to these portrayals, the Soviet Union's government often persecuted its people for engaging in homosexual acts or relationships. Beginning in the early 1930s, Joseph Stalin imposed harsh penalties to stamp out the homosexuals who had previously been tolerated. In fact, the Communist Party viewed such proclivities as remnants of the decadently effeminate behavior of the ruling class of Czarist Russia. Stalin and the party even aligned homosexuality with fascism which in turn linked it with even greater ideological and military threats to the Soviet Union. After Stalin's death in 1953, Nikita Khrushchev did not liberalize anti-gay laws. Prohibition of homosexuality remained in force throughout the Cold War. One of the main reasons for homophobia among Soviets mirrored the same attitude among their contemporaries in America: Just as pure heterosexual man could

---

64 Dean, *Imperial Brotherhood*, 68.
65 *Ibid.*, 9–16, 43–49, 74–76, 149–53. See also Judith Adkins, " 'These People are Frightened to Death': Congressional Investigations and Lavender Scare," 48 (Summer 2016), https://www.archives.gov/publications/prologue/2016/summer/lavender.html (Accessed 3 April 2018).

be the only good American capitalists, so too could heterosexual men be the only pure Soviet communists.[66]

Conclusion

The United States entered the post-World War II era as the more powerful and prosperous nation on earth. On the surface, those few years of peacetime marked a more successful return to normalcy than had occurred in the 1920s. The U.S. military demobilized, and American industry retooled for its post-war economic boom. American men and women exchanged their uniforms for civilian clothes, got married, and started families. However, beneath the façade of stability lay several crises regarding race, gender, and sexuality that percolated during the late 1940s running up to the start of the Korean War in 1950. That conflict, though not often examined through cultural lenses, exemplified how race and gender could be added to the mix of strategy, operations, tactics, and logistics. Americans brought with them pre-conceived notions of race based on past experiences that were ultimately disproven and discredited by its Asian enemies. Fears of North Korea and China as the latest iteration of the "yellow peril" added to the American dread of "red peril" of communist and Soviet expansion. During the Korean War's three years, the post-war fault lines of race, gender, and sexuality helped create the context of the Cold War, a titanic struggle between this United States and the Soviet Union. The battlefields stretched into the families, households, and lives of Americans where their idyllic Caucasian middle-class heterosexual paradigm faced assaults on all cultural fronts, whether psychologically in unmet expectations of the American dream, physically in deviant sexual behaviors, or ideologically in communist subversion. The United States barely weathered the 1950s only to be thrust into a still more turbulent decade for racial, gender, sexual, and Cold War tensions in the 1960s.

---

66 Igor S. Kon, "Russia," in *Sociolegal Control of Homosexuality: A Multi-Nation Comparison*, ed. Donald J. West and Richard Green (Plenum Press, 1997), 221–43; Laura Essig, *Queer in Russia: A Story of Sex, Self, and the Other* (Duke University Press, 1999); and Dan Healey, "Masculine Purity and 'Gentlemen's Mischief': Sexual Exchange and Prostitution between Russian Men, 1861–1941," *Slavic Review* 60 (Summer 2001): 233–65.

9 Race and Gender During Decolonization

Introduction

The Second World War unseated Western Europe as the wealthiest, most dominant region in the world turned the Europeans into a collection of debtor nations in the interwar decades, leaving the continent a battleground for the ascendant United States and Soviet Union after 1945. At the same time, Europeans possessed neither the moral will nor the material ability to maintain their far-flung imperial holdings. No more were those old world powers be omnipotent; their colonies' indigenous peoples sensing the weaknesses in their overlords and doubling their efforts to escape imperialism. Although independence, liberation, and unification movements sprang up across the European empires earlier in the twentieth century, it took the Cold War to set strategic, ideological, and economic conditions for decolonization efforts to succeed.

This chapter outlines the process of decolonization by focusing on how and why opposing discourses on race and gender affected the colonized and elicited tragic reactions by the colonizers. Among the many examples in the Cold War were those indigenous peoples seeking independence from Western imperial influence in China, Cuba, India, Malaya, Palestine, Vietnam, Indonesia, Burma, Rhodesia, Algeria, Cyprus, Egypt, Kenya, the Congo, the Philippines, and others. However, two case studies stand out because they illustrated the diverse spectra of race and gender dynamics on both sides: The Mau Mau Rebellion in British-controlled Kenya in the 1950s, and the Viet Cong and the North Vietnamese Army in American-supported South Vietnam during the 1960s and early 1970s. Each case study highlights the complex, often contradictory, combinations of political, economic, geographical, religious, and ideological factors, tied together with race and gender. The Kenyans and Vietnamese brought particular cultural identities to their fights for independence. In the former case, the British recognized that role of Kenyan women and adjusted their strategy to counter the women's contributions to the Mau Mau Rebellion. In the latter example, however, the Americans never recognized the many significant roles of Vietnamese women in the fight in the South, and thus never found ways to stop their efforts. Race and gender profoundly influenced the ways the British and Americans assessed the resourcefulness and audacity of those indigenous peoples.

Of all the imperial home fronts during decolonization, the United States stands out because tropes of race and gender figured so prominently when the cultural rumblings in the 1950s exploded into protests during the 1960s and 1970s. The Women's Rights Movement and Civil Rights Movements gained numbers and

https://doi.org/10.1515/9783110477467-009

visibility as they pushed for equality with Caucasian males. These two less-than-equal groups drew inspiration from the Anti-War Movement's protests against the "draft" during the Vietnam War, and so too did this movement gain power outflowing from synergies among African Americans and women. Compounding the social and political unrest was the moral unrest caused by the Sexual Revolution and the Counterculture. The fabric of American race and gender ripped apart at the seams under the dual pressures of an unsuccessful war in Vietnam and rampant upheavals at home. To one degree or another, other nations in the West also experienced trauma during decolonization, but the United States provides a unique example because of the American moral rhetoric about equality and freedom was put on trial at home during the Vietnam War.

Inside the U.S. armed services, the advances by African Americans and women between the 1950s and 1975 should not be interpreted as the end of chauvinism or racism in the military establishment. Women and most minorities still endured discrimination based in part on personal bigotry and in part on institutional inertia. Nevertheless, the U.S. military did prove to be a laboratory for social engineering that broke new ground for more equitable, if never wholly equal, opportunities for women and minorities than were available in civilian life.

The Historiography of Decolonization, Race, and Gender

In their book of the same name published in 2017, German scholars Jan C. Jansen and Jürgen Osterhammel described the term "Decolonization" as

> a technical and rather undramatic term for one of the most dramatic processes in modern history: the disappearance of empire as a political form, and the end of racial hierarchy as a widely accepted political ideology and structuring principle of world order.[1]

Although the two authors rightfully mention racism as one crucial element in the imperial-colonial relationship, gender should be appended to their explanation because masculinity and femininity also formed rigid hierarchies that reinforced or paralleled those racism. Jansen and Osterhamml next add two essential qualifiers to their explanation of decolonization:

> The simultaneous dissolution of several intercontinental empires and the creation of nation-states throughout the global South within a short time span of roughly three postwar

---

1 Jan C. Jansen and Jürgen Osterhammel, *Decolonization: A Short History*, trans. Jeremiah Riemer (Princeton University Press, 2017), 1. This volume was revised and expanded from the original German volume *Dekolonisation* (Verlag C.H. Beck, 2013).

decades (1945–1975), linked with the historically unique and, in all likelihood, irreversible delegitimization of any kind of political rule that is experienced as a relationship of subjugation to a power elite considered by a broad majority of the population as an alien occupant.[2]

The explanation is necessarily vague because each instance of decolonization followed divergent paths, so more or less than others, in the process. What can be added to most of the instances is this: civil wars or revolutionary wars often precipitated, accompanied, or resulted from the decolonizing effort.[3]

Many indigenous peoples embraced violence as the necessary means to overthrow their imperial overlords, as in the Dutch colony of Indonesia and the French colonies of Algeria, Vietnam, Laos, and Cambodia. Elsewhere in India, Mahatma Gandhi used non-violence and civil disobedience protests to try to help achieve independence from the British Commonwealth. Despite his efforts, however, bloodshed did occur between Indians and British, and between Muslims and Hindus that during the partition of Pakistan and India. The religio-nationalistic differences ran too deeply in Indian society to avoid violence. In Africa, much bloodshed also occurred during an anti-colonial uprisings. In the cases of the Congo (Zaire) and Rwanda, independence movements precipitated brutal civil wars among ethnic, political, religious, and/or regional factions that resulted in the deaths of 100,000s of people. Genocide on a scale similar to Rwanda occurred in Cambodia in the decades following its independence from the French Empire. Frequently, it seemed that the fights for independence succeeded in expelling the imperial powers, but then filling those political vacuums meant more bloodshed and suffering. In sum, rarely were the decolonization's transitions from colony to nation smooth or peaceful. Seldom did stability take hold without indigenous authoritarian governments taking power, Tragically, too many of the newly independent nations suffered low living standards and human rights violations that rivaled the abuses of their imperial overlords. Long-standing internal antagonisms of indigenous groups could not be restrained by several new post-colonial governments in the Third World.[4]

---

2 *Ibid.*, 1–2.

3 See reprinted articles in James D. Le Sueur, ed., *The Decolonization Reader* (Routledge, 2003). For a general survey, see Anthony Clayton, "Wars of Decolonization, 1945–1975," in *War and the Modern War*, vol. 4, *The Cambridge History of Modern War*, eds. Roger Chickering, et al. (Cambridge University Press, 2012), 515–41.

4 John Darwin, lecture, "Decolonization: A History of Failure?" July 13, 2011, Library of Congress Kluge Center, http://www.loc.gov/today/cyberlc/feature_wdesc.php?rec=5246 (accessed April 3, 2018). See also Darwin, *The Empire Project*.

The bloody conflicts of decolonization occurred during the Cold War, when those underdeveloped or undeveloped colonies comprised the "Third World." This term likely originated as *"Tiers Monde"* first used by the French diplomat Alfred Sauvy in the early 1950s. It was a play on words using the famous pamphlet *"Qu'est-ce que le tier-état?"* ("What is the Third Estate?") written by the Abbé Emmanuel Joseph Sieyès in 1789 just before the start of the French Revolution. The words "third estate" referred to the lower-class social group encompassing some 90 percent of the French population yet owning only a tiny fraction of the nation's wealth. Sieyès' asked and answered three questions about this group: "What is the Third Estate? Everything. What has it been until now in the political order? Nothing. What does it ask? To become something." His answers resonated with those French peasants and city workers hoping for radical change and the leveling of their society. They then started a decade of bloody revolution.[5]

Switching to Cold War era, those poorer, undeveloped, or underdeveloped nations resembled the third estate as denoted by Abbé Sieyès. The Third World nations in Africa, Asia, and Central and South America compromised much of the global population living on most of the global land mass and holding, but not controlling, most of their resources. The colonies suffered exploitation and oppression for several centuries by the tiny minority of Europeans and more recently Americans.[6] Many of the colonies became proxy battlegrounds for the titanic struggle between the Soviet Union and its communist allies comprising the "Second World," and the United States and its industrialized democratic allies formed the "First World." In many cases, iterations of communist ideology provided the theoretical impetus for the indigenous peoples of the Third World to rebel against the established empires of the First World. As will be seen in the rest of this chapter, the clashing racial and gendered identities of the colonized and colonizers often magnified tragedies during these conflicts.

The symbology of the Third World as an anologue for the third estate helped drive one conventional historical interpretation of decolonization: Marxist theories positing class struggle and economic as determinant of history. Apart from the scholars themselves, Marxist agitators in the Third World called on the indigenous peoples in colonies threw off that control in acts of "self-determination"

---

5 For a classic study with a Marxist spin, see George Rudé, *The Crowd in the French Revolution* (Oxford Clarendon Press, 1959).

6 See Odd Arne Westad, *The Global Cold War: Third World Interventions and the Making of Our Times* (Cambridge University Press, 2007); Martin Shipway, *Decolonization and in Impacts: A Comparative Approach to the End of Colonial Empires* (Wiley-Blackwell, 2008); and Kwon, *The Other Cold War.*

to use Vladimir I. Lenin's term. For Lenin and his followers, ousting the impe-rialists should take the form of bloody revolution.[7] The conflicts pitted the cap-italistic home countries against workers and national liberation movements in the colonies. On the face of it, the revolutions and liberations in China, Vietnam, and Cuba from capitalist/imperialist control stood among the most conspicuous examples of this process during the Cold War.

Even so, the various stMarxist-Leninism Nationalism served not only as the central premise for another conventional interpretation of decolonization but also as a significant motivation in many anti-colonial movements.[8] Nationalism among indigenous peoples could be considered synonymous with national identity and "self-determination." President Woodrow Wilson appropriated this concept as one of his major hope for the post-World War I world. He meant this term to apply to minorities in nations or empires controlled by others as evinced in his "Fourteen Points" speech on January 8, 1918. Wilson stated in point five that

> A free, open-minded, and absolutely impartial adjustment of all colonial claims, based upon a strict observance of the principle that in determining all such questions of sover-eignty the interests of the populations concerned must have equal weight with the equitable claims of the government whose title is to be determined.[9]

The spirit and substance of Wilson's words legitimized decolonization by creat-ing a rallying point for liberation movements throughout the twentieth century. A young Ho Chi Minh (then known by the name Nguyen Ai Quo) imbibed the idea of self-determination when he attended the Paris Peace Conference as one of several

---

7 V. I. Lenin, "The Socialist Revolution and the Right of Nations to Self-Determination" (1916), reprinted in *Collected Works*, vol. 22, 4th ed. (Progress Publishers, Moscow, 1964), 143–56, at http://www.marx2mao.com/Lenin/SRSD16.html (accessed April 3, 2018). For more recent rhet-oric, see "The Right to Self-Determination is our Our Revolutionary Policy," *The Call* 4 (January 1975), at Marxist Internet Archive, https://www.marxists.org/history/erol/ncm-3/ol-self-det.htm (accessed April 3, 2018).
8 Jansen and Osterhammel, *Decolonization*, 35–70. For examples, see Anthony Reid, *Imperial Alchemy: Nationalism and Political Identity in Southeast Asia* (Cambridge University Press, 2010); Partha Chatterjee, *The Partha Chatterjee Omnibus: Nationalist Thought and the Colonial World, The Nation and its Fragments, A Possible India* (Oxford University Press, 2008); and Thomas Mar-tin, et al., *Crises of Empire: Decolonization of and Europe's Imperial States, 1918–1975*, 2nd ed. (Bloomsbury, 2015);
9 Woodrow Wilson, "Speech on the Fourteen Points," *Congressional Record*, 65th Congress 2nd Session, 1918, pp. 680–81. Digitized in Yale University Avalon Project, http://avalon.law.yale. edu/20th_century/wilson14.asp (accessed September 4, 2013). See also Wilson's 1917 Inaugura-tion Address in this same online collection.

Vietnamese nationalists. Tragically, however, the hopes of Ho, Mao Zedong, and Jawaharlal Nehru would come to naught for the next decades.[10] Ho took the idea of self-determination with him back to French Indochina, where it provided grounds for ongoing liberation and unification efforts during the Vietnam Wars from 1945 to 1975. It is also worth noting that Ho incorporated self-determination and conspicuously American notions of democracy in his "Declaration of Independence of Vietnam" in September 1945, leveraging the language heralding the first decolonization success – the United States of America.[11] While national identity could grip indigenous peoples by appealing to their uniqueness and merit, identities could likewise be challenged, if not undermined, in the home nations that previously controlled those colonies as part of their once-mighty empires. The French, for instance, went through identity crises as they lost colonies in African and Southeast Asia. Meanwhile the British felt similar angst elsewhere in South Asia and Africa.[12]

Ideological motivations like communism and nationalism, as well as economic, political, and strategic factors, saturate the conventional historiography on the dissolution of the old world's empires during the Cold War. Between 1945 and 1975, nearly every colony exercised agency against and eventually claimed independence from their imperial overlords. The bifurcated world with the United States facing off against the Soviet Union provided the Third World's colonies with ideal opportunities to place one superpower off against the other to secure resources for their independence movements.[13]

Whereas nationalism and other ideologies played prominent roles, neither race nor gender receives the attention that they deserve during the Cold War. The two components can be found not only in conflicts in the colonies but also in controversies in the imperial home countries. They combined with ideologies, as well as economics, religion, region, personality, and diplomacy to create a complex, confusing, or contradictory mosaic. Nevertheless, understanding decolonization, whether relatively violent or peaceful, requires that race and gender be inserted

---

10 See for example Erez Manela, *The Wilsonian Moment: Self-Determination and the International Origins of Anticolonial Nationalism* (Oxford University Press, 2007).
11 Modern History Sourcebook, "Vietnamese Declaration of Independence (1945)," https://sourcebooks.fordham.edu/halsall/mod/1945vietnam.html (accessed April 3, 2018).
12 Robert Aldrich and Stuart Wood, "Ends of Empire: Decolonizing the Nation in British and French Historiography," in *Nationalizing the Past: Historians as Nation Builders in Modern Europe*, eds., Stefan Burge and Chris Lorenz (Palgrave Mcmillan, 2010), 259–81; Todd Shepard, *The Invention of Decolonization: The Algerian War and the Remaking of France* (Cornell University Press, 2008); and M. Kathryn Edwards, *Contesting Indochina: French Remembrance between Decolonization and Cold War* (University of California Press, 2016).
13 Dane Kennedy, "Imperial History and Post-Colonial Theory," in *The Decolonization Reader*, ed. James D. Le Sueur (London: Routledge, 2003), 10–22.

into the discourses. In studying Southeast Asia, for example, diplomatic historian Robert J. McMahon offers one corrective:

> The inherently oppressive nations of the colonial systems imposed by the West, even taking important variations into account, served as the indispensable incubator for Southeast Asia's indigenous nationalist movements. The arrogance and haughtiness of so many colonial administrators, coupled with their frequently contemptuous, race-conscious attitudes bred strong native resentment.[14]

It is legitimate to replace McMahon's term "race-conscious" with "gender-conscious" because too often their own gender norms were projected onto the colonial peoples. Incorporating them into decolonization requires borrowing analytical tools employed in "Subaltern Studies" and "Postcolonial Studies" to deconstruct the many gendered and racial meanings of words, symbols, and actions in the decolonization process. The modes of inquiry concentrate on the colonial experience from the bottom up, rather primarily from the Eurocentric perspective of imperialists. In so doing, both fields share similarities with Marxist and World Systems interpretations of history.

Subaltern Studies began in the 1980s among Indian scholars, who wanted to write a new history of their nation that focused on the non-elite (labeled subalterns) and offered uniquely Indian interpretation. In the earlier Cold War years, much political and social upheaval erupted across India as the lower castes challenged the stratified social structure with an elite minority holding so much wealth and power. The efforts of Indian peasants to gain more equality, by violence if necessary, followed on India's bid for independence. When historians tried to tell the story of rebelling groups, they too often found that the narrative modalities remained too provincially "Western" and thus biased, patronizing, inaccurate, or irrelevant to those subaltern groups in Indian. To rectify this, subaltern scholarship sought to break the bonds of Eurocentric historical narrative and replace it with an Indian narrative with indigenous symbols, theories, models, and methodologies. Thus, just as India achieved independence from a British imperial yoke, so too could it exercise agency and achieve autonomy from the European historiographical yoke. Since the 1980s, Subaltern Studies spread throughout the world where indigenous peoples assert their own historical consciousnesses and empower themselves through their histories.[15]

---

14 Robert J. McMahon, *The Limits of Empire: The United States and Southeast Asia since World War II* (Columbia University Press, 1999), 7.
15 Jansen and Osterhammel, *Decolonization*, 166–70. For examples of scholarship, see Ranajit Guha, *Elementary Aspects of Peasant Insurgency in Colonial India* (Oxford University Press, 1983); Dipesh Chakrabarty, "Postcoloniality and the Artifice of History: Who Speaks for 'Indian' Pasts?"

Postcolonial Studies began in 1978 with the late Edward Said's publication of his seminal book *Orientalism*, which leveled stinging critiques of Western notions of the "East." He found that too many American and European perspectives on the Middle Eastern region, Arab culture, and Islamic religion suffered from prejudices based in deeply ingrained stereotypes. From as far back in history as Herodotus' *Persian Wars* up to the recent film *300*, these assumptions tainted the West's understanding of the Oriental "other" and impaired interactions with the peoples of the East. They needed to have their voices heard in what had otherwise been a one-sided dialogue. It must also be noted that, because the West sought to dominate the East since the 1800s, the relations between grew increasingly unequal and oppressive. In the years since *Orientalism* appeared, the field of post-colonial studies expanded to include interactions between the empires and colonies across the globe.[16] This scholarship sought answers to many questions about the colonial peoples during subjugation and then after liberation:

> How did the experience of colonization affect those who were colonized while also influencing the colonizers? How were colonial powers able to gain control over so large a portion of the non-Western world? What traces have been left by colonial education, science and technology in postcolonial societies? How do these traces affect decisions about development and modernization in postcolonies? What were the forms of resistance against colonial control? How did colonial education and language influence the culture and identity of the colonized? How did Western science, technology, and medicine change existing knowledge systems? What are the emergent forms of postcolonial identity after the departure of the colonizers? To what extent has decolonization (a reconstruction free from colonial influence) been possible? Are Western formulations of postcolonialism overemphasizing hybridity at the expense of material realities? Should decolonization proceed through an aggressive return to the pre-colonial past? How do gender, race, and class function in colonial and postcolonial discourse?[17]

Of all these questions, the last one about gender and race is most relevant to this chapter on warfare in the decolonization.

---

in James D. Le Sueur, ed., *The Decolonization Reader* (Routledge, 2003), 428–48; and Prasenjit Duara, "The Discourse of Civilization and Decolonization," *Journal of World History* 15 (2004): 1–5.
16 Jansen and Osterhammel, *Decolonization*, 166–70. See Bill Ashcroft, et. al, *The Empire Writes Back: Theory and Practice of Colonial Literatures,* 2nd ed. (Taylor and Francis, 2002); for excerpted writing of luminaries like Edward Said, see Bill Ashcroft, et al., eds, *The Post-Colonial Studies Reader,* 2nd ed. (Routledge, 2006); and Robert J.C. Young, *Empire, Colony, Postcolony* (Wiley-Blackwell, 2015).
17 Excerpted from Emory University, "Postcolonial Studies @ Emory," https://scholarblogs. emory.edu/postcolonialstudies/about-postcolonial-studies/ (accessed April 3, 2018). See also Amy Allen, *The End of Progress: Decolonizing the Normative Foundations of Critical Theory* (Columbia University Press, 2016).

Race, Gender, Insurgency, but not Marxism in Kenya

Among many examples of violent decolonization during the Cold War, Kenya stands out as an illustrative case study because this nation's struggle for independence defies conventional historical models and highlights the value of filtering decolonization through the lenses of race- and gender-consciousness.[18] Some context is necessary to under Kenya's importance. For hundreds of years before the nineteenth century, the east African-coastal region formed part of a commercial network of Africa, the Middle East, and the Indian subcontinent. Arabs and Persians settled along the coast where they established several major port cities that became conduits between the interior of Kenya and the outside world. The slave trade, iron production, fishing, and agriculture emerged as the leading fixtures in the Kenyan economy. The influx of Arabs and Persians combined with the indigenous peoples and migrants, some of whom were escaped or freed African or Middle Eastern slaves, to form a heterogeneous society that included some 40 ethnic groups. Of these, the largest was the Kikuyu tribe.

Among the Europeans, the Portuguese first tried to exert control over Kenya in the sixteenth century. They captured port cities, turning them into bases for their exploitation of the interior and domination of the East African coast. In 1630, an Arab leader united the Kenyan people in a violent effort to expel the Portuguese from the area. After that, the Muslim Sultan of Oman ruled Kenya until the rise of Europe's New Imperialism in the nineteenth century. By 1890, the British assumed control of Kenya, making it first a protectorate known as British East Africa and later a crown colony called the Kenya Colony in 1920. Europeans had never before ventured far beyond the coastline until British settlers moved deep into the nation, where they staked claims to large farms in the fertile interior, grew wealthy on raising coffee beans and tea leaves, and utilized railroads to transport their crops to market. The settlers began oppressing the Kenyans (including the Kikuyus) already farming that land. The Kenyans found themselves working as a mass labor force. The British colonial government further bolstered the white minority through labor laws, low wages, land acquisitions, heavy taxation, and racial discrimination. By the 1930s and 1940s, angry Kenyans started a decades-long struggle to create their own nation independent of the British Empire. In the post-World War II era, an armed insurgency by the Kikuyu

---

18 For starting points, see Wunyabari O. Maloba, *Mau Mau and Kenya: An Analysis of a Peasant Revolt* (Indiana University Press, 1993); Nicholas K. Githuku, *Mau Mau Crucible of War: Statehood, National Identity, and Politics of Postcolonial Kenya* (Lexington Books, 2015). Conversely, the Mau Mau Rebellion is seen as a national liberation movement similar others across the globe in Robert B. Edgerton's *Mau Mau: An African Crucible* (I.B. Taurus, 1990).

tribe, known as the "Mau Mau Rebellion," ran from 1952 to 1956, though violent remnants persisted until 1960. British official estimates put the death toll among the Mau Mau at 11,000 guerilla fighters, of whom 1,080 fighters were executed by hanging. Other sources put the numbers of deaths at between 25,000 and 90,000 people, as well as 160,000 incarcerations of Kenyans suspected of being insurgents or aiding them. The Mau Mau fighters referred to their movement as Land Freedom Army or the Freedom Struggle Association. Herein lay one of the key goals of the rebellions – land reform. Kenyan nationalism also provided some impetus for the Mau Mau. Just three years after the rebellion subsided, the nation of Kenya finally achieved independence from the British to become the Republic of Kenya in 1963. The British decided to allow this to happen in part because the new indigenous government seemed to be amenable to British interests in the region and because the once-mighty global empire had grown too weak to maintain its colonies by force.[19]

The historical debates center on the nature of the Mau Mau Rebellion and the degree of its influence on Kenya's eventual independence. Marxian critiques could be layered over the Mau Mau rebellion in which oppressed Kenyan insurgents fought against their British imperial landowners, but this lens is simplistic at best and ahistorical at worst. Elsewhere, some approaches in Subaltern Studies and Postcolonial Studies can help illuminate factors of class, power, and wealth concentration as precipitants for the Mau Mau rebellion. Kenya's peasant farmers, however, did not fill their ranks (though they did give some tacit support). Most of the fighters came from the margins of Kenyan society – landless squatters or the urban unemployed. Consequently, the Mau Mau rebellion did not fit precisely into peasant revolt models, especially in Subaltern Studies.

Constructions of race and gender can be seen in the conventional narrative in that British imperialists viewed the Kenyans through a paternalist lens. Because the colonized people were essentially child-like non-Caucasians and thus incapable of self-rule, the British believed their control of Kenya to be necessary to maintain order and improve standards of living. Imperialism thus represented a positive good for the colony.[20] Such paternalism was not unique to Kenya. It could be seen in other European empires across the globe, as well as in the American "empire" in Central America and the Philippines. Chapter 3 in this volume deals in detail with the long-standing constructions of imperial-self versus colonial-other.

---

19 Peter Baxter, *Mau Mau: Kenyan Emergency, 1952–1960* (Helion, 2012). The term "Mau Mau" was likely an allusion to the Mau Escarpment and the nearby Mau Forest (p. 8). See also "Mau Mau Uprising: Bloody History of Kenya," BBC News UK, April 7, 2011. http://www.bbc.co.uk/news/uk-12997138 (accessed January 18, 2014).
20 Maloba, *Mau Mau and Kenya*, 24–26.

Figure 9.1: Troops of the King's African Rifles carry supplies on horseback (c. 1954). They are escorted by armed soldiers on watch for Mau Mau fighters.
Source: Imperial War Museum (Public Domain) https://commons.wikimedia.org/wiki/
File:KAR_Mau_Mau.jpg

Nevertheless, the reality in Kenya proved to be more complicated, if not confusing. Indeed, that is why this nation's drive for independence stands out as such a useful case study. The Mau Mau fighters, for instance, were not steeped in Marxist or Leninist ideology, and their rebellion was never politicized in the ways that the movements led by Mao in China or Ho Chi Minh in Vietnam were. So, while a Marxian critique might provide an interesting interpretative lens through which to evaluate economic power relations in colonial Kenya, this critique does not make those fighters "Marxists." To do would so be ahistorical as argued by historian Wunyabari O. Maloba in his ground-breaking *Mau Mau and Kenya: An Analysis of a Peasant Revolt*. He writes that

> the Marxist scholars and sympathizers saw no characteristics of a genuine people's war of the kind their students and reflections had led them to believe in. Certainly, the [Mau Mau] movement had no Marxist ideology, nor did it have a cadre of revolutionary intellectuals propounding well-knit and stimulating ideological positions. Instead of the standard agents of propaganda and politicization of the masses, it was found, to the dismay

of radical scholars, that the Mau Mau fighters employed ancient oaths and even invoked deities. . . It was, therefore, a back-ward looking movement which did not pass the litmus test of ideological purity and methodological application of Marxism to its environment. Mau Mau rebels had never even heard of Marx![21]

Maloba also identifies other discontinuities between Marxism and the Mau Mau. He finds no proletarian surge because many employed Kenyan workers living in urban centers did not join the cause, nor did the educated Kenyan middle class see sufficient benefits of challenging the British imperial forces and risk bloody retributions. Rather, according to Maloba, the Mau Mau rebellion "was led and organized by a group of semiliterate men who chose to use traditional symbols to enlist support."[22] Simply put, there was no "there" there. Instead, during the 1950s, Caucasians in Kenya and elsewhere increasingly regarded that the Mau Mau as religious zealots, rather than communists or nationalists. For scholars Jan Jansen and Jürgen Osterhammel, the rebellion was a "domestic intra-Kenyan war."[23]

Stepping back for a moment, additional racial and gendered components can be teased out of the preceding narrative and its analyses. Kenya's white landowners puzzled over the barbarism of the Mau Mau because, from their paternalist perspective, they treated their black countrymen fairly and equitably. One episode in particular – the massacre of the Lari settlement in 1953 – caused much consternation among whites and blacks in South Africa. Mau Mau insurgents attacked black Kenyans in the settlement and killed the men, women, and children suspected of loyalty to the British imperial government. This blatant act of savagery undermined the credibility of the Mau Mau, making the movement seem more like a series of feuds, alienating possible allies among the black majority, and portraying the movement as anti-Christian. Thereafter, white settlers and neutral blacks gradually turned against the increasingly isolated rebels as menaces to Kenya's stability. Vicious reprisals by the British against the Mau Mau caused the deaths of some 11,000 Kenyans and the forced internment of many thousands more.[24]

Meanwhile, the British imperialist forces ratcheted up their counterinsurgency efforts by sending Army units to Kenya and enlisting support from Kenyan tribes

---

21 Maloba, *Mau Mau and Kenya*, 10. See also Baxter, *Mau Mau*, 8; and W. O. Maloba, *African Women in Revolution* (Africa World Press, 2007), 68–69. However, in his book *Mau Mau: An African Crucible*, Robert Edgerton ignores the oath-making as a significant factor.

22 Maloba, *Mau Mau and Kenya*, 10.

23 Jansen and Osterhammel, *Decolonization*, 109, see also 154.

24 John Lonsdale, "Mau Maus of the Mind: Making Mau Mau and Remaking Kenya," in *The Decolonization Reader*, ed. James D. Le Sueur (Routledge, 2003), 269–72, 277–79; Caroline Elkins, *British Gulag: The Brutal End of Empire in Kenya* (Cape, 2005).

opposed to the Kikuyu-dominated Mau Mau movement. The combined British-Kenyan forces protected the populace from attacks and chase down the Mau Mau fighters. For the British, Kenya split into a nation of hostile blacks fighting as insurgents and most blacks remaining neutral or even loyal to the British colonial government. This schism benefited the British because the rebels never achieved any level of unified effort or support with other Kenyans. The Mau Mau never capitalized on fundamental problems of race-based divisions of wealth and labor. Nor could they exploit class-based resentments among the masses of black farmers and workers against wealthier whites who controlled the economy. Consequently, the Mau Mau's influence began waning in 1955 and collapsed by 1960.[25]

Constructions of gender played important roles in the Mau Mau rebellion in ways that highlight the need to include this cultural category. The British forces with their Kenyan allies could not decisively defeat the male insurgents of the Mau Mau in terrain so favorable in guerrilla operations. The rebels could make hit-and-run attacks against blacks or whites almost at will. When the British-Kenyan Army units tried to react and bring the Mau Mau to battle, they escaped into forests to live to fight another day. The British needed to employ a less-direct means of combating this elusive enemy. The British rounded up would-be Mau Mau men and their children and detained them in re-education camps, thus depriving the rebellion of possible recruits.[26]

In addition to trying to kill, capture, or incarcerate the male rebels, the British recognized that the Kikuyu women provided the essential logistical support for the Mau Mau. According to African scholar Cora Ann Presley, "Their function was to supply information, to smuggle arms, food, clothing, and medicine to the guerrilla army, and to maintain lines of transit for recruits traveling from the urban and rural sectors of the Central Province to join the military forces in the forest."[27] These women achieved relatively high levels of agency in playing such integral parts in the rebellion. Presley argues that, "to defeat the Mau Mau militarily, it was crucial for the British to isolate the guerrilla fighters from their supplies. Mere isolation, however, was not sufficient. The non-combatant force, led and organized to a large degree by women, had to be engaged with force and persuasion."[28] The British could have ignored these seemingly passive, sometimes invisible,

---

25 Baxter, *Mau Mau*, 18–38. See also Daniel Branch, *Defeating Mau Mau, Creating Kenya: Counterinsurgency, Civil War and Decolonization* (Cambridge University Press, 2009).
26 Cora Ann Presley, *Kikuyu Women, the Mau Mau Rebellion, and Social Change in Kenya* (Westview, 1992), 123–49; and Maloba, *African Women in Revolution*, 18–22.
27 Cora Ann Presley, "The Mau Mau Rebellion, Kikuyu Women, and Social Change," in *The Decolonization Reader*, ed. James D. Le Sueur (Routledge, 2003), 296.
28 *Ibid.*, 310–11.

roles of Mau Mau women. Given Western stereotypes of gendered identities of men as warriors and women as nurturers, it would have been understandable for the British to concentrate on combating the male fighters. However, because they set aside their ingrained constructions of gender when these did not conform to reality, the British specifically targeted the Mau Mau's women by the thousands for incarceration and re-education. This helped doom the Mau Mau rebellion to eventual defeat by 1960.[29]

Race, Gender, Insurgency, and Ideology in Vietnam

The Europeans were hardly alone in feeling the effects of waves of decolonization during the Cold War. Although many Americans denied that the United States possessed a formal empire, they did acknowledge the need to utilize military force to protect nations aligned against the Soviet Union and communism.[30] Not long after the Korean War drew to a close in 1953, the United States slowly entered another proxy war in Southeast Asia: Vietnam.

The United States provided financial and material resources and eventually armed forces in a limited war to contain Communist revolutionaries led by Ho Chi Minh and his brilliant commanding general Vo Nguyen Giap. From the American perspective, maintaining the status quo in Southeast Asia was more important than supporting self-determination. Nevertheless, the Vietnamese expelled the French imperial forces from 1946 to 1954, when they achieved a major victory at the Battle of Dien Bien Phu. This heralded the possible unification and liberation of Vietnam from occupation by the western European imperialism. American military and political leaders, however, worried this defeat would be the start of a "domino effect" in which other nations in Southeast Asia might fall to Communist rule. The United States, therefore, intervened to ensure that at least half of Vietnam would remain squarely in the anti-communist camp. The American leadership, however, failed to account for the strength of nationalism in Vietnam. The United States committed more money, material, and manpower to preserve the allied client state of South Vietnam from Ho and the Communist menace of North Vietnam. Since its creation in 1954, the South Vietnamese government was never popular with most people in the South. A succession of

---

29 Maloba, *African Women in Revolution*, 84–85.
30 For an overview of American efforts to maintain control and contain communist revolutionary influences in Latin America, see Michael Grow, *U.S. Presidents and Latin American Interventions: Pursuing Regime Change in the Cold War* (University Press of Kansas, 2008).

dictators and puppets of the United States followed one after another, and for the next two decades, civil war and revolution ensued.[31]

By 1965, many Americans including President Lyndon Baines Johnson, Secretary of Defense Robert McNamara, and General William C. Westmoreland decided that containing Communism required a commitment of American ground and air forces in the "Americanization" of the conflict. Over the next few years, American involvement escalated to the point that by 1968 more than 500,000 American troops deployed in-country. What they found there was a lush, beautiful, exotic yet deadly land. The American leadership believed that killing ten enemy combatant for every one American lost would be a sufficient "kill ratio" to achieve victory.

The war in Vietnam, however, did not go as American military planners and political leaders anticipated. Many Vietnamese combatants served on the National Liberation Front (NLF), otherwise known as the Viet Cong (VC) to the American forces and the allies in the South. The VC proved to be much more tenacious and resourceful than any Americans could have imagined. Simply put, the VC was not the type of enemy – nor did the VC wage the high-intensity kind of conflict – that conventional American forces were designed or prepared to fight. The VC operatives mingled with the South Vietnam populace, only showing themselves during ambushes and hit-and-run attacks. This elusive enemy then blended back into the civilian populace in the city streets, village hootches, and rice paddies. Alternatively, the VC retreated into impenetrable jungles or escaped into massive tunnel networks. It was often impossible for Americans to tell friend from foe because the South Vietnamese looked, acted, and dressed alike. American counterinsurgency doctrines and applications evolved too slowly to recapture the hearts and minds of the majority of the South Vietnamese people who gradually stopped supporting the American client state of South Vietnam and started aiding the North Vietnamese. Such confusion and frustration led to many injuries and deaths of tens of thousands of innocent South Vietnam non-combatants resulting from American efforts to search out and destroy enemy operatives. Sadly, some exhausted, angry American troops led by incompetent officers lost discipline and committed a few large-scale war crimes like the My Lai Massacre on March 16, 1968, as well as more numerous small-scale atrocities. The acts of rape, torture, and terror were exacerbated by the American dehumanization of the Vietnamese race and objectification of Vietnamese women.[32]

---

31 See McMahon, *Limits of Empire*, 44–49.
32 For a recent, comprehensive study of the My Lai Massacre, see Howard Jones, *My Lai, 1968, and the Descent into Darkness* (Oxford University Press, 2017), 67, 77–82, 340–48.

The American troops won every major battle in Vietnam according to standard definitions of victory – inflicting greater casualties on the enemy and of holding the field of battle at day's end. However, Ho, Giap, and the North Vietnamese believed in different definitions of victory that entailed surviving to fight another day and winnowing down American troop strength and morale in a years-long war of attrition. Their strategies for achieving victory resembled those of George Washington and Nathaniel Greene in the American War for Independence. Just as Americans misconstrued the VC and PAVN's unconventional warmaking in the twentieth century, so too did the British fail to understand American strategic objectives and operational methods in the eighteenth century. Any useful historical comparison between these two examples, however, ran the risk of being lost because of American ideological and racial preconceptions regarding Ho, Giap, and their followers.

Following the Tet Offensive in 1968, the new American President – Richard M. Nixon – began withdrawing American combatants and turned combat operations back to the ARVN in what was termed "Vietnamization." Affecting this decision were massive anti-war protests along with the Counterculture and the Civil Rights and Women's Rights Movements back in the United States that shook the foundations of civil society. During years of negotiations, 58,000 Americans died in combat, and millions of Vietnamese lost their lives, the last American troops left South Vietnam in 1973; and South Vietnam succumbed to the North's forces two years thereafter.[33]

This brief account encapsulates the conventional historical interpretations of the Vietnam War, most of which fail to emphasize race or gender as significant influences on the causes, conduct, and consequences of that conflict. The two culturally-defined categories need to be written into the narratives and dissected through the analyses of the Vietnam War. They are keys to understanding the why and how both Americans and Vietnamese fought the way they did in this conflict.

The escalation to the major American commitment of troops to Vietnam from 1961 to 1965 reveals much about masculinity in the United States. After having grown soft in the late 1950s while facing challenges at home and abroad, American manhood experienced a renaissance in the persona of John Fitzgerald Kennedy. He assumed the mantle of redeemer of American manly virtue and the nation as

---

33 There are many studies of the Vietnam War, ranging from George Herring, *America's Longest War: The United States and Vietnam, 1950–1975*, 4th ed. (McGraw-Hill, 2002) to John Prados, *Vietnam: The History of an Unwinnable War, 1945–1975* (University Press of Kansas, 2009). For the North Vietnamese perspective, see Military History Institute of Vietnam, *Victory in Vietnam: The Official History of the People's Army of Vietnam, 1945–1975*, trans. Merle L. Pribbenow (University Press of Kansas, 2002). None of these books, however, delves into issues of race or gender in any conscious ways.

a whole, just as Teddy Roosevelt did for his generation at the turn of the century. Born into a wealthy, influential family from Massachusetts, Kennedy cultivated his image as the virile, manly warrior through his service in the Second World War. In that conflict, he was decorated for holding the crew of his patrol torpedo boat together after a Japanese warship rammed it. Despite a back injury, Kennedy demonstrated great personal courage when he helped a more severely wounded sailor through the water to safety. After the war ended, the Massachusetts Democrat won election to three terms in the House of Representatives and then two elections as U.S. Senator. In his years in the Senate, Kennedy added anti-communism to his masculine bona fides when he served on a Senate committee investigating communism and worked with Senator Joseph McCarthy to expose suspected communism subversives. When the censure vote against McCarthy occurred, Kennedy was absent, ostensibly recovering from one of several back surgeries. With Kennedy's status as a cold warrior fixed firmly in place, he ran against the Republican Richard M. Nixon in the 1960 presidential election. The less-photogenic but no less anti-communist Nixon failed to match Kennedy's style and substance in the first nationally televised presidential debates. Even so, Kennedy won the election by a small margin. Once he became president in 1961, he set about changing the image of the office and its trappings.[34]

Kennedy fancied himself to be King Arthur at Camelot, surrounded by the knights that made up his cabinet and adored by his supporters. Kennedy relied on what K.A. Cuordileone calls his "new frontierman's cult of masculine toughness." The new president's carefully cultivated persona included him "flexing (manly) muscles from Cuba to Vietnam."[35] Aside from his domestic agenda, Kennedy wanted to re-establish America as the preeminent bulwark against communism. His first major effort against that dreaded enemy turned into the poorly-planned and poorly executed Bay of Pigs invasion in April 1961. This fiasco saw American-supported Cuban exiles try to invade their homeland and expel Cuba's new communist leader Fidel Castro. Kennedy did not sanction much-needed American aerial support when the invasion forces landed on Cuba and got pinned down by Castro's forces. Next came Kennedy's attempt to redeem himself in the eyes of his nation and the world, when he faced down the Nikita Khrushchev and the Soviet Union in the Cuban Missile Crisis in October 1962. The American president could not tolerate nuclear missiles being placed on Cuban soil little more than 90 miles from Florida and within striking distance of

34 Dean, *Imperial Brotherhood*, 17–20, 43–49, 169–79; and Cuordileone, *Manhood and America*, 20–29.
35 Cuordileone, *Manhood and America*, 167, 180–82.

half the United States. Kennedy took the two nations to the brink of nuclear war. He appeared to win this second round against communism, but hindsight has shown that the Soviets backed down before the nuclear missiles started launching. Another crisis then erupted in Berlin in October 1962 where communist East Germany erected the Berlin Wall around free part of West Berlin. Finally, a growing threat of communism emerged in Southeast Asia in Vietnam. As with his earlier tests, Kennedy could not tolerate the possibility that another nation might fall to communist control. That same manly heroism that put American men into space and ultimately on the moon – the "new frontier" – could be focused on stopping the rising communist tide.[36]

Some 8.7 million Americans heeded the call to service of Kennedy, Johnson, and the nation to volunteer for service in the U.S. military during the Vietnam Era. They enlisted out of a sense of patriotic duty, need for adventure, means of avoiding incarceration, means of evading the draft, need to stop Communism, or proof of manhood, or combinations of these. Another 2.2 million were drafted in military service; and, just as those conscripts of earlier conflicts, they added the desire for survival to the list of motivations. In this way, the draftees resembled those of the Europeans conscripted in 1916 and thereafter in the First World War. Apart from race, social background proved to be another major factor in whom served in the armed forces. The preponderance of draftees came from lower-income backgrounds of Caucasian, African-American, or Hispanic-American descent. Indeed, estimates run as high as 80 percent of service personnel (draft or volunteers) came from blue-collar, agricultural, and single-parent backgrounds. Part of this class-bias came from the fact that the local Selective Service (draft) Boards were dominated by middle-class membership, who tended to favor their own economic strata for exemptions. Meanwhile, the men coming from middle-class or wealthier background avoided service through deferments as college students, family fathers, or stints in the National Guard or Reserve. From 1963 to 1968, President Lyndon Johnson never called these reserve components to active federal service. A few American men evaded the draft and fled to Canada, but these men tended to come from backgrounds with sufficient resources or educations to make "dodging the draft" (in the day's parlance) viable options. The poorer blacks and whites enjoyed no such luxuries. Taken as a whole, Vietnam could legitimately be considered a rich white man's war, but a poor man's fight.[37]

---

36 Dean, *Imperial Brotherhood*,179–87, 201–10; Kimmel, *Manhood in America*, 265–69; and Cuordileone, *Manhood and America*, 201–236.

37 Christian G. Appy, *Working-Class War: American Combat Soldiers and Vietnam* (University of North Carolina Press, 1993), 33–48, 220–28; Herman Graham III, *The Brothers' Vietnam: Black Power, Manhood, and the Military Experience* (University of Florida Press, 2003), 15–20; Kyle

Although the class distinctions in the U.S. military were compelling, understanding race and gender as factors in the Vietnam War reveals that conflict to be a clash between two culturally-influenced "ways" of war.[38] Whether white or black, Americans possessed ingrained perceptions regarding the "yellow"-skinned Vietnamese male or female "others" that shaped policy decisions of American military and civilian leadership and tactical decisions of low-ranking grunts in the jungles or rice paddies. Because North Vietnamese garnered little or no respect. Racial slurs directed at the Vietnamese became common parlance among those Americans in the Vietnam War. They used words like "slopes," "slants," "zipperheads," "dinks," and "gooks," as names for Vietnamese, whether they came from the North or South. Some of these terms dated back to the Korean War, World War II, or earlier as applied to any people of Asian descent.[39] In an oral history interview conducted in 2008, one retired African-American officer recalled his attitudes about the Vietnamese almost four decades after he served in-country as a young Army second lieutenant:

> It was just something that the troops just picked up and just said. Well, I mean gooks. I mean, every Vietnamese, it doesn't make a difference who they were, was a gook. And you know, I don't think that there was a very good respect for the civilian population. I'm not talking about the Viet Cong or the enemy now ... You know, a lot of cases in the heat of battle where you've been hurt or maimed or something by your enemy, well it's you know, there's no holds barred and you're not a good guy. But in the local population itself, you know, everything was almost as if they were inferior. I mean, not only among the white soldiers, but among African-American soldiers too... Where if you're going to win the hearts and minds you're got to start with the basics, and the basics is that, you know, you're a guest in this country even though we were there based on our ideology and what we perceive as a threat. Those folks are human as well. And if they're not directly tied or related to the

---

Longley, *Grunts: The American Combat Soldiers in Vietnam* (Routledge, 2008), 14–15, 20; Dean, *Imperial Brotherhood*, 210–40; and Goldstein, *War and Gender*, 278–80.

38 Several books demonstrate the true relevance of studying race and gender in the Vietnam War and military history as a whole: Westheider's *Fighting on Two Fronts*; Sandra C. Taylor's *Vietnamese Women at War: Fighting for Ho Chi Minh and the Revolution* (University Press of Kansas, 1999), Karen Gottschang Turner and Phan Thanh Hao's *Even the Women Must Fight: Memories of War from North Vietnam* (Wiley, 1998); Heather Stur, *Beyond Combat: Women and Gender in the Vietnam War* (Cambridge University Press, 2011) and most recently Maxwell's *Brotherhood in Combat*.

39 For examples, see Longley, *Grunts*, 50–51, 96–98; "Vietnam Veteran's Terminology and Slang," http://www.vietvet.org/glossary.htm (accessed September 15, 2009); and NandUPress, "USA Glossary."

enemy, who you are fighting, you are never going to gain respect for them because of the way that you act, your attitude, and your misunderstanding of the culture.[40]

Even at the highest of levels of American government, dismissive or derogatory attitudes about the Vietnamese emerged in quotes like President Lyndon Johnson calling North Vietnam a "damn little pissant country" and a "raggedy-ass fourth-rate country." His condescending remarks embodied American exceptionalism mixed with bigotry and hubris that formed the core of American foreign policies of the post-World War II era.[41] Neither Johnson nor his advisors could conceive that this inferior enemy would stand up to the technological capabilities and operational advantages enjoyed by the U.S. military. America's past experiences fighting wars against the Japanese, North Koreans, and Chinese offered few useful strategic and tactical lessons in the conflict with the Vietnamese. Conversely, like other Asians, the Vietnamese did not embrace the American or Western notions of life or the individual, nor did they believe Americans or Western Europeans to be superior. Indeed, the VC exploited the hatred of the Vietnamese people for outsiders as "force multiplier."[42] Any American atrocities were employed as means of denouncing the American presence or encouraging recruitment. The Vietnamese would willingly sacrifice themselves in what seemed to the Americans to be suicide attacks. Moreover, unlike the Pacific War and the Korean War, the Vietnam War did not play out in conventional battles using conventional tactics. Instead, the VC and to a lesser degree the PAVN utilized guerrilla tactics to fight an insurgent conflict against the Americans, who in turn believed this type of warfare showed the enemy's cowardice or inferiority. Either of these traits fed Americans' self-image as exceptional. In a tragically ironic twist, the projection of normative ways of warmaking onto the enemy all but doomed the American efforts in Vietnam to defeat.[43]

---

40 Clark W. Fuller, interview by Steven Brown, 11 July 2008, Cantigny First Division Oral History Project, Ball States University, transcript, pp. 23–24, http://libx.bsu.edu/cdm/ref/collection/CtgnyOrHis/id/48.
http://libx.bsu.edu/cdm4/item_viewer.php?CISOROOT=/CtgnyOrHis&CISOPTR=48&CISOBOX-=1&REC=9 (accessed 4 April 2018).
For a published collection of interviews, see Wallace Terry, ed., Bloods: Black Veterans in the Vietnam War: An Oral History (Presidio, 1985).
41 Op cited in Michael H. Hunt, *Lyndon Johnson's War: American Cold War Crusade in Vietnam, 1945–1968* (Hill and Wang, 1996), 105.
42 Ballard and McDowell, *Hate and Combat* Behavior, 235. See also Vito M. Solazzo, *An Analysis of the Origin and Basis of the Factors Motivating and Sustaining the Viet Cong in Combat* (Marine Corps Command and Staff College, 1968).
43 See William Darryl Henderson, *Why the Viet Cong Fought: A Study of Motivation and Control in Combat* (Greenwood, 1979).

Vietnamese notions of "self" and "other" likewise affected choices at all levels of warmaking. As integral parts of their insurgency, the VC and the PAVN utilized women and children much more than most Americans could have imagined. Americans viewed these women with suspicion as possible informants and spies, or with contempt as objects of sexual gratification. Either way, their contributions never merited the status as severe threats to the American cause in Vietnam. However, according to estimates, at least two million Vietnamese women mobilized against the Americans in many different roles, including recruiters, spies, saboteurs, couriers, sappers, porters, informants, laborers, and even combatants in the VC cadres and PAVN units. Tens of thousands walked thousands of miles on the Ho Chi Minh Trail carrying weapons, ammunition, food, and other supplies from the North to their comrades in the South. Untold numbers of women remain nameless to history because they died during these trips. Just as has been seen among women in resistance movements during the Second World War, many motivations drove the Vietnamese women to participate they called "American War." Some of their motivations, like ideology, may seem obvious; but, as Turner demonstrates in her book, other motivations sprang from very basic hopes and goals or from Vietnamese cultural factors. Regardless of their motives, these Vietnamese women exercised remarkable, not mention wholly unexpected, levels of agency as actors in the conflict.[44]

The failure by Americans to assess the Vietnamese women's contribution ran contrary to the British reaction to the Mau Mau rebellion in Kenya. The negation did irreparable harm to the American efforts in Vietnam on political, strategic, operational, tactical, and logistical levels. Not only did the British recognize the essential logistical support of women to the Mau Mau male fighters, they also targeted those women for incarceration, thereby eliminating key long-term support to the fighters.

Whereas women's involvement represented yet another foreign, strange, and unexpected practice to American outsiders, Vietnam's history includes a tradition of women taking up arms as "long-haired warriors" and "citizen-warriors" that ran parallel to the tradition of women as mothers and nurturers. Some women like Nguyen Thi Dinh rose to high levels of rank and wielded real influence. Dinh helped establish the NLF, served as chairwomen of the South Vietnamese Women's Liberation Association, and rose to the rank of major general and member of the Central Committee of the Vietnamese Communist

---

44 Turner with Hao, *Even the Women Must Fight*, 35. See also Mark W. McLeod and Nguyen Thi Dieu, *Culture and Customs of Vietnam* (Greenwood, 2001), 131–53.

Figure 9.2: Russian-made rifle, carried by this woman when she was captured in Nearby Brush, is slung around her neck by South Vietnamese soldiers before they began their interrogation of her as Viet Cong suspect near AP La Ghi in Vietnam, August 25, 1965.
Source: (c) picture alliance/ASSOCIATED PRESS

Party in the post-war era. Binh also played significant roles as a co-founder of the NLF, a member of the VC's Central Committee, and a negotiator at the Paris Peace Accords. They joined the Trung Sisters (A.D. 39), Trieu Tri Trinh (248), and Bui Thi Xuan (1802) as famous female soldiers and leaders in Vietnamese military history. These women, whether in antiquity or modernity, fulfilled a call made by a Vietnamese proverb variously translated as, "When war strikes close to home, even women must fight," or "When the enemy comes, even the women should fight."[45] Such expectations for Vietnamese women in wartime were intertwined with their culturally-defined roles as mothers. Their maternal duties to their families and their nation demanded that they be willing to make sacrifices for their children as well as be willing to fight, kill, and die for their nation. This Vietnamese paradigm combining the feminine and warrior roles was vastly different from the American paradigm subordinating the warrior role to the femi-

---

45 Turner, *Even the Women Must Fight*, 5; Arlene Bergman, *Women of Vietnam* (Peoples Press, 1974), 32.

nine role. Clearly then, the North Vietnamese and their allies in the South took advantage of Americans' ingrained presumptions that the enemy women were not warriors, killers, or heroes.[46]

Race, Gender, and Sexuality in the U.S. military during Vietnam

Apart from the implications of fighting a yellow enemy in the Vietnam War, race and racism played roles within the recently integrated American military and among its conscripted and volunteered troops. Vietnam was the first conflict fought by a racially-integrated American military. In addition to coming too frequently from lower-income, less-educated background, African Americans endured racism from the draft process through basic training and on to the battlefields of Vietnam. There would be residual problems from the earlier segregated era analysis by James Westheider in *Fighting on Two Fronts*, Lawrence Allen Eldrige in *Chronicles of a Two-Front War*, and more recently Jeremy Maxwell in *Brotherhood in Combat*. Westheider finds three typologies of racism still prevalent in the U.S. military during the conflict: "institutional racism," "personal racism," and "perceived racism." To some degree, institutional racism receded and perhaps personal racism was driven underground by integration in armed forces and by civilian measures such as *Brown v. Topeka Board of Education* (1954), the Civil Rights Act (1964), and the Voting Rights Act (1965). Nevertheless, racism in the military institution and among personnel also remained strong enough to block or slow efforts to make the American military more equal and equitable for minorities. Perceived racism – policies, structures, or practices that were coincidentally or unintentionally racist, prejudiced, or discriminatory in their effects – exacerbated the problems caused by institutional and personal racism in the late 1960s.[47]

As had occurred in previous conflicts, the African-American community supported the war in Vietnam. Patriotic service in wartime offered one means of achieving more equality and more civil rights. However, support for the war effort eroded among African Americans as the conflict dragged on. The draft proved to be the most contentious point because so many young black men did not receive deferments that some of their wealthier, better educated countrymen received. Moreover, for many blacks, skewed decisions of Caucasian-dominated

---

46 See Goldstein, *War and Gender*, 80–81; De Pauw, *Battlecries and Lullabies*, 269–72.

47 Taylor Branch, *At Canaan's Edge: America in the King Years, 1965–1968* (Simon and Schuster, 2007); Westheider, *Fighting on Two Fronts*; Lawrence Allen Eldridge, *Chronicles of a Two-Front War: Civil Rights and Vietnam in the African American Press* (University of Missouri Press, 2012); Maxwell, *Brotherhood in Combat*; and Fuller interview, 19–20.

draft boards, negative evaluations of mental capacities, slow promotions for minorities, and disproportionately high percentages of blacks in combat units and on casualty lists stood as incontrovertible evidence of racism. These factors drove Civil Rights leader, Rev. Martin Luther King, Jr., to label Vietnam a "white man's war, a black man's fight." This represented a departure from the previously dominant desire in the African-American community to encourage military service in wartime as a means of proving fitness for full citizenship. After the fiasco of the Tet Offensive and the assassinations of King and Robert F. Kennedy in 1968, more and more African Americans opposed involvement in the Vietnam War. Some African Americans embraced the "Black Power" movement and grew militant and violent. It was not uncommon to hear black radicals claim solidarity with the Vietnamese, another race being exploited by Caucasian racists from the United States. By the late 1960s, the Civil Rights Movement splintered into several sub-groups as many black activists joined the burgeoning Anti-War Movement. In this way, the Southeast Asian conflict constituted a catalyst for several movements that demanded social, political, and legal changes in the United States.[48]

Reactionary beliefs and actions spilled over into the armed services in the United States and those personnel deployed to Vietnam. Racial tensions exploded in violence at Camp Lejeune, NC, in 1969; aboard the USS *Kitty Hawk* in 1972; and in the U.S. military stockade at Long Binh in 1968. Once "in-country," African-American troops increasingly resented their Caucasian officers and resisted the policies and orders they issued. Some white troops made matters worse by displaying Confederate battle flags, dressing in KKK attire, or utilizing racist slurs such as "nigger" or "boy." The blacks, particularly of enlisted ranks, in Vietnam began withdrawing into their own insular groups, practicing the ritualized handshake called "dapping," and sometimes even "fragging" particularly racist or incompetent Caucasian officers. The self-imposed segregation between the races gave rise to still more tensions because of lack of communication the race-based groups caused. As morale and discipline declined after 1968, illegal substance abuse increased among black and white troops alike. The worst behaviors and incidents occurred on American bases where there was relative safety, if not boredom. Over time and especially after the Tet Offensive, the motivations among servicemen drifted from patriotism and self-fulfillment to draft requirements by law. Too many body bags and wounded men came home for too few permanent battlefield victories to be ignored. In fact, the support for the Vietnam

---

48 Longley, *Grunts*, 9–11, 160–61; Maxwell, *Brotherhood in Combat*, 106–113; and Appy, *Working-Class War*, 14–22, 223–33.

Figure 9.3 Vietnam War Protesters, Wichita, Kansas, 1967 Protesters carry signs and act out "Saigon Puppet" demonstration in front of Wichita City Building in 1967.
Source: National Archives and Records Administration, USA.
https://commons.wikimedia.org/wiki/File:
Vietnam_War_protesters._1967._Wichita,_Kans_-_NARA_-_283627.jpg

War – patriotic, anti-communist, or otherwise – declined among the service personnel and veterans alike after Tet. Philip Caputo's *Born on the Fourth of July* stands out as a poignant literacy example of one veteran's shift from patriotism to cynicism.[49]

Units in combat, however, experienced less racial tension because of the small unit *esprit* among the troops, the common enemy in the VC, and the shared goal of survival. It is also noteworthy that African-American officers, career NCOs or members of families with long-standing military traditions tended to avoid

49 Appy, *Working-Class War*, 220–28. For an overview of veterans' perspectives, see James Wood, *Veteran Narratives and the Collective Memory of the Vietnam War* (Ohio University Press, 2016), 46–73.

involvement in the active resistance. Instead, they viewed military service as a profession with benefits and potential for advancement that would be endangered by participating in or being perceived as a proponent of militancy and resistance.[50]

At home, American's self-image of their nation as "the city on a hill" became tarnished by the senseless waste of lives in an endless, winless conflict. Apart from anti-war protests, upheavals erupted across regions and lines of color, class, and race regarding problems during the 1960s. It is not easy to determine whether anti-war activism precipitated other movements or vice versa. Regardless, that decade saw swirling, intertwining, and overlapping calls for radical change because the heteronormative constructions of gender and race and accepted concepts of civil society in the 1950s were laid bare to expose cultural faults lines that, when put under pressure, rocked the nation. Women and African Americans agitated for equal rights with Caucasian men. Women took to the airwaves, voting booths, and streets to push for a Constitutional amendment to guarantee their status on par with men. Meanwhile, blacks recognized that the Civil Rights and Voting Rights Acts represented major milestones of a so-called "Second Reconstruction" in the mid-1960s, but they also knew that an end to discrimination on practical levels such as salaries or job opportunities still loomed in the distant future. So great was African American anger that many adopted militant rhetoric and sometimes violent tactics.[51]

The challenge to the 1950s notions of proper gender roles spread as far as the bedroom during that next decade. A small yet vocal minority Americans embraced the Sexual Revolution with its elevation of promiscuity to become acceptable, if not preferable, in specific segments of American society. Men and women enjoyed sexual relations unfettered by social conventions such as gender roles and marriage. Women could use the most modern contraception (the pill) to achieve sexual liberation from the previously male-controlled yoke of childbirth and childcare. Gay activism also experienced a resurgence in calls for legal equality and civil treatment.[52]

---

50 James E. Westheider, "African Americans, Civil Rights, and the Armed Forces during Vietnam," in *Integrating the U.S. Military: Race, Gender, and Sexual Orientation since World War II*, eds., Douglas Walter Bristol, Jr, and Heather Marie Stur (Johns Hopkins University Press, 2017), 96–121; Graham, *The Brothers' Vietnam*, 45–66, 120–21; and Nalty, *Strength for the Fight*, 303–17. See also Fuller, interview, 18–21.
51 Kwon, *The Other Cold War*, 39–41; Gerstle, *American Crucible*, 311–46; Longley, *Grunts*, 127–35; and William L. O'Neill, *Coming Apart: An Informal History of America in the 1960s* (Ivan R. Dee, 2004).
52 Bailey, *Sex in the Heartland*, 136–199; and Ruth Rosen, *The World Split Open: How the Modern Women's Movement Changed America* (Viking, 2000).

Such rejection of mainstream mores spread to other areas of American life in the form of the "Counterculture," which drew inspiration from Jack Kerouac, Allen Ginsburg, and William Burroughs of the 1950s "Beat Generation." During the next decade, the Counterculture appealed to young people who felt trapped by their Second World War-era parent's expectations for their futures, societal requirements in the present, and traditional codes of behavior in the past. Countercultural reactions included, among others, perpetuating the middle-class dream of a quiet home in the suburbs, serving in the U.S. military in Vietnam, and engaging in illegal activities like drug use and presumably immoral activities like open sexual relationships. The protests against all things normative found voices among musicians, artists, and authors. The movement (if it can even be called that) lasted from 1964 through 1972 which coincided with main American commitment of troops and resources in the Vietnam War.[53]

Meanwhile half a world away, the last American troops left Vietnam in 1973 in defeat. Those men had apparently not lived up to the wartime standards of victory of their fathers and grandfathers. Many tangible and intangible factors contributed to the American defeat in Vietnam; but, sadly for the returning generation of veterans whether they deserved it or not, losing that war brought shame and emasculation to their manly warrior ethos. Moreover, readjusting to post-war life particularly in the civilian world proved to be no easy task for whites or blacks. Because of the horrific experiences they endured, many veterans suffered from post-traumatic stress disorder (PTSD). Not unlike the generation of European veterans who survived the First World War, the Vietnam veterans comprised a lost generation. Making matters still worse was the high levels of discord among American people caused by the Vietnam War, and those anti-war elements did little to help integrate the returning troops in the post-war era. Those American veterans did not receive the goodwill and support from their countrymen that veterans from the world wars had enjoyed. It would take several decades and several conflicts to help restore some level of self-esteem to the Vietnam veterans.[54]

In the aftermath of the Vietnam War, minorities previously subjected to personal discrimination and institutional prejudice gradually made significant strides toward equality in military's ranks. The U.S. military increased its efforts to raise awareness of the problems of racism among its personnel and to promote greater educational and career opportunities for personnel of races and ethnic

---

53 See chapters in Peter Braunstein and Michael William Doyle, eds., *Imagine Nation: The American Counterculture of the 1960s and 1970s* (Routledge, 2002); and O'Neill, *Coming Apart*, 233–74.
54 Goldstein, *War and Gender*, 278–80. See also Jonathan Shay, *Achilles in Vietnam: Combat Trauma and the Undoing of Character* (Simon & Schuster, 1995).

backgrounds. As the institutionalized and personal racism weakened, the racial ceilings on advancement and promotion cracked and broke. Women and minorities have since advanced to the rank of full general and served in a variety of high-ranking commands and MOS's. This is not to say that they faced no problems or incidents of residual racism and chauvinism.[55]

Conclusion

Although infrequently examined through the dual lenses of race and gender by traditional military historians, decolonization in Kenya and Vietnam exemplified the efficacy of adding race and gender to the mix of strategy, operations, tactics, and logistics. Perceptions, policies, and practices regarding race and gender profoundly affected the experiences and consequences of these conflicts in implicit and explicit ways. Both conflicts pitted the Caucasian-dominated Western military powers against presumably inferior indigenous peoples. The British and the Americans brought pre-conceived notions of race and gender based on past colonial experiences to Kenya and Vietnam. Unlike the British who adapted to and minimized the contributions of Kenyan women to the Mau Mau Rebellion, American stereotypes of women as nurturers were disrupted by Vietnamese constructions of women as warriors. This disconnect between American gender assumptions and Vietnamese gender realities meant that Americans never fully grasped their enemy's capabilities and motivations. Thus, there existed no way to counter the Vietnam women.

Aside for race and gender on the battlefields, these categories also affected the United States military as female and African-American servicemen struggled against internalized prejudices to assimilate into that institution. The turbulent decade of the 1960s and the Vietnam War would, however, also reveal how racism and chauvenism remained entrenched in policies and procedures of the American military, as well as in the minds of some bigoted Caucasian military personnel. Following the establishment of the All-Volunteer Force in 1973, more and more opportunities and more and more equality for women and African Americans and other minorities in the U.S. military would be achieved, though not with ongoing setbacks and problems.

---

55 For observations about African-American officers advancing from company to field grade ranks, see Fuller interview, 20–37.

10 The Future of Race and Gender in Warfare

As the preceding chapters have demonstrated, wars have started and suffering in wars has been exacerbated by constructions of "self" and "other" with race and gender as identifiers. History – for our purpose modern Western history since the early 1800s – is tragically replete with examples of the racism and sexism inflaming the desires of one group to attack, subjugate, and kill opposing groups. When volatile ideologies like nationalism and religion are added into the mix, the bloodlust can reach fever pitches that nullify legal and moral inhibitors during conflicts. The twentieth century alone bears the terrible marks of the Holocaust, the Rape of Nanjing, and countless other genocides and atrocities, all of which included racial and gendered components. Even so, saying that, for instance, "War is the way it is, because men are the way they are" is too simplistic.[1] The factors of race, gender, sexuality, ethnicity, religion, region, ideology, morality among others are complex and often contradictory pieces in cultural mosaics that have evolved over time.

With these observations in mind, *Race and Gender in Modern Western Warfare* has examined warfare through the dual lenses of race and gender in hopes to depicting wars and the societies that fight them in illuminating ways.

More than two decades ago, historian John Lynn laid out a bleak forecast for military historians. With their relevance challenged on all sides by social historians, who accused (not exactly unfairly) them of clinging to outdated models of analysis, practitioners of traditional military history had become an insular, bitter cadre, taking offense at any challenge or suggestion to expand their scope beyond battle and campaign narrative. Without rejecting the idea that conflict *was* central to the military historian's mission ("To me, the essence of military history is combat; it is what makes our subject unique," he wrote),[2] Lynn acknowledged that the field's critics were correct in a 1997 article published in the *Journal of Military History*. The very context and nature of this field as practiced in the academic environment need to change if it were to remain viable in the field as a whole. Certainly, this would chafe the sensibilities of many existing practitioners, accustomed to a more grounded, archival-oriented approach. But, Lynn asserted, by adapting the best elements of social history, anthropology, sociology,

---

[1] For example, see Cynthia Cockburn, "Gender Relations as Casual in Militarization and War: A Feminist Standpoint," *International Feminist Journal of Politics* 12. 2 (2010): 139–57. Cockburn argues certain feminist theories are inherently "anti-war" since warfare is a male-oriented, gendered power construction.

[2] John Lynn, "The Embattled Future of Academic Military History," *Journal of Military History* 61 (October, 1997): 777–89, quote on 783.

https://doi.org/10.1515/9783110477467-010

humanities, and political science to the field, military history would not merely remain relevant, its reach and appeal would grow.[3]

One of the fields and methodologies Lynn suggested could be a model for incorporation into the practice of military history was gender studies. Considering the influence of masculinity as a cultural and social influence on war and military institutions in *grand siècle* France, Lynn argued that military historians should embrace gender studies as a natural adjunct to their other analytical and methodological skills. Understanding the behavior of French officers hailing from the nobility required understanding both what their normative sense of masculinity was and what it was not, and how femininity was understood in a direct opposition to male identity.

Whereas John Lynn did not make the same explicit pronouncement about race, it can be argued (and is frequently, within this textbook) that the ideologies of race and gender are so intertwined that they can not be separated. Racism appropriated gendered terms as validations just as sexism appropriated racial terms. For example, the supposedly racially superior groups – from the ancient Greeks to the twentieth century's Germans and Japanese – often bequeathed exceptional masculine and paternal traits to their own races, and degraded their enemy races with feminized and infantilized traits. Likewise, normative gender carried with them expectations for acceptable behavior by wealthy white women in the American south or British India, as opposed to black slaves or brown servants in these regions respectively. In the historical contexts, it mattered not that reality showed equality of skill, strength, endurance, or intellect across races or genders. Instead, aligning race and gender served a "self"-promoting, "self"-fulfilling narrative about superiority that in turn justified violent subjugation of the inferior "other."[4]

Much of this textbook has been devoted to expanding upon the mission staked out by John Lynn in his article now more than two decades old: we set out create a historiographic overview of how the field has progressed in adopting race and gender as lenses to frame the past. What has been presented thus far is a series of snapshots of new practitioners in the fields of gender, race, sexuality, and ethnicity have taken up Lynn's challenge. There remains the question, however, of where is military history – or rather, war and society studies – going from here? What new topics and areas of inquiry remain ripe for exploration and

---

3 *Ibid.*, 783–784.

4 See Glenda Gilmore, *Gender and Jim Crow: Women and the Politics of White Supremacy in North Carolina, 1896–1920* (University of North Carolina Press, 1992); Procida, *Married to the Empire*; Benesch, *Inventing the Way of the Samurai*; and Amy Carney, *Marriage and Fatherhood in the Nazi SS* (University of Toronto Press, 2018).

development? How do these rising and established academic historians make their work more relevant to the much larger public audience that views military history in large part as an entertainment commodity? This closing chapter consids these questions as it examines some current and proposed paths of research in war and society and military history.

It is worth noting, however, that considerations of race and gender within military history and culture splits into two distinct pathways. First, there are those works that, while focusing on assessing and analyzing the historical past exclusively, do so by introducing new arguments and lines of discussion to the debate. These may include questions related to sexual assault, female combat integration, and same-sex relationships within historical case studies. Second are the assessments of current issues relating to race and gender, not only to gain a firmer understanding of these issues, but to also identify how they are shaping the context of contemporary institutions and ideologies.

This concluding chapter thus presents several examples from both categories, with some insights into the state of the literature associated with them, as well as observations on future opportunities for research. In the section "Recent Trends in Historiography," short essays detail some more recent works in three topics – Sexual Assault in War; Genocide and War; and LBGTQ Personnel and Military Service. The second section titled "Areas for Further Consideration" examines several other topics of current note: Racial and Ethnic Intolerance in the U.S. Military; Sexual Assault in the U.S. Military; and the question of whether racial or gendered factors will remain relevant as war continues to evolve in the post-computer mainframe age.

Recent Trends in Historiography

Sexual Assault and War

Cultural historian Joanna Bourke admonishes us to avoid the temptation to deploy rape as a metaphor to describe deep national trauma during peace and war. "Rape is not a metaphor for the ruin of a city or a nation ("The Rape of Nanjing" or "The Rape of Kuwait"). It is not an environmental disaster ("the rape of our planet"). It is the embodied violation of another person."[5] Yet for centuries, it was a relatively ambiguous act, denied legitimacy on the balance of a series of patriarchal assumptions about male power and female compliance. All

---

5 Joanna Bourke, *Rape: Sex, Violence, History* (Counterpoint, 2017), 6.

too often it was treated essentially as a crime against property – that is to say, rape was defined as only occurring if the male provocateur had no filial or familial tie to the victim. This absence of a clear definition, the moralistic assumptions that women who were assaulted were in some degree complicit in the act, and the collective shaming of victims by society at large have all combined to make rape a silent crime, one that is deeply misunderstood and, accordingly subject to revision at the hands of clever advocates for those accused of perpetrating the act.

This ambiguity and manipulation of intent and victimhood have also affected the historical treatment of sexual assault in past conflict. Again, Bourke notes the inherent dilemmas posed in assessing rape and sexual assault via a historian's lens. Chief among these is the danger of normalizing sexual violence through casual discussions of the act. There is nothing normal about rape, Bourke states, yet poor discursive and linguistic treatments may trigger an acceptance of sexuality as a normative adjunct of war. Another hazard is in the temptation to focus analysis and narrative exclusively on the victim. Rape is a calculated act dependent upon the perpetrators exercising their own agency. While it is certainly appropriate to emphasize the plight of the victim, failure to address the person initiating the assault only fosters a singular narrative. Yet here again, unartful treatment of the rapist will only dissuade the reader from taking seriously the entire encounter, or worse, again serve to normalize sexual assault for some readers.[6]

Historians have traditionally found it difficult coming to grips with sexual violence in war, preferring to ignore it altogether or, at best, acknowledging it as an unfortunate side-effect of war. The rationale for the cavalier underplaying of rape in wartime is self-evident: calling greater attention to the issue only cluttered the narrative of battle and campaigns, while also raising significant doubts as to the conduct of individual soldiers in wartime. Yet as both the new military history and war and society sub-disciplines gain greater relevance in the profession, the centrality of sexual abuse and violence as an aspect of war relating directly to civilian societies becomes clear. Rape is neither universal nor total in war – it is not an inevitable fate nor do all soldiers take part in it – but it is still very real. One of the pioneering chroniclers of wartime sexual violence, Susan Brownmiller, records examples as distant as the Judean wars against the Philistines, and as recent as the Vietnam War. Indeed, "It has been argued that when killing is viewed as not only permissible but heroic behavior sanctioned by one's government or cause," writes Brownmiller, "the distinction between taking a human life and other forms

---

6 *Ibid.*, 10–11.

of impermissible violence gets lost, and rape becomes an unfortunate but inevitable by-product of the necessary game called war."[7]

One valid critique of Brownmiller's work rests on the extent to which she attempts to portray rape as being so normal in wartime as to be a common event. There is no question that sexual violence remains a constant to warfare, however she neglects to distinguish between false accounts (such as those drawn up by British propagandists during the First World War to portray the German army in Belgium as lust-crazed monsters) and the reality upon which they were based. As John Horne and Alan Kramer note in their more recent studies of the German atrocities in Belgium during the First World War, rape was a real aspect of the German military occupation. A precise reckoning is not possible; considering the shame experienced by the victims and the general acceptance that rape was an incidental, ad hoc crime, such a conclusion is not surprising. Post-war French and Belgian commissions, while drawing attention to the frequency of rape by German soldiers in the occupied territories, did acknowledge that at no time was sexual assault considered to be part of a reprisal policy targeting alleged *francs-tireur*, unlike the wholesale executions of civilians in both countries.[8] Nonetheless, the French Commission's conclusion that two percent of reported atrocity incidents in French territory were related to rape points toward a serious breakdown in restraint and moral control within the German army. Of course Allied propagandists did exaggerate these real outrages, in order to make a stronger case for German cultural brutality at large. By accepting these accounts at face value (to the point of attacking later historians who sought to revise these propaganda-motivated tales), Brownmiller falls into the trap of appearing to over-sensationalize her arguments.[9] These admissions not withstanding, though, sexual assaults raised many concerns in the First World War, although few incidents resulted any formal policy of coercion and ethnic cleansing with the obvious exceptions being the Armenian genocide or the invasion and occupation of Serbia.[10]

Since the late 1990s, military and social historians, many closely associated with the war and society sub-discipline, have begun to engage the troubled

---

7 Susan Brownmiller, *Against Our Will: Men, Women and Rape* (Fawcett Columbine, 1975), 31–33, quote on 32.

8 Horne and Kramer, *German Atrocities, 1914*, 71, 196. Also see Alan Kramer, *Dynamic and Destruction: Culture and Mass Killing in the First World War* (Oxford University Press, 2007), 138–139, 244–245.

9 *Horne and Kramer, German Atrocities, 1914*, 197; Brownmiller, *Against Our Will*, 40–47.

10 Philipp Ther, *The Darker of Nation-States: Ethnic Cleaning in Modern Europe*, trans. Charlotte Kreutzmüller (Bergahn, 2014), 59–66; and Norman M. Naimark, *Fires of Hatred: Ethnic Cleansing in Twentieth-Century Europe* (Harvard University Press, 2002), 17–56.

history of sexual violence in war more critically. Several insights emerge. First and foremost, the plurality of recent historians strive to clarify that, despite earlier claims, sexual assault is rarely a normal adjunct to organized state violence. And yet, an overwhelming majority of cases are not recorded, denying observers any clear view of the prevalence of rape and sexual violence in wartime.[11] Indeed, as Joanna Bourke and others explain, military institutions frequently serve to limit sexual violence. The formalized systems of justice, communal relationships, and the development of *esprit d 'corps* identities can reduce the impulsive drives that can foster sexual objectification and assault. This is of course by no means a constant – many military organizations rely heavily upon crude sexual oriented metaphors and prose imagery in training.[12] A significant modifier appears to be the social makeup of a military force, and the extent to which it represents the civilian society from which it is drawn. Outliers prone to embracing violence will exist in a citizen army, as it is drawn from the larger society as a whole. But the majority of servicemen will reject sexual violence as an abhorrent rejection of the social contract they have always known. "In other words," Bourke states, "rape is avoidable."[13]

A second observation can be made about the relationship between war and toxic masculine codes of behavior in select individuals. In a seeming contradiction to the idea that military cultures can limit the potential for sexual aggression, there is no question that they can also foster aberrant masculine behaviors and expectations. In both world wars, European civilian and military policy makers presumed that sexual desire was a normal aspect of the healthy male's well-being. Soldiers were often actively encouraged to satisfy their urges by visiting military brothels during rest and recovery periods between battle. Even in armies where the parent culture was restrained, if not repressive (like the United Kingdom and the United States during the First World War), individual soldiers found their own ways to solicit sex for hire. The ensuing liaisons were hardly romantic. Dagmar Herzog notably describes how the military brothel system "encouraged an even more, depersonalized, conveyor-belt quality of sex than had been typical

---

11 It should be noted that sexual violence in war is being treated as a separate topic from sexual violence in military cultures. This is not to claim a special distinction between the two, but rather is an attempt to preserve clarity.

12 One of the more commodified examples of this type of activity is the first half of Stanley Kubrick's 1987 film *Full Metal Jacket*. Set in Parris Island in 1967, it captivated audiences through its harsh and unflinching portrayal of U.S. Marine Corps boot camp training, with no shortage of misogynistic and highly chauvinistic references. Such language persists in the American military through to the current day, as revealed in Carol Burke's *Camp All-American, Hanoi Jane, and the High-and-Tight* (Beacon Press, 2004), xi–xii, 13–14, 28–42.

13 Bourke, *Rape*, 385.

in prewar prostitution."[14] By enlisting sexuality in wartime, states and military organizations enabled a climate of devalued female identity, essentially reducing women in warzones to the status of chattel property – or even worse. The result is a blurred, if not chaotic, line between sanctioned sexual promiscuity and overt sexual assault. Regina Mühlhäuser presents just such a fractured sense of wartime sexuality taking place within the *Wehrmacht* on the Eastern Front in the Second World War. Despite clear legal and social constraints on sexual interaction with "racial undesirables," soldiers regularly engaged in both brothel visits and sexual assaults against Soviet women. Military prosecutions of offenders were rare, as the need to preserve individual and collective morale took precedence over safeguarding the persons and honor of racial inferiors. Individual soldiers faced punishment only if their actions threatened unit cohesion or represented an outrageous breach of acceptable National Socialist codes of acceptable male conduct. Indeed, consensual relationships between German soldiers and Soviet women were considered far more grave transgressions than other, more abusive or violent encounters.[15]

Toxic masculinity could also be ingrained into soldiers through indoctrination or training. Japanese historian Saburō Ienaga describes how the conscript private soldier was subjected to a constant barrage of physical and verbal abuse following the first military plots against the civilian government in 1931. Junior officers were encouraged to heap insults and strike recruits, anything to strip dignity and agency from enlisted men and render them totally subservient to authority The intention, he notes, was to craft a callous, impassionate soldier who would follow any directive. The reality, however, was the process so infantilized and degraded many infantrymen to the point where violent expressions of rage against civilians and captured enemy soldiers were normalized.[16] In part such savage conduct – including mass gang rapes, sexual murder, and genital mutilations – reflected a tacit acceptance of sexual violence as an unavoidable consequence of total war. More telling for Ienaga, however, was the moral degeneration within the Japanese military that was itself partially associated with the brutalization of its own personnel. Officers in occupied garrisons and frontline units alike exerted little control over their own conduct, he states, let alone

---

14 Dagmar Herzog, *Sexuality in Europe: A Twentieth-Century History* (Cambridge University Press, 2011), 49.

15 Regina Mühlhäuser, "Between 'Racial Awareness' and Fantasies of Potency: Nazi Sexual Politics in the Occupied Territories of the Soviet Union, 1942–1945," in Dagmar Herzog, editor, *Brutality and Desire: War and Sexuality in Europe's Twentieth Century* (Palgrave Macmillan, 2009, 2011), 197–220.

16 Ienaga, *The Pacific War*, 52–54.

that of their men. In such a climate of dissipation and immorality, enlisted men conditioned to exhibit total obedience and submission to order were left with no moral model to follow. As a result, outrageous mass atrocities like those taking place at Nanjing in December 1937 and Manila in February 1945, not to mention the steady drumbeat of smaller scale incidents throughout China and Southeast Asia became routine. Indeed, Saburo Ienaga noted, "Rape was an accepted prerogative of the Imperial Army."[17]

Historians working in the area also consider another fact, namely the employment of rape as a coercive weapon. In the First World War, Turkish troops introduced sexual enslavement as a tool to punish and cement the subordinate inferior status of Armenian women.[18] The long marches from Turkish Armenia into the camps established in the Syrian desert have been identified as some of the particular loci for the brutalization of the captive women and children by the largely young, inexperienced cadre of Turkish conscripts employed as guards. This aspect of the Armenian atrocities is quite instructive, historian Matthias Bjørnlund observes. The marches were not merely intended for the exclusive use of savaging the victims, but also as a means by which to brutalize their escorting guards, so they would be less likely to show pity or tenderness toward their charges, thus completing the dehumanization of the Armenians.[19] Wholly unlike the cases cited previously in Belgium in 1914, the Turkish outrage appear to have received the formal sanction of the Ottoman military leadership, not only to demonstrate the alien otherness status of the Christian Armenians, but also to reaffirm the normative gendered social order within the empire. Bjørnlund explains:

> If women (as was often the case in the Ottoman Empire) are basically viewed as chattel, as male property by soldiers, gangs, or the general population who have been given more or less explicit permission to live off the land during war and genocide, sexual violence can be seen as a right, as a natural extension of the right to plunder. . . .[20]

The mass rapes of the Armenian women, therefore, was established as an organized activity intended to help secure the annihilation of this alien group (to the larger Ottoman perspective) through a dehumanizing campaign meant to also

---

17 *Ibid.*, 171–172, 186–187, 190–191, quote on 166. See also Chapter 7; and "Manila Holocaust: Massacre and Rape," by Dr. Benito J. Legarda Jr.," http://www.malacanang.gov.ph/75102-manila-holocaust-massacre-and-rape/. Accessed June 25, 2018.
18 Herzog, *Sexuality in Europe*, 47.
19 Matthias Bjørnlund, "'A Fate Worse Than Dying': Sexual Violence during the Armenian Genocide," in Herzog, *Brutality and Desire*, 16–58, 21.
20 *Ibid.*, 30.

guarantee the submission of the perpetrators to the larger vision of the state. "The aim of organized rape in such instances," Bjørnlund continues, "is to destroy family ties and group solidarity; to undermine military morale by inflicting trauma, humiliation, and fear; to block procreation of the group; and to impregnate women in order to affect the ethnic composition of populations."[21]

Elsewhere, sexual coercion and enslavement served less draconian and more specific purposes. Forced prostitution stands out as a particularly onerous, though common, practice in the twentieth century. During the Pacific War, the Japanese military's comfort stations were manned not only by Japanese peasant women but also thousands of Chinese, Korean, Filipino, and Western women, forced into sexual slavery. Compelled to service Japanese soldiers with no regard to their own safety or well-being, the victimized women were subject to draconian discipline and callous indifference from the military authorities. Oddly, senior Japanese officers responsible for organizing the first comfort stations cited the urgent need to reduce the frequency of rape perpetrated by soldiers against Chinese civilians in and around Shanghai. As Yoshimi Yoshiaki observes in her history of the comfort women, the decision itself was a perverse choice: why settle on forced prostitution, rather than actually enforce standing military justice codes? The rationale, she concludes, was born from the Japanese experience in its brief Siberian intervention, where the army had great success in reducing venereal disease incidence after assuming responsibility for inspecting and licensing brothel prostitutes in Vladivostok.[22] In Europe, not only did the Nazis coerce non-German women into working at military brothels, the SS also established a series of brothels at concentration camps to service guards and slave laborers. This last purpose was intended originally as part of an incentive regimen for slave laborers at munitions and heavy industrial factories located near the camps.[23]

No less outrageous was the wholesale rape of women by the advancing Soviet Red Army from 1944 through 1945. The collective accounts of Soviet rapes has become part of the stock and trade narrative of the end of the Second World War in Europe as well as the early Cold War. Historian Norman Naimark correctly notes that, while not all Soviet soldiers took part in the rapes in Poland, East Prussia, Austria, and Germany, the practice was, if not directly sanctioned by

---

21 *Ibid.*, 30.
22 Ienaga, *The Pacific War*, 184; Yoshimi Yoshiaki, *Comfort Women: Sexual Slavery in the Japanese Military During World War II*, trans. Suzanne O'Brien (Columbia University Press, 1995, 2000), 45–46.
23 Robert Sommer, "Camp Brothels: Forced Sex Labour in Nazi Concentration Camps," in Herzog, *Brutality and Desire*, 168–196; and Na'ama Shik, "Sexual Abuse of Jewish Women in Auchwitz-Birkenau," in *Op. Cit.*, 221–246.

Soviet military and political authorities, certainly tolerated and ignored for the short term. However, Naimark also notes how many German women also transferred their status as rape victims into willing sexual partners to obtain privileges and essential food and fuel during the first winter after the war's end. In this regard, the patterns of sexual power and manipulation by aggressors and victims alike were little different from those taking place earlier in wartime Europe.[24]

Lost in the American exceptionalist narrative of the end of the Second World War is the sexual aspect of the wartime and postwar occupations of Western Europe. Historian Mary Louise Roberts charts the American GIs quest for sensual gratification across France, noting that many young soldiers acquired a highly biased, prejudicial attitude toward French civilians that facilitated their exploitation as willing and unwilling sexual partners. Some of this was no doubt due to lingering misperceptions and stereotypes from an earlier war.[25] Susan Carruthers follows suit, noting that it was the very size of the American military effort, not least of which the immense rear echelon providing supply and services for the combat units in the line, that fostered a massive prostitution industry in Italy and France. In fact, civics affairs officers were regularly tasked with finding accommodations for prostitutes, whose primarily clients would obviously be American soldiers.[26]

One last factor considered by historians relates to how and why Western societies employed sexuality to both validate and undermine existing conventions of racial and class-oriented superiority. Sexual contact between white and nonwhite partners was commonly seen as a transgressive act. The introduction of colonial troops into the European core during the First and Second World Wars threw contemporary standards of racial hierarchy and sexuality into disarray. Many European governments and civilian groups sought to block casual interactions between white women and colonial soldiers through any means possible short of the vigilante mob violence commonplace in Jim Crow America. In both wars, French censors carefully monitored letters to and from imperial troops for descriptions of sexual liaisons with local women, using the gleaned details to punish the soldiers and to humiliate and harass the civilian partner.[27]

---

24 See Norman Naimark, *The Russians in Germany: A History of the Soviet Zone of Occupation* (Belknap Press, 1997), 69–140; also see Anonymous, *A Woman in Berlin: Eight Weeks in the Conquered City: A Diary* (Picador, 2006).

25 Mary Louise Roberts, *What Soldiers Do: Sex and the American GI in World War II France* (The University of Chicago Press, 2013), 20, 48–55.

26 Susan Carruthers, *The Good Occupation: American Soldiers and the Hazards of Peace* (Harvard University Press, 2016), 112.

27 Richard S. Fogarty, "Race and Sex: Fear and Loathing in France during the Great War," in Herzog, *Brutality and Desire*, 59–90, 74–75.

The American experience, as just alluded to, was far more violent and savage than that taking place within Western Europe. Sexual anxiety has long been understood as a key underpinning of racial stereotypes and white mob violence directed against African Americans. Indeed, as Joanne Nagel notes, "Sex is the whispered subtext in spoken racial discourse. Sex is the sometimes silent message contained in racial slurs, ethnic stereotypes, national imaginings, and international relations."[28] For centuries, African Americans were cast as sexually hyperactive beings, devoid of moral restraint and enslaved by their own biology. Such accounts became part of the foundational ideology in English colonies in the New World, the associated rape myths surrounding black men following the spread of slavery in the Caribbean and later the American colonies. By the early twentieth century, in America black men were the regular antagonist of lurid rape fantasies, threatening to overwhelm white society at any given moment if white vigilance were ever relaxed.[29] For the black soldier serving in the AEF, France was a hazardous space within which to negotiate and assert agency. Contrary to the popular narrative that identifies French civilian society as less racist, and thus, more welcoming to African Americans, the majority of people, especially outside of the Parisian metropolis, retained strong prejudices against non-whites. Historian Richard Fogarty identifies the extent to which the French military and political authorities strove to keep their own imperial *indigènes* isolated from allegedly vulnerable white French women. Sexual relations in particular were feared because they would not only create the perception of racial equality between French whites and the colonized, but also realize the prospect of colonial troops returning home with the experience and knowledge of power over white women. As Fogarty notes, these experiences and the subsequent loose talk about them:

> made clear the potential effect of interracial relationships upon the status of French women in the colonies. If these women were supposed to be the pillars of the community there, embodying French ideas about civilization and domesticity and defining the boundaries that separated colonizers from colonized, *indigènes* with such attitudes, many of whom would eventually return to their homes, presented a significant potential threat to the colonial order.[30]

---

28 Joane Nagel, *Race, Ethnicity, and Sexuality: Intimate Intersections, Forbidden Frontiers* (Oxford University Press, 2003), 2.
29 *Ibid.*, 93–94. Sell also Sharon Block, *Rape and Sexual Power in Early America* (The University of North Carolina Press, 2006), 163–165; and Bobby A. Wintermute, "'The Negro should not be used as a combat soldier': reconfiguring racial identity in the United States Army, 1890–1918," *Patterns of Prejudice* 46 (June 2012), 278–298, 293–295
30 Fogarty, *"Race and Sex,"* 66.

While Fogarty emphasizes the official response to the question of sex and presumptions of non-white racial equality, similar anxieties ran through the very core of French civilian society. It was one thing for prostitutes to engage with non-white soldiers; contact with regular citizens was frequently cast as non-consensual to preserve the personal and community sense of acceptable conduct. This informal bar to racial intermingling was extended with little objection to African Americans as well. Indeed, here the best solution was often found in acquiescing to American racial intolerance. Historian Andrew Huebner describes this in his account of the July 27, 1918, court martial of Private William Buckner, 313th Labor Battalion. On July 2, Buckner had sex with a local woman in a field near the town of Arrentières. The French woman alleged rape, while Buckner argued theirs was a consensual act. The tribunal convicted Buckner and sentenced him to death by hanging on charges of rape. Huebner concludes that the trial and its outcome reveal the "transportability of American sexual and racial politics."[31] Not only was American racial intolerance readily transferred to the rural French countryside to be applied to African Americans, it also influenced French authorities to impose their own version of Jim Crow. Shortly after the Buckner court-martial, the chief French military liaison with the AEF, Colonel Louis Albert Linard, issued a memorandum that essentially legitimized American racial intolerance. Accepting the premise that African Americans in France were unable to contain their sexual passions, Linard acknowledged an alleged increase in rapes by colored American soldiers. As a solution, he called for racial segregation on the American model, in order to prevent future transgressions. The presumption of sexual violence – not the actual perpetration of it – thus became a tool for imposing racial segregation and thereby promoting a culture of white superiority considered essential for the maintenance of the imperial project and French white masculinity.[32]

In the American experience of both world wars, sexual assault became, for all practical purposes, a "black crime" – that is to say, it was a charge that was levied unevenly against African-American soldiers. There are two considerations here: the first, which was assumed by the institutions at the time, was that African American soldiers were more likely to commit violent sexual crimes. This conclusion, which was widely shared at the time across civilian and military authorities (witness the aforementioned 1918 Linard memorandum), was patently false. This brings attention to the second consideration: that charges of rape and sexual assault were unfairly and unevenly brought against black soldiers in large part to

---

31 Andrew S. Huebner, *Love and Death in the Great War* (Oxford University Press, 2018), 172, 180–81, quote on 181.
32 Huebner, *Love and Death*, 181–82. See also Chad L. Williams, *Torchbearers of Democracy: African American Soldiers in the World War I Era* (University of North Carolina Press, 2013), 159–63.

both conform to existing racist precepts that were dominant in American society and to conceal the greater problem of sexual assault within the American military as a whole in the two world wars. African Americans in the AEF were far more likely to be accused of rape than their white counterparts; moreover, false accusations were rife. Even white officers attached to the two colored divisions spread false accusations about their own men. Yet AEF commander, General John J. Pershing, and his subordinates directed their focus almost exclusively on the largely made-up "problem" of sexual assaults by black soldiers on French civilian women. Throughout 1918, the French leveled many unsubstantiated accusations against black soldiers, reaching such a fevered crescendo that Pershing pressed for the return home of the 92nd and 93rd Divisions within weeks of the November 11, 1918 Armistice, entirely on the basis of their alleged sexual aggression.[33] Such slanders would persist in the next major war. Mary Louise Roberts notes that even in the Second World War, a racialized double standard existed with regard to sexual congress involving American troops and local women. In the summer of 1944, the US Army in France was developing a reputation as being more sexually active – and by extension, more likely to engage in rapes and assaults – than both the German and British/Commonwealth armies. As the criminal and medical cases mounted, the American military sought to shift culpability for sexual violence almost entirely to African-American soldiers, essentially, Roberts notes, "the US military used its own record of injustice to construct rape as a *fact* of racial depravity."[34]

As the war and society field develops further by incorporating more analytical tools and methodologies from gender and race historians, a clearer understanding of the interconnectivity between sexuality and war will take shape. This short overview of recent historiography reveals the extent to which historians working in the military history field have identified how war and the organized aggression associated with military institutions can foster climates of toxic masculinity and displaced power dynamics which in turn can target some of the most vulnerable members of wartime society. The case studies introduced here are limited, in large part because the field is evolving. No doubt it will grow more sophisticated and diverse regarding the depth and breadth of its scope as more historians and other researchers escape self-imposed and other external stigmas and anxieties over discussing the issues associated with sexual violence in war.

---

33 Sammons and Morrow, *Harlem's Rattlers and the Great War*, 372; and Williams, *Torchbearers of Democracy*, 167–70, 193.
34 Roberts, *What Soldiers Do*, 246–47, quote on 247.

Genocide and War

The word "genocide" combines the Greek word *"genos"* (race) with the Latin word *"cide"* (to kill). Taking its etymology in a literal sense, genocide can be understood as one race engaging in killing other races as evinced, for example, in the Nazi program to exterminate the Jews and others in Germany and across Europe. The post-war trials against German leaders labeled their heinous acts of the Holocaust are war crimes and crimes against humanity.[35] Over time, the uses of genocide have expanded beyond its association with the Holocaust to become applicable to any large-scale, systematic extermination of one group by another group. The roles of nationalism, religious fanaticism, and other factors ignite motivations, especially as criminologist Travis Morris observes, when those ideas are "weaponized," enemies are "manufactured," and demagogues take the reins in "racial holy wars" against those enemy peoples.[36] Religiously-motivated persecution is essentially an action aimed at denying victims not only dignity but their humanity as well.

The roots of genocides in the twentieth and twenty-first centuries can be tracked back into the 1800s when Social Darwinism, Lamarckian racial hierarchies, eugenics, and other models legitimized brutality as the United States devastated the Native Americans and the Western European nations conquered the world. Might made right: military power combined with a Western belief in inherent superiority to validate New Imperialism. Imagined differences in intellect and ability relegated non-white races to inferiority and sub-humanity.[37] Subsequently, racism has exerted ever greater influence during the twentieth and twenty-first centuries. According to one estimate, some 187 million men, women, and children perished in genocides in German South West Africa in 1904–1907, Armenia in 1915, the Ukraine in 1932–1933, the Holocaust in 1933–1945, Guatemala in 1966–68, Ethiopia in 1974–1991, Cambodia in 1975–1979, Rwanda in 1994, and Bosnia in 1995.[38] It must be noted that warfare – civil, revolutionary, and/or liberation – frequently helped create dangerous contexts that, according to Africana studies

---

35 For an overview of the historiographical debates and definitions, see Earl, "War, Genocide, and Atrocities," 224–26; Ther, *Dark Side of Nation-States*, 1–16; and R. Gellately and B. Kiernan, eds., *The Spector of Genocide: Mass Murder in Historical Perspective* (Cambridge University Press, 2003).
36 Travis Morris, *Dark Ideas: How Neo-Nazi and Violent Jihad Ideologues Shaped Modern Terrorism* (Lanham, MD: Lexington, 2016), 1–4, 25–27.
37 See Chapters 2 and 3.
38 Mark Levene, "Why is the Twentieth Century the Century of Genocide?" *Journal of World War* 11 (Fall 2000) 305–66, cited in Earl, "War, Genocide, and Atrocities," 226. Mark Levene is a prolific writer on comparative histories of genocide, ethnic cleansing, and war crimes. See also Paul Bartrop, "The Relationship between War and Genocide in the Twentieth Century: A Consideration," *Journal of Genocide Research* 4.4. (2002): 519–32.

scholar Edward Kissi, "led extremists to seize power or use history, mythology and pre-existing ethnic prejudices to plan and execute genocide."[39] Race and gender should be added to his list.

In the twenty-first century, genocidal death tolls continues to rise in the Sudan against the Darfuri and by the Islamic State against defiant Muslims, Christians, and Kurds in Iraq and Syria. Any number of other localized areas could degenerate into similar catastrophes. Given the necessary resources and political opportunities, there is little doubt that Neo-Nazi elements in the United States and across Europe would undertake ethnic cleansing and genocide against non-Caucasians. The linkage of these internationally-labeled crimes to non-state actors like terrorist groups will doubtlessly expand because creating intense anxiety over relocation, sexual assault, torture, and death are effective tactics in quelling resistance or coercing acquiescence to the goals of those terrorist groups.[40]

During the Cold War, the term "ethnic cleansing" entered the international legal vernacular to describe the forcible removal of unwanted ethnic groups from territories that could then be seized by more powerful, aggressor groups. Throughout the nineteenth century, the United States military's relocation of Native Americans from their ancestral homelands to faraway areas euphemistically called "reservations" comes to mind as one tragic instance of ethnic cleansing, or more accurately racial cleansing. During the 1930s and 1940s, the Nazis employed ethnic cleansing as part of the Holocaust when they swept more than 6 million Jews, Gypsies, homosexuals, and other unwanted groups from most of Europe. More recently during the early 1990s, the Bosnian Serb military engaged in a campaign to purge unwanted groups from their territory. The United Nations General Assembly reacted declaring ethnic cleansing to be one form of genocide.[41]

Racism or ethnocentrism certainly create hierarchies that tap into brutal impulses that may lead to genocides. These are hardly the only motivators, however. Ideological beliefs and cultural constructions of gender along with corollaries to sexuality have also played critical roles in crafting the messages and

---

39 Edward Kissi, "Rwanda, Ethiopia, and Cambodia: Links, Fault Lines and Complexities in a Comparative Study of Genocide," *Journal of Genocide Research* 6 (March 2004): 119.

40 See Morris, *Dark Ideas*, viii; and Anne-Marie de Brouwer and Sandra Ka Hon Chu, eds., *The Men Who Killed Me: Rwandan Survivors of Sexual Violence* (Douglas and McIntyre, 2013), 23–26.

41 United Nations General Assembly A/RES/47/121, December 18, 1992, https://www.un.org/documents/ga/res/47/a47r121.htm (Accessed June 25, 2018). See also Edward Kissi, "The Holocaust as a Guidepost for Genocide Detection and Prevention in Africa," *The Holocaust and the United Nations Outreach Program Discussion Papers Journal* (2009): 45–55.

practices of mass atrocities. Several chapters in this book offer insights into how and why gender and sexuality can increase violence to the point of genocide.[42]

Regarding femininity, one means of genocide was sterilizing women to stop them from expanding population in the targeted groups. This strategy takes into account the biological capacities of women to conceive and give birth. Rape and sexual assault can have similarly devastating effects on female victims. "The politics and psychology of rape as policy," according to sociologist Helen Fein, "functions as a ritual of degradation, to instill terror and demoralize the victim group, to destroy the continuity of their reproduction, and as symbolic reward and revenge to the participants."[43] The trauma to women's bodies caused by rapes can reduce pregnancies or permanently damage reproductive organs. The examples of sterilization and explanations of rape coincide with one element of the legal definition of genocide espoused the United Nations Genocide Convention: "Imposing measures intended to prevent births within the group."[44]

The brutality in the late twentieth century pointed to normalization and to sanction of sexual violence in genocides and ethnic cleansings. The Hutu tribal leaders, the Khmer Rouge, and the Serbian policies mandated these acts against females and males of all ages in the Tutsi tribe in Rwanda, the Vietnamese and other minorities in Cambodia, and the Bosnian Muslims and Bosnian Croats, respectively. These acts included vaginal penetration, genital mutilation, castration, sodomy, and gang rapes that Helen Fein argues are "often embedded in rituals of degradation" and are "attacks on the family and self-esteem of the husbands and fathers" by "publicly demonstrating their groups impotence and their inability to protect 'their women.'" Fein concludes that "perhaps, paradoxically, the latent function of the honor of women is to instigate enemies to dishonor women." The historical examples leave very little doubt of this last point.[45] In raw numbers, as many as 250,000 rapes occurred in Rwanda, 50,000 in Bosnia, and untold thousands in Cambodia, where cultural mores demanded that Cambodian women remain silent about being victims of sexual violence. Elsewhere in recent decades, hundreds of thousands of female victims suffered similar fates in East

---

42 October 29, 1929, Wall Street crash, economic distress

43 Helen Fein, "Genocide and Gender: The Uses of Women and Group Identity," *Journal of Genocide Research* 1.1 (1999): 43.

44 United Nations, "Convention on the Prevention and Punishment of the Crime of Genocide," Resolution 260 (III), 9 December 1948, http://www.hrweb.org/legal/genocide.html (Accessed June 28, 2018).

45 Fein, "Genocide and Gender," 58. See also Scott Straus, *The Order of Genocide: Race, Power, and War in Rwanda* (Cornell University Press, 2008), 52, 157–63.

Timor, Liberia, Sierra Leone, Bangladesh, the Congo, Haiti, Uganda, Kenya, and the Philippines, to name only a few.[46]

In a report on Rwanda, the group Human Rights Watch describes how rape as sanctioned by Hutu policy debased Tutsi women while simultaneously elevating the Hutu men. The following offers disturbing justifications for diabolical acts:

> Tutsi women were targeted on the basis of the genocide propaganda which had portrayed them as beautiful and desirable, but inaccessible to Hutu men whom they allegedly looked down upon and were "too good" for. Rape served to shatter these images by humiliating, degrading, and ultimately destroying the Tutsi woman. Even Tutsi women married to Hutu men were not spared, despite the custom that a wife was protected by her husband's lineage after marriage. Most of the women interviewed described how their rapists mentioned their ethnicity before or during the rape. Rape survivors recounted such comments as: "We want to see how sweet Tutsi women are," or "You Tutsi women think that you are too good for us," or "We want to see if a Tutsi woman is like a Hutu woman," or "If there were peace, you would never accept that."[47]

By tying together ethnic, gendered, and psychological threads in Rwanda, this quote demonstrates that sexualized rhetoric is integral to genocide.[48]

No argument can be made that this new century has seen even the slightest decline in the weaponization of rape and sexual assault. Quite the contrary, these brutal acts are taking on increased importance, especially for non-state actors like terrorist groups neither subscribe to international legal prohibitions nor show respect of basic human rights. The Islamic State (sometimes denoted as ISIS or ISIL) utilized sexual violence as one of many methods of instilling fear and establishing control of large sections of Iraq and Syria since 2014. These most radical of Islamicist sects linked sexual slavery and rape to their twisted religious doctrines. One victim – then a 12-year-old girl who was part of the Yazidi Christian minority in Iraq – recounted her experiences: "I kept telling him it hurts — please stop," said the girl. "He told me that according to Islam he is allowed to rape an unbeliever. He said that by raping me, he is drawing closer to God." The author of the *New York Times* article quoting the pre-teen girl added that the Islam State fighter explained that what he did to her "was not a sin. Because the preteen girl

---

46 Fein, "Genocide and Gender," 43–63; Brouwer and Chu, *The Men Who Killed Me*, 11–26; and Ben Kiernan, *The Pol Pot Regime: Race, Power, and Genocide in Cambodia under the Khmer Rouge, 1975–79* (Yale University Press, 1996).

47 Human Rights Watch/Africa, *Shattered Lives: Sexual Violence during the Rwandan Genocide and its Aftermath* (Human Rights Watch, 1996), 18, cited in Fein, "Gender and Genocide," 55.

48 Pamela DeLargy, "Sexual Violence and Women's Health in War," in *Women and Wars: Contested Histories, Uncertain Futures*, ed. Carol Cohn (Polity, 2012), 54–79.

practiced a religion other than Islam, the Quran not only gave him the right to rape her — it condoned and encouraged it, he insisted."[49] When taken together with massacre and torture in Iraq and Syria, the Islamic State's calculated uses of sexuality-based tactics against its enemies qualify as genocide.[50]

LBGTQ Personnel and Military Service

The justifications for excluding LGBTQ (Lesbian, Gay, Bi-Sexual, Transgender, Queer) men and women from military service argue that homosexuals and non-heterosexuals could disrupt unit cohesion, hurt discipline, undermine morale, and alter command structures. Similar points regarding women and minorities serving the uniform in general and in combat units in particular appeared throughout American history, as did apprehensions about women's minimal strength. In the twenty-first century, however, many of the developed world's militaries have gradually added more opportunities for women and minorities. The same can apply to LGBTQ service personnel, albeit at a much slower pace in the case of the U.S. military.[51]

As of 2018, the armed forces of Canada, Western Europe, and the United States have lifted pre-existing bans on homosexual men and women to serve in uniform. After eliminating mistreatment and expulsion of homosexuals in 1992, the Canadian government subsequently legalized civil unions and same-sex marriage in its military in 2003. France is not quite as open as Canada, but gay men and women can enlist. The French military is slowing equalizing the rights for full benefits and adoptions in marriage and civil unions. In 2005, the United Kingdom's military started permitting spouses in same-sex civil partnerships to receive life insure pension, immigration equality, and other benefits enjoyed by opposite-sex spouses. The civil partners could also reside in military base housing

49 Rukmini Callimachi, "ISIS Enshrines A Theology of Rape," *New York Times*, August 13, 2015, https://www.nytimes.com/2015/08/14/world/middleeast/isis-enshrines-a-theology-of-rape.html (Accessed June 29, 2018).

50 See the U.S. Holocaust Memorial Museum, "Confront Genocide," https://www.ushmm.org/confront-genocide (Accessed July 4, 2018).

51 For historical overviews of the U.S. military, see Randy Shilts, *Conduct Unbecoming: Gays and Lesbians in the U.S. Military* (St. Martin's Press, 1993); Aaron Belkin and Geoffrey Bateman, eds, *Don't Ask, Don't Tell: Debating the Gay Ban in the Military* (Lynn Reinner, 2003); and Steve Estes, "The Dream That Dare Not Speaks Its Name: Legacies of the Civil Rights Movement and the Fight for Gay Military Service," in *Integrating the U.S. Military*, eds. Bristol and Stur, 198–218; and relevant chapters in Donald Rohall, et al., eds., *Inclusion in the American Military: A Force for Diversity* (Lexington Books, 2017).

and obtain security clearances. Finally, 2014 saw the recognition of same-sex marriages in the UK's armed services. The Canadians and Western Europeans more quickly to accept bi-sexual and transgender personnel into service with spousal benefits. Lastly little or no negative effects have been recorded in unit cohesion, morale, discipline, and the like, although passage of time and collection of evidence may not yet substantial enough to support concrete conclusions.[52]

Throughout the twentieth and into the twenty-first century, controversies surrounding same-sex relationships among military personnel provoked the ire of many political, social, religious, and military groups in the United States. During the world wars, for instance, homosexuals and lesbians existed in a liminal category that blurred immorality, criminality, and psychopathology.[53] "'Mental Illness' was the moral equivalent of sin," observed cultural historian Beth Bailey. "Thousands of men rejected by or discharged from the armed forces on psychiatric grounds during World War II returned home with official documents (requested by all prospective employers) labeling them 'sexual deviants.'"[54] Among these discharges were victims of false allegations or unfounded decisions that ruined the lives of heterosexual men with effeminate traits and straight women with masculine traits.

Then at the close of the twentieth century opposition to the ban on same-sex orientations in the U.S. military grew more vocal. The opposition asserted that all Americans (especially males in terms of Selective Service) had obligations to serve and deserved right protecting open association, free speech, and due legal process. Conversely, the existing policies were discriminatory. President Bill Clinton tried to push legislation overturning the ban, but when facing stubborn resistant inside the military and among conservatives in the public and Congress, he issued Defense Directive 1304.26 in December 1993. Otherwise known as "Don't Ask, Don't Tell" (DADT), this new policy barred formal questions regarding sexual orientations yet allowed disciplinary actions to be taken gay men or women who admitted as such or were caught engaging in homosexual or lesbian intercourse. Similar policies also prohibited heterosexual adultery or fraternization. DADT did not provide any protection for homosexuals, let along bisexuals or transgender people, against unwanted harassment or abuse. Such secrets likewise ran serious

---

52 Suzanne B. Goldberg, "Open Service and Our Allies: A Report on the Inclusion of Openly Gay and Lesbian Servicemembers in U.S. Allies' Armed Forces," *William & Mary Journal of Women & Law* 17 (2011): 547–65, 590.

53 Lewis H. Loeser, "The Sexual Psychopath in the Military Service," *American Journal of Psychiatry* 102 (July 1945): 92–101, reprinted in *Gay Warriors: A Documentary History from the Ancient World to the Present*, ed. B. R. Burg (New York University Press, 2002; and Forrest M. Harrison, "Psychiatry in the Navy," *War Medicine* 3 (February 1943): 114–37.

54 Bailey, *Sex in the Heartland*, 54–55.

risks of hurting command and control, undermining discipline, and damaging morale within given units. As such, DADT represented a band-aide that failed to answer deeper questions about the sexual orientation and legitimate military service in the long term.[55]

Nearly two decades passed until a more decisive resolution emerged in December 2010, when President Barrack Obama signed legislation that ended DADT and opened American military service to openly gay men and women that next year. At the end of his second term, Obama also lifted the ban on transgender people serving in the U.S. Military. As Secretary of Defense Carter Ash stated on June 30, 2016,

> Our mission is to defend this country, and we don't want barriers unrelated to a person's qualification to serve preventing us from recruiting or retaining the Soldier, Sailor, Airman, or Marine who can best accomplish the mission...Starting today: Otherwise qualified Service members can no longer be involuntarily separated, discharged, or denied reenlistment or continuation of service just for being transgender.[56]

It is worth noting that the years-long Global War on Terror created a demand for personnel that simply could not satisfied by the traditional demographic of heterosexual men from all races. So, necessity drove in part the broadening the recruitment policies. Regardless, as commander-in-chief, Obama mandated a change that obligated the military to execute changes including revisions of the *Uniform Code of Military Justice*'s definition of sexuality and formulation of new procedures for investigating abuses and crimes relating to this new group. A whole host of other practical policies require changes in lodging arrangements, physical fitness standards, medical treatments, restroom designations, and the like. Additional guidance is also needed for unit commanders and staffs to ensure professional treatment of transgender personal and professional behavior by them.[57]

---

55 See B. Moradi, "Sexual Orientation Disclosure, Concealment, Harassment, and Military Cohesions: Perceptions of LBGT Military Veterans," *Military Psychology* 21.4 (2009): 513–33; and David Smith and Karin De Angelis, "Lesbian and Gay Service Members and Their Families," in *Inclusion in the America: A Force of Diversity*, eds. David Rohall, et al. (Lexington, 2017); 129–48.
56 U.S. Secretary of Defense Ash Carter, "Secretary of Defense Ash Carter Remarks Announcing Transgender Policy Changes," June 30, 2016, cited in U.S. Department of Defense, "Transgender Service in the U.S. Military: An Implementation Handbook," September 30, 2016, https://www.defense.gov/Portals/1/features/2016/0616_policy/DoDTGHandbook_093016.pdf?ver=2016-09-30-160933-837 (Accessed July 7, 2018).
57 Bristol and Stur, "Conclusion," *Integrating the U.S. Military*, 226–28. For straightforward explanations and advice commanders and fellow service personnel, see Judith Rosenstein, "The Integration of Trans People into the Military," in *Inclusion in the America: A Force of Diversity*, eds. David Rohall, et al. (Lexington, 2017); 149–68.

President Obama's decision to open military service to transgender men and women stood as an example of the American military reflecting and reacting to tensions over changing mores in civilian society that in turn supports that institution.[58] In fact, a recent book analyzing policies on transgender in the 2010s echoes the same prejudices identified in 1999 by Beth Bailey regarding homosexuality in the mid-twentieth century:

> Much like gay and lesbian personnel, transgender tendencies fell into mental health disorders except gender non-conformity came along much later among mental health experts. . . In was not until 2013 that transgender was removed as a formal pathology from the *Diagnostic and Statistical Manual of Mental Disorders.*, As of 2016, military men and women can transition and then become accountable to the standards of their new sex.[59]

It does seem that cliché – "There is not hing new under the sun" – fits the recycled arguments over inclusion and integration across transgender lines from those earlier debates of homosexuality, femininity, and race.

Although hotly contested by social and religious conservatives, the broader cultural values of the American people have tended to point toward more tolerant attitudes about transgender orientations. Obama's policy affected an estimated 6,000 to 15,000 transgender men and women among some 1.3 million Americans in uniform in 2017. However, this estimate remains uncertain because very few personnel have self-identified as transgender. Other shifts in policy also occurred in the intervening years since 2010, such as the legitimation of same-sex marriages and civil unions among American service personnel. These changes have brought the U.S. military into similar standing with eighteen other nations' armed forces.[60]

The future developments in the U.S. military and American society as a whole will test the degree to which homosexual and transgender personnel will face institutional or individual discrimination in advancing in rank especially in the key combat arms branches. Parallel to this will be a potential transformation of the warrior ethos that is tied so closely to particular brand masculine symbology and functionality. This ethos may or may not evolve to different degrees in given branches of the American armed forces. For example, when, if ever, will

---

58 See Morten G. Ender, et al., "Research Note: Cadet and Civilian Undergraduate Attitudes toward Transgender People," *Armed Forces and Society* 41 (April 2016): 427–35.

59 David Rohall, et al., "The Intersections of Race, Class, Gender, and Sexuality in the Military," in in *Inclusion in the America: A Force of Diversity*, eds. David Rohall, et al., (Lexington, 2017), 199; Bailey, *Sex in the Heartland*, 54-61.

60 *Ibid.*, 149. See also G.J. Gates and J.L. Herman, "Transgender in the Military Service of the United States," 2014, The Williams Institute, https://williamsinstitute.law.ucla.edu/wp-content/uploads/Transgender-Military-Service-May-2014.pdf (Accessed July 6, 2018).

a sufficient number of people (i.e. not Caucasian, heterosexual, and Christian) be the catalyst for a different version of "warrior" in the Army versus the Marine Corps? And, as a follow-up question: To who degree would that new warrior archetype be effective in wartime in a world filled with non-state actors, WMDs, and blurred borders? Just as contentious will be the politicized fight over extending the Selective Service requirement to women and eventually to transgender men and women. If gender equality ever becomes absolute, then should the obligation to register for the draft likewise be equalized?[61] The tentative answers to these question and the future outcomes will reveal as much about the innate nature of warfare as they will the race and gender in American military institutions and civilian societies during wartime and peacetime.

Contemporary Considerations: Racial Intolerance and Sexual Assault in the US Military

Looking forward from our vantage point in the first quarter of a new century, the influence of racial and gendered discourses on the practice of military history will doubtlessly increase. This is not merely a case of more persons trained in these methodologies entering the field. Events current to our researching and writing *Race and Gender in Modern Western Warfare* (between 2008 and 2018) reveal racialized politics and the ebb and flow of gender identities and the questions of legitimate access to civic institutions like the military, as well as the pushback against said opportunities. The heated debates about such issues will not end anytime soon. Historians working within the scopes of gender and race as applied to the history of conflict, military cultures, and their institutions must be prepared to follow new or long overlooked research initiatives as they take shape even today

In the U.S. military, combat service has long stood as the seminal barrier to equality between the genders and races and soldiers of all sexual orientations. The following quote by Mady Wechsler Segal focuses on women and gender, but it could likewise be applied to race and sexual orientation:

> For women to participate, either the military has to be perceived (by policymakers and the populace) as transformed to make it more compatible with how women are (or perceived to be) or women have to be perceived as changing in ways that make them more seemingly suited to military service. . . These perceptions are socially constructed. The discourse on

---

61 Bristol and Stur, "Conclusion," 233, 236.

the issues, indeed the salience given to specific arguments about women's military roles is not based on objective reality, but rather on cultural values.[62]

Keeping these words in mind, conceptions about race and gender and to a lesser degree sexual orientation have shifted over the last decades. Greater social acceptance for African Americans, other minorities, and women has taken shape as they have been permitted to serve in units or military occupational specialties (MOS) that place them in direct combat.

Although not equitable as yet, achievements of minorities and women have occurred after the end of the Vietnam War and in the wake of the advent of the All-Volunteer Force.[63] After a long career that included service as an African-American combat fighter pilot in Korea and Vietnam, Daniel "Chappy" James, Jr., received his fourth star and assumed command of North American Aerospace Defense Command in 1975. Colin Powell rose to the highest rank possible in the U.S. military when he became the first African American to serve as Chairman of the Joint Chiefs of Staff in 1989. Just this year in 2018, the Army's Lieutenant General Darryl A. Williams becomes the first African American officer to become Superintendent of the U.S. Military Academy. Other minorities also attained promotions to the highest tiers, as evinced by Richard E. Cavazos, a decorated Army veteran of Korea and Vietnam who was the first Hispanic American to become a brigadier in 1976 and later the first to reach general as commander of Army Forces Command in 1982. An American of Japanese descent as well as combat veteran of Vietnam, Eric Shinseki became the first Asian-American to reach the four-star rank and serve as the Army's Chief of Staff in 1999.

Women also enjoyed more opportunities as they advanced to higher ranks and expanded their MOS's in the post-Vietnam decades. Martha McShally was the first female combat pilot in 1995; and as a Lieutenant Colonel, she has more recently taken command of the 354th Fighter Squadron. In 2013, Michelle D. Johnson received her third star and became the first female general officer to serve as superintendent of a service academy – in her case the U.S. Air Force Academy. In 2000, Kathleen McGrath became the first women to command an American warship when she captained the frigate USS *Jarrett* in the Persian Gulf. Women have also achieved the highest flag ranks. Ann E. Dunwoody advanced to four-star general and took charge of the Army Materiel Command in 2008. Michelle Howard went from being the first African-African women to command a U.S. Navy ship in 1999 to attaining full admiral rank as only woman and African

---

62 Segal, "Women's Military Roles," 758.
63 See also Susan D. Hosek, et. al, *Minority and Gender Differences in Officer Career Progression* (RAND Corporation, 2001); and Margaret C. Harrell, *New Opportunities for Military Women: Effects Upon Readiness, Cohesion, and Moral* (RAND Corporation, 1997).

American to serve as Vice Chief of Naval Operations in 2014. She then again broke new ground by leading operational forces as the commander of the U.S. Naval Forces Europe and Naval Forces Africa until her retirement in 2017. These men and women stood on the shoulders of officers like Brigadier General Anna May Hayes, Brigadier General Elizabeth S. Hoisington, Brigadier General Benjamin O. Davis, Sr., and his son, Lieutenant General Benjamin O. Davis, Jr., all of whom advanced to flag rank from the World War II through the Vietnam eras.[64]

Although positive moves toward more equality, listing these developments cannot be seen as evidence for the end of all discrimination in the U.S. military or in civilian America. Incidents of sexual assault and harassment in the U.S. military have become more prevalent – or rather, more public. Likewise, race-oriented bias and hate crimes continue to occur, undermining attempts to make a case for ends to institutional and personal racism. Service in combat and assignment to the combat arms remains the primary access point to the upper echelons in the Department of Defense. The military ethos requires that uniformed personnel be willing and able to obey ordered and fight, kill, and if necessary die. If a given individual can fulfill these expectations, then should it matter what race or gender that person is? Servicemen of color broke through the threshold of rank after decades of false assumptions about their intelligence and leadership abilities because they overturned those assumptions by dutifully serving in America's wars. Once the preconceptions were stripped away, minority servicemen could attain those higher ranks.[65]

Another consideration is the transference of racial intolerance to other social categories in the post-9/11 military. Evidence from numerous observers and social commentators specializing in recent years point to the rising influence of a virulent blend of evangelical millennialism and Pentecostal Protestantism in the American military sphere. Not only has this sometimes manifested as internal peer pressures against "outsider" faiths within the military, but also through direct representations of an eschatological dimension of the War on Terror fought in Muslim-dominated Central Asia and Middle East. Are disparaging comments about Iraqi and Afghan civilians and the appropriation of direct and oblique

---

64 See Tanya L. Roth, "'An Attractive Career for Women": Opportunities, Limitations, and Women's Integration into the Cold War Military," and Isaac Hampton II, "Reform in the Ranks: The History of Defense Race Relations Institute, 1971–2014," both in Bristol and Stur, *Race, Gender, and Sexual Orientation*, 74–95, 122–41.

65 In his seminal book *Fighting on Two Fronts* (1997) that examines African Americans serving in the U.S. Military in the Vietnam War, historian James Westheider finds three typologies of racism in the U.S. Military: institutional, personal, and perceived. Just because a policy or decision-maker might fit one or two of these topologies did not mean that all three could apply. This is a useful model for understanding all types of prejudice and discrimination the U.S. military since the Vietnam War.

references to the Medieval Crusades just newer versions of typical American soldier talk disparaging their enemies and their own motivations? Or does this rhetoric represent an informalized and tacitly accepted blurring of racial prejudice with religious zealotry? If so, what does this portend for the future of civil-military relations in a modern democratic society? And regardless of the presence or lack of forethought and intent, how are the anti-Muslim dogmas perceived by the indigenous people and foes, and do such perceptions translate into a quantifiable moral advantage for one side or the other?[66] Answers to these questions have contributed to and played off of neo-conservative ideologies promoted by authors like Victor Davis Hanson and Max Boot in implicit and explicit ways. For instance, if White Anglo-Saxon Christian exceptionalism has been so dominant and so ideal for so long, then perhaps civilizational warfare between Christendom and Islam could or even should occur. Such xenophobic beliefs about the religions, races, and worldviews of "others" have dangerous potential affects on American military policy, strategy, and operations could easily spiral out of control.[67]

In his book *From Chivalry to Terrorism: War and the Changing Nature of Masculinity*, Leo Braudy uses "new tribalism" to describe this dynamic of demonizing, dehumanizing, and devaluing the "other." He cautions that tribalism – combined with the ideological goals of a radical religious terrorist group – is displacing nationalism with its loyalty to a nation-state and national group. This mutually reinforcing connection parallels those bonds made by ethnocentrism, exceptionalism, or racism as unifying power and destructive potential because the tribes' members blindly embrace particular beliefs and categorically hate opposing beliefs and believers. Global political events since 2008 attest to Braudy's warning. Evidence of his "new tribalism" is readily apparent in the rise of populist groups and parties in Asia, the Mideast, and Europe, not to mention the ongoing cultural divide within the United States, where tensions reached a fever pitch over race, gender, religion, economic, or political power, or

---

66 See Jeff Sharlet, "Jesus Killed Mohammed: The Crusade for a Christian Military," *Harper's Magazine*, May 2009, 31–43, http://www.harpers.org/archive/2009/05/0082488 (Accessed June 28, 2018).

67 Hanson. *Carnage and Culture*; Max Boot, *Savage Wars of Peace: Small Wars and the Rise American Power* (Basic Books, 2002); and the perilously divisive book, Samuel P. Huntington, *The Clash of Civilizations and the Remaking of World Order* (Simon and Schuster, 1996).

The criticisms of neo-conservatism during the Bush Administration come from many sources: Andrew Bacevich, *The New American Militarism: How Americans Are Seduced by War*, rev. ed. (Oxford University Press, 2013), 80–94; relevant chapters in Beth Bailey and Richard H. Immerman, eds., *Understanding the U.S. War in Iraq and Afghanistan* (New York University Press, 2015); and Muehlbauer and Ulbrich, *Ways of War*, 472–95.

some combination thereof. Sadly, tribalism also becomes enmeshed with seductive possibilities of victory offered by militarism. All these factors magnify one another as they spiral out of control.[68]

Racism remains a distasteful, and increasingly public, aspect of American society and character, both in dealings with foreigners abroad and with non-whites at home.[69] Since the turbulent events of the 1960s, racial intolerance has been treated as a mark of ignorance and inadequate judgment in American society – and rightfully so. Yet even as individuals are acculturated to reject such views, episodes of intolerance flare up at critical friction points of social change: the Boston busing crisis of the mid 1970s; the anti-Semitic rhetoric in New York City's Crown Heights neighborhood in 1991; or the violent riots in South Central Los Angeles following the Rodney King beating trial in 1992. More recently, the collective outrage over unwarranted displays of lethal force by police and white civilians against African Americans, the cumulative weight of hitherto ignored sexual exploitation and abuse in the workplace, the growing wave of white supremacism, and the questions of who is entitled to claim full recognition – and legal protection – in American society demonstrates that much of what has been heralded as social progress is illusory. Contrary to the rosy perceptions of its most fervent supporters, American military institutions are not immune to the basest impulses of racism – or "otherism" to draw on anthropologist C. Loring Brace's term – lurking under the stones in its parent society.[70] For example, in April 2009, the FBI and the Extremism and Radicalism Branch of the Homeland Environment Threat Analysis Division of the Department of Homeland Security conducted a study that identified direct and indirect efforts by white supremacist organizations to recruit disgruntled veterans returning home from war.[71] Likewise individuals with these sympathies and beliefs voluntarily entered have the U.S. military in growing numbers in part because they can carry out their racialist agenda at home the "others" and abroad against the Arabs, an inferior race with a pagan religion. This represents a twisted white supremacist inversion of the African-Americans' "Double V" campaign during World War II. Such beliefs prompted

---

68 Braudy, *From Chivalry to Terrorism*, 522, 542–47; and Bacevich, *The New American Militarism*, 19–20, 173–204.

69 For prejudices in the military and international arenas, see Nikhil Pal Singh, *Race and America's Long War* (University of California Press, 2017).

70 Brace, *"Race"*, 3, 165.

71 U.S. Department of Homeland Security, *(U//FOUO): Rightwing Extremism: Current Economic and Political Climate Fueling Resurgence in Radicalization and Recruitment*, IA-0257-09, http://www.fas.org/irp/eprint/rightwing.pdf (Accessed June 28, 2018).

researchers completing a Department of Defense 2005 study on terrorism in the American military to conclude:

> Effectively, the military has a 'don't ask, don't tell' policy pertaining to extremism. If individuals can perform satisfactorily, without making their extremist opinions overt through words or actions that violate policy, reflect poorly on the Armed Forces, or disrupt the effectiveness and order of their units, they are likely to be able to complete their contracts.[72]

Another concern can be seen in the rise in gang-related associations among military service personnel., Beginning with Operation Iraqi Freedom in 2003, American military recruiters have been under pressure to meet higher induction quotas in order to satisfy wartime force deployment needs. In January 2007, a Department of Justice report examining the years before the Global War on Terror stated:

> Gang-related activity in the US Armed Forces is increasing. Although gang members constitute only a fraction of military personnel nationwide, their presence can compromise installation security and force protection both internally and externally. Gang members in the military can disrupt good order and discipline and threaten military operations. Gang membership in the ranks may also result in a disruption of command, low morale, disciplinary problems, and a broad range of criminal activity. Gang-affiliated military personnel and dependent gang-affiliated children of service members facilitate crime on and off military installations, and are at risk of transferring their weapons and combat training back to the community to employ against rival gang members and law enforcement officers.[73]

Criminal gangs including the Bloods, Crips, Mara Salvatrucha (MS-13), Latin Kings, Mexican Mafia, Hell's Angels, and among others allegedly use the military – particularly the U.S. Army – as recruitment, training, and networking venues in which new and existing members gain weapons training, combat experience, and new skills in planning and logistics to further their enterprises. While several gangs include members from a variety of ethnicities, some are not restricted to one nationality, ethnicity, or race, but also take great pride in their exclusivity and racial or ethnic identity. The problem of gang recruitment inside the U.S. military, like that of white supremacists and domestic Islamicists, has prompted a

---

72 Matt Kennard, "Neo-Nazis are in the Army Now,"
https://www.theinvestigativefund.org/investigation/2009/06/15/neo-nazis-are-in-the-army-now/(Accesed June 28, 2018); and Defense Personnel Security Research Center, Department of Defense, *Screening for Potential Terrorists in the Enlisted Military Accessions Process*, https://fas.org/irp/eprint/screening.pdf (Accessed June 28, 2018).
73 National Gang Intelligence Center, *Gang-Related Activity in the US Armed Forces Increasing*, 12 January 2007, https://narcosphere.narconews.com/userfiles/70/ngic_gangs.pdf (Accessed June 28, 2018).

reassessment of existing pre-screening protocols at the point of recruitment and induction as well as a harsher policy toward behaviors and activities that reflect an unhealthy association with criminal gangs and extremists. The immediate difficulty is reconciling the need to preserve the integrity of the military's cadre from such intrusions without infringing upon personal liberties and stereotyping entire groups because of the activities of few members thereof.[74] At this time, such efforts are reminiscent of the post-Vietnam anti-drug efforts – the Navy's "not on my ship, not in my Navy" campaign, for example – and are generally limited to self-policing and increasing awareness among recruiters. However, if the military's anti-drug measures are a model, information dissemination will be followed by a zero-tolerance enforcement and remediation policy.[75]

Since the American withdrawal from Vietnam and the inception of the All-Volunteer Force (AVF) in 1973 as an alternative to the mass conscription military, American society has struggled to define the limits of gender identification and cross-gender participation in the armed forces. Perhaps more than any other occupational field, military service retained its strong masculine-exclusive cultural identity. Until the 1970s female participation in this sphere of activity was restricted to simple, if not superficial, tasks. With the exception of the medical nurse and technician, women only entered Military Occupational Specialties (MOS's) that were defined as "safe" and did not compromise their status as objects of heterosexualized desire – clerks, typists, office assistants, adjutants, etc. The AVF and the subsequent dismantling of the Women's Army Corps in 1978 initiated a new arena for the gender conflicts in the burgeoning culture wars of the coming decades.[76]

Sociologist Melissa Herbert notes that no less than the most basic seminal notions of gender identification in American society remain at stake. Even the act of opening up logistical and technical military occupation specialties that had previously been male-exclusive areas challenged the definition of manliness in a

---

74 Carter F. Smith, *Gangs and the Military: Gangsters, Bikers, and Terrorists with Military Training* (Rowman and Littlefield 2017), 68–78, 109–116. Smith examines examples of gang recruitment and violence at Fort Bragg, North Carolina since the 1990s (pp. 209–214).

75 An example of how the news about the military's anti-gang stance is disseminated to the rank and file is found in the New Jersey National Guard's official magazine *Guardlife*. The January 2007 issue included a short essay by Technical Sergeant Paul Conners, 177 FW/PA entitled "Gang Members: No Place for You in the Guard," which offered information on identifying gang members and cautions from local law enforcement on the prevalence of gangs, closing with the admonition, "once identified the gang member will very quickly become a 'former' member of the Air National Guard." See http://www.state.nj.us/military/publications/guardlife/volume32no6/10.html. (Accessed June 28, 2018).

76 See Heather Stur, "Mens' and Women's Liberation: Challenging Military Culture after the Vietnam War," in Bristol and Stur, *Integrating the U.S. Military*, 142–59.

masculine dominated institution. Thus a two-way exchange of identity transference and negotiation is at play in many non-combat specialties. Not only are there tensions over the prospect of women losing their femininity by taking on hitherto masculine occupations (mechanics, engineers, heavy machine operators, military police), but the very prospect of the shift from masculine exclusivity to a blended female/male occupational environment calls into question the gendered and sexualized preferences of men monopolizing some occupations. As logistical support services, for example, become staffed more frequently with women, those men remaining in these occupations may be considered "less manly" than their peers in other combat-oriented specialties.[77]

In response to the widening participation of women in the American military, opponents and critics unleashed a barrage of essays and books predicting the imminent collapse of the institution. Decrying the alleged influence of liberal politicians and women's liberation advocates, conservative and traditionalist critics assayed the recruitment of women as eroding the warrior ethos of the military, affecting its combat readiness and capacity to conduct its primary defensive role. Such attacks were not restricted to conservative intellectuals, however; more importantly, they reflected a powerful threads of misogynist hostility to women who dared cross into the military sphere of masculinity.[78] Just like a generation earlier, women who entered military service were castigated as sexual deviants. Sexualized slurs – "slut," "dyke," "whore" – are employed as tools of negative sanction to illustrate the transgression of the imaginary gender line. In response, female military personnel find themselves in a constant struggle from the point of their induction or commission to balance their femininity without sacrificing their utility as soldiers, sailors, and air personnel. Veer too far into one extreme – adopting traditional feminine trappings of makeup, lipstick, and hair styling – or the other – dressing down feminine characteristics and adopting male-oriented habits of casual cursing and heavy drinking to fit in – and the female soldier risks being dismissed by her peers as a sexualized exotic other, and hence, unfit for

---

77 Melissa S. Herbert, *Camouflage isn't Only for Combat: Gender, Sexuality, and Women in the Military* (New York: New York University Press, 1998), 14–15, 32–42. Of course, it is also true that logistical services have frequently been classified in gendered language and terms long before these positions were opened to female participation. Since 1978, however, the intensity of such comparisons has increased.

78 For example, see Brian Mitchell, *Women in the Military: Flirting with Disaster* (Regnery, 1998); as well as the unapologetically strident arguments against women in military service made by Martin Van Creveld in his "Less than We Can Be: Men, Women, and the Modern Military," *Journal of Strategic Studies* 24 (2000): 1–20; and *Men, Women & War: Do Women Belong in the Front Line?* (Cassell, 2002).

service on the grounds that she undermines the masculine heterosexual ethos of the institution.[79]

Such bias and violence against women in uniform hinders equality in the institution and society at large. Female service personnel are subjected to routine acts of sexual insults and come-ons, gender harassment, and other forms of workplace-oriented harassment. They are casually groped and touched in inappropriate ways, not only by their peers, but also by superior NCOs and officers. Female personnel have been coerced and compelled to engage in sexual acts against their will and often under threat of dismissal or other sanction. Physical violence has ranged from simple assault and battery to murder; likewise sexual violence remain regular, albeit tragic, occurrences. Incidents of abuse directed toward female military personnel are nothing new. In her essay for Tod Ensign's anthology *America's Military Today: The Challenge of Militarism* published in 2004, journalist Linda Bird Francke describes a 40-year saga of misogyny, overt hostility, sexual assault, rape, and murder of female military personnel by their peers, subordinates, and superiors in uniform.[80] Indeed, the 1970s was "open season" on female personnel. Women routinely were humiliated on the basis of their gender, and were regularly assaulted on and off base. No official records were kept, according to Francke, because the male chain of command refused to accept the problem – in part because, in the post-Vietnam early days of the All-Volunteer Force, racial discrimination constituted a more pressing issue than sexual harassment.[81]

Even after the 1970s, sexual misconduct and assault remained a hidden crime, only coming to light in the most outrageous cases. The extent of the problem came into full view during the September 8–12, 1991 "Tailhook" scandal. Over 100 Navy and Marine aviation officers ran amok during the 35th Annual Tailhook Symposium, assaulting 83 women and seven men over the weekend. The outrages included a "gauntlet" of drunken men groping, biting, and stripping women attempting to pass through it.[82] In 1997, one Army officer and two enlisted men were convicted of sexual assault, rape, and adultery for the regular

---

79 Herbert, *Camouflage Isn't Only for Combat*, 60–61, 65–77; and Goldstein, *War and Gender*, 300–301.

80 Linda Bird Francke, "Women in the Military: The Military Culture of Harassment; The Dynamics of the Masculine Mystique," in Tod Ensign, *America's Military Today: The Challenge of Militarism*. (The New Press, 2004), 135–167. A 1992 Senate report made the claim that 60,000 women were raped or assaulted while in the US military, though it did not offer a year by year breakdown nor a comparison with civilian statistic (Goldstein, *War and Gender*, 96).

81 Francke, "Women in the Military," 148–150.

82 "What Really Happened at Tailhook Convention: Scandal: The Pentagon report graphically describes how fraternity-style hi-jinks turned into a hall of horrors," *Los Angeles Times*. April 24,

abuse of five women under their direction and command at the Aberdeen Proving Ground, in Maryland.[83] In 2003, reports of sexual violence surfaced at the Air Force Academy, prompting a Pentagon investigation of all three service academies. The report revealed 18.8 percent of all female cadets experienced sexual abuse, ranging from verbal insults to rape. Only one in five of these incidents were reported.[84]

Whereas sexual assault has been a problem in the US military for decades, it only became the subject of close scrutiny in 2004, following a series of news reports detailing incidents in Iraq and Afghanistan. At that time, the Department of Defense had no standardized policy toward sexual assault; instead, each service branch implemented its own measures, which the 2004 Task Force Report on Care for Victims of Sexual Assault found lacking.[85] The report identified 1,913 cases of sexual assault against 2,012 female and male servicemembers in 2002–2003. These only constituted reported cases, the report acknowledging that inconsistencies in terminology and definitions, as well as victim reluctance to go public with their allegations, meant that the official tally was likely incomplete. Indeed, the Uniform Code of Military Justice did not include sexual assault as a specific offense in 2004.[86] Overall, the report found the Department of Defense's treatment of sexual assault within the ranks to be lacking, directly stating that "No overarching policies, programs, and procedures exist within DoD to ensure all functional areas responsible for dealing with victims of sexual assault provide an integrated response to reported cases of sexual assault."[87] In response to the report, the Pentagon created a Joint Task Force for Sexual Assault Prevention and Response, which in turn established a new prevention and response policy in January 2005. Assembling military chaplains, lawyers, police, and 1,200 new sexual assault response coordinators (SARCs), this scheme was made permanent in October 2005 with the inauguration of the Sexual Assault

---

1993, http://articles.latimes.com/1993-04-24/news/mn-26672_1_tailhook-convention (Accessed June 28, 2018).

83 "Drill Sergeant Gets 6 Months For Sex Abuse at Army Post," *The New York Times*. May 31, 1997. http://query.nytimes.com/gst/fullpage.html?res=9C01E7DF1E3AF932A05756C0A961958260 (Accessed June 28, 2018).

84 "Code of Dishonor," *Vanity Fair*, November 6, 2006. https://www.vanityfair.com/news/2003/12/airforce200312 (Accessed June 28, 2018).

85 *Department of Defense Task Force Report on Care for Victims of Sexual Assault, April 2004*, 9–11, 18–19. http://www.ncdsv.org/images/DOD_TaskForceReportOnCareForVictimsOfSexualAssault_4-2004.pdf (Accessed June 28, 2018).

86 *Ibid.*, 19–20, 23; According to the report, 9 percent of all victims (181 persons) were male.

87 *Ibid.*, 44.

Prevention and Response Office (SAPRO).[88] While well-intentioned, in practice SAPRO has proven to be only partially effective in preventing and responding to sexual assault within the American military. In 2016, the Pentagon estimated over 20,300 sexual assaults had occurred in the prior fiscal year, of which only 6,083 were reported, despite a "zero tolerance" policy. The same report indicated that 93 percent of assaults against women were committed by peers and acquaintances. Victims reporting assaults were frequently targets of reprisal, ostracized, blamed, and shamed by perpetrators and peers.[89]

Focusing on the statistical reality of sexual assault in the U.S. military is disheartening; it also fails to address the broader societal factors that create the climate for sexual misconduct and that validate the perpetrators. First, it goes without saying that masculinity is the cornerstone of American military institutional culture, and indeed, dominates throughout the West. Since ancient history, war and wartime service have been the traditionally exclusive male social venue. This has become so imprinted on the human psyche that it has assumed proto-biological legitimacy: "Women can not fight because of their upper body strength index," or "Women can not fight because their natural role is as nurturer, not protector," and similar arguments. Despite the evidence – again, with examples reaching back into the classical world, through the current conflict – that such biologically based arguments are false, they have become so ingrained as to defy reality. Thus a broad consensus of American society tacitly agrees that war is a "man's business," and that women have no business in combat – even as they experience combat daily.[90]

Another aspect of femininity in the military is its association with individual identity. Within military institutions, individuality is suborned by the group and repressed in the name of homogeneity and organizational cohesion. In fact, individuality is an alien concept that should be avoided when referencing the military as a cultural venue. The institution is valued more than the individual, who from their initial training and indoctrination are acculturated to become parts of the group. Conformity to the masculine ideal, which places military service in the dual role of rite of passage and qualifier of maleness – an ideal which in the United States is increasingly tied to the lower middle-class, working-class, and rural and urban poor conventions of gender identity and values. This in turn

---

88 "Department of Defense Sexual Assault Prevention and Response Office Mission and History," http://www.sapr.mil/index.php/about/mission-and-history (Accessed June 28, 2018).

89 *Department of Defense Annual Report on Sexual Assault in the Military, Fiscal Year 2015*, 7, 11–13. http://sapr.mil/public/docs/reports/FY15_Annual/FY15_Annual_Report_on_Sexual_Assault_in_the_Military.pdf (Accessed June 28, 2018).

90 See MacKenzie, *Beyond the Band of Brothers*, 98–133; and DePauw, *Battle Cries and Lullabies*.

translates into an institution that, even as some sixteen percent of its members are women, denigrates them as "weak," "indecisive," "fickle," and, of course, sexually active – regardless of their status as uniformed or civilian personnel. In this environment of a charged hyper-masculinity, in which the maturity level of both the majority of the enlisted cadre, *and* the entire junior officer corps, is between 18 and 24, young servicemen are constantly encouraged to display their manhood and repress their pre-service notions of decent restraint vis-à-vis public/private sexual identity.

The entire acculturation process for male recruits in the military is one long pathway toward asserting a hyper-masculine ethos in place of earlier identities. As noted, a major part of this is related to the traditional masculine-oriented culture of the military as a social entity; maleness translates into combat utility and effectiveness. The more strident and testosterone-fueled the recruit, the more aggressive and efficient he is purported to be. Rituals like cadence-calls, casual references in training to "Suzie Rottencrotch" and other euphemisms intended to isolate women – even loved ones – as corrosive forces threatening masculinity, rigorous physical fitness training, and the use of female/gender sensitive terms by authority figures – "wimp," "sissie," "lady," "faggot" – all emphasize a rigorous and physical maleness that views sexuality as an exclusively heterosexual act of female submission and male dominance. This boot-camp perspective may be relaxed in secondary training venues for specialists and non-combat MOS's, but it retains its appeal in encouraged (although non-sanctioned) after-hours leisure activities. Junior NCOs – themselves only a few years older than their new charges – facilitate and participate in free-time activities ranging from contact to extreme sports, from binge drinking to reckless driving, all competitive activities intended to foster male bonding. Female peers, alternatively, are either excluded or reduced to passive observers – lest they exhibit behaviors marking them either as sexually accessible or as lesbians, which in the world before the repeal of DADT was an automatic ticket to discharge.

None of these examples alone translates specifically into a culture of sexual violence against female soldiers. It is important to note that the overwhelming majority of male soldiers do not participate in the regular harassment of their female peers. However, it fosters a cult of unanimity and unspoken support among members of the small peer group (e.g.: Squad, Platoon) that in turn promotes a "cone of silence" around each other with reference to all but the most savage acts (and as we see in some examples in Afghanistan and Iraq, even with these acts). The misogynistic culture infecting the American military is self-regulating and self-sustaining, and it is also far more pervasive than even its members will care to admit – young, decent men who in civilian life would not say or act in such a demeaning manner are empowered, in part by training, in part by being members of a peer group, and at times, at the prodding of an alpha male(s) in their group, to engage in ethnic and gender slurs, insults, and crude locker-room come-ons without second thought.

What of the female soldier herself? Women in uniform share, with their male peers, a variety of reasons for enlisting in the service, including economic opportunity, social advancement, patriotism and family tradition, citizenship and assimilation, and ennui and boredom with life at home. Yet from the moment they enter the military, they are set apart as being "different" from the male recruits. Segregated through most of training, they must meet different standards of physical conditioning and demonstrate greater aptitude in rote learning in military culture and tradition – in part intended to emphasize the institutional differences between men and women in the military as a task-fulfillment oriented community. Gender segregation has mixed results, however. On the one hand, training company segregation is intended to both remove distractions from both male and female recruits, thus facilitating the breakdown of civilian identities and cultural norms. The reasoning is that, the period between induction and graduation from basic training is primarily about improving physical conditioning, instilling basic pride in one's self as member of the military community, and to remove civilian-based social and moral cues that would restrict automatic compliance with instruction. Gender integration may well affect the pursuit of these aims, proponents argue. At the same time, however, critical observers of the military's deeply flawed gender culture point out that gender integration only helps deconstruct and eliminate the misogynistic attitudes that are inculcated in segregated basic training. Simply put, if not trained together with women, male soldiers will be prone to continue to disrespect their female counterparts.[91]

After basic training, the ambiguous cues regarding women's place in the institutions continue, just as the trend toward misogynistic conduct escalates. Even amongst themselves, female service personnel struggle with the challenge over their gendered identity. Persistence in displaying feminine style while in uniform – careful attention to appearance, lipstick, makeup, etc. – can be taken as a sign of being too feminine, and being thus cast as willing to use appearance or sexuality to win support and advancement. Conversely, overt efforts to downplay femininity and to adopt masculine cues of vulgarity, overt aggression, and otherwise "being one of the boys" can result in being labeled too masculine. This balance between "whore" and "dyke," to borrow from sociologist Melissa Herbert, creates undue tension among female personnel who feel they are under constant

---

91 Erin Solaro, *Women in the Line of Fire: What You Should Know About Women in the Military* (Seal Press, 2006), 259, 264–272.

scrutiny by their male peers. This is particularly the case in the more physical MOS's that have traditionally been male-oriented: Military Police, mechanics, truck drivers, etc. – though it remains a problem throughout the service in all occupations – even after the demise of "Don't Ask Don't Tell."[92]

On a side note, it is worth noting how DADT has served a dual role for the military establishment. Intended to screen one group – homosexuals – who challenged traditional sexual and gender norms in the military, it was also used extensively to target uniformed women regardless of their sexual preference, by serving as a litmus test that simultaneously permitted a culture of sexual abuse and subjectification. Again turning to Francke, she describes testimony from dozens of women who were labeled lesbian merely because of conduct – either as being "too aggressive" and hence, masculine; or as "too feminine" and hence, overtly sexual and feminine. Female soldiers and officers who expressed support for their female subordinates and peers were cast as lesbians, as were those women who rejected the sexual advances of males. Giving in was no guarantee of safety, either; one female Marine officer was cast as the base whore after giving in to her commanding officer – ready for sex with any other officer, any time of day or night. Most sadly she was compelled to accept this status, as her career became tightly bound to her sexualitzation: reject or complain, and be denied promotion or discharged; accept and submit, and likewise be denied promotion or respect – and face the prospect of discharge if her abusers were found out by their own spouses.[93]

American military policies based on age-old assumptions about female's physical strength and emotional capacities persisted from 1973 when the All-Volunteer Force was instituted until after the attack on September 11, 2001. Controversies surrounding women in combat persist regarding the moral ambiguities, political ramifications, and physiological realities of women fighting, killing, and dying. Neither many men in the military nor many Americans in the civilian world can envision women in combat units. In some cases, their notions about prohibiting women from performing combat roles tend to be relatively benign or perhaps sentimental. This view relied on traditionalist roles for women that insulated or protected them from dangers of military service. In other cases, the taboo against women in combat reaches deep into the male psyche. This goes beyond discomfort with women in uniform or with worries about physical shortcomings. Some

---

92 Melissa S. Herbert, *Camouflage Isn't Only for Combat: Gender, Sexuality, and Women in the Military*. (New York University Press, 1998), 45–48, 55.
93 Francke, "Women in the Military," 135–167, 151–152.

men, civilian and military alike, fear the cultural, familial, political, legal, and military ramifications of women fighting, killing, and dying in combat.[94]

One of the most outrageous facets of the cultural backlash against female military personnel is how it is exacerbated by blind ignorance – which is the only way to classify it without making an indictment – by vocal conservative supporters of the military. Many male – and increasingly, among Republicans, female – critics openly doubt charges or cast female victims as willing participants and/or provocateurs. During and after the now-infamous Abu Ghraib incidents, Specialist Lynndie Englund became the favored scapegoat of critics, not only of the war in Iraq but also for conservatives opposed to gender integration in the military. In casting her as a backwoods sexual sadist, these critics have overlooked her own victimization by her sergeant (who coerced her into a sexual relationship and compelled her to share her sexual favors with other personnel) and others in her unit. To wax colloquial, Lynndie Englund was thrown under the bus by those wishing to paint her as evidence of the hazards of open gender integration.

The frequent conservative response to the Englund case aderes to a long tradition of obscuring the problem of sexual assault in the military. In what has become the typical litany among conservatives, rather than address the breakdown in military authority on the part of the unit's commanding officers and NCOs, they target female personnel exclusively. Over a decade ago, Brian Mitchell dismissed the 1997 charges of rape and coercive sexual abuse by senior NCOs at Aberdeen Proving Ground as patently false, made by a group of manipulative female trainees seeking to conceal their own misconduct.[95] Later, critics like Kingsley Browne decried reports of sexual conduct among units in Iraq as evidence that gender integration created a climate where sexual activity was bound to occur, because, as he put it, "Sex Happens."[96] Equally telling, critics blame the system that in their opinion has thrown women into the military in spite of common sense. In 2000, conservative journalist Stephanie Gutmann dismissed gender integration as a short-sighted exercise in political correctness. It was the "military brass themselves, who try to show that they are diligently trying to cleanse their diseased culture by ordering study after study, attempting to gauge the incidence of sexual harassment in the ranks" who fostered a culture

---

94 For perspectives on the Second World War, see Campbell, "Women in Combat," 321; and for the post-9/11 environment, see Solaro, *Women in the Line of Fire*, 15.

95 Brian Mitchell, *Women in the Military: Flirting with Disaster* (Regnery Publishing, Inc., 1998), 309–311.

96 Kingsley Browne, *Co-Ed Combat: The New Evidence that Women Shouldn't Fight the Nation's Wars* (Sentinel, 2007), 195.

of false accusation and exaggeration.[97] Citing another critic of gender integration ("'When you take young women and drop them into that hypermasculine environment, the sex stuff just explodes'") Kingsley Browne dismisses the issue of gender violence altogether, going on to say that "an environment in which sexual assaults . . . are common is not an environment conducive to cohesion."[98] By openly dismissing the charges of sexual assault in the military, these critics and others bolster the culture of misogyny and hypermasculinity that influences young male recruits. Mars is validated, as Athena lies moribund.

The preceding institutional, personal, and perceived examples of racism, chauvinism, homophobia, and others should not, however, be taken as signaling the imminent breakdown of the American military. Indeed the racial and ethnic diversity of the U.S. armed forces constitutes one of its greatest assets at home and abroad. Ever since its inception, for example, the Army served as a vehicle for ethnic assimilation and citizenship expansion in the Republic. For over two centuries, the Army provided opportunities for men and women of ethnic and national identities to advance their social, economic, and education status while serving with distinction and pride. In return, many used their service as the gateway to increased equality, fuller citizenship, and future prosperity in the United States after their military service ends. Morever as foreign observers – civilian and uniformed – witness the composition of the U.S. armed forces in service abroad, its multi-ethnic composition and the ability to maintain strong cohesion is one of the best indicators of the success of the American experiment in the world arena. Contrary to the claims of some extremists, diversity, not blood, is the sustenance of liberty. As an institution, the American military stands out among social institutions as an agent for great change and progress in this regard.

Whither Gender and Race in Future Wars?

Rooted in martial traditions of citizen soldiers risking life and limb on behalf of the Republic, America's military is also the heir to centuries of Western concepts of male identity and the collectivist "band of brothers" myth. The bonding of soldiers in combat units is not necessarily a harmful phenomenon in and of itself. It certainly can be leveraged to increase combat effectiveness, provide strength to individuals in uniforms, and imbue those individuals with willingness to fight,

---

97 Stephanie Gutmann, *The Kindler, Gentler Military: How Political Correctness Affects Our Ability to Win Wars.* (Encounter Books, 2000), 211–12.
98 Browne, *Co-Ed Combat*, 200.

kill, and willingly die for the unit as a whole. Nevertheless, the band of brothers myth has been appropriated to exclude "others" who are not deemed to be brotherly enough because of race, ethnicity, gender, religion, sexual orientation, region, and the like. The myth can take on cult-like characteristics. Rejecting participants in American society speaks to the realization that, for many participants and civilian observers, the military remains a gateway to attaining the fullest version of masculinity for young men. The band of brothers concept stands on three foundational truths as explained by Australian scholar of gender and security Megan MacKenzie:

> First, the myth casts the nonsexual, brotherly love, male bonding, and feelings of trust, pride, honor, and loyalty between men as mysterious, indescribable, and **exceptional.** Second, male bonding is treated as primary and an **essential** element of an orderly, civilized, society. Third, all male units are seen as **elite** as a result of their social bonds and physical superiority.[99]

MacKenzie further contends that the myth must "depend on the exclusion of women" to remain sacrosanct in the eyes of some men – and some women – who want to perpetuate the myth.[100] Apart from the dangers of this gender consciousness, MacKenzie's explanation of myth can be applied to historical periods when minorities could not achieve membership in the band.

Elsewhere, in a study of military culture, Carol Burke offers similar analyses of how vestiges of these earlier ideas resonate within the US military as an institution. From basic training, where the emphasis is on "remaking" civilian boys into military men, through their service in a highly paternal hierarchical social system, to the creation of a mythologized military past by veterans recounting their service and authors and historians so eager to preserve it, the emphasis rests unquestioningly upon the acquisition of a masculine identity. The presence of women as peers delimits the masculine ideal sought by so many in their service, and threatens the sanctity of thousands of years of tradition and identity. In response, the military compels women in its ranks to conform to traditions while governing their access to specializations that would further erode the masculine exclusivity of military service. Women remain the subject of harsh discourse forms – the violent objectification of women as sexual toys in cadence calls, the gauntlet of sexual aggression and harassment in the service academies,

---

99 Emphasis in text in Megan MacKenzie, *Beyond the Band of Brothers: The US Military and the Myth that Women Can't Fight* (Cambridge University Press, 2015), 3. See also Sebastien Junger, *War* (Twelve, 2010).
100 *Ibid.*

and, at the most extreme end of the spectrum, rape and sexual coercion by their peers and superiors.[101]

These persistent obstacles notwithstanding, women made significant advances in the U.S. military in the AVF decades since 1973. More recently during Operations Iraqi Freedom and Enduring Freedom, they served in Iraq and Afghanistan where no front lines exist and everyone is targeted. They were *de facto* combatants in both countries.[102] In her study on combatant experiences, Army historian Lisa M. Mundey quotes a female soldier as saying, "I did everything there. I gunned. I drove. I ran as a truck commander. And underneath it all. I was a medic." Mundey next cites a female NCO whose recollections are just as candid: "We've had grenades thrown at us, shooting at us with AK-47's . . . When someone is shooting at you, don't say, 'Stop the war. I'm a girl.'"[103] The Department of Defense recognized the courage of female combatants when, for example in 2009, Air National Guard helicopter pilot Major Mary Jennings Hegar took enemy ground fire before being shot down while flying a rescued mission in Afghanistan. Although wounded, she helped fight off enemy attacks and keep other wounded soldiers safe. Hegar received the Distinguish Flying Cross (second highest award below only the Medal of Honor) and the Purple Heart. Her experiences and many similar ones helped legitimize calls for lifting the ban on women in the combat arms of infantry, artillery, and armor. In fact, Hegar launched a lawsuit against the Department of Defense in 2012 that argued the "Combat Exclusion Policy" was not constitutional.[104]

The next year in January, President Barrack Obama ended the *de jure* restriction against women in combat units. This decision opened up nearly every MOS to female service personnel that comprised 14 percent (some 200,000 personnel) of the entire U.S. military. In 2015, Captain Kristen Griest and First Lieutenant

---

101 Carol Burke, *Camp All-American, Hanoi Jane, and the High-and-Tight: Gender, Folklore, and Changing Military Culture* (Beacon Press, 2004), 25–59. See also Cynthia H. Enloe's seminal works on gender and the military: *Does Khaki Become You? The Militarization of Women's Lives* (South End Press, 1983). and *Maneuvers: The International Politics of Militarizing Women's Lives* (University of California Press, 1997).

102 See also MacKenzie, *Beyond the Band of Brothers*, 42–73; and Jennifer G. Mathers, "Women and State Military Forces," *Women and Wars: Contested Histories, Uncertain Futures*, ed. Carol Cohn (Polity, 2012), 124–43.

103 Oral history interviews cited in Lisa M. Mundey, "The Combatants' Experiences," in *Understanding the U.S. Wars in Iraq and Afghanistan*, eds. Beth Bailey and Richard H. Immerman (New York University Press, 2015), 177.

104 May Jennings Hegar, *Shoot Like a Girl: One Woman's Dramatic Fight in Afghanistan and on the Home Front* (New American Library, 2017); and Douglas Walter Bristol, Jr., and Heather Marie Stur, "Conclusion," in Bristol and Stur, *Race, Gender, and Sexual Orientation*, 229–32.

Shaye Haver graduated as the first women from U.S. Army's 62-day long Ranger School. At the graduation ceremony, Major General Austin S. Miller awarded the "Ranger" tab to the two officers and remarked that, "We've shown that it's not exclusively a male domain here." Although there can be little doubt that Griest and Haver and those women who graduated in the years since experienced hazing that tested their mental, emotional, and physical mettle in Ranger School, their ground-breaking achievement ushered them into the elite group of warriors, previously only open to the most masculine men capable of completing the school.[105]

Earlier in American history, for example, similar arguments opposed integration of the military across racial and ethnic lines because these "others" were different and thus inferior. Real-world experiences demonstrated that those prejudices to be unreasonable; and although slow, progress has been made. Now in the twenty-first century, American society and its military wrestled with issues of sexual orientations of personnel that do not conform to normative heterosexuality. The cycles of skeptical questions about morale, discipline, combat effectiveness are replaying again.

The debates notwithstanding, the realities of modernization in the digital age and increasing prevalence of unconventional military operations beg new sets of questions about the ability, indeed the wisdom, to restrict participation in all areas. The future of warfare will not merely require the application of brute physical force against enemies, but rather it will surely require the careful employment of military personnel and weapons in cyber-space, on remote-controlled battlefields, or across culturally diverse borders. Questions of ideology, religion, and justice desperately need to be taken into account. The aligning of the strategic goals with tactical and operational means cannot remain monopolized by views on race and gender in a particular *Weltanschauug* that stereotypes and alienated allies and potential foes alike. History has demonstrated that myopia prompted poor decisions that in turn resulted in defeat in Vietnam during Cold War and likely failure in the Middle East now.

---

105 David Vergun, "First Women Graduate Ranger School," https://www.army.mil/article/154286/First_women_graduate_Ranger_School/ (Accessed July 4, 2018); Ray Sanchez and Laura Smith-Spark, "Two Women Make Army Ranger History," August 21, 2015, https://www.cnn.com/2015/08/21/us/women-army-ranger-graduation/index.htm (Accessed July 4, 2018).

Where Should the Scholarship Go From Here?

Race and gender, as well as closely related ethnicity and sexuality, will remain controversial topics in historical studies. Scholars working in these fields must take care to build more methodological bridges with historians of warfare, and vice versa. Intellectual exchanges must cross all boundaries back and forth among the historical discipline.[106] After all, it has been three decades since John Wallach Scott called for just such an amalgamation:

> The subject of war, diplomacy, and high politics frequently comes up when traditional polit-ical historians question the utility of gender in their work. But here, too, we need to look beyond the actors and the literal import of their words. The legitimizing of war – of expend-ing young lives to protect the state – have variously taken the forms of explicit appeals to manhood (to the need to defend otherwise vulnerable women and children), of implicit reliance on belief in the duty of sons to serve their leaders of their (father the) king, or of associations between masculinity and national strength.[107]

The same call can be made to the historians of race, ethnicity, sexuality, and other inquiries about cultural constructions. In the intervening years, the evolu-tion has come a long way as "War and Society" and the "New Military History" have gained traction in the larger field of military history in the intervening years. The rise of non-state actors as terrorists and combatants requires that many non-military factors be added to calculations of the costs of warmaking. Similarly new scholarship introduces other considerations – the role of popular mass media on promoting militarized culture, and its subsequent influence on gender norms in society; the growing tide of intolerance on the basis of race and gender and how it shapes the contours of legitimacy in Western society – that need to be considered.[108]

---

106 See the relevant chapters in Ann-Dote Christensen and Palle Rasmussen, eds., *Masculinity, War and Violence* (Routledge, 2016); Muehlbauer and Ulbrich, *The Routledge History of Global War and Society;* Vuic, *The Routledge History of Gender, War, and the U.S. Military;* Geoffrey W. Jensen, *The Routledge Handbook of the History of Race and the American Military* (Routledge, 2016).

107 Scott, "Gender," 1053–1075, quote on 1073.

108 Examples of this new scholarship include: Joanna Bourke, *Deep Violence: Military Vio-lence, War Play, and the Social Life of Weapons* (Counterpoint, 2015) [Originally published in the UK as *Wounding the World: Hoe the Military and War-Play Invade Our Lives.* Virago, 2014]; Nicholas Githuku, *Mau Mau Crucible of War: Statehood, National Identity, and Politics of Post-colonial Kenya* (Lexington Books, 2015); Will Jackson and Emily Mantelow, eds., *Subverting Em-pires: Deviance and Disorder in the British Colonial World* (Palgrave Macmillan, 2015); Elizabeth Cobbs, *The Hello Girls: America's First Women Soldiers* (Harvard University Press, 2017); Sabine Hirschauer, *The Securitization of Rape: Women, War, and Sexual Violence* (Palgrave Macmillan,

One should always refrain from speculating about future trends in historical scholarship; after all, researchers do retain no small agency over the choices they pursue, and usually uninformed guesses and hunches end in disappointment. Nevertheless there are enough clues in the course of existing scholarship, not to mention how the growing influence and importance of the war and society field continues to attract new scholars, to make some tentative forecasts. What is causal relationship between the constructions of race and/or gender as a state-sanctioned relationship and war? How do measured continuities and/ or changes identified in race, gender, and military history provide evidence of so-called "ways of war" for non-traditional conflict (e.g.: post-Cold War globalization; decolonization, the Global War on Terror)? How do local sources help expand the analysis of gender, race, and sexuality during wars of conquest and or liberation? What are the anticipated long-term consequences of racial, ethnic, and gender integration and segregation on military institutions in this era of fluid gender identity and ethnic migration? Is militarized sexual violence becoming more frequent as the reach of international law is tested by non-state actors? As state conflict becomes increasingly digitized, either via cyber-based proxy conflict, the ascendance of lethal remotely piloted vehicles, and the appearance of new nanite-based technologies, how relevant are existing cultural gender and race-based biases and perceptions toward national defense? These are but a few possible directions for future scholar inquiries.

Rarely for better and most often for worse, war has been part of the human condition since the first people crafted crude spears and bludgeoning weapons to protect themselves from threats human and animal. Traditional notions about human nature and feminist assumptions about masculinity cannot answer questions of why wars occur. Yet, warfare can tell us much about the societies, the soldiers, and the militaries that fight them. If one is open and willing to consider factors like race, gender, culture, or sexuality, then insightful observations can be made and lessons gleaned about the past. This should in turn help understand the

---

2014); Oleg Benesch, *Inventing the Way of the Samurai: Nationalism, Internationalism, and Bushidō* (Oxford University Press, 2016); Laura Sjoberg, *Gender, War, and Conflict* (Polity, 2014); Nikhil Pal Singh, *Racism and America's Long War* (University of California Press, 2017); Carol Cohn, *Women and Wars: Contested Histories, Uncertain Futures* (Polity, 2012); Travis Morris, *Dark Ideas: How Neo-Nazi and Violent Jihad Ideologues Shaped Modern Terrorism* (Lexington, 2016); Jeremy Maxwell, *Brotherhood in Combat: How African Americans Found Equality in Korea and Vietnam* (University of Oklahoma Press, 2018); Megan MacKenzie, *Beyond the Band of Brothers: The US Military and the Myth that Women Can't Fight* (Cambridge University Press, 2015); M. Kathryn Edwards *Contesting Indochina: French Remembrance between Decolonization and Cold War* (University of California Press, 2016); Tracy Rizzo and Steven Gerontakis, *Intimate Empires: Body, Race, and Gender in the Modern World* (Oxford University Press, 2016).

present. Feminist philosopher Jean Bethke Elshtain rejects polemical assumptions by some other feminists and more traditional scholars when she concludes that, "War is productive destructiveness, not only in the sense that it shifts boundaries . . . but in a more profound sense. War creates the people. War produces power, individual and collective. War is the cultural property of people, a system of signs that we read without much effort because they have become so familiar to us."[109] Her explanation defies the usual polemics about warfare emanating from the left and the right.

Elshtain, unknowingly echoes what our entire book, and many scholars cited herein, argue. Cultural constructions of gender and race reveal much about warfare in the past and the present. Failure to account for these cultural factors limits the analytical value of military history and likewise reduces the potential success in military operations.

---

109 Elshtain, *Women and War*, 167.

Bibliography

Adams, Kevin. *Class and Race in the Frontier Army: Military Life in the West, 1870–1890*. University of Oklahoma Press, 2009.

Adams, Michael C.C. *The Best War Ever: America and World War II*. Johns Hopkins University Press, 1994.

_____. *The Great Adventure: Male Desire and the Coming of World War I*. Indiana University Press, 1990.

Adas, Michael. *Machines as the Measure of Men: Science, Technology, and Ideologies of Western Dominance*. Rutgers University Press, 1990.

Addison, Paul, and Angus Calder, eds. *Time to Kill: The Soldier's Experience of War in the West 1939–1945*. Pamlico Press, 1997.

Adelman, Jeremy, and Stephen Aron. "From Borderlands to Borders: Empires, Nation-States and the Peoples in between in North American History." *American Historical Review* 104 (June 1999): 814–41.

Adkins, Judith. "'These People are Frightened to Death': Congressional Investigations and Lavender Scare," *Prologue* 48 (Summer 2016) https://www.archives.gov/publications/prologue/2016/summer/lavender.html

Adler, Jessica L. *Burdens of War: Creating the United States Veterans Health System*. Johns Hopkins University Press, 2017.

Alexander, Joseph H. *Utmost Savagery: The Three Days at Tarawa*. Naval Institute Press, 1995.

Allen, Amy. *The End of Progress: Decolonizing the Normative Foundations of Critical Theory*. Columbia University Press, 2016.

Allen, Peter Lewis. *The Wages of Sin: Sex and Disease, Past and Present*. University of Chicago Press, 2000.

Allen, Robert L. *The Port Chicago Mutiny: The Story of the Largest Mass Mutiny Trial in U.S. Naval History*. Heyday, 2006.

Ambrose, Stephen E. *Citizen Soldiers: The U.S. Army from the Normandy Beaches to the Bulge to the Surrender of Germany*. Simon & Schuster, 1998.

_____. *D-Day: June 6, 1944, The Climactic Battle of World War II*. Simon & Schuster, 1994.

Anderson, Benedict. *Imagined Communities: Reflections on the Origin and Spread of Nationalism*. Verso, 1998.

Anderson, Bonnie S., and Judith P. Zinsser, *A History of Their Own: Women in Europe from Prehistory to the Present*. Rev. ed. New York: Oxford University Press, 1999.

Anderson, Karen, *Wartime Women: Sex Roles, Family Relations, and the Status of Women during World War II*. Praeger, 1980.

Anderson, Warwick. *Colonial Pathologies: American Tropical Medicine, Race, and Hygiene in the Philippines*. Duke University Press, 2006.

Appy, Christian G. *Working-Class War: American Combat Soldiers and Vietnam*. University of North Carolina Press, 1993.

Arnold, David. *Colonizing the Body: State Medicine and Epidemic Disease in Nineteenth Century India*. University of California Press, 1993.

Asada, Sadao. *Culture Shock and Japanese-American Relations: Historical Essays*. University of Missouri Press, 2007.

https://doi.org/10.1515/9783110477467-011

Ashcroft, Bill, et. al, *The Empire Writes Back: Theory and Practice of Colonial Literatures,* 2nd ed. Taylor and Francis, 2002.

Ashcroft, Bill, et al., eds. *The Post-Colonial Studies Reader.* 2nd ed. Routledge, 2006.

Austin, Allen. "Eastward Pioneers: Japanese American Resettlement during World War II and the Contested Meaning of Exile and Incarceration." *Journal of American Ethnic Studies* 26 (Winter 2007): 58–84.

Bacevich, Andrew. *The New American Militarism: How Americans Are Seduced by War.* Rev. ed. Oxford University Press, 2013.

Ballard, John A., and Aliecia J. McDowell. "Hate and Combat Behavior." *Armed Forces and Society* 17 (Winter 1991): 229–41

Bailey, Beth. "The Army in the Marketplace: Recruiting the All-Volunteer Force." *American Historical Review* 94 (June 2007): 47–74.

_____. *Sex in the Heartland.* Harvard University Press, 1999.

Bailey, Beth, and David Farber, "The 'Double-V' Campaign in World War II in Hawaii: African Americans, Racial Ideology, and Federal Power." *Journal of Social History* 26 (December 1993): 817–43.

Bailey, Beth, and Richard H. Immerman, eds. *Understanding the U.S. War in Iraq and Afghanistan.* New York University Press, 2015.

Barber, John, and Mark Harrison. *The Soviet Home Front, 1941–1945.* Longman, 1991.

Barbusse, Henri. *Under Fire: The Story of a Squad (Le Feu).* E.P. Dutton & Co., 1917.

Barnes, Harry Elmer. *The Genesis of the World War: An Introduction to the Problem of War Guilt.* Alfred A. Knopf, 1927.

Barnhart, Michael A. *Japan Prepares for Total War: The Search for Economic Security, 1919–1941.* Cornell University Press, 1987.

Barton, Christopher P. "Tacking Between Black and White: Race Relations in Gilded Age Philadelphia." *International Journal of Historical Archeology* 16 (December 2012): 634–50.

Bartov, Omer. *The Eastern Front, 1941–1945, German Troops and the Barbarisation of Warfare.* 2nd ed. Palgrave, 2001.

_____. *Hitler's Army: Soldiers, Nazis, and War in the Third Reich.* Oxford University Press, 1992.

Bartrop, Paul. "The Relationship between War and Genocide in the Twentieth Century: A Consideration." *Journal of Genocide Research* 4.4 (2002): 519–32.

Bates, Keith, et al., eds., *Civil Religion and American Christianity.* BorderStone, 2015.

Baxter, Peter. *Mau Mau: Kenyan Emergency, 1952–1960.* Helion, 2012.

Beard, Mary. *Women as Force in History: A Study of Traditions and Realities.* Persea Books, 1946.

Beasley, Edward. *The Victorian Reinvention of Race: New Racisms and the Problem of Grouping in the Human Sciences.* Taylor and Francis, 2010.

Bederman, Gail. *Manliness and Civilization: A Cultural History of Race and Gender in the United States, 1880–1917.* University of Chicago Press, 1997.

Benesch, Oleg. *Inventing the Way of the Samurai: Nationalism, Internationalism, and Bushidō in Modern Japanese.* Oxford University Press, 2014.

Beorn, Waitman Wade. *Marching into Darkness: The Wehrmacht and the Holocaust in Belarus.* Harvard University Press, 2014.

Berg, Manfred. "Black Civil Rights and Liberal Anticommunism: The NAACP in the Early Cold War." *American Historical Review* 94 (June 2007): 75–96

Bergman, Arlene. *Women of Vietnam.* Peoples Press, 1974.

Berkin, Carol. *First Generations: Women in Colonial America*. Hill and Wang, 1997.

Bernstein, Gail Lee, ed. *Recreating Japanese Women 1600–1945*. University of California Press, 1991.

Bickers, Robert A. *The Scramble for China: Foreign Devils in the Qing Empire, 1800–1914*. Allen Lane, 2011.

Bickers, Robert, and R. G. Teidemann, eds., *The Boxers, China, and the World*. Rowman and Littlefield, 2007.

Biddiss, Michael. *Father of Racist Ideology: The Social and Political Thought of Count Gobineau*. Weybright and Talley, 1970.

Bielakowski, Alexander M., ed., *Ethnic and Racial Minorities in the U.S. Military: An Encyclopedia*. Two Volumes. 2 vols. ABC-Clio, 2013.

Billig, Michael. *Banal Nationalism*. Sage, 1995.

Birken, Lawrence. *Consuming Desire: Sexual Science and the Emergence of a Culture of Abundance*. Columbia University Press, 1989.

_____. *Hitler as Philosophe: Remnants of the Enlightenment in National Socialism*. Praeger, 1995.

Bisbort, Alan. *Beatniks: A Guide to an American Subculture*. Greenwood, 2009.

Bischof, Günter, and Robert L. Dupont, eds. *The Pacific War Revisited*. Louisiana State University Press, 1997.

Black, Jeremy. "Determinisms and Other Issues." *Journal of Military History* 68 (October 2004): 1217–32.

_____. *Rethinking Military History*. Routledge, 2004.

_____. *War and the Cultural Turn*. Polity, 2011.

Blanton, DeAnne, and Lauren M. Cook, *They Fought Like Demons: Women Soldiers in the American Civil War*. Baton Rouge: Louisiana State University Press, 2002.

Block, Sharon. *Rape and Sexual Power in Early America*. University of North Carolina Press, 2006.

Bock, Gisela. *Women in European History*. Trans. Allison Brown. Blackwell, 2002.

Boehm, Kimberly Phillips. *War! What is it Good For?: Black Freedom Struggles and the U.S. Military from World War II to Iraq*. University of North Carolina Press, 2012.

Bogle, Lori Lyn. *The Pentagon's Battle of the American Mind: The Early Cold War*. Texas A&M University Press, 2004.

Bogousslavsky, Julien, ed., *Hysteria: The Rise of an Enigma*. Karger, 2014.

Bolton, Herbert Eugene. *The Spanish Borderlands: A Chronicle of Old Florida and the Southwest*. N.P.: 1921; Reprint, Forgotten Books, 2012.

Boot, Max. *Savage of War of Peace: Small Wars and the Rise of American Power*. Basic Books, 2002.

Borstelmann, Thomas. *Apartheid's Reluctant Uncle: The United States and Southern Africa in the Early Cold War*. Oxford University Press, 1993.

_____. *The Cold War and the Color Line: American Race Relations in the Global Arena*. Harvard University Press, 2001.

Bourke, Joanna. *Deep Violence: Military Violence, War Play, and the Socia Life of Weapons*. Counterpoint, 2015. [Originally published in the UK as *Wounding the World: Hoe the Military and War-Play Invade Our Lives*. Virago, 2014.]

_____. *Dismembering the Male: Men's Bodies, Britain, and the Great War*. University of Chicago Press, 1996.

_____. *Rape: Sex, Violence, History*. Counterpoint, 2017.

_____. *Working Class Cultures in Britain, 1890–1960: Gender, Class, and Ethnicity*. Routledge 1993.

Bourne, Stephen. *Black Poppies: Britain's Black Community and the Great War*. The History Press, 2014.

Bowers, William T., et al., *Black Soldier, White Army: The 24th Infantry Regiment in Korea*. U.S. Army Center of Military History, 1996.

Brace, C. Loring Brace. *"Race" is a Four-Letter Word*. Oxford University Press, 2005.

Brack, Gene M. "Mexican Opinion, American Racism, and the War of 1846." *Western Historical Quarterly* 1 (April 1970): 161–74.

Branch, Daniel. *Defeating Mau Mau, Creating Kenya: Counterinsurgency, Civil War and Decolonization*. Cambridge University Press, 2009.

Branch, Taylor. *At Canaan's Edge: America in the King Years, 1965–1968*. Simon and Schuster, 2007.

Brandt, Allan M. *No Magic Bullet: A Social History of Venereal Disease in the United States Since 1880*. Oxford University Press, 1987.

Braudy, Leo. *From Chivalry to Terrorism: War and the Changing Nature of Masculinity*. Vintage, 2005.

Braunstein, Peter, and Michael William Doyle, eds. *Imagine Nation: The American Counter-culture of the 1960s and 1970s*. Routledge, 2002.

Brewer, Susan A. *Why America Fights: Patriotism and Propaganda from the Philippines to Iraq*. Oxford University Press, 2009.

Bridenthal, Renate, et al. *Becoming Visible: Women in European History*. 2nd ed. Houghton Mifflin, 1987.

Bristol, Douglas Walter, Jr., and Heather Marie Stur, eds. *Integrating the U.S. Military: Race, Gender, and Sexual Orientation since World War II*. Johns Hopkins University Press, 2017.

Bristow, Nancy K. *Making Men Moral: Social Engineering During the Great War*. New York University Press, 1997.

Brittain, Vera. *Testament of Youth: An Autobiographical Study of the Years 1900–1925*. Reprint. New York: Penguin, 1994.

Brokaw, Tom. *The Greatest Generation*. Random House, 1998.

Brown, Kathleen M. *Good Wives, Nasty Wenches, and Anxious Patriarchs: Gender, Race, and Power in Colonial Virginia*. University of North Carolina Press, 1996.

Browne, Kingsley. *Co-Ed Combat: The New Evidence that Women Shouldn't Fight the Nation's Wars*. Sentinel, 2007.

Browning, Christopher R. *Ordinary Men: Reserve Police Battalion 101 and the Final Solution in Poland*. HarperPerennial, 1992.

Brownmiller, Susan. *Against Our Will: Men, Women and Rape*. Fawcett Columbine, 1975.

Buttar, Prit. *Germany Ascendant: The Eastern Front 1915*. Osprey, 2015.

Burg, B.R. *Gay Warriors: A Documentary History from the Ancient World to the Present*. New York University Press, 2002.

Burge, Stefan, and Chris Lorenz, eds. *Nationalizing the Past: Historians as Nation Builders in Modern Europe*. Palgrave Macmillan, 2010.

Burke, Carol. *Camp All-American, Hanoi Jane, and the High-and-Tight*. Beacon Press, 2004.

Bussey, Charles M. *Firefight at Yechon: Courage and Racism in the Korean War*. University of Nebraska Press, 2002.

Butler, Judith. *Gender Trouble: Feminism and the Subversion of Identity*. Routledge, 1990.

Callimachi, Rukmini. "ISIS Enshrines A Theology of Rape." *New York Times*. August 13, 2015. https://www.nytimes.com/2015/08/14/world/middleeast/isis-enshrines-a-theology-of-rape.html.

Calloway, Colin G. *New Worlds for All: Indians, Europeans, and the Remaking of Early America*. Johns Hopkins University Press, 1997.

Cameron, Craig M. *American Samurai: Myth, Imagination, and the Conduct of Battle in the First Marine Division, 1941–1951*. Cambridge University Press, 1994.

Campbell, D'Ann. *Woman at War with America: Private Lives in a Patriotic Era*. Harvard University Press, 1984.

————. "Women in Combat: The World War II Experience in the United States, Great Britain, Germany, and the Soviet Union." *Journal of Military History* 57 (April 1993): 301–323.

Canada ALPHA. "Rape of Nanking." http://www.alpha-canada.org/testimonies/about-the-rape-of-nanking.

Canaday, Margot. *The Straight State: Sexuality and Citizenship in Twentieth-Century America*. Princeton University Press, 2009.

Carnes, Mark C., and Clyde Griffen, eds., *Meanings for Manhood: Constructions of Masculinity in Victorian America*. University of Chicago Press, 1990.

Carney, Amy. *Marriage and Fatherhood in the Nazi SS*. University of Toronto Press, 2018.

Carruthers, Susan. *The Good Occupation: American Soldiers and the Hazards of Peace*. Harvard University Press, 2016.

Cecil, Hugh, and Peter Liddle, eds. *Facing Armageddon: The First World War Experienced*. Leo Cooper, 1996.

Central Intelligence Agency. "The Kitchen Debate – Transcript." July 24, 1959. https://www.cia.gov/library/readingroom/docs/1959-07-24.pdf .

Chang, Iris. *Rape of Nanking: The Forgotten Holocaust of World War II*. Penguin Books, 1997.

Charles, Daniel. *Master Mind: The Rise and Fall of Fritz Haber, the Nobel Laureate Who Launched the Age of Chemical Warfare*. Ecco, 2005.

Chatterjee, Partha. *The Partha Chatterjee Omnibus: Nationalist Thought and the Colonial World, The Nation and its Fragments, A Possible India*. Oxford University Press, 2008.

Chauncey, George. *Gay New York: Gender, Urban Culture, and the Making of the Gay Male World, 1890–1940*. Basic Books, 1994.

Checkland, Olive. *Humanitarianism and the Emperor's Japan, 1877–1977*. St. Martin's Press, 1994.

Cherry, Bruce. *They Didn't Want to Die Virgins: Sex and Morale in the British Army on the Western Front, 1914–1918*. Helion & Company, 2016.

Chickering, Roger, et al., eds. *War and the Modern War*. Vol. 4. *The Cambridge History of Modern War*. Cambridge University Press, 2012.

Christensen, Ann-Dote, and Palle Rasmussen, eds., *Masculinity, War and Violence*

Citino, Robert M. "Military Histories Old and New: A Reintroduction." *American Historical Review* 112 (October 2007): 1070–1090.

Clark, Alan. *The Donkeys: A Controversial Account of the Leaders of the British Expeditionary Forces in France, 1915*. Morrow, 1962.

Cobbs, Elizabeth. *The Hello Girls: America's First Women Soldiers*. Harvard University Press, 2017.

Cockburn, Cynthia. "Gender Relations as Casual in Militarization and War: A Feminist Standpoint." *International Feminist Journal of Politics* 12 (2010): 139–57.

"Code of Dishonor." *Vanity Fair*. November 6, 2006. https://www.vanityfair.com/news/2003/12/airforce200312.

Coffman, Edward M. "The New American Military History." *Military Affairs* 48 (January 1984): 1–5.

Cohen, Deborah. *The War Come Home: Disabled Veterans in Britain and Germany, 1914–1939.* University of California Press, 2001.

Cohn, Carol ed. *Women and Wars: Contested Histories, Uncertain Futures.* Polity, 2012.

Cole, Sarah. *Modernism, Male Friendship, and the First World War.* Cambridge University Press, 2003.

Collar, Peter. *The Propaganda War in the Rhineland: Weimar Germany, Race and Occupation after World War I.* I. B. Tauris, 2013.

Colley, Linda. *Britons: Forging the Nation, 1707–1837.* Rev. ed. Yale University Press, 2009.

Colley, David. *Blood for Dignity: The Story of the First Integrated Combat Unit in the U.S. Army.* St. Martin's Griffin, 2004.

Collingham, Lizzie. *The Taste of War: World War II and the Battle for Food.* Penguin Books, 2011.

Conners, Paul. "Gang Members: No Place for You in the Guard." *Guardlife* (January 2007). http://www.state.nj.us/military/publications/guardlife/volume32no6/10.html.

Cook, Theodore, and Haruko Cook, eds. *Japan at War: An Oral History.* The New Press, 1992.

Cooper, Frederick, and Ann Laura Stoler, *Tensions of Empire: Colonial Cultures in a Bourgeois World.* University of California Press, 1997.

Cope, Robert S. *Carry Me Back: Slavery and Servitude in Seventeenth Century Virginia.* Pikeville College Press of the Appalachian Studies Center, 1973.

Cosmas, Graham A. *An Army for Empire: The United States Army in the Spanish-American War.* Texas A&M University Press, 1998.

Costogliola, Frank. "'Unceasing Pressure for Penetration': Gender, Pathology, and George Kennan's Formation of the Cold War." *Journal of American History* 84 (March 1997): 1309–1339.

Cottam, Kazimiera J. "Soviet Women in Combat in World War II: The Ground Forces and the Navy." *International Journal of Women's Studies* 3 (July-August 1980): 345–57.

Crook, Paul. *Darwinism, War, and History.* Cambridge University Press, 1994.

Crosby, Alfred. *The Columbian Exchange, Biological and Cultural Consequences of 1492.* Greenwood, 2003.

Crouthamel, Jason. *An Intimate History of the Front: Masculinity, Sexuality, and German Soldiers in the First World War.* Palgrave Macmillan, 2014.

Crowe, David M. *The Holocaust: Roots, History, and Aftermath.* Westview Press, 2008.

Cuordileone, K.A. *Manhood and America: Political Culture in the Cold War.* Routledge, 2005.

Curtin, Philip D. *Disease and Empire: The Health of European Troops in the Conquest of Africa.* Cambridge University Press, 1998.

Mary. *Gyn/Ecology: The Metaethics of Radical Feminism.* Beacon Press, 1978.

Daniel, Uta. *The War from Within: German Working-Class Women in the First World War.* Berg, 1997.

Daniels, Daniel. *The Japanese American Cases: The Rule of Law in the Time of War.* Lawrence: University Press of Kansas, 2013.

Darrow, Margaret H. *French Women and the First World War: War Stories from the Home Front.* Bloomsbury Academic, 2000.

Darwin, John. Lecture. "Decolonization: A History of Failure?" July 13, 2011. Library of Congress Kluge Center. http://www.loc.gov/today/cyberlc/feature_wdesc.php?rec=5246

David, Saul. *The Indian Mutiny.* Penguin Books, 2003.

Davis, Belinda J. *Home Fires Burning: Food, Politics, and Everyday Life in World War I Berlin.* University of North Carolina Press, 2000.

Davis, John W. "The Negro in the United States Navy, Marine Corps, and Coast Guard." *Journal of Negro Education* 12 (Summer 1943): 347–48.

Dawson, Graham. *Soldier Heroes: British Adventure, Empire and the Imagining of Masculinities.* Routledge, 1994.

de Beauvoir, Simon. *The Second Sex.* Trans. H. M. Parshley. Reprint, 1949; Knopf, 1953.

de Brouwer, Anne-Marie, and Sandra Ka Hon Chu, eds., *The Men Who Killed Me: Rwandan Survivors of Sexual Violence.* Douglas and McIntyre, 2013.

De Pauw, Linda Grant. *Battlecries and Lullabies: Women in War from Prehistory to the Present.* University of Oklahoma Press, 1998.

Dean, Eric T., Jr. *Shook over Hell: Post-Traumatic Stress, Vietnam, and the Civil War.* Harvard University Press, 1999.

Dean, Robert D. *Imperial Brotherhood: Gender and the Marking of Cold Foreign Policy.* University of Massachusetts Press, 2001.

"Declaration of Causes of Seceding States." Civil War Trust. https://www.civilwar.org/learn/primary-sources/declaration-causes-seceding-states

DeGroot, Gerard J. *Blighty: British Society in the Era of the Great War.* Longman, 1996.

Dendooven, Dominiek, and Piet Chielens. *World War I: Five Continents in Flanders.* Lannoo, 2008.

Dennis, Routledge M. "Social Darwinism, Scientific Racism, and the Metaphysics of Race." *Journal of Negro Education* 64 (Summer 1995): 243–52.

DeRosa, Christopher S. *Political Indoctrination in the U.S. Army from World War II to the Vietnam War.* University of Nebraska Press, 2006.

Despatino, Todd. *Citizen Hobo: How a Century of Homelessness Shaped America.* University of Chicago Press, 2003.

Diamond, Jared. *Guns, Germs, and Steel: The Fates of Human Societies.* W.W. Norton & Company, 1997.

Dighton, Adam. "Race, Masculinity, and Imperialism: The British Officer and the Egyptian Army, 1882–1899." *War and Society* 35 (February 2016): 1–18.

Dombrowski, Nicole Ann, ed. *Woman and War in the Twentieth Century: Enlisted With or Without Consent.* Garland, 1999.

Donaldson, Laura E. *Decolonizing Feminisms: Race, Gender, and Empire-Building.* University of North Carolina Press, 1992

Dobak, William A. *Freedom by the Sword: The U.S. Colored Troops, 1862–1867.* Skyhorse Publishing, 2013.

Dolski, Michael R. *D-Day Remembered: The Normandy Landings in American Collective Memory.* University of Tennessee Press, 2016.

Dorinson, Joseph, and William Pencak, eds. *Paul Roberson: Essays on His Life and Legacy.* McFarland, 2002.

Doubler, Michael D. *Closing with the Enemy: How GIs Fought the War in Europe, 1944–1945.* University Press of Kansas, 1994.

Doughty, Robert A. *Pyrrhic Victory: French Strategy and Operations in the Great War.* Belknap Press, 2005.

Dower, John. *War Without Mercy: Race and Power in the Pacific War.* Pantheon, 1987.

Drea, Edward, et al., *Researching Japanese War Crimes Records: Introductory Essay.* Nazi War Crimes and Japanese Imperial Government Records Interagency Working Groups. National Archives and Records Administration, 2006.

"Drill Sergeant Gets 6 Months For Sex Abuse at Army Post." *The New York Times.* May 31, 1997. http://query.nytimes.com/gst/fullpage.html?res=9C01E7DF1E3AF932A05756C0A961958260

Duara, Prasenjit. "The Discourse of Civilization and Decolonization." *Journal of World History* 15 (2004): 1–5.

Dubois, W.E.B., *A W.E.B. DuBois Reader.* Ed. Andrew G. Paschal. Macmillan, 1971.

Dundink, Stefan, et al., eds. *Masculinities in Politics and War: Gendering Modern History.* Manchester University Press, 2004.

Duus, Peter, and Kenji Hasegawa, eds. *Rediscovering America: Japanese Perspectives on the American Century.* University of California Press, 2011.

Dyer, Theodore G. *Theodore Roosevelt and the Idea of Race.* Louisiana State University Press, 1980.

Earhart, David C. *Certain Victory: Images of World War II in the Japanese Media.* Routledge, 2007.

Eckstein, Modris. *Rites of Spring: The Great War and the Birth of the Modern Age.* Houghton Mifflin, 1989.

Edgerton, Robert B. *Mau Mau: An African Crucible.* I.B. Taurus, 1990.

Edwards, M. Kathryn. *Contesting Indochina: French Remembrance between Decolonization and Cold War.* University of California Press, 2016.

Ehrenreich, Barbara. *Blood Rites: Origins and History of the Passions of War.* Metropolitan, 1998.

Ehlert, Hans, et al., eds., *The Schlieffen Plan: International Perspectives on the German Strategy for World War I.* University Press of Kentucky, 2014.

Eliav-Feldon, Meriam, et al., eds. *The Origins of Racism in the West.* Cambridge University Press, 2009.

Elkins, Caroline. *British Gulag: The Brutal End of Empire in Kenya.* Cape, 2005.

Ellis, David. *The Rise of African Slavery in the Americas.* Cambridge University Press, 2000.

Elshtain, Jean Bethke. *Women and War.* Basic Books, 1987.

Ely, H.E. *The Use of Negro Man Power in War.* U.S. Army War College. October 30, 1925. Memorandum to the Army Chief of Staff. Franklin D. Roosevelt Presidential Library and Museum. http://www.fdrlibrary.marist.edu/TCGui.pdf

Emory University, "Postcolonial Studies @ Emory" https://scholarblogs.emory.edu/postcoloni-alstudies/about-postcolonial-studies/.

"Employment of negro man power in war." November 10, 1925. AWC 127–25. Franklin Delano Roosevelt Library. https://fdrlibrary.org/documents/...doc.../4693156a-8844-4361-ae17-03407e7a3dee

Ender, Morten G. et al., "Research Note: Cadet and Civilian Undergraduate Attitudes toward Transgender People." *Armed Forces and Society* 41 (April 2016): 427–35.

Engel, Barbara Alpern. "Women in Russia and the Soviet Union." *Signs* 12:4 (Summer 1987): 781–796.

Enloe, Cynthia H. *Does Khaki Become You? The Militarization of Women's Lives.* South End Press, 1983.

_____. *Maneuvers: The International Politics of Militarizing Women's Lives.* University of California Press, 1997.

Ensign, Tod, ed. *America's Military Today: The Challenge of Militarism.* The New Press, 2004.

Erickson, Edward J. *Ordered to Die: A History of the Ottoman Army in the First World War.* Greenwood Press, 2001.

Essig, Laura. *Queer in Russia: A Story of Sex, Self, and the Other.* Duke University Press, 1999/

Evans, Andrew D. *Anthropology and War: World War I and the Science of Race in Germany.* University of Chicago Press, 2010.

Evans, Richard J. *The Third Reich at War.* Penguin Press, 2009.

Faludi, Susan. *Stiffed: The Betrayal of the American Man.* William Morrow, 1999.

Fanon, Frantz. *Black Skin, White Masks.* Grove Press, 1998.

Faulkner, Richard S. *Pershing's Crusaders: The American Soldier in World War I.* University Press of Kansas, 2017.

Fein, Helen. "Genocide and Gender: The Uses of Women and Group Identity." *Journal of Genocide Research* 1 (1999): 43–63.

Ferrante, Joan, and Prince Brown Jr., eds. *The Social Construction of Race and Ethnicity in the United States.* Longman, 1998.

Fieseler, B. et al., "Gendering Combat: Military Women's Status in Britain, the United States, and the Soviet Union." *Women's Studies International Forum* 47 (November-December 2014): 115–126.

Fogel, Joshua, ed. *The Nanjing Massacre in History and Historiography.* University of California Press, 2000.

Fogarty, Richard S. *Race & War in France: Colonial Subjects in the French Army, 1914–1918.* Johns Hopkins University Press, 2008.

Foner, Eric, ed. *The New American History.* Rev. ed. Temple University Press, 1997.

Foos, Paul. *A Short, Offhand, Killing Affair: Soldiers and Social Conflict during the Mexican-American War.* University of North Carolina Press, 2005.

Foote, Lorien. *The Gentlemen and the Roughs: Violence, Honor, and Manhood in the Union Army.* New York University Press, 2011.

Frader, Laure L., and Sonya O. Rose, eds. *Gender and Class in Modern Europe.* Cornell University Press, 1996.

Frantzen, Allen J. *Bloody Good: Chivalry, Sacrifice, and the Great War.* University of Chicago Press, 2004.

Frederick, Sharon. *Rape: Women and Terror.* Association of Women for Action and Research, 2001.

Frederickson, George. *Racism: A Short History.* Princeton University Press, 2002.

Friedan, Betty. *The Feminine Mystique.* Norton, 1963.

Friend, Craig Thompson. *Southern Masculinity: Perspectives on Manhood in the South since Reconstruction.* University of Georgia Press, 2009.

Fuller, Clark W. Interview by Steven Brown. July 11, 2008. Transcription. Cantigny First Division Oral History Project. Ball State University Digital Media Repository. http://libx.bsu.edu/cdm/ref/collection/CtgnyOrHis/id/48.

Fussell, Paul. *The Boys' Crusade: The American Infantry in Northwestern Europe, 1944–1945.* Modern Library, 2005.

_____. *The Great War and Modern Memory.* Oxford University Press, 1976.

_____. *Wartime: Understanding and Behavior in the Second World War.* Oxford University Press, 1990.

Gaddis, John Lewis. *Strategies of Containment: A Critical Appraisal of Postwar American National Security.* Oxford University Press, 1982.

Gates, G.J., and J.L. Herman, "Transgender in the Military Service of the United States" (2014). The Williams Institute. https://williamsinstitute.law.ucla.edu/wp-content/uploads/Transgender-Military-Service-May-2014.pdf

Gatewood, William B. , Jr. *Smoked Yankees and the Struggle for Empire: Letters from Negro Soldiers, 1898–1902.* University of Illinois Press, 1971.

Gellately R., and B. Kiernan, eds., *The Spector of Genocide: Mass Murder in Historical Perspective.* Cambridge University Press, 2003.

Genesis (New International Version).

Gerstle, Gary. *American Crucible: Race and Nation in the 20th Century*. Princeton University Press, 2001.

Gerwatch, Robert, and Erez Manela, eds., *Empires at War: 1911–1923*. Oxford University Press, 2014.

Getz, Trevor R., and Heather Streets-Salter. *Modern Imperialism and Colonialism: A Global Perspective*. Prentice Hall, 2011.

Giangreco, D.M. *Hell to Pay: Operation DOWNFALL and the Invasion of Japan, 1945–1947*. Naval Institute Press, 2011.

Gilbert, James. *Masculinity in the Middle: Searching for Masculinity in the 1950s*. University of Chicago Press, 2005.

Gilder Lehrman Institute of American History. "History Now: Historical Context: Facts about the Slave Trade and Slavery." https://www.gilderlehrman.org/content/historical-context-facts-about-slave-trade-and-slavery.

Gilmore, Glenda. *Gender and Jim Crow: Women and the Politics of White Supremacy in North Carolina, 1896–1920*. University of North Carolina Press, 1992.

Ginio, Ruth. *The French Army and Its African Soldiers: The Years of Decolonization*. University of Nebraska Press, 2017.

Ginzburg, Benjamin. *The Adventure of Science*. Simon & Schuster, 1931.

Githuku, Nicholas. *Mau Mau Crucible of War: Statehood, National Identity, and Politics of Postcolonial Kenya*. Lexington Books, 2015.

Goldberg, Suzanne B. "Open Service and Our Allies: A Report on the Inclusion of Openly Gay and Lesbian Servicemembers in U.S. Allies' Armed Forces." *William & Mary Journal of Women & Law* 17 (2011): 547–90.

Goldhagen, Daniel Jonah. *Hitler's Willing Executioners: Ordinary Germans and the Holocaust*. Vintage, 1997.

Goldstein, Joshua S. *War and Gender: How Gender Shapes the War System and Vice Versa*. Cambridge University Press, 2001.

Goldstein, Phyllis. *A Convenient Hatred: The History of Antisemitism*. Facing History and Ourselves National Foundation, 2012.

Grady, Tim. *A Deadly Legacy: German Jews and the Great War*. Yale University Press, 2017.

Graham III, Herman. *The Brothers' Vietnam: Black Power, Manhood, and the Military Experience*. University of Florida Press, 2003.

Gramsci, Antonio. *Prison Notebooks*. Columbia University Press, 1992.

Graves, Joseph L. *The Emperor's New Clothes: Biological Theories of Race at the Millennium*. Rutgers University Press, 2003.

Gray, J. Glenn. *The Warriors: Reflections on Men in Battle*. Harcourt, Brace, and Company, 1959.

Greenberg, Amy S. *Manifest Manhood and the Antebellum American Empire*. Cambridge University Press, 2005.

_____. *A Wicked War: Polk, Clay, Lincoln, and the 1846 U.S. Invasion of Mexico*. Alfred A. Knopf, 2012.

Grenier, John. *The First Way of War: American War Making on the Frontier, 1607–1814*. Cambridge University Press, 2005.

Griffin, Roger, ed. *Fascism*. Oxford University Press, 1995.

Griswold, Robert L. *Fatherhood in America: A History*. New York: Basic Books, 1993.

Grow, Michael. *U.S. Presidents and Latin American Interventions: Pursuing Regime Change in the Cold War*. University Press of Kansas, 2008.

Guha, Ranajit. *Elementary Aspects of Peasant Insurgency in Colonial India*. Oxford University Press, 1983.

Gullace, Nicoletta F. "Sexual Violence and Family Honor: British Propaganda and International Law during the First World War." *American Historical Review* 102 (June 1997): 714–47.

Gump, James. *The Dust Rose Like Smoke: The Subjugation of the Zulu and the Sioux*. University of Nebraska Press, 1994.

Gutman, Herbert. *Work, Culture, and Society*. Vintage, 1977.

Gutmann, Stephanie. *The Kindler, Gentler Military: How Political Correctness Affects Our Ability to Win Wars*. Encounter Books, 2000.

Haber, L.F. *The Poisonous Cloud: Chemical Warfare in the First World War*. Clarendon Press, 1986.

Habermas, Jurgen. *The Structural Transformation of the Public Sphere: An Inquiry into a Category of Bourgeois Society*. MIT Press, 1991.

Hagemann, Karen, "Women's War Service in the Two World Wars." *Journal of Military History* 75 (October 2011): 1060–73.

Hagemann, Karen, and Stefanie Schüler-Springorum, eds., *Home/Front: The Military, War and Gender in Twentieth Century Germany*. Berg, 2002.

Halberstam, David. *The Coldest Winter: America and the Korean War*. Hyperion Books, 2007.

Halberstam, Judith. *Female Masculinity*. Duke University Press, 1998.

Hannaford, Ivan. *Race: The History of an Idea in the West*. Johns Hopkins University Press, 1996.

Hanson, Victor Davis. *Carnage and Culture: Landmark Battles in the Rise of Western Power*. Doubleday, 2001.

Hapke, Laura. *Daughters of the Great Depression: Women, Work, and Fiction in the American 1930s*. University of Georgia Press, 1995.

Harrell, Margaret C. *New Opportunities for Military Women: Effects Upon Readiness, Cohesion, and Moral*. RAND Corporation, 1997.

Harris, J. P. *Sir Douglas Haig and the First World War*. Cambridge University Press, 2008.

Harrison, Forrest M. "Psychiatry in the Navy." *War Medicine* 3 (February 1943): 114–37

Harrison, Mark. *Public Health in British India: Anglo-Indian Preventive Medicine, 1857–1914*. Cambridge University Press, 1994.

Harrison, Simon. "Skull Trophies of the Pacific War: Transgressive Objects of Remembrance" *Journal of the Royal Anthropological Society* 12 (2006): 817–36.

Hart, Peter. *The Great War, 1914–1918*. Profile Books, 2014.

Hartman, Susan H. *The Home Front and Beyond: American Women in the 1940s*. Twayne, 1984.

Headrick, Daniel R. *Power Over Peoples: Technology, Environment, and Western Imperialism, 1400 to the Present*. Princeton University Press, 2010.

_____. *The Tools of Empire: Technology and European Imperialism in the Nineteenth Century*. Oxford University Press, 1981.

Healey, Dan, "Masculine Purity and 'Gentlemen's Mischief': Sexual Exchange and Prostitution between Russian Men, 1861–1941." *Slavic Review* 60 (Summer 2001): 233–65.

Hegar, Mary Jennings. *Shoot Like a Girl: One Woman's Dramatic Fight in Afghanistan and on the Home Front*. New American Library, 2017.

Hegarty, Marilyn. *Victory Girls, Khaki-Wackies, and Patriotutes: The Regulation of Female Sexuality during World War II*. New York University Press, 2008.

Heinrichs, Waldo. and Marc Gallichio, *Implacable Foes: War in the Pacific, 1944–1945*. Oxford University Press, 2017.

Heller, Joseph. *Catch-22*. Simon & Schuster, 1981.

Henderson, William Darryl. *Why the Viet Cong Fought: A Study of Motivation and Control in Combat.* Greenwood, 1979.

Henrickson, Margot A. *Dr. Sranglove's America: Society and Culture in the Atomic Age.* University of California Press, 1987.

Herbert, Melissa S. *Camouflage isn't Only for Combat: Gender, Sexuality, and Women in the Military* New York University Press, 1998.

Herf, Jeffrey. *Reactionary Modernism: Technology, Culture, and Politics in Weimar and the Third Reich.* Cambridge University Press, 1986.

Herring, George. *America's Longest War: The United States and Vietnam, 1950–1975.* 4th ed. McGraw-Hill, 2002.

Herwig, Holger H. *The First World War: Germany and Austria-Hungary, 1914–1918.* Arnold, 1997.

_____. *The Marne, 1914: The Opening of World War I and the Battle that Changed the World.* Random House, 2011.

Herzog, Dagmar, ed. *Brutality and Desire: War and Sexuality in Europe's Twentieth Century.* Palgrave Macmillan, 2009, 2011

Herzog, Dagmar. *Sexuality in Europe: A Twentieth-Century History.* Cambridge University Press, 2011.

Higonnet, Margaret, et al., eds. *Behind the Lines: Gender and the Two World Wars.* Yale University Press, 1987.

Hirshauer, Sabine. *The Securitization of Rape: Women, War, and Sexual Violence.* Palgrave Macmillan, 2014.

Hobson, John A. *Imperialism: A Study.* George Allen & Unwin, 1902, 1905. Reprint. Cosimo Classics, 2005.

Hochschild, Adam. *King Leopold's Ghost: A Story of Greed, Terror, and Heroism in Colonial Africa.* Houghton Mifflin, 1999.

Hofstadter, Richard. *Social Darwinism in American Thought.* University of Pennsylvania Press, 1944.

Hoganson, Kristin L. *Fighting for American Manhood: How Gender Politics Provoked the Spanish-American and Philippine-American Wars.* Yale University Press, 1998.

Holcomb, Thomas. Personal Papers Collection. Marine Corps University Archives. Quantico, Virginia.

Holm, Jeanne. *Women in Combat: The New Reality.* Wadsworth, 1996.

Holmes, Richard. *Soldiers: Army Lives and Loyalties from Redcoats to Dusty Warriors.* Harper Press, 2011.

_____. *Tommy: The British Soldier on the Western Front, 1914–1918.* HarperCollins, 2004.

hooks, bell, and Amelia Mesa-Bains. *Homegrown: Engaged Cultural Criticism.* South End Press, 2006.

Hopkins, Donald R. *The Greatest Killer: Smallpox in History.* University of Chicago Press, 1983.

Horne, Gerald. *Race War !: White Supremacy and the Japanese Attack on the British Empire.* New York University Press, 2003.

Horne, John, and Alan Kramer. *German Atrocities 1914: A History of Denial.* Yale University Press, 2000.

Horsman, Reginald. *Race and Manifest Destiny: Origins of American Racial Anglo-Saxonism.* Rev. ed. Harvard University Press, 1981.

Hosek, Susan D., et. al, *Minority and Gender Differences in Officer Career Progression.* RAND Corporation, 2001.

Howe, Glenford. *Race War and Nationalism: A Social History of West Indians in the First World War*. Ian Randle Publishers, 2002.

Huebner, Andrew S. *Love and Death in the Great War*. Oxford University Press, 2018.

_____. *The Warrior Image: Soldiers in American Culture from the Second World War to the Vietnam Era*. University of North Carolina Press, 2011.

Hughes, Matthew. and William J. Philpott, eds, *Palgrave Advances in Modern Military History*. Palgrave McMillan, 2006.

Hull, Isabel. *Absolute Destruction: Military Culture and the Practices of War in Imperial Germany*. Cornell University Press, 2006.

Human Rights Watch/Africa. *Shattered Lives: Sexual Violence during the Rwandan Genocide and its Aftermath*. Human Rights Watch, 1996.

Hunt, Michael H. *Lyndon Johnson's War: American Cold War Crusade in Vietnam, 1945–1968*. Hill and Wang, 1996.

Huntington, Samuel P. *The Clash of Civilizations and the Remaking of World Order*. Simon & Schuster, 1996.

Hurtado, Albert L. *Herbert Eugene Bolton: Historian of the American Borderlands*. University of California Press, 2012.

Hutchinson, John. *Champions of Charity: War and the Rise of the Red Cross*. Routledge, 1997.

Hyde, Anne F. *Empires, Nations, and Families: A History of the North American West, 1800–1860*. University of Nebraska Press, 2011.

Imperial War Museum. "Nine Women Reveal the Dangers of Working in a Munitions Factory." https://www.iwm.org.uk/history/9-women-reveal-the-dangers-of-working-in-a-first-world-war-munitions-factory.

Janicki, David A. "The British Blockade During World War I: The Weapon of Deprivation." *Inquiries Journal: Social Sciences, Arts, & Humanities* 6:6 (2014). http://www.inquiriesjournal.com/articles/899/the-british-blockade-during-world-war-i-the-weapon-of-deprivation.

Jackson, John P., and Nadine M. Weidman, eds. *Race. Racism, and Science: Social Impact and Interaction*. Rutgers University Press, 2005.

Jackson, Kenneth T. *Crabgrass Frontier: The Suburbanization of the United States,* Oxford University Press, 1987.

Jackson, Will, and Emily Mantelow, eds., *Subverting Empires: Deviance and Disorder in the British Colonial World*. Palgrave Macmillan, 2015.

Jansen, Jan C., and Jürgen Osterhammel, *Decolonization: A Short History*. Trans. Jeremiah Riemer. Rev. ed. Princeton University Press, 2017. [Originally published in Germany as *Dekolonisation*. Verlag C.H. Beck, 2013.]

Jarvis, Christina S. *The Male Body at War: American Masculinity during World War II*. Northern Illinois University Press, 2004.

Jensen, Geoffrey W., ed., *The Routledge Handbook of the History of Race and the American Military*. Routledge, 2016.

Jensen, Kimberly. *Mobilizing Minerva: American Women in the First World War*. University of Illinois Press, 2008.

Johnson, David K. *The Lavender Scare: The Cold War Persecutions of Gays and Lesbians in the Federal Government*. University of Chicago Press, 2004.

Jones, Howard. *My Lai, 1968, and the Descent into Darkness*. Oxford University Press, 2017.

Jones, James H. *Alfred C. Kinsey: A Public/Private Life*. W.W. Norton, 1997.

Jones, John Bush. *Songs That Fought the War: Popular Music and the Home Front, 1939–1945*. Brandeis University Press, 2006.

Joseph, Gilbert, and Catherine C. LeGrand, eds. *Close Encounters of Empire: Writing the Cultural History of U.S.-Latin American Relations*. Duke University Press, 1998.

Jünger, Sebastien. *War*. Twelve, 2010.

Kaplan, Amy. "Romancing the Empire: The Embodiment of American Masculinity in the Popular Historical Novel of the 1890s." *American Literary History* 4 (Winter 1990): 659–90.

Karlin, Jason G. "The Gender of Nationalism: Competing Masculinities in Meiji Japan." *Journal of Japanese Studies* 28 (Winter 2002): 41–7.

Karsten, Peter, ed. *The Military in America: From the Colonial Era to the Present*. Rev. ed. Free Press, 1986.

Karsten, Peter. "The 'New' American Military History: A Map of the Territory, Explored and Unexplored." *American Quarterly* 36 (1984): 389–418.

Kaufman, Jesse. *Elusive Alliance: The German Occupation of Poland in World War I*. Harvard University Press, 2015.

Kay, Alex, et al., eds., *Nazi Policy on the Eastern Front, 1941: Total War, Genocide, and Radicalization*. University of Rochester Press, 2012.

Keegan, John. *The Face of Battle: A Study of Agincourt, Waterloo, and The Somme*. Penguin, 1976.

Keene, Jennifer. *World War I: The American Soldier Experience*. University of Nebraska Press, 2011.

Kennard, Matt. "Neo-Nazis are in the Army Now." June 15, 2009. https://www.theinvestigativefund.org/investigation/2009/06/15/neo-nazis-are-in-the-army-now/

Kennedy, David M. *Over Here: The First World War and American Society*. Reprint. Oxford University Press, 2004.

Kerber, Linda K. "The Meanings of Citizenship." *Journal of American History* 84 (December 1997): 833–54.

Kiernan, Ben. *The Pol Pot Regime: Race, Power, and Genocide in Cambodia under the Khmer Rouge, 1975–79*. Yale University Press, 1996.

Kimmel, Michael Kimmel. *Manhood in America: A Cultural History*. The Free Press, 1996.

Kinder, John M. *Paying with Their Bodies: American War and the Problem of the Disabled Veteran*. University of Chicago Press, 2015.

Kindsvatter, Peter S. *American Soldiers: Ground Combat in the World Wars, Korea, and Vietnam*. University Press of Kansas, 2003.

Kinsey, Alfred, et al., *Sexual Behavior of the Human Female*. W.B. Saunders, 1953.

_____. *Sexual Behavior of the Human Male*. W.B. Saunders, 1948.

Kinzer, Stephen. *The True Flag: Theodore Roosevelt, Mark Twain, and the Birth of American Empire*. Henry Holt and Company, 2017.

Kissi, Edward. "The Holocaust as a Guidepost for Genocide Detection and Prevention in Africa." *The Holocaust and the United Nations Outreach Program Discussion Papers Journal* (2009): 45–55.

_____. "Rwanda, Ethiopia, and Cambodia: Links, Fault Lines and Complexities in a Comparative Study of Genocide." *Journal of Genocide Research* 6 (March 2004): 115–33.

Klein, Christina. *Cold War Orientalism: Asia in the Middlebrow Imagination, 1945–1961*. University of California Press, 2003.

Klinek, Eric. "The Army's Orphans: The United States Army Replacement System in the European Campaign, 1944–1945." Ph.D. diss., Temple University, 2014.

Knaft, Donna B. *Beyond Rosie the Riveter: Women of World War II in American Popular Graphic Art*. University Press of Kansas, 2012.

Kohn, Richard H. "The Social History of the American Soldier: A Review and Prospectus for Research." *American Historical Review* 86 (June 1981): 553–67.

Koonz, Claudia. *Mothers in the Fatherland: Women, the Family, and Nazi Politics*. St. Martin's Press, 1987.

Kramer, Alan. *Dynamic of Destruction: Culture and Mass Killing in the First World War*. Oxford University Press, 2007.

Kramer, Lloyd S. *Nationalism in Europe and America: Politics, Cultures, and Identities since 1775*. University of North Carolina Press, 2011.

Kramer, Paul A. "Race-Making and Colonial Violence in the U.S. Empire: The Philippine-American War as Race War." *Diplomatic History* 30 (April 2006): 169–210.

Kren, George M., and Leo Rappaport, *The Holocaust and the Crisis of Human Behavior*. Rev. ed. Holmes & Meier, 1994.

Kryder, Daniel. *Divided Arsenal: Race and the American State During World War II*. Cambridge University Press, 2001.

Krylova, Anna. *Soviet Women in Combat: A History of Violence on the Eastern Front*. Cambridge University Press, 2010.

Kuhl, Stefan. *The Nazi Connection: Eugenics, American Racism, and German National Socialism*. Oxford University Press, 2002.

Kusmer, Kenneth L. *Down and Out, On the Road: The Homeless in American History*. Oxford University Press, 2002.

Kwon, Heonik, *The Other Cold War*. Columbia University Press, 2010.

Laqueur, Walter, ed. *Fascism, A Reader's Guide: Analyses, Interpretations, Bibliography*. University of California Press, 1976.

Larson, Jason. *Greek and Roman Sexualities: A Sourcebook*. Bloomsbury, 2012.

Last, Dick van Galen, with Ralf Futselaar. *Black Shame: African Soldiers in Europe, 1914–1922*. Trans. Marjolijn de Jager. Bloomsbury, 2015.

Le Sueur, James D. ed., *The Decolonization Reader*. Routledge, 2003.

Leahy, William D. *I Was There*. McGraw-Hill, 1950.

Lee, Wayne E. *Barbarians and Brothers: Anglo-American Warfare, 1500–1865*. Oxford University Press, 2010.

_____. *Waging War: Conflict, Culture, and Innovation in World History*. Oxford, 2015.

Leed, Eric J. *No Man's Land: Combat and Identity in World War I*. Cambridge University Press, 1979.

Legarda, Dr. Benito J., Jr. "Manila Holocaust: Massacre and Rape." http://www.malacanang.gov.ph/75102-manila-holocaust-massacre-and-rape/

Lenin, V.I. *Imperialism: The Highest Stage of Capitalism* in *Selected Works*. Progress Publishers, 1963, 667–776. http://www.marxists.org/archive/lenin/works/1916/imp-hsc/index.htm

_____. "The Socialist Revolution and the Right of Nations to Self-Determination" (1916). Reprinted *Collected Works*. Vol. 22. 4th ed. Progress Publishers, 1964, 143–56. http://www.marx2mao.com/Lenin/SRSD16.html

Leonard, Thomas C. *Illiberal Reformers: Race, Eugenics, and American Economics*. Princeton University Press, 2017.

Lerner, Gerda. "The Lady and the Mill Girl: Changes in the Status of Women in the Age of Jackson." *American Studies* 10 (Spring 1969): 5–15.

Levene, Mark. "Why is the Twentieth Century the Century of Genocide?" *Journal of World War* 11 (Fall 2000): 305–366.

Levine, Philippa. *Gender and Empire*. Oxford University Press, 2004.

Lewis, Carolyn Herbst. *Prescription for Heterosexuality: Sexual Citizenship in the Cold War Era.* Chapel Hill: University of North Carolina Press, 2010.

Library on Congress. Prints and Photographs Online Catalog. http://www.loc.gov/pictures/item/2010652057/.

Linden, Stefanie Caroline, and Edgar Jones, "'Shell shock' Revisited: An Examination of the Case Records of the National Hospital in London." *Medical History*, 58:4 (October, 2014): 519–545.

Linder, Ann P. *Princes of the Trenches: Narrating the German Experience of the First World War.* Camden House, 1996.

Linderman, Gerald F. *The World Within War: America's Combat Experience in World War II.* Free Press, 1997.

Linker, Beth. *War's Waste: Rehabilitation in World War I America.* University of Chicago Press, 2011.

Linn, Brian McAllister. *The Philippine War, 1899–1902.* University Press of Kansas, 2000.

Lipstadt, Deborah. *Denying the Holocaust.* Plume, 1994.

Liulevicius, Gabriel Vejas. *War Land on the Eastern Front: Culture, National Identity and German Occupation in World War I.* Cambridge University Press, 2000.

Loeser, Lewis H. "The Sexual Psychopath in the Military Service." *American Journal of Psychiatry* 102 (July 1945): 92–101.

Longley, Kyle. *Grunts: The American Combat Soldiers in Vietnam.* Routledge, 2008.

Loughran, Tracey. "Shell Shock, Trauma and the First World War: The Making of a Diagnosis and Its Histories." *Journal of the History of Medicine and Allied Sciences* 67:1 (January 2012): 94–119.

Lovel, Julia. *The Opium Wars: Drugs, Dreams, and the Making of Modern China.* Overlook Press, 2015.

Lutz, Tom. *American Nervousness, 1903.* Cornell University Press, 1991.

Lynn, John A. *Battle: A History of Combat and Culture from Ancient Greece to Modern America.* Westview, 2003.

_____. *Bayonets of the Republic: Motivation and Tactics in the Army of Revolutionary France, 1791–1794.* Westview, 1996.

_____. "The Embattled Future of Academic Military History." *The Journal of Military History* 61 (October, 1997), 777–89.

_____. *Women, Armies, and Warfare in Early Modern Europe.* Cambridge University Press, 2008.

Maloba, W.O. *African Women in Revolution.* Africa World Press, 2007.

_____. *Mau Mau and Kenya: An Analysis of a Peasant Revolt.* Indiana University Press, 1993.

Manela, Erez. *The Wilsonian Moment: Self-Determination and the International Origins of Anticolonial Nationalism.* Oxford University Press, 2007.

Mangan, J.A., and James Walvin, eds., *Manliness and Morality: Middle-Class Masculinity in Britain and America, 1800–1940.* St. Martin's Press, 1987.

Marine Corps General Correspondence, RG 127, National Archives and Record Administration, College Park.

Martin, Thomas. et al., *Crises of Empire: Decolonization of and Europe's Imperial States, 1918–1975.* 2nd ed. Bloomsbury, 2015.

"Mau Mau Uprising: Bloody History of Kenya." BBC News UK/ 7 April 2011. http://www.bbc.co.uk/news/uk-12997138.

Maus, L. Mervin, "Injurious Effects Resulting from the Moderate Use of Alcohol." *Journal of the Military Service Institute* 54:187 (January-February, 1914): 1–8.

Maxwell, Jeremy. *Brotherhood in Combat: How African Americans Found Equality in Korea and Vietnam.* University of Oklahoma Press, 2018.

May, Elaine Tyler. *Fortress America: How We Embraced Read and Abandoned Democracy.* Basic Books, 2017.

_____. *Homeward Bound: American Families in the Cold War Era.* Basic Books, 1988.

MacGregor, Morris J. *Integration of the Armed Forces, 1940–1965.* U.S. Army Center of Military History, 1981.

MacGregor, Morris J., and Bernard C. Nalty, eds., *Blacks in the United States Armed Forces*, 13 vols. Scholarly Resources, 1977.

MacKenzie, Megan. *Beyond the Band of Brothers: The US Military and the Myth that Women Can't Fight.* Cambridge University Press, 2015.

Mangin, Charles. *La Force Noire.* Hachette et Cie, 1911.

Mansoor, Peter R. *The G.I. Offensive in Europe: The Triumph of American Infantry Divisions.* University Press of Kansas, 1999.

Marshall, Heather Pace. "Crucible of Colonial Service: The Warrior Brotherhood and the Mythos of the Modern Marine Corps, 1898–1934." M.A. thesis, University of Hawaii, 2003.

Mayer, Holly A. *Belonging to the Army: Camp Follower and Community during the American Revolution.* University of South Carolina Press, 1996.

McClintock, Anne. *Imperial Leather: Race, Gender, and Sexuality in the Colonial Context.* Routledge, 1995.

McDevitt, Patrick F. *"May the Best Man Win": Sport, Masculinity, and Nationalism and the Empire, 1880–1935.* Palgrave McMillan, 2004.

McEuen, Melissa. *Making War, Making Women: Femininity and Duty on the American Home Front, 1941–1945.* University of Georgia Press, 2011.

McLeod, Mark W. and Nguyen Thi Dieu, *Culture and Customs of Vietnam.* Greenwood, 2001.

McMahon, Robert J. *The Limits of Empire: The United States and Southeast Asia since World War II.* Columbia University Press, 1999.

McPherson, James M. *Drawn with the Sword: Reflections on the American Civil War.* Oxford University Press, 1996.

McPherson, James M. *The Negro's Civil War: How American Negros Felt and Acted During the War for the Union.* Pantheon Books, 1965.

Megargee, Geoffrey P. *War of Annihilation: Combat and Genocide on the Eastern Front, 1941.* Rowman & Littlefield, 2006.

Melmanm, Billie, ed. *Borderlines: Genders and Identities in War and Peace, 1870–1930.* Routledge, 1998.

Menning, Bruce W. *Bayonets Before Bullets: The Imperial Russian Army, 1861–1914.* Indiana University Press, 1992.

Meyer, Jessica. *Men of War: Masculinity and the First World War in Britain.* Palgrave Macmillan, 2008.

Meyer, Leisa D. *Creating G.I. Jane: Sexuality and Power in the Women's Army Corps in World War II.* Columbian University Press, 1996.

Meyerowitz, Joanne. *Not June Clever: Women and Gender in Postwar American, 1945–1960.* Temple University, 1994.

Michaels, Jonathan, *McCarthyism: The Realities, Delusions and Politics behind the 1950s Red Scare.* Routledge, 2017.

Mitchell, Brian. *Women in the Military: Flirting with Disaster.* Regnery, 1998.

Mitchell, Silas Weir. *Short Works of Silas Weir Mitchell.* BiblioBazaar, 2008.

Middlebrook, Martin. *The First Day on the Somme/* Allen Lane, 1971.

Military History Institute of Vietnam. *Victory in Vietnam: The Official History of the People's Army of Vietnam, 1945–1975.* Trans. Merle L. Pribbenow. University Press of Kansas, 2002.

Miller, Arthur. *Death of a Salesman.* Viking Press, 1949.

Miller, Edward S. *War Plan Orange: The U.S. Strategy to Defeat Japan, 1897–1945.* Naval Institute Press, 1991.

Miller, Stuart Creighton. *"Benevolent Assimilation": The American Conquest of the Philippines, 1899–1903.* Yale University Press, 1982.

Millett, Allan R. *The War for Korea, 1945–1950: A House Burning.* University Press of Kansas, 2005.

_____. *The War for Korea, 1950–1951.* University Press of Kansas, 2010.

Mjagkij, Nina. *Loyalty in Time of Trial: The African American Experience during World War I.* Rowman and Littelfield, 2011.

Montgomery, David. *The Fall of the House of Labor: The Workplace, the State, and American Labor Activism, 1865–1925.* Press Syndicate of the University of Cambridge, 1987.

Moore, Deborah Dash. *GI Jews: How World War II Changed a Generation.* Harvard University Press, 2006.

Moore, James E. "Hysteria from a Surgical Stand-Point." *Annals of Surgery: A Monthly Review of Surgical Science Since 1885.* 28 (August 1898): 177–186.

Moradi, B. "Sexual Orientation Disclosure, Concealment, Harassment, and Military Cohesions: Perceptions of LBGT Military Veterans." *Military Psychology* 21 (2009): 513–33.

Morden, Bettie J. *The Women's Army Corps, 1945–1978.* Center of Military History, 1990.

Morillo, Stephen, with Michael F. Pavkovic, *What is Military History.* 3rd ed. Polity, 2017.

Morris, Travis. *Dark Ideas: How Neo-Nazi and Violent Jihad Ideologues Shaped Modern Terrorism.* Lexington, 2016.

Moss, Mark. *Manliness and Militarism: Educating Young Boys in Ontario for War.* University of Toronto Press, 2001.

Mosse, George L. *Fallen Soldiers: Reshaping the Memory of the World Wars.* Oxford University Press, 1990.

_____. *The Image of Man: The Creation of Modern Masculinity.* Oxford University Press, 1996.

_____. *Nationalism and Sexuality: Respectability and Abnormal Sexuality in Modern Europe.* Howard Fertig, 1985.

Muehlbauer, Matthew S., and David J. Ulbrich, eds, *The Routledge History of Global War and Society.* Routledge, 2018.

_____. *Ways of War: American Military History from the Colonial Era to the Twenty-First Century.* Routledge, 2017.

Nagel, Joane. *Race, Ethnicity, and Sexuality: Intimate Intersections, Forbidden Frontiers.* Oxford University Press, 2003.

Naimark, Norman M. *Fires of Hatred: Ethnic Cleansing in Twenthieth-Century Europe.* Harvard University Press, 2001.

_____. *The Russians in Germany: A History of the Soviet Zone of Occupation.* Belknap Press, 1997.

Nalty, Bernard C. *Strength for the Fight: A History of Black Americans in the Military* (New York: Free Press, 1989.

Narrett, David. *Adventurism and Empire: The Struggle for Mastery in the Louisiana-Florida Borderlands, 1762–1803*. University of North Carolina Press, 2015.

National Gang Intelligence Center. *Gang-Related Activity in the US Armed Forces Increasing*. January 12, 2007. https://narcosphere.narconews.com/userfiles/70/ngic_gangs.pdf

Naztavlenie dlia deistvii pekhoty v boiu. vysohaishe utverzhdeno 27 fevralia g. St. Petersburg, 1914.

Neely, Mark E., Jr., *The Civil War and the Limits of Destruction*. Cambridge: Harvard University Press, 2007.

Neiberg, Michael. *Dance of the Furies: Europe and the Outbreak of World War I*. Harvard University Press, 2013.

Noer, Thomas J. "Truman, Eisenhower, and South Africa: The 'Middle Road' and Apartheid." *Journal of Ethnic Studies* 11 (Spring 1983): 75–104.

Norton, Mary Beth. *Separated by Their Sex: Women in Public and Private in the Colonial Atlantic World*. Cornell University Press, 2011.

Novak, William J. "The Myth of the Weak American State." *American Historical Review* 113 (June 2008): 752–72.

Nye, Robert A. *Masculinity and Male Codes of Honor in Modern France*. University of California Press, 1998.

_____. "Western Masculinities in War and Peace." *American Historical Review* 112 (April 2007): 417–38.

Olusoga, David. *The World's War: Forgotten Soldiers of Empire*. Head of Zeus, 2014.

O'Neill, William L. *Coming Apart: An Informal History of America in the 1960s*. Ivan R. Dee, 2004.

Ormand, Kirk. *Controlling Desires: Sexuality in Ancient Greece and Rome*. Praeger, 2008.

Paine, S.C.M. *The Wars for Asia, 1911–1949*. Cambridge University Press, 2012.

Painter, Nell Irvin. *Standing at Armageddon: A Grassroots History of the United States, 1877–1919*. W.W. Norton, 2008.

Pasher, Yaron. *Holocaust Versus Wehrmacht: How Hitler's "Final Solution" Undermined the German War Effort*. University Press of Kansas, 2014.

Payne, Stanley. *Fascism: Comparison and Definition*. University of Wisconsin Press, 1980.

Pennington, Reina. *Wings, Women, and War: Soviet Airwomen in World War II Combat*. University Press of Kansas, 2002.

Percy, William Alexander. "Jim Crow and Uncle Sam: The Tuskegee Flying Units and the U.S. Army Air Forces in Europe during World War II." *Journal of Military History* 67 (July 2003): 773–810.

Perez, Louis A. *Cuba: Between Reform and Revolution*. Oxford University Press, 1995.

_____. *Cuba in the American Imagination: Metaphor and the Imperial Ethos*. University of North Carolina Press, 2008.

Piehler,G. Kurt. *Remembering War the American Way*. Smithsonian Books, 2004.

Pinion, René. "Le Guerre Russo-Japonaise et l'Opinion Européene." *Revue de Deux Mondes* 21 (May 1, 1904): 218–19.

Poliakov, Léon. *The History of Anti-Semitism*, vol. 4, *Suicidal Europe, 1870–1933*. Trans. George Kiln. University of Pennsylvania Press, 2003.

Porch, Douglas. *Wars of Empire*. Smithsonian Books/HarperCollins, 2000.

Prados, John. *Vietnam: The History of an Unwinnable War, 1945–1975*. University Press of Kansas, 2009.

Prager, Dennis, and Joseph Telushkin. *Why the Jews? The Reason for Antisemitism, The Most Accurate Predictor of Human Evil*. Touchstone, 1983, 2003, 2016.

Presidential Commission on the Assignment of Women in the Armed Forces, *Women in Combat: Report to the President, November 15, 1992.* Brassey's, 1993.

Presley, Carol Ann. *Kikuyu Women, the Mau Mau Rebellion, and Social Change in Kenya.* Westview, 1992.

Procida, Mary. *Married to the Empire: Gender, Politics and Imperialism in India, 1883–1947.* Palgrave, 2002.

Putney, Clifford. *Muscular Christianity: Manhood and Sports in Protestant America, 1880–1920.* Harvard University Press, 2003.

Quétel, Claude. *A History of Syphilis.* Trans. by Judith Braddock and Brian Pike. Johns Hopkins University Press, 1992.

Ramold, Steven J. *Slaves, Soldiers, Citizens: African Americans in the Union Navy.* Northern Illinois University Press, 2002.

Read, Piers Paul. *The Dreyfus Affair: The Scandal that Tore France in Two.* Bloomsbury, 2012.

Reid, Anthony. *Imperial Alchemy: Nationalism and Political Identity in Southeast Asia.* Cambridge University Press, 2010.

Remarque, Erich Maria. *All Quiet on the Western Front.* Reprint. New York: Ballantine, 1989.

Renda, Mary. *Taking Haiti: Military Occupation and the Culture of U.S. Imperialism.* University of North Carolina Press, 2001.

Richardson, Riché. *Black Masculinity and the U.S. South: From Uncle Tom to Gangsta.* University of Georgia Press, 2007.

"The Right to Self-Determination is Our Revolutionary Policy." *The Call* 4 (January 1975). Marxist Internet Archive, https://www.marxists.org/history/erol/ncm-3/ol-self-det.htm

Riley, Glenda. *Confronting Race: Women and Indians on the Frontier, 1815–1915* (University of New Mexico Press, 2004).

_____. "Frederick Jackson Turner Forgot the Ladies." *Journal of the Early Republic* 2 (Summer 1993): 216–30.

_____. *Frontierswomen: The Iowa Experience.* Iowa State University Press, 1981.

_____. *Taking Land, Breaking Land: Women Colonizing the American West and Kenya, 1840–1940.* University of New Mexico Press, 2003.

Ritter, Gerhard. *The Schlieffen Plan: Critique of a Myth.* Wolff, 1958.

Rizzo, Tracy, and Steven Gerontakis. *Intimate Empires: Body, Race, and Gender in the Modern World.* Oxford University Press, 2016.

Robinson, Carson. "We're gonna have to slap the Dirty Little Jap." https://www.historyonthenet.com/authentichistory/1939–1945/3-music/04-PH-Reaction/19420218_Were_Gonna_Have_To_Slap_The_Dirty_Little_Jap-Lucky_Millinder.html

Robinson, Charles M., III. *The Fall of a Black Army Officer: Racism and the Myth of Henry O. Flipper.* University of Oklahoma Press, 2008.

Robinson, Greg. *By Order of the President: FDR and the Internment of Japanese Americans.* Harvard University Press, 2003.

Robinson, Paul. *The Modernization of Sex: Havelock Ellis, Alfred Kinsey, William Masters, and Virginia Johnson.* HarperCollins, 1977.

Roeder, George H., Jr., *The Censored War: American Visual Experience during World War Two.* Yale University Press, 1993.

Rohall, Donald, et al., eds., *Inclusion in the American Military: A Force for Diversity.* Lexington Books, 2017.

Rome, Adam. *The Bulldozer in the Countryside: Suburban Sprawl and the Rise of American Environmentalism*. Cambridge University Press, 2001.

Roosevelt, Theodore. *The Strenuous Life* (1899). http://www.bartleby.com/58/1.html

Rosen, Ruth. *The World Split Open: How the Modern Women's Movement Changed America*. Viking, 2000.

Rossino, Alexander B. *Hitler Strikes Poland: Blitzkrieg, Ideology, and Atrocity*. University Press of Kansas, 2003.

Rotundo, E. Anthony. *American Manhood: Transformations in Masculinity from the Revolution to the Modern Era*. Basic Books, 1994.

Roy, Kaushik. *Brown Warriors of the Raj: Recruitment and Mechanics of Command in the Sepoy Army, 1859–1913*. Manohar, 2008.

_____. ed., *War and Society in Colonial India*. 2nd ed. Oxford University Press, 2006.

Rudé, George. *The Crowd in the French Revolution*. Oxford Clarendon Press, 1959.

Said, Edward. *Culture and Imperialism*. Vintage, 1993.

_____. *Orientalism*. Vintage, 1979.

Sammons, Jeffrey T., and John H. Morrow, Jr. *Harlem's Rattlers and the Great War: The Undaunted 369th Regiment and the African American Quest for Equality*. University Press of Kansas, 2015.

Santayana, George. *The Life of Reason: Or the Phases of Human Progress*. Scribner, 1953.

Schneider, Carl J., and Dorothy Schneider, *An Eyewitness History: World War II*. Facts on File, 2003.

Schrijvers, Peter. *The GI War against Japan: American Soldiers in Asia and the Pacific during World War II*. New York University Press.

Scott, Joan Wallach. "Gender: A Useful Category of Historical Analysis." *American Historical Review* 91 (December 1986): 1053–1075.

Segal, Mady Wechsler. "Women's Military Roles Cross-Nationally: Past, Present, and Future." *Gender & Society* 9 (December 1995): 757–775.

Segars, J.H., et al., eds. *Forgotten Confederates: An Anthology About Black Southerners, Journal of Confederate History* Series, Vol. XIV. Southern Heritage Press, 1995.

Sharlet, Jeff. "Jesus Killed Mohammed: The Crusade for a Christian Military." *Harper's Magazine* (May 2009) 31–43. http://www.harpers.org/archive/2009/05/0082488.

Shaw, Henry I., Jr., and Ralph W. Donnelly. *Blacks in the Marine Corps*. USMC History and Museums Division, 1975.

Shay, Jonathan, *Achilles in Vietnam: Combat Trauma and the Undoing of Character*. Simon & Schuster, 1995.

Sheffield, Gary. *The Somme*. Cassell, 2007.

Shellum, Brian G. *Black Cadet in a White Bastion: Charles Young at West Point*. Bison Books, 2006.

_____. *Black Officer in a Buffalo Soldier Regiment: The Military Career of Charles Young*. University of Nebraska Press, 2010.

Shepherd, Ben. *War in the Wild East: The German Army and Soviet Partisans*. Harvard University Press, 2004.

Shepard, Todd. *The Invention of Decolonization: The Algerian War and the Remaking of France*. Cornell University Press, 2008.

Shibusawa, Naoko. "The Lavender Scare and Empire: Rethinking Cold War Antigay Politics." *Diplomatic History* 36 (September 2012): 723–52.

Shipway, Martin. *Decolonization and in Impacts: A Comparative Approach to the End of Colonial Empires*. Wiley-Blackwell, 2008.

Showalter, Dennis, ed., *History in Dispute. Vol 9: First World War, Second Series*. St. James Press, 2002.

Showalter, Dennis. *Instrument of War: The German Army 1914–18*. Osprey, 2016.

Showalter, Dennis, et al. *The German Failure in Belgium, August 1914*. McFarland, 2018.

Shy, John. "The Cultural Approach to the History of War." *Journal of Military History* 57 (October 1993): 13–26.

Siegel, Lee. "Death of a Salesman's Dreams." *New York Times*. 2 May 2012. https://www.nytimes.com/2012/05/03/opinion/death-of-a-salesmans-dreams.html

Siemens, Daniel. *Stormtroopers: A New History of Hitler's Brownshirts*. Yale University Press, 2017.

Silber, Nina. *Gender and Sectional Conflict*. University of North Carolina Press, 2008.

Silbey, David J. *The Boxer Rebellion and the Great Game in China*. Hill and Wang, 2012.

_____. *A War of Frontier and Empire: The Philippine-American War, 1899–1902*. Hill and Wang, 2007.

Singh, Nikhil Pal, *Race and America's Long War*. University of California Press, 2017.

Sinha, Mrinalini. *Colonial Masculinity: The "Manly Englishman" and the "Effeminate Bengali" in the Late Nineteenth Century*. Manchester University Press, 1995.

Sitkoff, Harvard. *The Struggle for Black Equality, 1945–1980*. Hill and Wang, 1981.

Sledge, E.B. *With the Old Breed at Okinawa and Peleliu*. Presidio Press, 1981.

Slotkin, Richard. *The Fatal Environment: The Myth of the Frontier in the Age of Industrialization, 1800–1890*. MacMillan, 1985.

_____. *Gunfighter Nation: The Myth of the Frontier in Twentieth Century America*. Atheneum, 1992.

_____. *Regeneration Through Violence: The Mythology of the American Frontier, 1600–1860*. Wesleyan University Press, 1973.

Smelser, Ronald, and Edward J. Davies II, *The Myth of the Eastern Front: The Nazi-Soviet War in American Popular Culture*. Cambridge University Press, 2008.

Smith, Carter F. *Gangs and the Military: Gangsters, Bikers, and Terrorists with Military Training*. Rowman and Littlefield, 2017.

Smith, John David. *Black Soldiers in Blue: African American Troops in the Civil War Era*. University of North Carolina Press, 2002.

Smith, Leonard V. *Between Mutiny and Obedience: The Case of the French Fifth Infantry Division during World War I*. Princeton University Press, 1994.

Smith, Ralph. *Jamaican Volunteers in the First World War: Race, Masculinity, and the Development of National Consciousness*. Manchester University Press, 2004.

Smith-Spark, Laura. "Two Women Make Army Ranger History." August 21, 2015. https://www.cnn.com/2015/08/21/us/women-army-ranger-graduation/index.htm

Snyder, Jack. *The Ideology of the Offensive: Military Decision Making and the Disasters of 1914*. Cornell University Press, 1984.

Snyder, Timothy. *Bloodlands: Europe Between Hitler and Stalin*. Basic Books, 2010.

Soh, C. Sarah. *The Comfort Women: Sexual Violence and Postcolonial Memory in Korea and Japan*. University of Chicago Press, 2008.

Solaro, Erin. *Women in the Line of Fire: What You Should Know About Women in the Military*. Seal Press, 2006.

Solazzo, Vito M. *An Analysis of the Origin and Basis of the Factors Motivating and Sustaining the Viet Cong in Combat*. Marine Corps Command and Staff College, 1968.

Spackman, Barbara. *Fascist Virilities: Rhetoric, Identity, and Social Fantasy in Italy.* University of Minnesota Press, 1996.

Spurgeon, Ian Michael. *Soldiers in the Army of Freedom: The 1st Kansas Colored, The Civil War First African American Combat Unit.* University of Oklahoma Press, 2014.

Stanhope, Philip Henry. *Notes of Conversations with the Duke of Wellington.* London: 1886.

Statistical Abstract on the Sickness and Mortality of the Army of the United States . . . , From January, 1839 to January, 1855. A.O.P. Nicholson, Printer, 1856.

Statistical Abstract on the Sickness and Mortality of the Army of the United States . . ., From January, 1855, to January, 1860. George W. Bowman, Printer, 1860.

Stearns, Peter. *Be a Man: Males in Modern Society.* Homes and Meier, 1990.

Stephenson, Jill. *Women in Nazi Germany.* 3rd ed. Longman, 2001.

Stevenson, David. *Cataclysm: The First World War as Political Tragedy.* Basic Books, 2004.

Stockdale, Melissa. "My Death for the Motherland is Happiness: Women, Patriotism, and Soldiering in Russia's Great War, 1914–1917." *American Historical Review* 109 (February 2004): 78–115.

Stoff, Laurie. *They Fought for the Motherland: Russia's Women Soldiers in World War I and the Revolution.* University Press of Kansas, 2006.

Stoler, Anna Laura. *Carnal Knowledge and Imperial Power: Race and the Intimate in Colonial Rule,* 2nd ed. University of California Press 2002.

Stovall, Tyler, and Georges van den Abbeele, eds., *French Civilization and Its Discontents: Nationalism, Colonialism, Race.* Lexington Books, 2003.

Strachan, Hew. *The First World War. Volume I: To Arms.* Cambridge University Press, 2001.

Streets, Heather. *Martial Races: The Military, Race and Masculinity in British Imperial Cultures, 1857–1914.* Manchester University Press, 2004.

Stur, Heather. *Beyond Combat: Women and Gender in the Vietnam War.* Cambridge University Press, 2011.

Tadayoshi, Sakurai. *Human Bullets: A Soldier's Story of Port Arthur.* Archibald, 1908.

Takaki, Donald. *Double Victory: A Multicultural History of America in World War II.* New York: Back Bay Books, 2001.

Tanaka, Yuki. *Hidden Horrors: Japanese War Crimes in World War II.* Westview Press, 1997.

_____. *Japan's Comfort Women: The Military and Involuntary Prostitution during War and Occupation.* Routledge, 2002.

Taylor, Sandra C. *Vietnamese Women at War: Fighting for Ho Chi Minh and the Revolution.* University Press of Kansas, 1999.

Taylor, William A. *Every Citizen a Soldier: The Campaign for University Training after World War II.* Texas A&M University Press, 2014.

Tchen, John Kuo Wei. and Dylan Yeats, eds. *Yellow Peril!: An Archive of Anti-Asia Fear.* Verso, 2014.

Terry, Wallace, ed. *Bloods: Black Veterans in the Vietnam War: An Oral History.* Presidio, 1985.

Ther, Philip. *The Darker of Nation-States: Ethnic Cleaning in Modern Europe,* trans. Charlotte Kreutzmüller. Bergahn, 2014.

Theweleit, Klaus. *Male Fantasies. Volume I: Women, Floods, Bodies, History.* Trans. Erica Carter, et al. University of Minnesota Press, 1987.

Thomas, Evan. *The War Lovers: Roosevelt, Lodge, Hearst, and the Rush to Empire, 1898.* Little, Brown and Company, 2010.

Thompson, E.P. *The Making of the English Working Class.* Victor Gollancz, 1963.

Thorpe, Rebecca U. *The American Warfare State: The Domestic Politics of Military Spending.* University of Chicago Press, 2014.

Tickner, J. Ann. *Gendering World Politics: Issues and Approaches in the Post-Cold War Era.* Columbia University Press, 2001.

Tillman, Ellen D. *Dollar Diplomacy by Force: Nation-Building and Resistance in the Dominican Republic.* University of North Carolina Press, 2016.

Todd, Lisa M. *Sexual Treason in Germany during the First World War.* Palgrave Macmillan, 2017.

Tocqueville, Alexis de. *Democracy in America.* Trans. Henry Reeve. Reprint. Barnes & Noble, 2003.

Todman, Dan. *The Great War: Myth and Memory.* Hambledon and London, 2005.

Townshend, Charles. *Desert Hell: The British Invasion of Mesopotamia.* The Belknap Press of Harvard University Press, 2011.

Treadwell, Mattie. *Women's Army Corps.* Government Printing Office, 1953.

Truman, Harry S. "E.O. 9981," 1948. http://www.ourdocuments.gov/doc.php?flash= true&doc=84&sortorder=

Tunstall, Graydon A. *Blood on the Snow: The Carpathian Winter War of 1915.* University Press of Kansas, 2010.

Turner, Karen Gottschang, and Phan Thanh Hao, *Even the Women Must Fight: Memories of War from North Vietnam.* Wiley, 1998.

Twain, Mark. "Mark Twain – The World of 1898: The Spanish-American War." Hispanic Division, Library of Congress. http://www.loc.gov/rr/hispanic/1898/twain.html

Ulbrich, David J. "A Male-Conscious Critique of *All Quiet on the Western Front.*" *Journal of Men's Studies* 3 (February 1995): 229–40.

_____. *Preparing for Victory: Thomas Holcomb and the Making of the Modern U.S. Marine Corps, 1936–1943.* Naval Institute Press, 2011.

Ulrich, Laura Thatcher. *Good Wives: Image and Reality in the Lives of Women in Northern New England.* Vintage, 1991.

United Nations, "Convention on the Prevention and Punishment of the Crime of Genocide." Resolution 260 (III). December 9, 1948. http://www.hrweb.org/legal/genocide.html

United Nations General Assembly. A/RES/47/121. December 18, 1992. https://www.un.org/ documents/ga/res/47/a47r121.htm

United States Army. *The Medical Department of the United States Army in the World War.* Vol. IX. *Communicable and Other Diseases.* Government Printing Office, 1928.

United States Department of Defense. *Department of Defense Annual Report on Sexual Assault in the Military, Fiscal Year 2015.* http://sapr.mil/public/docs/reports/FY15_Annual/FY15_ Annual_Report_on_Sexual_Assault_in_the_Military.pdf

_____. *Department of Defense Task Force Report on Care for Victims of Sexual Assault, April 2004.* http://www.ncdsv.org/images/DOD_TaskForceReportOnCareForVictimsOfSex- ualAssault_4–2004.pdf

_____. Defense Personnel Security Research Center. *Screening for Potential Terrorists in the Enlisted Military Accessions Process.* April 2005. https://fas.org/irp/eprint/screening.pdf

_____. "Department of Defense Sexual Assault Prevention and Response Office Mission and History." http://www.sapr.mil/index.php/about/mission-and-history.

_____. "Transgender Service in the U.S. Military: An Implementation Handbook." September 30, 2016. https://www.defense.gov/Portals/1/features/2016/0616_policy/ DoDTGHandbook_093016.pdf?ver=2016-09-30-160933-837

United States Department of Homeland Security. *(U//FOUO) Rightwing Extremism: Current Economic and Political Climate Fueling Resurgence in Radicalization and Recruitment*, IA-0257-09. April, 7, 2009. http://www.fas.org/irp/eprint/rightwing.pdf

United States Holocaust Memorial Museum. "Confront Genocide." https://www.ushmm.org/confront-genocide.

U.S. War Department. *Handbook on Japanese Military Forces*. TM E 30-480. Government Printing Office, 1944.

Urban, Mark. *Fusiliers: The Saga of a British Redcoat Regiment in the American Revolution*. Walker and Company, 2007.

Urwin, Gregory J.W., ed., *Black Flag over Dixie: Racial Atrocities and Reprisals in the Civil War*. Southern Illinois University Press, 2005.

Van Creveld, Martin. "Less than We Can Be: Men, Women, and the Modern Military." *Journal of Strategic Studies* 24 (2000): 1–20.

_____. *Men, Women & War: Do Women Belong in the Front Line?* Cassell, 2002.

Van Norwick, Thomas. *Imagining Men: Ideals of Masculinity in Ancient Greek Culture*. Praeger, 2008.

Vapnek, Lara. *Breadwinners: Working Women and Economic Independence, 1865–1920*. University of Illinois Press, 2009.

Vergun, David. "First Women Graduate Ranger School." August 21, 2015. https://www.army.mil/article/154286/First_women_graduate_Ranger_School/

Verhey, Jeffrey. *The Spirit of 1914: Militarism, Myth, and Mobilization in Germany*. Cambridge University Press, 2000.

"Vietnamese Declaration of Independence (1945)." Modern History Sourcebook. https://sourcebooks.fordham.edu/halsall/mod/1945vietnam.html.

Volkov, Shulimit. *Walther Rathenau: Weimar's Fallen Statesman*. Yale University Press, 2012.

Vonnegut, Kurt. *Slaughterhouse Five, or the Children's Crusade*. Dell Publishing, 1969.

Vuic, Kara Dixon, ed., *The Routledge History of Gender, War, and the U.S. Military*. Routledge, 2017.

Wackerfuss, Andrew. *Stormtrooper Families: Homosexuality and Community in the Early Nazi Movement*. Columbia University Press, 2015.

Walker, George. *Venereal Disease in the American Expeditionary Forces*. Medical Standard Book Co., 1922.

Walker, J. Samuel. "The Decision to the Use the Bomb: A Historiography Update." *Diplomatic History* 14 (Winter 1990): 97–114.

Walkowitz, Judith. *City of Dreadful Delight: Narratives of Sexual Danger in Late-Victorian London*. University of Chicago Press, 1992.

Watanabe, Kasuko. "Trafficking Women's Bodies, Then and Now: The Issue of Military 'Comfort Women.'" *Women's Studies Quarterly* 27 (Summer 1999): 19–31.

Ward, Julie K., and Tommy Lee Lott. *Philosophers on Race: Critical Essays*. Wiley-Blackwell, 2002.

Watson, Alexander. *Ring of Steel: Germany and Austria-Hungary in World War I*. Basic Books, 2014.

Watts, Sarah. *Rough Rider in the White House: Theodore Roosevelt and the Politics of Desire*. University of Chicago Press, 2006.

Weigley, Russell F. *A Great Civil War: A Military and Political History, 1861–1865*. Indiana University Press, 2004.

_____. ed. *New Dimensions in Military History: An Anthology*. Presidio Press, 1975.

Weingartner, James. "War against Subhumans: Comparisons between the German War against the Soviet Union and the American War against Japan, 1941–1945." *Historian* 58 (March 1996): 557–72.

Wesseling, H.L. *The European Colonial Empires, 1815–1919*. Pearson Longman, 2004.

Wesseling, H.L. *Soldier and Warrior: French Attitudes toward the Army and War on the Eve of the First World War*. Trans. Arnold J. Pomerans. Greenwood Press, 2000.

West, Donald J., and Richard Green, eds., *Sociolegal Control of Homosexuality: A Multi-Nation Comparison*. Plenum Press, 1997.

Westad, Odd Arne. *The Global Cold War: Third World Interventions and the Making of Our Times*. Cambridge University Press, 2007.

Westheider, James E. *Fighting on Two Fronts: African-Americans in the Vietnam War*. New York University Press, 1997.

Wette, Wolfram. *The Wehrmacht: History, Myth, Reality*. Trans. Deborah Lucas Schneider. Harvard University Press, 2006.

"What Really Happened at Tailhook Convention: Scandal: The Pentagon report graphically describes how fraternity-style hi-jinks turned into a hall of horrors." *Los Angeles Times*. April 24, 1993. http://articles.latimes.com/1993-04-24/news/mn-26672_1_tailhook-convention

Whyte, William H., Jr., *The Organization Man*. Doubleday, 1957.

Wiesner-Hanks, Merry. *Gender in History: Global Perspectives*. Malden, MA: Wiley-Blackwell, 2010.

Wilhelm II. "Hun" Speech. German History in Documents and Images. http://germanhistorydocs.ghi-dc.org/sub_document.cfm?document_id=755.

Williams, Chad L. *Torchbearers of Democracy: African American Soldiers in the World War I Era*. University of North Carolina Press, 2013

Wilson, Woodrow. "Speech on the Fourteen Points." *Congressional Record*. 65th Congress 2nd Session, 1918. pp. 680–81. Yale University Avalon Project, http://avalon.law.yale.edu/20th_century/wilson14.asp

Wingfield, Nancy M., and Maria Bucur, eds. *Gender and War in Twentieth Century Eastern Europe*. Indiana University Press, 2006.

Winter, Jay., ed., *Cambridge History of the First World War*. Vol. III. *Civil Society*. Cambridge University Press, 2014.

Wintermute, Bobby A. "'The Negro should not be used as a combat soldier': Reconfiguring Racial Identity in the United States Army, 1890–1918." *Patterns of Prejudice* 46 (June 2012): 278–95.

_____. *Public Health and the U.S. Military: A History of the Army Medical Department,1818–1917*. Routledge, 2010.

Wittig, Monique. "The Point of View: Universal or Particular." *Feminist Issues* 3.2 (1983): 63–69.

Wohl, Robert. *Generation of 1914*. Harvard University Press, 1979.

"Women at Arms: G.I. Jane Breaks the Combat Barrier." *The New York Times*. August 16, 2009. http://www.nytimes.com/2009/08/16/us/16women.html?_r=1

A Woman in Berlin: Eight Weeks in the Conquered City: A Diary. Picador, 2006.

Wood, James. *Veteran Narratives and the Collective Memory of the Vietnam War*. Ohio University Press, 2016.

Woodruff, Charles E. *Medical Ethnology*. Rebman Company, 1915.

World War I Centenary, "The British Army's fight against Venereal Disease in the 'Heroic Age of Prostitution.'" http://ww1centenary.oucs.ox.ac.uk/body-and-mind/

the-british-army%E2%80%99s-fight-against-venereal-disease-in-the-%E2%80%98hero-ic-age-of-prostitution%E2%80%99/

World War I Propaganda Posters. http://www.ww1propaganda.com/

Wyatt-Brown, Bertram. *The Shaping of Southern Culture: Honor, Grace, and War, 1760s–1890s*. University of North Carolina Press, 2001

Yamamura, Kozo. "Success Illgotten?: The Role of Meiji Militarism in Japan's Technological Progress." *Journal of Economic History* 37 (March 1977):113–35.

Yamashita, Samuel Hideo. *Daily Life in Wartime Japan, 1940–1945*. University Press of Kansas, 2015.

Yoshimi, Yoshiaki. *Comfort Women: Comfort Women: Sexual Slavery in the Japanese Military during World War II*. Trans. Suzanne O'Brien. Columbia University Press, 2002.

Young, Robert J.C. *Empire, Colony, Postcolony*. Wiley-Blackwell, 2015.

Zuber, Terrance. *Inventing the Schlieffen Plan: German War Planning, 1871–1914*. Oxford University Press, 2014.

Zuckerman, Larry. *The Rape of Belgium: The Untold Story of World War I*. New York University Press, 2004.

Index

https://doi.org/10.1515/9783110477467-012